Political Murder

Political Murder

From Tyrannicide to Terrorism

Franklin L. Ford

Harvard University Press
Cambridge, Massachusetts, and
London, England   1985

This book is printed on acid-free paper, and its binding materials
have been chosen for strength and durability.

Library of Congress Cataloging in Publication Data
Ford, Franklin L. (Franklin Lewis), 1920–
Political murder.
Includes index.
1. Assassination—History. I. Title.
HV6278.F67 1985   303.6′2   85-5837
ISBN 0-674-68635-7 (alk. paper)

To the Memory of

Guy Stanton Ford
and
William Leonard Langer

Teachers by Example

Preface

THE IDEA FOR THIS BOOK was born in 1970, toward the end of America's worst outbreak of political assassination and near the beginning of an unprecedented epidemic of terrorism worldwide. To that extent, the study was called into being not just by intellectual interest but also by a sense of shock. The passage of time consumed in research and writing has brought a certain fading of the visceral component, but no decline in a felt and urgent need to understand. Assassination and other human actions often categorized as "accidents of history" may become more familiar to one age than to another simply through repetition. But precisely because their incidence has varied throughout mankind's recorded experience, they pose an urgent challenge to our capacity for learning from the irregular course of events.

Prior to the present undertaking, my involvement with matters of political violence, both official and insurrectionary, had been largely confined to the history of Nazi Germany, including the baleful record of Hitler's regime and the eventual attempt to kill the Führer himself on July 20, 1944. Fully a quarter of a century after that event, however, a combination of research in Vienna on aspects of the Thirty Years' War, including the slaying of Wallenstein in 1634, and the spate of news then pouring in from all over the globe concerning lethal acts attributed to political motives produced a sudden but persistent impulse to find out what history might have to tell about homicide in pursuit—or defense, or merely defiance—of power in the state.

The resulting book would never have been completed without generous help received from many sides. A comprehensive list of all the individuals who have given of their time and expertise would be too long for inclusion here, but some at least should be mentioned by name. They include Isadore Twersky and John H. Finley for their careful reading of the chapters dealing, respectively, with Judaic and Greek antiquity, as well as Mason Hammond, who supplied penetrating and constructive criticism of the pages devoted to ancient Rome. Ephraim Isaac introduced me to rarely exploited materials concerning Ethiopia's past, while the late Kenneth Onwuka Dike offered rewarding insights into other aspects of African history.

From Judith Shklar I received perceptive comments on medieval and early modern tyrannicide theory, from Felix Gilbert the same concerning Renaissance thought, and from Wallace T. MacCaffrey the benefit of his detailed knowledge of Tudor and Stuart England. Robert Bireley, S.J., is owed a special debt for having located, and in some cases copied by hand, valuable documents bearing on the seventeenth-century European debates over political murder. Finally, John V. Kelleher merits my lasting gratitude for his guidance through some of the most perplexing problems of modern Irish history. These and a number of other learned consultants deserve credit for having diminished the incidence of error in the chapters to follow. The flaws that remain are my own responsibility.

Among the institutions for whose precious resources and accommodating staffs I am grateful are the libraries of Harvard, Princeton, and Duke universities, the University of North Carolina at Chapel Hill, Bennington College, Vienna's Universitätsbibliothek, and in London both the British Library and the Public Record Office. To the Institute for Advanced Study at Princeton, New Jersey, and the National Humanities Center, in Research Triangle Park, North Carolina, I am indebted for the opportunities they have afforded to read, reflect, and write amid congenial surroundings and in the company of wonderfully thoughtful people.

Three individuals have contributed in signal fashion, at different times and in different ways. Archibald MacLeish offered initial interest, followed by criticism and enthusiastic support, often at junctures when my own energy and optimism showed signs of faltering. Mairi McCormick, near the beginning of the enterprise, supplied indispensable collaboration, finding relevant readings and summarizing their contents with quick intelligence. Ann Louise McLaughlin, at Harvard University Press, has taken things the rest of the way, so to speak, bringing to the effort her practiced editorial eye and her ability to manage with equal skill both the copy and the author.

To my wife, Eleanor, who has shared in many earlier projects and trials, let me say simply that none of them has resulted in a book more fully "hers too" than this, as she must know.

F.L.F.

Contents

Illustrations

Political Murder

Introduction

A historical inquiry, like any other, begins with questions, which in turn give rise to the need for some initial agreement concerning definitions. Without that, no search for intelligible answers is likely to have much success. In the present case, three pivotal concepts demand clarification at the start. They are, in descending order of generality, political murder, assassination, and tyrannicide.

Political murder, homicide related to the body politic and its governance, includes everything from the most narrowly targeted assassination to random killings designed to intimidate opponents, while calling attention to a given cause. It comprises the effect of impersonal bombs, official and unofficial "death squads," the work of the occasional killer with a private grievance—be he outraged husband, hard-pressed debtor, or irreconcilable family foe—whose act may be political only in the sense that its victim happens to be a public figure. It includes programs of genocide aimed at entire races or ethnic groups, attempts to decimate class enemies, and, in the eyes of some at least, formal warfare itself. Others hasten to call murder the execution of even a convicted killer whose defense has rested on claims of political purpose.

This book touches repeatedly, if at times obliquely, on all these categories; not to do so would be to renege on the promise implicit in its title. Nevertheless, the chapters that follow will concentrate on an area far less extended, that of assassination as a particular species of the genus. The word itself, since its Arabic original entered Western European languages at the time of the Crusades, has been variously defined and, even in our own day, is used in sometimes quite divergent senses. The Islamic *Hashishiyyin* slew "enemies of the Faith," readily identifiable as enemies of their own order, but in the West a negative connotation persisted, suggesting guileful action and motives which, if not always base, were at best amoral. Thus, Dante used the term "assassin" to describe any "professional secret murderer,"[1] in

1

short a hit man. *The Oxford English Dictionary* currently in use still refers to an assassin as "one who undertakes to put another to death by treacherous violence," and a few lines further on introduces the hallowed but scarcely universal figure of the "hired mercenary."[2] Thus, contemporary usage often remains too narrow, while the older, since it frequently extended to wholly private homicide, could be too broad. Max Lerner's use of assassination as "the killing of a person in public life from a political motive and without legal process" marked a distinct improvement, though his final phrase raises interesting questions about the occasional use of judicial action as a surrogate for outright murder.[3]

For my purposes what is needed is a definition that eliminates such fortuitous elements as the resort to ambush or the hiring of an agent, stressing instead the personalization of both doer and victim, together with the relevant range of motives. Any description that meets those requirements is bound to be somewhat cumbersome, but the following is at least comprehensible: "Assassination is the intentional killing of a specified victim or group of victims, perpetrated for reasons related to his (her, their) public prominence and undertaken with a political purpose in view." That formula obviously does not exclude the occasional substitution of judicial action for murder in defiance of the law. In other respects, however, it will be seen to be comparatively restrictive, as it is meant to be.

If assassination represents only one kind of political murder, tyrannicide denotes a category more limited still, a circle within a circle within a circle. The reason for paying special attention to the tradition of striking down illegitimate, capricious, or impious rulers on grounds of principle is that for at least two and a half millennia it has constituted in the eyes of philosophers the only respectable link between ethics and political violence. That being so, the ideal of tyrannicide needs constantly to be compared, and not infrequently contrasted, with the reality of actual events, motives, and consequences.

With these conceptual elements in mind—political murder in general, assassination as its most individualized expression, and tyrannicide as the latter's ostensibly justifiable subcategory—it is possible to start making sense out of some initial questions:

(1) Why do humans kill, and risk being killed, for political reasons at all? Politics is itself so much a matter of life, of cooperation in order to survive and prosper, that linking it to death seems almost paradoxical. What at first glance may appear morbid, however, ceases to be so easily dismissable if one considers the history of organized societies.

(2) Is murder thus motivated endemic, more or less continuous, and in that respect an inevitable feature of the human condition? As seen from the politician's point of view, is assassination just another hazard of the trade displaying nothing more than what a recent commentator calls "a deadly randomness"?[4]

(3) Or does history record the opposite, an uneven oscillation between high and low incidence of political murder? If so, can these "highs" and "lows" be explained by recurrent configurations of social, psychological, institutional, or other circumstances? Are there, in short, "things to watch for"?

(4) In that record as a whole, do enigmatic loners or elaborate conspiracies predominate? So much has been said and written on this subject in recent times that, if not an impossibly exact tally, a dispassionate overview would seem to be in order.

(5) What connections are there between political murder, on the one hand, and, on the other, only tangentially political concerns including religion, sex, exhibitionism, self-fulfillment, and suicide? Is there in fact any such thing as a purely political crime?

(6) Do such purportedly ethical concerns as those to be found in classical tyrannicide and in some expressions of modern anarchism belong to the realm of political theory? What can be said for the ethical justification of any slaying at all?

Further queries would not be hard to formulate, but the foregoing half-dozen should serve to launch the investigation. There remains to be considered, however, the way in which that investigation itself has been conceived, as well as the book's resulting strategy. The method employed, as will at once become apparent, is frankly episodic and is pursued without apology to those who find all narrative inconsequential and who therefore retire into something, anything, other than *l'histoire événementielle*. It is hard to see how a work devoted to the phenomenon and the problems of political murder could refuse to concern itself with actual political murders. And that calls for an unembarrassed attention to the details of the story itself, as best it can be reconstructed out of testimony both old and new. After all, it does no lasting good to ponder the causes, the symbolic significance, or the "message" of an event which, upon closer inspection, turns out not to have occurred.

At the same time, using selected vignettes to shed light on shifting tendencies and periodic trends in both behavior and attitudes is very different from proposing an exhaustive catalogue. This book includes a few lists, most of them short, and a handsome total of two tables, summarizing major assassinations in the sixteenth and twentieth centuries. In other respects the approach, while clearly dependent on illustration, could scarcely be called encyclopaedic. Almost every reader will miss some, and more than a few may miss many, time-honored examples of tyrannicide, assassination, and political murder. Redemption for such sins on an author's part can come only from the demonstration that certain less familiar episodes also have a surprising amount of relevant history to impart.

In the handling of these case studies a conscious effort has been made to avoid laboring analogies. Forebearance in this regard is not always easy; there is a seductive temptation to play such games as starting a discussion about two articulate and energetic young brothers, who rose to high office in a republic still savoring victory in a major war, only to fall victim, one after the other, to memorable assassinations. Once the reader has the Kennedys firmly fixed in his or her mind, it is all too easy to step back and introduce Tiberius and Gaius Gracchus, Roman tribunes of the second century before the Christian era. The trouble with comparisons between the Gracchi and the two slain Kennedy brothers is that, while some are apt, others are strained, and still others pure nonsense. Generally speaking, if historical parallels work, they tend to announce themselves; and if they do not, no amount of anxious matchmaking on the part of a speaker or writer is likely to do much good. On the other hand, it would be foolish to deny that certain almost eerily recurrent patterns can and do appear, especially when allowance is made for timebound differences in detail.

Despite some unavoidable disappointment at not being able to include more frequent and extensive references to the place of other disciplines than history—law, philosophy, social sciences, literary fiction, and the arts, both graphic and dramatic—in this study of assassination, it is my conclusion that the most pressing questions concerning political murder are neither aesthetic nor ethical, but pragmatic. To say this is not to minimize the importance of taste, much less of morality, but only to suggest that what we need to ponder most of all is whether assassination *works*. Does it, in even a tiny minority of cases, promise results otherwise achievable only by revolution or by war? Can it forestall evil acts or prevent irreparable damage inflicted by misguided leaders? In other words, is assassination ever a valid option, a bargain at the going rates? In order to reply to operative questions such as those, it is necessary to address a prior one, namely: "How often in history have assassinations produced results even close to what their perpetrators were seeking to achieve?" And that requires one to contemplate a vast array of times, places, actions, and outcomes.

PART ONE

The Lessons of Antiquity

THE ANCIENT WORLD, in particular the Middle East and the Mediterranean basin, gave birth to mankind's earliest known efforts at political organization. That being so, it also experienced and with increasing care recorded instances of political homicide still able to hold our interest, born only in part of a reverence for classical models.

To antiquity we owe a number of evocative terms, among them "tyrannicide," "proscription," "zealot," and, last of these ancient words to appear, the Arabic root from which "assassination" is derived. Examples of unforgotten deeds include those of Jael and Joab in Israel, the stabbing of Hipparchus the Athenian by Harmodius and Aristogiton, the deaths by violence of the Gracchi, Pompey, Caesar, and Cicero against the background of Rome's Republic in decline, not to mention the destruction of countless Roman emperors and pretenders in the ensuing centuries. Less familiar to a Western reader, but just as revealing, were the attempts on the life of the Gautama Buddha and the harsh dynastic struggles around the throne of Ethiopia.

Perhaps even more important than the march of events was the emergence of certain patterns of political thought and behavior. In the case of the devoutly monotheistic Jews, some notorious wielders of earthly power were struck down for having betrayed the Lord God Jehovah. Greek tyrannicide theory developed from more secular roots. The Hellenic ruler deemed worthy of assassination was not condemned for ungodliness but for having either usurped his position or abused an office legitimately his by being a capricious despot. In actual practice, Athens and the other major city-states of mainland Greece witnessed very few political murders during their golden age; the more turbulent public life of the colonies abroad provided Aristotle and other definers of tyranny with most of their case studies.

The Roman Republic throughout almost the first four centuries of its existence saw even fewer assassinations, over a much longer period, than had the *poleis* of Periclean Greece. When political murder erupted in Rome, with the deaths of the brothers Tiberius and Gaius Gracchus, it signaled the beginning of the Republic's own disintegration, to be followed by rampant intrigue and bloodshed under the Empire. Even while that imperial power was still strong, it encountered bitter resistance in the Palestine of the Zealots and Masada, featuring lethal attacks on Roman officials and Jewish "collaborators." When the Empire crumbled, there appeared in its wake new structures of power and new models of political homicide from the German kingdoms of western Europe to the Muslim realms of the Middle East and northern Africa.

1

Jehovah's Children and His Enemies

The Bible as Source

In his last work, posthumously published as *The Origins of History,* Sir Herbert Butterfield reserves a special place for ancient Israel. Previous historical literature, he remarks, had mixed the barest of annals with epic poetry and pure mythology: "Then, suddenly [he goes on], one finds oneself confronted with what must be the greatest surprise in the whole story. There emerges a people not only supremely conscious of the past but possibly more obsessed with history than any other nation that has ever existed."[1] Beginning with the Exodus from Egypt, the figure of Jehovah, God of the Israelites and their deliverer "out of the house of bondage," occupied a *historical* role unique among the deities of antiquity. In order to use biblical accounts for the study of any such phenomenon as political murder, one therefore has to appreciate both their narrative interest and their religious message. The Old Testament in particular, through all its translations and despite past debates over its proper content, survives as a literary gift we may read with an absorption not necessarily confined to reverence. The place of the Lord God, however, at once guide and admonisher, rewarder and punisher, is paramount in the annals of His children. His is a constant presence in the shaping of their laws and their explanations of behavior.

Scriptural evidence, for all its richness, poses some undeniable difficulties. The component texts are at once solemn and openly didactic, purporting to be as changeless in content as they are unswerving in their religious purpose. They were nonetheless products of endless retelling before they were ever written down, with the resulting embellishment, mutation over time, and occasional ambiguity that characterize all oral tradition. There is a further problem, not only of selecting relevant anecdotes from the wealth of those at hand but also of grouping them in such a way as to lend coherence to the whole.

Concentrating for now on the Old Testament, we can identify three fairly distinct clusters of politically motivated or at any rate politically significant murders. The first is found in the Book of Judges and comprises episodes dating from the twelfth century before the Christian era. The second belongs to a time about two hundred years later, the era of the united monarchy under David and Solomon, as recounted in the Second Book of Samuel and the First of Kings. The final grouping forms part of the story of the subsequent ruin of Israel and Judah, become separate kingdoms after Solomon's death. For that we must rely primarily on the Second Book of Kings.[2]

In the Days of the Judges

By about 1200 B.C. the Jewish tribes had achieved a reasonably stable geographical identity and a discernible, though shifting, pattern of alliances among themselves. With Egypt in confusion and the Hittite empire destroyed, the most serious threat in the Hebrew part of Canaan was sporadic pressure from the Philistines on the Mediterranean coast, based on Gaza and its sister cities. Hardly less worrisome was the rivalry with "the seed of Aram," the Arameans who had pushed into present-day Syria and Jordan. Although warfare with these neighbors east and west was not constant, it seems almost never to have subsided entirely on both fronts at the same time. Despite their wars and their own chronic disunity, however, the people of Israel had managed to settle down in ways not possible before and to increase their prosperity through sheepherding, agriculture, and the growth of commerce both on the Mediterranean (despite the Philistines) and overland through the use of what was then still a novelty, the camel train.

For the Jews, resisting as they did the use of royal titles already common among their neighbors, the "age of kings" still lay in the future. Instead, what now appeared in Israel was an institution rooted in the Mosaic tradition and adumbrating the later political roles of such mighty prophets as Samuel, Elijah, and Elisha. This was rule by judges, leaders in peace and war who claimed to have special guidance from the Lord God. The first such, Othniel son of Kenaz, was credited with throwing back a "Mesopotamian," that is, Aramean, invasion, emerging in the process as a new kind of Hebrew commander-in-chief.[3] His successor, Ehud of the tribe of Benjamin, carried out the first righteous assassination, defined as such by the Old Testament.

The precise date of this exploit is not known, but the author of the relevant account shows no uncertainty about what was done and what it achieved. According to scripture, the children of Israel "did what was evil in the sight of the Lord; and the Lord strengthened Eglon the king of Moab against [them]." [4] Eglon, leading a host composed of Moabites, Ammonites, and Amelekites, overran Israel from the east and proceeded to rule it for eighteen years. Only at the end of that time were his subjects finally vouchsafed a leader to free them from foreign oppression. Ehud the Benjamite, who had been commissioned as bearer of tribute to Moab, took along something else, a two-edged sword fully a cubit (twenty-one inches) in length. Having presented the specified gifts to Eglon, Ehud sent away his own retainers and then went back to the king, saying, "I have a mesage from God for you," whereupon he ran him through. The chronicler, meticulous in matters of physical detail, points out that the assassin was left-handed and his victim "a very fat man." Fleeing the scene, Ehud escaped to Israel with glad tidings of a liberation which reportedly lasted for eighty years.

Sad to relate, more exact dating indicates that in much less than those eight decades the Israelites were back doing "what was evil in the sight of the Lord." This time the chastiser sent against them was the king of Canaan, whose general Sisera overran the country and "oppressed the people of Israel cruelly for twenty years." [5] At the end of that term of suffering the prophetess Deborah, who was now "judging Israel," prevailed upon a general, Barak by name, to attack Sisera and all his chariots. Barak seems to have had some doubts about the project and finally agreed to march against the Canaanites only if Deborah came along. She did; and the Israelites won a great victory by the river Kishon, which Deborah, in her subsequent hymn of praise and thanks to the Lord, says reached flood stage at the crucial, divinely appointed moment.[6]

Following this battle there occurred the second case of tyrannicide celebrated in the Book of Judges. The defeated general, Sisera, trying to escape from the pursuing Israelites, trudged southward on foot into the land of the Kenites, west of the Dead Sea, seeking the tent of his ally Heber. When Sisera arrived, only Heber's wife, Jael, was at home. She invited Sisera in, gave him milk when he had asked for water, offered to stand guard at the door while he rested, and then, once he was sound asleep, took a hammer and a tent-peg and drove the latter through his temple into the ground. "So," to nobody's surprise, save obviously Sisera's, "he died." [7]

These related episodes, with females playing key roles—Deborah as a Jeanne d'Arc before the letter, Jael as the slayer of an alien tyrant—make clear the importance of their sex throughout the history of the ancient Jews. Their importance for my topic is no less clear. Some of the politically active women yet to be encountered will be righteous, others evil; but all will be formidable in their resolve.

Jael's act in particular was to have a powerful and continuing influence on the imaginations of writers and painters for many centuries to come. Take the most obvious example: Judith and her killing of Holofernes after a night together in his tent. It is a tale apocryphal in two senses: first, it is surely a fabrication; and second, it has been consigned by Judaic and Chris-

Judith with the Head of Holofernes,
by Bernardo Cavallino (1616–1656)

tian theology alike to the Apocrypha, beyond the scriptural pale. Popular imagination, however, has remained impervious to evidence that the Book of Judith cannot be dated earlier than the fourth century B.C. or that most authorities place it as late as the second.[8] No matter that it is impossible even to identify Holofernes with any known enemy of Israel. Was he an Assyrian, as is commonly assumed? If so, what was he doing in Palestine so many hundreds of years after all his troops had left? For poets, painters, and dramatists alike, the figure of the tousled heroine exhibiting a tyrant's newly severed head has been far more satisfying than the primitive story of Jael and Sisera, brutal in its simplicity, ambiguous in its motivation, and devoid, or nearly so, of sexual suggestion.

The other tale which, unlike that of Judith, really does belong to the twelfth century before the Christian era differs both in tone and in meaning from those that came before. It concerns the horrendous exploits of Abimelech, whose father, Gideon (more commonly called Jerubbaal), had been so great a judge that he had been offered the title of king over the Israelites.[9] He had declined the opportunity, but his son saw things differently. Abimelech after Jerubbaal's death agreed to be called "King of Shechem," after the hometown of his mother; and while this was only a local designation, its holder soon revealed notions of royal authority going far beyond the powers previously claimed by any judge. The late Gideon had left behind him no fewer than seventy sons born of his wives and concubines; but sixty-eight of these sons were quickly slain by brothers of the concubine from Shechem, mother of the new king. This massacre, since it was carried out by Abimelech's up-country uncles, was assumed to have been planned by Abimelech himself; further proof of his cruelty came at once, when he began to attack independent towns, slaughtering all opponents on whom he could lay hands.[10]

Abimelech's triumph, fortunately for just about everyone in Israel, turned out to be short-lived. He had taken the city of Thebez in one of his siege-massacres, driving many of the inhabitants to the top of a tower. When, however, the conqueror appeared at its foot, to direct the burning out of his enemies, "A certain woman threw an upper millstone upon Abimelech's head, and crushed his skull. Then he called hastily to the young man his armor-bearer, and said to him, 'Draw your sword and kill me, lest men say of me, "A woman killed him." ' And his young man thrust him through, and he died."[11] How Abimelech managed to shout these orders despite the adverse effects of a millstone, even an *upper* millstone, is not clear. In any event, the sanguinary "King of Shechem" was gone, and his slayer took her place in the register of female tyrannicides.

The sequel, too, deserves notice. In one of the earliest variations upon the theme of the doomed-prince-hidden-and-saved, another son of Gideon, Jotham by name, had been overlooked in Abimelech's fratricidal purge. On this survivor's recommendation, "God . . . made all the wickedness of the men of Shechem fall back upon their heads."[12] Whether Jehovah or a vengeful populace carried out the actual punishment of the uncles, the "curse of Jotham" signaled the end of a false start toward monarchy. What is significant from a political point of view is that the wretched memory of Abimelech lived on, discrediting the idea of kingship among the Jews for at least another century.

The Life and Times of Joab

About 1020 B.C., when Saul received the previously unused title of king over Israel, appeared the dawn of a new era. It was not a gentler time, and some people appear never to have stopped looking back nostalgically toward the rule of judges. Nevertheless, the issues posed for the Hebrews by the succession Saul–David–Solomon represented something undeniably different.

Nowhere do those issues appear more starkly than in the career, not of a Hebrew king, but of a soldier and counselor of kings, as told in the Second Book of Samuel. This Joab lived through parts of all three reigns. He was a son of David's sister Zeruaiah and an officer under Saul. He remained a prominent figure under both David and Solomon until the latter finally had him killed. Not least important, he participated in, or at least knew a great deal about, all the important political murders of that tumultuous time.

Joab makes his first appearance as a serious actor during the struggle for succession after the death of Saul. David's rival in that showdown, which came just before 1000 B.C., was Saul's only surviving and acknowledged son, the ineffectual Ishbosheth (or Eshbaal). The latter's principal asset was the loyalty of a veteran officer, Abner, whom one authority has called "the only capable person on the side of Saul's family."[13] It was Abner, not Joab, who had identified David for Saul, when the young man marched off with his slingshot to meet the Philistines; and it was Abner who had escorted the victor, carrying the head of Goliath, into the king's presence after the battle.[14] Despite his role in the elevation of David, however, the general never wavered in his loyalty to Saul's own son, whose army commander, or "captain of the host," Abner became when the succession struggle broke out. After the old king, beaten by the Philistines at Gilead, chose to fall on his sword, the southern tribes, those of Judah, declared for the hero David; but it was Abner's army that set Eshbaal over Samaria and the north, the future separate kingdom of Israel.[15]

At the time, concern for a distant future was scarcely the order of the day. The man of the hour was Joab, a military commander who defeated Abner and the enemies of David at Gibeon and sent his opponents fleeing for their lives. The soldier who ran fast enough to overtake Abner was Joab's own brother Asahel, youngest of the three sons of Zeruaiah. Brought to bay,

Abner turned and slew Asahel, purportedly in self-defense. Joab, as later events would prove, was not one to forget such things; but for the moment Abner rallied enough of his army to turn back the pursuing victors, and the blood feud had to be suspended.

There followed a curious interlude, cutting across this family quarrel between generals. Abner, with or without political motives, chose to take to bed Rizpah, a former concubine of Saul. It is abundantly clear from other episodes in the Old Testament that sexual intercourse with a royal mistress was regularly taken as a gesture symbolizing a claim to power. Thus, when Eshbaal learned of the affair a violent quarrel erupted, and Abner shortly announced that he was going over to the side of David.

Before this defection could be completed, sex again invaded politics; for the pretender informed Abner that the latter must arrange to have Michal, Saul's daughter, sent to David as his wife. Part of the justification given for David's demand was that he had earlier offered the lady marriage, bestowing as an engagement gift calculated to catch her attention the foreskins of a hundred captured Philistines.[16] This demand for Michal's person raised difficulties, for by this time she was married to one Paltiel, son of Laish. However, the thoroughly intimidated Eshbaal authorized her delivery to the camp of David, Paltiel was brusquely told by Abner to stop complaining, and Abner himself announced that David was now *his* king.

Reenter Joab, returning from a military tour to discover that David had not only accepted Abner's allegiance but also sent him north as a royal commander. Here was an unforeseen and dangerous political rival, as well as a personal enemy, and Joab wasted no time in addressing his new problem. Pretending to act in David's name, he called Abner back to Hebron, the temporary capital, met him at the gates of the town, asked him aside to talk quietly, and stabbed him to death. Though political concerns must have been at least equally important, Joab's explanation was that this act had at last avenged the death of his brother Asahel. David, for his part, denied all knowledge of the plot and delivered a fulsome lament at Abner's funeral. He also complained to his servants about "the sons of Zeruaiah," among them Joab and Abishai.[17]

Yet Joab, the eldest of those royal nephews, retained his military command—to David's good fortune as things turned out. It was Joab, more than anyone else, who was destined to suppress the most serious, as well as most famous, revolt launched against the king in the entire course of his reign: the conspiracy of Absalom. The Old Testament contains few characters more opaque than this third of David's sons, a young man able both to charm the crowd and to hold the unreasoning devotion of his father, yet a figure of shallow ambition and at best unreliable morals. It is no exaggeration to say that every story written since biblical times about the rebellion of a son, including William Faulkner's, has owed a debt to that of Absalom.

We first meet him engaged in a lurid family quarrel. His older brother Amnon had conceived a passion for their sister Tamar (half-sister certainly in Amnon's case, full sister perhaps in Absalom's). Feigning illness, so that Tamar was sent to prepare him food, he attempted to seduce her. Then, in the face of her shocked resistance, "being stronger than she, he forced her, and lay with her." [18] Thereafter, *he* ordered *her* out of his house. Tamar went, with ashes on her head, to the home of Absalom. The latter sheltered her but took no immediate action against his half-brother. David too, though reportedly angry when he heard the news of trouble among his children, did nothing about it. To some modern readers at least, it may come as a surprise to find that the inappropriate use of force, *not* the element of incest, was what offended Absalom, and his father as well, when confronted with the rape of Tamar. Despite religious taboos, incestuous relationships had no great shock effect upon a royal court teeming with wives and concubines, cousins and half-siblings.

Whatever the sources of his reaction to Tamar's plight, Absalom did watch for a chance to dispose of the culprit. After two years of waiting he persuaded his father to send all the brothers, taking a picnic lunch, to help with the shearing of sheep; then, assuring his own servants that it is easy to kill a man while his "heart is merry with wine," he had the unsuspecting Amnon stabbed to death.[19] Faced with urgent need to escape, in part because the first, garbled report to reach King David was that all of Absalom's brothers had been slain, the prodigal fled into Syria. There he remained for three years until Joab once more took center stage. Perceiving that David yearned to be reunited with his favorite son, the canny general arranged to provide his master with a moral and at least quasi-religious basis for relenting.

The scene that followed would make good theater. Indeed, it *was* good theater. Joab dispatched to the palace a "wise woman" from Tekoa, carefully briefed to tell the king a trumped-up story about two imaginary sons of her own. She begged protection for one of them, who she said had killed the other while they were working in the fields and who was now being threatened by the rest of his relatives. Once David had granted her suit she turned, without need for further explanation, to the matter of his own bereavement; by the time the day was over, he had called in Joab and ordered him to send for Absalom. The latter returned to Jerusalem from the east, though he was still forbidden to see the king.[20]

This state of affairs lasted for two years, during which Absalom worked hard at making himself admired by the populace for his beauty, virility, and seeming concern for the people.[21] As soon as he felt secure enough to do so, the prince summoned Joab to him, so that they might discuss a lifting of the irksome ban which still forbade him to enter the king's presence. Joab appears to have been playing a cautious game, for he ignored both the first and second of these summonses. Thereupon Absalom ordered his servants, possibly the same ones who had killed Amnon five years before, to burn Joab's barley field, which bordered on his own princely portion. Joab quite naturally came to Absalom's house to complain, and stayed to discuss the larger issue of an audience with the king. David, now urged by his best general and always tempted in any event to favor Absalom, agreed to receive his son.

The reconciliation was complete but short-lived. Absalom kept building up his own popularity, at the same time pressing his father to name him judge, a title having more than simply judicial significance.[22] After four years of preparation he obtained his father's permission to go worship the Lord in Hebron and set off from Jerusalem with agents going ahead to prepare the proclamation of his own kingship. He also called into his service a counselor of David, Ahithophel the Gilonite, an Iago-like figure in his own right. When news of the uprising in support of Absalom reached Jerusalem, David fled toward Jordan, naming ten of his concubines to keep up the royal household while he was away.

Appropriation of concubines seen as a political act is nowhere more emphatically illustrated than in Absalom's action—taken on Ahithophel's advice—soon after the rebel forces had occupied Jerusalem. The pretender at once proceeded to demonstrate how completely he had supplanted his father by copulating in public with all of the ten concubines David had left behind to maintain his residence. "They pitched a tent for Absalom upon the roof," the Old Testament tersely informs us, "and Absalom went into his father's concubines in the sight of all Israel." [23]

This exercise in image-building completed, the young prince began to seek council concerning further steps to be taken in the civil war. Ahithophel urged hot pursuit of David, with himself in command of the rebel army. The king, however, had taken the precaution of sending back into Jerusalem men loyal to the royal cause, though they professed allegiance to Absalom. One of these was a veteran counselor, Hushai, who persuaded Absalom to overrule Ahithophel's counsel and to take personal charge of his own forces. Hushai then sent other loyalists, the priests Zadok and Abiathar, to warn David that in view of the impending attack he should take his troops east across the Jordan.

Joab, all this time, stood by Absalom, the pretender he himself had managed to have called back from exile. However, the coalition of rebel leaders was showing signs of disintegration. Ahithophel, upon learning that he would not lead the host, went home to his city of Gilon and hanged himself. Joab, though never self-destructive, also responded angrily to the announcement that Amasa, a son of King David's sister Abigail, would be field commander of Absalom's army. What Joab did recalls the action of his old enemy, Abner, years before. Denouncing his ill-treatment by an ingrate, he went over to David's side and was shortly given command of a third of the royal forces.

Ignoring these defections, Absalom and Amasa marched out of Jerusalem and crossed the Jordan in pursuit of the king. In the forest of Ephraim, the decisive battle was joined between Amasa's army and the forces now led by Joab. It resulted in a crushing defeat for the rebels, and though Amasa escaped, his prince did not. As a matter of fact, the fleeing Absalom in his final appearance achieved a truly memorable level of bad luck: "Absalom was riding upon his mule, and the mule went under the thick branches of a great oak, and his head caught fast in the oak, and he was left hanging, between heaven and earth, while the mule that was under him went on." [24] Suspended in midair, the prince had to await the consequences. These included his being identified by a passerby, the arrival of Joab, and the latter's businesslike disposal of Absalom with three stabs to the heart. The body was thrown into a pit in the forest, and the Davidite forces were ordered to cease their pursuit of rebel survivors, presumably to let the work of reconciliation begin. Informed of his son's death, the king fell into a fit of weeping: "O my son Absalom, my son, my son Absalom! Would I had died instead of you, O Absalom, my son, my son!" [25] Not even Joab's indignant but sensible reminder that this was precisely what the young man too had had in mind could stifle the father's famous lamentation.

Absalom's rebellion had one more chapter, in effect a violent epilogue. Joab, loyal defender of his king—if not unwaveringly at least in time to qualify as the military savior of the royal cause—was soon to receive yet another rude shock. For David proceeded not only to forgive his nephew, the rebel commander Amasa, but also to make him captain of the host in Joab's place, and this even before returning to Jerusalem from the battlefield of Ephraim. The older general's reaction was predictable. When Amasa's suppression of a revolt by Sheba the Benjamite appeared to lag behind schedule, the king decided to send out Joab with a supporting army. Joab caught up with his rival—once under Absalom and now again under David—"at the great stone which is in Gibeon" and, feigning a kiss of welcome, seized Amasa's beard and killed him with a sword. [26]

Joab, whatever weakness he may have exhibited for vendettas, was an able commander. He now pursued the rebel leader, Sheba, caught up with and besieged him in the city of Abel, and arranged with the terrified inhabitants to cut off the head of the fugitive and throw it over the wall. The king's army then returned to Jerusalem in triumph. [27]

Like so many other figures of violence, whether fictional or historical, Joab showed a marked capacity for first helping, then in due course alienating, the very people who would eventually contribute to his downfall. Consider certain of his earlier services to King David. When that ruler with an ever-roving eye saw Bathsheba bathing in a place overlooked by the palace roof, her husband, Uriah, was actually serving under Joab's command in Ammon, at the siege of Rabbah. It was therefore Joab who, on his master's orders, sent Uriah to "the forefront of the hardest fighting," there to be killed.[28] The irony of the tale of course lies in the fact that this left David free to bring Bathsheba into his house and to "beget of her a son," the future King Solomon. And it was Solomon who would destroy Joab.

The old soldier, save for his brief enlistment under Absalom, had been faithful, not to say accommodating, to David the king. As the monarch sank into his last illness, however, the question of succession posed difficulties for Joab, as it did for everyone else involved. Of David's sons the eldest, Amnon, had been killed by Absalom and Absalom by Joab, while Chileab, second in age, simply disappeared from history. This seemed to leave the fourth son, Adonijah, as heir apparent. So, at any rate, things appeared to Joab, captain of the host, as they did to David's old supporter against Absalom, the priest Abiathar, and—needless to say—to Adonijah himself.[29] All three, however, underestimated the power of Bathsheba and of the prophet Nathan, who now joined forces to remind the dying king of his promise to make Solomon successor to the throne. David formally acknowledged that pledge before death brought an end to his forty-year reign, and Solomon was duly anointed king. As for Adonijah's encampment outside the city, it immediately broke up at the sound of the coronation horns. There was no repetition of Absalom's futile revolt.

Solomon announced that he would spare Adonijah, "if he prove to be a worthy man," but no such assurance was given Joab or Abiathar.[30] It is a revealing but not very flattering fact that David on his deathbed advised Solomon to destroy Joab, citing the murders of Abner and Amasa, even though the king had never seen fit to punish those acts in his own time. Still, despite his father's counsel, Solomon was not ready to move against the old retainer without clearer grounds than the admonitions of a dying monarch. The pretext, when it came, took the by now familiar form of Adonijah's invading the royal harem. Specifically, he went to Bathsheba, told her that he coveted Abishag, a former concubine of David, as a wife, and asked the queen mother to intervene with Solomon on behalf of his suit. Bathsheba, whether innocently or not, carried this plea to the king, who flew into a rage. Was this not a move by Adonijah to possess a woman of the king's own bed and thus raise himself to power after the fashion of other pretenders past?

Moving swiftly, the monarch launched the type of purge familiar to oriental courts throughout recorded history. He called in a loyal general, Benaiah son of Jehoiada, and ordered him to slay Adonijah. Next he summoned the priest Abiathar and banished him from the court. Finally, when Benaiah returned from dispatching Adonijah, he was instructed to kill Joab as well. That veteran of violence around the throne must have guessed his time had come, for he "fled to the tent of the Lord and caught hold of the horns of the altar."[31] Benaiah hesitated in so holy a place and went back to apprise Solomon of the dilemma; but the king had no doubts, so Benaiah returned to the temple and slew Joab with his sword. Thereafter, Benaiah, on royal orders, murdered still another past enemy of David, one Shimei who had cursed the king during Absalom's revolt. "So the kingdom was established in the hand of Solomon." [32]

It would be hard to find, even in the grimmest of Greek tragedies, a tale more steeped in cruelty and in the brooding sense of inevitability than that of Israel's first kings. At the same time, it would be unfair to view the reign of David in these terms only, ignoring his flashes of courage in adversity or the spiritual qualities and sheer beauty of the Psalms. By the same token, Solomon's reign was destined to contain better things than feigned anger over a concubine, and the brutal slaying of his brother and of his dead father's old friends and unpunished enemies. Nevertheless, without this look at the career and adventures of Joab, the significance of the Old Testament's place in the history of political murder might easily elude our grasp.

Division and Fall of the Monarchy

Just as the main themes of the age of judges were supplanted by those of the age of three kings, so both those dramas differed from what was to follow. This segment began with Solomon's death in 922 B.C. and ended with the Babylonian conquest of Jerusalem over three centuries later. In place of heroic judges such as Deborah and Gideon, instead of violent but usually loyal soldiers in the mold of Abner, Joab, and Benaiah, we now confront a raging general, Jehu, and the dark horror contained in the stories of Jezebel and Athaliah, queen-priestesses of Baal.

The central fact of Palestine's history during the ninth and eighth centuries before Christ is the split between the southern kingdom, Judah (with Edom), and the northern secessionist kingdom of Israel, including rich Samaria. At Solomon's death the Judaeans remained loyal to the Davidite line. Israel, on the contrary, revolted at once—apparently releasing ill-contained resentment against long years of royal impositions—and elected as king a successful army commander, Jeroboam, like Napoleon Bonaparte some twenty-seven hundred years later just back from campaigning in Egypt. Thereafter, Judah was to remain comparatively stable for a much longer time than rebellious Israel, the latter destined to stagger through a series of crises.

One reason for this was that the northern kingdom lived under a turbulent succession of rival warlords. When Jeroboam died in 901 B.C., his son Nadab was murdered within a year by Baasha, an officer in the siege camp before Gibbethon. Religion's role is not made explicit here, beyond the scriptural assurance that Nadab, like his father before him, had done "what was evil in the sight of the Lord." [33] The amphictyonic role, on the other hand—the weight given to tribal decisions—runs throughout the saga of Israel's kings. Baasha, however he defined legitimacy, religious or consensual, killed Nadab and reigned in his stead. "And as soon as he was king, he killed all the house of Jeroboam." [34] Although successful in wiping out the traces of that brief dynasty, Baasha had less luck in founding one of his own. At his death his son Elah tried to succeed him, only to be killed almost at once by still another military commander, Zimri, who thereupon did to Baasha's other offspring precisely what that worthy had done to Nadab's.

Zimri, a usurper with no prophet to vouch for him, was easily defeated by Omri, captain of the host, and in despair took his own life, leaving Omri free to consolidate his own family in power. This he did, though it required a civil war to complete the task. The new king and his son Ahab after him managed to give Israel a couple of decades of the nearest thing to domestic peace it had known since the division of Solomon's kingdom. In 850 B.C., however, Ahab was killed in battle; and his first son, Ahaziah, died in an accident a year later, to be succeeded by his brother Jehoram. The stage was set for the Omrides' own debacle. [35]

Several causes converged to produce Jehoram's ruin. One was that the new ruler impressed no one as a soldier. The war against the Moabites, earlier conquered by his father but now in the field again, went badly from the start; and to this danger was added a growing threat from Syria. Another difficulty was that certain conservative denominations, notably that of the nomadic Rechabites, had opposed the monarchy since the days of Solomon. Most important of all, however, was the judgment of the prophets, expressed in the fiery messages of Elijah and, after him, Elisha. Their repudiation of the Omrides is easily understood if one considers the defiance of Jehovah shown by the queen mother, Jezebel.

This daughter of the king of Tyre and Sidon had been a priestess of Asherah (Astarte) in her Phoenician homeland. When she married King Ahab, she brought to Israel not only the cult of that lurid goddess but also temples raised to a still mightier figure of pagan worship, Baal himself. [36] Whether her royal husband abandoned completely his personal allegiance to the Lord of the Jews is not clear, but he did respect his wife's religion and gave orders to execute her wishes. When her influence not only continued but actually increased under the rule of her two sons, pious indignation against the queen mother soared out of control. Was this not the whore-priestess of the fertility goddess, Asherah, whose temple housed ritual prostitution? Was it not the wicked queen who had contrived to have Naboth of Jezreel stoned to death on false charges of blasphemy and treason, so that his vineyard might pass into the hands of King Ahab? Had she not seen to the hounding of the prophet Elijah into oblivion in the desert? [37]

Her son King Jehoram seems to have had some inkling of a political and religious crisis in the making. Early in his reign, to be sure, he had done "what was evil in the sight of the Lord"; but to his credit, in the eyes of the devout, could be set the fact that he had "put away the pillar of Baal which his father had made." [38] He was, however, no man to stand up to Jezebel. And it seems likely in any event that things had gone too far for the dynasty to be saved by half-measures. The end of the Omrides, as recounted in the Second Book of Kings, was both swift and terrible.

In 842 B.C., urged on by Elisha, successor to the prophet Elijah, yet another military commander decided to act. This was Jehu, whom Elisha had arranged to have proclaimed and anointed king in the eastern army camp while King Jehoram, wounded in one of his many aimless battles, was recuperating back home in Israel. Amid the cheers of the soldiers, Jehu set off for Jezreel, his intended victim's place of convalescence. There another Jewish ruler, Ahaziah, king of Judah and Jehoram's ally against the Arameans, strode forth with his royal kinsman to welcome the presumably loyal general. Jehu, meeting them before the walls, first killed Jehoram with bow and arrow, then ordered Ahaziah pursued and slain as well. The pretender next entered Jezreel, had the queen mother Jezebel thrown to her death from a window, and proceeded to slaughter the surviving relatives of Jehoram, along with all members of the court there present. The house of Omri was no more. Followers of Baal, however, still worshiped him in Samaria, the capital; so Jehu took his army there, massacred the Baalites, and demolished their temple. For more than a quarter-century, with the blessing of the prophet Elisha but obviously without support from either Phoenician or Judean allies against Syrian pressure, Jehu would retain his precarious place on the throne.

The story of Israel's destruction as an independent state requires at least summary reference to what happened in its sister kingdom, Judah. The southern realm, possessed of mighty Jerusalem and its heights, less torn by the tribal and sectarian strife that kept the Israelites of Samaria in turmoil, seems relatively calm—or did until the period just described. As noted earlier, Judah had stayed with descendants of David and Solomon for their royal succession. Instead of the continual military coups and purges in the north, Judeans had witnessed less violence in the form of coups and murders, in fact enjoying relative stability throughout the long reigns of Asa (913–873 B.C.) and Jehoshophat (873–849). When the latter died, however, there ensued a time of troubles, responding at least in part to events in Israel.

King Jehoshophat, though sworn to military collaboration with Israel's Omride monarchy, never wavered in his apparent devotion to Jehovah. He was a ruler as careful in his fiscal and judicial as in his religious policies. Thus, he had earned, and received, the approval of his subjects, including their priests and prophets. The one mistake with which the scriptures charge him—and it was a fateful one—grew out of the alliance with Israel: he married his son, another and different Jehoram, to Athaliah, a princess of the Israelite ruling house and a kinswoman of Jezebel. [39] It was she who was widely suspected of inciting her husband to have all his brothers killed when he mounted Jehosophat's throne in 849.[40] Whether she was truly to blame or whether that blood purge (mentioned only once in the Bible) took place at all, there seems to be no doubt that she brought the Phoenician worship of Baal into Jerusalem itself.

Whatever the exact nature of her previous crimes, the queen of Judah faced a crisis when her husband, Jehoram, died after a reign of barely seven years and was succeeded by his young son Ahaziah. The latter survived only a few months after his accession until, as described above, he was cut down at Jezreel by Jehu's bowmen and his body carried home to be buried in Jerusalem.[41] Athaliah, either out of ambition or from fear of her dead husband's and son's kinsmen, moved quickly to secure the throne. She declared herself ruler over Judah, ordered all remaining heirs of the house of David summarily murdered, and went on vigorously promoting the worship of Baal while persecuting the people of Jehovah. The resemblance of this coup d'état to the earlier performance of Jezebel in the north is evident. So is the familiar theme of yet another escape by a single prince from a mass assassination.[42]

This time it was the child Joash, rescued by his aunt Jehoshabeath, wife of the chief priest. Spirited away first to a bedchamber during the slaughter of Davidite princes, he was kept safe in the Temple, where Queen Athaliah the Baalite was not likely to come visiting. When Joash reached the age of seven the chief priest himself, Jehoiada, took over his wife's task, presenting this only male descendant of David to the officers of the army as their rightful king. Athaliah made an appearance in time to cry treason, but as a woman, a usurper, and a follower of false gods, she had no real chance to retain power in conservative Judah. "So all the people of the land rejoiced; and the city was quiet; after Athaliah had been slain with the sword at the king's house." [43] Once again Jehovah stood triumphant over Baal.

According to scripture, the rescued prince ruled for forty years, initially under the watchful eye of Jehoiada. However, this seemingly happy state was not destined to last throughout the reign. After his stern adviser, the chief priest, died in the fullness of years, Joash turned to more relaxed religious behavior. Equally serious, he proved to be a poor general, forced almost at once to begin paying tribute to Syrian invaders. At last, he, too, died by the sword, reportedly murdered by his own army officers in 800 B.C. For more than two centuries after this anticlimactic epilogue to the story of Athaliah and her struggles the Judean monarchy would live on, beleaguered by various enemies, until the capture of Jerusalem by the Babylonians in 587 B.C. Here there is no reason to follow its history any further, beyond remarking that periodic murders continued to occur for as long as remnants of the kingdom survived.

Much the same observation might describe Israel's later decades as well, except that here the record ends more abruptly, amid even greater violence than is to be found in Judah. So far as ancient Israel (that is, the northern monarchy) was concerned, the chronicle ends almost a century and a half before the fall of Jerusalem, and does so with yet one more series of atrocities.

These events took place against a background of impending disaster at the hands of Assyrian conquerors from beyond the eastern lands of Aram and his seed. It is no doubt a coincidence, but not an insignificant one, that the final rash of assassinations in sovereign Israel began at almost the same time as the accession of a new and energetic Assyrian king. He was Tiglath-pileser III, destined to revive his previously weakened empire and to launch the westward drive that in a few years would reduce the Israelites to tributary status and soon thereafter occupy their capital city.

Just as this ominous force began to gather in the valleys of the Tigris and Euphrates, the long reign of Jehu's heir, Jeroboam II (786–747 B.C.), finally reached its end. He seems to have been an able king, at any rate a successful general; but for his heirs and for his people, the way ahead lay steeply downward. His son Zechariah, within six months of assuming the throne, was murdered by Shallum son of Jabesh, who was himself assassinated a month later by Menahem son of Gadi.[44] Little is known of these men, their backgrounds, motives, or support; but Menahem managed to rule for eight years, in the course of which he sought to buy off the Assyrians, promising Tiglath-pileser annual tribute to be raised by a land tax in Israel.[45] If Menahem hoped thereby to establish a lasting dynasty, he miscalculated badly. After his own death in 738 and the accession of his son Pekahia, the latter was killed almost at once by any army officer, Pekah son of Remaliah.[46]

From here on the denouement comes quickly. Six years after murdering the son of Menahem, King Pekah was slain by Hoshea son of Elah, presumably another soldier, who abandoned his predecessor's brief resistance to the Assyrians and surrendered to them most of what was left of his nation's territory.[47] Even Hoshea, the kingdom's last native ruler, could not resist the temptation to defy the foreign conquerors when informed that Tiglath-pileser had died and was to be followed on the throne of Ashur and Babylon by his son Shalmaneser V. Hoshea's disastrous strategy was to withhold the annual tribute and to seek an alliance with an all-but-impotent Egypt. When Shalmaneser launched his inevitable assault on these enemies in the west, Hoshea sued for peace and was himself imprisoned by the unforgiving Assyrian. Whether it was the short-lived Shalmaneser himself (died 722 B.C.) or his successor, Sargon II, who finally captured the city of Samaria, its fall marked the end of the northern kingdom. Pursuing the policy of deportation already established in the conquest of Damascus and other strongholds— one which would be imitated by the Babylonians as well in the more famous "captivity" of the Judeans years later—the Assyrian victor shipped thousands of Samarians eastward to Mesopotamia.[48]

Governance under the Lord

This chapter has relied heavily on fragments of narrative to be found in the Old Testament, a source that will be used again later with reference to Palestine in the time of the Maccabees and Romans. For now it is enough to have pondered the books of Judges, Samuel, Kings, and Chronicles. Together they constitute a rich mine of examples, exhortations, and explanations that for three millennia have influenced thinking about murder and statecraft throughout much of the world. Butterfield's recognition of "something different" which began with the Hebrews' telling of history is surely valid. The place of factual accuracy in all this must nevertheless be termed problematic at best. For example, the heroism of Judith is a creation of fable, not of history; yet its power to influence minds and imaginations has in large measure rendered irrelevant its apocryphal nature. Historical or imaginary, the annals of the ancient Jews are at once circumstantial and provocative. Their chief weakness for the student of political homicide may lie in the very profusion of murders of invaders and brothers, kings and pretenders, occurring at a rate that threatens to outrun the observer's memory.

A few points deserve to be made, however. In many of the assassinations discussed here the motives were not in any meaningful sense "political" at all. Time after time personal passions, differing pieties, and the answering of personal calls from the Lord God Jehovah have seemed to leave little room for the demands of a body politic.

In terms of political criteria yet to be defined in Greece, the writers of the Hebrew scriptures doubtless merit the label "barbarous," so quickly applied by the thinkers of Hellas to anyone who did not speak their language and to anything that lay outside their world of ideas. To what extent was such dismissal justified? The answer cannot be categorical. By Greco-Roman standards Jehovah's children produced no definitions of legitimacy, leadership, or representation likely to sustain enduring institutions of state. They did not, for example, produce any coherent notion of how authority might be transferred in the face of conflicting personal interests. Where then is to be found the contribution they made to arguments over assassination?

Perhaps their greatest significance in this regard lay in what they did not even try to say about it. In this, as in some other important respects, the ancient Jews were less nearly unique than they and their opponents alike would have us believe. There was, for instance, no significant difference between their ruthless treatment of prisoners and the standard practice followed by their enemies. Similarly, the murder of sibling princes, potential heirs to a throne, was no Hebrew peculiarity. It was a common expedient among the peoples of antiquity who believed in hereditary succession, and it continued to be the custom of the Ottoman Empire well into modern times. The harsh world of the Middle East has never left much room for familial affection.

Once that has been said, the Bible deserves to be viewed as the source of several important ideas about murder and politics. One in particular. What makes the Old Testament secure in its condemnation of idolatrous foes is the unswerving devotion to a transcendental source of judgment—the Word of the Lord, pronounced by a bearer, self-announced but necessarily acknowledged by some consensus. It may be a priest of the hierarchy who assumes this role, as when Abiathah encourages Absalom to rebel against King David or when Jehoiada grooms Joash to destroy the power over Judah of the idolatrous Queen Athaliah. More often it is a prophet, raised by his own self-confidence and eloquence, who challenges one ruler or legitimates another's right to govern. When Nathan intervenes with King David on the latter's deathbed, it is Solomon, choice of the prophet (and the queen mother), who is named heir apparent, overriding the rights of his elder brother. When Elijah is driven into exile by Jezebel, he leaves behind a call for her destruction and that of the house of Omri, to be carried out by Elisha and Jehu.

All of this could and did contribute to the creation of great literature. Still more important in other terms, it produced the most emphatic and lasting assertion of monotheism as a guide to public action the world has ever known. But it represented a political theory only to the extent that theocracy is recognized as a self-validating form of government. Even for those who accept that form, it is necessary to acknowledge the capriciousness and unaccountability inherent in eulogies or condemnations of rulers when uttered by prophets. Ahead, in the clearer, colder light of Greek thought and then Roman practice, lay formulations which the ancient Israelites, despite the grandeur of their epic, would scarcely have recognized, much less accepted.

2

The Greeks

Darkness and Light in Hellas

On a southeastern headland of Attica stands the famous temple of Sunium built to Poseidon, god of the sea. Raised in Periclean times, around the middle of the fifth century B.C., it was not yet standing when the Assyrian armies swarmed over Israel or when most of the other events of the previous chapter were taking place among the Jews. Thus, though the temple's once-white marble has been darkened by time, Sunium may still be seen as an expression of novelty in its own age. The very fact that it honored not only a deity but also the ships and men of Athens, victors over the Persian fleet at Salamis, made the temple a human monument, rather than solely a place of worship. More than that, especially when seen for the first time by a traveler approaching Greece by boat, the graceful pillars have the power to evoke an insistent sense of change. With silent eloquence they suggest an atmosphere far different from that of exhortation, condemnation, dedicated monotheism, and righteous violence portrayed in the Old Testament. Presumably not every observer shares that sensation; but anyone who does is bound to ask whence it comes.

Part of the answer lies in the impression of *light*—intense, penetrating, even pitiless—cutting through the somber canvas of events that occurred in this land as they did in other parts of the antique world. Admittedly, such an impression may obscure more than it illuminates. The Greeks' impulses, like their assumptions and their motives, are not always so clear as a modern observer might wish. Behind even the most compelling passages of Thucydides and Aristotle there is always some murkiness, some depths we plumb, if at all, only with the greatest difficulty. Yet, in combination, the voices of classical Greece tell us so much more about the action and thought of their civilization than we shall ever know about those of their predecessors and contemporaries elsewhere that the Hellenic achievement shines forth as

25

matchless. And because so much modern knowledge of ancient Greece relies on Athenian writings and inscriptions, art and architecture, as well as because it was Athens that presented mankind with the oldest fully reported experiment in constitutional government, it is only natural to turn first to the Agora, the Acropolis, and the Academy.

The Strange Case of Athens

Almost at once there appears a surprising fact. The famous age of Pericles, indeed the entire fifth century B.C.—though it began with the Persian invasion, was filled with civic turmoil, and ended in the deadly war against Sparta and her allies—produced in Athens almost no political murder at all. Major figures rose and fell on shifting waves of public opinion. Violent death, however, was not the standard penalty for defeat. Cimon, Pericles, Alcibiades, all had to face threats of trial, ostracism, exile—in short, loss of power—but none of their stormy careers ended either in execution or in assassination. How can one explain this? Why does Athens in the Golden Age present us with the first of those major remissions, to borrow a medical term, in the otherwise malignant history of man's readiness to kill for "reasons of state"?

One way to approach the question is to consider the most famous assassination in all of Greek history, just a few years before the start of the century in question. The story begins in 527 B.C., when Pisistratus, tyrant of Athens, fell sick and died after two decades in power, leaving three sons as heirs to his authority. While restoring order to Attica and confronting the threat of a Persian onslaught, the old man had clung stubbornly to a policy of peace with neighboring Greek states and vigorous encouragement of Athenian commerce. His successes could not be denied, but neither could his autocratic suppression of popular liberties and his banishment of numerous political opponents, including especially the aristocratic clan of Alcmeonids.

Exactly how his sons Hippias, Hipparchus, and Thessalus divided the power he had left them remains a matter of dispute among ancient writers. Some treat Hippias, the eldest, as virtually an autocrat, alone at the top. Others suggest that all three shared responsibility in a triumvirate of sorts. Still a third view, that of Herodotus writing some years later, is that primacy lay with Hippias, but that at times the second son, Hipparchus, also exercised considerable power in his own name.[1] It is Hipparchus whose assassination concerns us.

The history of that event appears first in the form of a highly colored legend. According to tradition, Hipparchus was a tyrant stabbed to death in 514 B.C. by two heroic friends of freedom, Harmodius and Aristogiton. His slayers were cruelly executed for their courage; but after the defeat of the other sons of Pisistratus a few years later, a statue of the tyrannicides was erected, reputedly the earliest Greek representation honoring not gods but mortals.[2] How a more skeptical and ultimately more informed view of the episode emerged over the next couple of centuries is an important case study of Greek political and historical analysis.

The process of correction seems to have begun about seventy-five years after Hipparchus' death. It was then that Herodotus referred to the victim not as a full-fledged tyrant but merely as "son of Pisistratus and brother of Hippias the despot."[3] Note that Herodotus in writing this did not soften the judgment against Pisistratid rule; but he went on to make a significant revision in the previously accepted estimate of the deed's political effect. Speaking of the Alcmeonids and their decisive role, he concluded that "it was they who freed Athens much more than did Harmodius and Aristogiton, [who] did but enrage the rest of Pisistratus' kin by killing Hipparchus, and did nought to end the rule of the rest of them."[4] This squares with the record of events, which saw Hippias crush the revolt of 514 without difficulty, only to be deposed four years later by the Alcmeonidae and their Spartan allies.

Herodotus showed why the victorious enemies of Hippias were moved to resurrect the memory of Harmodius and Aristogiton, but he did nothing to elucidate the motives of the assassins themselves. That task was left for Thucydides, writing near the end of the fifth century and seeking to understand the political history of Athens before the terrible Peloponnesian War in which it, and he, found themselves embroiled. This further revision expressed both its author's dislike of sentimental fables and his objections to violence directed at public officials.[5] As a result, the account of Hipparchus' murder provided by Thucydides differs from the legendary version far more sharply than does the summary left behind by Herodotus.

According to Thucydides, relying on documents in combination with a critical use of oral tradition, Harmodius and Aristogiton had been moved neither by partriotism nor by love of liberty but by the passions born of a homosexual triangle. Like the older historian, he observes that Hippias rather than Hipparchus had been the actual tyrant of Athens, in most respects at any rate.[6] He then takes up the course of events. Harmodius, a handsome youth beloved of the older, less aristocratic Aristogiton, had attracted the attention of Hipparchus. In repelling Hipparchus' advances, Harmodius assumed that he was risking the vengeance not only of his pursuer but of Hippias as well. As Thucydides points out, the Pisistratids were not much given to acts of violence; but what Hipparchus had recourse to instead may well have been even more provocative, given the sensitivity of his society where points of honor and status were involved. He chose to use his power as a marshal of the great festival of the Panathanaea to denounce a sister of Harmodius, in public, as unworthy to carry a sacred basket in the procession which would mark its close. That, says Thucydides, was enough

Harmodius and Aristogiton

to convince the lovers, previously frightened but now outraged, that they must act, making such use as they could of the festive excitement.

At this point the narrative, so lucid in most respects, becomes briefly confusing. For Thucydides writes that Harmodius and Aristogiton intended to attack Hippias, the real tyrant, while he was watching the procession form at the so-called Ceramicus, outside the city. If their motives were indeed personal and their hatred directed at Hipparchus, why strike at his elder brother? The question, left unanswered, appears to challenge the writer's contention that political motives had no place in the drama. One could, however, imagine that the murderers were afraid to punish Hipparchus without first eliminating his brother, their intended victim's most dangerous ally. Certainly any other course threatened to call down upon them a terrible vengeance; and that, as things turned out, is what did ensue.

Arriving at the Ceramicus and finding Hippias not merely surrounded by guards but actually questioning one of their coconspirators, Harmodius and Aristogiton, Thucydides tells us, assumed themselves betrayed. Impulsively they rushed back into the city, found Hipparchus near the Leocorium, and stabbed him to death. Was this a rational response to having seen the older brother in full command and, so they thought, forewarned of the uprising? Perhaps, if sharing the fantasy of many later assassins, the two still hoped to set off a popular uprising against the tyrant and thus save their own lives. Instead, Hippias promptly disarmed all suspicious-looking members of the civic militia and assumed personal charge of the search for Aristogiton (Harmodius having already been killed by the crowd when he was seized at the Leocorium).[7] Aristogiton was soon captured and, in Thucydides' laconic conclusion, "not very gently handled."[8] According to Aristotle, in his still later reconstruction, the elder assassin suffered long torture, in the course of which he implicated many alleged collaborators among the city's leading families. Finally he was killed by Hippias in person.[9]

Although the tyrant had reestablished control over Athens, his new harshness perhaps contributed to the reaction which overthrew him only a few years later. In that sense the episode may, after all, despite Thucydides' dismissal of the slayers and their motives, deserve attention from students of Athenian political history. The reference to Aristotle is in itself enough to show that the famous murder and its aftermath continued to interest Athenian thinkers throughout most of the century following the great historian's treatment. It also reveals a kind of analysis different from that in which Thucydides had been engaged.

Not that the philosopher from Stagira, drawn in his youth to Athens from that northern colonial town by the fame of Plato and his Academy, admired Harmodius and Aristogiton or despised the Pisistratids. On the latter point a mature Aristotle wrote of Pisistratus: "His administration was temperate, as has been said before, and more like constitutional government than a tyranny." [10] It is scarcely surprising to find the former counselor of Alexander the Great of Macedon less hostile to autocratic rule than Herodotus had been in the golden age of Athenian democracy. This is not yet the place, however, for examining the debate in Greece over just what constituted tyranny or what means might rightly be adopted to defeat it. For now, it is enough to remark Aristotle's contribution to the story of Athens' only memorable assassination.

To begin with, historians of philosophy and philosophers of history should be interested to note, he shows a lively interest in getting things straight. For example, it was neither Hippias nor Hipparchus, but the youngest brother, Thessalus, Aristotle concludes, whose violent, headstrong character was to blame for "all the evils . . . which befell the house." [11] He chides Thucydides for having said that Harmodius and Aristogiton had only a few confederates, when in fact they had quite a number.[12] Finally, he insists that Hippias had no need to disarm potential dissidents within the civic guard, "since at that time they did not bear arms in the processions." [13] What then, beyond corrections, did Aristotle bring to the legend of Harmodius and Aristogiton? In order to appreciate his full contribution we have first to ponder the record of Greek experience both within and beyond the narrow confines of Attica.

After the expulsion of Hippias in 510, the triumphant Alcmeonids moved at once to institute a series of democratic reforms. They reduced the power of aristocratic families (other than their own, of course), established the *demes* as township political units, and created an expanded council of Five Hundred. The head of their clan, Cleisthenes, took effective control, and his model, one of authority calling for mass support, was not lost on his descendant Pericles. In spite of the disruption brought by the Persian Wars, old issues of the oligarchy versus the people and of civil constitution versus military dominance were still very much alive in the 460s. By then the ideal of the hero-general, the *strategos autokrator,* was Cimon, the Athenian field commander since 476, when Themistocles had been dismissed. A gifted soldier and unchallenged spokesman for the aristocratic faction, Cimon in effect ruled the city.[14] In 463, however, despite his victorious siege of the island of Thasos, he was brought to trial in Athens on charges of having accepted bribes from the ruler of Macedon. He was acquitted, but the emergence of the Alcmeonid Pericles as leading spokesman for the prosecution signaled new directions in Athenian politics.

Cimon's downfall came two years later, not because of charges of corruption but from a dispute over military alliances and strategy. In the Peloponnesus, Sparta was faced with a mass revolt by its subjects, the helots. Cimon's decision was to go to the assistance of the Spartan rulers, allies he considered indispensable to Athenian security. In 462, having secured a favorable vote in the Council, he took an army south to join Lacedaemonians,

Plataeans, and Aeginetans in the siege of the rebel stronghold atop Mount Ithomé.[15] The Athenian popular party, led by Ephialtes, clung to the view that Sparta and its leaders were unreliable and that the Athenian hoplites, or heavy infantry, had in any case no business serving in the Peloponnesus.

Ephialtes had lost the Council's initial debate over dispatching that expedition, but he won the subsequent campaign for popular support. The Spartan government, for reasons difficult to reconstruct, abruptly dismissed Cimon and his army of four thousand men before Ithomé. Thus, the *ephors* of Sparta, although this can hardly have been what they intended, overturned their political allies in Athens. The Athenian Council and Assembly angrily voted to withdraw from the anti-Persian league and to form an alliance with Thessaly, as well as with Argos, Sparta's foe in the Peloponnesus. In the same wave of indignation, Cimon was formally ostracized. With its leader in exile, the oligarchic party fell into disarray. Notice, however, that through all this not a single attack against a political leader had occurred.

The stage was now set for Ephialtes to introduce his democratic reforms, resuming the efforts of Cleisthenes several decades before. The new leader brought charges against numerous members of the aristocratic law court, the Areopagus, stripped that body of jurisdiction over all cases save those of murder, and divided its previous powers between the Council of Five Hundred and the Assembly.[16] Before he could pursue his program further, however, Ephialtes was himself struck down by one Aristodicus of Tanagra. The assassin almost certainly acted on behalf of the secret societies of oligarchs. The result, however, not for the first or last time in history, turned out to be the opposite of the one he and his sponsors had hoped to achieve. For it was Pericles, leader of the popular faction, who now stepped into control of the government, beginning more than thirty years in the course of which he would combine the administrative vigor of Pisistratus with the popularity both Cleisthenes and the fallen Ephialtes had sought.[17]

Now is the time, before looking beyond Athens, to ask why that city-state witnessed so few political murders. Something must surely be said about institutionalized alternatives. Trial, dismissal by vote of the Council and/or the Assembly, ostracism proposed by any citizen—all these were potential threats to the position of a leader. At times they were misused, but they were safety valves for the registering of opposition without resort to poison or the knife. The two assassinations that did occur are instructive in this regard. Hipparchus was killed by enemies at once resentful and frightened, personal foes who seem to have had no settled intention of killing his brother Hippias for reasons of state. Ephialtes in turn was the victim of patrician wrath, engendered by anti-aristocratic reforms, which would have denied his opponents a fair, nonviolent hearing before the Areopagus.

Institutional provisions cannot channel all forms of hostility and rebellion into orderly channels; but they can help. Perhaps most important in the

Athenian experience was a set of emerging habits of mind, and hence of behavior. Even Pisistratus and his sons after him are described as quite restrained, generally exiling their enemies instead of killing them. Ephialtes and Pericles did not ask for the death of their great opponent, Cimon, once they had defeated him in the political arena. Neither Herodotus nor Thucydides nor Aristotle showed any subsequent inclination to romanticize assassination. Among them, only Aristotle even bothered to express implied disapproval of the way in which the Aristogiton died: Hippias "lost control of himself and snatched out his dagger and dispatched him." [18]

Colonial Tyrants: Phalaris of Acragas

Athens, for all its elegance, was not immune to outbursts of cruelty. Thucydides' account of the Melian debate, to cite a famous instance, reveals naked power, rationally explained to be sure, but then applied with utter ruthlessness against a defeated island people at the mercy of the Athenians.[19] At almost the same time, however, in the midst of the Peloponnesian War, there were signs that his compatriots were capable of registering disgust at betrayal and brutality, whoever was at fault. In 425 B.C., when a mob in Corcyra (Corfu) massacred its patrician prisoners after the latter had surrendered in return for the promise of a fair trial, the men of the Athenian fleet which had given the rebels their victory looked on aghast at the butchery.[20] Since no early reference is ever wasted in Thucydides, the Melian and Corcyran episodes may help to explain the atmosphere of horror surrounding the Athenians' own disaster in Sicily a few years later, at the hands of the Syracusans and their Spartan allies.[21]

It has been argued that reactions in haughty Athens to the treatment of the city's captured army at Syracuse foreshadowed those of nineteenth-century Englishmen receiving the news from Cawnpore during the Sepoy Mutiny. What concerns us here, however, is the reminder that it was in the Greek diaspora, the colonies scattered across more than half of the Mediterranean and all the way to the Black Sea, that one encounters the highest level of political violence to be found anywhere in Hellenic history.[22]

On the beautiful island of Sicily, with its ebullient people and its somber history, an early and undeniably effective tyrant, Phalaris of Acragas, ruled from 570 to 554 B.C. His city was a new settlement, dating only from 583, when immigrants from Rhodes had established a Greek community on the south Sicilian coast. The colony's initial prospects cannot have been very bright, for to the resistance of inland tribes such as the Sicanians was added the greater challenge of Phoenicians based on Eryx, Segesta, Entella, and other towns farther to the west, reinforced at times by ships and men from dreaded Carthage, across the "African Sea."

Beset by internal quarrels, even as they faced these alien threats, the

Greek settlers of Acragas were easily seduced by an enterprising troop commander. Phalaris began by securing the right to employ, ostensibly for innocent public works, a large number of prisoners of war. Using them, he built a fortress where none had stood before, high above the town, then he armed his former slaves to control the citizenry should force be needed. Alone, this "prisoner-army" could not have withstood an onslaught by Sicanians or Phoenicians; but using his taxing power to the full, the tyrant added enough fresh mercenaries to create a formidable array of regular troops. At no time did its leader show any inclination to rely on a militia of citizen soldiers.

With his self-made army Phalaris successfully defended the colony against its external foes, but his record of domestic oppression was marked by appalling brutality. The writer of a modern work on the Greek tyrannies says that he "seemed to embody for antiquity in general, as scarcely anyone else did, the type of the cruelly frantic tyrant." [23] It may or may not be true that he had recourse to a hollow bronze bull, which could be partially filled with glowing coals and into which his enemies were thrown, their cries from the bull's belly amusing him as simulations of a live animal's bellowing. The Moloch theme, familiar not only to Phoenician/Carthaginians but also to the people of Rhodes, whence the Acragans had come, doubtless appealed to any dissident looking for stories to discredit the despot. [24]

To suggest that Phalaris may not have owned and operated this ugly plaything falls short of making him a genial character. In fact, the only recorded attempt to show him thus is an improbable tale of his relations with two would-be assassins, Chariton and Melanippos. The story, spread by the early Peripatetics, involves a supposed attempt on the tyrant's life by young Chariton, whose male lover Phalaris had offended. Chariton, captured by the bodyguards before he could act, was put to torture but would identify no collaborator. At that point, so runs the legend, Melanippos came forward to confess that his had been the grievance and his the real guilt. Phalaris, supposedly overcome by such loyalty, pardoned both culprits, in recognition of which the god of Delphi granted him a postponement of his own death. [25]

Whatever extension the tyrant of Acragas may have bought ran out in 554 B.C., when he succumbed to the onslaught of a second wave of refugees from Rhodes. They were led by one Telemachos, a member of the Emmenid clan who had fled the eastern Mediterranean island in some force after a serious quarrel there. Establishing themselves along the coast east of Acragas, these new Rhodian-Sicilians, aided by many of the earlier settlers who had turned against Phalaris' harsh regime, took the city and killed the despot, his mother, and all his immediate entourage. The great-grandson of Telemachos of Rhodes would later be called the best ruler in the stormy history of Acragas. That success, however, served as no more than an epilogue to the story of Phalaris, his triumph, his atrocities, and his fall.

Dionysius and Dion of Syracuse

Unconvincing as the history of Phalaris may seem as an advertisement for tyranny, the Sicilian Greeks went on producing others. Without question the most important of such case studies centered in Syracuse and reached its climax in the career of Dion, friend and student of Plato.[26] Nowhere else in ancient times, not even in the relationship between Aristotle and Alexander, did the persistent vision of a philosopher-king, or at least of a philosopher at a ruler's side, appear to be so close to realization. Nowhere else, one must add, did the failure of that dream cost the ruler more.

Bear in mind that the Syracusans had only recently, in 413 B.C., defeated the siege army of Athens and so tipped the scales of the Peloponnesian War in Sparta's favor. Syracuse had become, almost overnight, no longer just a western colony of Greece but an imperial power in its own right. That is how its most successful tyrant, Dionysius I (c. 405–367 B.C.), saw it, and few contemporaries would have disagreed with him. During a long reign he built a domain that covered most of Sicily, much of southern Italy, and even a northwestern sector of mainland Greece. Several ancient writers quote him as having expressed an interest in central Italy as well, including Etruria in particular, but also the little town of Rome.

Dionysius was a successful general and an intelligent administrator. Under the first heading can be entered his ability to resist the Carthaginians, the standard by which any Greek leader in Sicily had first to be measured. In domestic matters Dionysius' apparent distaste for repression, popular though this undoubtedly was, did not amount to timidity in dealing with domestic opposition. Some historians have credited him with the vision of Greek empire, adumbrating that of Alexander the Great, though modern scholarship does not support anything quite so grand. Still worth pondering, however, is J. B. Bury's judgment: "Dionysius stands out as the ablest and most important Greek statesman between Pericles of Athens and Philip of Macedon." [27]

Not the least of Dionysius' achievements was his survival until a peaceful death at a ripe old age. He succumbed even then allegedly only as a result of having celebrated too late and too hard the prize awarded a play he had written for the Lenaean festival at Athens. During his lifetime, however, this interest in culture appears not to have been entirely reliable, as witness his treatment of Plato. The celebrated philosopher was first welcomed to Syracuse (in 389 B.C.), only to be turned over to the Spartan fleet when the tyrant became bored with him and thereafter sold in the slave market at Aegina—a warning to all academics of the hazards of visiting appointments. Plato's freedom was bought back by friends, but not until after permanent damage had been done to his feelings toward the Syracusan tyrant and the latter's favorite intellectual, a local historian, magnate, and future admiral named Philistus.

When Dionysius died the succession was even more complicated than usual. His son and heir apparent, destined to rule as Dionysius II, was most notable for his triviality. The real power figure in the wings was a leading aristocrat, Dion, hopeful of acting as regent if the dying ruler could be persuaded to name as his successor not Dionysius II but one or both of the two small boys he had sired upon another wife, Aristomache, Dion's sister. Even that circumstance did not exhaust the complexities. Brother-in-law to the late tyrant through Aristomache, Dion was also his son-in-law, having been given Dionysius' daughter Arete in marriage. In regard to young Dionysius II, he was thus both a brother-in-law and a stepuncle of sorts.

Dion's initial attempt to block the accession of Dionysius II failed, and for a time he seemed resigned to ingratiating himself with the new tyrant. In particular, he undertook to secure for Dionysius the counsel of Plato, whom Dion had come to know during the philosopher's first, ill-starred visit to Sicily. Plato, rather surprisingly, agreed to return to Syracuse not once but twice. The first time, in 366, he was there when Dion was suddenly exiled by the tyrant, at the instigation of Philistus, enemy of Plato and Dion alike. Yet the Athenian returned for a final visit in 361, only to be hustled out of town following another quarrel with Dionysius II. Not until then, belatedly one might have thought, did the Academy's founder conclude that travel in Sicily was unrewarding.

Dion meanwhile had temporarily exchanged places with Plato, reveling in the cultural ambience of Athens, frequenting the Academy, and at one point traveling to the Peloponnesus in order to accept from Sparta the title of honorary citizen. His interest in politics, however, was undiminished; and when Plato finally came home to stay, the Syracusan exile again reversed their destinies, setting out to rebuild his own in Sicily. This could not be accomplished instantly, but in August 357 he set sail from Greece with 1,500 men in a fleet of galleys. The flotilla, though considerable, was not strong enough to challenge at once the naval forces of Dionysius; so Dion chose a devious route to his homeland, avoiding the heavily patrolled coast of Italy. Behind him, on the island of Zacynthus (Zante), he left the other half of his invasion force, with orders to follow under the command of a certain Heraclides, his henchman at the time.

Capturing Syracuse turned out to be almost ridiculously easy. Dion was able to land his advance force on the south coast and move overland toward his target, not only without resistance but with welcome support, including military recruits, from the local population. When even the mercenaries defending Syracuse began to desert as he approached, all defense collapsed, and the rebel army marched into the city amid joyous demonstrations.

Dion's problems, however, were just beginning. Dionysius II was still at large, having been absent on a trip to a Syracusan outpost in Italy; and while awaiting his return, the mercenaries loyal to him had seized the fortified harbor island of Ortygia, a stronghold from which they might counterattack at any time. Last but not least, Dion was still receiving no help from the other ships and troops he had left behind in Greece, under Heraclides, who had already shown himself dilatory and eventually would prove traitorous. Within Syracuse itself the lull in military operations brought a marked increase in political acrimony. Dion, loyal Platonist that he was, denounced "lawless tyranny" and populist anarchy alike, asking for himself only the title of general with full powers, *strategos autokrator*. In so doing, he assumed the role of dictator pro tem, for the duration of the crisis, a position later institutionalized by Rome. In the Assembly, however, a growing number of critics dwelt on the danger that he might at any time convert such a commission into a mandate to rule indefinitely as tyrant.

This is not the place to recount all the intricacies of the civil war in Syracuse, rich though the story is in those details of political fortune and human choice recounted by Plutarch in his famous life of Dion. The rebel fleet, when it finally arrived from Zacynthus in the summer of 356, did manage to defeat the navy of Dionysius II, in the process capturing and putting to death Philistus, the despot's chief supporter. The fort in the harbor still remained a threat, however, with its garrison under the command of Apollocrates, son of the tyrant (who had escaped once more to Italy). Charged in the Assembly with having let Dionysius elude the blockade, Heraclides sought to redeem himself by defecting from Dion to the popular party, which, though divided over the choice of rulers, was united in its demand for a redistribution of property. In disgust, Dion left the city, moving his household and his troops to Leontini, some twenty miles to the northwest.

Should he have done so? It seems clear that the local politicians in Syracuse were repeating a mistake familiar throughout history, rushing to slice up the victory pie in the premature belief that the real enemy had been defeated. It is less clear that Dion should have walked out of the debates. Scarcely had he and his forces moved to Leontini than Dionysius II, from Italy, launched a new drive of his own, sending a convoy of troop transports to reinforce the garrison on the island of Ortygia. The thin screen of war galleys escorting these ships was easily defeated by Heraclides at sea; but the faithless admiral, hastening to claim credit for this victory, neglected to report that the troopships themselves had slipped through, debarking their fresh cohorts of mercenaries on the island fort. That night, while the citizens celebrated an apparent triumph, the soldiers from Ortygia poured over the city walls and rampaged through Syracuse, raping, looting, and killing as they went.

Terrified and helpless, the Syracusans begged Dion to return. This he did, though his initial hesitation allowed the troops from the island fort a second night of pillaging. Once reinstalled, far from meting out harsh punishments, he pardoned Heraclides and allowed Apollocrates to sail away from Ortygia under parole, to join his father Dionysius in Italy and even to take with him five triremes filled with troops. The internal political tumult persisted, at last producing the murder of that seemingly indestructible intriguer, Heraclides, struck down by order of his old leader if Plutarch's version is correct.[28]

Strangely enough, given the wealth of detail available concerning most of his career, Dion's own death remains shrouded in mystery. We know only that he was assassinated in June 354 B.C. by agents of a former friend named Calippus, once a fellow member of the Platonic circle. Calippus himself lasted only about a year as Dion's successor, before losing control of Syracuse to a nephew of Dion (one of those younger sons of Dionysius I). This too, however, failed to provide a lasting solution for the problems of the faction-torn city. Within a decade the famous Timoleon would set out from Corinth, answering the appeal of a number of Syracusan citizens to restore order and freedom in their polis. Timoleon's story is an almost cheerful one, certainly as compared to what had gone before, since he appears to have been at once brave and sensible. Years before his coming, however, Syracuse had yielded to others its prominent place in the history of Hellenic struggles.

Tyrannies North and East

Was there emerging what could be defined as a Greek view of political murder? Before an answer is possible, one more base needs to be touched, the world of the "northern marches," as defined by the perspective of the mainland Greek city-states. This world, soon to be dominated by the power of Macedon, was foreign to those older communities in some very significant ways. Speaking of the work of King Philip II of Macedon and that of his son, Alexander the Great, the German scholar Berve explains what was different in these words: "The great Hellenistic empire did not grow from the soil of the *polis,* nor did the citizens of any polis call it into being. . . . Monarchically inclined Macedonians were its founders and support, its subjects for the most part not Greeks but people accustomed to autocracy."[29] This implies not only that the Athens which Demosthenes strove to rally by his *Philippics* had of necessity to suffer from the Macedonian advance, but also that the record of the Greek city-states offers no help at all in seeking to understand what the empire of Philip and Alexander would become.

Convincing though Berve is in many respects, his second implication seems so broad as to be misleading. There were several Greek communities whose records suggest that, if not the classical polis of Attica or the Peloponnesus, at least the smaller colonial tyranny may tell us about the role of the house of Macedon, and how it developed. The first of these was Pherae, a city whose ruins are in Thessaly, to the south of Macedonia. Its ruler, Jason, during four years beginning in 374 B.C. faced problems not very different from those of the Sicilian tyrants following the Peloponnesian War. Like them, he had to ponder the uncertain effects of that still-unfinished struggle between Sparta and the North. Jason tended at first, though seemingly without much enthusiasm, to gamble on an eventual Spartan victory. His real interest, however, centered on the task of creating a large Thessalian state. And so, in the summer of 371 when the Spartans, temporarily at peace with Athens, set out to conquer Thebes and its Boeotian hinterland, the tyrant of Pherae reversed himself and joined the Theban confederation.

The latter's stunning victory at Leuctra left Jason in something of a quandary. Refusing to join Thebes in pursuit of the Spartans, whose retreat was surely welcome, he turned his attention to the conquest of Thessaly. Yet all these plans collapsed within a year. Just as Jason of Pherae was about to announce his imperial dreams to the Pythian festival at Delphi, in September 370 B.C., he was, in the words of a laconic modern account, "struck dead by some conspirators whose motives have never come to light." [30]

What lent importance to Jason's meteoric rise and fall was the emergence of the northern lands upon the stage of fourth-century Greek history. The career of Clearchus of Heraclea, who died a few years later, is also relevant to that phenomenon, albeit in a different way. The very location of Heraclea, on the south shore of the Black Sea, the Pontus Euxinus, made events there if anything even more significant than those in Thessaly. For it was on the northeastern frontier where Greeks still faced Persians, and would face them again, that the seeds of Macedonian conquest were being sown, sometimes admittedly at very oblique angles.[31]

Clearchus came to power around 365 B.C. in Heraclea Pontica, to give its full name—a Greek colony at the base of a peninsula thrusting northward into the sometimes beautiful, sometimes ominous expanse of the Black Sea. He succeeded at the outset for no apparent reason save that his fellow oligarchs wanted a leader to defy popular demands for the redistribution of property. The new tyrant, for such he clearly was, has been described as a cultivated man, stepping into the struggle between the *demos* and the patricians from a background of study in Athens, where he had listened to Plato and been tutored by Isocrates.

Once he had, so to speak, "taken office," his first concern was to shore up his position, since he did not entirely trust even the men who had called him to power. The solution he settled upon was an arrangement with Mithridates, the Persian king of Pontus, who agreed to supply troops on the promise that Heraclea would acknowledge his overlordship, at a time to be arranged. Clearchus, under the terms of the treaty, would thereafter continue to rule the colony, but as the king's vassal. Mithridates, who ascended the Persian imperial throne shortly after this bargain had been struck, seems to have found it highly satisfactory. But he was badly misled. When he visited Heraclea to receive the allegiance pledged him by Clearchus, he was taken prisoner and released only after committing himself to a ransom large enough to pay the new tyrant's army of mercenaries.

The rest of Clearchus' story, though its pattern is too familiar to require much detail in the retelling, nevertheless deserves a place in the pre-Alexandrian background. After holding power for twelve years, during which time he drove out aristocratic rivals, freed serfs, and in general played the role of a popular dictator, he was slain in 353 B.C. His assassins were two young men of the Heraclean intelligentsia, Chion and Leonidas by name, who, like their victim, had studied in Athens. By the time they struck him down, Clearchus reportedly was demanding to be worshiped as a god and dressing as such on festive occasions.

Even his old teacher Isocrates had despaired of this experiment in authoritarian rule, no longer guided by philosophy. In about 346, the Athenian magus wrote a letter to Timotheus, son of Clearchus and by that time his father's successor as tyrant of Heraclea. In its own way the epistle is as interesting as Plato's three letters concerning Syracusan affairs a few years earlier. Isocrates salutes the young ruler for having reportedly thrown off the legacy of "harsh and cruel progenitors." At the end of the letter, however, the tone of a proud yet wary old mentor insinuates itself:

> Almost all who have sailed hither from your court say that you resemble my best pupils. But as for Clearchus when he visited us, all who met him agreed that he was at that time the most liberal, kindly, and humane of the members of my school; but when he gained his power he seemed to change in disposition so greatly that all who had previously known him marvelled. For these reasons I was estranged from him . . . Farewell; if you wish anything from here, write.[32]

The Macedonian Adventure

Episodes featuring Jason of Pherae and Clearchus of Heraclea, combined with what is known of disarray in the mainland Greek states, help to explain the swift rise of "barbarous" Macedon. Its king, Philip II, came to power in 359 B.C., after he had his half-brother Archelaus put to death and drove all his other rivals, relatives or not, into exile. From then on he reigned over a kingdom that had no constitutional tradition and no apparent interest in political niceties. In that regard, surely, the judgment of Berve quoted earlier is correct. Demosthenes of Athens may have assured his own place in the history of oratory by his brilliant speeches denouncing the Macedonian king before the Areopagus, but to King Philip the *Philippics* must have counted for little more than a noisy irritant.[33]

He was right in believing that neither Greek politics nor Greek resistance on the battlefield could halt the advance of his armies. The latter, adapting the phalanx of Leuctra, won victories from the northern marches to Sparta's domain in the Peloponnesus. It was family trouble that brought him down. In 337 B.C., on the occasion of Philip's marriage to a certain Cleopatra (this is when the famous and much-used name seems to have entered the roll of Hellenistic princesses), the king quarreled with young Alexander, his son by another and older wife, Olympias. A reconciliation of sorts was patched up betwen Philip, on the one hand, and, on the other, Olympias and their son Alexander, though the latter spent some time in exile among the Illyrians of the Adriatic coast. The family accord did not in any event prove lasting.

Olympias is deserving of special interest. If nothing else, she recalls those earlier women of power who carved their names into the Hebrew scriptures. It was at the wedding of her (and King Philip's) daughter—another Cleopatra—to Olympias' brother, Alexander king of Epirus, that Philip was murdered by is own guardsmen. The queen was a suspect, but Persian agents were also implicated.[34] Whether or not she had arranged her husband's death, however, there seems to be no doubt that Olympias quickly ordered the murder of Philip II's young wife, with her infant son and a number of the dead king's closest associates.

All this occurred in 336 B.C. It is some indication of Olympias' capacity to survive even the brisk pace of Macedonian politics that she lived another twenty years. Throughout the first thirteen of them she presided over an otherwise almost womanless household; for Alexander the Great took no concubines and only two queens, both tied to him by political, and purely formal, marriages. When he died, in June 323 B.C., worn out by incredible journeys and furious military campaigning, his mother was compelled to watch, with one can imagine what emotions, as the conqueror's generals contested his inheritance, the huge Macedonian empire: Persia, Babylonia, Egypt, Syria, and Greece. Eventually she entered the battle in person, called by one of the successors to save Macedonia itself. With the armies of Epirus and of Polyperchon, the general who had appealed for her aid, she reoccupied the home kingdom, ordered more than a hundred rebel officers executed, declared her grandson king, and engineered the assassination of the self-styled Philip III, an illegitimate son of her deceased husband. To rid herself of the pretender's wife, daughter of another of Philip II's bastards and a young woman as forceful as her husband had been incompetent, the queen-grandmother chose gentle persuasion. She had delivered to the cell of this Eurydice a knife, a rope, and a cup of poison. The young widow, in what has come down to us as a final display of independence, scorned all three gifts, hanging herself instead by her own silken girdle.

The destruction of Philip III and Eurydice constituted the last political victory of Olympias' tempestuous career. A disaffected general named Cassander, who had been away campaigning in the south, hurried home with his army and found ample support from a Macedonian population grown rebellious under the old queen's bloody purges. In quick succession he defeated in battle what was left of her forces, killed her principal commander, and placed Olympias herself on trial, with his entire army serving as the jury. The queen refused to appear for what could only be called a judicial farce. Even after having been convicted of treason, she still managed to cow the soldiers sent to execute her. When they refused to act, a group of men personally related to her former victims came forward and put her to death. Thus ended the epic of Philip, Alexander, and, more especially, Olympias.

The Birth of Tyrannicide Theory

In the book he wrote with Oscar Jászi, *Against the Tyrant,* John D. Lewis opens discussion of Greek contributions by referring to Herodotus and his reflections on hubris, "the unbridled, defiant arrogance of the tyrant." [35] This feature alone, argued the "father of history," was enough to justify condemning tyranny. Elsewhere, using a rich and high-born Persian named Otanes as his spokesman, Herodotus stated the case against autocrats in more detail:

> What right order is there to be found in monarchy, when the ruler can do what he will, nor be held to account for it? Give this power to the best man on earth, and it would stir him to unwonted thoughts. The advantage which he holds breeds insolence, and nature makes all men jealous. This double cause is the root of all evil in him; sated with power he will do many reckless deeds, some from insolence, some from jealousy. For whereas an absolute ruler, as having all that heart can desire, should rightly be jealous of no man, yet it is contrariwise with him in dealing with his countrymen ... Of all men he is the most inconsistent; accord him but just honour, and he is displeased that you make him not your first care; make him such, and he damns you for a flatterer. But I have yet worse to say of him than that; he turns the laws of the land upside down, he rapes women, he puts high and low to death. [36]

This speech deals not with Greek civic tyrannies but with oriental kingship. That, at any rate, is its declared subject. Herodotus must nevertheless have had in mind a larger issue, one closer to the recent and contemporary history of Hellas itself. For this is by no means the only instance of his using the Persians, as Tacitus would one day use the Germans against Rome, to warn and to scold his fellow citizens. In the case of the passage just quoted, the device may have commended itself for a special reason, namely, that the word "tyranny" is most probably Asian, certainly not Greek, in origin. Might the historian not have sought to make the institution appear especially distasteful by emphasizing its alien roots?

Another chronicler often concerned with things Persian was Xenophon, born at about the time Herodotus presumably died (ca. 430 B.C.). Xenophon's *Anabasis* tells of the revolt by Cyrus, satrap of Anatolia, against his brother, King Artaxerxes II. The author himself took service with many other Greeks in the army of Cyrus, shared its defeat by Artaxerxes in Babylonia, and then joined in the flight northward to the Black Sea, the "up-country march" that gave his book its title. Despite this hard-earned familiarity with Asian power struggles, Xenophon, unlike Herodotus, made no effort to conceal his thoughts about tyranny behind a Persian veil of references to kingship. By birth a wealthy Athenian, and like Plato a student of Socrates, he knew enough about Sicilian and other Greek despotisms to abhor the usurper who seizes power by misuse of mercenary troops and by self-serving appeals to the *demos,* or populace.

In his famous dialogue *Hiero* he has the poet Simonides argue with a "king of Syracuse" over "the condition of royalty." The Syracusan locale, remember, had more than colonial associations for an Athenian of the fifth and fourth centuries; and a phrase such as "the rule of one man" describes monarchy and tyranny alike. More significant still is the fact the Xenophon quickly turns from Sicilian affairs to Athens' own legend of Harmodius and Aristogiton. Having spoken approvingly of the Greek's customary feelings of repugnance toward violence aimed at subverting constitutional government, he goes on to say, still through his protagonist, Simonides: "But with tyrants the very reverse is the case; for states, instead of avenging their deaths, bestow great honour on him who kills a tyrant; and instead of excluding tyrannicides from their temples, as they exclude the murderers of private citizens, they even place in their temples the statues of those who have been guilty of tyrannicide." [37]

As a group, the historians probably did most to advance Greek thought on the subject of tyranny and tyrannicide prior to Aristotle and his embarking upon a still more determined inquiry into the intellectual problems involved. Thucydides, as we have seen, tried to straighten out the facts about Hipparchus' murder and the subsequent fall of the Pisistratid dictatorship. On the other hand, he chose without explanation to ignore Athens' only recent assassination, that of Ephialtes in 461 B.C. Was this because of his distaste for the populist reforms espoused by Ephialtes? Did it constitute a cool dismissal of the victim and his death as simply unimportant? Or was it simply an expression of that skepticism concerning political motives shown by Thucydides on occasion? There is no way of knowing for sure. Despite this rather puzzling omission, however, it was without question the author of *The Peloponnesian War* who made the clearest and most influential contribution by a historian to the first debate over tyrannicide.

What of the playwrights? Aeschylus, Sophocles, Euripides, and other Greek dramatists of the fifth century B.C. exploited the theatrical possibilities of murder in high places, and they did so in a fashion characteristic of the religiopolitical culture of which they were a part. This applies, as might be expected, to tragedy, not to the comedies of Aristophanes, though he indulged in political satire at times, making the war party in Athens his target of choice. Assassination is hardly a comic theme, however ludicrous its manifestations have at times appeared.

It is Aeschylus, who spent his youth in Athens under the Pisistratids and his mature years amid the alarums of the Persian Wars, whose concern over serious political issues makes him particularly important for the historian. In *Prometheus Bound,* as one leading commentator puts it, "Zeus is a modern tyrant as seen by the contemporaries of Harmodius and Aristogiton." [38] Among other plays by the same ancient author, *Seven against Thebes,* the trilogy of the *Oresteia,* and *The Persians* all bristle with evocations of violence, glory, and tragedy in the life of the state. Bear in mind, however, that Aeschylus—and this is true as well of Sophocles and Euripides after him—showed a deep commitment to the older religious values of Greek tradition and their meaning for human existence. Hence their characters stood opposed not so much to human rivals as to fate and ultimately to the gods themselves. The crisis of risk and trial, parricide and incest, that Sophocles unrolls in the *Oedipus* cycle involves hopes, passions, and grief which contemporaries must have found as immediate as audiences still do today. In the end, however, it is the gods who intervene to determine destinies. The Greek tragic theater is rich in allegory but not in the direct use of history. The importance of that distinction becomes apparent when one considers dramatists such as Shakespeare and Schiller, who make repeated use of explicitly historical plot lines.

The discipular succession of philosophers, culminating in Aristotle, propounded what was genuinely new in Greek thought with respect to political homicide. Here, as in many other areas of inquiry, it is impossible to say with confidence how much the Stagirite owed to Plato, apart from known passages in the latter's work, or how much both of them owed to Socrates. To take one example, the emphasis on caprice in the definition of tyranny was apparently a Socratic tenet. Xenophon remembered his and Plato's old teacher telling them: "Government with the consent of the people and in accordance with the laws of the state was monarchy, whereas government without consent and in accordance not with laws but with the whim of the ruler was despotism." [39]

Accepting that essential distinction, the Athenian thinkers pushed further along the path which led from a once almost value-free use of the term "tyrant" among the Greeks to the definition that still dominates most discussion of misrule and of justifiable resistance.[40] To Socrates' emphasis on tyranny as an embodiment of capricious authority, however, both Plato and

Aristotle added their insistence that in some cases even a ruler who did not rule by whim might still be called a tyrant, *if* he had come to power by other than legitimate means. Henceforth, usurpation would be counted alongside lawless misrule as the other pillar of classical tyrannicide theory. For it was as *usurpers* that such colonial despots as Phalaris of Acragas, Dionysius of Syracuse, and Clearchus of Heraclea seemed most distasteful to political theorists observing them from the relative security of Athens. No less important, this genetic flaw had been compounded by the tyrant's reliance on both mercenary troops and misguided mobs won over by demogogic promises.

At virtually every point the Greek condemnation of tyranny contained an ethical component. Plato in *The Republic* sees the tyrant not only as an embodiment of bad government but also as someone whose private life is miserably disordered. And Book V of Aristotle's *Politics* contains a famous passage in which its author spells out how a despot keeps himself in power by debauching his people.[41] What is less commonly remarked, however, about this concern for morality in questions of government is that these philosophers did not stop with ethical judgments passed only upon rulers. Their strictures extended to the opposition as well. There is an absolutely crucial belief—reportedly shared by Socrates, explicitly set forth by Plato and Aristotle—that tyranny must be seen as a debasement of the political process, not as an excuse for abandoning it. Despotism was a perversion, a perversion of monarchy, as oligarchy was of aristocracy and mob rule (ochlocracy) of democracy. With this in mind, the Greeks achieved a high level of agreement around the proposition that to exchange one perversion for another is no solution at all.[42]

It was Aristotle who fulfilled what earlier was referred to as the culminating role, selecting, evaluating, and reframing older arguments while almost surely adding some of his own. It was he, more purposefully and coherently than any other thinker known to history, who strove to assemble the necessary elements in a definition of justifiable tyrannicide, even as he drew a line between it and the assassination of a political figure chosen on less defensible grounds. The second effort, making that distinction, was for him no less important than the first. To it he brought an Attic candor which warned against admiration for pseudo-tyrannicide and its bogus heroes.

His treatment of Harmodius and Aristogiton offers a case in point. Like Thucydides before him, he was fully aware that the victim had died not for any exalted political cause but because of sexual passion, further envenomed by injured family pride and at last by fear, which led to what might today be called a "preemptive strike." To that knowledge is added, in Aristotle's *Consitution of Athens,* an assertion that the sons of Pisistratus were not, by his definition, really tyrants at all. They were immune to charges of usurpation, having inherited their father's power without any eruption of civil strife. As for misrule, while Hippias admittedly refused to acknowledge elected representatives, what the Stagirite had written of Pisistratus presumedly applied to the son as well, that his administration had been "more like constitutional government than a tyranny." [43]

Despite his cold dismissal of the two famous assassins enshrined in Athenian legend and his refusal to see in the house of Pisistratus an example of unbridled despotism, Aristotle did concede that either usurpation or misrule might offer grounds for tyrannicide. Even then, his tone, as befitted a believer in orderly government, was restrained. Like most of his continuators in later centuries, he insisted that to raise one's hand against a ruler, any ruler, was serious business, to be undertaken only when there was no other discernible remedy for a malignant growth in the vitals of the body politic. Furthermore, as a number of modern critics rightly point out, Aristotle generally assumed that resistance, if and when it came, would almost certainly take the form of an elite action. His disciples reply that such an assumption was based not on social prejudice but on observation, popular rebellions having throughout history produced a poor record of success. Smaller groups—noblemen at court and in the army, religious leaders, magistrates, senators—enjoyed better opportunities to strike at a despot, if only because they had access to him. This doctrine of the *melior pars,* as it would come to be known, rested on the premise that such groups, while admittedly having a self-centered interest in protecting their own rights, would also recognize an obligation to act on behalf of the community as a whole.

When to that motive is added a deep mistrust of the demagogue—the rabble-rouser—as tyrant par excellence, the so-called "elitist" tilt of classical theory on the subject is not surprising. Given the existence of a disenfranchised population of freemen, and a still larger mass of slaves, the entire body of active citizens in an ancient Greek city-state—and this would be no less true of the Roman republic—was itself an elite by any modern definition. To imply that the error of Socrates or Plato or Aristotle, when wrestling with the problem of political violence, lay in being "undemocratic" by the standards of Abraham Lincoln, not to mention those of a twentieth-century egalitarian, is to convert ignorance of history into a partisan virtue.

One last point about Greek antiquity must be made. It does not arise from questions of democracy versus the *melior pars,* nor from the demands of accuracy against those of the "useful myth." Instead, it involves what the Greeks meant by *nomos,* the combination of tradition, restraint, and acceptance by the community which gave meaning to a social-political entity and to the place of every member within it.[44] What made assassination, including even the special category of principled tyrannicide, so sensitive an issue was the unblinkable fact that the sword of the killer cut both ways. The tyrant deserving of death had condemned himself as a "lawless person," living outside society by his own cruel and arrogant choice. But so had the assassin, *unless* he could claim to hold that narrow ground on which the true tyrannicide may stand without slipping into the despot's own quagmire of egoism and anomie.

The ancient Greeks, with their taste for difficulty and discipline, warned men to defend the political order against usurpers of power and monsters of misrule—but to do so without damaging the painfully acquired set of restraints lacking which *good* rule, too, could easily become impossible. By so doing, they added maturity to the list of qualities required by responsible citizenship. In Athens, as the brilliant French classical scholar and anthropologist Vidal-Naquet has shown, the mysterious tradition of the *ephebeia* drew a sharp line between, on the one hand, the eighteen-year-old future citizens who in their black cloaks—themselves aids to guile and stealth—were assigned to serve as frontier guards and, on the other, the heavy infantry of the hoplite battle line.[45] Much remains unclear about the *ephebeia,* but that is not true of the Spartan *krypteia* (a useful reminder that Athens was never the only Greek community important for the student of political behavior). Under Sparta's rules the young initiate, before becoming a real soldier, was required to serve time as a guerrilla in the hills, living off the countryside by stealthy foraging and *by murdering the unfortunate helots* he found violating the curfew or simply robbed for his own sustenance. As Bernard Knox has put it: "The oppositions in this case are many: light or unarmed against heavily armored hoplite; separate small-group operations as opposed to the massed phalanx; young man on the mountain and fully grown soldier on the level ground . . . the stealthy assassin of helots against the frank and loyal warrior of the pitched battle; the young man in the night, the grown man fighting in the light of day."[46]

Misgivings about the inherent furtiveness of assassination are thus no recent feature of the argument, though they will find their clearest expression much later in history. For the time being, it must be said of the ancient Greeks that their precocity never ceases to amaze. Even as they were outlining the right of resistance to tyranny, they staked out the position that political murder equals bad politics far oftener than its momentary admirers care to admit. Or, to put things in more positive terms, any political system able to dispense, even if only partially, with mindless violence deserves our respectful attention, however far it may still have been from a theory of freedom for all.

3

Rome

A Republic of Laws

The riddle of ancient Rome, a city-state whose influence still affects a world its people never knew, defies simple explanation. Roman conquests offer only a partial answer—they are at least equally a part of the question. At a deeper level of causation lies the record of ordered power, sustained over a very long period of time, uncommonly consistent in its application, and hence able to produce a balancing of force with restraint unknown to other empires of Mediterranean and Middle Eastern antiquity. This restraint, whence it sprang, and what at last became of it deserve the most serious attention from anyone concerned with aspects of political violence.

The Romans' prolonged success in containing the threat of assassination is less widely recognized than the fact that it was an ability they eventually lost. For lose it they did. While the old ways survived, however, their effect was remarkable. Mainland Greece, as we have seen, knew very little political murder in the course of the fifth century before Christ. But the Roman Republic lived for almost exactly *four* centuries without the politically motivated slaying of a leading public figure, from well before the traditional founding date of 509 B.C.—the last king, Tarquin the Proud, having murdered his predecessor, Servius Tullius, in 534—until the assassination of Tiberius Sempronius Gracchus in 133.

By the latter date there were obvious signs that an age of relative stability in domestic governance was slipping away; and some of these signs were not new. Nevertheless, it was the assassination of the elder Gracchus, coming so soon after Rome's victory in the Punic Wars and followed by the murder of his brother Gaius twelve years later, that most startlingly announced the onset of bloodshed and disarray. Stewart Perowne introduces his *Death of the Roman Republic* with an ironic contrast between the appearance of triumph and the reality of trouble to come. Rome, in his words, had become the mistress of East and West, of the cities of Greece, the kingdoms of Asia Minor, of the Levant, of the Holy City of Jerusalem, of the fabled and numinous land of Egypt, of the opulence of Carthage, of the ranches and mines of Spain, of the fields of France ... The satrapies of Cyrus and Alexander became its provinces: Roman consuls and praetors administered what had been the appanages of kings and pharaohs. Rome was unprecedented, Rome was supreme. Her republic had subdued all her enemies—except one, herself.[1]

As some of the items in his recital make clear, however, Perowne is speaking of a time which extended even later than the premonitory shocks of the Gracchi's murders. For that reason, and because the achievement of the early and middle Republic should not be passed over too quickly in favor of the vicissitudes of the late, it is worth pausing a moment to consider three features of Roman history which may help to explain its prominence in the present study. The first of these was its military organization; the second, its structure of public law; the third, and most specific in its relevance, the respect accorded Roman officials entrusted with the administration of government.

Roman armies, facing many different enemies over the course of a millennium (half of it preimperial), changed their tactics and even their composition a number of times. They suffered humiliating defeats, some of them inflicted long before the final collapse. Despite later tributes to their tenacity and discipline, their cadenced marching, their combined use of both phalanx and line, their integration of different weapons, their methodical construction of siege walls and fortified camps, the legions did not fight every battle by the rules of a single manual. Julius Caesar, one of the greatest and easily the most literate of all their generals, conceded as much. Nevertheless, to a Roman civilian of the second century B.C., probably no feature of the state represented more consistency or more nearly approached an appearance of changelessness than did the army.[2]

For here was something that expressed the "old virtues" of loyalty, unselfishness, and rational organization, in short, the very embodiment of *res publica,* the "public affair." Roman citizens were as much a civilian elite as those of a Greek *polis,* surrounded by the disenfranchised and the literally enslaved, had ever been. Yet these same Romans subscribed with apparent willingness to the disciplinary model and demands of an essential military ethos. Men knew they would probably serve, if they had not already done so—and might die—in the ranks of the army. Female citizens too, seen in the formidable person of the Roman mother, embraced its values and its heroes. What is of special interest about those values is the high place they accorded civil order and respect for established procedures. Thus, the armies of the Republic had shown restraint in domestic politics even in the most desperate times of threatened disasters, as when Hannibal's host was closing in on the city. Pondering this dual legacy of iron discipline under arms combined with a deep civilian distrust of military dictatorship save in the direst emergencies, a modern observer is tempted to suggest that Rome became mistress of an empire not in a fit of absence of mind but in the awareness of an intermittent state of siege.

Part of the reason for the Roman performance must therefore be sought in a second of its features, the respect for a civil law without which victory in war might itself prove unattainable or, if won, not worth the sacrifice. Legal constraints, demanding not so much heroism as patience, in the long run proved more fragile than the structure of military command. Without the vitality of the public law over the space of several centuries, however, there would be no explaining the Republic's record of conservative yet flexible institution-building, and of efforts to accommodate conflicting social demands. The "political genius" of Rome, like that of England later, no doubt contained something cold, impersonal, and in the eyes of many moderns unexciting, but its resiliency was long unmatched.

The genius of republican Rome no doubt was somewhat cold, at least in comparison with the exhortations of an Old Testament prophet or the clamor of a Carthaginian crowd watching defeated sea captains and their crews nailed on crosses along the North African coast—as Voltaire would have said, "to encourage the others." The Romans of the early and middle Republic seem to have acknowledged a number of inhibitions, some of them matters more of custom than of legislation, which nonetheless offered great security to the representatives of government. Like every other people, they indulged in brawls, vendettas, and occasional group attacks, especially the stoning of individuals condemned by public opinion for private transgressions. The *public* sphere, however, was long considered beyond the permissible reach of lynch mobs or wreakers of personal vengeance. One result of this crucial distinction was that from the end of the sixth century before Christ until two-thirds of the way through the second, the persons of Rome's political officials were virtually immune to assault.[3]

Hence a third attribute, restraint in behavior toward figures of public authority, takes its place as the most important of all for any student of assassination. The web of mutually reinforcing attitudes toward violence in the conduct of the *res publica* appeared to include a singular distrust of legendary assassins and other would-be resistance heroes of the past, contrasting sharply with the honor paid by many Greeks to the memory of Harmodius and Aristogiton. The story of Lars Porsenna, allegedly slain by a brave young man, was by Romans largely abandoned to the mists of Etruscan folklore.[4] That of Tarquinius Superbus has survived thanks to Shakespeare's poetic celebration of the rape and suicide of Lucretia. Her violator, however, as contemporaries well knew, was in fact not the tyrant but his son.

(Tarquin himself had subsequently been allowed to leave Rome unhindered, even though Lucretia's bereaved husband was one of the new Republic's first two consuls.) The myth of Spurius Maelius, the would-be "king of Rome" in the next century, who, according to some versions, was assassinated by an ancestor of Caesar's Brutus, does not bear serious scrutiny despite its popularity in later times.

In short, there was almost no political assassination of moment until the Republic at last entered upon its season of troubles. Was this because Rome, as has been alleged concerning certain authoritarian regimes both earlier and more recent, simply crushed all incipient attacks upon its leaders? Had that been the case, the government would scarcely have shied away, as it did repeatedly throughout the period in question, from either mass repression or individual proscription aimed at dissidents. What seems more likely is that a widely shared sense of the need for restraint merged with a consensual pressure opposing self-promotion to keep purposeful killing from the stage of Roman politics for a remarkably long time.

The Gracchi

Most historians take as their boundary dates for the "late Republic" the years 133 and 44 B.C., those of Rome's two most important assassinations. Well they might, for the murders of Tiberius Gracchus and Julius Caesar were more than sensational episodes. Each in its own way gave dramatic expression to a constitutional and social crisis, en route to the climax of the Republic's mortal illness.[5]

Stewart Perowne, earlier quoted on the subject of Roman triumphs, must have had in mind especially the *annus mirabilis* of 146, when Carthage was at last destroyed, Macedonia reduced to the status of a Roman province, and rich, disloyal Corinth in Greece captured, looted, and leveled to the ground. Spoils from the east, added to the silver from newly conquered Spanish mines, brought such an influx of wealth that the treasury, to its own amazement, announced a surplus and suspended for a time the *contributio,* the principal direct tax upon Roman citizens. For the better part of a decade, public and private spending soared, as did employment for the urban poor. It was a time when everything one dreamt of doing seemed easy to pay for, using loot and foreign tribute.

Unfortunately for its beneficiaries, this proved to be a classic postwar boom, followed by a demoralizing bust. By about 138 B.C. public works and the jobs they had created were in sharp decline. The treasures of Corinth and Syria had been dissipated; and far from being able to continue tax relief, the government was scrambling to find new revenues. The city's population of unskilled labor had almost certainly been rising, because of urban attractions and because of the migration of farm workers forced off the large estates or *latifundia* by a seemingly endless influx of slaves, those other spoils of conquest. Although census figures remain problematic, there is archaeological evidence that after 146 many high-rise tenements had gone up in Rome, pointing to an increase in the number of poor urban residents.

All of this, it bears repeating, was obvious no later than 138. Within three years thereafter, a massive slave rebellion broke out in Sicily, Rome's most important source of grain, and in Spain the sputtering Numantine War took a bad turn, demanding large commitments of troops and supplies. Signs of economic and political confusion seemed to be everywhere. There was a crisis in public finance, triggered by the need to pay and provision Roman forces throughout the Mediterranean world. There was a rural crisis, produced in part by the competition of slave labor that had ruined many small farmers, while periods of absence for military service had bankrupted many others. And finally there was a crisis within Rome's own walls, engulfing a people caught between unemployment and an inflation spawned by extra spending money, but perpetuated by the high cost of food and other commodities for a growing population.

To the front of a stage darkened by the cruelty of Roman behavior abroad and tense with the hatreds of competing interest groups at home, there stepped in 134 B.C. the first of two brothers who gave their name to an era of disarray that culminated in tragedy. Tiberius Sempronius Gracchus, then about twenty-eight years old, was the scion of a family linked to several of the most prestigious bloodlines within Rome's patrician order. On the paternal, Sempronian side he was the son, great-nephew, and great-grandson of three generations of consuls. His father had been a successful general, administrator, and diplomat in various posts from Spain to Asia Minor. His mother, Cornelia, was the daughter of no less a figure than Scipio Africanus, victor over Hannibal and the Carthaginians at Zama. Another of Scipio's grandsons, Aemilianus, who had completed the destruction of Carthage in 146, was both first cousin and brother-in-law to T. Sempronius, whose sister he had married. Finally, Gracchus was joined by his own marriage to yet another great house, the Claudian.

The ambitious young man at the center of all this had received the usual upper-class education, including in his case some Greek philosophy at the feet of the Stoic Blossius of Cumae and the democratic rhetorician Diophanes of Mitylene. By the time he was fourteen, however, Tiberius had already begun ten years of military service, and in 146 he was serving under his cousin Scipio Aemilianus before the walls of Carthage. For personal bravery in that successful siege he won the coveted "mural crown"—a gold circlet in the form of battlements—together with sufficient notice back in Rome to assure a promising start in political life as soon as he left the army. Elected a *quaestor* for 137, he took the first step on the *cursus honorum*, the progression of advancement through the chief offices of the Republic.

In this capacity Gracchus was assigned to service in Spain, where the consul Mancinus was about to suffer a tremendous defeat at Numantia. By office only a financial administrator, the young quaestor was in fact a member of the commanding general's personal staff; and as such he negotiated the release of some twenty thousand Roman prisoners taken by the Celto-Iberians in that battle. This diplomatic achievement was a considerable one, but it went sour almost at once. Back in Rome an indignant Senate repudiated the armistice terms, ordered the war resumed, and delivered the unfortunate Mancinus, naked, to the Numantians as evidence that their offer of amnesty was not welcome. The Iberians, doubtless puzzled by the Roman way of doing things, decided after some debate merely to send Mancinus back across the battle lines with instructions to get dressed again and stay there.

So the bitter war dragged on; but Tiberius Gracchus, once his year as quaestor had expired, returned home to an uncertain future. By his own account, he had been troubled by the large slave-operated ranches, set among languishing smaller farms, he had seen while passing through Italy en route to Spain, as well as by the poor quality of the Roman troops whom he had observed once he got there. Perhaps just as important was his resentment over the repudiated Numantine peace, poisoning relations between the young patrician and a suspicious Senate. After a couple of years devoted to family business he abruptly announced his candidacy, not for an aedileship or praetorship, which would have been the usual next step in the sequence of magistracies, but for election as one of the ten tribunes of the plebs. The latter class, through its representatives in the Tribal Assembly (*comitia tributa*), responded by choosing him one of its tribunes to take office in December 134 B.C.

A tribune was not a magistrate in the regular sense. Nevertheless, he was empowered to veto, on his sole authority and without reference even to any of his nine peers, any action proposed by an official of the state. He could enter the Senate at will in order to monitor its deliberations; and his right to initiate legislation before the Assembly gave him a range of political opportunities for which men might well interrupt, as Tiberius had done, even the cursus honorum. His constituents, the plebs, included a number of prosperous citizens and landholders, technically members of "the people" but certainly not part of anything a modern analyst would call "the masses." Yet they continued to rely for leadership on members of a privileged stratum of Roman society, that of the powerful families who still dominated the councils of the consular-senatorial oligarchy. Among such leaders Tiberius Sempronius Gracchus was not the only one of note. He was, however, the first to play the political game so roughly as to bring about his own destruction.

The disaster that overtook him probably sprang less from his substantive proposals than from his tactics, a paradoxical mixture of attempts to revitalize the Republic and of challenges to the very constraints on which its system of checks and balances relied. The centerpiece of his program was unveiled early in 133, in the form of a new agrarian law which, far from being a hasty concoction of his own, owed a great deal to earlier drafts, among them the one composed by Publius Mucius Scaevola, an incumbent consul at the time. It dealt specifically with the fate of those public lands acquired by Roman conquests in central Italy but not as yet leased or granted to new owners, though many of the tracts were being actively cultivated by squatters. The new law would leave every such tenant, if he were a Roman citizen, something over three hundred acres, plus half that much land for each son, up to a limit of two. Once that division had been made, the remaining public lands were to be assigned to other citizens by a commission of three members. (Those elected by the Assembly after passage of the law were Tiberius Gracchus, his brother Gaius, and Tiberius' father-in-law, Appius Claudius.)

The measure purported to meet several needs at once. According to its sponsors, many of Rome's urban poor would return to the land, strengthening the depleted ranks of old-fashioned yeomen. Increased small farming promised in turn to produce more in the way of subsistence crops, especially grain, than could ever be expected of the big latifundia, whose owners displayed a marked preference for raising livestock, olives, and grapes, with slaves rather than citizens supplying the labor. Because the army was supposed to enlist only owners of a stated amount of land, the dejected units which Tiberius remembered from Spain would receive a transfusion of real citizen-soldiers. And just to make sure that landless men did not accept allocations from the commission only to sell them to rich neighbors, pocketing quick money and at the same time escaping liability for military service, the law provided that every such grant, once accepted and registered, would be nontransferable, forever!

No doubt the program had other, less altruistic ends in view. If adopted, it promised to make Tiberius a personal hero of the recipients of free land, their relatives, and their immediate friends. That it was at the same time part of a factional thrust for power at the highest levels was revealed by the concerted support it received from the Claudian and Licinian as well as Sempronian connections. In view of the stakes, small wonder that within the senatorial class there was strong opposition to the eloquent and impatient young man who had thrust himself into the forefront of Roman politics. Nor was that the only kind of opposition. Tiberius Gracchus was not a spokesman for all humble men. His reform would have dispossessed thousands of "Italians," noncitizens of Rome, who were occupying public lands but would not benefit from its being distributed to the citizenry; and his hasty assurance that he also favored certain concessions to noncitizens only blunted one kind of animosity by sharpening others inside Rome.

The deterioration in this political debate and the resulting slide toward deadly violence can be traced through four stages, each initiated by a tactical decision on Tiberius' part. The first was his failure to consult the Senate concerning his agrarian law before taking it to the Assembly. In theory, to be sure, legislation was proposed by the magistrates or tribunes and enacted by the Assembly of once geographically defined "tribes" or by the Plebeian Council on its own authority, the Senate having only an advisory role. In hallowed practice, however, views of the Senate were formally placed on record before any bill came to a formal vote. Whatever hostility Gracchus may have carried over from his experience with the Numantine treaty, he must have known that simply to brush aside the *senatus consultum* as an empty formality was something no Roman politician could do with impunity. After some delay he did take his bill to the Senate for discussion; but by then the damage had been done.

The second stage began when the bill's opponents persuaded another of the tribunes, the respected Marcus Octavius, to veto it before the Assembly could vote. Gracchus brought it back, after only a brief delay, for another reading and, when Octavius again interposed his veto, moved a vote of recall to deprive the opposing tribune of his very office. The vote carried, Octavius was replaced by a candidate presumably hand-picked by the Sempronian party, and the bill was enacted into law without further delay. Bypassing the Senate had been bad manners and probably bad politics, but this latest stroke was a truly revolutionary departure. Granted that Octavius' stubbornness in twice vetoing a colleague's proposal was itself unusual, no tribune had ever been ousted on the motion of one of his peers.

Third, even with his project approved, Gracchus faced the difficulty of financing its operation. The state commission might award land to thousands of poor Romans, but how were the latter to cover their "start-up costs"—housing, tools, seed, animal power, sustenance for themselves and their families until the first crops could be harvested? The problem of capital outlay could not have been posed more urgently, and this at a time when the Roman treasury contained no reserves to be used for any such purpose. Then there occurred a windfall. King Attalus of the rich kingdom of Pergamum in Asia Minor died, leaving "the people of Rome" as his heirs; his personal fortune was shipped to Italy without delay.

Tiberius may have possessed early knowledge of the bequest, for his father had been a friend and ally of Attalus, and the Sempronians were known for their patronage of clients in the East.[6] Whether or not he had warning, he moved swiftly to convert the new riches into support for his land resettlement plan. He moved, and the Assembly voted, that since the gift had been made to the people of Rome, not the Senate but the Assembly should assume both control of the cash and direction of future relations with Pergamum.

And so, as the tribune's year in office passed its midpoint, the stage was set for his fourth and, as it turned out, crucial decision. He announced himself a candidate for reelection. His opponents, faced with the prospect of another whole year of what seemed to them his impulsiveness and contempt for political order, responded by charging that his reelection would be illegal. It is not clear that such was the case; for although a recent law had prohibited *magistrates* from serving second terms, an exception had just been made for the consul Scipio Aemilianus in 135, and in any case the prohibition might not apply to tribunes.

Under these circumstances the resistance to Tiberius Gracchus became more and more a campaign to cast doubt on his judgment, his integrity, and his disinterestedness as a reformer. Below the level of political bombast, however, still another and more ominous element had entered the discussion, a growing conviction among his opponents in the Senate that the tribune simply could not be allowed to serve another term, whatever steps might be required to prevent it. On election day Tiberius assembled a crowd of his followers on the Capitoline Hill, whence they proceeded to attack anyone who baited them or in any other way showed opposition to their candidate. As rioting spread and temples were hastily closed to avoid pillage and sacrilege, the Senate was summoned to convene, also on the Capitoline within sound of the uproar. Its debate commenced amid various wild rumors, including one that the tribune was now demanding a royal crown.

Presiding over the Senate that day was the consul Mucius Scaevola, an old ally of Gracchus, albeit one who had shown increasing disapproval of his friend's impulsiveness. Whatever his personal feelings, the consul maintained his composure, refusing to call out the troops against Tiberius' unruly supporters and saying that he would recognize nothing done illegally—presumably by either side. Infuriated by the chairman's caution, Scipio Nasica, a consul five years before and now *pontifex maximus* (high priest) of Rome, jumped up shouting that all who would save the state should follow him. He was joined by more than enough of his colleagues to make up an assault force. Though its members had come unarmed into the Senate, they now broke up benches and fashioned makeshift weapons outside the chamber, at the same time being joined by their retainers and other sympathizers, some of whom were more heavily armed.

The end came swiftly, almost anticlimactically given the seriousness and complexity of issues involved. The phalanx of senators and their henchmen, led by the furious Nasica with his purple-edged toga pulled up over his head after the fashion of a priest performing a religious sacrifice, beat its way through the confused mob to where Tiberius and a number of his supporters were trapped before the temple of the Capitoline Jupiter. The tribune and those around him were clubbed to death, either on the spot or after a brief effort at flight, and their bodies thrown into the Tiber.[7] As many as three hundred victims may have succumbed that day; and in the Senate-ordered investigations that followed, certain others were put to death, among them Diophanes, the dead tribune's old tutor.

Despite the numbing shock of this first political assassination in republican Rome, public life quite rapidly, if only temporarily, resumed its normal course. This occurred partly because the moderates led by Mucius used their influence first to postpone and then to limit the duration of the anti-Gracchan purge, at the same time opposing any effort by the popular assembly to conduct its own prosecution of Tiberius' killers. Partly, too, the calming of passions was aided by the Senate's decision to send Nasica, instigator of the lynching, to Asia Minor as commissioner charged with the integration of Pergamum. But above all, the resumption of day-to-day operations showed that Rome's government was still far too resilient and too firmly based on a consensus among interested (not to say self-interested) parties for it to come tumbling down after just one disruption, however sensational. Almost a century more would be required to achieve its surrender to the "imperial peace."

With respect to the brothers Gracchi, there has long been a tendency to treat Gaius, the younger by some seven years, as the more doctrinaire, the more effective (if only because he managed to have not one but two years as tribune), and hence the more "politically interesting" of the two. Even if that judgment were valid—and it is challenged by those who see the brothers as more alike than different—the second case study could be treated more briefly than the first. Although the tragedy of Gaius was no mere replay of Tiberius' downfall, the two episodes have a great deal in common.

Gaius Sempronius Gracchus had not only identical ancestry and similar relations by marriage but also very much the same upbringing as the "martyred tribune" of 133. Of the two men, Gaius is reputed to have been the more polished and persuasive orator, as Tiberius was the more admired soldier. Indeed, it is difficult to establish the facts about Gaius' army record; for although he claimed in 124 B.C. to have served as an officer for twelve years prior to that date, one must ask how that accords with his having functioned as a (presumably civilian) member of the three-man public land commission set up in 133, after which he was elected a questor in 127, and three years later won a tribuneship.

There can be no doubt that Gaius Gracchus, during his two terms as tribune of the plebs, initiated an unusual volume of legislation. In the first year he addressed himself to a host of technical problems, ranging from the sale of public grain supplies and regulations governing clothing for the army to reforms in the criminal court system and the creation of a special tribunal to look into charges of official corruption. Though he took the opportunity to settle a few old scores with the enemies of the slain Tiberius, vengeance seems not to have seriously diverted the younger brother's attention away from political affairs.

Reelected easily to serve a second year (the Assembly having in 130 confirmed the right of tribunes to do so), Gaius began to branch out into more ambitious projects. Reviving an old Sempronian interest in resettling the Roman poor, he pushed through laws creating several new colonies in southern Italy and, at the risk of being charged with sacrilege, one in North Africa near the ruined and accursed site of Carthage. His daily business still included close attention to grain distribution, the building of roads and bridges, and other fairly routine tasks. On a more controversial front, however, Gaius put forward several institutional proposals guaranteed to enrage much of the officeholding class. First, he announced a broadening of jury selection for his special court to try cases of corruption, augmenting the original pool of three hundred senators by the addition of three hundred knights, clearly distinguishable from politically active members of senatorial families. Second, he struck a blow against the voting rules observed in the hallowed *comitia centuriata,* which each year chose consuls and praetors for the next. Finally, to this issue and to that of the impaneling of equestrian jurors there was added, in his campaign for reelection to a third term, still another proposal: that full voting rights be extended to many non-Roman Italians, thus threatening the urban patricians on yet another front.

Gaius Gracchus was defeated in his bid to be reelected one more time. We cannot be sure just what overturned the previous Sempronian majority in the Assembly, but it is clear that Gracchus' reelection was strongly opposed by one of the consuls, Gaius Fannius, and by a fellow tribune of Gracchus, Marcus Livius Drusus, both members of the Scipionic bloc. These men were not brutal reactionaries—the Scipionians were among Rome's most cultivated and moderate patricians—but their differences with Gaius appear to have become irreconcilable. Once his time in office expired, at the end of the year 122, he was at the mercy of his enemies now assuming power, especially the new consul Opimius, unlike Fannius and Drusus a violent type, as events were soon to demonstrate.

The showdown began with a motion offered by an incumbent tribune but inspired by Opimius and designed to repeal the law authorizing Gaius' new colonies, especially the controversial one outside Carthage. On the day appointed for the Assembly's vote, Gracchus and his supporters poured onto the Capitoline Hill; in the ensuing turmoil a fight broke out in which a herald of Opimius, having directed an obscene gesture at Gaius, was stabbed to death by some of the latter's henchmen. That was all the pretext the consul needed to ask for, and receive from the Senate early the next morning, a "final decree" giving him emergency powers to defend the state (itself a revolutionary departure). Tiberius Gracchus had died at the hands of a lynch mob; Gaius, by contrast, was now formally declared to be an enemy of the Republic, in effect an outlaw whose followers were disrupting the body politic through riot and murder.

Opimius set to work at once using cavalry and mercenary units, including a force of the dreaded Cretan bowmen. Besieged in the temple of Diana on the Aventine Hill, Gaius sought in vain to open negotiations with Opimius. In response the consul offered only to let the culprits surrender for trial by the Senate, before which they could "beg for mercy." Then he turned his archers loose against the Aventine temple. It took them little time to massacre most of the defenders, Gaius himself managing to escape briefly, only to perish after having been pursued across the Tiber. His closest ally and sometime fellow tribune, the ex-consul Marcus Fulvius Flaccus, was also killed that day, along with his two sons. Before the blood purge ended, an indeterminate number of other followers of Gracchus lost their lives (though Plutarch's estimate of three thousand deaths is surely much too high).[8] Opimius was triumphant. Though he was brought to trial, after his year as consul, for having killed Roman citizens without due process, the special tribunal set up to try his case decided that the need to protect the Republic had been paramount—and he was acquitted.

So ended the two-part drama of the Gracchi, history's first well-documented case of major political homicide in a state both powerful and institutionally "developed"—hence its eerily modern quality. To some it has seemed a morality tale in which idealistic young reformers were struck down by selfish defenders of established privilege. Others have seen it as a parable revealing the disaster that awaits the hubristic challengers of either gods or time-tested governmental systems. Neither characterization does full justice to the facts.

The Gracchi were by no means hopelessly visionary. Both were recognizable Roman politicians of their day, not least in the pragmatic approach they brought to a host of problems besetting the Republic in the first decades following its defeat of Carthage. Neither were they open to the charge of thoughtless rabble-rousing, as might have been true had they consciously incited armed mobs to attack public officials or attempted to make use of mutinous troops. Despite some of the rhetoric indulged in by both at times, they could not fairly have been labeled tyrants in the Aristotelian sense of being either illegitimate usurpers or unprincipled demagogues. For their support came not from the disenfranchised masses, much less from the slave population Spartacus would seek to mobilize a half-century later. Instead, these two representatives of the Sempronian house relied on their own connections with powerful patrician families and with substantial plebeians in the Tribal Assembly. Even Gaius' eventual appeals to Italian farmers, through land distribution and enfranchisement bills, were aimed at enlisting not vagrants but men he considered deserving yeomen unjustly excluded from the rolls of Roman citizens.

At the same time, most of the opponents of the Gracchi showed themselves to be not blind reactionaries, but principled conservatives who honestly disagreed with some or all of the brothers' expedients, and feared still more the precedential dangers arising from their tactics. To balloon the powers of the tribunate out of all proportion to those of the Senate and the magistrates did indeed threaten to unbalance the complex constitution Rome had evolved through centuries of travail and danger, forbearance and compromise—and previously unheard-of political success.

What seems genuinely tragic, but nonetheless instructive, about the Gracchi's meteoric careers is that in the end the serious debates they aroused were drowned in blood. The two ill-fated tribunes may have been cavalier about reordering institutional relationships, as well as arrogant in their dismissal of even the most reasoned opposition, but it was neither they nor their opponents who did Rome the greatest damage. In part the Republic declined because of economic and social (including demographic) changes that no politician could have wholly controlled, especially given the climate of boundless expectations which so often have followed total victory in a long and dangerous war. But a large share of the blame must also be borne by individuals—Nasica the high priest with his sacrificial frenzy, Opimius the consul with his merciless proscription—men who chose to answer the most complex political questions with the simplest of answers: political murder.

Pompey, Caesar, Cicero

It is important to inquire not only into the causes of historic assassinations but also into their sequels. Following the destruction of the Gracchi the commission set up to administer Tiberius' agrarian law continued functioning (and was in fact strengthened under Gaius Gracchus), only to lose its power by degrees, as important features of the program, especially the inalienability of homesteads, proved unenforceable. On the other hand, the right of a tribune to run for reelection, challenged by Tiberius' senatorial opponents in 133, was reconfirmed by the Assembly soon thereafter. The dead brothers' concern over military manpower was carried forward by successive consuls until in 107–105 the reforms of Marius and of Rutilius Rufus produced the "new model" Roman army with its reorganized legions, its parallel detachments of auxiliaries, and its professional cavalry. Finally, after the War of the Allies in 91–88 B.C., another old cause of the Gracchi finally triumphed when all Italians were offered Roman citizenship if they applied for it within sixty days, and towns as far north as the Po Valley acquired the so-called "Latin rights" once reserved to Rome's nearest neighbors and oldest associates.

In most of these respects the violence directed against Tiberius and Gaius had failed to achieve its purpose. Nevertheless, the Gracchi's efforts and their deaths as popular martyrs had not broken the power of the oligarchy, nor had the tribuneship been converted into the kind of all-powerful ministerial post that they had tried to create. The consuls still ruled; and the law of 151 forbidding any consul to serve for more than one year was simply ignored—as witness the celebrated case of Marius, elected seven times! Lastly, despite the slain men's efforts, senatorial control over both the courts of law at home and diplomatic-colonial services abroad was quickly and firmly reestablished.

In a wider sense the political heirs of the Gracchi *and* their enemies alike came upon increasingly bad times. The republican institutions they had taken for granted were during the ensuing century eroded by waves of innovation and reaction. The Republic nearing its end was very different from that which had destroyed Carthage a hundred years before. The franchise had been broadened and Roman citizenship diluted almost beyond recognition. While its extension of equality was in spirit commendable, and in political terms probably inevitable, the effects on decision making were bewildering. Meanwhile, the "responsible" political class of old showed signs of corruption, as well as polarization between the often reactionary *optimates* and frankly demagogic *populares.* The ballooning of officialdom—hundreds of senators, forty quaestors, sixteen praetors by 45 B.C.— matched the collapse of any meaningful electorate and the disarray of the assemblies. Finally, as Caesar showed when his soldiers crossed the Rubicon and headed south, the proconsuls and the armies could no longer be counted upon to obey the law.

Hand in hand with these general signs of lost form and purpose went another ominous indicator: a marked increase in political violence, including murder. From about 90 B.C. onward virtually every year brought some lethal outbreak.[9] Even earlier, in 100 B.C., a consular candidate had been murdered by agents of two demagogues, Saturninus and Glaucia, tribune and praetor respectively. Thereafter, praetor Asellio was assassinated in 89; the son of the consul Pompeius Rufus was slain in 88; the consul Gnaeus Octavius died at the behest of a vengeful Marius in 87; and from then on an almost unbroken annual recurrence of personal attacks on candidates for election and on movers of legislation darkened the political record.

This final agony of the Republic reached its climax with three violent deaths which occurred in the space of only five years, to be followed by a widening civil war and the creation (in fact if not yet in theory) of the Empire by 23 B.C. Beginning a couple of decades earlier, Gnaeus Pompeius Magnus, Gaius Julius Caesar, and Marcus Tullius Cicero had all fallen victim to assassination. Although the circumstances surrounding their murders differed markedly, their careers had been closely intertwined in the pattern of contemporary events. Hence the three cases assume added significance when looked at together.

Caesar ordered his army of Gaul south from Ravenna, saying at the Rubicon "the die is cast," in late November 50 B.C.[10] Almost at once the lines of conflict with his former son-in-law Pompeius began to harden. In Caesar the republican government faced a redoubtable foe, skilled as a diplomat, politician, and general, conqueror of unnumbered Celtic and Germanic foes from Provence to Britain. Not that Pompey, commanding the senatorial army in Rome, had much to concede in terms of military renown. Behind him lay nearly three decades of victories—over anti-Sullan rebels in the north of Italy, over the last of the Spartacist insurgents in the south, over Mithridates' Greco-Persians in Asia Minor, over other foes all the way from Spain to Palestine. Called by some the "organizer of Asia," he was more generally known as Pompey the Great.

By 50 B.C. Caesar's ten-year term as proconsul, effectively military governor, of both Gauls—Transalpine and Cisalpine, the latter encompassing modern Liguria, Piedmont, Lombardy, and Venetia—as well as Illyricum, that is, the Dalmatian coast of what is now Yugoslavia, was drawing to a close. Looking ahead, he made clear his intention to seek election in 49 for another year as consul in 48 (he had served an earlier term in 59). This knowledge, together with the imminence of Pompey's departure to take up proconsular duties in Spain, confronted the Senate with some urgent and potentially dangerous choices. Most senators, including Cicero and the younger Cato, distrusted Caesar's record as an ambitious politician in the populist mold of Marius and Cinna. Hence, although Pompey, too, was viewed with suspicion in many influential quarters, there appeared to be no alternative but to make him the Republic's defender. The plan agreed upon in Rome was to maneuver Caesar out of his governorship and field command before he could be elected consul, thereby creating an interval of some months during which judicial action could be taken against him as a private citizen charged with having broken various laws during his consulship a decade before.

The crucial time period would be the fall and winter of 50–49 B.C. In mid-November (Julian style) the Senate, with Pompey's approval, voted that the governor of the Two Gauls and Illyricum should in effect be outlawed unless he immediately laid down his office and disbanded his troops. Seen against this background, crossing the Rubicon did indeed mark the beginning of the Civil Wars, for it was a double act of defiance: it made clear that Caesar would not relinquish his military command; and it took his Thirteenth Legion, and himself, across the southern boundary of Cisalpine Gaul, in violation of the law restricting generals, to their assigned provinces.

For the time being the Thirteenth was his only army—probably no more than three thousand soldiers, for Caesar liked his legions spare, swift, and experienced. This one, having crossed into "Italy," stopped at Ariminum (Rimini) a few miles down the Adriatic coast from the Rubicon and waited for reinforcements from the north. One might suppose that immediate counteraction would have ended the threat posed by forces still so weak. Several things, however, conspired to undermine Pompey's position guarding Rome. First, other veteran legions of the Army of Gaul caught up with their commander in a remarkably short time, some marching all the way from beyond the Alpine barrier. Second, Pompey's own best troops were in far-off Spain. Third, other units already in Italy began to declare for the invading general, and even some of the Pompeian soldiers, having surrendered to Caesar, were integrated into the latter's forces.

Under the circumstances, Pompey vindicated his own reputation for skill as a tactician by managing to bring his threatened army to Brundisium, on the heel of the Italian boot, and there embark it to Greece, accompanied by both of the consuls as well as many senators and other civilian officials. Because of the conscription ordered by the Senate, the "republican" forces were increasing in numbers, though the troops needed field experience before they could face Caesar's with much hope of success. Perhaps more important, Pompey's fleet was larger than any his former father-in-law could send into action. Instead of trying at once to cross the Adriatic in pursuit, therefore, Caesar turned his army around and set off to strike at Pompey's generals and legions in Spain.

This is not the place for a detailed recapitulation of the next four years of military operations and political maneuvers. Suffice it to say that the former covered immense distances, from Ilerda in northeastern Spain, where Caesar first crushed a Pompeian army at the beginning of June 49, to battles in western Greece and in Thessaly, at Alexandria in Egypt and Zela in Asia Minor not far from the Black Sea, at places in present-day Tunisia on the North African coast, and finally, back on Spanish soil, at Munda, in the extreme south, where on March 17, 45 B.C., Caesar won his final victory in the field, defeating the last organized remnants of Pompey's and the Senate's once considerable host.

By that time Pompey himself was dead, the victim of Middle Eastern intrigue. After transporting his troops out of Brundisium, he had established a base in Dyrrhachium, on the Greek Adriatic coast. Caesar meanwhile, back from Spain as the victor of Ilerda, saw to his own election as a consul for the year 48 and accepted the additional title voted him by the Assembly: dictator for the duration of the crisis. He showed himself restrained in dealing with former enemies in Rome, but remained determined to hunt down the fugitive Pompey. Leaving his docile fellow consul Publius Servilius to monitor the political situation at home, and with his trusted lieutenant Mark Antony, who had administered Italy while Caesar was in Spain, now commanding a follow-up invasion force, the consul-dictator and several of his legions slipped past the Pompeian sea blockade and landed on the Greek coast not far south of his enemy's base. When, in February 48, Antony also crossed the Adriatic with four more legions and some badly needed cavalry, the land armies were at last ready to join battle.

They did so on June 6, 48 B.C., near the small Thessalian town of Pa-laeopharsalus (Pharsalus, as it is more commonly called today). Caesar's account puts his total forces, shrunken by casualties and disease, at only about 22,000, his opponent's at more than 45,000.[11] The second figure is almost certainly exaggerated, but the performance of the hardened Gallic legions was all their commander could have demanded of them. Pompey's cavalry, as was to be expected, drove back its outnumbered opponents but then, when attacked by a column of infantry that Caesar had held in reserve for the purpose, fell into a panic and left the field, abandoning their luckless foot comrades. More than 24,000 Pompeians reportedly surrendered; but their defeated leader escaped up the coast to Thrace, and thence by sea to the Aegaean island of Mitylene, there to ponder where best he might start rebuilding his fortunes. The choice he made, a fateful one, was Egypt.

In the ancient empire on the Nile political affairs were even more than usually unsettled. Ptolemy XI Auletes, a tenth-generation descendant of one of Alexander the Great's generals, had died in 51 B.C., leaving the Hellenistic kingdom to his young son Ptolemy XII and the latter's older sister, Cleopatra. The girl-queen who had tried, and failed, to seize sole power through an abortive military coup, was precariously encamped with her makeshift army beyond the eastern edge of the delta. Her brother, although the titular ruler, was controlled by three would-be regents: the eunuch Pothinus, the rhetorician Theodotus of Chios, and a military adventurer named Achillas—a trio loftily dismissed by Sir Charles Oman, who believed they were half-castes despite their Greek names, as "miserable Levantines." [12] Of greater moment was the fact that the undeniably mixed Egyptian army contained many Roman veterans who had served under Pompeius Magnus in the eastern wars and might now, or so he hoped, enlist with him again.

The hard-pressed general's decision to come to Egypt posed a frightening dilemma for the regime at Alexandria. If the three councilors advised King Ptolemy not to receive Pompey, what would happen to them if he eventually won? But if Pompey were given asylum and support, only to lose in the end, what pitiless retribution might not await them at the hands of a victorious Caesar? The solution they settled upon joined ruthlessness with caution. "If we lure him ashore and kill him," Theodotus is alleged to have concluded, "we do Caesar a favor, and have nothing to fear from Pompey. For a dead man cannot bite."[13]

That is what they did. Achillas, accompanied by two Roman officers turned mercenaries, was rowed out to meet Pompey's trireme as it neared the Egyptian coast. The general's wife, Cornelia, and numerous aides on board were frightened by the sight of royal troops on shore and boats in the water; but the welcoming party assured the new arrivals that sandbars made it dangerous for a seagoing vessel to come any closer to the beach. So Pompey, accompanied by a couple of his own centurions and two personal servants, stepped down into the small boat, expecting to be rowed to an audience with the young king of Egypt. He reportedly tried to start some conversation with his hosts and, failing in that, took out the Greek text of the speech he meant to give on meeting Ptolemy. Studying this kept him occupied until the boat touched shore. Upon stepping out of the barge, he was stabbed from behind by Achillas and the two legionaries. "Drawing his toga down over his face with both his hands," so Plutarch tells us, "he neither said nor did anything unworthy of himself, only groaned a little, and so ended his life in his sixtieth year and only one day after his birthday." [14]

When Caesar arrived in Alexandria shortly after, bringing with him two legions and his small force of cavalry, he reacted in a predictable way. Presented by Theodotus with Pompey's head and signet ring, he sent the former to the victim's widow, the latter to Rome as confirmation of the murder. Had Pompey been captured alive, self-interest and reasons of state would surely have dictated the prisoner's execution. In the event, however, Caesar revealed a patrician's sense of outrage at the killing of a Roman by foreigners and renegades.

Pompey died the victim of intriguers who feared either to acknowledge or to defy a beaten but still dangerous actor in the affairs of mighty Rome. Caesar died four years later at the hands of fellow participants in those affairs, most of whom owed him their positions and some, their very lives. By the spring of 44 B.C. he was in his sixth year as consul and his fifth as dictator, though there is evidence that he had begun to consider giving up the latter title now that the Civil Wars appeared to be over. Since the climactic victory at Munda and the lavish ceremonies of triumph upon his return from Spain, he had devoted himself to a broad array of legislative projects. These dealt with matters as diverse as financial policy, citizenship, colonization, the reordering of procedure in criminal trials, and so on, continuing the work he had begun with his calendar reform and other measures in 47. He had also, in the autumn of 45, made a will to replace the old one (which had named Pompey his heir) and placed it in the keeping of the Vestal Virgins. This testament designated three grandnephews as his principal beneficiaries and declared one of them, young Octavius—the future Emperor Augustus—to be his adopted son.

The same instrument provided for a second set of heirs, should Caesar outlive the first. Among this group of nonrelatives in reserve, so to speak, were Mark Antony, the consul's old Commander of Horse, and another former comrade in arms, the admiral Decimus Brutus. (It is this circumstance that has led some to suggest that Caesar's famous dying words, "Et tu, Brute?" were meant not for Marcus Junius Brutus, as generally assumed, but for Decimus, also one of the assassins.) Two other steps were taken by Caesar in the closing weeks of his life: he declined the royal diadem offered him at the festival of the Lupercalia by Antony, newly installed as his fellow consul for the year 44; and he announced his decision to undertake a military campaign in the east against the stubborn Parthians.

Neither decision reveals Caesar as a would-be subverter of the Republic, though there is no way of knowing whether he would have restored it. The Lupercalia offered an ideal opportunity for seizing a crown, if that is what he wanted; and his determination to take the field against Rome's most dangerous foreign enemy hardly squares with selfish domestic ambitions. No doubt Caesar expected to hold power in some form for the rest of his life, but his repeated reelection as consul combined with a free hand in military affairs would not have been very different from the solution to Rome's political troubles favored by a number of responsible citizens. Certainly it would have been a far cry from the Greek and Oriental models of tyranny conjured up by the whispers of his enemies.

What he did place in jeopardy by clinging to the emergency title and powers of dictator was the Senate's hallowed superiority over all magistrates, including consuls. His policies, though perhaps not so revolutionary as his critics had feared, nevertheless ran counter to the narrow interests of the most defensive and privileged wing of the oligarchy, the *optimates*. Not all opposition to Caesar, however, was reactionary or self-serving. To an intelligent and well-briefed conservative such as Cicero, senator for life since his own consulship in 63 B.C., the roots of Caesar's power and the direction of its growth continued to look menacing in the extreme. With the frequent and orderly rotation of elective government once broken by a military and political genius, how could anyone save the Republic from eventual oblivion?

What has tended to befog the case of principled Romans against Julius Caesar is the extent to which it has been identified with the person of Marcus Junius Brutus. Even those aware that Caesar does not qualify as the worst tyrant in history sometimes hail Brutus as the greatest of all tyrant-killers. Heir to one of the proudest family traditions in all of Rome, appointed governor of Gaul by Caesar himself in 46 B.C., and elected praetor for the year 44, he was a man of culture whose background invited the suspicion that he was one of the dictator's hostages from the high aristocracy. Lacking the fierce ambition of his coconspirator Cassius (the Pompeian admiral pardoned by Caesar), Brutus appeared to have no selfish motive for turning on the leader whom he defended loyally as late as the summer of 45. This apparent independence has contributed to his reputation for republican virtue. Yet he left behind not enough traces of his mind at work to make one certain even about his vaunted purity of motive. More troubling still is the lack of a discernible *positive* motive, pure or not. In the words of F. E. Adcock, "he had no eyes for anything beyond the negative duty and the dull simplification of tyrannicide." [15]

The conspiracy began to assume definite shape after Caesar's victory at

Munda had erased any lingering possibility of his being defeated in battle. Its fruition occurred on the Ides (15th) of March, 44 B.C., when the circle of assassins thrust daggers into their victim, striking repeatedly until his helpless staggering ended outside the Senate House. According to the common account, Caesar received no fewer than twenty-three wounds, while his killers accidentally inflicted a number of injuries on each other.[16]

One of the most sincere among those who hoped that Caesar's death might liberate believers in the "good old ways" was Cicero. He was growing old himself, but remained nonetheless a power to be reckoned with by the late dictator's political heirs, Mark Antony in particular. With Cato now dead by his own hand in Africa, Cicero must have seemed the one remaining "conscience of the Republic." He had, to be sure, taken no part in the conspiracy, its prime movers having probably distrusted his well-known independence of mind. Once Caesar was dead, however, the veteran orator's voice was raised in the Senate, urging clemency for the assassins and the appointment of Brutus and Cassius, the former a close personal friend of the speaker, to proconsulships in the provinces. When it became clear that not the slayers but the avengers of Caesar were gaining in public support, Cicero retired to his country estate for several months, only to reenter Rome that autumn and deliver the speeches against Mark Antony he proudly labeled "Philippics," after the famous Athenian orations of Demosthenes in opposition to Philip of Macedon.

The senatorial party under Hirtius and Pansa, consuls for the year 43, had by now come to share these misgiving about Mark Antony, who was busily engaged in preparations for an all-out attack on the army of Decimus Brutus in northern Italy. The hope of the "republicans" lay in keeping Octavius, Caesar's adopted son, on their side by giving him a share in commanding the forces being sent under the two consuls to oppose Antony's legions besieging Mutina (Modena). The consular forces had some initial success in this effort; but both Hirtius and Pansa died of wounds received in the fighting, and Octavius turned back upon Rome at the head of an army now "his" as it had not been while the consuls lived. By June 43 he had cowed the Senate into calling special elections, in which he was chosen as one of the consuls to fill the vacancies created on the battlefield, and also into solemnly confirming his adoption.

From this point events moved swiftly toward the definitive stage of the Republic's dissolution and the tragic finale of Cicero's career. Decimus Brutus having been killed by a chieftain in Cisalpine Gaul (the more famous Brutus was for the time being safe in Greece), Octavius unexpectedly reversed himself and in November reached an agreement with Mark Antony and the latter's ally, Marcus Lepidus, governor of Transalpine Gaul. This Second Triumvirate was as solemnly established as the first one, Caesar's and Pompey's, had been informal. It was also far more menacing to what remained of the Republic. The triumvirs marched on Rome and by the end of the month had the vote of the Tribal Assembly empowering them to issue decrees and to command all magistrates for a period of more than five years. Then they turned to the outlawing of their political enemies, in which Mark Antony showed himself the most vengeful. Because the bounties for killing proscribed individuals were generous, the death toll mounted rapidly; according to one modern estimate, it reached three hundred senators and two thousand equestrians before the reign of terror had run its course.[17]

That Cicero would be among the first members of the Senate marked for death went without question, if Mark Antony's wishes were to be respected. Octavius, toward whom the old orator had been friendly, almost fatherly, held out against his fellow triumvirs for a couple of days, but then gave in as part of an arrangement by which each of the three conquerors agreed to the execution of someone he had previously sought to have exempted. Late the previous summer Cicero had returned to his villa at Tusculum, where he must have followed reports from Rome with a growing sense of inevitability.

When word of their proscription arrived, he and his brother Quintus decided to try to reach the Adriatic coast, whence they might escape to safety with the anti-Caesarean forces in Greece. Quintus, fearing that he was not carrying enough money to pay for the flight, turned back to pick up additional funds from his home, only to be betrayed and killed by bounty-hunters. Cicero did reach the sea but seemed to have been indecisive, perhaps because he still retained some faith in Octavius. Going ashore at Gaieta, where he had a summer home, he virtually surrendered to his pursuers. Two of them, army officers named Herennius and Popillius (men he was said to have defended in a murder trial years before), caught up with his litter as he was being carried toward the shore and, in the absence of any resistance on his part, cut his throat. This was on December 7 in 43 B.C., the sixty-fourth year of Cicero's life. His head and his hands were carried to Mark Antony.[18]

The Empire as Epilogue

To the casual reader it may seem strange that my discussion of Rome, including its special place in the history of political murder, should have been so heavily weighted in favor of the final century of the Republic, from the end of the Punic Wars to the deaths of Pompey, Caesar, and Cicero. This allocation of emphasis leaves relatively little available space for the record of what ensued, despite the fact that the Empire lasted longer than the Republic and featured many more assassinations. At issue here is the matter of qualitative as opposed to quantitative significance. Some of the prominent individuals slain in imperial times were politicians. Others were not. But of only a handful could it have been said that their deaths compared, in the gravity of questions raised, with the principal homicides committed in the age of the Gracchi and the Civil Wars.

In the uneven but growing series of political homicides which occurred under the Empire, a certain number are well worth noting. Earliest among them was the killing of Gaius Caesar Augustus Germanicus, better known as Caligula. When the first emperor, Augustus, died in A.D. 14, he left the throne to an adopted son, Tiberius Claudius Nero. Tiberius having in turn succumbed in 37, at the ripe old age of seventy-nine, it was announced that one of his designated heirs was his young grandson Tiberius Gemellus. The other was a great-nephew, already a successful army commander, Gaius Caesar, whose nickname "Caligula" meant "little boot," after part of the soldier's uniform he had worn in his youth. Gaius, after what can only have been a halfhearted attempt to rule jointly with his cousin, had Gemellus killed and thereupon began a reign marked by increasingly mad self-deification. Having begun by alienating the Senate and the nobility, he proceeded to make the fatal mistake of offending the military as well. In 41 Cassius Chaerea, tribune of the praetorian guard and victim of one of the unbalanced emperor's many insults, killed him as Caligula was about to leave Rome for a campaign in Asia. His wife and daughter were also slain, and the Senate, hastily summoned, was told by the perperator to salute "the return of liberty." Rome had witnessed its first assassination of an emperor.[19]

The Senate, apparently taking too literally Chaerea's words, tried in vain to reassert its own prerogatives and to reestablish the Republic. But the guardsmen, who held the real power, insisted on another emperor of the Julian-Claudian line, a rather bookish uncle of Caligula, Tiberius Claudius Drusus, destined to rule for thirteen years. Claudius' public relations suffered from, among other things, his bad judgment in selecting wives (one of them, Messalina, was a sadistic nymphomaniac whose execution he had to order in 48), but he was in most other respects an intelligent and conscientious administrator. While his expansion of the imperial bureaucracy may have given too much power to ambitious secretaries of the household, he dealt fairly with the provinces, even giving nobles from the most favored among them, such as Gaul and Macedonia, access to membership in the Senate. After Messalina's death, however, with senatorial approval, he married a niece, Agrippina, and shortly thereafter adopted her son, the future Emperor Nero.

This choice was the last, and worst, of Claudius' surrenders to women. Earlier in this book, in considering the feats of Jezebel and Athaliah, it was suggested that in due course the Romans of the imperial epoch would produce a number of murderous ladies rivaling those of the Old Testament, since among Greeks, Alexander's mother, Olympias, is the only serious candidate for that distinction. In the case of Rome, Agrippina may be said to clinch the agrument. Her first husband, Domitius Ahenobarbus, sired Nero and then prudently died. Her second spouse, one Passienus Crispus, she poisoned in 49, clearing the way for her marriage to Claudius the following year. Thereafter she set out to eliminate all threats to herself and her son.

She hounded into exile a hostile astrologer, Scribonius, who soon either committed suicide or was murdered. Statilius Taurus, a distinguished proconsul whom she arranged to have indicted by the Senate for alleged misdeeds during his years of service in Asia and Africa, killed himself rather than suffer the indignity of trial. The women she considered dangerous fared no better: a divorced wife of the late Caligula, Lollia Paulina, was driven to suicide; Domitia Lepida, another potential rival, was executed after a mock trial. Finally it was the turn of the Emperor Claudius himself, poisoned in 54 by Agrippina with the help, Tacitus and others assure us, of his own physician.[20]

The way was now clear for the accesssion of Nero, his mother's darling but a ruler who, after five years in power, tired of her constant interference and, urged on by certain courtiers (including Seneca) and by his mistress Poppaea, had Agrippina herself killed in gruesome fashion by a group of sailors dispatched to her lakeside villa. The wheel that began to turn with her poisoning of Passienus ten years before had come full circle. One more fatal episode must be mentioned, however, before closing the grisly record of Nero's times. That worthy, last of the Julian-Claudians, had by 68, following his absence on a tour of Greece, been declared a public enemy by the Senate. In June, learning that the praetorian guard had recognized the general Servius Sulpicius Galba as emperor, Nero killed himself at a country place near Rome.

Galba's elevation had actually begun when two legions proclaimed him in Spain, and he had to return to Italy before receiving the confirmation of a powerless Senate. That winter one of the lieutenants who had come home from the provinces with him, Marcus Salvius Otho, seized upon a vote of the legions in Germany to reject Galba in favor of their commander Vitellius, then secured his own recognition by the now seemingly aimless praetorians. At Otho's command the guard murdered Galba in January 69; and two rival pretenders, Otho in Rome and Vitellius marching down from the Rhineland, faced each other in a new civil war. Otho, defeated in the Po Valley, committed suicide; but the Danubian legions entered that arena, supporting still another provincial leader, the imperial legate in Judea, who would rule as the Emperor Vespasian. Beaten in northern Italy, Vitellius fell back on Rome, only to die there on December 20 fighting in the streets. By the time Vespasian entered the capital the next summer he had already been recognized for months as emperor by vote of the Senate.

Galba might have offered some hope of order and restraint after the idiocy of Nero, but he had been given no time in which to produce any lasting results. More significant than his abrupt end, however, was the evidence of A.D. 69 that, with the original imperial line extinguished, there remained no basis for dependable action by the military in support of any new ruler. Within the space of a single year legions from different provinces, with the concurrence in Rome of both the praetorians and a demoralized Senate, had destroyed three successive emperors proclaimed by other troops—Galba, Otho, Vitellius—and launched a fourth, Vespasian, on a ten-year reign. Clearly the sword alone now offered succession, without the promise of stability.[21]

Before the end of the first century one more important emperor, Titus Flavius Domitianus (Domitian), was slain. He had come to the throne in 81 as successor to his elder brother, another son of Vespasian. Seemingly an able manager of domestic affairs and unquestionably a successful field commander on the Rhine and the Danube (he organized the fortification of both great valleys), Domitian was nevertheless petty and vengeful, especially in his dealings with the Senate. After fourteen years in power he finally let his personal hatreds and suspicions propel him into an action which crystallized the opposition. He ordered the execution of his cousin Flavius Clemens, *Consul ordinarius* and the husband of Domitian's niece Domitia. The victim was not only the tyrant's kinsman but also, by all accounts, such a harmless bumbler that his death gave warning to all that no degree of insignificance could make a Roman safe. With the approval of the eminent senator and respected jurist Cocceius Nerva, a plot was contrived and Domitian slain in 96 by a freedman, one Stephanus, who stabbed his victim while handing him a document. Stephanus was killed at once by the imperial guard, but the other conspirators slipped away, leaving the elderly Nerva to serve as emperor for the two years he had to live.

There remain just two more outbreaks of assassinations serious enough to demand attention. One began with the death of Commodus, son of Marcus Aurelius and himself emperor since 180, when at the age of only nineteen he succeeded his famous father. Unlike his predecessors, Trajan, Hadrian, and Marcus Aurelius, the young ruler lacked political sense and personal restraint. He had able and faithful ministers put to death in deference to factional hatreds; he terrorized the Senate after discovering an ineffectual plot against him in 182; and he came increasingly to pose as, at the very least, a demigod. His hope of survival lay in keeping the loyalty of the praetorian guard, on whose members he bestowed high salaries and countless gifts. In 192 that hope failed him. Suffering the same mischance which would doom Robespierre in Paris almost exactly sixteen hundred years later, Commodus let fall into the hands of potential conspirators—the Egyptian chamberlain Eclectus and the praetorian prefect Laetus—a draft proscription list. Moved wholly or in part by this knowledge, they arranged, with the aid of his concubine, to poison Commodus and then, when the dosage failed, had him strangled in his bath by the wrestler Narcissus, a member of the palace staff supposedly charged with seeing that the emperor kept up his daily exercises.

Commodus having left no heir, the praetorian guard, at the behest of

Laetus, proclaimed as emperor one Publius Helvius Pertinax. Pertinax, though destined to occupy the throne for less than three months, beginning in December 192, stands out as one of the more engaging of Rome's short-term rulers. Of modest Italian origins, he had served with distinction as a military commander on several fronts and had had a term as consul before settling, at the age of sixty-six, into the less demanding post of city prefect. Like Galba and Vespasian before him, Pertinax seemed to offer some hope of personal sanity and good administration in contrast to the profligate reign so recently ended. But like Galba in this respect as well, he was given no chance. The busy Laetus, when he discovered that the supposed puppet had ideas of his own, including economy projects which enraged senators and guardsmen alike, went back to plotting. The praetorians themselves carried out Pertinax's murder in the spring of 193.

Once more the legions in various provinces rushed to enter the game, proclaiming no fewer than three different pretenders to the succession. One of these, L. Septimius Severus, a Roman commander in Pannonia (today's Hungary and Yugoslavia), prevailed and inaugurated a stern rule of eighteen years with the prudent decision to disband the existing praetorian guard and reconstitute it using loyal legionnaires from the field armies. When he died in 211, leading his troops against the Britons near York, he was succeeded by his eldest son, originally Septimius Bassianus but better known as Caracalla.

Thus opened the last round of Roman state killings to detain us here. The reign began in some confusion because Caracalla's younger brother, P. Septimius Geta, expected to share the imperial dignity. Geta, only twenty-two when their father died, proved no match for his ruthless sibling, who had him and several of his supporters murdered almost at once.[22] Now sole emperor, Caracalla established a reputation for largesse by sponsoring public works such as the luxurious baths in Rome whose ruins still bear his name; and he successfully commanded the Empire's defense against the Alamanni, Goths, and other German foes. Like more than a few of his predecessors, however, Caracalla fell victim to palace intriguers, in particular another praetorian prefect, Marcus Opellius Macrinus. Macrinus, reportedly startled by word that a soothsayer had named him future emperor and fearful lest Caracalla hear of the prophecy, seized the opportunity to kill him on his way to visit a religious sanctuary in the east. This happened on April 8, 217.

Macrinus did succeed Caracalla, but only briefly, succumbing in June 218. Thereupon, with the backing of legions stationed in the Levant, a truly exotic figure seized the crown. Born in Syria, he had been named Varius Avitus Bassianus, though most historians know him as Elagabulus or, incorrectly, as Heliogabalus. Although a great-nephew of the late Emperor Septimius Severus, he was more Syrian than Roman, choosing upon his accession the name of the god Baal of Emesa—Elah-Gabal—whose priestess his mother had been and whose worship the new emperor brought to Rome. Elagabulus in one sense personified the highly controversial appearance in the capital of various cults imported from the East, cults with which Christianity was sometimes bracketed, to its disadvantage; but it was his homosexual excesses which appear to have contributed most to his rapid decline in public standing. (To have offended imperial Rome, they must have been excessive indeed!) In spite of this and the growing fear he aroused in the minds of the established orders, he clung to power for four years with the help of his strong-willed grandmother Julia Maesa. In 221 it even began to appear that he might find a degree of respectability, having at Julia's urging adopted a comparatively harmless cousin, Alexander or Alexianus, as his son and heir.

Elagabulus, however, shortly abandoned the idea of sharing power and let it be known, with a characteristic lack of discretion, that he intended to disinherit the young man. Faced with the prospect of being ruled once more by an unrestrained despot, the opposition decided to act. On March 11, 222, a group of praetorian guards killed the emperor, together with his Baalite mother, Julia Soaemias, and threw his body into the always convenient Tiber.[23]

The assassinations recalled here constitute only a small fraction of the many to be found in the annals of imperial Rome. Most of the ones included, and virtually all of those omitted, are better characterized as products of palace intrigues or military mutinies than events revealing serious political conflict within acknowledged institutional boundaries. The murders of Caligula, Domitian, Commodus, and Elagabulus no doubt deserve to be considered tyrannicides in keeping with the classical definition of usurpation or flagrant misrule, or both; but even they showed traces of other and less principled motives. Eventually, in the lurid twilight of the Empire, it became difficult to identify any principle at all, save personal vengeance or self-interest savagely pursued. In 453 Atilla, king of the Huns, was reportedly killed by a woman acting on orders from the Roman general Aëtius, erstwhile victor over a Hunnic army in Gaul and a Visigothic force in Spain. The following year Aëtius was slain by an ungrateful emperor, Valentinian III, who within another six months died in his turn, allegedly at the hands of two of the late general's old retainers. At this point one becomes acutely aware of having ventured beyond documentable Roman history into the legends of still darker ages.

What the Romans Showed

Rome's contributions to an understanding of political murder contrast with those of Greece in a manner consistent with much else bequeathed by those two societies to the modern world. That is to say, between them the relation of theory to practice seems almost reversed. The Greeks had a few famous assassinations, comparatively speaking only a few, which they proceeded to analyze and to debate at length, endeavoring to distinguish tyrannicide from other, less justifiable resorts to personal violence. It remained for the Romans to test such definitions by repeatedly enacting dramatic episodes on a vastly expanded stage. To signal this contrast is not to ignore the Greek case histories, nor to belittle the intellectual efforts of those citizens of Rome, Cicero among them, who thought and wrote about the ethical problems of tyrannicide. The proportionate difference in emphasis, however, is sufficiently marked to suggest the need for care in the application of such terms as "*the* Greco-Roman tradition."

On the Roman side there is another distinction, that between the republican and imperial eras. The Republic, I have suggested, posed more difficult questions concerning violence in politics than did the Empire. Later ages have with good reason studied the Empire's record of bloodshed, not only because of its sensational aspects but also because it was, after all, the record of the most powerful state the world had ever seen. The fact remains that one must look earlier, to the Gracchi, Pompey, Caesar, Brutus, Mark Antony, Cicero, for the names and destinies that still loom large in any discussion of political violence in the ancient world.

This book's attempt at such discussion has not yet proceeded to the point of offering an answer to the question whether assassination, including principled tyrannicide, is ever "good politics." Roman history, however, at least suggests that political murder often proves destructive of more than its victim's life and threatens, even under circumstances of apparent success, to unleash consequences far removed from its author's expectations. The cost of killing a Gracchus, and helping thereby to undermine a tradition of balance and restraint, or a Julius Caesar, unleashing in the process a military stampede toward wholly autocratic power, calls for painstaking appraisal of many factors. That process was temporarily checked by Augustus, who openly and it appears sincerely, attempted to revive the Republic, albeit in the general sense of *res publica* under an emperor charged with mediating the divisive forces that had undermined the old structure. No such solution proved viable under successors who in any case gave no indication of wishing to pursue it. Instead, the Empire, over the course of its long but deteriorating existence, provided one of history's most imposing demonstrations of how political violence perpetuates itself long after its supposed rationale has ceased to be a subject for reflection.

4

Other Peoples, Other Lands

Reports from the Neighbors

Mention of Attila calls to mind the difficulties awaiting anyone who ventures beyond the familiar sources and chronological structure of Hebrew scripture and classical Greco-Roman history. Political murder is nevertheless a worldwide phenomenon whose traces must be sought wherever they survive. Even the Huns, of whom it has with good reason been said that they built nothing, wrote nothing, and strove to leave no witnesses, can be glimpsed through the eyes of more sedentary and literate foes. Sometimes these include Chinese and Persian chroniclers of invasions by Asian nomads. In general, however, a well-tried centrifugal principle, that of proceeding from the more to the less familiar, justifies beginning with what the Jews, the Greeks, and the Romans had to say about other ancient peoples whose lands and interests touched their own.

The Old Testament, specifically the Second Book of Kings, contains an episode involving Ben-Hadad II, the Syrian ruler of Damascus in the ninth century B.C. This son of the conqueror Ben-Hadad I shared his father's hatred of the Jews, who returned the hostility with all the ardor their prophet Elisha demanded. Up to a point the plot that eliminated Ben-Hadad recalls Elisha's successful effort within Israel to destroy Ahab and Jezebel with the help of Jehu (see Chapter 1). This time it was Hazael, an ambitious subject of the king, who met secretly with Elisha at a place near Damascus and there heard the prophet's assurance that Ben-Hadad, who was ill at the time, would soon either die or voluntarily surrender the throne to none other than Hazael himself. Returning to Damascus, Hazael delivered courteous greetings from the holy man to the ailing sovereign, then smothered him with Ben-Hadad's own bedclothes. Sad to relate, having assumed the royal title, as Elisha had prophesied, Hazael proceeded to become yet another abomination in the sight of the Lord, attacking Jehu and the Israelites at every opportunity.[1] So much, the Bible implies, for Syrian gratitude.

An episode involving the kingdom of Lydia in Asia Minor during the seventh century before the Christian era introduces a despot about whom we might never have learned had he not appeared in a famous Greek source, Herodotus' *History*. Its author, by the way, dismissed the king's Persian name, Sadyattes, preferring to use Candaules, meaning "dog-strangler." Early in the first book of his great work Herodotus reproduces the dog-strangler's story, featuring a plot worthy of that master of ribald invention, Boccaccio, two thousand years later.

"This Candaules," reports the historian in a tone of at least mild surprise, "fell in love with his own wife, so much so that he supposed her to be by far the fairest woman in the world." [2] His pride in the queen eventually led him to conclude that she must be displayed in the nude, albeit without her knowledge, before one of his favorite guardsmen, Gyges by name, who would be secretly admitted to the royal sleeping quarters. Gyges appears to have had serious misgivings about the wisdom of hiding in a ruler's boudoir. He begged his master to forget the project, saying: "With the stripping off of her tunic a woman is stripped of the honor due her . . . As for me, I fully believe that your queen is the fairest of women." The king, however, insisted, leaving a mere soldier in the palace guard no choice but to obey.

According to Herodotus, Gyges was introduced into the bedroom as planned and did in fact watch the queen disrobe; but as he was tiptoeing away, she recognized him and without apparent hesitation decided that her husband should pay with his life for this affront. Summoning Gyges the next day, she offered him another of those choices that seemed to bedevil his early career: "You have two roads open before you . . . You must either kill Candaules and take me and the throne of Lydia for your own, or yourself be killed without further ado." Her new consort-designate having demurred as usual, which is to say briefly, she led him back to the royal bedchamber, where the king was sleeping. With a dagger supplied by the queen, Gyges carried out the murder and went on to rule for thirty-two years. In the nineteenth-century version by the German dramatist Hebbel, the wronged lady kills herself as the curtain falls, her need for vengeance satisfied. [3] In the less moralistic text of Herodotus there is no suggestion of any such denouement.

Elsewhere in the Mediterranean world, the Carthaginians might have preferred themselves to inform posterity of their experience with murder as an aspect of ancient statecraft; but they were not given the chance. Once the Scipios had done their work in North Africa, killing soldiers, enslaving civilians, leveling walls, and sprinkling the ruins with salt, all that remained of Rome's most dangerous rival was to be found in Greek and more especially Latin commentaries. Even these, however, were enough to show that Carthage, like Rome, had had its military-patrician factions and its political infighting between oligarchic and popular parties. It also had commanders slain by their subordinates, the admiral Hannibal (not the famous general) having been crucified by his own men in 259 B.C. after ordering his triremes beached to avoid battle with a Roman fleet off the coast of Sardinia. The later Hannibal was not murdered or lynched, but his brother-in-law Hasdrubal, governor of Spain, fell victim in 221 to a Celto-Iberian said to have harbored a wholly personal grudge. Despite the seemingly trivial circumstances of his death, Hasdrubal was unquestionably a figure of genuine importance, active, as was his father-in-law Hamilcar Barca, in Cathaginian politics on the populist side. In at least one respect even his murder qualifies as a political event, since it resulted in Hannibal's elevation to the position of commander in Iberia, the base for his momentous campaigns against Rome itself.[4]

Latin sources have something to say about other denizens of Spain, not just its Carthaginian occupiers. The fateful Numantine revolt, earlier seen adding to Rome's colonial worries after the Punic Wars and helping to shape the career of Tiberius Gracchus, might never have erupted had not the Lusitanian leader Viriathus been assassinated by men who had been offered Roman bribes. He was reportedly a remarkable "leader of barbarians," so respected by the Romans that in a burst of rage, perhaps combined with parsimony and certainly influenced by the slaying's ominous consequences, the Senate refused to pay his killers the money promised, sending them into exile instead.[5] There is not enough additional evidence bearing on ancient cases of murder for hire to support any confident guess as to how frequently the Romans may have had recourse to it. From what is known about Rome's treatment of barbarian leaders other than Viriathus, however, it seems unlikely that the Senate's repudiation of his slayers sprang from any deep-seated moral revulsion.

Some of the time Romans appear as observers, wary but claiming to be detached, at least until events took an unacceptable turn. It was in this capacity that they recount events in the North African kingdom of Numidia—roughly equivalent in location and extent to present-day Algeria—where Jugurtha launched his bloody campaign to succeed King Micipsa. The latter was an illegitimate son and heir of Massinissa, the ruler whose quarrel with Carthage had been Rome's pretext for launching the Third (and final) Punic War. Jugurtha, an adopted nephew of Micipsa, was therefore initially regarded in Rome as an ally. Even when, in 117 B.C., he arranged the murder of Hiempsal, a son of the late king, and then drove into exile Hiempsal's brother Adherbal, reports of the coup d'état failed to alarm policymakers on the far-off Capitoline. The rection there was entirely different a few years later, when the Senate received news that the African king had rebelled openly against the Roman protectorate, killing legionaries and civilian officials alike. Defeated and captured by Marius and Sulla after a ferocious war, Jugurtha was lucky enough to die in prison before alternative arrangements could be completed for his inevitably brief future.[6]

At various other points along the perimeter of Rome's spreading domain the Republic helped to cause, even when it did not consciously will, a number of political killings. In 47 B.C., following Pompey's death, the advance of Caesar's legions into Asia Minor touched off a chain reaction of violence, not all of it confined to the battlefield. Their victory at Zela shook the foundations of power along the entire south coast of the Black Sea. Pharnaces, a son of Pompey's old foe Mithridates and himself king of Bosporus prior to the Roman conqueror's death in Egypt, decided on hearing of the assassination that the time had come to throw off the restraints previously imposed upon Near Eastern rulers. This gamble proved disastrous on two counts, one military (Pharnaces having traded Pompey for Caesar as a foe), the other personal. At Zela the Bosporan army was cut to pieces; and soon after, as the king was fleeing westward in a vain effort to reach safety, he was murdered by one of his own governors now in revolt.[7]

Mention of Egypt recalls still another action spun off by the Roman Civil Wars: the supposed elimination of King Ptolemy XIII by his sister Cleopatra. That energetic woman might earlier have moved against Ptolemy XII, her ostensible coruler under their father's will, had the sickly boy not drowned in the course of a military exercise. Julius Caesar had taken the precaution of associating her with a second brother, the ill-fated thirteenth of his name, who was murdered following the Ides of March and Cleopatra's hasty return from Rome. Contemporaries, whether rightly or wrongly, seem to have entertained no doubts as to who had instigated the crime.[8]

To cite additional cases of political murder on the margins of the Roman world would be easy, but needlessly repetitious. Many of them, in any case, were "political" in only the most limited sense of the term, having resulted from mere palace intrigues or dynastic struggles within families as closely, not to say incestuously, related as Egypt's Ptolemies. A word of caution is also in order with respect to even the best accounts transmitted by the Jews, the Greeks, or the Romans, the first a people with their own unique application of monotheism to public affairs, the remaining two much given to theorizing about tyranny and justifiable resistance to it. Not surprisingly, all three tended to belittle any action not readily definable in their particular terms, be they scriptural or philosophical—terms used self-confidently and often with intelligence, but inevitably ethnocentric. The killing of Viriathus in Spain was unquestionably an act of political significance, not against a tyrant, to be sure, but against an opponent who both in life and in death posed serious problems for the Roman Senate. What little is known about Carthaginian government suggests that fuller knowledge of its workings might reveal features not necessarily pleasant to contemplate but interesting in comparative terms, as parts of a narrative almost wholly obliterated because it ended in total defeat.

Rival Powers

Three ancient empires—Assyria, Egypt, and Persia—demand what might be called an intermediate approach, for all left quite extensive records of their own, more or less fully corroborated by Hebrew, Greek, and Latin writings. The crisis involving the Assyrian throne in 745 B.C. is a case in point. Mystery continues to surround some of its details, despite efforts by students of Assyrio-Babylonian history and Judaic texts to clarify the narrative by pooling their archaeological and documentary resources.[9] There is even disagreement over the royal title of the military commander who seized power that year—should he be called Tiglath-Pileser III or IV? Regarding more important aspects of his coup, however, there is substantial agreement. Since the death of Adadnirari III in 782, Assyria had suffered chronic misrule as well as recurrent defeats inflicted by the kingdom of Van to the north. Military humiliation led to an army mutiny and the extinction of all members of the ousted dynasty. Their successor's name appears to have been Pul or Pulu; and it is known that after his troops took Babylon and Ashur, he decreed that the Babylonians should crown him as Pul, perhaps to avoid arousing their antipathy to the unmistakably Assyrian name Tiglath-Pileser. Whatever sensitivity he may have displayed in the matter of names did not extend to the matter of killing off possible rivals from the past.

Or consider Egypt before it fell under foreign domination. One episode in particular is established by a remarkable combination of sources: not only local hieroglyphic inscriptions but also Hebrew scriptures and the account written in Greek by Herodotus.[10] However, Egyptians do not depend on the Hellenic evidence for this segment of their ancient history; and as for the Old Testament, its rendering in the books of Jeremiah and Ezekiel is at best confusing.[11]

The story begins with the death of King Psammis in or about 589 B.C. His son and heir, Hophra, the "Apries" of the Bible, enjoyed good fortune through the first two decades of his reign, until a military defeat suffered while attacking the Greek colony of Cyrene in modern Libya produced revolt at home. Faced with the need to quiet rumors that through fear of his army he had purposely exposed it to disaster, the beleaguered monarch chose a supposedly loyal officer, Amasis by name, to explain matters to the populace. When, however, someone interrupted the negotiations by thrusting a helmet on Amasis' head, thereby suggesting a royal coronation, Hophra's supposed advocate underwent a sudden conversion to the rebel cause. The king first tried to temporize. Then, enraged at learning that Amasis would not obey a royal summons to appear, he ordered the unfortunate messenger's ears and nose cut off. In the civil war that followed Hophra was taken prisoner and brought to the palace of Sais. There his captors turned him over to a shouting crowd, which strangled him forthwith, leaving

Amasis to reign for forty-four years—or so the chronological calculations of antiquity would have it.

Another prominent Egyptian who paid with his life for having lost at politics was Inaros (Ienharou in Hebrew), leader of an abortive revolt against Persian power in 465 B.C. Surrounded and forced to surrender by the armies of Artaxerxes I, Inaros nevertheless secured from the victor a solemn guarantee of amnesty. Unfortunately for him, the mother of Artaxerxes, a formidable dowager queen named Amestris, did not consider herself bound by surrender terms granted in the field—and she wanted the rebel dead. Unable to move immediately against Inaros, who remained in confinement, she waited patiently for five years until the royal order was issued to proceed with his execution by that most hideous of all Eastern means, impalement.[12]

Inaros' fate was not directly connected to other political killings in Persia, heir to the Egyptian, Assyrian, Babylonian, Median, and other crumbling empires. The need to augment a people's own records through the use of foreign sources is in this case imperative, for the Greeks watched the rising power in the East with a fascination sharpened by foreboding. The Persian accounts, however, are often of unique value. Among other things, they point to a political tradition which prior to the disastrous collision with the Greeks had not been particularly cruel. In 550 or 549 B.C., for example, when the Persian rebels under Cyrus the Achaemenian defeated and captured the Median King Astyages, they spared his life, a gesture which may surprise some students of Middle Eastern power struggles but which is not treated as exceptional by Persian chroniclers of the time. Even the assassination of Cyrus the Great's son Cambyses in 522 did not immediately overturn the older mores, supported by the Zoroastrian religious opposition to blood sacrifice and comparable in some respects to the relative mildness of political behavior in mainland Greece at about the same time.[13]

How shocking, then, must have been the onset of murders which began in Achaemenian Persia shortly before the middle of the fifth century B.C. In 465 King Xerxes, still a powerful monarch despite his reverses at the hands of the Athenians, was slain by a leading courtier, Artabanus, who also put to death one of his victim's sons in preparation for his own assumption of the crown. Another son of Xerxes, destined to rule as Artaxerxes I, apparently waited until Artabanus had cleared the path to the throne, then within a few months defeated and killed his father's assassin. Almost simultaneously, as the history of Inaros the Egyptian shows, Artaxerxes crushed insurgents in widely separated parts of the Persian Empire.

The end of his long reign, in 424 B.C., brought more bloodshed in its wake. The legitimate heir, Xerxes II, was murdered by his half-brother Sogdianus, who reigned for a few months, only to be put into a slow furnace by another of these interesting half-brothers, Ochus, who on his coronation assumed the name Darius II. Throughout his twenty-year rule Darius was dominated by an uncommonly ruthless half-sister, Parysatis, whom he married. A half-sister of the couple, seen as a rival by the vigiliant Parysatis, was buried alive on suspicion of disloyalty.

The saga of Persia's Achaemenid kings had not much longer to run before giving way to that of the Seleucid despotism. Before that change was effected, however, three more monarchs of the old line would die by violence. In 338 Artaxerxes III was poisoned by persons unknown to history. His son Arses was murdered two years later through the machinations of one Bogoas, a eunuch who arranged to have a collateral heir named Codomannus crowned as Darius III. Finally this last descendant of Cyrus the Great was slain in 330 by an adventurer known as Bessus, who briefly claimed the deteriorating legacy of the Achaemenids. Before he could enjoy it came invasion by Alexander the Great, followed by the latter's premature death and the ensuing scramble among Macedonian generals for shares in the fruits of his conquests. The Persian share quickly fell to the self-crowned Seleucus I, founder of the new Hellenistic dynasty that bore his name.

The preceding debacle, as described by Persian and Greek historians, calls to mind the fall of royal houses, earlier, in Israel and Judah, as well as the extinction of the Julian-Claudian line, yet to come in imperial Rome. The Persian story, however, differs, if not in kind at least in degree, because of the amount of sustained and apparently calculated sadism it contains. The prominence of this feature poses a further question of significance for the entire record of political violence. Why did the Persians, despite a previous record of rather less cruelty than stereotypic thinking might lead one to expect, come to rely on such lavish use of impalement, immolation, entombment alive, and related horrors? No simple answer is possible, but Persia under the Achaemenids does seem to have experienced a dreadful application of psychological warfare practiced by its rulers at the expense of any and all potential resisters.

Ancient history—and later history as well—suggests that official terror is usually the mark of a regime that may appear brutally self-confident but is in fact insecure. Thus, in the Greek colonies, where political institutions were undeveloped and sometimes all but nonexistent, the ferocity of political behavior, including the use of murder as a tool of intimidation, contrasted sharply with the mores prevalent in Athens or Sparta. In Rome, only as the old framework of rules and attitudes crumbled did gratuitous slaughter come to replace firmer bases for authority. Ancient Persia, after the death of Xerxes I never again would have a government sufficiently sure of itself and its subjects to dispense with frightful forms of killing, intended not only to eliminate individual dissidents but also to paralyze by fear their would-be sympathizers. Such a policy has drawbacks, most obvious being the near certainty that each new leader of a successful revolution will repay the vanquished tyrant in his own coin, using some form of death penalty more ingenious than any the victim himself had been able to devise while in power. Presumably, however, the Achaemenids and others like them fatalistically numbered such reprisals among the occupational hazards of despotism.

Greater Asia: The Sins of Devadatta

The size of the Asian land mass and the variety of its peoples' past existence combine to challenge, and not infrequently to discourage, modern inquiry. The problem lies not so much in the paucity of sources as in the difficulty of integrating them into patterns comprehensible to the non-Asian mind. One result of their apparent incomparability is a tendency, natural enough but nonetheless unfortunate, to assume that the historical experience of all these peoples is as idiosyncratic as their ways of describing it may at times appear. China's number of acknowledged assassinations is so small as to convince some observers that Chinese political behavior, when compared to Mediterranean, Mesopotamian, or Iranian, has been unbelievably mild. Brief reflection leads one to wonder just how decorous were the clashes of aristocratic factions, the competition among warlords, or especially the prolonged civil strife that marked the end of the eastern Chou dynasty and its replacement by the Ch'in, a process extending by occidental reckoning from the fifth to the third century B.C.

The fact remains that descriptions of even these struggles are often resolutely bland. According to Chinese accounts, the notable Chou Emperor Wang III, a contemporary of Confucius, in 478 B.C. simply "passed away with dignity," though his dynasty was already in serious—Westerners might have said terrible—peril. Still more notable was the adjustment to adverse circumstances made by one of Wang's successors, Wang Nan, who, after ruling for fifty-nine years, reportedly gave up the imperial title and stepped down to become a humble vassal of the Ch'in who replaced him. Ancient scribes do remark that Nan Wang "died covered with ignominy"; but after almost sixty years on the throne, he cannot have greeted death with much surprise. One can easily think of losers in Persia or Numidia who would have gladly settled for such an end.[14]

Japan's past, allowance made for there being no reliable information about it dating from before the third century of the Christian era, inspires less uneasiness than does China's, insofar as the relation of myth to reality is concerned. Japanese legends, annals, and imaginative literature (the *bunraku* puppet dramas, for instance) all point to an extremely violent society.[15] Here too, however, a Western observer is struck by certain peculiarly Japanese features. The power struggles were ruthless, but political assassination was complicated, and in some instances inhibited, both by a rigid code of knightly honor and by the aura of divinity surrounding most figures of authority. All one can say with any confidence at this point is that some of the features of East Asian political history are as easily grasped as others are elusive to Europeans and Middle Easterners alike.

In the religious scriptures of India appears one of the few reports involving assassination to be found in the ancient history of southern Asia. It involves a plot around the year 500 B.C. to murder the Gautama Buddha. Admittedly, not even the fullest use of surviving fragments will yield anything like a consecutive biography of Prince Siddhartha Gautama (or Gotami as his family name is sometimes given); but the story of his miraculous escape from three attempts on his life contained in the *Cullavagga* makes that collection of Pali texts the best available source.

Among the members of the original Buddhist community was a Gautama cousin, Prince Devadatta, reputedly devout and well-regarded until he revealed an unseemly desire to replace his kinsman as head of the newly founded order. Devadatta is supposed to have launched his conspiracy by agreeing with a certain Prince Ajatasattu that the latter's father, King Bimbisara, should be killed in order that, under the protection of Ajatasattu, an attack might be made on the Buddha. Some versions of the story assert that Bimbisara was murdered according to plan, others that the entire plot miscarried; but all agree that Devadatta's part of the operation failed utterly. First, some archers hired to kill the Buddha were so impressed by him that they became his followers and refused to have any part in the crime. Next, Devadatta tried to throw a stone down from a peak upon the Buddha's head, only to have another piece of rock arrest the fall of the missile (a reasonable modern reading of how two mountains "leaned together" to protect the intended victim). Turning next, we are told, to still different means, "Devadatta made another unsuccessful attempt to kill the Buddha by dispatching the elephant Nalagiri after infuriating him with liquor, against the Teacher. When the ferocious elephant approached the Buddha, the Venerable Ananda stepped forward to sacrifice his life for the sake of his Master, but the Buddha subdued the beast by His loving-kindness."[16] By reason of these activities, according to the Pali source, "Devadatta became extremely unpopular." But he managed one more attempt to unseat the Buddha, this time by championing a set of five avowedly fundamentalist interpretations of the religious law, intended to expose what he called the Teacher's own laxity. This effort having failed, the frustrated cousin went more or less directly to hell, the jaws of which, according to certain traditional accounts, simply opened and swallowed him alive.[17]

Whether Devadatta passed living into the flames or was otherwise punished, the extent to which this narrative centers on the adventures of a dangerous heretic will not have been lost on its reader. It is primarily a religious document, bearing not only on the question of quasi-divine leadership but also on a collision between fundamentalist and broader interpretations of early Buddhist doctrine. Its other message extols the gentleness of the Buddha in refusing to have his opponent punished by mortal hands, even after three murder attempts and an abortive revolt. In its emphasis on mercy the *Cullavagga* differs most sharply from comparable writings, even the most profoundly religious, bequeathed to the future by the pre-Christian West.

Continents Known and Unknown

About the Americas before the age of discovery a good deal of speculation is still required where political patterns are concerned, despite what may be gleaned from early European observations, archaeological evidence, and elements of Amerindian folk memory that survived long enough to be copied down in lasting form. The growth of knowledge about the Andean Incas in particular suggests that in their mountainous domain they achieved a remarkably orderly succession of rulers, the result in part perhaps of their heavy reliance on priestly sanctions. The same may have been equally true of the Mayan, Toltec, and Aztec civilizations, although their practice of ritual human sacrifice has aroused more modern curiosity than have less lurid aspects of authority. It is futile, however, to speculate as to whether or not such sacrifice at times had a bearing on contests for secular power, since the identity of victims has never been established. The notion that native rulers might have used ostensibly religious ceremonies for the purpose of killing their rivals rests on no foundation save that of plausible inference—and in the history of political murder, plausibility is not always the most reliable guide.

Concerning the greater part of Africa, beyond the ken of ancient Egyptians, Greeks, and Romans, the student of political behavior faces many of the problems that beset efforts to reconstruct the early history of the Western Hemisphere. With the help of Arabic travel literature one can make out at least the dim outlines of the African scene in the early Moslem era. Oral history has also made increasing contributions to modern knowledge. Nevertheless, the questions most likely to be asked by an investigator seeking to draw parallels with Europe and the Middle East are seldom answered by sources of that nature. The circumstances attending succession from one local chieftain to another are often impossible to reconstruct from the customarily terse references that have survived. Even in the annals of larger states, including the Mandingo Empire of West Africa, neither successful nor unsuccessful assassins find much place. References to purposeful homicide appear to have been discouraged by the winner of a political struggle, inhibited from boasting about it if the tactic had been his, and reluctant to perpetuate its memory, if there had been an unsuccessful attempt against him. The most that is likely to be said is that the losers were allowed to kill themselves or, more commonly, to flee the country.

A partial exception to this pattern is Abyssinia. Considerably more is known about the fabled realm of Prester John, as Europeans referred to it, than about any other portion of Black Africa in antiquity. This is not to say that there are no problems of reconstruction and interpretation. For one thing, Abyssinian documents, though relatively numerous, are often difficult to read. For another, the customary division between "ancient" and "medieval," conceived in European or even Middle Eastern terms, had no comparable meaning for a land whose ruler continued until our own century to style himself not only Christian but also "King of Kings" after the Persian *shah-in-shah* and "Lion of Judah" out of pride in his Semitic heritage. The survival of slavery down to almost the present day was further proof that in this home of intertwined Judaic, Christian, and Muslim influences neither social nor political history conformed to outsiders' notions of periodization.

A glimpse of dynastic troubles in the twelfth century (Christian era) helps to show what Abyssinia's records do contain. For a long time before those troubles the Zāgwē family, devoutly Christian since the conversion of Täkle-Hāymānot, one of its early members, had seemed firmly ensconced in power with continuing support from the church hierarchy. King Lālībalā, though his accession was surrounded with pagan superstition, subsequently won renown as the builder of amazing "monolithic churches" into mountainsides of solid stone and, like his ancestor Täkle-Hāymānot, in time came to be regarded as a saint.

Before his local canonization, however, Lālībalā's fame rested on the dramatic circumstances of his route to the throne. The ruling monarch, King Harbāye, is said to have discovered that his crown was in danger only upon being informed, belatedly, of a legend that Lālībalā had been destined from birth to rule in his place. Here is the relevant passage from a manuscript biography in the British Library:

> Lālībalā was the son of Djān Sheyūm, a rich man who was a native of Rōha, and he was born in that town. When his mother had brought him forth, a dense cloud of bees surrounded him, and when she saw this the spirit of prophecy came upon her, and she cried out: "The bees know that this child is a king," and she called him Lālībalā, which means "The bee recognizes his sovereignty." She thought also that the bees represented the soldiers of the army that would serve her son.[18]

There is a difference of opinion among contemporary chroniclers as to whether King Harbāye himself took action against this unforeseen claimant. Most witnesses point to his half-sister as the would-be assassin. She supposedly sent Lālībalā a cup of poisoned beer, which he in turn offered to a "deacon of his household" as a gesture of good-fellowship. The deacon promptly expired, as did a dog who wandered in and lapped up some of the spilled beer. Filled with remorse at the spectacle of these innocent victims,

Lālībalā decided to end his own life by finishing the draft. What remained of it, however, was not enough to kill him, only to end the life of a large tapeworm which had been troubling him for some time. The French translator adds a note, explaining the passage in the reassuring tones of a nineteenth-century rationalist: "This detail may strike the reader as singular, but it is altogether natural . . . for one must not forget that Abyssinia is the land of the tapeworm." [19]

Lālībalā apparently came to power, as his mother had foretold. But about A.D. 1270 Na-akuto La'ab, one of his successors, lost the crown to Yekūnō 'Amlāk of the rival house of Shoa. Their struggle was not just military; it also involved a combination of religious and genealogical arguments put forward by the rival parties on behalf of their favorites. Na-akuto's supporters insisted that he was a legitimate heir of both Täkle-Hāymānot and Lālībalā. On the other hand, legitimate monarchs of Abyssinia were supposed to be direct descendants of King Solomon and the Queen of Sheba. A legend grew up around this particular coup d'état, relying for authority on the *Kebra-Nagast,* the sacred book of Judaic continuity, and telling how the spirit of Täkle-Hāymānot the Christianizer had returned to earth in order to persuade the king that his own relationship to Solomon came only through a serving maid in ancient Israel and that Yekūnō 'Amlāk was the true heir to the Queen of Sheba.[20]

This entire incident, quite apart from questions about its supernatural resolution, suggests confusion with the previous one; for Lālībalā, too, was identified as a pretender breaking the dynastic succession. We are left asking just when the Zāgwē line was extinguished and whether the truth about its end has not been lost in overlapping legends. With respect to the later version, two further observations must be added, which, if only by their seeming realism, lend support to its authenticity. The first is that Yekūnō 'Amlāk, whatever the truth about his ancestry, possessed much the larger army; the second, that Na-akuto La'ab is said not to have abdicated, as a result of his pious vision, but to have been murdered by his rival in the church of Saint Qirgos.[21]

A final episode from Abyssinia's past, considerably later than those just recounted but still relevant to the issues at hand, involves an effort to secure a ruler's abdication as an alternative, in theory at least, to his assassination. The principal figure was King Dawīt, whose reign (1380–1412) features one of several miracles ascribed to the Virgin Mary in Africa. Sometime around 1402 Dawīt is supposed to have been informed by certain holy men that divine word had reached them to the effect that he must surrender his crown to his son Téwodros. The king, instead of acceding at once to the priests' demand, sought the advice of his former tutor, the venerable Aqabé-Sa'at Säräqä-Birhan, who with other supporters of the king volunteered to pray to the Mother of God herself. Her response was that the king would reign until his death. With so reassuring a second opinion in hand, Dawīt decided he could safely disregard the call for his abdication and instead continued to rule for the remaining ten years of his life.[22]

Taken together, these episodes from the annals of non-Judeo-Greco-Roman antiquity bear witness to the universality of political murder as a feature of human societies throughout recorded time. On the other hand, they give proof of its variety as experienced in parts of the world largely unaffected by either Old Testament teachings or the earliest formulations of classical tyrannicide theory. If one is to harness the power of past in the service of understanding lethal violence in relation to statecraft, both the universality and the variety of its manifestations, from Lydia to China and from the India of Buddha to the Ethiopia of the Zāgwē kings, deserve to be borne in mind.

5

Zealots, Barbarians, and Assassins

A Time of Transition

Abyssinia, its mixture of Judaic heritage and African folkways further complicated by the impact of Christianity, provides only one example of political strife in a world no longer either "biblical" or "classical" as those terms are generally understood. Further illustrations are needed to bridge the gap between Judeo-Greco-Roman antiquity on the one hand and, on the other, an altered set of patterns taking form among peoples strewn around the shores and hinterland of the Mediterranean basin.

The first case again involves the Jews, no longer as the people of Judges or Kings but as subjects of foreign domination, struggling to retain their religious heritage and to recover their territorial independence. The second adopts a very different angle of vision, that of the migrant Germans who overran the western Empire, alternately compromising with past authority and slaughtering their opposition (including each other) as they hacked out the first crude units of a new European state system. The third section turns to yet another fateful departure, the Arab crusade and the famous Order of Assassins who would seek to enforce upon it the Islamic purity envisioned by their chieftains.

All three groups—Zealots terrorizing Palestine, Teutonic "barbarians" endowing the term with a meaning no longer merely supercilious, *Hashishiyyin* who made their name a synonym for the premeditated slaying of rulers—contributed to the shaping of attitudes and behavior no longer those of antiquity. In another sense, these Judaic, Muslim, and Teutonic vignettes speak to concerns not only modern but vividly contemporary. Their several legacies can be found in today's news of Middle Eastern crises, in yesterday's reports of conspiracies to assassinate in widely scattered parts of the globe, and in day-before-yesterday's memories of "Germanic hardness" as practiced by minions of the Third Reich.

Palestine and the Roman Imperium

During the first century of the Christian era, what was to become the Holy Land of three great religions, and was already that of two, witnessed a major crisis some features of which recalled the Judaic past while others were unprecedented. At its center was the hatred that had replaced once friendlier relations between Judaea and Rome. The very name applied by the conquerors to ancient Israel—"Palestine," after the hated Philistines—bespoke a desire to humiliate the descendants of Jacob and David, as did the inclusion of Judaea in the Roman province of Syria. Despite these slurring references, official accounts and correspondence make clear that, as seen from Rome, the Jews continued to enjoy more respect than did most other subject peoples, making them comparable only to the Greeks and perhaps the stubborn Iberians in that regard. The sources of hostility have to be sought in the earlier collaboration and its souring, a sequence which lent to the eventual Jewish War, as Roman annalists would call it, that special bitterness associated with civil wars and with struggles between former allies.

Not that the old relationship had been very close or, especially in Roman eyes, suggestive of anything like equality. It had, nevertheless, been born out of a coincidence of interests within the arena of Middle Eastern power politics strong enough to be remembered as mutually beneficial. In 168 B.C., after many generations of suffering under other foreign powers, the Jews found themselves subjects of Antiochus of Syria, who that year wrested Jerusalem from the Ptolemies' Greco-Egyptian forces. Antiochus was not himself a Syrian but a Seleucid descended from the general who had succeeded Alexander the Great in the formerly Persian sector of the Macedonian empire. In taking Judaea he was simply capitalizing on the misfortunes of other such heirs. Earlier that same year, at Pydna in Asia Minor, the legions of Lucius Aemilius Paulus had crushed the army of Philip V, the Macedonian king who was shipped back to Rome and there paraded in chains. This allowed Antiochus to move on Jerusalem. He was not the only beneficiary. Shock waves from the Roman victory spread across the old Macedonian domain in ways not even the distant Senate could have foreseen; and among several peoples who were inspired to rebel against their Hellenistic overlords, the Jews were the first and most successful. In that sense at least, it can truly be said that the Hebrew epic of the Maccabees began at Pydna.

The spark that ignited resistance inside Judaea was struck by the Syrian king at the outset of his rule there. Though brought up in the faith of Baal, the deity once adored by Jezebel and Athaliah, Antiochus had turned to other gods whose credentials accorded better with his own pride in Greek ancestry, however remote. At Jerusalem he proclaimed the Temple a home for the Olympian Zeus, imposing worship of that deity upon all his new

Jewish subjects. The revolt that followed almost immediately broke out in the small town of Modein, where a priest named Mattathias struck down a Jew who had bowed before an idol erected on orders from the Seleucid monarch. Mattathias next slew a royal officer, and the war was on. After two years of leading the rebel army Mattathias died, to be succeeded in command by his third son, Judas, nicknamed Maccabeus, "the Hammer," in recognition of his strength and daring.[1]

Another two years elapsed before the army of Judas Maccabeus was able to surround Jerusalem; but when he did, his careful preparations brought success. Late in 164 B.C. the holy city fell, Antiochus fled, and in the Roman month of December the Temple was reconsecrated to the worship of the Lord God Jehovah. From the eight-day commemoration of that event came Hanukkah, the "festival of light," a holiday nonetheless joyous for lacking scriptural sanction.

Judas was a brave soldier and, judging from his record, a shrewd commander. He was relentless in pursuing all whom he considered to be enemies of his people and of his God. Having freed Jerusalem and cleansed the Temple, he turned his forces north and east, driving the demoralized Syrian army from the shores of Galilee and beyond the Jordan. This continuation of the war demanded new resources, and before being killed on the battlefield, in 161 B.C., Maccabeus had sent a message to Rome in the hope of securing guarantees against future counterattacks against him. Not only his death but the state of affairs in the central and western Mediterranean prevented this initiative from being more than a portent; for the Romans, committed to their deadly struggle with Carthage, refused to become further involved on the side of the Maccabees. It would be almost another century before the beat of the legions' drums would be heard in Judaea.

Throughout that interval the most urgent question facing the Jews was whether or not successive Maccabean heirs, increasingly referred to as Hasmoneans after an ancestor of the dead Judas, could sustain themselves as heads of state. They sought to do so while employing not a royal but an ecclesiastical title, that of high priest, assumed in order by the two younger brothers of Maccabeus, Jonathan and Simon, and then by the latter's son Hyrcanus. Not very circumstantial reports of how both Jonathan and Simon were eventually assassinated, in 153 and 134 respectively, if nothing else boded ill for the future stability of a Jewish nation.[2] Worse was to follow, for the record of Hyrcanus' successors was a dreary one of growing weakness made worse by dynastic egoism. At last, in 64 B.C., one of these kings, as they now called themselves, threw himself on the mercy of Pompey, fresh from his great victory over Mithridates; and a Roman garrison took up positions in Jerusalem.

It is important not to misrepresent the form of this newest foreign occupation of the Holy Land, for the Romans were no mere continuators of Ptolemaic or Seleucid rule. The latter in particular, under Antiochus, had desecrated Jewish temples, scorned the sabbath, and ridiculed such holy observances as circumcision. In calling for resistance to these sacrilegious insults, the first Maccabees had won the support of a devout and stubborn people. The Romans, more disciplined and more practical than most of the Eastern despots who had preceded them, offered far less ammunition to would-be rebels. Particularly in the matter of religion, they followed their usual practice and, once assured that their dominion was unchallenged, administered the Judaean protectorate in accordance with the principle "live and let live."

Did this make it easier to bear than previous subjugations? One might have assumed it would, but only until the tragic paradox of Roman-Jewish relations manifested itself. For the conqueror's law, while superior to most others in its sophistication and consistency, was still *his* law. As for issues of faith, what to Rome seemed tolerant, even generous, the most uncompromising Jews saw an an extension of Hellenistic values, secular, polytheistic, self-evidently threatening to the reverence due Jehovah and Him alone.[3] For such Jews, two obvious difficulties would not readily yield to their deeply felt convictions. One resulted from the power of an experienced, vigilant Roman administration and the military forces at its disposal: a proconsul sent by the Senate was no Oriental dynast, and a veteran legion could not be safely confused with even the previously much larger cohorts of Syrians or Egyptians. The other problem, doubtless even more painful to contemplate, lay in the collaborationist policies of Israel's own monarchs, last of the Hasmoneans, policies seemingly supported by a majority of their subjects. Faced with the impossibility, at least for the time being, of rekindling organized resistance, those who cherished the memory of Maccabeus went underground.

By the time of King Herod's reign (37–4 B.C.) three politically vocal factions had defined themselves within the Jewish population with respect to the military presence of the Romans.[4] Supporting the Herodian court was the party of Sadducees, who favored collaboration and raised no objection to the building of theaters and baths as past conquerors had raised temples to Baal and altars to Astarte. More conservative in religious terms, but not opposed to the political status quo, were the Pharisees, who accepted Roman control so long as it did not interfere—as it generally did not—with established Judaic ritual. Then there were the Essenes, anti-Roman but too ascetic and otherworldly to combat the physical presence and power of Gentiles in Israel.

In revulsion against all these positions, writes Jewish historian Flavius Josephus, there was born at last a "fourth party" soon to be called, by friends and some enemies as well, the Zealots in recognition of their intransigent dedication to Judaism and their merciless hatred of the foreigner.

Later to be known by the Romans by a different name—*sicarii,* "dagger men"—they first signaled their defiance in A.D. 6 with a revolt against the census ordered by Roman authorities that year for the entire province of Syria, including of course Judaea. The campaign of assassination they launched was all the more chilling because its victims included not only occupation officials but also Saducees and other Jews identified as complaisant toward Rome. Josephus, a Jew but also a Roman sympathizer by training and conviction, saw in the Zealots nothing but creatures in the grip of murderous and self-destructive madness, whose only function in the history of his people would be to call down upon it the full wrath of an empire that, despite its own internal problems, remained an enemy no less to be feared than the republic that had preceded it.

The main outlines of the Jewish War of 66–70 are well known: how the Zealots launched their revolt with the massacre of several considerable Roman troop units; how the inevitable reprisals were visited upon Jerusalem, and particularly on the Temple, torn down stone by stone to mark the end of the emperor's forbearance; and finally the siege of the citadel at Masada, ending with the mass suicide of the Jewish leaders and their families trapped within its walls. This uprising, both longer and bloodier than most against Rome, testified to the desperate courage of the rebels. Yet without adopting Josephus' negative position in all particulars, we must consider carefully the adulation heaped upon the Zealots by some modern Israeli patriots and perpetuated on American television in 1981 by a lavish but uncritical dramatization. For one thing, the Zealots gave the world one of its most startling examples of murderous certainty in the absolute moral rightness of a cause. Their targets were not only Roman oppressors but all Judaean compatriots who failed to share their vision of god-sent fury.[5] As a result, countless Jews died at the hands of the *sicarii.* Such killings continued, according to Josephus and other sources, at Jerusalem and in the villages surrounding Masada, until almost the last moment before the Romans completed their circumvallation of the doomed mountain stronghold. Even the suicide pact of Masada raises a question not about the death of the Zealot leaders, who were surely right to expect no mercy if taken by the besiegers, but about the inclusion of all the women and children in the defenders' last dagger-work, completed as the legionaries swarmed over the parapets.

That the Romans took this rebellion very seriously cannot be doubted. Their nervousness about the epidemic of assassinations during the years before the outbreak of full-scale military operations must have had a great deal to do with the ferocity of their actions, not least against the Temple, once the Jewish War began. Seen as a whole, the crisis comprised much more than that war alone and included countless incidents antedating the tragedy of Masada. The famous episode in which Paul the Apostle saved his own life by a timely assertion of Roman citizenship becomes in this context an interesting segment of political history. Paul had been arrested just outside the once sacred precincts of the ruined Temple at Jerusalem. A Roman tribune, to whom he appealed, asked in reply, "Are you not the Egyptian who recently stirred up a revolt and led the four thousand men of the murderers out of the wilderness?"[6] The famous prisoner swore that he was no Egyptian, adding the all-important "Civus Romanus sum." That claim, once verified, earned him immediate release; but the anecdote reveals the extreme tension besetting Judaea at the time.

Considered from at least two points of view, even the death of Jesus of Nazareth at an earlier point in the background of the Jewish War takes on some of the coloration of a political execution. It was in the calculated interest of the Jewish religious establishment embodied in the leadership of the Sanhedrin to eliminate a disruptive and unpredictable prophet, as Christ was regularly portrayed. The standpoint of Roman officials in Palestine is somewhat different, both from that of the Pharisees whose support Rome accepted and from those later historians who have stressed the Empire's fear of anyone whom patriots might call Messiah and King of the Jews. The latter consideration no doubt did weigh on Roman judgment of the case and its implications, but the anxious question put to Paul by the tribune invites further reflection.

To the Roman rulers of Judaea, Jesus must have seemed an impressive man, gifted with intelligence, eloquence, and serene courage. In what sense was he dangerous? Not just as a teacher or even as a prophet, it would appear. His death on the cross, remember, came some three decades before the great revolt and the destruction of the Temple, at a time when Rome still tolerated Jewish holy men of many different types as a matter of policy. The Romans during Christ's lifetime evinced no great interest in his religious message, but neither had they any cause to fear its purely spiritual implications, assuming that they could not have foreseen what Gibbon would in retrospect describe as its corrosive effect on the power of Rome. The one connection that might have alarmed them at the time would have been any suggested link between a popular hero and the most violent expression of Jewish resistance to the Empire, the *sicarii*. A point worth noting in this regard is that the dreadful form of Jesus' execution, crucifixion, was not so widely used under Roman rule as is sometimes assumed. It had been learned, with contempt, from the Carthaginians and was generally reserved for rebel slaves and for murderous outlaws, which is what imperial officials considered the Zealots to be. The precise relation between the death of Jesus and the political atmosphere of his lifetime remains a highly controversial point among New Testament scholars. The secular record of resistance and repression in first-century Palestine nevertheless has its place in any study of the death on the cross.[7]

German Invaders and Their Ways

Nowhere else in this book, whatever the continuing problems of selection and excision, does the need to compress impose itself more urgently than in treating the Teutonic tribes which overran the Roman Empire from the northeast. An earnest German scholar, Paul Liman, confessed three-quarters of a century ago that, for all his natural interest in his forebears, he could not begin to enumerate their acts of political murder.[8] They were barbarians in the full meaning of the term, not necessarily more sadistic than some of those who applied it to them, but unreflective and even ostentatious in displaying savagery. Their own chroniclers, ancestors though they may have been to Shakespeare and Goethe, were capable of describing, without a trace of moral or practical misgivings, how some Visigothic or Frankish warlord had ordered the trunk of a sturdy, growing tree split open with wedges a few feet above ground level, the body of a living enemy inserted, and the wedges pulled, leaving the tree to do the rest.

One such anecdote from the sixth century is reminiscent of Herodotus' tale of Gyges and the Lydian King Candaules, though it lacks that story's intriguing ambiguities. It concerns Alboin, a famous king of the "longbeards," who gave their name to the part of northern Italy they overran: Lombardy. King Alboin had killed another German chieftain, Kunimund, king of the Gepids, and had taken his daughter Rosamund to wife. Toward the end of a Lombard version of a state banquet, Kunimund's empty skull was brought out and filled with wine which Alboin ordered his consort to drink as a toast to future victories. The lady's reaction was literally murderous. According to the eighth-century historian Paulus Diaconus, Rosamund swore mortal vengeance and, with the help of Alboin's jealous foster brother Helmichis, identified a "powerful man" named Peredeo as the best agent to carry out her wishes.[9] Here the ancient tale of Gyges does appear to enter German legendry, for when first approached Peredeo, too, supposedly voiced misgivings about the project. Rosamund, however, knew him to be the lover of one of her own maids, and, sending the maid away, she slipped into the girl's bed and waited for Peredeo, unaware of the change in partners, to join her. Once he had done so, he was asked how he dared to lie with the queen. Faced with a penalty he either knew in advance or could readily imagine, Peredeo agreed to kill Alboin while he was having a nap and did so with a sword Rosamund had obligingly hung over the royal bedpost. This murder in A.D. 572 presumably opened a bright future for the principal conspirators, but instead, Helmichis and Rosamund poisoned one another not long thereafter. What happened to the reluctant Peredeo is not known.

Is there a political message in Alboin's end? None that Paul the Deacon seems eager to impart, beyond implying that forcing one's wife to drink from her father's skull is potentially dangerous. Admittedly the account was composed in the second half of the eighth century, about two hundred years after the events described. Nevertheless, a reader may still find puzzling the absence of curiosity about possible motives more calculating than vengeful. The episode, recounted merely as a family quarrel, has no greater resonance than that of a Roman emperor drowned in his bath by a hired wrestler; in fact it has less, since Rome's place in history compels us to ponder the fate of Commodus, while Alboin's death in the master bedroom of a probably dilapidated Italian villa is easily reduced in modern parlance to just another "gangland killing."

This very quality of triviality so often encountered in the slaying of barbarian chieftains poses at least one question of undeniable importance. In the absence of a governmental structure worthy of the name, can there be *political* assassination at all, as generally understood, or only private murder writ large? Even in highly developed polities the killing of a leader may, under some circumstances, fail to qualify as a crime of state. All the stronger, then, is the temptation to dismiss violence among the rude precursors of medieval and modern Europe as nothing more than mindless thuggery. The knowledge that Tacitus' vision of the German communities as primitive democracies populated by noble savages is a moralistic fabrication has reinforced the tendency of many historians to hurry through the twilight of Rome as though anxious to get safely past the night to another sunrise.[10]

What warns against turning away too quickly is the fact that political murder, to qualify as such, requires only some discernible connection with political institutions, no matter how undeveloped. The barbarian invasions may at first have appeared to bring nothing but capricious carnage in place of Roman law, but apart from the fact that the Empire itself had gone far in that direction before the Germans poured across its frontiers, it is worth remembering that out of the great *Völkerwanderung* would come in time the new structures of Europe's High Middle Ages. And with changed political realities would emerge renewed concern for such concepts as sovereignty, due process, justifiable resistance, and hence assassination as something more than a muscular reflex.

Looking ahead in that way helps to explain the special interest modern scholarship has shown in one among the several German tribal groups, that of the Franks. Some of the attention paid to Frankish Merovingians and then to Carolingians must no doubt be credited to their uncommonly industrious chroniclers, especially Bishop Gregory of Tours in the sixth century and the Emperor Charlemagne's biographer, Einhard, who wrote more than two hundred years later. Another part of the explanation must lie in the knowledge that the Franks were destined both to give birth (not to mention their name) to one of Europe's most powerful nation-states and to produce the first Germanic revival of the Roman Empire in the person of this same Charles the Great.

So seductive is the wisdom of hindsight that Frankish history requires a certain amount of deglamorizing. Pregnant as it is with portents of modern French, German, and other national developments, so far as political violence was concerned it probably did not differ very much from that of Germanic invaders who went elsewhere, be it North Africa, Spain, Italy, Scandinavia, or the British Isles. Gregory's portrayal of murders around the Merovingian court is illustrative in this respect, paralleling as it does the annals of other contemporary barbarian kingdoms.

Take the sad fate of Queen Amalsuntha, daughter of Theodoric king of the Ostrogoths in sixth-century Tuscany, murdered in her bath on orders of her cousin and coregent Theodahad. The political results of this event were in some respects unrelated and in others diametrically opposed to its author's purpose. For Amalsuntha's death affected Mediterranean history in her day to the extent that it touched off the invasion of Italy by Byzantine forces in A.D. 535. The connection lay in her having been an ally of the formidable Eastern Emperor Justinian, who used her murder as a pretext for moving against the Germans.[11] Theodahad suffered for having her slain, by seeing his Byzantine enemies triumphant on the battlefield before he in turn fell victim to assassination when the husband of a woman he had abducted stabbed him to death. Most important of all from the point of view of world history, in 540 Justinian's commander, Belisarius, took Ravenna and established there the permanent outpost of Greek culture whose influence would be felt for centuries throughout Western Europe.

Another cluster of events, beginning about a half-century later in Frankland, can lay claim to even greater significance as part of the Merovingian prelude to the rise of a royal house destined to produce in succession Charles Martel, King Pepin, and finally the Emperor Charlemagne. Dominating this pre-Carolingian stage were two women, Brunhild and Fredegund, barbarian queens who for sheer ferocity invite comparison with Jezebel, Olympias, Messalina, and other sanguinary adventuresses of antiquity.[12] By birth Brunhild was not Frankish but Visigothic, having been brought from her father's kingdom in Spain to marry Sigebert of Metz, the eastern Frankish realm soon to be the core of an expanded Austrasia. Her husband's brother Chilperich, ruler of the emerging kingdom to the west, Neustria, thereupon arranged to wed Brunhild's sister Galswintha, only to have her strangled a short time later so that he could marry his demanding mistress Fredegund. Chilperich was assassinated by an unknown assailant in 584, as his brother Sigebert had been some nine years earlier. Henceforward the widowed sisters-in-law faced one another as the deadliest of rivals.

In the rash of murders instigated by Brunhild and Fredegund, the former appeared for a long time to have had much the better of their struggle. She managed to outlast her enemy by a number of years, living to become a grandmother and making Austrasia the temporary center of an almost

united Frankland. At last, however, defeated in about 613 by one of Fredegund's surviving sons, Brunhild was dragged to her death behind a horse to
which she had been tied by her hair, an arm, and a leg before the animal was
lashed into a frenzy. Her fate, like that of Amalsuntha in Lombardy a century earlier, stands for more in the annals of tribal consolidation than just
a case of gruesome vengeance, signaling as it did the victory of Fredegund's
heir, Chlotar II of Neustria, and his temporary consolidation of all three
warring kingdoms of the Franks (Burgundy being the third). It was in this
realm that the son of Arnulf of Metz and the daughter of Pepin of Landen
by their union founded the dynasty destined to be called Carolingian after
its greatest representative.

If one adds to all this the Anglo-Saxon bloodshed recorded in scraps of
English folklore and the better-known list of Norse chieftains assassinated
in Scandinavia—Magnus Henrickson, Birger der Folkung, Haakon the
Elder, and many others—the roll of German tribal violence seems almost
endless. It would be laboring the obvious to do more than point out that the
ferocious energy and often reckless courage of these northern Europeans
were not matched by political judgment or restraint. Yet the eventual coming of greater sanity must be explained at least in part by the fact that the
Teutons proved after all not to be incurably self-destructive. When the combination of the Roman Catholic Church and the painfully developing
framework of feudal institutions, including feudal monarchy, offered them a
marginally safer and more predictable way of life, they took it. By that time
their record of cruelty had been matched—and with regard to assassination,
actually surpassed—by other heirs to Roman dominion in a very different
part of the disintegrating ancient world, men who worshiped neither Jesus of
Nazareth nor the gods of Valhalla.

Islam: Victories and Divisions

Following the destruction of the Temple and the taking of Masada, Rome's
grip on Palestine seemed unshakable, an appearance further strengthened
by the failure of the Bar Kochba revolt of A.D. 132–135. Jerusalem became
an exclusively Roman colony from which Jewish settlers were excluded by
law; and little Galilee in the north could scarcely replace the former capital
as a center of Judaic worship and culture. What followed of course was the
creation of a Jewish diaspora, with emigrant communities scattered from
Babylonia to Spain.

Rome continued to face serious, indeed deepening, problems in the Levant and beyond. As the western Empire sank into impotence, the conquerors from Italy gave way in the Middle East to other "Romans—most of them
Byzantine Greeks and recruits from Asia Minor—who sought to withstand
the military pressure of peoples once subjugated or at any rate cowed by the

legions. Among these were ancestors of future Muslims, not yet welded into advancing armies by the message of the Prophet but heirs nonetheless to the warlike traditions of those eastern tribes and kingdoms whose exploits fill the pages of the Old Testament. As in modern times, so too in the period when Roman power was visibly crumbling, Israel's influence on its enemies, be they Phoenicians, Syrians, Moabites, or even the peoples of Arabia and Egypt, was more profound than its recipients were willing to admit. Long before Mohammed adapted for his followers the words, the style, and many of the doctrines of Hebrew prophets, the torch of resistance to "Hellenism," and with it the examples of the Maccabees, Masada's garrison, and the rebels of Bar Kochba, had passed from the hands of the Jews to those of other Semites.

Roman imperial forces kept an especially close watch on the fierce tribes in the province of Arabia, comprising southern portions of modern Syria and Jordan as well as Iraq and the Arab desert lands themselves. Strings of fortresses, though not continuous walls, were built in an effort to separate the areas of supposedly direct imperial control from others belonging to more or less reliable client tribes. As in dealing with German and Celtic "barbarians" on European soil, the Empire strove to make viable bargains with the puppet rulers beyond the *limes,* the Asian pale.[13] Political struggles within Arab states repeatedly led to assaults upon these military bases, causing Rome to monitor and sometimes to intervene in the affairs of such states, if only to ward off potential threats. Thus, a walled camp was built in 529 at Hallabat, called by a modern scholar "the last precisely datable fortification in Roman Arabia," in response to reports that Harith the Kindite had been slain by Mundhir the Lakhmid a year earlier.[14] The victim, called Arethas in Greek, was a phylarch or magistrate with duties in Palestine, and at the same time a prince of Kinda, an Arabian kingdom supposedly allied to Constantinople. For both reasons officials of the eastern Empire decided on a harsh punitive assault upon Mundhir and his followers, after the completion of which a new treaty was concluded with Kindite compatriots of the unfortunate Harith.

Up to that time, and for a century thereafter, Arabs and other non-Jewish Semitic peoples figured in Roman and Byzantine annals only as stubborn particularists, willing to fight and to murder for the sake of tribal goals but constituting no integrated or dangerously aggressive force comparable to the Carthaginians or Parthians in the past. All this was to change dramatically with the appearance of Mohammed the Prophet and his fateful move from Mecca to Medina in the early 620s.

In theory, whatever may have been its actual effect, the appearance of Islam threatened no dramatic increase in personal violence, even on Allah's behalf. Although sterner than the Christian Gospels and closer in tone to the Old Testament, the Koran is an intensely legalistic document, prescribing orderly behavior and respect for established forms.[15] However, just as over time harsh things were done in the name of Jehovah and of Christ, so the creation of a warlike movement followed close upon Mohammed's call for selfless devotion to God.

In 644, only a dozen years after the founder's death, his second successor, or caliph (literally "deputy of the Prophet"), fell victim to the earliest recorded assassination of a Muslim leader. This Omar, who had come to power in 634 following the brief reign of the first caliph, Abu Bakr, is best remembered as the organizer of Islam's initial military victories. Although he had the services of such gifted commanders as Khalid ibn al Walid, conqueror of Syria, it was Omar himself who directed the Moslem invasions of Persia, Egypt, and Babylonia, in the process destroying Constantinople's power over everything south and east of Asia Minor. His death at the hands of a Christian Persian slave who stabbed him as he was entering a mosque in Damascus, has never been fully explained; but its effects proved to be as profound as they were sanguinary.

Omar's successor, Othman, the first caliph named by a committee of electors, devoted most of his energy to advancing the fortune of his family, the Omayyads of Mecca. His avarice and corruption helped to bring about his death, for he was assassinated at Medina in 656, to the accompaniment of a rebellion by veteran Arab army units. During his lifetime Othman had striven to protect himself against Mohammed's only surviving male relative, Ali—cousin and son-in-law of the Prophet, whose daughter Fatima he had married—by keeping alive the rumor that this rival had been to blame for Omar's murder in 644. Once Othman was gone, however, Ali was able to step forward as the fourth and last of the "Orthodox caliphs."

It was a short, troubled reign, beginning with a revolt at Basra led by two of Mohammed's personal friends and by the Prophet's preferred wife, Aisha. These opponents had scarcely been defeated before rebellion erupted in Syria, under the leadership of the provincial governor, the Omayyad Mo-awiya, posing as the belated avenger of his kinsman Othman's death. Civil war dragged on inconclusively, with Ali first seeking then rejecting arbitration, while his enemy gradually maneuvered him out of control of Egypt. Yet when Ali was killed in 661 it was not by an agent of his powerful enemy Mo-awiya, but by a disaffected soldier, one of the Kharijite sect that had supported him but whose ranks the caliph had decimated as punishment for insubordination.

With three successive caliphs eliminated by the dagger, the way was at last clear for the foundation of Islam's first secular dynasty, that of the Omayyads. During Mo-awiya's reign of almost twenty years the Muslims would mount their initial efforts to seize Constantinople, while other crusading hosts swept eastward as far as the Indus and westward into present-day Morocco. His immediate successors took Bokhara and Samarkand, Sind and much of India's Punjab. In Europe, Spain and southern Frankland were overrun by the rampaging desert armies. Yet by the middle of the eighth century what had happened to Rome over a much longer period was already happening to the Arab empire. Mutinies in Yemen, in North Africa, in Mesopotamia, even in Arabia's own Mecca and Medina first shook and then fatally undermined Omayyad military power. In 750, following a major uprising in the Persian province of Khorasan, Marwan II, the dynasty's last caliph, was pursued into Egypt and killed, whereupon there ensued a slaughter of other Omayyad princes. One of them escaped to found the kingdom of Cordoba in Spain; but in all of Islam east of Morocco, supremacy passed to Abu Muslim, leader of the Khorasan revolt, and to the Abbasid caliphs who came after him.

By the time the Omayyads were massacred Islam had begun to display several features of major importance to its future as a faith and as a political structure. For one thing, the strictly Arabic component, impressive though its initial outburst of martial energy had been, was proving too small and perhaps too inexperienced in governmental matters to maintain control over a sprawling empire of Asian, African, and European peoples. As a result, that empire had hardly come into existence before it began to splinter into historically recognizable units: Persia, Mesopotamia, Syria, Egypt, North Africa, Spain, and smaller subdivisions as well. Second, by the middle of the eighth century the great age of expansion was over. Defeat at the hands of Charles Martel and his Frankish army between Poitiers and Tours in 732 had turned back the Muslim advance into Western Europe, while in the East successive failures to capture Constantinople, followed by Byzantine victories at sea and in Anatolia, signaled a corresponding loss of Arab momentum. The coming centuries would be marked by unsuccessful efforts to repel attacks by Seljuk Turks, Mongols, and finally Ottoman Turks. Third, division into numerous political entities was matched by religious splits that paralleled in some ways the early Christian quarrels and heresies but were far more serious because more lasting than anything Christendom would undergo until the Reformation.

A fourth characteristic had to do with the place violence came to occupy in Islamic history. It consisted in the absence of any clear distinction between religious beliefs and political loyalties, or among "church, state, and society" as these came to be defined in Western thought. No such differences appear to have troubled the sons of the Prophet, with the result that a social grievance might prove readily definable in theological terms, while religious disagreements were almost automatically translated into political actions. This feature of the Islamic scene needs to be borne in mind when considering the role of a Muslim brotherhood remembered all over the world not by its original Persian name, the "deviators," but by an Arabic slang word, which in French and English became the "assassins."

Ismailis and the Hashishiyyin

The politico-religious movement from which the Order of Assassins emerged originated in a struggle over the caliphate, an issue bloodied from the start by the murders of Omar, Othman, and Ali. Beginning with the Prophet's own death, there had been disagreement as to how and on what basis a caliph should be chosen. Abu Bakr took office because of general respect for his age and past closeness to Mohammed, Omar because Abu named him, Othman because a small cluster of electors chose him, and Ali because his hereditary claims as cousin, son-in-law, and adopted son of the Prophet at last received formal recognition.

This belated adoption of a hereditary caliphate, without authorization from the Koran, produced conflicts deep enough to divide Islam down to the present day. For a time after Ali was murdered in 661, the faction which had supported him—the *Shi'a,* originally *Shi'atu Ali* or "party of Ali"—remained sullen but quiescent. Then, in 680, at the Iraqi town of Karbala a military force of the Omayyad caliphate seized and murdered Husayn, Ali's and Fatima's son and hence Mohammed's own grandson, together with scores of Husayn's relatives and retainers, whereupon the Shi'a broke into furious revolt. When the son of the murdered Husayn died some twenty years later, his followers adopted the position that not the caliphs of Baghdad, whether Omayyads or Abbasids, but only a semi-mystical "leader of the people," an *imam* to be found among the descendants of Ali and Fatima, could preside over the faithful.

This division between Shi'ite and Sunnite Muslims was the first of three schisms which eventually led to the creation of the Order of the Assassins, a product of that progressive splintering of a once-broad front characteristic of many other revolutions known to history.[16] The second division drove a wedge between, on one side, the orthodox Shi'a, today comprising the majority in Iran as well as a number of important minorities elsewhere, and, on the other, the Ismailis, who follow the Aga Khan. The latter take their name from Ismail, who in 765 at the death of his father, the sixth imam, was (unjustly in their view) passed over for the succession in favor of a younger son of the late ruler. The descendants of this second son nevertheless continued to be recognized by Shi'ites in general until 873, when the twelfth imam died without an heir. At that point the party of Ismail broke away completely, insisting that only descendants of him who had been wrongly disinherited in 765 henceforth deserved the title.

The Ismailis, now wholly separated from the majority Shi'ites, offered religious fervor, a consuming interest in questions of theology and law, and the promise of overt action against the Abbasid caliphs, whom both branches of the Shi'a continued to denounce. For a time, however, the Ismaili faction remained largely out of sight, keeping up their missionary efforts but otherwise biding their time until a lineal descendant of Fatima through Ismail could be identified as *al-Mahdi,* "the rightly guided one." That happened early in the tenth century, when a successful revolt in North Africa brought the proclamation of a Fatimid caliph, the long-awaited Mahdi, Obaydullah. At first his Ismaili dynasty controlled little beyond present-day Tunisia and parts of Algeria; but in 969 its armies conquered the Nile Valley and built a new capital named Cairo, where the rebel caliphate would rule for some two hundred years.

Conquest of Egypt launched the Ismailis into what appeared to be a golden age of power. By the second half of the eleventh century their caliph held dominion over not only Egypt and North Africa but also Syria, the African Red Sea coast, the Yemen and other parts of Arabia (including Mecca and Medina), and even the island of Sicily. Yet the older caliphate of the Abbasids survived in Baghdad, and after about 1050 its Sunnite armies, laced by tough, conservative converts from Asia, the Seljuk Turks, began to roll back the Ismaili empire. Within a century thereafter, as a modern authority puts it, the Fatimids "successively lost their Empire, their authority and their following."[17]

During these years, with Seljuk military power bearing down on all Muslim dissidents and a new threat looming in the shape of Crusaders from Europe, the third split occurred in Islam. The first had divided Shi'ites from Sunnites in the seventh century; the second, Ismailis from the orthodox Shi'a in the ninth. Now the culminating division occurred, between those Ismailis willing to accept the Fatimids' defeat and those who turned to other than conventional battlefield tactics. By the end of the eleventh century the marshaling of irreconcilables within the Ismaili movement had given birth to the Order of the Assassins.

Its founder, Hasan-i Sabbah, was born in Qom and educated in Rayy, Persian cities south of the Caspian Sea. He began his career not as an Ismaili but, like his father, as a majority Shi'ite. However, as he studied Moslem history and argued with Ismailis he became convinced of their rightness and ended by giving his allegiance to the Fatimid imam. After travels in Mesopotamia, Egypt, and more distant parts of North Africa he returned to Persia and began the organization of an underground force of missionaries and murderers. Their task, as he conceived it, was to carry the Ismaili word to the many and strike down the powerful few among the Sunnite majority, including especially its hated Seljuk generals and governors. (In choosing this course Hasan did not repudiate the original Ismailis' religious doctrines, only their tactical moderation.) His own plans called for a series of strong fortresses, mountain retreats which he believed could be made virtually impregnable through the commitment of devoted men, and in 1090, with the taking of a Seljuk stronghold, Alamut in northern Persia, he had his first castle. The program then beginning relied heavily on the activities of preachers, and Ismaili *da'is* (literally "summoners") carried the message of Hasan, now called "the Master," throughout western Asia. But their leader remained equally determined to unleash organized terrorism, destroying selected enemies and thereby intimidating others among the unconverted. In 1092, only two years after the capture of Alamut, the first team of assassins rode out through its gate and took the road to Baghdad. Their target, Nizam ul-Mulk, vizir of the Sultan Malik Shah, was a noted political economist, founder of two universities, but also a ruthless suppressor of dissent—and of course a Seljuk Sunnite. He was stabbed to death while being borne in his travel chair from a place of audience to the tent of his women.

From that time on, throughout the period of its organized existence, Hasan's Order slew literally innumerable victims, innumerable because some murders of the time may have been wrongly attributed to the Assassins, while others they probably committed were never formally acknowledged.[18] Outside Persia there was a second, virtually autonomous network established by their "mission" in Syria; and within these two principal areas separate castles had their own commanders, empowered to order strikes not all of which can have been recorded on the murder rolls of Alamut. Caliphs, sultans, ministers, governors, and generals were slain from eastern Persia to the Mediterranean coast. Although for many years the victims were Sunnite Muslims, the presence of the Christian crusaders in the Holy Land made it inevitable that some of their leaders would be attacked. The first such "Frankish" unbeliever was Count Raymond II of Tripoli in Syria, cut down in 1129 or 1130. The highest placed, whose death sent shock waves across Europe, was Conrad Marquis of Montferrat and ruler of the Latin Kingdom of Jerusalem, slain by Assassins disguised as monks when he visited Tyre in 1192. The Order also forced both Muslim and Christian monarchs (the latter including Saint Louis IX, king of France, and Frederick II, Holy Roman Emperor, while on separate crusades) to pay tribute as a price for not being stabbed by assailants too well disguised to be avoided.[19] Even the great Seljuk leader Saladin was said to have paid his share.[20]

This last point raises the question whether financial greed may not have rivaled and eventually surpassed religious conviction as a motivating force in the Assassins' history. If so, that history anticipated much of what is known about certain modern terrorist organizations. On the other hand, one cannot safely assume that such extortion was either altogether cynical or clearly distinguished in the minds of devout Muslims from other aspects of the holy war against Sunnites and Christian infidels. By the same token, claims that novices in the Order were prepared for future service by being introduced to luxurious "gardens of paradise" in remote castles stocked with the finest foods and most beautiful women must also be approached with a certain amount of skepticism. In the late thirteenth century Marco Polo, who had visited Persia itself, whereas most of the previous Western chroniclers had encountered only the Assassins' Syrian branch, insisted that Muslim boys did indeed receive such indoctrination from a Master who promised them bliss for eternity in return for unquestioning obedience.[21] Neither Marco Polo nor his predecessors, however, showed much insight into the Order's religious fervor, nor did they make allowance for the degree to which the Islamic heaven was regularly described, to members of *all* sects, in distinctly sensuous terms. Of one thing there can be little doubt: each of the known killings by Assassins was carried out in a genuinely ritualistic way, dependent on stabbing with a dagger or daggers which a medieval Christian observer describes as having been "so to speak, consecrated to this affair."[22]

A word is in order about the term "assassin," especially about the idea that it refers to the use of hashish or Indian hemp (*cannabis sativa*) to produce dreams of heavenly rewards while removing the fears and inhibitions of selected killers. Modern textual research casts serious doubt on any such colorful origins. The Arabic original generally found in medieval documents is *Hashishiyyin,* not the related but different word denoting users of hashish. What European chroniclers accompanying the crusaders probably heard was a Syrian colloquialism meaning "wild men," pejorative to be sure but not exotic or unfamiliar to a region that had known Zealots and *sicarii* in Roman times. In a similar fashion, Western visitors appear to have adopted the sobriquet "Old Man of the Mountain" for the Order's Master, though the term was unknown in Persia and was possibly just another scrap of Syrian patois. To suggest that the Assassins were more fanatical than calculatingly extortionate and that they had no need for narcotics to add fuel to their religious fervor is not to embrace the kind of relativism which argues, in effect: "Anyone so sincere must have been at least partly right." Quite the contrary, the addition of that protean element "sincerity" to a list of otherwise murderous attributes makes them no less chilling, or more deserving of emulation.

The fairest way to sum up what can now be said of the movement and its legacy may be to quote a highly qualified authority Sir Bernard Lewis:

> Concerning the place of the Assassins in the history of Islam, four things may be said with reasonable assurance. The first is that their movement, whatever its driving force may have been, was regarded as a profound threat to the existing order, political, social and religious; the second is that they are no isolated phenomenon, but one of a long series of messianic movements, at once popular and obscure, impelled by deep-rooted anxieties, and from time to time exploding in outbreaks of revolutionary violence; the third is that Hasan-i Sabbah and his followers succeeded in reshaping and redirecting the vague desires, wild beliefs and aimless rage of the discontented into an ideology and an organization which, in cohe-

sion, discipline and purposive violence, have no parallel in earlier or in later times. The fourth, and perhaps ultimately the most significant point, is their final and total failure. They did not overthrow the existing order; they did not even succeed in holding a single city of any size. Even their castle domains became no more than petty principalities, which in time were overwhelmed by conquest, and their followers have become small and peaceful communities of peasants and merchants—one sectarian minority among many.[23]

Even if one is inclined to argue with Lewis about the lack of parallels in *later* times, it cannot be denied that in its own day the Order of the Assassins represented something unprecedented. The example of the Jewish Zealots, it is true, suggests earlier attempts to organize secret clubs of killers; and one may wonder whether in his mountain fastness at Alamut the well-educated Hasan himself did not occasionally recall that other, even more famous fortress, Masada by the Dead Sea. But there had never before been such disciplined, concerted, and sustained commitment to political terrorism demanding the murder of individual opponents.

Their period of organized power lasted for two centuries—a long time when compared to other outbursts of terrorist violence. The castle of Alamut fell to Hasan in 1090; it was stormed by Mongol conquerors and demolished in the late 1270s. At roughly the same time the Mamluk invaders from Egypt were tearing to pieces the order's structures in Syria. As a hostile Sunnite chronicler, the Persian Juvayni, wrote with unconcealed relief: "So was the world cleansed which had been polluted by their evil . . . It was a cup that had been filled to overflowing; it seemed as a wind that had died."[24] Only their name and their example survived.

PART TWO

The European Centuries

FROM NO LATER than the middle of the eleventh century of the Christian era until well into the nineteenth, the world's next-to-smallest continent was by far its most turbulent political arena. In the wake of the Crusades, European travelers such as Marco Polo, followed by a host of explorers, missionaries, colonizers, and merchants, brought back news of distant lands and different societies. Nevertheless, it was Europe, with its bewildering variety of political entities and its peoples' seemingly inexhaustible energy in pursuit of power, that left the most telling marks on the history of assassination throughout much of the second millennium.

One reason for the area's hold on our attention is that its story is so rich in paradox and puzzles. None is more challenging than the fluctuation, easier to document than to explain, in the incidence of political murder. Both medieval civilization at its height and the Old Regime in its latter stages were characterized by relatively low rates of assassination. By contrast, the intervening period of religious conflict and religious strife, as well as the nineteenth century to come, witnessed outbursts of personal violence destined to be surpassed only by still greater waves of bloodshed occurring on today's enlarged world stage.

In the "high" Middle Ages (the twelfth and thirteenth centuries in particular) the Church, feudalism, and possibly the emergence of strong municipalities shared credit for the reduced frequency of homicide as a feature of politics. In this respect medieval Europe deserves to be compared with Periclean Athens and Republican Rome. By historical standards, however, this remission, like the earlier ones, was brief. With the fragmentation of western Christendom and the reassertion of princely power at its most egoistic came the rise in sanguinary episodes we associate with the Renaissance, the Reformation, and the ensuing Wars of Religion.

The return to less violent political mores, extending from the second half of the seventeenth century through nearly all of the eighteenth, puzzles many observers, for the phenomenon constitutes a threat to their image of brutal oppression and deep hatred of rulers throughout the pre-French Revolutionary era. A number of behavioral, attitudinal, and institutional factors must be taken into account if the early modern interlude is to be understood.

Far less mysterious is the swelling roll of assassinations, European and non-European, during the nineteenth century. Beginning in the 1790s, new secular causes, ranging from nationalism and egalitarianism to anarchism and nihilism inspired more and more deeds of political violence. At the same time an older motive, religion, continued to press its claims. With quantitative increase came geographical proliferation. By the end of the 1800s Europe had projected its example far beyond its shores. Henceforth only a global view would suffice for a phenomenon long perceived in primarily European terms.

6

The High Middle Ages

Causes and Limits of Change

It would be wrong to suppose that a European world groping toward reconstitution after Rome's downfall achieved quickly anything resembling freedom from political terror. It did not. But neither did it remain helplessly mired in the conditions of the Empire's collapse and the struggles among barbarian chieftains over the loot. Instead, what followed was a slow and often interrupted movement away from seemingly unlimited violence, a movement that eventuated in another of those *relative* declines in the assassination rate encountered in Greek and in Roman history. The medieval case differed from these earlier ones, as they had differed one from the other. Nevertheless, at least the "high Middle Ages," from roughly the second half of the eleventh century through the first half of the fourteenth, demand inclusion among the major periods of remission that have marked the annals of political murder.

For a very long time the example of the late Roman Empire combined with that of the Germanic invaders to project a baleful message from the past. One forceful reminder of that past was the murder of the Holy Roman Emperor Berengar, a Frankish descendant of Charlemagne slain by his own henchmen in 924. Berengar has been called a nonentity;[1] the same could not be said of a later claimant to the imperial title, Philip of Swabia, killed at Bamberg in 1208 by the Count Palatine, Otto von Wittelsbach. Exactly one century after Philip's demise the second in the long line of Hapsburg emperors, Albrecht I, died at the hands of a nephew, Johannes Parricida, in a quarrel over the latter's demand that he be designated successor while Albrecht still lived. Violent deaths among magnates of the Empire are sometimes found inscribed in sources so obscure as to suggest that others may have remained unknown because they left no lasting record at all.

Medieval Europe had additional examples neither Roman nor German, but reported from more distant places. The murders of Count Raymond of Tripoli and Conrad of Montferrat, both slain during the twelfth century by the Assassins in Syria, were denounced throughout western Christendom as outrages attributable to Muslim evil. Less easily dismissed were similar crimes committed by Byzantines who were Orthodox worshipers of Jesus. In A.D. 602 the Emperor Maurice, or Marikios, having been driven from his capital by an army officer named Phocas, was ambushed and slain together with his five sons and a number of loyal retainers. Phocas was thereupon cordially welcomed as emperor by Pope Gregory the Great in letters from Rome. In 668 Emperor Constans II, who had earlier put to death his brother Theodosius, was himself assassinated by a hostile courtier while on a visit to Syracuse to organize the defense of Sicily against the Arabs in North Africa. The turmoil of the eighth-century iconoclastic controversy triggered a new round of murders in the eastern Empire, beginning after the death of the formidable Leo the Isaurian. Leo's son managed to succeed him on the imperial throne in 743 as Constantine V, but only by dint of having had his rival (and brother-in-law) blinded and many of the latter's partisans slain. In 867 the Emperor Michael III was stabbed to death, presumably at the behest of a trusted favorite who assumed the imperial purple as Basil I.[2]

One of the most celebrated political murders committed in the eastern Empire was that of Emperor Nicephorus II Phocas in 969. The episode is also among the most illuminating in what it reveals about how word of such events might find its way westward. The *Chronicon* compiled by Adémar of Chabannes, a French monk at the monastery of St. Cybard in Angoulême, contained, in addition to knowledgeable comments on the affairs of southwestern France almost down to the author's death date (1034), four much less reliable but still interesting excursions into Byzantine history. The first had to do with the abovementioned assassination:

> At that time [presumably just after the accession of Louis IV as king of France in 936] the Emperor Nicephorus, who was bringing up the children Basil and Constantine at Constantinople, invaded the realm of the Saracens, took Antioch and other strongholds . . . and restored them to the Greeks. The empress [Theophano], mother of Basil, feared that Nicephorus would behave tyranically to her children, and while he was besieging Tripoli ordered that he be summoned by a trick, for she told him that the barbarians were besieging Constantinople, which was altogether false; and on Holy Saturday while he was pouring forth his prayers on bended knee in the basilica of the sacred palace of Constantinople, she ordered that he and four of his slaves be run through with a sword. And to all the lords (proceribus) of the Greeks she pretended that he had suddenly died of an illness. The deed remained a secret for a long time

until the chiefs (satrapae) of the Greeks became suspicious, opened up his tomb, and found his body run through with swordblades.[3]

The evaluation of this passage by a modern scholar reveals a good deal about the imprecision of medieval news coverage, at the same time providing a corrected version in its own way no less dramatic than that of Adémar himself:

> Of course Nicephorus Phocas was murdered at Theophano's order not in the 930s but in 969, not at prayer in the imperial chapel on Holy Saturday, but in his new specially-chosen bedroom in the Great Palace immediately adjoining the south wall of the Church of the Virgin, between ten and eleven o'clock on the snowy night of 10 December. Adémar apparently does not know that the empress was married to Nicephorus. He does not mention her co-conspirator, John Tzimiskes, who was hoisted up in a basket from the dock of the Boukoleon onto the terrace outside the palace and who personally participated in the murder. Adémar is wrong in thinking that the crime was hidden; it became public at once. But he does know that Nicephorus was the guardian of the two young princes, that he invaded the lands of the Muslims and scored successes, and that he was treacherously murdered . . . There is, then, an incrustation of ignorance and legend over the truth, but the episode as recounted by Adémar is not untrue.[4]

Robert Lee Wolff, the author of that passage, went on to produce a persuasive hypothesis as to how the story of Nicephorus' fall and three other approximations of Byzantine history came to be known in Western Europe before the Crusades. The answer, he argues, involves a Greek Orthodox monk, the future Saint Symeon of Sinai, who spoke Latin, had been educated in Constantinople, and traveled to France in the late 1020s, when he spent "a long time" in Angoulême according to its resident chronicler, Adémar.[5] What the future saint had to tell lost a good deal of accuracy in translation (assuming that he had not provided a garbled version in the first place), but it provides a significant illustration of how literate Europeans began to learn about such episodes in the East even before the First Crusade. In the case of Nicephorus, be it added, Westerners had a special interest; for the daughter (and namesake) of Empress Theophano was married in 972 to the future Holy Roman Emperor Otto II.

Part of the reason for intervals of relatively effective control over public violence in ancient Greece and Republican Rome had lain in a combination of institutions and popular conceptions of what constituted acceptable behavior. If medieval civilization, despite Roman imperial, Teutonic, Arab, and Byzantine examples, produced another period in which assassination became comparatively rare, the explanation presumably must again be sought in its institutional and behavioral patterns. Two influences—one religious, the other social, economic, and ultimately political—deserve attention.

The Roman Catholic Church—its papacy, episcopal hierarchy, monastic orders of "regular" and parishes under "secular" clergy—was in many respects the most determined as well as most successful adapter of Europe's classical birthright in matters of law and administration. Under the guidance of the Church and relying on a combination of scriptural and pagan authorities, western Christianity slowly developed a set of practical restraints upon political violence. Of these, none were more important, admitting that sometimes they were honored more in the breech than in the observance, than the Truce of God and the Peace of God, which forbade bloodshed at stated times and in specified locales, respectively. A spiritual mediator, or clergyman, designated to arbitrate a given dispute could demand that the parties abstain from lethal action during a holy season, in a place of worship, or under other circumstances earlier agreed upon. The power of the Church to impose the sanction of interdict against offending states or of excommunication against recalcitrant individuals lent practical weight to such prohibitions, often in the absence of effective support from the secular arm. By extension, those same penalties might be levied against tyrannical governments or unjust assassins.

Outside the ecclesiastical confines, feudalism's role in setting limits on lawlessness is less easy to characterize; but in the long run it was no less important than that of the Church. Neither feudalism nor any other sociopolitical system has ever eliminated exploitation or violence among men. Nevertheless, over the course of the past century or so, historians have come to recognize in feudalism the basis for an undeniable regularization of behavior among members of what had been an all but unbridled fighting caste. Other relations, affecting treatment of non-nobles in general and the peasantry in particular, were marked by arrogance and oppression. Feudalism, technically speaking, refers only to relationships between noble suzerains and their vassals, who were noblemen too. Since, however, most fiefs by their very nature involved the subordination of serfs or other tenants, it has long been customary to equate manorial abuses with feudal privilege. Yet peasants appear to have been no better treated in Italy, where feudalism remained weak, and to have fared even worse in vast stretches of eastern Europe, where it never took root at all.

The civil law of the Romans had been public law par excellence, with the procedures that affected private citizens not neglected but nonetheless subordinated to those defining the interests of the state. The canon law of the medieval Church, though it owed a great deal to ancient Rome, was also indebted to the inspiration of the Scriptures and the Early Fathers. Feudal law, as it had emerged by the eleventh century, differed from both civil and canon law in that it was essentially private and above all contractual. It had begun as little more than a rough pattern of understandings between vassals and suzerains, understandings which included among other matters the definition of wrongful violence committed by either party. Oaths of fealty and the originally simple ceremonies of homage defined reciprocal obligations to aid and to protect, as well as rights to damages in case of default.[6]

As entire feudal kingdoms began to take form and to develop their own official hierarchies, these contracts between rulers as suzerains and their most important subjects as vassals became more and more complex, affecting a range of interests too broad to be called exclusively private. They tended, through reliance on equity and the common law, to create new principles of public law as well. When that began to happen feudalism took its place in the history of political behavior, nudging it toward something still harsh and not infrequently violent, but far more predictable than the ways of power in the Dark Ages that had gone before. A vassal, conscious of his contractual rights, had acquired in his capacity as subject a genuinely novel basis for resisting tyranny. (It has been pointed out that whoever first said or wrote "a man's home is his castle" presumably *lived* in a castle!) On the other hand, a nobleman's memory of his oath of fealty to a feudal monarch might cause the vassal more misgivings about assassination than would have occurred to, let us say, an officer of the praetorian guard ordered to kill a Roman emperor.

Kings, Lords, and Churchmen

The medieval experience with political murder varied greatly in accordance with the status of victims and perpetrators. Around royal thrones dynastic infighting repeated itself in ways familiar to ancient, or for that matter more recent, history. A case in point was the Neapolitan succession in southern Italy and the Hungarian in central Europe which converged in the brutal murder of King Charles (of Durazzo), wearer of both crowns until he was struck down in 1386 at Buda castle by agents of the dowager Queen Elizabeth, who was subsequently killed by his allies.

Quite different were the royal struggles of Great Britain, more isolated and perhaps for that reason often less complex than those of many realms on the Continent. The conquest of 1066 and its extension northward all the way to the Scottish marches brought the uncommonly developed and formalized feudalism of Normandy across the Channel, accompanied by the initial power resulting from a military victory. This produced a conjunction between feudal obligations, which Norman rulers never failed to invoke, and a potentially more absolute conception of royal sovereignty implicit in William the Conqueror's Domesday Book, surveying and cataloguing all he now ruled as king of England.

The Scottish side of things differed in many ways from the English, but even the clans could not escape the impact of Norman victories which extended from the Mediterranean to the Irish Sea. True, the best remembered of early Scottish political killings—those of Duncan I by Macbeth in 1040 and of Macbeth by Duncan's son Malcolm on the battlefield in 1057—had barely preceded that impact. Yet Malcolm, though he had spent his exile in an England still under Anglo-Saxon control, was soon obliged as king to pay tribute to William the Conqueror and to the latter's son William Rufus after him.

As for England itself, one of the two most significant royal murders in its history was that of Edward II (the other being Richard II's, three generations later). In 1307 the crown had passed to this untrained and indolent son of a masterful father, Edward I. Disaster came early to the new monarch in the form of crushing defeat by the Scottish clans under Robert the Bruce at Bannockburn in 1314. Not even that humiliation could arouse in King Edward the will to survive and govern. Drifting from one favorite to another, and treated with open contempt by Isabella, his French-born consort, he was obliged to abdicate in 1327, surrendering to an aristocratic cabal which centered around the queen and had at its disposal the foreign army her lover, Roger de Mortimer, had recruited on the Continent. Edward II lingered for some eight months confined at one place after another, only to be murdered in Berkeley Castle.

Edward III, son of Edward II and Isabella, was only fifteen at his accession. He began his reign as no more than a puppet under the control of his mother and a regency council dominated by Mortimer. Foreign dowagers and their paramours, however, have a long tradition of misfortune. In 1330 Edward III's barons called upon him to assume power in his own name and, to aid him in making the transition, hanged Mortimer and drove Isabella into exile. The mild-mannered king would rule for the eventful half-century which witnessed the outbreak of the Hundred Years' War, great English victories at Crécy and Poitiers, and at midcentury the arrival of the plague. Conceding much to the baronage and basking in the reflected glory of his son, the intrepid Black Prince, Edward for a time enjoyed great popularity; but he died in 1377, a lonely and exhausted monarch who had outlived even the Black Prince and, while exploiting to the full his position's feudal components, had underestimated the growing disaffection among his non-noble subjects.[7]

The slaying of Edward II in England, like those of Philip of Swabia in Germany and Charles of Durazzo in Hungary, showed that even during centuries of relative stability dynastic rivalries could and did take their toll. How did the rest of society, including members of the feudal aristocracy, fare with respect to lethal violence? In many kingdoms the restraints imposed by religion and by contractual obligations were reinforced through the increasing intervention of royal courts on the side of order. Yet for the most part the nobility was still composed of fighters, made such by oath no less than by inclination. In addition to the endemic violence of local feuds and the activities of robber barons, both trial by battle and the jousting that passed for entertainment remained perfectly legal reminders of a warlike heritage. Special interest, therefore, attaches to the occasional assassination within the feudal complex and to the contemporary reactions which seem to have made it less common than is often assumed.

One such episode survives in the chronicle of a certain Galbert, notary in the Flemish city of Bruges, which tells of a shocking murder committed there on March 2, 1127. The victim, Charles the Good, Count of Flanders, was killed by a number of swordsmen while kneeling at Lenten prayer in the church of Saint Donatien—a circumstance sure to outrage religious feelings and for that reason not without its political importance. The assassins were acting for one Borsiard and other members of the powerful Erembald family, sworn enemies of the count. Charles's death, although the outgrowth of a clan feud, had extensive repercussions, for the ensuing turmoil turned into a genuine civil war between rival claimants to the comtal dignity. Galbert, a man of his times, makes numerous references to feudal relations, including his disapproving observation that among the murderers were "knights of Borsiard's household," who became mere mercenaries by accepting payment in cash for their exertions. On the other hand, loyal vassals of Charles the Good were among those who perished with him. Feudal obligations played their part in the aftermath as well. One of the count's would-be successors, William of Ypres, citing his own oath of fealty to the deceased but also acting in response to public indignation, ordered the execution of Provost Bertulf and several others of the Erembald faction when they fell into his hands. In the end, not William of Ypres but William of Clito gained majority support among the barons and was duly invested with the title and powers of count of Flanders by his royal suzerain, King Louis VI of France.[8]

Dignitaries of the Church, the other privileged component of medieval society, seem to have enjoyed no greater immunity from violence than had secular potentates, that is to say, very little in the early Middle Ages but considerably more beginning in the eleventh century. The papacy itself continued to exist under the threat of homicide until long after the barbarian invasions. In 914, when Rome was experiencing what unfriendly observers called the "pornocracy," or rule by harlots, a woman named Theodora, wife of the senator Theophylact, succeeded in getting her favorite local aristocrat elected as Pope John X. Unfortunately for him, Theodora's daughter Marozia, former mistress of Pope Segius III and the mother of at least one future pontiff, had plans of her own. In 928 she engineered the arrest and subsequent murder of John X.[9] Some years later, in 999 and 1003 respectively, Gregory V, the first German pope, and the famous French Pope Sylvester II (Gerbert of Aurillac) died under what many contemporaries viewed as suspicious circumstances. In neither case were charges of foul play proved beyond doubt, but the atmosphere of suspicion that surrounded both was characteristic of the times.

As with crowned heads of state and titled laymen, so with princes of the Church, the great centuries of both feudal monarchy and the medieval papacy brought important changes. Wearers of the episcopal miter or even the papal tiara still suffered indignities from time to time, and more than a few had reason to fear for their lives. Very seldom, however, did such menaces eventuate in outright killing; and on those rare occasions when a prelate was the victim of physical violence, the reactions it produced were very different from the impotent whisperings of Roman society over the deaths of Pope John X and Pope Sylvester II. Political murder can be found throughout most of recorded history, but the palpable shock it has produced during certain respites is what lends them special significance.

Shock is certainly the right word for the response to Pope Gregory VII's abduction on Christmas Eve 1075, while he was saying mass in Rome's Santa Maria Maggiore. A group of swordsmen opposed to papal reform efforts—and presumably allied with German imperial interests, since this occurred early in the Investiture Controversy—dragged Gregory off to the fortified palace of one of the conspirators, the City Prefect Cencius. This time the elements of sacrilege were unblinkable, and the popular uproar was such that Cencius and his confederates released the pontiff after a single night's confinement. In the sequel, Gregory VII was defeated by the power of Emperor Henry IV, despite the latter's temporary humiliation at Canossa; for despite Norman help from the south of Italy, the papal forces could not withstand the imperial army's assaults on Rome, and the pope died in 1085, a fugitive in Salerno. The fact remains that his abduction eight years before had been a miserable failure by the emperor's bungling partisans.

However one strikes the balance of wins and losses in the struggle over lay investiture, the example of Gregory VII, driven from Rome rather than assassinated, seems to have influenced several later opponents of the papacy. In 1118 the newly elected Gelasius II, having announced his rejection of imperial demands for shared control over ecclesiastical appointments, was subjected to physical intimidation by a hostile Roman family, the Frangipani, and forced to leave the Eternal City. The pontiff thereupon excommunicated Emperor Henry V, who in turn dictated the election of his own anti-pope; and the beleaguered Gelasius fled to France, abandoning both Rome and the Keys of Peter. His successor, Calixtus II, followed a different course, making the compromise governing lay investiture that ended a half-century of struggle over that contested right.

The last humiliation of a medieval pope in Italy marked the beginning of the "Babylonian captivity," when seven successive pontiffs resided in Avignon, an enclave within the kingdom of France, and the ensuing Great Schism, which extended into the fifteenth century with the Church divided between rival papacies, Avignonese and Roman. The opening signal had been the response of France's King Philip IV (the Fair) to Boniface VIII's bull *Unam Sanctam*, dated 1302. That proclamation embodied the most defiant claim of papal supremacy ever thrown into the teeth of secular rulers. The reaction of the French monarch was prompt, ruthless, and, at least in intent, no doubt predictable. Guillaume de Nogaret, one of Philip's most energetic ministers, was dispatched to Italy with instructions to secure allies, of whom Sciarra Colonna proved to be one, for a personal assault on the pontiff. Boniface was staying in the papal palace at Anagni on the night in 1303 that Nogaret, Colonna, and their henchmen broke in, dragged him from his bed, declared he was their prisoner, and threatened to kill him. A popular reaction not unlike the earlier one in Gregory the Great's favor drove the conspirators into flight. Boniface VIII died within a year, having apparently never fully recovered from the shock and humiliation of Anagni, but once again threats of murder had evaporated in the face of public outrage.[10]

Although the Babylonian captivity and the Great Schism did not subject the Roman Catholic hierarchy once again to the abject terror which had often surrounded it during Christianity's first millennium, the changing conditions of the fourteenth century were evident in the decline of deference shown clergymen. Skeptical rulers, of whom Philip the Fair was only one, no longer demonstrated that fear of ecclesiastical censure which once had brought Henry IV to heel at Canossa or John of England to formal homage for all of England and Ireland, figuratively on bended knee before Innocent III in 1213. Failure of the "bishop of Rome" to maintain control over his See and the subsequent spectacle of rival ecclesiastical parties openly disputing control of the Church eroded its spiritual position almost continuously until the sixteenth-century Catholic Reformation brought a revival of papal authority.

Precisely because of the return to factionalism and physical coercion, it is important not to forget the interval during which medieval civilization had offered something more sophisticated in its response to violence. That response can best be seen in terms of a single episode, an assassination that like those of the Gracchi, Henry of Navarre, Abraham Lincoln, Anwar Sadat, and Indira Gandhi, brought into sharp focus important characteristics of an entire society. It involved two powerful figures, previously the closest of friends, one a king, the other an archbishop. It was the work of a genuine, if haphazard conspiracy. And it was played out, as on a stage, in one of the world's great cathedrals.

Murder at Canterbury

On December 29, 1170, the day of his death, Thomas Archbishop of Canterbury had just turned fifty-two.[11] He was the son of Gilbert Becket, a successful merchant and future royal sheriff of London.* As a boy he received a good, though not unduly rigorous education, at Merton School in Surrey, followed by several years on the Continent. By 1154, when Henry Plantagenet ascended the English throne as Henry II, Thomas was ensconced as archdeacon of Canterbury, barely a clergyman in any spiritual sense of the term but a favorite adviser to England's most honored prelate, Archbishop Theobald. The archbishop recommended his protégé to King Henry, who appointed him chancellor, adding to that high office a degree of personal confidence that grew until Thomas of London was being referred to as "second in the realm." While retaining his ecclesiastical title and income as archdeacon, he served his liege in battle against the king of France, accepted the homage and fealty of his own knightly vassals, and tended to the crown's fiscal as well as legal affairs.

In 1161 Thomas' old patron, Theobald, died at Canterbury, leaving vacant the great see. After a year's hesitation the king, though reluctant to lose his able chancellor and congenial partner in distinctly nonreligious pursuits, named him archbishop, primate of England. With no more diffidence than Christian self-effacement required, Thomas accepted the awesome commission. His election as archbishop, voted by the cathedral chapter at the king's command and confirmed by Pope Alexander III, launched a momentous decade in the history of disputes between church and state. From the moment he assumed the archepiscopal office Thomas was transformed into a determined—his opponents would say fanatical—advocate of the clergy's rights in opposition to the crown. Between two personalities as forceful and at times volatile as those of Henry II and this rival he had fashioned for himself, the collision course seemed inalterable.

The issues now separating them involved the whole range of claims and counterclaims already familiar from papal-imperial confrontations and similar tests elsewhere in Europe. The English case, however, had a peculiarly distinct point of focus. It was the question of trial, and more particularly of punishment, for members of the clergy charged with offenses against the law, "criminous clerks" as they were called. Henry, pursuing the logic of the sovereign's rights as supreme justiciar, might well have insisted that the cloth conferred no immunity whatever from prosecution in the royal courts. In fact, he demanded only that a cleric tried by an episcopal tribunal and there found guilty of murder, rape, or other recognized felony (including the most controversial, treason) should be surrendered to the "secular arm," that is to say, officials of the crown, for punishment. Since the time of Arch-

* Though his father used the patronymic "Becket" and passed it along to his famous son, the medieval practice was to identify a clergyman by title or by place of origin—in this case, as "Thomas of London" until as archbishop he became "Thomas of Canterbury." The insertion of "a" or "à" in later renderings of his name is an affectation not used in his lifetime.

bishop Anselm and the king's grandfather Henry I at the beginning of the century, spokesmen for the Church had regularly maintained that only religious courts could judge *or punish* miscreants able to show proof of ordination as clergymen. Although many of the churchmen's arguments were heavily traditional, not to mention self-regarding, one rested on undeniably genuine grounds for concern. It went to the Church's role as arbiter and pacifier of potentially violent laymen, an obligation that might seem far removed from any case of individual crime but required, at least in theory, complete and unconditional freedom from governmental coercion.

The issue was an old one, but not even in the great Anselm's day had it been contested by two such adversaries as this king and this archbishop. Most English prelates, and with them Pope Alexander, deep in his troubles with the Empire, favored a conciliatory stance. Just the opposite was true of Thomas, possibly made more intransigent by the awareness of his non-noble background and his dependence on ecclesiastical privilege to sustain his dignity, but seemingly nonetheless sincere in his devotion to the cause he had adopted. At the council of Clarendon in 1164 the assembled knights and bishops agreed to "constitutions" ostensibly confirming customs of the realm but actually endorsing a royalist interpretation of nearly every point at issue. In reply, the Archbishop of Canterbury made clear his refusal to yield; by year's end he had left England for a long exile, partially self-imposed, in France.

Not until December 1, 1170, did Thomas return to his homeland. During the intervening six years his opponents at court and in the English clergy had taken full advantage of his absence. The Archbishop of York, Canterbury's traditional rival but an avowed enemy on other and more personal counts as well, had been especially active. As recently as the preceding summer he had welcomed the task of presiding at the coronation of King Henry's eldest son, a precautionary formality borrowed from German imperial practice but in the circumstances a manifestly calculated affront to Thomas. The latter in return, although he was having little success in mobilizing support on the Continent, at least managed to secure from a beleaguered pope confirmation of the right to excommunicate numerous transgressors back home in England, most of them "disloyal" bishops who had deserted his cause. And so the fight went on until finally, in the autumn of 1170, through the mediation of Alexander III's envoys from Rome a truce of sorts was patched together between the king and the archbishop. Thomas returned to Canterbury on the first day of what was to be his last month alive.

Henry II was still in France, where lay a large part of his holdings, including the Angevin-Plantagenet patrimony and the southwestern lands inherited by his queen, Eleanor of Aquitaine. This produced the anomaly of a ruler who, while sovereign in England, held his fiefs across the Channel as a vassal of the French king. An English monarch's decisionmaking in the twelfth century was thus complicated by the difficulty of maintaining communication across one of the world's most troublesome stretches of water. In 1170 the controversy's central figure had betaken himself to Canterbury in eastern Sussex. His king meanwhile awaited Christmas at the castle of Bures in Normandy.

There he was joined by three high clergymen, the excommunicated bishops of London and of Salisbury together with Roger Archbishop of York. They informed Henry, falsely, that Thomas was now engaged in the excommunication of all his remaining enemies, at the same time defying the royal law courts without exception and surrounding himself with a rebel army. (In reality, his bodyguard consisted of five knights.) The king, lacking the means of verifying these charges, reacted in a manner consistent with other outbursts known to have punctuated the entire career of this enigmatic man, one of the greatest among medieval state-builders but at times almost neurotic in his anger. The precise words he used in venting his rage upon the nobles and prelates staying with him at Bures remain subject to dispute, like many other aspects of the case. This is how an excellent modern study collates several versions current at the time:

"The man ate my bread and mocks my favors. He trampled on the whole royal family.* What disloyal cowards do I have in my court, that not one will free me of this lowborn priest?"[12] Despite all efforts by scholars intent on establishing a true text, no one can be certain that every word of the famous speech has survived as spoken. Henry may have said not "lowborn" but "ignoble," since he was probably less interested in the archbishop's lineage than in his loyalty. But there can be no doubt about the reaction of at least four of the Anglo-Norman nobles in attendance there at Bures.

Reginald FitzUrse, William de Tracy, Hugh de Moreville, and Richard Brito were representative of the baronial order frequently at odds with the Church over questions of property rights, legal jurisdiction, financial dues, and social status. A cleric of Becket's strong opinions and uncompromising partisanship must have seemed threatening in the extreme, despite the fact that FitzUrse, Tracy, and Moreville had been his vassals since the days when he was royal chancellor. Indeed, FitzUrse and Moreville were later implicated in a baronial revolt which counted the murder of Thomas among its grievances against the king!

Whatever their motives and misgivings at the time, the four barons quietly left Bures, crossed the Channel to England in separate boats, and on December 28 reassembled at Saltwood Castle, between Dover and Hastings

---

* One of the false reports brought from England by Thomas' enemies was that he was refusing to recognize the coronation of Prince Henry.

some fifteen miles from Canterbury. There, with their hosts, Robert and Ranulf le Broc, they set about assembling a force of local men-at-arms. Their plans must still have been quite vague, for there was talk of merely arresting the archbishop and bringing him before the king for judgment. This is only one of several indications that the climactic encounter might have ended less tragically had not Thomas been determined to earn martyrdom. His slayers were men accustomed to violence; but three of them recognized in their victim an erstwhile liege, and all must have perceived the danger inherent in an attack upon the highest churchman of the realm. They may even have harbored some lingering doubt as to how the king himself would view their enterprise once his notorious temper had had time to cool. About that, one can only speculate.

What is known is that on the morning of December 29, with a small troop of retainers, they rode to Canterbury and set up headquarters in the abbey of St. Augustine, whose abbot was an old opponent of the archbishop in the nearby cathedral. Having taken the precaution of enlisting additional recruits in the town, the knights laid aside their own weapons and set forth to parley with Thomas in the private apartment of his residence. They found him conducting business, after the midday meal, with the help of his administrative and legal aides, one of whom was the foremost political philosopher of the day, John of Salisbury. (Having *his* firsthand account of what followed can only be likened to possessing an eyewitness report of Caesar's death written by Polybius or Plutarch.) The argument that developed was not well-joined but eventually became so heated that the four visitors stormed out and returned to their base in the abbey where, according to some versions of the story, they proceeded to bolster their resolve with wine. Late in the afternoon they buckled on full battle harness and with swords drawn returned to the cathedral.

Thomas had just walked through the cloister to five o'clock vespers. Near the altar of the cold, echoing church he faced his assailants and their band of supporters, while his own flock of aides and other would-be worshipers retreated into the shadows of the great nave. Even at this climactic moment, the barons and the prelate argued over his duty to the king, until William de Tracy, overcome by rage, swung his sword at the uncovered head before him. Within a few moments and after several more blows, the archbishop was dead.

Consider the elements of medieval politics interwoven in the fabric of this episode: church versus state, the power of excommunication versus that of the king's will, the ecclesiastical versus the feudal hierarchy (not to mention the tensions and rivalries within each); the violent impulses of a fighting nobility versus the claims of fealty and homage. And throughout run the errant threads of personality. The outcome of the crisis proved to be as complicated as its antecedents. Within three years an uneasy pope, beset by reports of miracles attributed to the Church's newest martyr, proclaimed his canonization. Almost as quickly King Henry, having done penance and solemnly condemned the murder, began to speak of the irreplaceable Saint Thomas, while pious benefactions honoring the slain archbishop poured into Canterbury. Needless to say, however, the English monarchy did not retract its assertion of supremacy over the Church in judicial matters. With regard to that issue, the Tudor Reformation three-and-a-half centuries later may be said to have sealed the defeat of ecclesiastical claims for which Thomas Becket had seen fit to die. Even so, it is hard to recall another political murder's stamping its imprint so firmly on the image of an age.

Some Early Christian Views

Up to this point medieval Europe's place in the history of political homicide has been dealt with primarily in terms of events. Attitudes toward authority, allegiance, and permissible violence have for the most part, as in the Becket affair, been treated less as products of theory than as ingredients of the narrative. But what was taking place at the level of ideas?

There are at least two ways in which to approach the period's reigning system of thought, Christian doctrine derived from the Bible and from the writings of the Church Fathers. The first is to point out that Christ's message had been one of nonviolence and that its interpreters for centuries preached obedience to secular authority almost as though it were indistinguishable from personal piety. In the West at least, neither tyrannicide nor any other form of active defiance received canonical sanction. Peter, destined to perish at the hands of the state, told his flock: "Submit yourselves to every ordinance of man for the Lord's sake."[13] Paul, founder of what has been called the magisterial view of Christian discipline, wrote the faithful in Rome that "there is no power but of God" and he who "resisteth the power resisteth the ordinance of God."[14]

Paul's famous admonition to "render unto Caesar what is Caesar's" was no doubt a prudent rule for survival in the period before Emperor Constantine's adoption of Christianity, though even then the Apostle reserved "what is God's." By the early fifth century Augustine was using good and bad Roman rulers to demonstrate that God had set all of them over men, in some instances to punish, in others to protect, in all to curb and regulate. For confirmation the most learned of the Fathers turned to the Book of Proverbs: "Through Me kings reign, and tyrants through Me hold the earth."[15] Finally, Gregory, last of the patristic authors (he died in 604), declared: "Those who murmur against the rulers set over them speak . . . against Him who disposes of all things."[16]

If one were to stop there, the break between classical and early Christian thought in the matter of tyrannicide might seem unbridgeable. Another as-

pect, however, has to be considered: the less literal but perhaps more challenging message found in the lives of the apostolic-patristic spokesmen
themselves. Neither Peter nor Paul could be called a long-suffering or submissive man. Gregory's concern for the rights of rulers was understandable
in one who saw himself as the true heir of imperial Rome; but this founder
of the medieval papacy showed little deference in his dealings with Lombard kings or other barbarian lords of Italy.

Augustine of Hippo, as scholar and as preacher, transmitted the most
significant message of all, readable between the lines of his pronouncements
on civil authority. His insistence that human destiny lies in the other, heavenly city breathed a withering contempt for the powers of this earth. Did not
his *City of God* invoke the image of a *latrocinium* or band of robbers to characterize all secular government? Yet Augustine's breadth of classical knowledge led him repeatedly to reveal his debt to pagan philosophy, especially
that of Plato, thus tacitly encouraging an interest in political phenomena
which the bishop did not purposely endorse. Either way, he avoided telling
his reader to submit abjectly to power enthroned.

Once the question of classical survivals is raised, other considerations
propel the observer beyond any simple reading of apostolic-patristic doctrine. He discovers, for instance, that its possible range was far from being
exhausted by its Western formulators, the Greek Fathers having not embraced the most extreme authoritarian views of their Latin counterparts. As
early as the fourth century Saint John Chrysostom, bishop of Constantinople, observer, and moralist, asserted that Paul's strictures on civil power
could only be interpreted to mean that "the power of the office was ordained
by God, but not necessarily the ruler." Whether or not this reading is proof
of the close tie between Byzantine-Orthodox thought and that of ancient
Greece, it supports McIlwain's contention that here, more than in Western
patristic writings, are important sources of later Christian theories concerning resistance to tyranny.[17]

Not that Roman Catholic spokesmen, including others beside Augustine, ignored pre-Christian antiquity. In the seventh century Isidore of Seville, whose *Book of Sentences* and *Etymologies* would serve for many
hundreds of years as links between Europe and the classical world, injected
into the discussion of tyranny a note reminiscent of centuries long past.
Commenting on the evolution of the word "tyrant," he explained that its
earliest, all but value-free definition had over time acquired connotations of
illegitimacy, cruelty, and selfish caprice. "By doing right," wrote this spokesman of Latin Spain, "the title of king is kept; by wrongdoing it is lost."[18]

Soon after A.D. 1000, another classical strand began to reemerge in the
pattern of European thought: Greek Stoicism's insistence on the autonomy
of ethical judgments.[19] Given the Stoics' emphasis on intent, not outcome, as
central to the moral evaluation of any act including one of resistance, it is

not easy to say just how far their application of natural law would alone have advanced the discussion of tyrannicide. Did it prescribe only the use of rationality and equity as benchmarks for deciding whether to offer or to withhold the obedience demanded by a ruler? Or were its implications more far-reaching, conferring upon the subject even the right to kill, in the name of a "higher law," any figure of authority he deemed unjust?

Inevitably, as Europe's secular politics became more complicated and, for some at least, more absorbing, these early amalgamations of Christian and classical views had increasingly to face questions of that kind. Theorists loyal to the pope, to the Holy Roman emperor, or to any of several national monarchs raised doubts about the legitimacy of other rulers, not of course their own. Far more important, spokesmen for nonroyal but powerful interests, those of the clergy and the nobility in particular, began to assert the right of subjects to do more than just withhold obedience in a doubtless edifying but often ineffectual display of moral autonomy.

At that point, when the demand was voiced that kingship be justified in terms comprehensible to mortals, that the contractual rights of subjects be respected, and that rulers acknowledge a world in which "God and nature worked through the reason of man," the distance traveled since the days of Gregory, let alone those of Paul, became apparent.[20] Looking back at the sealing of Magna Carta in 1215, Henry de Bracton, England's great legal commentator, concluded that the king "ought not to be subject to any man, but subject to God and the law . . . There is no king where will rules and not law."[21] This was a sweeping formulation, applicable to property rights and to due process for persons. It was also a clear indication of how far the Aristotelian definition of tyranny had come toward the shaping of a political theory endowed with medieval features.

Two Schoolmen on Tyrannicide

When Bracton made his monarch subject to God as well as to the law, he was showing no greater deference to religion than was to be expected from an intellectual of that day. Theology's place as "queen of the sciences" was acknowledged by even the most secular legists and political theorists of the High Middle Ages. What is perhaps less self-evident is the growing concern over problems of legitimacy and order, as well as their opposites, expressed by ecclesiastical writers ostensibly preoccupied with theological matters. Among such learned clerics there were two in particular—the first working in the twelfth century, the second in the thirteenth—who best personified the resumption of ancient debates over the nature and correct response to tyranny.

John of Salisbury, an Englishman born in 1115, was educated partly on the Continent, not only at the famous school of Chartres but also in other centers of learning, and rose through the ecclesiastical hierarchy at least far enough so that on the fateful day at Canterbury he was present as secretary to Thomas Becket. Although that experience testified to a career of involvement in England's church-state conflict, his contemplative side showed itself to be less insular. He admired the great French reformer Saint Bernard of Clairvaux, came after considerable hesitation to embrace much of Platonic idealism in its medieval guise, and—a choice especially relevant to the discussion of tyrannicide—took Cicero as his favorite among ancient writers. From these eclectic mental travels he returned with an engaging ability to comment pungently, at times even humorously, on some of the most hallowed among scholastic themes. In examining the distinction between logic and philosophy, for instance, he noted the former's heavy investment in hair-splitting and concluded that the logician's categories "are not to be transposed from the world of knowledge to the world of reality."[22]

It would be neither useful nor fair to see a body of thought as profound and wide-ranging as John of Salisbury's exclusively in terms of the author's biography. It is nevertheless worth pointing out that he was a man of the Church, a loyal lieutenant of the murdered Becket, and hence, at least in the last two decades before his own death in 1180, all but inevitably a sharp critic of King Henry II. Even that animosity did not make him contemptuous of laws and institutions. When in 1167 the French commune of Reims drove its archbishop from the city, John condemned the revolt as "disorder" and "sedition." Yet his greatest treatise, the *Policraticus,* contained a denunciation of tyrants; and the terms he used became stronger still in subsequent writings. Specifically, in seemingly unabashed defiance of Pauline and Augustinian tenets, he stripped away the shelter of consecration from any ruler unworthy of honor. A king, to quote the *Polycraticus,* is "a kind of likeness of divinity," but a tyrant is fashioned in "the likeness of the devil." Could a pious author have defined the polarity in more emphatic terms?'

The two most significant scholastic commentators on the issue of tyranny, Saint Thomas Aquinas and John of Salisbury, shared very little else, apart from their priestly calling and their erudition. John was the servant of a martyr in England, a detractor of a powerful feudal monarch, but also a Platonist whose ideals included an organic state in which the parts of a corporate society could be represented best by parts of the human body. Although he saw in tyranny the work of the devil, he could not lightly propose the amputation of a political structure's "head." Thus his condemnation of bad rulers, while always explicit, at times seemed almost more visceral than truly philosophical.

Thomas of Aquino was different both in background and in political impulses, insofar as the latter had any place at all in his intellectual universe. Born in south-central Italy, around 1225, at Roccasecca in the lands of his father, Count Landulf, he was through his mother a nephew of the Holy

Roman Emperor Frederick Barbarossa. Trained in law at Monte Cassino and at Naples, become (against the wishes of his family) a Dominican friar, a student, and later a professor at the University of Paris, he died before reaching the age of fifty. To those present-day Christians, by no means all of them Roman Catholic, who see in Thomas Aquinas the culminating figure in the development of medieval theology, a treatment centering on his thoughts concerning tyrannicide may seem fragmentary or tangential, or both. Detailed analyses of his oeuvre, however, can be found elsewhere. What is needed here is at least a brief appraisal of his thought as it intersects with the topic at hand.

John of Salisbury had reflected the Platonism current in some of his century's greatest schools; Thomas Aquinas shared the new enthusiasm for Aristotle, which, with the help of Moorish scholars from Alexandria to Spain, gripped Paris at the time he was studying and teaching there. His problem with Aristotelian texts (including the recently translated *Politics*) was not simple: how to use them in the service of Christian theology without adopting the Islamic interpretations of Averröes and other Arabic transmitters. His solution was to develop around a Christianized reading of Aristotle a system that included the concept of Eternal Law, expressed to man by nature through reason, which ever since has occupied a hallowed place in the official thinking of his Church.

What has Saint Thomas to say about tyrannicide? As one might expect, he begins by asking where resistance to unjust rulers fits into the divine scheme of things revealed by rational analysis. This product of a career divided between the imperial-papal-princely world of Italy and a France ruled by the saintly Louis IX characteristically spoke in measured terms—again no surprise—when the subject was secular rule. His reflections on it proceed from two central notions: his definition of injustice and his concept of the common good. With respect to injustice, he says in the *Summa Theologica* that "human law . . . insofar as it deviates from reason, is called an unjust law, and has the nature, not of law, but of violence."[23] In all his writings the common good constitutes the ruler's main responsibility, though the definition varies between the advancement of man's rational ends, a distinctly Aristotelian proposition advanced in the *Summa,* and the nurturing of the True Religion, the demand that appears in Aquinas' work on *The Rule of Princes.*[24]

Saint Thomas on tyranny and resistance raises two points crucial to the continuing debate. The first had been mentioned, but not emphasized, by John of Salisbury and other medieval writers in the twelfth and thirteenth centuries. In Aquinas it is enunciated with full force: opposition to misrule is the task of certain groups who have both a duty and a right to attack unjust princes.[25] This famous doctrine of the *melior pars,* far from sanctioning impulsive action by an individual tyrannicide, confined its endorsement to what can best be described as "institutional rebellion." That is, it called upon holders of offices, wealth, and privileged rank to assume responsibility for the overthrow of a despot.

The second argument bequeathed by Thomas of Aquino is very different from his appeal to an idealized political and social elite, resting instead on a commonsensical view of mankind. In several earlier writings the future saint had conceded that unjust, violent laws were a constant threat and spoke of proper means by which to "change magistrates"; but only in *De Regimine Principum* does he face squarely the question of tyrannicide. From the pages of that treatise the shrewd realist, nephew of a German emperor and son of a Neapolitan count, peers out at us, unencumbered by his Dominican cowl or the robes of a doctor of the Sorbonne. Previously he had written, in deference to Cicero and other ancients, that "he who kills the tyrant for the liberation of his country is praised and receives a reward."[26] Now, in the *Rule of Princes,* he appears to entertain serious doubts about the justice of killing a legitimate monarch for any reason whatsoever. And, lest those doubts appear to spring from excessive legalism or unabashed sycophancy, he offers his readers a quite different set of considerations: first, that a failed attempt at tyrannicide makes its target more oppressive than ever; that, conversely, the successful assassin has all too often become a tyrant even worse than his victim; and that—here words seven centuries old have the snap of present truths—"good kings would be likely to be slain more often than tyrants, for the rule of good kings was hard on evil-doers and evil men were more likely than good men to resort to such a desperate measure as tyrannicide."[27] With those few lines the greatest scholastic Doctor of the Church seems to step forward, out of his own time and into an era soon to follow.

7

A New Age of Princes

English Dynasts

The assassinations of Edward II at Berkeley Castle and Charles of Durazzo at Buda on the Danube were medieval not just in a chronological sense. The hapless Plantagenet died partly because he had failed to master the role of a feudal monarch; the murdered king of Naples and Hungary had aroused deadly animosity by breaking his oath of fealty to an old liege and benefactor, Louis the Great, by seizing the Crown of Saint Stephen from Louis' heiress. Both killings typified the fourteenth century, a time of terrible wars and plagues in much of Europe, whose records convey a feeling of disorientation, of departure from hallowed assumptions and restraints, so strong that a sense of change still permeates its history. But was it change to something new, perhaps even "progressive"—to anticipate the use of a term which would then have had little if any meaning—or did it represent reversion to patterns much older than those of the High Middle Ages? These two Angevin rulers, one in Britain, the other on the Continent, had been struck down with seeming contempt for monarchy itself. And what of public reactions? They were, to say the least, far weaker and more confused than the indignation that had greeted Count Charles's slaying in twelfth-century Bruges, let alone that of Thomas à Becket at Canterbury.

The fourteenth and fifteenth centuries, like the rest of human history, produced a mixture of continuity and change, archaism and innovation. The very term "renaissance," whether applied to Charlemagne's empire, twelfth-century Europe, or the Italy of Petrarch, Raphael, and Michelangelo, means not just birth but rebirth. Hence the famous Italian city-states witnessed events recalling the accounts of ancient writers, while at the same time giving expression to startlingly novel theories of political behavior. No less pregnant with significance for the future, although today less well remembered than the legacy of the turbulent peninsula, were certain develop-

126

ments occurring at about the same time in lands to the north and west of it, specifically in Britain and France.

For the English monarchy, the cost of protracted combat abroad and confusion at home, persisting decade after decade as the Hundred Years' War dragged on across the Channel, had been clearly discernible in 1377, at the time of Edward III's inglorious end. The old king died not violently, but surrounded by portents of violence to come. Richard II, son of the late Black Prince, was only ten years of age when he succeeded his grandfather; he was still a minor, under the tutelage of his uncle John of Gaunt (and duke of Lancaster), when the popular revolt of 1381 broke out under Wat Tyler and other leaders. Richard did assert himself in dispersing the rebels; but the repression that followed, like the murder of Tyler which had preceded the revolt's collapse, left the boy king deeply unpopular in many quarters. In 1389 he began the eight years of his so-called "constitutional period," when the ruler's own efforts at conciliation profited, however briefly, from relative prosperity and an armistice of sorts between him and Parliament.

The political truce, however, could not survive Richard's quarrels with the Lords and Commons over fiscal control, followed by harsh proscription of his opponents in all walks of life. Branded anew as a tyrant, especially by spokesmen for the aristocracy, and above all by Henry of Bolingbroke, John of Gaunt's exiled son, the still young but prematurely enfeebled ruler was unable to save his crown. Hurrying home from an ill-timed expedition to Ireland upon hearing of Bolingbroke's return to England, he was easily captured by the rebel army in 1399, imprisoned in the Tower of London, and the following year either murdered or allowed to die of exposure and neglect.

This famous instance of regicide inspired the soliloquy on "the death of kings" placed in Richard's mouth two centuries later by a playwright whose eloquence the real-life actor could never have approached. It was in some ways a familiar scene, at least to Englishmen who remembered that the victim's great-grandfather, too, had died in confinement. On the other hand, Richard II, unlike Edward II, left no heir, no figure for loyal vassals to acclaim; and his destroyer, become Henry IV, launched the monarchy into almost a century of dynastic conflict scarcely alleviated by the continental victories of his son and successor, Henry V.

Even before the red rose of Lancaster's banner and the white rose of York's gave their names to England's own "thirty years' war," from 1455 to 1485, the adverse effects of French military revival at midcentury were being felt on the British side of the Channel. John de La Pole, duke of Suffolk and leader of the peace party, was impeached by Parliament in January 1450 on charges of having signed away the rich French province of Maine under the terms of a brief truce he had sponsored two years before. In February, King Henry VI, always erratic though not yet insane, in effect pardoned his minister and favorite by "reserving the case" to his own judgment. Both Lords and Commons promptly reenacted the impeachment, causing Suffolk to flee in the hope of evading punishment. At Ipswich the ship in which he was attempting to slip through the blockade was intercepted by vessels whose captains took their orders from Parliament, and the duke was taken prisoner. Without even the semblance of a hearing, he was beheaded with a rusty sword, a fitting symbol of internecine strife at the end of a hopeless war.

In one respect the Wars of the Roses were paradoxical, marking as they did the failure of a traditional type of baronial resistance, yet still seeming to express the feudal aristocracy's demands for greater influence over royal policy. The long and bitter conflict saw great families vie for access to the throne, at the same time lesser nobles and burgesses were striving to gain full recognition of Parliament's medieval rights. Yet it ended with the feudality decimated by assassination and battle, and with Henry Tudor hailed by Lords and Commons alike as King Henry VII, father of a still more autocratic namesake and grandfather of England's greatest queen. Here indeed had begun a "new age of princes."

During the savage in-fighting of the decades before the Tudor victory on Bosworth Field, a number of additions had been made to Europe's experience with the death of kings. Henry VI, deposed in 1461 by Edward IV, his Yorkist cousin, though not captured until some time later, languished for several years in the Tower of London where both he and his son the prince of Wales finally died, unattended though probably not murdered. The more celebrated deaths in the Tower, those of twelve-year-old Edward V and his younger brother, the duke of York, in 1483, are if anything even less well documented than the case of Henry VI. The end of the "little princes" created a polemical storm centering about the figure of their uncle and alleged assassin, the duke of Gloucester, who assumed the throne as Richard III. The slaying of dynastic rivals, even when mere boys, was not unknown to the fifteenth century; and the princes' disappearance in effect handed the crown of England, if only for two years, to Richard Crookback, as he was called because of his lameness. On the other hand, contemporary sources portray Gloucester as a prince possessed not only of ambition but also of considerable courage and, according to some testimony, a capacity for magnanimous actions, certainly not as the monster with which Shakespeare capped a century of Tudor propaganda.

For the historian of political violence, however, the precise allocation of responsibility for every death in the bloody Tower is of less moment than the mass of evidence showing that neither religious nor feudal restraints seemed any longer to exert the considerable, if not always decisive, force they had demonstrated for several centuries prior to the Hundred Years' War. In the British case, a duke of York murdered in 1460 by Lancastrians ignoring the Christmas Truce of God, or a duke of Clarence drowned in a wine barrel by other noblemen in 1478 offered dramatic proof of the level to which political relations descended before Richard III perished at Bosworth—for the want, one may safely say, of far more than just a horseshoe nail.

Fifteenth-Century France

The French kingdom sustained even greater damage than the English in the course of their seemingly endless struggle, not only because it was fought entirely on the Continent but also because for the Valois monarchy it was a civil no less than a foreign conflict. The ducal house of Burgundy, allied to Britain, threatened the very existence of a France laboriously pieced together by the medieval Capetian rulers. By the end of the fourteenth century that structure was in danger of crumbling into autonomous principalities, as the Holy Roman Empire of German states had long since done. At the top of the French feudal pyramid not a single monarch but the great noble families made a mockery of allegiance, alternating between assertions of haughty indifference and efforts to dictate royal policy.

In the early 1400s the rivalry between the most powerful of these "connections"—the Burgundian and the Orleanist, or "Armagnac"—dominated the political stage, soon to be bloodied by two of the most celebrated assassinations in the nation's history. First to be struck down was Louis duke of Orleans, younger brother of the feebleminded King Charles VI and leader of the war party determined to end the temporary lull in fighting with England. The king had installed this talented but ostentatious "first prince of the blood" in a position approaching that of regent, to the displeasure of the Bavarian-born Queen Isabella, who encouraged John the Fearless of Burgundy. The latter, capitalizing on Orleans' unpopularity in Paris, arranged to have his opponent murdered there as a would-be tyrant seeking to usurp the crown. On November 23, 1407, he was cut down in the narrow Rue des Poulies.

Duke John, having survived an inquest by the royal council, and still supported not only by the queen but also by the adoring crowds of Paris, appeared to have attained a station more nearly regal than even that formerly imputed to his victim. The latter's son, young Charles of Orleans, nevertheless continued the fight with help from his energetic father-in-law, the count of Armagnac (whence the name increasingly applied to the anti-Burgundian party). More important still, the victory by Henry V's English army at Agincourt in 1415 threw the entire situation facing the Valois monarchy into what for a time seemed hopeless confusion.

Agincourt's immediate results, including the English capture of Rouen, Normandy's capital, tended to confirm Burgundian ascendancy within

France. A popular massacre of Armagnac supporters occurred in Paris, while the helpless king and his son, the future Charles VII, fled southward. All of these dramatic developments set the stage for another assassination, that of John the Fearless. Having grown suspicious of his dangerous allies, the English, he opened negotiations with the royalists (though not with the Orleanists), looking toward some sort of compromise. It was at the site of a scheduled parlay with the Dauphin Charles, on the bridge over the Seine at Montereau in September 1419, that the Burgundian duke was slain by a zealous Armagnac anxious to avenge the murder twelve years before.

The sequel to this killing was in many ways as misleading as its antecedents. The enraged Burgundian leaders, still with Queen Isabella's blessing, renewed their faction's support of England, forcing Charles VI to declare illegitimate his own son, name Henry V as both heir to the throne and regent of the kingdom, and give his daughter in marriage to the English ruler. But once more death, this time nonviolent, upset all these arrangements and in doing so opened the war's concluding phase. In 1422 Charles VI of France, then Henry V of England succumbed, leaving Charles VII monarch, at least in name—an uninspiring figure but one well served by both fortune and his own lieutenants. Not even the John of Burgundy's vindictive stroke in capturing Jeanne d'Arc and turning her over to an English ecclesiastical court for burning in 1431, could reverse the patriotic momentum she had personified.

Confronted with so intricate a tapestry of personalities and events, a modern reader might easily miss the full significance of the era's two major assassinations. The deaths of Louis of Orleans and John of Burgundy had to compete for attention with a world-famous battle, the witch-trial and judicial murder of a saint, the consignment of a dauphin to bastardy, and the unfolding of what in French eyes remains a hallowed struggle for national liberation. But until the two dukes were murdered France had known no comparable occurrence throughout the more than four hundred years since the founding of Hugh Capet's dynasty. With these killings a different and in some respects deadlier political game began. Small wonder that correspondingly radical ideas concerning attacks upon the mighty began to be uttered by the mouths and inscribed by the pens of Frenchmen.

The earliest—and for hundreds of years the most controversial—of these commentators was Jean Petit, who died in 1411 after a lifetime devoted to serving the dukes of Burgundy. Little is known about his background, except that he studied liberal arts and theology at Paris and dabbled in law at the University of Orleans without, however, earning a degree in that subject as he had in the others. Through the influence of the Burgundian house he became a priest, comfortably supported by the "livings" of two parishes without having to devote much time to their spiritual needs. Instead, as a master of arts and of theology on the rolls of the Sorbonne, he wrote treatises on various issues of the day, including the Great Schism of the Church. When his patron, John the Fearless, required an apologist for the murder of the duke of Orleans, Petit was available.[1]

The situation that gave rise to this call for his services was symptomatic of the kingdom's troubles. Having at first disclaimed all responsibility for the death of the king's brother, Duke John had left Paris with his private army of retainers and, once safe on his own estates, made clear through spokesmen in the capital that the act had indeed been committed by his order, and that for it he deserved not the kingdom's condemnation but its thanks. The king might have been expected to unleash all the power of the French state against Burgundy, but conditions dictated a milder course.

To begin with, "the power of the French state" was in Charles VI's time a phrase containing more traditional grandeur than actual substance. The Valois, though they held the royal title, disposed of little more, and in fact sometimes less, authority backed by military resources than did several other families and factions. The house of Burgundy in particular, with its massive holdings in eastern France and the Low Countries, not to mention its demonstrated capacity for playing off the English invaders against the French court, could not be brusquely called to account. Furthermore, the disappearance of the duke of Orleans, an erratic spendthrift and in the eyes of many a dangerous adventurer where war with England was concerned, had produced no widespread public mourning. On the contrary, the common people of Paris revered the name of the duke of Burgundy, as they would cheer his person when at the end of February 1408 he reentered the city with a large contingent of troops—barely three months after his masked swordsmen had ambushed their victim in the Rue des Poulies.

The setting for Jean Petit's address to the royal council, his "Justification" as it was called, had elements both of pomp and of mummery, as befitted the occasion. On March 8, after a week of planning by John the Fearless and his advisers, who had received the king's permission to make all arrangements, a carefully selected audience assembled in the great hall of the Hôtel Saint-Pol. On a bench in the center sat the princes of the blood, eight of them in all, including the exiled Angevin king of Sicily, the duke of Guyenne, and of course that most interested of royal cousins, the duke of Burgundy. In the absence of King Charles, ailing as usual, John the Fearless was in effect the presiding officer at his own arraignment. Having taken his place and surveyed the ranks of nobles present, most of whom were his supporters, he asked that Master Jean Petit of the University be allowed to mount the improvised pulpit of scaffolding and from there explain the case.

The nature of that explanation cannot have surprised the speaker's audience; its main points had been made in manifestos circulated earlier among courtiers and townspeople. Petit's thesis, stripped of the rhetorical adornments of scholastic disputation, was that the duke of Orleans had been a criminal, a devil in human form. Crimes ranging from plots to supplant the king, through numerous acts of sorcery, to others of murder—including, the excited cleric assured his listeners, that of the monster's own son—were charged to the deceased. Few of those present, having known the late duke as an often foolish but scarcely villainous prince, can have taken all this very seriously. Still, things being as they were, one nodded sagely and kept silent.

When Petit concluded his four-hour harangue, he knelt before the duke of Burgundy and humbly asked him to acknowledge his instigation of the Orleans assassination, which by then might as well have been called an execution. John the Fearless complied, begged forgiveness for having had to use admittedly distasteful means in order to save the realm, and left a free man, exonerated by a silent assembly within the chamber and greeted by a popular ovation when he stepped outside. As a contribution to legal and political theory there remained Jean Petit's ringing assertion: "It is lawful for any subject, without any order or command, according to moral, divine, and natural law, to kill or cause to be killed a traitor and disloyal tyrant."[2] This opinion, resting on the assumption that the duke of Orleans had intended to seize the crown and then to *become* a tyrant, was wreathed in subjunctives and adorned with references to earlier authorities from Aristotle to Thomas Aquinas.

Less than a decade after the meeting in the Hôtel Saint-Pol, and only three years after the death of its orator, a far greater representative of the Sorbonne, the conciliarist Jean Gerson, took advantage of a brief respite from Burgundian domination in Paris to attack Petit's arguments. In particular, he condemned the idea that an alleged tyrant could be slain without due process, by anyone who felt impelled by moral, divine, or natural urges to undertake the action. Gerson dismissed such claims as incitement and ill-considered bombast, laying down in their place a set of firm conditions for the elimination of even an undoubted tyrant. There should be no stealth, no recourse to poison, no killing without a chance for the victim to purge his soul of guilt before meeting his Maker. Such admonitions may sound quaint and ineffectual, but Gerson, in the short time he had before the Burgundians returned in force and cowed the University into repudiating his remarks, tried to enlighten his contemporaries regarding the real teachings of several predecessors, among which those of Aquinas had perhaps suffered most from Jean Petit's methods.

The remaining French case from the fifteenth century lacks the complexity of the Burgundian-Armagnac crisis, but it still evoked memories of that savage feud. In 1465, only four years after the accession of King Louis XI—shrewd, patient, undramatic, and hence distasteful to romantics in his own time and ever since—there took form against him one of those seemingly endemic cabals of princes. Its members included the dukes of Alençon,

Lorraine, Bourbon, Berry, and, one need scarcely add, Burgundy (now the aging Philip the Good, who had succeeded his father, John the Fearless, nearly half a century earlier). The League of the Public Weal, as it called itself, enjoyed some success at the outset, defeating a royal army at Montlhéry near Paris and forcing Louis to cede various towns to rebel leaders. Indeed a full decade was required for the king to overcome the combination of threats confronting the crown, especially that posed by Burgundy under Duke Philip's son and successor, Charles the Bold. Overcome they finally were, however, with some opportune help from Swiss militia who slew the Burgundian conqueror in battle at Nancy, and by 1477 the Valois monarch was more securely enthroned than any of his predecessors had been since soon after the beginning of the Hundred Years' War. Nevertheless Louis XI lived out his life aware that plots to kill him had for years been openly discussed.

These circumstances lent more than the usual amount of interest to an antagonistic history of the reign written by Thomas Basin, bishop of Lisieux, in defense of the princes' roles (and his own) in the league of the Public Weal. The author was not only an influential Norman clergyman but also a former adviser to King Charles VII. What he had to say reveals a corresponding mixture of ecclesiastical and secular arguments directed against a monarch he portrays as equally threatening to the Church and to the lay nobility. His *History of Louis XI,* apparently completed by 1471 or 1472, also contained a great deal of second-guessing about ends, means, and outcomes, all introduced to exonerate the insurgents of charges that their efforts to destroy the king were bringing nothing but misery to themselves and to many others. At one point Bishop Thomas becomes most explicit about the right to overthrow and, if necessary, to kill a tyrant, reviving in the course of his argument a long-popular metaphor, that of a ship, its captain, and its crew:

> But, say these same persons [critics of the rising against Louis XI], the princes and all the other adherents of the League were subjects and vassals of the king . . . in no wise permitted to take up arms against [him] . . . We shall reply with a question: If they were on a boat, supposing even that they were the captain's slaves by birth or by purchase, and this captain, through incapacity or malice, sought to wreck his boat and to sink it in the shoals of Scylla and Charybdis, ought they nevertheless to submit to him? [There follows a passage about the need to remonstrate and, if unsuccessful in that, to resist with force.] If they could not save themselves otherwise, because of the captain's obstinacy, would one deny them the right, for the common salvation, to bind him . . . or even to use with respect to him still greater rigor?[3]

The rhetoric was not new, but the classical argument had been resumed in terms which, though more measured than Jean Petit's, were very different from those employed by Gerson before him—or by Thomas Aquinas before them both.

Renaissance Italy

When the curtain rises on the Italian scene in the fifteenth and sixteenth centuries, one perceives at once the difficulties involved in periodization. Here was papal Rome, the center of western Christendom by virtue of its spiritual role but also in effect a secular state competing with Venice, Milan, Florence, and Naples as one of the peninsula's leading powers. Here too, in the monuments of that other, pagan Rome, and perhaps still more in the memory of its greatness, were to be found the strongest ties linking an emergent Europe with the ancient past.

Italy's own past was special in other respects as well. The former Byzantine stronghold of Ravenna was only one of the cities which for centuries had witnessed the coming and going of soldiers and scholars, merchants and artists, from the Greek East. Their influence had helped to offset that of the Germanic invaders, who found themselves subdued and then assimilated earlier in Italy than anywhere else. The Muslim world, even after the Norman conquest of Sicily and southern Italian provinces drove the armies of the Crescent back across the Mediterranean, remained no farther away than the shores of North Africa. And finally, that most characteristic of Western European institutions, feudalism, never penetrated Italian society deeply enough to supplant the urban complex of city-states far closer in form and spirit to ancient *poleis* and *civitates* than to the Paris of Charles VII or the London of Henry V.

It should be no surprise to find in the Italian political record of the *quattro-* and *cinquecento* much that is more reminiscent of ancient times and exotic lands than of the new courts of Europe. Sometimes this affinity with classical civilization can be overstated. It is possible to compare Lucrezia Borgia with a Macedonian queen or Roman empress, but to pursue the parallel too far runs the risk of misunderstanding a real-life woman of her own time. Beautiful, Lucrezia is reported to have been; sensuous she definitely was; and murderous she proved to be on occasion. But the equivalent, either in power or in bloodlust, of an Olympias or a Messalina, she was not. Nor can she serve even as the exemplar of female ruthlessness in her day, Caterina Sforza of Milan and Isabella d'Este of Mantua having at least matched and probably surpassed her in that respect. (Both of them also expressed contempt for one they called a "Spanish slut" because of the Borgias' roots and "daughter of a priest," her father having become Pope Alexander VI.)

Although the importance of Lucrezia Borgia can easily be exaggerated, the same does not apply to her formidable brother Cesare. An able troop commander and a smiling diplomat, he was also a killer whose victims seldom received the slightest warning. In 1500 he celebrated his capture of Ravaldino by raping its mistress, Caterina Sforza, before throwing her into prison. He then told friends that she had defended the fortress more stoutly than her virtue, adding cynically that the fortress had never before been taken. The figure of Cesare Borgia will reappear several times in these pages, his own activities and the accounts of them by Machiavelli having made him a prototype of the Renaissance prince in all his egoistic, bloodstained glory. Here it need be added only that his services to Lucrezia almost certainly included the slaying in 1500 of her second husband, Alfonso duke of Bisceglie, so that she might marry into Ferrara's ruling house.[4]

Reference to Machiavelli in connection with the Borgias illustrates the extent of political history's debt to Renaissance art and literature. Italian painters of the fifteenth and sixteenth centuries were especially prolific in their representation of individuals who were either assassins or victims of assassination, and in some instances successively both. With comparable zeal, contemporary writers combined the description and analysis of such events, displaying a clarity all but unmatched from classical antiquity to modern times.

This spate of uncommonly vivid source material imposes on the historian an obligation not to let visual and verbal effects overwhelm his sense of probability. Not every brilliantly expressed suspicion deserves to be greeted with instant and total credulity. Did Cesare Borgia actually murder his elder brother Giovanni in 1497? Often charged, but never proven. Did the Sforza regent of Milan, Ludovico, called "the Moor" because of his swarthy complexion and hated by Italian patriots for having summoned the French invaders in 1494, poison Gian Galeazzo, his nephew and ward, that same year? Probably not, but the legend remains. As for the doings of King Ferrante (Ferdinand I) of Naples,[5] or the provision by the Venetian Council of materials and money for the support of assassins, what can ever be known for certain?[6] Present-day readers, impatient to be fully informed about more recent political crimes, have reason to reflect on the timelessness as well as the intractability of their problem.

Among the cases that do qualify as significant and relatively well-documented, the first, involving the murder of Duke Galeazzo Maria of Milan, is also one of the least complex. This ruler had been sired by the remarkable Francesco Sforza, a *condottiere,* or military entrepreneur, who had fought his way up through the tangle of papal-imperial and related hostilities to seize a ducal tiara. The son apparently bore little resemblance to his father. Indolent, voluptuous, and petulant, he acquired in the course of his ten-year reign a reputation so bad that when his mother, Bianca Maria, died, in all likelihood of natural causes, he was widely suspected of having arranged for her to be killed. At last, on December 26, 1476, as he was entering the

Church of Saint Stephen, he was stabbed to death by three young members of the Milanese aristocracy. Two of them were slain on the spot by guards. The third, a would-be poet named Girolamo Olgiati, was captured sometime later and executed after horrifying tortures, but not before he had talked at length about Brutus, Cassius, and his own right to be honored as a classical tyrannicide.

No testimony, the condemned Olgiati's included, suggests at all convincingly that Ludovico the Moor planned either the murder of his brother Galeazzo Maria or that of the latter's son Gian Galeazzo eighteen years later. Ludovico benefited from both to be sure, the first having permitted him to usurp control of the government as regent for his ineffectual nephew, while the second cleared the way for him to assume the title as well as the powers of duke. Nevertheless, the *cui bono* argument, pointing the finger of guilt at whoever has profited from a crime, is often deceptive when applied to political assassination. In any event, a quite different aspect of Gian Galeazzo's death in the porch of Saint Stephen's seems more important than its perpetrators' motives, namely, its locale.

The recurrence of political murders committed in the vicinity of altars may by now have caught the reader's attention, seeming as it does to mock medieval Christianity's efforts to control political violence. The Church had, it is true, achieved some notable successes in the cause of restraint, but at times the odor of sanctity appeared only to heighten the drama of an act that openly defied religious admonitions. As a matter of practical calculation, the would-be assassin could count on enjoying a distinct advantage in a place of worship, where the intended victim was almost certainly to be unarmed, probably bareheaded, and possibly on his knees. The most arresting consideration, however, had nothing to do with such operational details. It arose from the fact that a political murderer, as will emerge more clearly from certain modern case histories, is often bent on nothing so much as shock effect. Where better could that be achieved than in a sanctuary consecrated to peace and mercy?

The same question is germane to another episode, the attack on the Medicis of Florence, carried out in 1478 by a cabal formed around their rivals, the Pazzis. Important as several members of that powerful family unquestionably were in hatching the enterprise, to call it simply the "Pazzi conspiracy," as is usually done, does less than full justice to its complex genesis and wide ramifications. Several Italian powers outside Florence actively supported the plan for an assault upon Lorenzo the Magnificent and his younger brother Giuliano de' Medici, while several others were kept closely informed. One of the most active conspirators was the archbishop of Pisa. Another was Girolamo Riario, current husband of the redoubtable Caterina Sforza (then still years away from her disastrous encounter with Cesare Borgia). The pope in Rome, Sixtus IV, was privy to the arrangements and had such high hopes for their success that he flew into a frenzy upon learning of Lorenzo's escape.

The attempt was peculiar in several respects. The Pazzis and their associates decided to attack not only in a church, Florence's magnificent cathedral, but on Easter Sunday, a day even holier than Christmas in the minds of many Christians. The brothers Medici had made known their intention to worship in the Duomo, and there Giuliano was fatally stabbed by Francesco de' Pazzi and one Bernardo Bandini. Lorenzo was supposed to have been killed by another conspirator named Montesecco; but Montesecco had sudden qualms of religious conscience (or more probably, according to skeptical contemporaries, simply lost his nerve), and his two last-minute replacements, one of them a priest, bungled their assignment. The young ruler having been rescued from the sacristy, into which he had fled, the majority of his Florentine subjects rose in fury against the conspirators. Francesco de' Pazzi and Archbishop Salviati of Pisa were apprehended in the town hall, the Palazzo Pubblico, and hanged from its windows; Lorenzo's assailants were torn to pieces by the crowd. Their fate was shared by other known or suspected culprits before the day was over. Riario, allegedly the pope's bastard son, escaped with his life, only to be slain by two aristocratic enemies at his wife's castle of Forlì some ten years later. Sixtus IV, meanwhile, vented his rage with more energy than logical consistency, excommunicating Lorenzo de' Medici and placing the city of Florence under interdict for having lynched the archbishop. The pontiff's impotence was nevertheless revealed for all to see, since the Florentine government, ignoring his fulminations, granted still more power to the surviving Medici prince.[7] Seldom has an assassination attempt recoiled so disastrously on its planners and sympathizers.

Details of another instructive episode, which took place in 1501 at Fermo near the Adriatic coast, are supplied by Machiavelli in a chapter of *The Prince* entitled "Of Those Who Have Attained the Position of Prince by Villainy."[8] Young Oliverotto da Fermo, raised by an uncle, Giovanni Fogliani, as in effect a foster son, made up his mind to remove all constraints, using the most violent means, and to seize full control of "his" city. He invited his uncle and numerous local dignitaries to a dinner, enticed them into a side room, and there had them all murdered by soldiers who had been hiding for that purpose. By so doing, Oliverotto did indeed "attain the position of prince by villainy," though his tenure was extremely brief. About a year later he was strangled at another dinner party, given at Sinigaglia by a still more accomplished subscriber to this form of hospitality, Cesare Borgia.[9]

A final case history resumes the story of the Medici family, after its return to power following the republican interlude of 1494–1512. In 1513 two young men named Capponi and Boscoli, irreconcilably opposed to the reestablishment of princely rule, decided to assassinate Giovanni Cardinal de' Medici (later Pope Leo X) and his younger brother, Giuliano, the surviving sons of Lorenzo the Magnificent. The attempt failed, and both culprits were executed after a perfunctory trial.[10] While he was awaiting death, however, Pier Paolo Boscoli earned a degree of fame by expressing about as clearly as possible the interplay of Christian and classical ideals in the fantasies of a Renaissance tyrannicide. As reported in a letter by Luca della Robbia, the great ceramicist and a friend of the condemned man, Boscoli's last words when della Robbia visited him in prison had included the following: "Oh, Luca, pray get Brutus out of my head, so that I may make this step entirely as beseems a good Christian."[11] Nothing could have better characterized the collision between incompatible ideals in the Florence of his time than this evocation of the Roman who slew Caesar, by a failed assassin who also considered himself a pious disciple of the revolutionary monk Savonarola.[12]

From Polemics to Analysis: Guicciardini

Only at long and irregular intervals throughout recorded history have dramatic events elicited commentaries by participant observers capable of lending both depth and resonance to what would otherwise be only timebound reminiscences. Thucydides remains the classical, as John of Salisbury is the medieval, and Churchill perhaps the modern, paradigm of such reflective chroniclers.

That Renaissance Italy produced at least two of its own is not surprising, given the convergence there of several influences: the maturing of Humanistic scholarship; the development of a lettered class of public officials; and the impact of harsh and unsettling events, culminating in the successive interventions by foreign powers which began with the French invasion of 1494. This last, more than any other single occurrence, added a new dimension to the already complex interplay of forces within the Italian state system. An observer who previously had only read about comparable struggles among the ancients found them being reenacted before his eyes on a political, diplomatic, and military stage suddenly expanded beyond easy recognition.

Nowhere more strikingly than in Florence did this mixture of established tendencies and unfamiliar shocks come together to inspire a quality of realistic appraisal which was, if not without precedent in human experience, genuinely new to the emerging Europe of the post-medieval era. And among Florentines none revealed more clearly the effects of that interaction than two well-positioned public officials, one commonly viewed as a historian, the other as a political philosopher, though in reality each deserves to be counted among the early modern masters of both disciplines. In order to appreciate Guicciardini's and Machiavelli's full significance for the understanding of assassination's place in political history, one must reflect for a moment on what might be called the state of the argument in Italy prior to the appearance of their writings in the early sixteenth century.

Long before then, in the mid-thirteenth century, Thomas Aquinas had brought to the scholastic treatment of tyrannicide his pious yet rationalistic view of divine law, plus a commonsense awareness of the distance that often separated announced from actual motives behind the murder of kings. Without abandoning this quality of prudential caution, Marsiglio (Marsilius) of Padua sixty or seventy years later—his *Defender of the Peace* was completed in 1324—took what appeared to be a much harder line with regard to oppressive rulers. Yet Marsiglio, for all his Bracton-like references to legal restraints on potential tyrants, remained a diligent controversialist on the side of the Holy Roman Emperors, the Bavarian Wittelsbach Ludwig IV in particular, and a political adviser of sorts to the pro-imperial, anti-papal Ghibelline party in Italy. Thus, when he wrote about tyrants he was generally aiming his remarks at popes far more than at secular princes. Even his insistence on the right of the community's "dominant part" to take action against a bad ruler appeared in a context which marked its author as precisely what he was, a progenitor of the conciliar movement within the Church, not as a prophet of parliamentary, let alone democratic resistance.

Both Saint Thomas and Marsiglio, one a theologian, the other a legist, had accorded normative elements a prominent place in their respective pronouncements on government. They discussed how governors *ought* to behave and, in the event of their behaving otherwise, what *entitled* responsible representatives of an abused society to raise the standard of revolt. To this talk of divine law, ethical judgment, obligations, and entitlement, however, was conjoined in the works of both men a distinctly measured quality that contrasted sharply with the bombastic sentiments appropriate to a heroic stance.

Marsiglio's younger contemporary, the literary humanist Giovanni Boccaccio, showed no such inhibitions in his use of rhetoric, untempered by any reminder of how things are apt to turn out in real life. What the author had to contribute on the subject of tyrannicide is well represented by the following: "Shall I call the tyrant king or prince, and obey him loyally as my lord? No, for he is the enemy of the commonwealth. Against him I may use arms, conspiracies, spies, ambushes, and fraud; to do so is a sacred and necessary work. There is no more acceptable sacrifice than the blood of a tyrant."[13] These were not the words of a fictional character; they appeared in a relatively scholarly, albeit popular, collection of biographical vignettes composed in Latin.

Admittedly the passage was written neither by a philosopher nor by an official privileged to observe at close range the workings of the state. Despite his early experience as a businessman and some study of canon law, Boccaccio was essentially a man of letters, a friend of Petrarch, and an interpreter of Dante. His works of imaginative literature, including not only *The Decameron* but numerous others as well, place him in the first rank of fourteenth-century Humanists. It would be a mistake to cudgel one's brain in an effort to find deeper meaning in his utterances on the subject of tyrannicide. Nevertheless, their tone and content help to provide a backdrop for the entry of more matter-of-fact observers and analysts.

The same value, as well as limitations, may be discerned in certain other emotional views that found expression in the Florence of Guicciardini's and Machiavelli's own youth. Following the French invasion and the expulsion of the Medicis in 1494, the new regime planted before the Palazzo Vecchio a statue of Judith with the severed head of Holofernes. On its pedestal appeared a strangely irrelevant inscription: "The citizens have erected this example of the salvation of the Republic." All tyrannicides, it seemed, were to be not merely remembered but venerated.

The contrast between such eulogistic sentiments and the distinctly restrained views on the subject of assassination expressed by Francesco Guicciardini (1483–1540) brings to mind Thucydides' deglamorization of Harmodius and Aristogiton nearly two thousand years before. If anything, the Florentine case had even greater potential than the Athenian for arousing indignation then and ever since, especially since Guicciardini's personality, described as sly, unsympathetic, and boundlessly ambitious, excited a repugnance in many quarters which had until recently shown few if any signs of abating. Neither the acknowledged brilliance of his penetrating mind nor the evidence of its having ranged far beyond the limits of *The History of Florence,* evidence that became available in the mid-nineteenth century when his descendants at last made the family archives available to scholars, has shaken the lingering belief in the essential unpleasantness of his character. John Addington Symonds' judgment, delivered many years after the opening of the archives, was redolent of Victorian disapproval: "Guicciardini," he wrote, "was the product of a cynical and selfish age, and his life illustrated its sordid influences."[14]

Ironically, it is the very directness with which the Florentine illuminated the issues of his time that has led other authorities to accord his works increasing respect, if not for high moral tone at least for a lack of obtrusive partisanship. Close reading, too, has worked in Guicciardini's favor by convincing not a few twentieth-century students of his thought that he did not in fact, whether from cynicism or opportunism or cowardice, defend tyranny. When he wrote cynically, which he often did, it was just as likely to be in criticism as in praise of authority. "Every government," he remarked in a famous passage, "is nothing but violence over subjects, sometimes moderated by a form of honesty."[15] But his condemnation of more than ordinarily bad government arose less from ethical outrage than from the conviction that a brutal, capricious regime was more likely to encompass its own downfall than a patient and consistent one. He praised Lorenzo de' Medici's refusal to unleash ferocious repression in order to secure his hold on Florence, explaining that "such a procedure would, in the course of time, emerge as being full of difficulties, of suspicion, and finally of cruelty."[16]

Nevertheless—and this his detractors prefer to emphasize—he praised dramatic acts of resistance very seldom, and then only with the most careful qualifications. Symonds quotes the following sentence from Guicciardini's *Government of Florence* as evidence that its writer was essentially hostile to decisive acts of resistance: "Very few indeed have these been, whose motive for tyrannicide was a pure love of their country's liberty; and these deserve the highest praise."[17] Though the sentence ends with a conventional tribute, its real message, critics argue, lies not there but in the opening clause. Presumably the coldness with which he, like Machiavelli, appraised the disaster of the Pazzi conspirators was further proof of his complete lack of sympathy for all dissidents.

What made Guicciardini something of a transitional figure in the evolution of Florentine thought concerning tyrannicide was that he continued to observe many of the old forms—without carrying them to the rhetorical heights attained by Boccaccio—while at the same time introducing the kind of ambivalence apparent in the sentence quoted above. Another instance of that sometimes irritating stylistic device appears at the end of his discussion of the decision by Lorenzo the Magnificent to make greatly increased use of armed guards, this in partial reaction to the Pazzis' attempted coup. Guicciardini declares that he can understand why the Florentine ruler was tempted to rely on "mercenaries," those instruments of despotism so hated by its enemies since time immemorial. On balance, however, the Italian scholar seems to conclude, regretfully, that the decision was unfortunate: "Nevertheless, it was not the mark of a free city or of a private citizen but of a tyrant and a city in subjection." But *then* consider the final twist he supplies by adding one more sentence: "In short, one must conclude that under him the city was not free, although it would be impossible to find a better or more agreeable tyrant."[18]

Here Guicciardini echoes, no doubt consciously, not just the message but almost the exact words of Aristotle discussing Pisistratus. Yet nobody would seriously call Aristotle a defender of tyranny as he defined it. The Florentine was, it appears, somehow more suspect in that regard. Perhaps Guicciardini's career as a supple and possibly at times unscrupulous public official, in capacities ranging from an embassy to Spain to the governorship of a province within the Papal States, makes it easy to imagine him as a sycophant wherever governmental power was involved. Or perhaps this results from bracketing his memory with that of a fellow Florentine, who was a greater political philosopher, but one even more maligned for his supposed "heartlessness."

Machiavelli

The distinction frequently drawn between Guicciardini as primarily a historian and Machiavelli as the more important theorist is valid, one of their ablest interpreters has pointed out, only within limits.[19] Guicciardini, in seeking to understand the disaster that had befallen Italy in his lifetime, recalled more persistently and in greater detail the intricate narrative of the power struggles affecting the peninsula before as well as after the French invasion in 1494. Machiavelli, on the other hand, seemed to define his task as one of the extracting general principles of political life from the swirl of contemporary events. Both, however, showed an ability to harness historical reconstruction in the service of theoretical inquiry, and each brought to bear an insider's knowledge of political, diplomatic, and military affairs far beyond the borders of their native Tuscany. Not only the principal states and leading personalities of Italy but also major foreign courts, including those of the Empire, France, and Spain, attracted their fascinated gaze.

This reliance on current events as a source of instructive experience is worth bearing in mind when one considers Niccolò Machiavelli's contributions to the study of violence, and especially of tyrannicide. At the same time it must be remembered that he was a classically trained Humanist to whom doctrines borrowed from classical antiquity were part of the common currency of intellectual enterprise. In a curious way this deference to ancient strictures on tyranny may have contributed to his reputation for hypocrisy and guile. The solemn opinions found especially in his "republican treatise," *Discourses on the First Ten Books of Titus Livy,* seem difficult if not impossible to reconcile with the calculating remarks about assassination familiar to readers of his other works, *The Prince* above all.

In the *Discourses* the author expressed a horror of despotism which would have done credit to Cicero, entitling a whole chapter "In Proportion as the Founders of a Republic or Monarchy Are Entitled to Praise, So Do the Founders of a Tyranny Deserve Execration."[20] In the same tract he warns against the danger that even the best "founders" may yield to enticements of ambition, citing Julius Caesar as an illustration of its power. Praising the spirit of resistance epitomized by Brutus, the Florentine commentator intones the judgment that "no tyrant can secure himself against such attacks, except by voluntarily giving up his usurpation."[21]

Is it any wonder that the cool advice to usurpers that appears elsewhere in Machiavelli's writing should have been so widely accepted as proof of his cynical duplicity? *The Prince* alone contains enough approbation of ruthless power, applied swiftly and with surgical precision, to offset whatever condemnation of such behavior is to be found in the *Discorsi*. Assigned in 1502 to serve as Florentine representative at the military headquarters of Cesare Borgia, Machiavelli heard from the duke's own lips the story of perhaps the most celebrated of banquets culminating in murder. Consider the tone in which this episode at Sinigaglia two years earlier is recalled in chapter 7 of *The Prince:* "He [Borgia] dissembled his aims so well that the Orsini made their peace with him, being represented by Signor Paulo whose suspicions the duke disarmed with every courtesy, presenting him with robes, money, and horses, so that in their simplicity they were induced to come to Sinigaglia and fell into his hands."[22] Two of the condottieri who had been part of the alliance against their host were strangled on the spot; others, including the leaders of the Orsini and Colonna parties in Rome, lost all stomach for further resistance. "The duke," concludes Machiavelli, "had laid a very good foundation for his power."

But was this otherwise unsentimental believer in reason of state the victim of uncritical hero-worship where the purposeful Borgia was concerned? In the eyes of an increasing proportion of modern scholars, the reverse appears more likely to have been true. Machiavelli, they argue, took his case histories where he found them. The accident of his having been posted to Cesare's tempestuous court in the Romagna naturally made its central figure one of the emissary's favorite objects of study. It is certainly true that when the loss of his office as municipal secretary forced him to seek reinstatement by currying favor with the Medici family, Master Niccolò made good use of Borgia's memory. Who better could he have found to personify the alternation of swift violence and patient cultivation of popularity, of playing at one time the lion and at another the fox, than the redoubtable lord of Urbino?

Even when Machiavelli's works appear to have been colored by his need to cultivate the favor of potential benefactors, they rely heavily on instances of shrewd realism in action. *The Prince* has as its primary aim the examination of various tactics rulers must adopt in order to survive, depending on how they came to power and what particular problems confront them. Less familiar, but no less significant, are the statements made even in the "republican" *Discourses* to the effect that wielders of political power and responsibility cannot be bound by ethical restraints valid for private individuals.

In assaying Machiavelli's importance for the student of political murder, it is less important to dwell on his fascination with Cesare Borgia's career, or to seek in vain for some reconciliation between the Florentine's realism and those conventional moral restraints whose force he would not have acknowledged, than to ask what resulted from his treatment of actual assassinations. And treat them he did, sometimes with unexpected results. Even his *History of Florence* includes a famous passage which requires an excursion to Milan and the murder of Galeazzo Maria Sforza in 1476. He follows the development of the plot hatched by the youthful zealots Lampognano, Visconti, and Olgiati and stresses the influence on all three of "an ambitious man of letters," Cola Montano (who as their tutor in Latin might have hoped for a gentler description from his fellow-humanist). The passage makes no effort to conceal the Sforza duke's cruelty and rampant lechery; and the conspirators' motives, the noble and the trivial alike, receive what appears to be a fair hearing. Finally, however, having described the murder and the grisly fate of the assassins, Machiavelli concludes with his customary matter-of-factness:

> These unfortunate young men's plot was secretly laid and boldly executed. They came to grief when those they hoped would follow and defend them neither defended nor followed ... Let princes learn to live so that they are honored and loved and so that no one hopes to save [himself] by killing them. And may the rest realize how futile it is to trust too much in a mob to follow and help them, however discontented it may be.[23]

If there lingers in those sentences a reminder of the author's preference for Borgia's style of violence, it lies in the implicit contrast between the mistakes of both the victim and his slayers, on the one hand, and, on the other, the lightning coup of Sinigaglia, followed by Cesare's equally swift reassurance of the momentarily startled populace. The same lesson, this time directed more at Galeazzo Maria's inept tyranny than at Olgiati and his companions, appears in Machiavelli's comments on the way in which Cesare Borgia announced the joyous termination of the reign of terror which he had unleashed on his subjects in the Romagna. Remirro de Orco, the duke's brutal steward there, was found one morning in the town square of Cesena, cut in half and with a blood-stained knife by his side, this, as explained a few lines earlier in *The Prince*, "to show that if any cruelty had taken place it was not by his [Cesare's] orders, but through the harsh disposition of his minister."[24] The local population reportedly was too relieved at the outcome to worry over the logic of the message.

Nowhere else in the works of Machiavelli is there a passage offering greater rewards than the brilliant analysis, in his *History of Florence*, of the Pazzi conspiracy of 1478.[25] Above all, it offers a fascinating illustration of the ability of the ex-secretary of the Council of Ten to reconcile objectivity with self-interest. In 1520, though still excluded from office, he had received from Pope Leo X and Cardinal Giulio de' Medici a commission to write the social and political history of the city, as a basis for possible changes to be instituted by the restored Medici regime. Given the identity of his patrons, it cannot have been easy to give an impartial account of the crime committed against two other Medici princes only slightly more than forty years ago. In addition, one of his patrons, now pope, and the other's father, Giuliano de' Medici, had been the objects of the intervening attempt by Boscoli and Capponi in 1513.

Given the circumstances, Machiavelli's achievement in constructing a balanced narrative can only be described as astounding. The lucidity of the reconstruction, the vivid portrayal of different personalities (among the numerous members of the Pazzi connection in particular), the meticulous attention to intentions, results, and the meddling of Fortuna, goddess of chance, all come together in an account fully deserving of comparison with the best of Guicciardini, or Thucydides. Point after point found elsewhere in Machiavelli's reflections on the deadly game of power finds an echo in his examination of the *cosa de' Pazzi*. At the end, having pondered the momentous aftermath of the attempt and its failure—Lorenzo the Magnificent having escaped with his life—the author takes yet another step back from his emerging canvas of the Florentine past in order to append a final observation: "Because conspiracies rarely succeed, they most often bring about the ruin of those who plan them, and they bring greatness to those against whom they are directed."[26]

Little more needed to be said. The transition from Christian teachings to a reborn classical realism as the principal check on assassins seems complete. And yet, almost as Machiavelli was writing those lines, Christianity was about to revive an ancient reason for slaying magistrates—their godlessness—which no Renaissance Italian, except Savonarola of course, would have hurried to embrace.

8

Religious Warfare and Reason of State

A Century of Bloodshed

In Europe the period between roughly the mid-1500s and the mid-1600s, variously referred to as that of the Wars of Religion, the Counter Reformation or the Catholic Reformation, occupies a special place in the history of political murder. It inherited, and continued to apply theories of tyrannicide as old as Aristotle's and commentaries as recent as Machiavelli's; but it witnessed as well the effects of a religious revolution upon the already violent behavior of emergent modern states. This mixture of sectarian conflict, state-building, dynastic egoism, and constitutional arguments left a distinctive imprint on the record of events and the evolution of ideas.

Little would be gained by recapitulating in detail all the plots, assassinations, trials, and executions of that sanguinary epoch. Lest their quantitative aspect be overlooked, however, I have included a table showing the principal fatalities. An overview of this kind has several advantages:

(1) It demonstrates that the mortality rate among political and religious leaders was very high, compared with that for the Middles Ages or for the era beginning about 1650.

(2) It warns that neither the chronology nor the geography of the matter is as simple as first approximations might suggest. Instead of a fairly consistent incidence of killings, one finds them distributed over the entire time span, though with clusters occurring in certain decades such as the 1560s, 1570s, and 1580s, and 1911–1920 of the ensuing century. The geographical pattern is more striking still. An age that witnessed no assault on a Hapsburg ruler, Austrian or Spanish, nor on a member of any primarily German house (that of Orange-Nassau being Dutch by adoption) produced a singular concentration of such incidents in France, the Low Countries, and the British Isles.

(3) The table illustrates the growing use of judicial or quasi-judicial

Major political murders and executions in the Age of the Wars of Religion

Date	Place	Victim(s)	Circumstances
July 1535	London, England	Sir Thomas More, former lord chancellor	Beheaded by order of a special royal commission, on charges of high treason
July 1540	London, England	Thomas Lord Cromwell of Wimbledon, earl of Essex, former royal secretary, lord privy seal, etc.	Beheaded under parliamentary bill of attainder on charges of treason and heresy, by order of Henry VIII
May 1546	Saint Andrews Castle, Scotland	David Cardinal Beaton, archbishop of Saint Andrews	Slain by Norman and John Leslie, William Kirkcaldy, James Melville, and other Fife lairds favorable to the Calvinist Reformation
August 1546	Paris, France	Etienne Dolet, Humanist scholar	Burned at the stake for heresy
January 1547	London, England	Henry Howard, earl of Surrey	Beheaded for high treason against Henry VIII
October 1553	Geneva, Switzerland	Michael Servetus (Miguel Serveto)	Burned at the stake for heresy by order of the Council of Geneva
February 1563	Siege camp outside Orléans, France	Francis, duke of Guise	Shot by Poltrot de Méré, Protestant nobleman
March 1566	Holyrood House Palace, Edinburgh, Scotland	David Rizzio (Riccio), secretary to Mary Queen of Scots	Stabbed to death by earls of Morton and Lindsay and others with support from the prince consort, Darnley
February 1567	Kirk o'Field, Edinburgh, Scotland	Henry Stewart, Lord Darnley, prince consort	Strangled and house blown up. Responsibility never proven, but James Hepburn, earl of Bothwell, and James Stewart, earl of Moray, clearly implicated
June 1568	Brussels, Spanish Netherlands	Edmond Egmont, count of Lamoral, prince of Gavre; and Philip II, count of Hoorne, admiral of Flanders	Beheaded for treason by order of Duke of Alva's "Council of Blood"
March 1569	Battlefield of Jarnac, southwestern France	Louis I, prince of Bourbon-Condé	Fatally shot by Montesquiou, Catholic army officer

Major political murders and executions in the Age of the Wars of Religion   (*continued*)

Date	Place	Victim(s)	Circumstances
February 1570	Linlithgow, Scotland	James Stewart, earl of Moray, regent of Scotland	Killed by Hamilton of Bothwellaugh (with knowledge of John Hamilton, Archbishop of Saint Andrews)
June 1572	London, England	Thomas Howard, duke of Norfolk	Beheaded by order of a royal commission on charge of high treason against Elizabeth I
August 1572	Paris, France	Gaspard II de Coligny, admiral of France	Killed by royal swordsmen under orders of Henry I of Lorraine, duke of Guise, with royal approval
December 1581	London, England	Edmund Campion, S.J.	Hanged following conviction on charge of high treason, following indictment for having conspired in Rome and France against Elizabeth I
July 1584	Delft, Holland	William the Silent, count of Nassau, prince of Orange, stadholder of Holland, Zeeland, and Utrecht	Shot to death by Balthazar Gérard
July 1584	London, England	Francis Throckmorton	Hanged following conviction for complicity in Catholic-Spanish plot against Elizabeth I
September 1586	London, England	Anthony Babington, with six fellow conspirators	Hanged following conviction for complicity in a similar but unrelated plot against Elizabeth I
February 1587	Fotheringhay Castle, England	Mary Stewart, queen of Scots	Beheaded under a royal warrant, for repeated acts of high treason against Elizabeth I
December 1588	Castle of Blois, France	Henry I of Lorraine, duke of Guise; and his brother, Charles of Guise, cardinal of Lorraine	Stabbed to death on successive days by royal guardsmen on orders of Henry III and under the command of their captain, Lorignac

Major political murders and executions in the Age of the Wars of Religion   (*continued*)

Date	Place	Victim(s)	Circumstances
August 1589	Saint-Cloud, France	King Henry III of France	Stabbed to death by a Dominican monk, Jacques Clément
February 1601	London, England	Robert Devereux, 2nd earl of Essex	Beheaded by order of a special commission for high treason against Elizabeth I
July 1602	Paris, France	Charles de Gontaut duke of Biron, marshal and admiral of France	Beheaded by order of the Parlement of Paris on charges of high treason "at home and abroad" against Henry IV
January 1606	London, England	Guy Fawkes, Ambrose Rokewood, Robert Keyes, and Thomas Winter (four others executed later)	Hanged following conviction for the Gunpowder Plot to blow up James I and both Houses of Parliament
May 1610	Paris, France	King Henry IV	Stabbed to death by François Ravaillac
April 1617	Paris, France	Concino Concini, marquis and marshal of Ancre	Stabbed to death by a royal guardsman, Vitry, on orders from Louis XIII and the duke of Luynes
July 1617	Paris, France	Leonora Galigai, widow of Concini	Beheaded by order of a special court following conviction on charges of lese majesty
October 1618	London, England	Sir Walter Raleigh	Convicted of conspiracy and treason by a jury in 1603; beheaded fifteen years later by order of James I
May 1619	The Hague, Holland	Johan van Oldenbarneveldt, advocate of the Estates of Holland	Beheaded following conviction by a special court of the States General, at the behest of the Stadholder, Maurice of Nassau
August 1628	Portsmouth, England	George Villiers, duke of Buckingham	Stabbed to death by John Felton, former naval lieutenant

Major political murders and executions in the Age of the Wars of Religion (*continued*)

Date	Place	Victim(s)	Circumstances
October 1632	Toulouse, France	Henry II, duke of Montmorency, governor of Languedoc	Beheaded for treason, by order of the Parlement of Toulouse, endorsed by the Parlement of Paris
February 1634	Eger, Bohemia	Albrecht Wenzel Eusebius von Wallenstein, duke of Friedland, etc.	Stabbed to death by Captain Walter Devereux, with Imperial authority
May 1641	London, England	Thomas Wentworth, earl of Strafford, privy councilor, president of the Council of the North	Beheaded under royal death warrant, following passage in Parliament of a bill of attainder
January 1645	London, England	William Laud, archbishop of Canterbury	Beheaded, failing royal pardon, after passage of a parliamentary bill of attainder, charging high treason
January 1649	London, England	Charles I, king of Great Britain and Ireland	Beheaded following conviction by a special High Court of Justice on charges of high treason and other crimes

measures to eliminate prominent figures, a reminder that throughout history jurisprudence, like foreign policy and taxation, has relied upon violence in the form of coercive power at the disposal of the state.

(4) Finally, it shows that in a time of solemnly declared religious and political causes, the role of deviant behavior, in the form of seemingly mindless attacks, had not faded into insignificance.

The Monarchomachs

The sixteenth century, which had begun with the unblinking political realism of Machiavelli and Guicciardini, produced before it ended a very different set of theories concerning tyrannicide and resistance. This change arose from the reinfusion of religious elements thrust into prominence once more by the crisis of western Christianity. Theories of resistance called "monarchomachist" had exponents on both sides of the line between the forces of the Reformation and those of Roman Catholicism. Protestant monarchomachs appeared first, for reasons not difficult to understand, though in the long run their Catholic opposites, including not just theorists but also popes and at least one powerful king, had greater influence on events. Yet both parties must be seen not only as antagonists but also as counterparts if one is to reach any informed judgment of their combined impact on European thought.

What was a monarchomach? Meaning literally a "fighter against monarchs," the term is used by modern historians of political theory to signify a believer in defiance of oppressive rule and, more specifically, one who tends to concentrate on the ruler's alleged offenses against a "true" religion. It was this emphasis on questions of faith that distinguished such thinkers from champions of republican ideals more broadly defined. The best and simplest way to characterize the shared message of Protestant and Catholic monarchomachs is by citing the fundamental assumption on which that message rested: that a heretical prince or princess was an outcast in the eyes of God and hence enjoyed no divine protection against a would-be slayer.[1]

There are two reasons why such a principle appealed first to certain Protestant controversialists. One is that by the mid-sixteenth century the Reformation had given rise to its "second wave," the Calvinist movement, most of whose members opposed the religious policies of the governments under which they lived and, as a result, were viewed as dangerous rebels. Many Lutherans, by contrast, were accustomed to obeying German or Scandinavian rulers of their own confession. Catholics, for the time being anyway, had correspondingly little reason to equate political with religious repression, save in Henry VIII's England and in some of the German and Swiss city-states. Hence it was the followers of John Calvin who as minorities in France, the Dutch Netherlands, and Scotland, or as a precociously powerful ruling elite in theocratic Geneva, most willingly declared war on "tyrants" in whom they saw enemies of God.[2]

The other explanation for the emergence of Calvinist monarchomachs has to do with elements of their theology, as well as, especially in France and Holland, their social base. Prophets of the Reformed faith had from the outset accorded the Old Testament so much reverence that it was only natural for them to combine certain Judaic teachings on the subject of ungodly rulers with the Aristotelian and Roman tenets dear to medieval scholastics and most of the Renaissance humanists. At the same time Calvinists in Western Europe relied for what political strength they could muster on the feudal nobility, the judiciary, and the magistracy of important towns. Hence they tended quite naturally to embrace every notion of corporate resistance, be it feudal or bourgeois, bequeathed to them by the Middle Ages. The result was a doctrine of justified and presumably militant opposition to misrule which invoked biblical authority and medieval rights in a genuinely novel way.

An execution at Geneva in 1553 first offered startling proof of the lengths to which a Calvinist regime in power would go in combating what it considered heresy. Miguel Serveto (Michael Servetus), a Spanish fugitive from the Inquisition, ran afoul of Swiss Protestant authorities as well by publishing a critique of trinitarian doctrine. Although Calvin himself later wrote that he personally deplored the burning, his objections seemed to be largely concerned with the mode of execution, not with the death sentence as such. In any event, his powerful deputy Theodore de Beza defended Servetus' punishment as one befitting a criminal found guilty of a capital crime.[3]

The next, and much larger question was how Calvinists should proceed when they were not the governing party but a persecuted minority. Calvin had advised the young Scottish exile John Knox against opposing Catholic rulers with force. It was not Calvin, however, but the redoubtable Beza who traveled to France in 1561 to address the Colloquy of Poissy, a disputation on current religious problems convened in the presence of the young Valois King Charles IX and the queen mother, Catherine de' Medici. The theological arguments presented there by Catholic and Protestant spokesmen are less important for present purposes than the fact that French Calvinists received their most resounding lesson in confessional advocacy not from the Founder but from his truculent heir apparent.[4] Not all *Huguenots* (as they called themselves after the Swiss-German term for sworn comrades, *Eidgenossen*) would prove as dogmatic as Beza. Nevertheless, his message of resistance without compromise and without quarter demonstrated its power when religious extremists on both sides shouldered aside the proponents of reconciliation and went to war.

Calls to battle in the Lord's name were not the only voices, Protestant or Catholic, heard in France during the latter half of the sixteenth century. The spirit in which Catherine and her chancellor, L'Hôpital, had sought compromise at Poissy was never wholly extinguished. In the writings of Jean Bodin, to mention only the most famous of the pragmatic *Politiques,* the state's responsibility for domestic order was given precedence over the rights of any religious party.[5] Sebastian Castellio, Geneva's most eloquent Protestant critic in the Servetus case, died in 1563, but not before he had constructed a moving appeal to Christian restraint and love as a rebuke to sectarian cruelty. And from Bordeaux came the skeptical reflections of Montaigne, suggesting that it was placing a very high value on one's conjectures to burn a man alive for them.[6]

Despite such views, a grim dogmatism held sway for several decades. French Catholics had the greater power to kill, and used it; but French Protestants retained their ability and willingness to apply violence when opportunity arose. More important, the minority faction had a good deal to *say* about resistance, including of course the venerable expedient of tyrannicide.

The earliest major work of Huguenot oppositional theory could not by any stretch of the imagination have been called incitement to political murder. François Hotman's *Franco-Gallia* of 1573, attacking the Catholic crown and especially the queen mother, was in essence a solemn appeal to that aristocratic constitutionalism its author erroneously attributed to German tribal practice. Hotman, though he justified political resistance by "magnates," does not even mention the name of the leading fifteenth-century apologist for tyrannicide, Jean Petit.[7] *Franco-Gallia* sanctioned civil war, to be waged by Protestants on behalf of old freedoms; and it argued in favor of mixed government, defending in particular the special role of the judiciary but also pleading the case of provincial legislatures. A call to assassinate Catholic rulers it was not.

The *Vindiciae contra Tyrannos* (officially anonymous but almost certainly the work of Protestant scholar Philippe Duplessis-Mornay) struck a bolder note.[8] After all, a "justification against tyrants" invited the question: justification of *what* against tyrants? Mornay's answer is not an endorsement of violence, but the tone has become more strident than that of *Franco-Gallia*. Hotman's earlier treatise was conceived and all but completed before the massacre of French Protestants on Saint Bartholomew's Day, 1572. The *Vindiciae*, on the other hand, drafted in the mid-1570s though not printed until 1579, had time in which to register the full shock of that horrifying operation, launched as it had been under royal auspices.

Mornay's most significant departure probably was his expansion of the doctrine of *political contract* to include godly rule. A prince who betrayed God and embraced a false religion violated the prior covenant with his own subjects and forfeited all claim to their allegiance. This was still no call for a spontaneous democratic uprising, a *jacquerie* against an anointed monarch. Instead, a justified rebellion will, it is assumed, be undertaken by the officers of the realm, including the provincial and municipal leaders on whom the Huguenots relied so heavily. Yet on this point the *Vindiciae* clung to one classical distinction, that between a usurper and a legitimate prince whose tyranny consisted in his or her illegal acts. It was only against the latter that, according to Huguenot theory, resistance was reserved to "officers"— the *melior pars* again. The illegitimate autocrat, having come to power through usurpation, remained, as in times past, an outlaw whom anyone might slay with impunity.

The *Vindiciae contra Tyrannos* devoted as much time and space to the secular obligations of princes as it did to religious matters. In so doing it expressed the grievances not just of Protestant Frenchmen but also, as had *Franco-Gallia,* those of nobles, justices in the courts of law, and local "notables," irrespective of denominational ties. Nevertheless, the secular aspects of the Huguenots' resistance to royal authority could easily be exaggerated. For when in the 1590s King Henry IV, although now a Catholic, guaranteed their safety, civil rights, and only slightly regulated freedom of worship, they quickly abandoned anti-monarchist claims and accepted the end of the civil war on those terms. Not until late in the seventeenth century, after Louis

XIV had revoked his grandfather's Edict of Nantes, would the banner of revolt against tyranny be raised again, this time by French Protestants living abroad. As for the actual Wars of Religion, even in their grimmest years and despite the example of a Huguenot officer who in 1563 killed the powerful Duke Francis of Guise, no member of the "Pretended Reformed Religion" raised a hand against a French monarch.

A second major branch of Calvinist regicide theory found its fullest expression not in the Netherlands, despite Dutch Protestant opposition to the Spanish monarchy, but in Scotland. Whatever Calvin supposedly said to John Knox on the subject of resistance, his cautious advice appears to have fallen on deaf ears.[9] It was Knox's fate, a dire one for so confirmed a misogynist, to have been born into an age of powerful women. Three of the most prominent were communicants of the Church of Rome: Mary of Guise, the French-born widow of James V of Scotland and regent following his death; Mary Queen of Scots, James's successor and briefly queen of France as well; Mary Tudor, queen of England (1553–1558) and consort of Spain's Philip II. Two others, with whom the Presbyterian divine had less to do, but of whom he was very much aware, were Catherine de' Medici in France and Margaret of Parma, sister to Philip II and his representative as Spanish regent in the Netherlands. Finally—a Protestant to be sure, but of much the wrong kind—there was Elizabeth I of England. The sentiments aroused in the reformer by this array of leading ladies he made clear in his *First Blast of the Trumpet against the Monstrous Regiment of Women* (1558).[10]

To a Scottish Calvinist the most menacing female appeared at the outset to be "Bloody Mary," as she was called by her Protestant subjects in Great Britain. Against her, as was his wont, Knox invoked the Old Testament: "God, for his great mercies sake, stirre up some Phinees, Helias, or Jehu, that the bloude of abominable idolaters maye pacifie Goddes wrath, that it consume not the whole multitude."[11] Since Phinees (Phinehas) had slain Zimri, an Israelite officer, as he lay abed in camp with a Midianite idolatress (Numbers, 25), and since both Elisha and Jehu had shared in the destruction of Jezebel, the religiopolitical significance of the passage was as unmistakable as its sexual overtones.

Knox was no less willing to denounce his and Jehovah's other enemies, men and women alike. Yet he never produced a doctrine of resistance having any broader base than his own choleric piety. Several English Protestants among the "Marian exiles" of the 1550s were more coherent. John Ponet, a former Anglican bishop who had fled to Strasbourg, wrote in 1556 that a tyrant might indeed be killed, but only if legal forms had been suppressed or if the assassin was inspired to defend God.[12]

It was left to one of Knox's compatriots, however, to formulate most broadly the sixteenth-century case for tyrannicide. George Buchanan, although he too was a Scottish Calvinist, was in addition a well-educated humanist who had studied at the Sorbonne in Paris. Perhaps for that reason, his principal work, *De Jure Regni apud Scotos*, published in 1579, contains relatively little on the subject of heretical misrule. Instead, its author addressed himself to man's natural inclination toward political association and, in terms reminiscent of Aristotle no less than of Aquinas, described a monarch as both the law's defender and its subject, on commission, so to speak, from those under his care. A ruler who breaches the contract by failing loyally to discharge that commission becomes a tyrant at war with his people. "Once war with the enemy has begun for just cause," concludes Buchanan in one of the most uncompromising formulations of a vehement period, "not only the whole people but also individuals have the right to kill the enemy."[13] All the accompanying words of caution against frivolous abuse of such a right could not alter the startling effect of Buchanan's message. Lucid and erudite, his Latin text stands, in the words of Harold Laski, as possibly "the most influential political essay of the century."[14] In opposition to Saint Thomas' warning that the killer of a king was likely to claim, but less likely to possess, a worthy excuse for his action, Buchanan declared the doctrine of tyrannicide sufficiently grand to survive its possible misapplication.

The situation of Catholics with respect to tyrannicide differed from that of Protestants in several important respects. In the eyes of the Roman Church the Reformation was seditious, its followers guilty of treason against both Christian law and civil authority, the utterances of its spokesmen anathema. Hus had been burned at Constance as a traitor and felon. So would Luther have been, but for the power and influence of Saxony's elector. At Paris in 1546 Etienne Dolet went to the stake condemned by the Sorbonne's faculty for his secular humanism. Until non-Catholic princes and princesses had established themselves as serious threats to the Church, there was little reason for Catholic spokesmen to explore the possible virtues of tyrannicide. When they did begin to do so, the issue was frequently posed in terms of the culprit's having led, incited, or supported an unlawful insurrection. To a monarch such as Philip II of Spain it must have seemed only a step from the execution of the highborn dissidents Egmont and Hoorn at Brussels in 1568 to the placing of a price on the head of Holland's leader, William the Silent, and only a short step further to giving Madrid's blessing to conspiracies aimed at the life of the meddlesome queen of England.

While the role of Spain, its king, its saints, and its polemicists was crucial throughout the period, the initial sanction for slaying Protestant rulers on purely religious grounds—irrespective of alleged rebellion—came not from the Escorial but from the Vatican. The great councils of the Church also played their part. That of Constance in the fifteenth century had only grudgingly withheld formal approval of selective tyrannicide, acceding thereby to the debating skill of Gerson; and the Council of Trent in the sixteenth century had no qualms about denouncing heresy in terms which could only be read as demanding death for false Christians of whatever rank or station. In the event, however, conciliar decisions counted for less than the pronouncements of successive popes: Pius V (1566–1572), Gregory XIII (1572–1585), and Sixtus V (1585–1590). Whatever their personal merits in other respects, the three pontificates together produced a near-disaster in the historical development of the Church's relation to political murder. Although Protestant historians were long content to see in Philip II the worst villain of the Counter-Reformation, a fuller and fairer understanding of the Spanish king's record shows that much of the time it embodied greater caution and restraint than that of Gregory XIII, for example, who celebrated the memory of the Saint Bartholomew's Day massacre and ordered Te Deums sung for the murder of William of Orange.[15]

Signals of this kind, emanating from Rome, were enthusiastically picked up by extremists within the Church, notably including French preachers of the Catholic League. One of these, Rossaeus of Paris, was especially vitriolic in his attacks on the *Politiques* and their counsels of restraint. Another, Jean Boucher, eulogized Jacques Clément, the feebleminded slayer of King Henry III in 1589, as a martyr inspired by Christ to avenge the deaths of the Guise brothers, leaders of the Catholic party of *dévots,* at Blois the previous year.[16]

Nevertheless, not French pulpit oratory but the scholarly writings of two Spanish Jesuits were what presented the Church's case for tyrannicide in its most fully developed form. Relying on both ancient and medieval authorities, these spokesmen, one a theologian, the other primarily a historian, took aim at Protestant and purportedly suspect Catholic rulers alike. Following in the footsteps of their Calvinist antagonists—but also fellow-monarchomachs—they appended to Aristotle's dual definition of tyranny as usurpation or selfish caprice a third and for them decisive element: deviation from the true religion.[17]

Francisco Suarez, who died in 1617 after a lifetime of teaching theology at the universities of Segovia, Valladolid, Alcalá, Salamanca, Rome, and Coímbra, was the milder of the two, not only in temperament but also in his admonitions to holders of royal power. Considered by some to have been the last of the great scholastics, he was influenced in his own day by an older contemporary, Father Bartolomé de Las Casas, and shared the Dominican's humanitarian concern over such issues as the treatment of native inhabitants of the Indies. He shared as well many classical and Thomistic views on regicide, including the belief that wrongs done by a legitimate prince were often better borne with patience than forcibly resisted with unpredictable results. It is in fact hard to find in Suarez on kingship much that goes beyond Aquinas' insistence on the primacy of divine law and the rights of the governed except—and here the Spaniard was a man of his times—the assertion that heresy, disbelief, and religious compulsion in a false cause were signs of tyranny even in an anointed ruler.

The situation in France obviously weighed on the devout observer's mind. Henry IV was legitimate by any reading of his genealogy. But was he also a crypto-Protestant, his public conversion to Catholicism notwithstanding? Had he, as was reported, explained away that act with the cynical remark that "Paris was worth a mass"? If so, Suarez implied, this king was a religious hypocrite and his title a false one. The Jesuit scholar's book *Of Laws and Legislators* was published only in 1612; but, as its contents make clear, it had been conceived and essentially completed prior to Henry's assassination in 1610, whence the widely held suspicion that its author had prayed for the monarch's death. Whether he welcomed or deplored it when it came, there is no way of saying with confidence.

Although Juan de Mariana outlived Suarez by several years, he was the elder of the two; and his book *Of the King and His Instruction* appeared in 1599, well before publication of the other's principal work. Mariana, too, endorsed the traditional condemnation of usurpers, but he went on to applaud still more the slayers of princes "who hold the laws and holy religion in contempt."[18] Here again, chronology is of some importance. Five years before this manual appeared the Jesuits had been exiled from France, by order of the predominantly Catholic Parlement of Paris and following several unsuccessful attempts on the life of Henry IV. In 1605, just as ten additional chapters of Mariana's magnum opus, a *History of Spanish Affairs*, were published, King Henry welcomed the Society back into his kingdom. In 1610 the king was stabbed to death by Ravaillac. The assassin was not a Jesuit and apparently had no Jesuit ties. Still, the timing of Mariana's writings, both historical and political, could not have been more damaging to the reputation of his order. More to the point, their author's name would be firmly linked with that of Buchanan in the coming revulsion against perpetrators and theorists of tyrannicide.

Coligny and William the Silent

Despite the massive intrusion of religious issues into the political struggles of the early modern era, not every assassination of that period could be traced to sectarian hatred. As the table of events has shown, other and more worldly motives cannot be ignored even when considering the record of those hotbeds of doctrinal warfare, Scotland and France.

North of the Tweed, murdering kings and pretenders had long been sufficiently common to make Shakespeare's contemporaries receptive to his portrayal of the Macbeths, husband and wife. In the time of Mary Queen of Scots that tradition retained its vitality without apparent need for inspiration from a Knox or a Buchanan.[19] There was the queen's favorite secretary, the Italian Rizzio, dragged from the royal apartment in Edinburgh's Holyrood House and butchered at the behest of her husband, Lord Darnley, and her illegitimate half-brother, the earl of Moray. That was in March 1566. Within a year it was the turn of Darnley, the ornamental but neurotic prince consort, strangled in his garden. That same night his house was destroyed by a mysterious explosion, the purpose and authorship of which has never been clearly established.

Moray, the most obvious beneficiary of the Rizzio and Darnley murders, since they left him regent of Scotland, had just three more years to live before he in turn was slain at Linlithgow. His assassin, a disaffected nobleman and self-proclaimed patriot, Hamilton, claimed to have proof that the regent was a traitor to Queen Mary and a paid agent of Elizabeth I. Not even the fact that the archbishop of Saint Andrews, Hamilton's kinsman, had supported the plot against Moray could make it a primarily religious undertaking, for the Hamiltons were among the Scottish queen's most devoted dynastic followers. There is no need to invoke motives of faith to explain the effects of palace intrigue combined with hatred of the Anglo-Saxon enemy.

A similar observation, albeit with different terms of reference, is in order concerning France, Scotland's old and frequent ally. The murder of the duke of Guise by a Huguenot in 1563 and that of the prince of Bourbon-Condé by a Catholic soon thereafter, although initiated in part by the antagonism dividing Christian parties, also represented episodes in the struggle between powerful aristocratic families and the political factions that had formed around them.[20] In that respect they recalled the vicious duel between "Burgundians" and "Armagnacs" a full century before the Reformation had been heard of in France. As for the Valois Henry III's decision to have two of the next generation of Guises slain at Blois in 1588, it is true that the king would die the following year by the hand of a religious zealot crying vengeance. Seen in its own terms, however, the extinction of the Catholic Guises by a Catholic ruler had been an act of sovereign power and dynastic guile, a Borgian application of reason of state without recourse to piety.

Having once eliminated from consideration a number of political crimes which, although they displayed traces of the epoch's pervasive religious coloration, were essentially secular in nature, one can see more clearly the outlines of certain others whose victims really were seen as Christian martyrs by one or more of the warring denominations. On the Catholic side Sir Thomas More, beheaded in England for opposing Henry VIII's personal version of church reform, must be counted as such a tragic hero. So must Scotland's Cardinal Beaton, murdered a half-dozen years later by a group of Calvinist sympathizers. Two other cases, both involving Protestant standard-bearers, affected European attitudes and alignments so powerfully that they deserve special attention.

In the summer of 1572 Gaspard count of Coligny, admiral of France, leading member of the all-but-royal house of Montmorency, veteran of wars from Italy to Flanders, and since Condé's murder acknowledged leader of his nation's Protestants, came to Paris in something approaching triumph. The population of the capital was overwhelmingly Catholic, but at court great courtesy was being lavished upon Huguenot magnates in general and the admiral in particular. The cause of this unaccustomed lull in civil and religious strife was to be found in a decision arrived at by the king, young Charles IX, and momentarily endorsed by his mother, Catherine de' Medici, to adopt the foreign policy espoused by Coligny. Simply stated, his proposal was to throw down the gauntlet to Spain, mobilizing for that purpose all Frenchmen regardless of faith, lending support to the Dutch rebels against Philip II and his viceroys, seeking help from Italian cities, German princes, and—who knew?—even the queen of England. Henry duke of Guise naturally denounced the proposal, invoking against heretics the memory of his slain father and pressing for an entirely different course, a crusade directed against Protestant England, where the king's former sister-in-law (and Guise's cousin) Mary Queen of Scots was confined, facing possible martyrdom.[21]

The sweltering heat, which held Paris in its grasp that August, was made the more oppressive by storm clouds of religious and political hostility. Coligny's confident arrival, far from signaling détente, seemed to underscore the dangers inherent in the situation. Protestants in the capital flaunted their royal favor by mounting public demonstrations, among them the destruction of a cross recently erected by Catholics in celebration of the execution of several "Huguenot criminals." More ominous, though less obvious, was Queen Catherine's growing resentment of the admiral's influence over her son. As abruptly as she had endorsed the plan to make war on Spain, she was now swinging to the opposite view. A well-schooled Italian princess, she gave no warning of her change of heart even to her son the king. Instead, she quietly sent word to the embittered Guises that she would welcome their cooperation in defense of the throne and the faith.

On the morning of Friday, August 22, still assured, or so he thought, of royal protection, Coligny was walking, with a few retainers, from the Louvre to his lodgings in the Rue de Béthisy. Along the route stood a house occupied by a henchman of the Guises, from which another of their agents, Maurevel by name, fired a harquebus at the Huguenot leader, striking him in the hand and shoulder. The wounded man, more familiar with pain than with fear, rushed at the head of his attendants to an upstairs bedchamber where the curtains could be seen still swaying; but all their search uncovered was the clumsy gun, lying where Maurevel had dropped it in his flight.

Word of the attempt spread quickly across Paris, igniting fear and anger as it went. King Charles, interrupted while playing *paume*, indoor tennis, hastened to the Louvre and dispatched a body of guards to protect Coligny's quarters. The queen mother, however, responding to the dangers she fore-saw stemming from the botched ambush, moved swiftly to counteract her son's initial remorse. Although for many hours no word issued from the pal-ace, arguments were in progress there, leading to serious deicsions. By Sat-urday afternoon, the day following the shooting, Charles IX had been converted to the need for ruthless measures. That evening, with Queen Ca-therine at his side, he received the duke of Guise, summoned in the king's name to concert military plans for the morrow.

Sunday was Saint Bartholomew's Day. Coligny died first, stabbed by a swordsman brought to the victim's apartment by Guise (henceforth, for Protestants, the malevolent figure of Christopher Marlowe's plays) with no resistance offered by the royal guards supposedly assigned to defend the place.[22] At the Louvre a large number of Huguenot nobles and their ser-vants were herded into the courtyard, there to be slaughtered by soldiers, while others of the condemned were surprised in corridors and sleeping quarters. Then the gates were flung open and armed units poured out to seek and destroy virtually all the remaining Protestant leaders resident in Paris. Less prominent members of the proscribed faith were slain by uncontrolled mobs whose like would not be seen again until the September Massacres of 1792. Even the first prince of the blood, young Henry of Navarre, and his cousin the prince of Condé survived only because they hastily agreed to at-tend mass that morning.

The death toll in Paris on Saint Bartholomew's Day can only be esti-mated. Approximations range from as low as two thousand to as high as three or even four times that number. Word of the massacre spread to the provinces, where some two hundred Huguenots lost their lives at Meaux, five hundred at Orleans, seven to eight hundred at Lyon. Comparable fig-ures have been compiled for Troyes, Rouen, Toulouse, and Bordeaux. Bells of thanksgiving sounded in Rome and Madrid. Those of London and Am-sterdam were silent in mourning.

The public figure whose death, not long after that of Coligny, was to shake Europe most deeply was a posthumous son-in-law of the murdered admiral. In 1584 William of Orange, count of Nassau and military com-mander (stadholder) of the United Provinces, had returned home to Delft after a visit to Paris with a new wife, his fourth, daughter of the late Hugue-not hero. There was, or so it seemed to him, no fresh cause to anticipate dan-ger in Holland. He had to be sure led the Dutch insurgents against the armies of Spain. In 1568 when counts Egmont and Hoorn were executed in Brussels, William had been publicly condemned by the same Spanish-Flem-ish imperial tribunal. And in 1580 King Philip II had solemnly placed him under ban as "the plague of the Christian community," announcing as he did so a sizable reward for the death of this Protestant rebel.[23]

Despite such solemn warnings, William, called "the Silent" in English but more commonly "the Sly" in Dutch, remained unmoved. He was not a pious Calvinist and stubbornly refused to ally himself too closely with the Dutch Reformed ecclesiastical establishment, preferring to chart his own course through the shifting currents of German, French, and English policies. About those of the Vatican and Madrid there was little he could do, save defy them, but the knowledge of powerful enemies abroad left him seemingly unperturbed. Spain and Italy were far away, and the Dutch regiments he had trained to defend their deceptively gentle terrain had shown themselves remarkably tenacious in doing just that, even in the face of the dreaded Spanish *tercios* and other units of the Army of Flanders.

Despite this show of nonchalance, the stadholder had more cause for misgivings than he chose to admit. Only two years earlier he had barely survived, gravely wounded, the murder attempt by a Basque adventurer named Jean Jaureguy. On July 10, 1584, the Dutch leader's previous good luck deserted him. Getting up from the lunch table in his house at Delft, William had strolled past a number of acquaintances and petitioners, acknowledging questions as he went, and started into a narrow stairwell leading up to the floors above. There, at close quarters, he was shot and fatally wounded by a pistol in the hands of Balthazar Gérard, one of a new breed of assassins converted to the uses of gunpowder.

Gérard was arrested on the spot and prior to his execution revealed enough about himself to provide a picture of religiosity mixed with greed. A French-speaking Catholic subject of Spain from the Free County of Burgundy, he had learned with excitement of Philip II's proclamation of 1580, including the famous offer of bounty money:

> So that this . . . destruction of the said Orange may be achieved more promptly and our people may be delivered more quickly from this tyranny and oppression, and wishing to reward virtue and punish crime, we promise upon the word of a king and as a servant of God that if there be someone, either our subject or a foreigner, with such good will and so strong a desire for our service and the public good that he can enforce our said ordinance and rid us of this plague, delivering Orange to us dead or alive or even just killing him, we will give and furnish to him and to his heirs the sum of 25,000 gold crowns, in land or cash at his choice, immediately after the accomplishment of the deed. If he has committed any crime or breach of the law whatever, we promise to pardon him and do pardon him as of now. Further, if he is not a nobleman, we grant him nobility for his valor.[24]

Gérard's trail northward, from what now is eastern France through the Low Countries to his fateful encounter in Delft, was punctuated not only by theological discussions with sympathetic clergymen but also by nervous requests for assurance from officials in Brussels and elsewhere about the certainty of payment. On the latter count at least, he need not have worried. The Spanish king, apprised of William the Silent's death, ordered public rejoicing, then bestowed on the slayer's parents a cluster of landed estates in the Free County and on the father a title of Burgundian nobility. This reaction by the most powerful Catholic monarch, coming as it did only a dozen years after Saint Bartholomew's Day and accompanied once more by jubilant Te Deums in Rome, seemed to many of Europe's Protestants a declaration of warfare to be waged not on the battlefield but in the shadows.

The Queen in Danger?

Elizabeth I of England, a target of John Knox's denunciations, occupied a position parlous in other respects as well. This is not to suggest that all alleged plots against her were equally menacing, nor that evidence pointing to manipulation of assassination scares by certain of her ministers should be ignored. Nevertheless, it would be an equally serious mistake to assume that she was never in genuine danger. She ruled, in a distinctly informal manner, a kingdom whose religious divisions tempted, as its foreign policies often infuriated, the great powers of Catholic Europe. Neither opportunities nor motives for assaults upon her were lacking.[25]

In fairness to Philip II it must be said that the Spanish ruler supported projects of that kind for only a relatively short period during the 1580s—his "bad decade" on so many fronts—and never with the *ad feminam* virulence of Elizabeth's papal or native foes. In the long run the latter—the British Catholic followers of two crowned Marys, one the queen's own sister and predecessor on the English throne, the other her Scottish cousin—proved to be her most dangerous personal enemies. She had, almost from the moment of her coronation, overturned the short-lived Marian reaction, resuming the Anglican Protestant course of her late brother, Edward VI. For that the Escorial could forgive her only as long as there was hope of an English-Spanish alliance. The Vatican and its communicants in Great Britain could not forgive her at all.

The year 1570 is significant in the present context because that is when Pope Pius V, in his bull *Regnans in Excelsis,* declared the "bastard daughter of Henry VIII and Anne Boleyn ... excommunicate and deposed." Ten years later, in reply to the query of certain English Catholics, a high official in Rome became more explicit: "Since that guilty woman ... is the cause of so much injury to the Catholic faith and loss of so many million souls, there is no doubt that whoever sends her out of the world with pious intention of doing God service not only does not sin but gains merit."[26] The attitude of the papacy toward British affairs was at this point marked not only by wrath but also by frustration, there being no means available to enforce the Vatican's judgment unless and until Spanish military power was committed. When *Regnans in Excelsis* was promulgated and even when the supplementary declaration just quoted was made in 1580, there was no assurance that a Grand Armada would set forth on "the enterprise of England."

Meanwhile, in the early 1570s there had been born a plot against the queen, centering around an incorrigibly optimistic and talkative Italian businessman in London, Roberto Ridolfi by name.[27] He was eventually charged by English authorities with having carried letters written by the pope to Mary Queen of Scots and to the duke of Norfolk, that veteran intriguer in Scottish politics. Much of the evidence produced by the crown was unconvincing. Ridolfi appears to have been not much more than a busybody; and Norfolk, though he had hoped to wed Queen Mary and was known to have corresponded with the Spanish court, was a Protestant who showed little enthusiasm for the Italian's schemes. As for the Scottish queen, whatever suspicions her wide correspondence may have excited, on this occasion her actual role was neglible.

Norfolk, to the surprise of many observers, was condemned and beheaded for "commerce with the enemy," that is to say with Spain, which had not been shown to have intervened and was not then at war with England. After the duke's execution in 1572, through Elizabeth's decree, the kingdom had no more holders of that rank throughout the rest of her reign. Ridolfi, the extent of his culpability not proven, slipped away to the Continent, where he survived to the age of eighty-one. Mary Queen of Scots, despite angry demands by royal councilors and members of Parliament for her condemnation, remained as she had been, at once a refugee and a prisoner in comfortable confinement, receiving innumerable messages and, unfortunately for many people ultimately including herself, answering them with a minimum of discretion.

The elements of absurdity in the Ridolfi affair and the seeming miscarriage of justice with respect to the duke of Norfolk may explain why some commentators dismiss too casually more serious plots against Elizabeth I that began to surface a few years later. If history often records tragedy subsequently replayed as farce, it also contains examples of the reverse, as two episodes of English history in the decade of the Armada will illustrate. Both revolved around young gentlemen of birth, members of a new generation of English Catholics. In the course of their educations they, like many of their contemporaries, had been strongly influenced by Jesuit missionaries, notable among them Edmund Campion and Robert Parson, newly returned from the Continent in 1580. Neither man, it should be pointed out, was an exponent of regicide. Campion in particular, who belonged to the humane school of Christian missions that in France would soon produce Saints François de Sales, Vincent de Paul, and Marie de l'Incarnation, appears to have harbored no malice toward the queen. The trouble was that his devout message appeared dangerous to Protestant Englishmen; in 1581, having been arrested as an unlawful missionary, he was executed for treason.[28]

The first conspiracy associated with this Catholic revival bears the name of an individual very different from Campion, the Oxford scholar and activist Francis Throckmorton. Determined to add militancy of purpose to the message of the Jesuit missionaries, he corresponded from his comfortable London home not only with Mary Queen of Scots but also with Catholic *Ligueurs* in France. This time there was a real connection with the Spanish government, through its ambassador to England, Bernardino de Mendoza. Either because of his frequent visits to Mendoza or because of a possible informer among the conspirators who met at his house, Throckmorton was taken into custody, while actually encoding a message to Mary of Scotland. He was executed for high treason, his confession having already led to the expulsion of Spain's envoy as *persona non grata*.

Throckmorton was thirty when he perished at Tyburn Gallows on July 10, 1584, the very day of William the Silent's assassination at Delft. His successor among plotters against Elizabeth was only twenty-five when he in turn was executed in September 1586. Anthony Babington had among his accomplices a priest named John Ballard, who shared the belief of Throckmorton's doomed contingent that Mary Queen of Scots must be freed by a Spanish army and crowned ruler of a joyously re-Catholicized Britain. Ballard, first of the conspirators to be arrested, revealed the names of six others, including Babington; all perished together in Lincoln's Inn Fields. Elizabeth's principal minister, the aging Sir Francis Walsingham, had followed the project through his agents for some time and had in his possession an exchange of correspondence between Babington and Mary Queen of Scots. This time the English ruler could not gainsay the evidence of an explicitly murderous plan, known to her royal prisoner at Fotheringhay Castle and enjoying the support of the Spanish king. The long, unhappy saga of Queen Mary had reached its end. In February 1587, still at the castle where she had lived in genteel confinement, she was beheaded in compliance with the royal death warrant.

These successive fiascoes involving Ridolfi, Throckmorton, Babington, and their luckless collaborators recall Machiavelli's observations on the subject of conspiracy to commit assassination. A still more famous illustration of such undertakings—and their frailty—was the Gunpowder Plot in 1605. The ignominious collapse of that attempt—undertaken after Queen Elizabeth's death but an extension of the religious struggles of her reign—seems to bear out the Florentine's contemptuous judgment. The plotters around Guy Fawkes were fervent Catholic opponents of the English establishment. They had assembled enough explosives beneath Parliament's chambers in Westminster to have destroyed the new King James I and both Houses with a single blast. Unfortunately for the conspirators, though fortunately for everyone else, some of them talked too much. A few hangings settled the matter, with nothing but an annual celebration of Guy Fawkes Day to show for it. Despite later struggles and false alarms inspired by religious hatred, England would never again confront a genuine "popish plot."

Henry of Navarre

The first, and most popular, of France's Bourbon kings was crowned at Chartres in 1594, five years after Henry III, the last Valois, had been murdered by Clément. Henry IV had abjured his Protestant faith, doubtless never so deep as his ambition; but soon after his coronation he provided Europe with a model of politically inspired toleration, the series of enactments which in combination are known as the Edict of Nantes. Those decrees conferred on French Huguenots not only freedom of conscience but also nearly complete freedom of public worship, military control of more than a hundred fortified towns, and various guarantees of nondiscrimination under the law. A leading Protestant, the duke of Sully, remained in effect first minister of the crown and custodian of the royal finances. At the same time the king reaffirmed the fundamental rule that only a Catholic could occupy the throne. He went out of his way to ingratiate himself with leaders of both sides in the civil war just terminated, revealing in the process a combination of jovial charm and deliberate calculation.

Henry's personality is important for an understanding of his career and of reactions to his eventual assassination. This king of France and of Navarre (inherited from his mother) saw himself as a gentleman-soldier, a dashing if not always prudent field commander, initially of Huguenot forces and now of national armies. He was also a gallant, who loved women almost as much as he loved cavalry mounts—a taste that contemporaries brought up on Rabelais and unenamored of the last Valois monarchs found not only forgivable but positively welcome. He had shown himself firm and equitable, though never selfless, in implementing the type of religious settlement long espoused by the *Politiques*. In foreign affairs, although he mistrusted Spain, he generally avoided confronting its power directly. For the rest, he offered kind words but little material support to his Dutch allies and temporized with England, whose "virgin queen" he detested. In all this, until almost the end of his life he differed from the earlier idol of French Protestants, Coligny, having instead built, with Sully's help, a reputation for shrewdness and caution born of early reverses and narrow escapes.

In the spring of 1610, however, there were signs that Henry was abandoning that moderate course. He had previously taken pride in serving as a peacemaker in Italy, Alsace, and elsewhere. Now he suddenly appeared intent on leading his troops against those of both the Spanish crown in the Netherlands and the Holy Roman Emperor along the Rhine. His erotic pursuits, admired in the young warrior, were beginning increasingly to represent nothing more statesmanlike than petulant self-indulgence. The Princess of Condé, object of the king's latest infatuation, had been removed by her husband to Brussels, whence the French ruler was demanding her return, even at the cost of a showdown with Spain's legendary Army of Flanders. That was something Richelieu too would risk, a quarter of a century later, but more deliberately and with the support of more promising allies. Given the situation, one wonders whether the assassin of Henry IV did not, with the worst will in the world, rescue his victim's fame.[29]

Paris was humming on May 14. Everywhere there were reports of armies forming. The queen, Marie de' Medici, had been consecrated at Saint-Denis the previous day and was scheduled to make her triumphal entry into the capital on May 16. After years of temporizing she had at last been named regent by her husband, who had no confidence in her political judgment but knew that she had forgiven him much. He appears even to have liked her; and now he was putting his affairs, including the succession of the eight-year-old Dauphin, in order before embarking on a campaign likely to be long and dangerous.

Henry rode out of the Louvre in an open carriage, accompanied by one of his former Catholic opponents, the duke of Epernon, with a handful of listless guards. Their destination was the Arsenal, where Sully awaited them, probably to complain over the cost of preparations for the visibly approaching war. Not far from the palace, in the narrow Rue de la Ferronerie, the carriage was halted by the sort of traffic jam to be expected in the vicinity of Les Halles, the public markets. During that stop François Ravaillac, who had been watching all day outside the palace, darted from a doorway and stabbed the king twice. The second thrust was almost instantly fatal. Epernon, a good soldier, tried in vain to protect his sovereign, then rescued the assassin from being lynched by a furious crowd of onlookers.

Ravaillac proved to be another fanatic in the mold of Henry III's slayer two decades before. He came from Angoulême in southwestern France, where he had earned a living of sorts by running errands for the local tribunals and teaching prayer classes for children whose parents were willing to pay a modest tuition. He had also tried unsuccessfully to enter a branch of the Order of Saint Benedict, whose members had rejected him, apparently because of doubts about his loudly announced sense of mission. Among other things, he claimed to have been ordered to destroy a king of France who was no better than an apostate, a traitor to the Church. Ordered by whom? The brothers in Angoulême had put the question to him, and it was repeated with greater insistence and suspicion by members of the Parlement of Paris who conducted his interrogation following arrest. Had it been the Jesuits? Partisans of Condé or of Spain? Irreconcilable Catholics of the defeated *Ligue?* The prisoner doggedly replied that it had been God.

Roland Mousnier points out, in one of the best published studies of an

Ravaillac's murder of Henry IV

assassination, that we might know more about the perpetrator if his inquisitors had been less determined to establish the existence of a conspiracy.[30] Not for the first or last time in history, both public and official opinion began by resisting the awful simplicity of a deranged killer's impulse, searching instead for an explanation more nearly befitting the magnitude of the consequences. Ravaillac insisted, even under torture, that he had acted at the instigation of no other mortal or mortals. A fortnight after his crime, the disgusted judges ordered that he be executed according to the prescriptions for parricide, embellished to take account of regicide as well. His hand was burned off and his body was broken on the wheel, then torn apart by teams of horses with assistance from spectators. But he never changed his story.

Wallenstein

It is possible to describe the slaying of Albrecht Wenzel Eusebius von Wallenstein in 1634 as the last major assassination of the Wars of Religion. In doing so, however, we must not oversimplify political history. The reaction of Protestants and Catholics alike to the Gunpowder Plot in England almost thirty years before had served notice of a revulsion against homicide justified by faith, and Ravaillac's stroke in 1610 had been still more roundly condemned. The killing of Concino Concini, marquis and marshal d'Ancre, at the entrance to the Louvre in 1617, though a political act of importance, had been bereft of religious motives; Orest Ranum is right to see in it simply an instance of ruthless but rational statecraft on behalf of an insecure monarch.[31] So why not explain Wallenstein's death in the same way, as the result of just one more act in defense of sovereignty, in this case the sovereignty of a Holy Roman emperor, Ferdinand II?

No doubt the deed was that in part; but it represented something more. Like the fall of Coligny, the Guises, and Henry IV in France, it was an episode not fully understandable without reference to the long struggle between Christian denominations. In the Germanies when Wallenstein perished, that struggle was not yet over, though its violent phase soon would be. After the Peace of Prague in 1635 the religious components of the Thirty Years' War were almost totally eclipsed by the dynastic and incipiently national duel between the two great Catholic powers, France and Spain. That, however, had not yet occurred when Wallenstein succumbed, victim of court cabals, personal jealousy, and his own ambition, to be sure, but also of sectarian hatreds not yet departed from the political stage in his lifetime.[32]

He came of an old but not particularly wealthy or influential family of the Bohemian gentry. It was a social order which, like its French counterpart, had supplied many recruits to the Protestant cause, including several generations of Wallensteins. Albrecht, however, seems to have concluded that allegiance to the Reformed faith was a poor basis for success in life and accordingly returned to Catholicism at an early age. He married twice, both times wealthy women, and, having shrewdly bought up confiscated properties of the emperor's outlawed enemies after the battle of White Mountain in 1620, proceeded to go into the business of building his own army. The most successful military contractor of his age, he created a force second to none in the Empire, including that of Ferdinand II's devout but jealous cousin Elector Maximilian of Bavaria. Wallenstein did not distinguish himself as a tactical commander, but he was a gifted administrator, especially in the field of logistics, and a generous employer who rewarded his troops with the spoils of many campaigns on the emperor's behalf. For himself he secured the titles and emoluments first of count (using his family name) and then duke of Friedland, a Bohemian town and district he acquired through a combination of real estate transactions and extortion. He received as well, once his regiments had overrun them, the lands of the distant Lutheran duchy of Mecklenburg on the Baltic coast.

This was the condottiere—the Capo or "Old Friedlander," as his men called him—who in 1629, at the summit of his power and prestige, entered upon the troubled final years of his life. Several factors, easy to identify but less so to weigh against one another, combined to undermine his position and ultimately to bring about his downfall. One was his curious decision to absent himself from the seats of imperial power. After 1627 Wallenstein never again visited either the Hapsburg court in Vienna or the Diet of the Holy Roman Empire in Regensburg. The latter body was often ineffectual, but in those years it provided the setting for negotiations among the seven powerful electoral princes as well as other influential "estates of the Reich." It may be that the duke of Friedland, failing despite his titles and wealth to qualify as a great hereditary noble, preferred to the snobbery of Vienna and the elaborate protocol of Regensburg the deference he could count on at his own military headquarters. Whatever its cause, this avoidance of personal contact with the emperor and the electors made life that much easier for his enemies, of whom there were a growing number.

Concerning his aims, contemporaries had little to go on, and historians have little more, for Wallenstein spoke guardedly in his own lifetime and left few records of any kind in writing. This inscrutability opened wide the door to flights of hostile imagination, including the evocation of another Caesar, waiting with his legions for the chance to overthrow the constitution. Just how he visualized the future in general, and his own in particular, has become no clearer with the passage of time, though his actions and a scattering of authentic documents offer some basis for appraising his calculations, if not his long-range intentions.

Wallenstein seems to have respected but never trusted Spain. What the government in Madrid and the Bohemian generalissimo had in common was a marked distaste for the "Catholic imperialism" that until 1635 dominated all discussion of German policy in Austrian and Bavarian circles.[33] It was clear to the Spanish court that a total war against Protestantism could be waged in Germany only at the sacrifice of effective help from the Empire against Spain's own rivals, the French and the Dutch. Wallenstein opposed Catholic extremists without embracing Spanish aims, preferring a policy of integration and self-sufficiency for the Holy Roman Empire as then constituted. This approach implied no fervent German nationalism, but it did reveal a pragmatic approach to religious divisions recalling the views of the French *Politiques* on the proper ends of government.

It was also a position that left its enigmatic architect exposed to charges of disloyalty, especially with regard to the emperor's Edict of Restitution in 1629, the highwater mark of the Counter-Reformation in Germany. Still worse, it roused suspicions that his cautious ecumenicism was proof of a willingness to negotiate in secret with Protestant leaders. It was all very well to consider peace with Saxony or inclusion of the Hanseatic port cities on the North Sea and Baltic coasts in an imperial power combining land and sea forces, but how could such ends be pursued without repudiating the fondest dreams of the Catholic party?

The discrediting of Wallenstein as an imperial war lord did in fact begin

with his alleged betrayal of the Edict of Restitution's spirit, if not its implementation. Under the Edict's terms the emperor restored to the Church's
control two archbishoprics (Bremen and Magdeburg), a dozen bishoprics,
and ten times that number of monasteries, convents, and other foundations,
all in Protestant hands prior to the imperial victories of the 1620s. Wallenstein's troops were called upon to carry out the transfers, despite their
leader's widely reported distaste for the policy involved. Among the accusa-
tions leveled against him by a hostile majority of the Diet and, more important, the bench of electors during the summer of 1630, when for the first time
his removal was openly discussed at Regensburg, the most bizarre was that
he had shown excessive cruelty in carrying out the Edict of Restitution!

Stranger still was the timing of Emperor Ferdinand's decision in September to accept the Diet's demand that Wallenstein be expelled as supreme
commander, for it followed by only two months the landing on Germany's
north coast of the most dangerous Protestant army the Empire would ever
face, the Swedes under Gustav Adolf. Within a few months, in January
1631, an alliance had been concluded between the Swedish warrior-king
and the still technically neutral France of Louis XIII and Richelieu. Before
the end of that year, one of frightening reverses for imperial forces from
Saxony and Bohemia to Mainz and the Rhenish Palatinate, Wallenstein had
been hurriedly reinstated as the Empire's general.

Swedish victories had compelled the emperor to recall his old defender.
Conversely, the death of Gustav Adolf on the battlefield of Lützen in November 1632 started the train of circumstances which led to Wallenstein's
second, and final, fall from grace. A Vienna terrified had been unable to get
along without the generalissimo. A Vienna believing itself saved revealed at
once that to get along without him was its dearest wish. Nevertheless, it was
Wallenstein's own inability to convert the gift of the Swedish monarch's demise into the coin of victory that finally emboldened his enemies even as it
disillusioned his friends. In November 1633, almost on the anniversary of
Lützen, another Protestant conqueror, Bernhard of Saxe-Weimar, briefly
the heir to Gustav Adolf's role and to French patronage, captured Regensburg, scattering in undignified flight the members of the Imperial Diet itself.
The loss of that city appears to have convinced Wallenstein and the emperor
alike that peace negotiations must be opened with Saxony and Brandenburg, if not at once with alien Sweden. This momentary consensus was misleading, for to many of Ferdinand's advisers it had begun to appear that the
Capo was neither necessary nor reliable, and that if he had not yet turned
traitor he would do so very soon.

In Vienna by late December the emperor had decided that some new action must be taken with respect to his commander. Ferdinand was not adverse to talking peace with Saxon and other North German spokesmen, but
he had come to share the fear that clandestine contacts were also being in-

augurated from the military headquarters in Pilsen with other interested parties—the Swedes, the French, Czech nationalists, who could be sure?—and his misgivings were crystallized during the first fortnight of January by two documents. The first was a scurrilous bill of particulars signed by one of Wallenstein's own field marshals, the Italian Piccolomini, who accused his chief of plotting treason for the purpose of securing the Bohemian crown. The other, probably taken more seriously by His Imperial Majesty, had been written by Prince von Lichtenstein, former president of the privy council and a tribune of sorts for aristocratic Catholic opinion at court. His contribution was the suggestion that Wallenstein be tried by some legally qualified body.

Ferdinand postponed formal arraignment by sending the case to a commission of three imperial councilors, members of the Reichshofrat but not, it would appear, selected for their known hostility to the generalissimo: one was his relative by marriage; the second a bishop who had supported him in the past; and the third a less friendly but nonetheless responsible jurist. All the more weight, therefore, attached to their unanimous recommendation on January 24, 1634, that Wallenstein be stripped of military authority and replaced not by the eager Piccolomini but by Marshal Matthias Gallas; that all imperial soldiers be absolved of any obligation to their former chief; and that said chief, with his alleged accomplices counts Ilow and Trčka, "be taken into custody and brought to a secure place so that he may defend and purge himself from all that has been spoken against him."[34] To this was added a grammatically nonparallel phrase, "or to seize him dead or alive." This last provision, which close analysis suggests was appended by the emperor himself, did not appear in the commission's recommendations as shown to certain privileged readers but was included in the proclamation of proscription issued on February 18. Two days later dispatches went off to the pope, the king of Spain, and the elector of Bavaria, informing them that Wallenstein had been dismissed and his lands declared forfeit.

Meanwhile, at Pilsen the generalissimo was keeping busy that winter despite a serious and apparently progressive illness. He continued to extend peace feelers in several directions—just how many will probably never be known. He considered an eleventh-hour proposal from the Spanish that in return for their full support in Vienna he join in the creation of a long military frontier roughly following the Rhine Valley and, true to his old misgivings on that score, rejected it. Finally, and somewhat mysteriously, he sent the emperor another of his periodic offers to resign, an action sandwiched between two demands that all officers give him in writing their personal oaths of loyalty. Then on February 21, presumably aware of the imperial warrant issued against him in Vienna three days before, he left Pilsen for Franconia, where a Swedish army under his old adversary Bernhard of Saxe-Weimar was encamped.

Wallenstein's death

Moving across Bohemia in the dead of winter, the commander and his party with their light escort, a depleted regiment most of whose officers were Catholic émigrés from Britain, paused for a night in the little garrison town of Eger, where a Scottish colonel named Gordon was in command. Exactly how the order to seize Wallenstein dead or alive reached Eger is not known. Gallas or Piccolomini may have relayed it to Gordon through Colonel Butler, who was in charge of the military escort, so that unbeknown to the generalissimo it had been accompanying him all the way from Pilsen. In any event, on the night of February 25 Trčka, Ilow, and the prominent Czech Protestant Count Kinsky were stabbed to death when assassins burst in upon a dinner party at the senior officers' temporary billet. Wallenstein, too sick to attend, was resting in a room above the banquet hall. He was slain there by a Captain Walter Devereux, who had rushed upstairs with Butler.

Vienna, along with other European capitals, learned the news as quickly as express riders could carry it. Although Wallenstein's estates yielded nothing like the riches expected from their confiscation, there were rewards for Gallas, Piccolomini, Gordon, Butler, Devereux, and numerous accomplices.

Ferdinand II declined to accept responsibility for any desire to have his once indispensable commander killed, but the court's relief and gratification were manifest.

There followed a desultory effort to prove the existence of a major conspiracy, led by Wallenstein and directed against the Empire. Despite several arrests and at least one summary execution, this line of prosecution attracted little interest. Charges of secret Protestant cabals attracted even less. The dangerous Capo was gone, that was the important thing; and anyway, the imperial government was itself moving toward the religious compromise which in 1635 would bring Ferdinand's abandonment of his vaunted Edict of Restitution. Initiative thus passed from the original antagonists in the Thirty Years' War to the non-German courts of France and Spain. It seems fitting, therefore, to grant Cardinal Richelieu, the leader of one of those powers, the last word on the most sensational episode of what might be called the "German phase": "Wallenstein's death remains a monstrous precedent . . . for in a life frought with perilous incidents the Emperor found no second servitor whose resourceful performance, even from afar, attained to the services rendered him by Wallenstein."[35] Given the Cardinal's own situation, he could scarcely be blamed for disliking this demonstration of princely ingratitude to a loyal "servitor."

Trial and Punishment

As Ferdinand II's use of a review board in the case of Wallenstein suggests, assassination without due process by no means constituted the only mode of political killing known to early modern Europe. Courts and commissions also had significant parts to play. Little would be gained from debating the technical legality of every capital sentence—that passed upon the duke of Norfolk under Queen Elizabeth, for example, arbitrary and indeed unjustified as that action appears to have been. Taken as a whole, however, the British experience gives rise to an especially challenging set of questions about "judicial murder," forcing us to ask whether certain capital trials expressed a genuine respect for the law or only the ruthless misapplication of its formalities.

Legal correctness is not always the decisive criterion. What appears to be an impulsive act may on occasion result from protracted, even anguished consideration, as in the long-postponed decision to execute Mary Queen of Scots. The earl of Essex was beheaded in 1601 after having been condemned by a special commission whose procedure was irregular but not patently unjust in view of the defendant's well-attested and repeated acts of treason. Conversely, eagerness for political advantage at times counted for more than the rules of judicature, even when the latter were formally observed. Sir

Walter Raleigh was beheaded in 1618, fifteen years after a jury had found him guilty of treason and conspiracy, during which time he had been at liberty to continue his voyages to the Spanish Main and the West Indies. There can be no doubt that, whatever may have been the specifics of his death warrant, he was in the end a victim of his king's desire to propitiate a new-found ally, Philip III of Spain. In that country Raleigh, once Drake was gone, loomed as the most feared and hated of all Englishmen. His execution by James I's order was nothing more nor less than a diplomatic gesture.

On the Continent the existence of a body of administrative law, inherited from Rome and reserved to the purposes of the state, freed governments from the common-law restraints that in England may not always have altered behavior but did seem to engender a great deal of nervous rationalization. Philip II felt no need to explain, much less apologize for, the decapitation of Egmont and Hoorne in Brussels, prominent nobles though they were. He may have looked upon the murder of William the Silent as only a belated execution of that same judgment in Belgium, confirmed by his own proclamation of the Dutch stadholder's outlawry.

In France, Henry IV chose to have another dissident nobleman, the duke of Biron, more reminiscent of England's Essex than of the Netherlandish aristocrats, sentenced by the Parlement of Paris and beheaded at the Bastille in 1602.[36] Fifteen years later Louis XIII and Luynes might have preferred to handle Concini the same way but concluded that only his assassination could be relied upon to end his influence over the queen mother and hers over French public policy. With Concini dead, the crown completed the process more sedately, by bringing his widow to trial, still in 1617. A special court found Leonora Galigai guilty of lese majesty but not of sorcery, crypto-Judaism, and other crimes initially imputed to her—so instead of being burned alive she was beheaded in the Place de Grève before her body was consigned to the flames.[37]

Richelieu's use of capital sentences was an unsentimental as it was frequent. His most dangerous opponent at court, Louis XIII's younger brother Gaston of Orleans, stood too close to the throne to be punished under the law; and there is no evidence to suggest that Richelieu ever sought to have him assassinated, tempting though the idea may have been. What the great minister could and did do was use the law as his weapon against a series of aristocratic opponents, beginning with the marquis of Chalais, executed in 1616 for an abortive plot to kill the Cardinal, and continuing until Cinq-Mars and De Thou went to the block on similar charges in 1642. The complexities that such cases entailed arose from the fact that the defendants were almost invariably personal favorites of the king.

Their implacable pursuer's motives were not always confined to mere self-preservation. Another and much larger issue was the feudality's pretended right to wage private warfare, a claim inherited from the Middle

Ages but discredited in France by the recurrent anarchy of the sixteenth century. The Cardinal's aim, as set forth in his contrived but in substance genuine political testament, was to show that the crown would no longer countenance rebellion.[38] A lordly territorial magnate, a swaggering young duelist in the capital, a courtier hatching conspiracies against government officials in the midst of salon chatter were in Richelieu's opinion equally dangerous to the state. So he bullied his master not only into signing death warrants but also on occasion into witnessing executions, as in the famous case of Henry II duke of Montmorency, governor of Languedoc and cousin of the king, beheaded at Toulouse in 1632 while his royal kinsman looked on aghast.

Of all the state trials in seventeenth-century Europe prior to the English Civil War, however, the most celebrated took place neither in France nor in the British Isles but in the Dutch Netherlands. For it was there that Johan van Oldenbarneveldt was sentenced and executed in 1619. The United Provinces, temporarily relieved of military pressure by the twelve-year truce with Spain, was approaching the end of that armistice to the accompaniment of bitter debates over foreign policy, Calvinist theology, and internal government. The seventy-one-year-old "Advocate of the Estates of Holland," as his principal title read, had long since taken a stand on each of these issues. He was an Arminian, that is, a latitudinarian in matters of religion; he was a partisan of peace, even at the cost of concessions to the Spanish; above all, he combined an intense loyalty to his province with ill-concealed skepticism concerning the role of the house of Orange. This combination of attitudes cost him his life.[39]

His trial on charges of treason was conducted before a court packed with his personal rivals and buffeted by the winds of theological conflict. Oldenbarneveldt, a genuine *Politique,* insisted on the state's obligation to maintain domestic peace, a position supported by his brilliant young contemporary, the international lawyer and theorist of sovereignty Hugo Grotius. Partly for that reason he decried what seemed to him the narrow sectarianism of the Dutch Gomarist party and its stern predestinarian doctrine, preferring the more forgiving views of the so-called Remonstrants, as both Bodin and Montaigne would have done had they still been among the living. To many preachers of the orthodox Dutch Reformed persuasion, however, the cool rationalism inherent in this Calvinist "heresy" seemed an affront to God Himself.

Still, religious differences might not have been equatable with treason had not Oldenbarneveldt's foreign policy also been portrayed by his critics as a sellout to the hated Catholic power of Madrid. The truce of 1609, arrived at in large part through the efforts of the accused minister, had become increasingly unpopular in the Netherlands as the years of uneasy peace wore on. His argument that the Dutch could expect no dependable support from either France or England remained as valid as ever, but in the light of new opportunities for the Protestant cause arising from the outbreak of the Thirty Years' War in Germany, what had seemed shrewd calculations a decade before could be made to appear outdated. And always there was the aristocratic stadholder, son of William the Silent, eager to fight Spain again. From that quarter, as things turned out, came the final impulse that doomed Oldenbarneveldt.

A genuine constitutional conflict was involved: not just between the house of Orange and an indigenous parliamentary tradition, but no less signally between provincial and federal rights in the United Provinces.[40] The defendant on trial had devoted his entire life to serving Amsterdam and the Estates of Holland, traveling the few miles to The Hague only when compelled to do so. He never tired of pointing out that his province and his city paid more than half of the national assessments. In return, Maurice of Nassau, whose power as stadholder lay primarily outside the great commercial ports, was able to play on the inevitable resentment aroused by Amsterdam's regents —their wealth, their hauteur, and their relatively sophisticated views concerning religion. In the end, Oldenbarneveldt was isolated by a political process that shifted control within town after town until at last Amsterdam itself passed under the domination of his opponents.

Perhaps by this reading Maurice of Nassau and the forces he represented did serve a national purpose by their attack on Oldenbarneveldt and the Remonstrants. Even if that were so, it would be more difficult to prove that their campaign required a human sacrifice to seal its victory. When the advocate of the Estates of Holland—the "second father of Dutch Independence," as his admirers called him, and by any definition the country's first native political leader—removed his jacket in the Binnenhof at The Hague and knelt to face the pale sunlight as his executioners requested, customarily unemotional observers felt, by their own report, a sense of tragedy.[41]

If Coligny's, William the Silent's, Henry IV's, and Wallenstein's were the classic assassinations of the early modern epoch, and Oldenbarneveldt's death its clearest instance of what can only be termed judicial murder, the execution of England's Charles I supplied a telling example of institutionalized regicide. It also marked the climax of more than a hundred years of rampant bloodshed, inspired by varying combinations of religious and political motives.

C. V. Wedgwood, in one of her volumes on the Puritan Revolution and the Civil War, writes that by 1648, six years after fighting broke out between royalist and parliamentary forces, "the king had to die. As Oliver Cromwell said, in a confused and cryptic speech defending the act before the House of Commons, 'providence and necessity had set them upon it.' "[42] The author is quick to remind her readers, however, that Charles's opponents had not begun their struggle with that end in view. On the contrary, in 1642 they had claimed only to seek "his honour and safety," by resisting the acts of his ministers. True, by that time a parliamentary bill of attainder had already sent the earl of Strafford to the headsman's block, and in 1645 his old colleague Archbishop Laud followed him there. Both had in theory been condemned for subversion and high treason, but in fact for their identification with unpopular royal policies. For the crown's sake the king had felt compelled to let them die. Now it was his turn to perish, in the nation's interest as his judges defined it.

The road from Nottingham, where the ruler's war flags were unfurled in August 1642, to the scaffold at Whitehall in January 1649 had been a long and twisting one. Its course, insofar as it was not determined by confusion and chance, had been set by Oliver Cromwell, one of history's undeniable and for that reason rare military geniuses, precise as an organizer of men, swift and inventive as a tactician, yet when away from the battlefield seemingly unable to explain his purposes without substituting the Lord's will for any humbler authority. Argument with this East County gentleman, of whose famed cavalry a Scottish enemy said, "Europe has no better soldiers," would have been difficult under the best of circumstances.[43] His self-assigned role as Jehovah's personal representative on earth made it all but impossible. Backed by his troops and uncompromising in his dealings with royalists, Anglicans, and Presbyterians alike, the victor of Marston Moor, Naseby, and Preston Pans dominated the scene as if divinely ordained to do so.

There were many other personalities involved and an almost equal number of intersecting motives. The Scots, Charles's own people, defied him and the Anglican Church alike as early as the First Bishops' War of 1639, joined Fairfax and the parliamentary army against the king and his Irish allies in 1644, accepted his personal surrender in 1645, turned him over to Parliament in 1647 in return for some 400,000 pounds back pack owed their troops, but then rose in his name against the English a year later. By that time Scottish Presbyterians and English Independents (Congregationalists) were treating one another as ferociously as were royalists and Cromwell's Roundheads. Add to those conflicts the animosity between Anglicans and Dissenters within English Protestantism, the impact of radical political-economic movements such as the Levellers and the Diggers, the mounting hostility between army leaders and the civilian majority in the House of Commons, and it is easy to see why the Civil War remains a source of seemingly endless debate over matters of interpretation.

Still, it is possible without oversimplifying this tangle of issues to identify four that by the end of 1648 had emerged as pivotal. They were: the predominance enjoyed by the army's spokesmen in parliament; the determination of the military to put Charles I to death; the recurrence of royalist uprisings in various parts of the land; and, not least important, the personality of the king. There he sat in Carisbrooke Castle on the Isle of Wight, a brooding and at fifty a prematurely aged man, described in courtly language as a royal guest of the governor but in reality a prisoner. Even as such, like his grandmother Mary Queen of Scots at Fotheringhay, he continued to receive and respond to letters concerned with action against the Roundheads. He saw in this neither treason or tyranny, but simply the defense of royal rights, a sacred trust to be upheld for as long as he lived.

So he made the final and fatal pact with the Scots, as well as with other foes of Cromwell. After the latter's victory at Preston Pans the king was brought to London and tried by a specially constituted High Court of Justice between January 20 and 23, 1649. Scorning that tribunal's competence—what "peers" had he to try him?—Charles declined to speak in his own defense until the death sentence was handed down, after which the lord president, John Bradshaw, refused to permit him to do so on the grounds that he now stood condemned. On January 30 he met his fate as "a Tyrant, a Traitor, and Murderer, and a public enemy of the Commonwealth of England," a ruler who had made war upon his own people. His demeanor was impressive, judging from eyewitness accounts, from the time he walked calmly upstairs in the Banqueting House and over a low windowsill onto the scafford until the headsman, with his deferential "an' it please Your Majesty," struck with the axe.

The execution of a reigning monarch, carried out in public after a full if unavoidably irregular trial, was an all but unique event. Not even imperial Rome, despite slayings of emperors by hired assassins and praetorian guards, had witnessed its like. And rarely has it been repeated since. Unless one considers Maximilian of Mexico in 1867 an emperor real enough to be counted, it is possible to cite only one close parallel: the fate of Louis XVI in 1793. Earlier in our own century, the Bolsheviks, although their leaders secretly condemned Tsar Nicholas II to death, decided against trying and executing him in his former capital.

This caution on the part of later tyrannicides, preferring stealth to publicity, reflects their awareness of the sequel to Charles I's decapitation. Within little more than a decade the dynasty was back on the throne, in the person of his son. Of the sixty-nine "Regicides," members of Parliament who had signed the king's death warrant in 1649, forty-one were still alive in 1660. Fifteen escaped from England (three of them to the American colonies), but one such fugitive was killed by a royalist sympathizer in Switzerland and three others were betrayed in Holland by a former comrade and dragged home to be hanged, drawn, and quartered. In all, nine Regicides suffered the death penalty, along with four officers who had taken part in the king's execution. The rest received sentences of varying degrees of severity. Three major figures—Cromwell, his son-in-law Ireton, and Bradshaw, late president of the High Court of Justice—were already dead from natural causes by the time of Charles II's restoration. But not even they escaped retribution. Their bodies were exhumed from Westminster Abbey, exposed on gibbets at Tyburn, and thrown into the ditch reserved for condemned felons.[44]

A less grisly, but in the larger historical sense more important aspect of England's beheading of its king is the place that memories of the scene at Whitehall came to occupy in the seventeenth-century revulsion against tyrannicide throughout Europe. That is not to say that the events of 1649 in London caused that revulsion. Quite the contrary. Considering the shock waves created by Henry IV's assassination in Paris and by Oldenbarneveldt's execution at The Hague, there is reason to see in Charles I's death much that was already anachronistic. Whatever the extent of its displacement in time, however, it continues to provide a dramatic punctuation mark, separating an age of rampant homicide for religious and political ends from the singular moratorium that followed.

9

The Early Modern
Interlude

The Dog That Did Not Bark in the Night

History's muse is full of surprises and scornful of confident predictions. An illustration is the abrupt decline in political assassination which extends from about the middle of the seventeenth century until the final decade of the eighteenth. This was not a total interruption. Even qualified, however, it calls to mind the plot line of Conan Doyle's famous story, "Silver Blaze," in which Sherlock Holmes identifies the murderer by observing that a dog— the culprit's own, of course—failed to bark at his stealthy approach in the night. The early modern lull poses a similar problem, that of trying to account for the *nonoccurrence* of something past experience had led one to expect.[1] Instead of explaining "why," the observer must ask "why not?"

There had been other instances of this sort, notably in Periclean Athens, the Roman Republic until almost the end of its long life, and Europe's High Middle Ages. These were by no means times or places singularly peaceful in other respects. The same was true of the century and a half preceding the French Revolution. Mob violence did not disappear, nor did private crime; and the decline in ferocity of punishments was at best sporadic. Yet the fact remains that only a few generations ago our ancestors proved themselves able to conduct their political business with little or no resort to individual homicide. How and why did this happen?

Framing an altogether satisfying answer will not be easy, and finding a monocausal one is impossible. It may help if we keep clearly in view the role of political institutions, the attitudes required to sustain them, and the opportunities they provide for peaceful change as well as the restraints they place on violent protest. External conflict and internal tension abounded in ancient Greece, republican Rome, and medieval Europe; the same was true of the period separating the end of the English Civil War from the onset of the French Terror in the 1790s. In all four epochs, however, governmental machinery seems to have been relatively effective in providing the domestic security that populations normally demand. Modern platitudes regarding the uniformly abhorrent repression practiced by past governments tend to obscure the fact that individual regimes have varied in their ability and their willingness to recognize major grievances. Just as obviously, the amount of public support on which authorities could rely when confronted by defiance of the law has differed from one setting to another. Finally, each of the four eras being compared followed times of frightening disorder, memories of whose anarchy contributed to a climate more than a little friendly to the forces of order—until the next swing of history's pendulum.

Signs of Revulsion

During the bloodiest decades of the sixteenth and early seventeenth centuries some commentators had not hesitated to condemn the lethal violence of their contemporaries. Thoughtful reactions of this kind could not at once alter the direction of events, but they raised some serious questions. One can discern a body of opinion hostile to political murder taking shape even before the case *in favor* of such killing had been fully developed and published by spokesmen for religious orthodoxy. Castellio, Bodin, and Montaigne were, after all, contemporaries of Beza and Buchanan, not to mention later monarchomachs such as Suarez and Mariana.[2]

Still more characteristic of that time than the views of the French skeptics and pragmatists were those of their compatriot Innocent Gentillet.[3] What makes this sixteenth-century Huguenot refugee in Geneva important is the way in which he attacked not so much concrete examples of political homicide as earlier theories he viewed as having defended, or in some instances merely rationalized, its use. Today his fame rests almost entirely on his *Anti-Machiavel* of 1576, in which he misquoted and misinterpreted the Florentine so thoroughly that later generations of readers were left to conclude that *The Prince* had been nothing but a manual for assassins. Less familiar is Gentillet's equally sharp denunciation of another controversial figure from the past, Jean Petit, apologist in 1409 for the duke of Burgundy's crime against the duke of Orleans.[4] Gentillet did not rule out assassination in the service of religion. Given his loyalties and his situation, he would scarcely have felt inclined to do so. Nevertheless, Gentillet's repudiation of Petit and the latter's famous *Justification,* combined with his expressions of horror at Machiavelli's works, place him among the initiators of the reaction against political murder, for secular ends at any rate.

Theory alone was for a long time selective, because partisan and subject to qualifications deemed appropriate to an age of militant faith. Much broader was the response to actual horrors enacted or prepared in the name of religion: Saint Bartholomew's Day in Paris; William the Silent's murder in Delft; the Gunpowder Plot at Westminster. Finally, in 1610, came the stunning climax: Henry IV's death among the carts and carriages in the Rue de la Ferronnerie. Single events often invite exaggeration of their effects, but this was one whose repercussions, not only immediate but lasting, would be hard to overstate. Its timing, the murderer's motivation, the victim's popularity and ecumenical rule, affected opinion and subsequent behavior to a degree unmatched by any other assassination in history. Even those of Abraham Lincoln and Mahatma Gandhi, while profoundly shocking to contemporaries, were followed not by reversal but by more of the same.

Had it done nothing else—and actually it did much more—the slaying of Henry of Navarre would be notable for having crystallized a nagging debate within the councils of the Society of Jesus. Many sixteenth-century Jesuits, disciplined and loyal to Rome but at the same time observant and shrewd, probably had doubts about the bombastic utterances of the Counter-Reformation popes, even before the appearance of the famous treatises of Suarez and Mariana. But it was not until the summer of 1610 that the General himself, Father Claudio Aquaviva, obviously aware of the Society's tenuous hold on legal recognition in France, denounced the theories of the Spanish monarchomachs and all who agreed with them. His Decree on Tyrannicide, issued at Rome on July 6 (less than two months after Henry IV's death), reads in part:

> Superiors of the Society and theologians . . . need not only to understand the contents of books by other authors but also above all to ponder them carefully, lest opinions, even though they be safe, approved, and well-founded, give rise in any way to scandal or other difficulties. Consequently . . . by the present decree we command in virtue of holy obedience and under pain of excommunication . . . and other penalties reserved to our judgment, that no religious of our Society is to presume to affirm, either publicly or privately, in teaching or in giving advice, much less in written works, that it is lawful for any person, under whatever pretext, to kill kings or princes or to plot their death . . . Indeed, we intend that Provincial Superiors who learn of any activity of this kind on the part of Ours and do not correct them or who do not forestall difficulties of this kind by seeing to it that this decree is piously observed, [should] not only incur the aforementioned penalties but be deprived of office; thus all will understand what the feeling of the Society is in this matter, and the error of one private person will not render the whole Society suspect.[5]

Further evidence of the Jesuits' anxiety over the danger of being linked to assaults on rulers appears elsewhere in their archives. One of the two

French delegates to the Society's international Congregation of Procurators held at Rome in 1625 was Father Pierre Coton, Provincial of "Gallia," that is, Paris and the surrounding area. He carried with him proposals from the French Congregation to the General, now Father Vitelleschi, seeking to give still fuller effect to the fifteen-year-old repudiation of tyrannicide. Coton's *proposita* began by lamenting the calumnies being circulated by enemies of the Society and begged the Father General to renew Aquaviva's famous decree "in the most effective and clear terms, so that at a single reading the innocence of the Society in this respect is clearly evident."[6] The petition went on to urge that, in addition, "our same Reverend Father write to the Most Christian King [Louis XIII]," thanking him for past favors, formally advising him that the pronouncement of 1610 had been renewed, and asking that "he issue a document or edict indicating to all his subjects that he and his council are agreed that the teaching of the Society . . . not only is not harmful to kings and kingdoms but . . . eminently favors them."

The response from the Father General displays a certain acerbity, beginning as it does on a note of surprise that confirmation of so well-known a position should be thought necessary, since "those of us who are impartial judges of the situation are satisfied with matters as they are."[7] Nevertheless, "the decree will be renewed in accordance with the thinking of the Procurators of France, so that nothing possibly can be thought lacking in the future." Having made that concession, Vitelleschi would go no further, advising the petitioners that it did not "seem at all opportune at this time to ask the said Most Christian King that he state his position about the doctrine of the Society in a public edict or royal rescript." A good deal of political shrewdness finds voice in the first reason given for not making too much of the matter in correspondence with Louis XIII—lest "an annoying memory be revived." There is also, however, in an ensuing clause some evidence of the coolness that existed between Rome and Paris in the time of Richelieu: "nor does it seem probable that [the king] or the royal ministers would give study and effort to it."

Whatever tactical, not to mention temperamental differences still existed between Catholic leaders in the first quarter of the seventeenth century, the preceding epoch of Philip II, Gregory XIII, Sixtus V, and the Jesuit monarchomachs appeared to have receded into a past at once remote and potentially embarrassing. The denunciation of assassins and their admirers rapidly became a chorus in which the pious as well as the skeptical appeared eager to join. In France the magistral *History of the Great Schism* by Louis Maimbourg, S.J., dealt another blow to an already badly damaged fifteenth-century reputation by referring to Jean Petit as having "sold his tongue and his pen to . . . Burgundy, against honor and conscience . . . to vindicate this execrable parricide."[8] Maimbourg's work was published in 1678. Some twenty years later Pierre Bayle, the book's severest critic in most other regards, found no quarrel with this judgment, agreeing in his *Diction-ary* of 1697 that Petit had "abused his talents to sustain some bad causes," and adding that "the honor of the [slain] duke of Orleans was ripped asun-der with more fury than his body had been by the assassins."[9] Not even Louis XIV's Huguenot opponents were eager to applaud political murder.

Concurrence on that point was natural enough throughout much of con-tinental Europe in this, the triumphant age of divine-right monarchy. Across the Channel, however, observers might have expected more difference of opinion among the "terrible English." If so, the absence of any significant deviation from an emerging European norm must have come as a surprise. For not even the memory of George Buchanan, learned, plausible, unques-tionably the most influential of Protestant monarchomachs in his own life-time, could not escape the overwhelming countermovement in the century that followed.

Predictably, supporters of the Stuarts continued to deplore Buchanan's *De Jure Regni apud Scotos,* as they had started to do when the Scottish Par-liament condemned the book in 1584. Royalist Oxford was only following suit when a century later it ordered the work burned by the common hang-man in answer to the rising tide of resistance to Charles II and the future James II. Infinitely more revealing as evidence of a changing climate of opinion was the fact that not even the Puritan regicides of 1648–49 had turned to Buchanan's views on the slaying of impious tyrants for support in disposing of Charles I. Neither the Cromwellian Parliament nor the tribunal it created for the purpose of passing judgment on the king explained his condemnation by accusing him of ungodly rule. Whatever may have been their private sentiments on the score of religion, the enemies of Charles I found him guilty of a specific act of secular treason: waging war against his own people. Similarly, while Buchanan's strictures on the political contract between sovereign and society must have commended itself to John Locke and other apologists for the Glorious Revolution of 1688, its consummation owed nothing to monarchomachs, either Catholic or Calvinist.

Some Likely Victims Spared

Among the most convincing indications of assassination's faltering appeal was, appropriately enough, a cluster of "non-events." Several leaders whose vulnerability seemingly matched their importance—Spain's Olivares, France's Richelieu, Sweden's Gustav Adolf, England's Cromwell—escaped becoming objects of lethal action during the second quarter of the seven-teenth century, the contemporary murders of Buckingham and Wallenstein notwithstanding. Considering the general level of violence in much of Eu-rope during this, the Baroque's "season of evil" par excellence, as well as precedents readily available from the recent past, the fact that such prominent figures of the Thirty Years' War and the Puritan Revolution were not slain by stealth offers a prelude of sorts to the long remission in political homicide that followed.

The example of Gaspar de Guzmán de Olivares, favorite minister (*privado*) of two Spanish kings for twenty-two years before he was dismissed in 1643, may at first appear typical of his nation's history.[10] Since the outset of the Reconquista, the late medieval counterattack upon Moorish power in Iberia, the discipline surrounding Spain's monarchy had been proverbial; it may indeed deserve the credit for having shielded Olivares as effectively as it did his royal masters, Philip III and Philip IV. However, the risks he ran cannot be lightly dismissed. The sacred mantle of Castilian-Hapsburg kingship did not cover his shoulders. He had always to fear—apart from the unforeseeable fanatic—the congeries of jealous rivals whose intrigues did at last drive him from power a couple of years before he died. His long ministry saw Spain involved in foreign ventures involving Italy, the war-torn Germanies and Low Countries, and above all implacable France. His brusque manner offended Castilian and Aragonese courtiers; his efforts at centralization enraged particularists from Andalusia to Catalonia; and before his ministry had run its course, Portugal, with French help, successfully rebelled against Spanish rule. These, surely, were potentially murderous sources of opposition. Yet the best-informed among modern students of Olivares' career can find no evidence that the *conde-duque* was ever the object of an assassination plot.[11]

The Privado's greast adversary in Paris presided over the councils of a kingdom even more deeply divided than Spain, though along somewhat different lines. Richelieu, from the moment he became Louis XIII's principal minister in 1624 until he died in 1642, still occupying that position, was never free from the threat of at least three possible types of assailant: a religious zealot, either Protestant or Catholic; an aristocrat striking for one of the cabals at court; or an agent of the king himself, who might at any time decide in exasperation to get rid of his imperious servant as in his youth he had shed Concini.[12]

In the face of these disquieting possibilities, Richelieu came through unscathed by human malice. His closest brush with disgrace or perhaps worse, the so-called "Day of Dupes" in 1630, began with portents of victory for the circle of courtiers, two queens, and the Bourbon heir presumptive to the throne who together had sought his downfall. It ended with those same enemies in the throes of panic, as king and minister emerged arm in arm from the royal apartment. Later projects instigated by Gaston of Orleans, the duchess of Chevreuse, and their various confederates fared no better. Whatever outbursts of resentment, however many flirtations with other would-be favorites Louis XIII may have permitted himself, his dependence on the forbidding presence at his side could not be overcome.

On the religious front there remained Catholic extremists who held in cherished memory the slayer of Henry III and even, albeit more furtively, the assassin of Henry IV. The threat of Protestant vengeance also had to be considered, especially during the bitter siege of La Rochelle in 1627 and 1628. In dealing with potentially recalcitrant members of the Roman Church, however, the king's chief counselor enjoyed the great advantage of being associated in the public's mind with his fellow cardinal, the revered Bérulle, and with other figures of the French "century of saints." As for the Huguenots, their military power undermined by defeat in battle and the defection of growing numbers of noblemen, Richelieu emerged from La Rochelle as a prudent guarantor of what remained of Protestant rights. Especially after French entry into the war against Spain and the Empire in 1635, the "pretended Reformed religion" had little to gain and much to lose from an attack on this Catholic clergyman, or for that matter on his successor as first minister, Cardinal Mazarin.

Returning to the possibility of assassination attempts inspired by nonreligious motives, a postscript is in order concerning the years of the Fronde, that confused flurry of rebellions in France extending from 1648 to 1653. The princes and ladies whispering more busily than ever once Richelieu was gone offered a spectacle difficult to associate with tyrannicide in the classic mode; and despite the vulnerability of an Italian prelate known to be the lover of a Spanish-born queen mother, there is little evidence of any serious plan to slay Mazarin (save perhaps by trying him for treason).[13] Nevertheless, political murder had been too familiar a feature of the French past to be easily ignored by a Bourbon monarch's councilors.

Richelieu and Mazarin, whatever dangers surrounded them, were civilians and, more important, high clergymen of the Church of Rome in a predominantly Catholic nation. Consider by contrast the dangers surrounding Gustav Adolf of Sweden, a soldier-king who spent much of his adult life campaigning in foreign lands amid political and, at least part of the time, religious enemies. Coligny in 1572, William of Orange in 1584, Henry of Navarre in 1610, all had died as Protestant champions in the eyes of both their slayers and their survivors. Now the Swedish ruler, from the day in 1630 when with his army he waded ashore on the Baltic coast of Pomerania and began a storied campaign of conquest, must have seemed to any Catholic opponent the most dangerous Protestant since Luther. Eventually supported by Brandenburg, Saxony, and apostate France, winning victory after victory as his troops pushed westward to the Rhine, eastward to Bohemia, and southward to the Danube, shredding the Hapsburg emperor's forces and the proud Edict of Restitution they were supposed to enforce, this "Goth," as his enemies called him, personified a war gone disastrously wrong from their point of view. Why then did they not assassinate him?

Part of the answer may lie in timing, for Gustav Adolf was killed in the battle of Lützen less than two and a half years after his march through the Germanies began. Nevertheless, there would have been ample time for the murder of a field commander by no means inaccessible to the many would-be recruits and other visitors who frequented his camp. Why was Vienna, where Wallenstein's murder was soon to be countenanced, not still more taken up with plans to kill the Antichrist from Stockholm?

As a matter of fact there were such plans; but nothing happened. Despite the impending resolution of Wallenstein's case, the minds of princes showed signs of changing with respect to tyrannicide more narrowly defined. This is how Emperor Ferdinand II's Jesuit confessor, Father William Lamormaini, a leader of the Catholic-imperialist faction at court, recalled the dark times following the Swedish victory at Breitenfeld in September 1631:

> The evil increased from day to day, and one war grew out of another. But because it was believed that only a few were to blame for all this misfortune, some people recommended that these leaders of the rebels be put out of the way. One man asked only that if in the execution of this project he be captured or lose his life, the monarch would look after his wife and child. The answer was: this would be neither Christian nor imperial in concept [*weder christlich noch kayserlich gedacht*]. His Majesty wished to do the just thing openly and with the sword [i.e., in battle]. The outcome, and all else, he had ever entrusted to God and intended to do so in the future as well.[14]

Whether or not the Emperor's scruples pleased his most energetic retainers, the very same decision was reached less than six months later by his Hapsburg cousin Philip IV of Spain. On March 2, 1632, a letter was sent in the King's name from Madrid to father Quiroga, the Capucin monk who was Spain's confidential envoy in Vienna. From the archives at Simancas here is the central paragraph:

> In your letter of January 3 to the Count-Duke [Olivares] . . . I have noted the plan a certain person told you he had for killing the King of Sweden, for which 30,000 *hungaros* [Hungarian ducats] would be paid when the business was done, and that after having discussed the matter with Her Most Serene Majesty, my sister the Queen of Hungary [the Infanta Maria, wife of the future Emperor Ferdinand III] and with my ministers who are present there, you pledged your word . . . that the sum referred to would be paid. I charge you, if the matter should be brought up again, to avoid acknowledging any such words; because even if what is so unscrupulously proposed could be carried out, which is in any case doubtful, the business would be unworthy of a great and just king, nor would it

be proper to make any promise about it even with the advice and counsel of my ministers. For, it being left to God to punish His enemies, and there remaining to us appropriate and legitimate means to resist and humiliate them according to what prudence and just intention will advise, God will favor [such means], and conscience and reputation will continue to be protected.[15]

No doubt Gustav Adolf's death in battle six months later was greeted by his foes as divine vindication of the restraint shown by Ferdinand II and Philip IV (or by Olivares on the latter's behalf). Even the Emperor's subsequent condemnation of Wallenstein probably appeared in the ruler's eyes to be something quite different: the result of a quasi-judicial decision reached against a subject who could no longer be trusted. In any event if the caution exhibited with regard to Gustav Adolf is compared with the celebrations at Madrid and Vienna when Coligny and William the Silent were slain, it is clear that something quite fundamental had altered Hapsburg views about how to deal with the most heretical among rebels and foreign foes.*

Oliver Cromwell remains to be considered. Whether viewed as one more Protestant standard-bearer or as a villainous perverter of legitimate rule, he could scarcely fail to incense dangerous enemies well schooled in classical theories of tyrannicide. By definitions as old as Aristotle's, Cromwell was the worst kind of tyrant. He was a usurper whose eventual title, Lord Protector, was itself a startling novelty, and the misgivings felt by Hapsburg rulers concerning a Gustav Adolf did not extend to this English commoner. He was not even a loyal first minister, an Olivares or a Richelieu or a Mazarin, touched by the reflected majesty of an anointed ruler. On the contrary, he had sent his own king to the headsman's block.

As one might expect, a number of plots were hatched against him. In 1654 an apparently well-financed group of royalists advertised a reward for whoever would kill "by pistol, sword, or poison . . . a certain mechanic fellow."[16] Even more famous were the efforts of Edward Sexby, a former officer in the Lord Protector's forces, to organize a conspiracy aiming at Cromwell's murder and comprising elements as seemingly incongruous as

---

* By a curious and little-known twist of history, the position taken by the Hapsburg monarchs on this occasion had been foreshadowed as early as 1605 by their family's great opponent, Henry IV of France. Having learned that the Spaniards' feared Genoese general, Ambrosio Spinola, might be traveling within easy reach of French forces, the king toyed with the idea of having him captured by a force of cavalry, a stroke that "would be worth a battle gained." A little later, however, Henry decided that Spinola must not be attacked or even kidnaped while visiting Paris, on the grounds that any such action would be reprehensible if committed inside France. See David Buisseret, *Henry IV* (London: Allen & Unwin, 1984), p. 170.

Cavaliers and Levellers! Yet Sir Charles Firth, who in *The Last Years of the Protectorate* pays close attention to these and other assassination plans, concludes that none of them came close to succeeding.[17]

For all the threats to Cromwell's survival, we should not underestimate his advantages. By the time his danger was at its greatest, he was a military dictator, less vulnerable than any civilian politician and less easygoing with respect to personal approaches than a Henry IV of France or a Gustav Adolf of Sweden in their royal self-confidence. Unlike Caesar centuries before, Cromwell refused to abandon the stern manners that went with the wearing of armor in favor of those befitting a toga, and he never lost the devotion of his military henchmen. Surrounded by the vigilant Ironsides, he presented a difficult target. Even so, he might have been killed had his enemies been willing to buy success at the cost of their own lives, but this they declined to do. Hence it was not until 1660, two years after its interment, that his body was symbolically "slain," that is, torn from its crypt at Westminster and subjected to public desecration.

Remnants of Violence

Like any other flood, that of political murder in early modern Europe receded unevenly, leaving backwaters where there once had been torrents. The law courts in particular continued to offer those in power a lethal weapon for use not only against private malefactors but also against rivals in the public sphere. It is possible to see in the increased importance of capital trials and occasional lynchings compensation of sorts for the decline in the incidence of assassination. Yet the observer must beware of false conclusions hastily arrived at. In particular, it would be a mistake to assume that wherever there had previously been numerous assaults upon prominent individuals there was now a corresponding plethora of trials for sedition or treason.

In France, despite the triumph of an autocratic monarchy under Louis XIV, accompanied by more outbursts of local resistance than historians used to recognize, the number of fatalities resulting either from mob action or from official repression appears to have decreased. This is not to make light of harsh measures adopted by the Sun King's government, especially during the consolidation of his personal rule, nor is it to deny that during the later years of the reign, years of desperate warfare against a formidable array of European powers, French subjects faced very grim conditions indeed.[18] Yet from first to last the record was considerably less blood-spattered than that of the later Valois epoch, or even of Richelieu's time. The severe application of royal justice, as in the use of special courts, the *Grands Jours,* sent to crush baronial resistance in the once lawless Auvergne, was not unwelcome to all segments of the population. The only example of a conspiracy to commit assassination at Versailles, the celebrated *affaire des poisons* of 1680, resulted in a long trial and a total of thirty-six death sentences, but none of the convicted could reasonably be called politically important figures. Even Madame Monvoisin—"La Voisin," the accused sorceress at the center of the case—was convicted and executed amid circumstances far less macabre than those surrounding the judgment of Leonora Galigai earlier in the century.[19]

The same pattern of relative restraint emerges from the annals of the Hapsburg empire, of the Hohenzollern lands under Brandenburg's Great Elector, of a Spanish kingdom fast losing its former power but not become less law-abiding or demonstrably more oppressive on that account. It was in northwestern Europe, especially in the Dutch Netherlands and in Great Britain, that the most ruthless public behavior was concentrated during the later decades of the seventeenth century. These neighboring nations—maritime, Protestant, freer no doubt than most other realms but nonetheless subject to constitutional crises and occasionally ferocious political struggles—produced more than their share of mortal peril.

It is interesting to contrast the United Provinces' experience with that of Sweden, another embattled Protestant power, during the same period. The Swedes had known no parallel to the case of Oldenbarneveldt in 1619 and had managed to survive even the troubled reign of Queen Christina until her abdication in 1654 without having recourse either to assassination or to civil war. Holland, on the other hand, unique in its government's singular mixture of republican and quasi-royal institutions, continued to be racked by periodic spasms of violence.

The most notable of these to occur after the Arminian-Gomarist conflict in the early 1600s and before the demise of the Republic at the end of the following century was the lynching of the brothers John and Cornelius de Witt in 1672. Its background included the war of 1665–1667 against England, followed after a five-year respite by a far greater military crisis, Louis XIV's all-out attack on the United Provinces. By that time the younger brother, John, though only forty-seven, had served for almost twenty years as Grand Pensionary of Holland, a technically provincial title which in fact made him the nation's chief civilian officer. With uncommon tact and flexibility he had steered his homeland through a succession of dangers, making war with foreign powers when unavoidable but seeking peace whenever there was a choice, holding the ambitious Orangists in check, and all the while defending Dutch commercial interests with unflagging care.

The French onslaught in 1672 overwhelmed the Grand Pensionary and his accustomed methods, dooming him to expulsion from office, followed by a miserable death. With the support of Cornelius, who had been more active than he in naval affairs but was involved as well in domestic and foreign policymaking, John had forged the Triple Alliance of 1668 against Louis XIV's ambitions. These diplomatic precautions appeared to have gone for nought, however, when Louvois's powerful army invaded Holland, and a terrified people turned as if by reflex to the traditional military leadership of the House of Orange, in the person of William III. The ambitious young stadholder was about to have his revenge for years of political eclipse, for in its panic the Dutch public seized upon the notion that the de Witts where wholly to blame for the nation's peril.

Pamphlets, placards, and streetcorner diatribes joined in accusing the brothers of incompetence, venality, possibly even connivance with the invaders. Cornelius was arrested late in July 1672, charged with conspiracy against the state, questioned under torture, and given a hasty trial which ended with his being sentenced to exile. On August 4 John, having resigned his office, came to The Hague to be with his brother in the Binnenhof, the place of his supposedly temporary confinement. On the afternoon of August 20, while the two men were together there and with the building surrounded but not protected by the stadholder's troops, a number of self-appointed executioners broke in and hustled both de Witts down to the street, where they were literally torn to pieces by a cursing mob.[20]

Admirers of the victims likened them to the Gracchi of old. In most respects the de Witts bore little resemblance to the Roman brothers, but after this demonstration of blood-lust, a sequel to the execution of Oldenbarneveldt a half-century earlier, the Republic was never again the same. It survived, at great cost, the protracted series of wars against France but slipped increasingly under the domination of English naval and commercial power, succumbing by the end of the eighteenth century first to the princely rule of Orange and then to the forces of the Revolution. Whatever share of responsibility for the killing of the de Witts in 1672 must be borne by William III, their deaths served his purposes at the time and perhaps those of his dynasty in the long run.

On the British side of the Channel not just a sudden outburst of popular hysteria, manipulated for partisan advantage as in Holland, but a whole series of episodes revived bitter memories of the Civil War. Beginning in 1678, backlash from the so-called Popish Plot doomed a number of alleged conspirators, successors, or so they were portrayed, of Guy Fawkes's band of Catholic incendiaries. In 1683 came the purge of defendants charged with complicity in the Rye House Plot. Less than two years after that Lord Jeffreys carried out his "bloody assizes" in the wake of Monmouth's Rebellion against James II. By comparison, the unseating of the king in 1688 was remarkably smooth and orderly—in that sense truly "glorious" as revolutions go, but a surprising sequel to a decade filled with perjury, parliamentary and ministerial incitement to violence, renewed eruptions of religious hatred (including a Catholic archbishop's murder by Scottish Covenanters in 1679), and merciless use of the crown's power to impose capital punishment.

Titus Oates, the man who "revealed" the Popish Plot, was a shadowy character, apparently as vengeful as he was self-aggrandizing. In September 1678 he swore before a justice of the peace that Jesuits and other traitors were planning to murder the king, place his brother James duke of York upon the throne as a Roman Catholic monarch, and invite French-Spanish forces to invade the British Isles. Charles II greeted these charges with disbelief, but the opposition in the House of Commons made the most of Protestant fears in order to secure passage of the Disabling Act, which excluded Catholics from Parliament for more than one hundred and fifty years. King Charles meanwhile came to the conclusion that the earl of Shaftesbury, leader of the nascent Whig faction, had personally invented the counterfeit plot, which he had not, and was capitalizing on the furor for partisan advantage, which he undoubtedly was.

At this point a mysterious, and quite possibly unrelated, tragedy occurred. Sir Edmund Godfrey, the justice of the peace who had taken Oates's deposition, was found murdered in one of London's peaceful parks. This happened just six weeks after the initial allegations and was almost unanimously assumed to be connected with them. The mystery of Godfrey's death has never been solved, but in a country filled with memories of Ridolfi and Babington, Throckmorton and Fawkes, it was readily accepted as proof of Catholic villainy. Five Jesuits, together with the Society's legal adviser in England, were arrested, tried, and hanged. In addition, the earl of Danby, though a Protestant and the king's lord high treasurer, was impeached in December, forcing his erstwhile master at last to dissolve the so-called "Cavalier Parliament," which for almost eighteen years had obediently deferred to royal wishes. Five Catholic peers were sent to the Tower, and one of them, Viscount Stafford of the prestigious Howard family, from there to the scaffold. Also beheaded was Edward Coleman, secretary and confessor to the duchess of York, on similar charges of high treason and criminal dealings with foreign governments. At least fifteen executions were attributable to religious animus.[21]

Finally, in March 1681, confronted by an Exclusion Bill designed to bar his own brother from succession to the throne, Charles II dissolved the House again and put an end to the proceedings. In so doing, he was supported by mounting evidence that Oates was a liar. The king had scarcely terminated one witch-hunt, however, than he launched another of his own, aimed at saving the Stuart dynasty. For that purpose he seized upon the alleged Rye House Plot. This purported conspiracy was denounced in June 1683 by one Josiah Keeling, an informer seen by some as nothing more than a continuator of Titus Oates wearing different political colors. Before the resulting purge was over, Whiggish suspects as prominent as the republican playwright Algernon Sidney, brother to the earl of Leicester, and Lord William Russell, son of the earl of Bedford, had been executed on the flimsiest evidence of traitorous intent. The earl of Essex, imprisoned in the Tower, chose to commit suicide, thereby lending credence in the eyes of the king's party to suspicions that he had been involved in a conspiracy to strike down his sovereign.[22]

The most important result of the Rye House panic may have been not the specific executions it produced, sensational as some of them were, but the revived fear of a royal assassination. Such a fear was soon reinforced in the opinion of Stuart partisans by the rebellion launched in the name of the duke of Monmouth, generally (though in all likelihood wrongly) reputed to be Charles II's illegitimate son. It was to the purported imminence of another regicide that Monmouth's "uncle," newly crowned as James II, and his lord chief justice baron Jeffreys appealed in carrying out the latter's ferocious effort to eradicate insurgency by the use of courtroom proceedings. Monmouth was quickly captured and beheaded at London in July 1685, as was his Scottish henchman the earl of Argyll at Edinburgh in June. Thereafter, as Jeffreys moved his assizes from town to town in the West Counties, headsmen and hangmen seemed even busier than in Henry VIII's time.[23]

In combination, the Popish Plot, the Rye House Plot, and the Monmouth Rebellion produced at least 175 executions, about 150 of them carried out in the course of Lord Jeffreys' Bloody Assizes.* The victims included Catholic peers, Jesuit clergymen, politicians rightly or wrongly identified as Whigs (some of them titled, others not), and a number of relatively obscure men. The numerous acquittals and commutations notwithstanding, and despite the probability that some of those who died were guilty as charged, the manifest miscarriage of justice in a sizable proportion of cases was perhaps the clearest indication that the "restoration settlement" had failed.

What ensued in 1688–89 was not so puzzling as it may have appeared to observers on the Continent, awaiting with a mixture of fascination and foreboding the next installment of English horrors. The Glorious Revolution, far from being one more blood bath, unseated another Stuart in a manner very different from that in which his father had been eliminated forty years before. James II, although an avowed Catholic and more unpopular than Charles I in other respects as well, was nevertheless actively assisted in his escape to France by opponents determined to avoid any repetition of a royal trial. He was replaced by a parliamentary monarchy after some rioting in

---

* Jeffreys had played an earlier, less prominent, role in the punishment of some of the Rye House defendants. All the more indicative, therefore, of the judge's broad definition of guilt is his presiding over the trial and conviction of Titus Oates on charges of perjury concerning the Popish Plot. Oates was sentenced to flogging in the expectation that it would prove fatal, but once again he demonstrated his unpredictability by surviving the lash and, after several years in prison, succeeded in living into the eighteenth century. Jeffreys, by contrast, was arrested during the Glorious Revolution and sent to the Tower, where he died in the spring of 1689.

London and a scattering of local clashes elsewhere, but without any full-scale battle on the order of Naseby or Marston Moor.

In January 1689 the self-constituted Convention Parliament voted not only to acknowledge the accession of William and Mary but also to charge that their predecessor on the throne, "by the assistance of divers evil counsellors, judges and ministers . . . did endeavor to subvert and extirpate the Protestant religion and the laws and liberties of this kingdom."[24] The English had by no means lost their taste for resistance, as witness the vigorous debates at Westminster over royal prerogative and parliamentary privilege under the new rulers, followed shortly by John Locke's published reflections on conditions for transferring power in the state. What the Glorious Revolution did signify, however, was the acceptance in England, later than in most of the rest of Europe, of a new restraint in the application of sanguinary means to the achievement of political ends.

The Eighteenth Century

During the hundred years that began with these events in Great Britain and ended with the great upheaval of 1789, Europe came closer than at any other time in modern history to rejecting assassination. This, like all generalizations of comparable scope, is subject to exceptions, beginning with an abortive Jacobite plot shortly after Queen Mary's death in 1694 to ambush and kill William III. The attempt was thwarted, and, as was characteristic of the times, a Parliament which so recently had deposed a king rallied to this one with virtually unanimous indignation at the very thought of such a plot.[25] Fifteen years later England was shocked by an unsuccessful attempt on the life of Robert Harley, soon to be the earl of Oxford, made by a French spy, the marquis de Guiscard, while undergoing interrogation by Harley and other members of the privy council. Between 1710 and Spencer Perceval's death in 1812, however, no subsequent British minister would be the object of a lethal attack.

On the Continent two other victims were not so fortunate. In 1707, during a session of the Hungarian estates at Önod, a prominent Magyar nobleman named Melchior Rakovsky, speaking for his county of Thurocz, strongly opposed the urgent call of Francis Rákóczi II, prince of Transylvania, for the Hapsburgs' expulsion and for acceptance of Louis XIV's offer of French support in prosecuting the civil war which he, Rákóczi, had launched. The response of the latter's aristocratic partisans was to draw their swords and kill Rakovsky where he stood in the assembly's meeting hall. Less than forty-eight hours later the son of another foe of Rákóczi's uprising was dragged from the same place and beheaded in a nearby field after being found guilty of "treason against Hungarian freedom."[26] The ill-fated revolt dedicated to that cause went forward, to disaster.

These Hungarian atrocities, like the attacks in England on William III and Harley, were to varying degrees the offshoots of Europe's last great war with the Ludovican France. By contrast, the sensational slaying of Tsar Peter III at St. Petersburg in 1762, by a clique of officers around Alexis Orlov was to a much lesser degree connected with the international conflict then drawing to a close. True, the erratic emperor had played some part in the Seven Years' (or, as Germans called it, the Third Silesian) War, principally by taking Russia out of the alliance with Austria and France that had threatened to overwhelm his personal idol, Frederick the Great of Prussia. Peter had gone further and in May 1762, only a couple of months before his murder, entered into a full treaty of alliance with the former enemy in Berlin. The action that destroyed him, however, was no simple effort to reverse a foreign policy decision. It was in part a quasi-oriental stroke of state reminiscent of numerous deaths in the realm of the Ottoman Turks and in part a Byzantine palace coup, with the victim's wife, Empress Catherine II, if not an active accomplice, an undoubted beneficiary of his disappearance.

The fact remains that even in an eighteenth-century Europe expanded to include the Hungarian countryside and the Russian capital, there were no successful political murders other than those of Rakovsky and Peter III until assassination returned to favor in the 1790s. Failed attempts, too, were infrequent, those aimed at reigning monarchs during the period having reached a total of only three. One was the superficial stabbing of Louis XV of France by Robert-François Damiens at Versailles in 1757. The second, in 1758, comprised two separate but coordinated efforts by gunmen to ambush Joseph I of Portugal outside his palace in Lisbon. The third was the ineffectual dagger attack upon George III by Margaret Nicholson in 1786 at the entrance to Saint James's palace (foreshadowing the more serious assault upon the British monarch in 1800).[27]

The long remission has given rise to a number of explanations varying greatly in their claims to credibility. It has been suggested that the technology of the age did not offer much chance of killing a highly placed personage. Why? Daggers, swords, and firearms more primitive than those of the eighteenth century had taken the lives of Coligny, William the Silent, Henry IV, and countless others in the past; with only minor alterations they would meet the needs of numerous assassins yet to come.

A more convincing answer is that the eighteenth century was notably lacking in "causes" and correspondingly scornful of "enthusiasm" of the kind displayed by zealots. The period, so runs this argument, lay between one of religious fanaticism and another in which people would be willing to kill and be killed for their choice among secular faiths: nationalism, libertarianism, egalitarianism, socialism, even anarchism. Throughout most of the 1700s what would now be called opinion-leaders seldom expressed anything other than contempt for homicide as a political expedient. In France the

Encyclopedists, while generally subscribing to "useful servitude" in place of capital punishment for all major crimes including assassination (in the process displaying at times a blithe indifference to the realities of human behavior not shared by the great Beccaria),[28] nevertheless referred to Henry III's killer as a demented monk acting for the Catholic League and dismissed Henry IV's as a "monster."[29]

If a compendium so critical of the existing order's most salient features could exhibit nothing more than distaste for famous regicides, was there any defense at all of "justified" political murder? Very little, one must answer, though diligent inquiry yields a few scattered examples. A German jurisconsult, Augustin Leyser, in his *Meditationes ad Pandectas* of 1717 labeled one section "The Doctrine of Jean Petit . . . Vindicated."[30] Leyser argued that this "honest and learned man" had not espoused the slaying of a sovereign prince but only sought to explain why an occasional usurper within a ruler's family, such as the duke of Orleans three hundred years before, might in good conscience be struck down. Doubt is cast on Leyser's objectivity, however, by the obsequious manner in which he sought to flatter the Hapsburgs of his own day, applauding the famous apologist for their ancestor, the duke of Burgundy. An equally partisan defense of Petit's memory was composed in 1755 by a French Dominican, Jean-Jacques Proville. What distinguishes Proville's work is that, while criticizing attacks aimed at the Burgundian spokesman in the fifteenth century, its real aim seems to have been to discredit the *History of the Council of Constance* published by a contemporary Protestant, Jacques Lenfant.[31]

That tracts such as these are remembered today almost solely as curiosities is natural, given the manner in which most other eighteenth-century commentators and publicists treated political homicide. David Hume described the killer of the duke of Buckingham in 1628 as having had "a sullen, unsociable mind."[32] Edward Gibbon identified assassination contemptuously as "the last resource of cowards."[33] Moufle d'Angerville, a gossipy but often refreshingly sensible Parisian, found in the attempt by Damiens merely an invitation to ridicule the perpetrator of such an act in the age of enlightenment.[34]

Given remarks of that kind, one might expect to find old assassinations and the two attempts that occurred in the 1750s receiving as little publicity as they did approbation. Yet the evidence, as intractable as ever, stubbornly points the other way. Early in the 1720s there appeared at Leipzig twelve folio volumes entitled *Annales Ferdinandei* and written during the first half of the *seventeenth* century by an Austrian diplomat, Franz Christoph Khevenhüller.[35] This work contains items of interest for each year of Emperor Ferdinand II's life (1578–1637), interspersed with illustrations from what appear to have been a supply of old copperplates at the publisher's disposal. Many of the illustrations show battles, ceremonies, processions, and the like in various parts of Europe; but prominently displayed as well are the assassinations of William of Orange, the brothers Guise, Henry of Valois, Henry of Navarre, and of course Wallenstein. The age and availability of the engravings have been noted because, like the vernacular German text, they suggest a relatively inexpensive, which is to say, by eighteenth-century standards, a popular edition.

Whatever may be concluded about Khevenhüller and his posthumous reading public, the overt attacks on Louis XV and Joseph I at midcentury released a torrent of pamphlets and broadsides, some libelous in their undocumented charges of conspiratorial guilt, others merely gruesome in their attention to details of the punishments meted out. The French government of Louis XV paid a tribute of sorts to the energy being expended on publications devoted to Damiens' futile attempt. The same Paris Parlement that sentenced the poor dull-witted culprit to torture and dismemberment "after the manner of Ravaillac" and ordered the demolition of his birthplace in Artois as well as the exile of all his close relatives, also condemned to be burned by the hangman several pamphlets lest they keep alive "the memory of the horrible attempt."[36]

As the French case suggests, contemporaries seized almost gleefully upon the events in Paris and Lisbon. One reason was that they lent support to the recently resumed practice of denouncing the Society of Jesus and its supposed machinations. Portugal's ferocious chief minister, the marquis of Pombal, used the "conspiracy of the Tavoras," as the plot against Joseph I came to be known, in order to smash two sets of domestic opponents. First, he ordered tried and publicly executed, by decapitation, strangulation, or breaking on the cross, nine lay defendants, including the duke of Aveiro and the marquis of Tavora, his wife, and two of their sons. Soon thereafter, the Jesuit spokesman Father Malagrida was burned at the stake in an auto-dafé, following which Pombal proceeded to expel all members of the Society from the Portuguese kingdom.[37]

It would serve no purpose here to linger over the legal details or the political effects of these attempts at assassination, standing all but alone in a self-proclaimed Age of Reason. The Damiens and Tavora affairs nevertheless shed light on that era's attitudes toward political murder. There is the evidence, already noted, of a great deal of excitement, some though by no means all of it expressed in the form of morbid curiosity. Within a few months after the executions in France and Portugal, to cite a curious example, Germany's enterprising publishers were busy once more. The year 1759 brought the publication of a 96-page booklet at Leipzig and Frankfurt am Main entitled *Conversation in the Realm of the Dead between the Author of the Conspiracy against the King of Portugal, Joseph de Mascarenhas, Former Duke of Aveiro, and Robert Francis Damiens, Notorious Regicide in France.*[33] In this fantasy the assassins drone on, lecturing one another about their own monstrous lives and ending in agreement that they should never have listened to the Jesuits. Though longer and perhaps slightly more censorious than most, the German potboiler was by no means atypical. Whatever else may be said about the eighteenth century in this regard, lack of popular interest in crimes of state was not what made it different.

A related point is that treatments both lurid and dignified usually condemned assassination. Considering this negative tone, one might be tempted to announce the puzzle solved by the hostile force of public opinion. Unfortunately, any such conjecture contradicts one of the few things that can be said with some confidence about the mind of the political murderer. There is no reason based on historical evidence to suppose an assassin acts out of the belief that his gesture will win general approval or, indeed, to think that approval as such matters very much to him one way or another. Attention, even if only in the form of notoriety, is what does interest him. So the question resurfaces, now in slightly altered form: What was it in the atmosphere and social mores of this period that blunted the attractions of criminal fame?

The Damiens and Tavora episodes provide a valuable albeit obvious insight into the peculiarity of the early modern moratorium. It arises from the fact that as events, regardless of motives or repercussions, they stand so nearly alone in their own day and age. Excluding, for reasons already noted, Margaret Nicholson's still more trivial attempt against George III, the only Western European entries on the roll of assassination attempts involve the stab of a penknife beside a waiting coach at Versailles and a pair of volleys fired at a coach approaching a palace in Lisbon. (Louis XV must have felt that of the two kings he had been the less fortunate, since he had been interrupted by Damiens when about to leave for an amorous assignation, whereas Joseph I of Portugal was on his way home from one.)

Assuming that human nature does not change beyond recognition on a time scale of hundreds of years, and remembering that the eighteenth century was not at all a peaceful one—the incidence of other crimes and occasional riots having long since dispelled any notion of an era pale in its colors, calm in its speech, or mild in its behavior—we still confront a stubborn problem of explanation. Did widely shared patterns of acceptance and aspiration set that age apart? Did a more rational, or at least more utilitarian view of government strip tyrannicide of any claim to self-sacrificing heroism? Or, quite the opposite, did enough of the sanctity of kingship suvive to make regicide (and by extension attacks on servants of the crown as well) repugnant to most people?

Such questions are easier to formulate than to answer. One suggestion that seems worthy of consideration entails asking not just how and why the eighteenth century was different but, more specifically, what experience or experiences eighteenth-century Europeans did not share with either their ancestors or their descendants after about 1790.

Part of any thoughtful reply would have to be: mass warfare, including especially civil war. The age of Louis XIV featured some long and wide-ranging conflicts. It also witnessed the lynching of the de Witts in Holland, the murder of Rakovsky, the plot against England's King William III, and the subsequent attack upon the future earl of Oxford. Even after the end of the Ludovican epic and the death of the Sun King in 1715, there were wars in Europe and outbursts of popular violence. But the wars were fought by relatively small and well-disciplined professional armies, and the riots generally had little or nothing to do with them.

After the rampaging *Landsknechte* and armed mobs of the Religious Wars, before the French Revolution's *levée en masse* and the conscript hordes of the Napoleonic era, there was an interval during which most people did not observe at firsthand the most horrendous aspects of war, in particular the spectacle of humans slain by the hundreds, even thousands. Contrast in this regard the experience of later generations, if not always as participants, then as the audience for increasingly graphic journalism, still photography, motion pictures, radio, and television. Is it not reasonable to suppose that modern warfare, especially given these methods of extending its psychological effects, has done something quite fundamental to general ideas of death in relation to political life?

Revolution in France

What I have referred to as "eighteenth-century" conditions came to an abrupt end before that century had completed its full course. Scenes enacted during the 1790s in locales as widely separated as Stockholm, London, and Saint Petersburg clearly demonstrated that what was changing in Europe, even with respect to political murder, could not all be traced to the great upheaval in France. Nevertheless, the abandonment of the early modern surcease from assassination and regicide was so crucial a feature of the French Revolution that it would be foolish not to look first at that historic drama.

Much of what took place in the course of that tumultuous decade represented a mixture of genuinely new departures with a partial return to older patterns, including those of lethal violence. Illustrative of the combination were two quite different occurrences. One was an unexpected murder that appeared to some (including its perpetrator) to be the act of a latter-day Judith or female Brutus, but which befell a standard-bearer of popular journalism and mass politics in their emerging modern form. The other was the execution of a king amid furious arguments about the powers of the people's delegates and the right of the populace as a whole.

In the summer of 1793, when the Jacobin Terror still had a year to run, Jean-Paul Marat had recently observed his fiftieth birthday. Not yet an old man, the former physician, half-Swiss and half-Sardinian, was weary enough after years of frantic activity to have toyed with the idea of retiring from political life. He was also suffering from an agonizing skin disease contracted during years of underground existence, a disease so serious as to make him start warning friends that he could not survive much longer. Founder of an influential newspaper, *The Friend of the People,* and its successor, the *Journal of the French Republic,* he claimed in more self-effacing moments to be only a humble editor and columnist. That, however, was false modesty in which he indulged less and less frequently, for his merciless war upon all he considered enemies of the Revolution had carried him to a prominent place among the leaders of the Convention, since September 1792 France's national parliament.

Marat continued to criticize the decision to go to war against England, the United Provinces, and Spain. He demanded an end to every vestige of royal power, won acquittal of treason in April 1793 before the Revolutionary Tribunal, and the following month had the grim satisfaction of seeing his erstwhile accusers themselves consigned to execution by the overthrow of the Girondist party in the legislature. Despite having submitted a letter of resignation from his own seat (the request was duly rejected by his fellow members), he retained enough energy to keep on urging the extermination of all Girondists still at large, anywhere in France. His power had never appeared more nearly unassailable. Proscription by the pen of Marat had come to be viewed as tantamount to a sentence of death.

The sultry evening of July 13, 1793, did justice to the name of the month in which it fell according to the new Revolutionary Calendar: *Thermidor.* Marat was in his Parisian apartment, 30 Rue des Cordeliers, soaking in the writing tub he had devised in the search for at least temporary relief from itching. Earlier that day a note had been left him by one "Marianne Corday," who identified herself as a resident of Caen in Normandy and promised information about fugitive Girondist deputies at large in that province. Marat, his curiosity aroused, ordered his housekeeper and common-law wife, Simone Evrard, to admit the visitor. After a few minutes devoted to talk about traitors in and around Caen, the prim-looking young female suddenly produced a long knife and fatally stabbed her half-submerged host, then surrendered to several neighbors brought running by Madame Evrard's screams.

The assassin was a handsome woman of twenty-five whose aristocratic name, Marie-Anne-Charlotte Corday d'Armont, betrayed her roots in the Norman gentry. She did indeed know something about Girondin sympathizers in her native canton, and her resolve to kill Marat had been born of conversations with some among them. One in particular, a man named Barbaroux, had supplied her with a letter to a kindred spirit, a Convention deputy who thus far had escaped expulsion and trial and who gave her directions and introductions when she reached the capital. Her thoughts on tyrannicide seem to have come from reading Plutarch, the Bible, and the classical tragedies of a seventeeth-century relative, the playwright Corneille. For a Norman girl, folklore concerning Joan of Arc, the martyr of Rouen, must also have suggested heroic sacrifice. Only a few days after the murder Corday was sent to the guillotine, following a hasty trial during which she made no effort to defend herself or her deed, beyond expressing satisfaction over its success. The rest of France plunged deeper into the Terror, with the executions of Marie Antoinette, Hébert, Danton, and at last Robespierre himself (in Thermidor again) just a year after Marat's death. By that time the slain editor had been memorialized on canvas by Jacques Louis David and in the words of eulogies delivered before the Convention, which installed his bust to look down on its remaining months of what could no longer be called deliberations.[39]

By the time Marat died at the hands of his celebrated assailant, the early modern lull in tyrannicide and other forms of political killing was already a thing of the past. As the reaction to Charles I's death in London had helped to usher in that moratorium, so the beheading of another king in what is now the Place de la Concorde emphatically signaled its end. For that as well as other reasons, the trial of Louis XVI had exercised a continuing hold on the historical imagination.[40]

To judge from the *cahiers* of 1789, those local and regional catalogues of grievances presented to the revived Estates General at Versailles, French public opinion had not been predominantly anti-royalist on the eve of the Revolution, or for that matter throughout its early phases. Hostile to antiquated privileges, certainly, and in that sense, anti-noble, anti-ecclesiastical, anti-corporative with respect to municipal and guild hierarchies, impatient over governmental corruption and ineptitude, suspicious of the king's Austrian-born wife, critical of his ministers and satin-clad courtiers—yet touchingly loyal to the monarch himself, the father-figure of his people. Habits of thought ingrained through long centuries of Capetian rule and nurtured by memories of Saint Louis IX and Henry of Navarre still underlay a considerable degree of reverence, even affection for the crown. The squandering of that capital had required a combination of foolish advice from such counselors as Louis XVI's brother, the count of Artois, self-defeating rivalry among privileged groups throughout the country, intervention by foreign rulers ostensibly on the royal family's behalf, and the king's own incorrigible tendency to oscillate between inaction and attacks of misdirected energy.

The first of the Revolution's successive experiments in constitution-making, accepted in principle by Louis on Bastille Day 1790, had envisaged a limited monarchy—eliminating hereditary titles and all ecclesiastical orders save those devoted to healing and teaching, but reserving a by no means inconsiderable role for the crown. Given the tendency of most revolutions eventually to become narrower in base and more radical in direction until reversed by internal resistance or external counteraction or both, it can be argued that this early attempt at conciliation was doomed, and would have been even under a prince as shrewd as Charles II of England or as imposing in will and intellect as Frederick the Great of Prussia.

The new constitution had not yet been adopted when the court circle began to act as though determined to play into the hands of its most implacable enemies. An increasingly indiscreet and easily intercepted correspondence was carried on by Artois and the queen with the irreconcilables around them on the one side and, on the other, foreign autocrats hostile to the Revolution as well as Frenchmen who had joined the swelling ranks of *émigrés*. Although the group of voluntary exiles as a whole was by no means entirely—or in numerical terms even predominantly—aristocratic, those invited to maintain contact with the court seem to have been almost invariably of noble birth. Meanwhile, in Paris and the provinces, forces opposed to every vestige of the Old Regime kept up their attacks upon it, through legislative speeches, resolutions passed by Jacobin and other political clubs, harangues delivered in cafés and on streetcorners, and articles in such newspapers as Marat's *L'Ami du Peuple*.

The resulting disintegration of the constitutional monarchy can be followed through a succession of events that occurred over the course of the ensuing two and a half years. On the night of June 20–21, 1791, the king took an action comparable, in propagandistic effect at any rate, to Charles I's raising of the royal battle standard at Nottingham in 1642. This "flight to Varennes" consisted not only in Louis XVI's slipping out of the Tuileries palace at Paris which his queen and their son, using an unmarked and closely shuttered coach, but also his effort to repudiate collaboration with the national government. Whether he was seeking Austrian protection in Luxembourg or asylum with royalist French army units in Lorraine has never been definitively established, but the precise intention is unimportant. Whatever its destination, the coach was recognized at Varennes-en-Argonne, and its occupants were returned to stricter confinement in Paris.

Three months later, in September 1791, the king went through the formalities of approving the new constitution, considerably altered since his acceptance of its draft in principle a year earlier. On October 1 the new Legislative Assembly elected under its terms was convened, replacing the *Constituante* but still containing, if no longer an aristocratic-clerical bloc, at least a number of *Feuillants,* as the relatively conservative members were called. The centrist majority continued to resist Jacobin demands for more explicitly anti-monarchist action. The following April, however, the assembly did agree on a declaration of war against the rulers of Austria and Prussia, a measure that had two portentous results. First—and somewhat ironically, since leading Jacobins, including Robespierre, had opposed the declaration of war, seeing in it an unwelcome diversion—the advent of hostilities increased the power of the most extreme and, equally important, most authoritarian revolutionaries. Second, it heightened an anxious population's fear of treasonable royal collusion with the Austrian and Prussian dynasts now identified as enemies of France.

By the first week of August 1792, Jacobin delegations from the radical wards or *sections* of Paris were calling upon the Législatif to strip "Louis Capet" of all privileges, not to mention the title itself. On the night of August 9–10 a revolutionary Commune elected by the sections to replace the capital's established city government led a huge crowd of radical *sans-culottes* and others in an assault on the Tuileries. Before the night was over the Swiss Guards assigned to the palace, numerous aristocrats with quarters there, and a substantial number of servants were slaughtered, though the king and his family temporarily found safety under the protection of the Assembly.

The focus of action then shifted to that national body. In an effort, purposeful in the case of some deputies, panicky in that of others, to mollify the *sans-culottes,* it declared the king to be not just protected but "in custody" and decreed that there should be immediately elected, under a greatly expanded definition of male suffrage, a new legislature to be called the National Convention. Membership in this body, which convened on September 21, included no avowed Feuillants nor, obviously, any identifiable supporters of the monarchy. In their place had been returned a phalanx of republicans committed to the pursuit of a variety of more or less extreme goals: Robespierre, Danton, Marat, Desmoulins, Saint-Just, and their short-lived opponents hailing from the Gironde in the Southwest and clustered about Brissot.

The monarchy was now a thing of the past; its restoration no longer seemed worth dreaming or worrying about. A fortnight before the Convention assembled the September Massacres, triggered by news of military defeats and rumors of betrayal, occurred in Paris and numerous provincial cities, claiming at the very least a thousand lives of "aristocratic" prisoners torn from their jail cells and butchered by the rampaging mobs. No such orgy had occurred since Saint Bartholomew's Day. Then, on September 22, 1792, the first day of Year I on the Revolutionary Calendar, the Republic was solemnly proclaimed. In December, with the Paris sections still clamoring for blood, the deputies took up the case of a royal defendant whose guilt was taken for granted, but whose punishment had still to be decided.

Among all the political and forensic details of the trial of Louis Capet, sometime king but now a citizen accused of treason, two points stand out as particularly revealing. One is that there was no effort, as there had been in England when Charles Stuart was brought to trial, to create a special judicial body for the purpose. Instead, the Convention voted to give itself, as a committee of the whole, the powers of a court extraordinary. Under the circumstances, political concerns took even clearer precedence over judicial ones than they had in the English case. Relatively moderate suggestions offered by the Girondins and certain spokesmen for the center, or Plain, were denounced by Jacobin orators of the Mountain, especially Robespierre and his handsome young colleague Saint-Just—called the "Angel of Death"— on grounds of anti-revolutionary deviationism and voted down.

Politicization of the trial had the further effect, and this constitutes the second major point, of producing some reversals so bizarre that under less somber conditions they could have appeared amusing. Here were the Girondins, usually accused by their opponents of being not sufficiently democratic, urging a national plebiscite to decide the king's sentence, in the transparent belief that a popular referendum would support them in substituting exile or imprisonment for the death penalty. Knowing that such was indeed likely to be the result of any such appeal to the people, especially those outside Paris, the orators of the Mountain abruptly dropped their usual glorification of the popular will, insisting that members of the Convention had been elected to interpret that will and must now bravely vote their own convictions without seeking issue-by-issue guidance at the polls.

On January 15, 1793, solid majorities were recorded in favor of declaring the defendant guilty and against any appeal to the people. The next day, however, brought a very different tally on the issue of Citizen Capet's punishment. Of the 760 deputies present and voting, 360 rejected the death penalty, 361 favored immediate execution, and 39 voted for death subject to a variety of reservations or delays for further deliberation. Only by that margin was the fateful issue decided. On January 21 the former king, convicted of conspiracy against the Republic and correspondence with its foreign enemies, calmly submitted to the great blade of the guillotine.

Some political effects of the regicide were specific, others diffuse. Taking the event as a signal for all-out war against the powers of Europe, the Convention voted in February to add England, Spain, and the United Provinces to its list of declared enemies, thereby, in the words of the motion, "throwing down the head of a king as a gage of battle." On the domestic front the execution, coming only a few months after the September Massacres, marked the end of all restraint in dealing with anyone charged with subverting the new dispensation of Liberty, Equality, and Fraternity. From March through October 1793, an average of 500 individual death sentences were carried out each month. In January 1794 the monthly figure soared to more than 3,500. By August of that year the total number of officially recorded executions, excluding unnumbered local massacres ordered by Deputies on Mission from the Convention or simply incidental to civil warfare in the provinces, had reached something over 14,000 for the year and a half following the king's death.[41] History had heretofore offered no documentable precedent for proscription carried out on such a scale. In the stampede of the Terror, Marie Antoinette's decapitation nine months after her husband's caused only passing excitement inside France.

The End of the Remission

Earth-shaking as the French explosion in the 1790s unquestionably was, it did not alone encompass all aspects of the renewal of political violence that, with only brief and localized interruptions, has continued until the present day. Other political killings of those years demand attention. Still more than events in France, some of these episodes recalled a half-forgotten past, reenacting scenes from it in the altered setting of a revolutionary age.

Probably the most important of such assassinations was that of King Gustav III of Sweden. Since his accession in 1771 Gustav had been the tireless defender of royal prerogatives acquired by his autocratic forebears, among them Gustav Adolf and Charles XII, over the course of more than two hundred years. He muzzled the nobility's spokesmen in the Riksdag, or national diet, while actively pursuing a foreign policy antagonistic to Russia in the east and Denmark in the west. Domestic and external issues came together in 1789, when the aristocratic opposition sought to block new taxes in support of his war against Tsarina Catherine II. The king's response was to expel noble deputies from the legislature.

To the extent that he attacked privilege, increased freedom of expression, moderated the penal code, and exercised a leveling influence of sorts on Swedish society, Gustav III might appear to have shared many of the aims of his era's democratic revolution, rivaling in this regard his contemporary, the Holy Roman Emperor Joseph II. On the other hand, even as his coup d'état was proceeding in Stockholm, he deplored the calling of the French Estates General, as he would denounce their successors, the National and Legislative assemblies. No egalitarian utopia enthralled Gustav. On the contrary, during the final weeks of his life he was actively attempting to organize a league of monarchs determined to crush the Revolution with all possible dispatch.

These facts, combined with the deed's dramatic circumstances, gave the death of Gustave III European-wide importance. But his views on events in Paris had little or nothing to do with its cause. The attack upon him was an expression of the hatred he had aroused among members of the Swedish nobility. One of them, James of Anckarström, acting for what turned out to have been a sizable conspiracy, chose the occasion of a masked ball in the royal opera house on the evening of March 16, 1792, to approach the tall, imposing king and shoot him in the back. The wounded man lingered in pain for almost a fortnight before succumbing, while his assassin under interrogation was spelling out the detail of one more aristocratic regicide of a most familiar kind. The ruler's death removed Sweden from the forefront of anti-Jacobin diplomacy, though that was not the chief aim of this original murder at a *ballo in maschera*. Gustav III died as he had lived, an enlightened despot in the full sense of both words.[42]

Another significant assassination at court was that of Russia's Tsar Paul I in March 1801. The Romanov emperor was in chronological terms the first royal casualty of the nineteenth century, but in other respects his murder belonged to the preceding decade of revolution and regicide. During his early years on the throne, when he was vehemently opposed to Jacobinism in every imaginable form, Paul had found a friend among European rulers in a most surprising place, the royal palace at Stockholm. Sweden's Gustav IV, who had come to the throne at the age of thirteen when his father was slain, originally shared with his correspondent in Saint Petersburg the darkest premonitions of anarchist threats arising from French developments. This shared fear of revolutionaries, however, did not unite their separate destinies for very long.

Gustav IV would end his reign as a madman, forced by yet another cabal of Swedish aristocrats to abdicate in 1809. Insanity and ruin came more swiftly to his counterpart in Russia.[43] Paul I occupied the throne for only slightly over four years, beginning with the death of his mother, Catherine the Great, in 1796. During that brief span he took his empire into the Second Coalition against France in 1799 and out of it in 1800, having by that time become both a great admirer of the First Consul Bonaparte and a confirmed Anglophobe, for reasons ranging from England's naval policies to her presence in India. More serious than this reversal in foreign policy, in the view of many courtiers and officials, was mounting evidence of the tsar's deteriorating mental balance. Some of that evidence was merely embarrassing, such as his simultaneous infatuation with two of the tsarina's maids of honor, or the growing deference he accorded the political opinions of his barber—not quite a Rasputin, but a strange intruder nonetheless. Other signs were deadly serious, especially the capricious expressions of sadism which frightened more and more of the people around him.

At last even his son and heir, the future Alexander I, fearing for his own and his mother's safety as Paul's unpredictable cruelty increased, was persuaded to endorse a cabal of high officers under Saint Petersburg's military governor, Count von der Pahlen, and another general, Count Levin von Bennigsen. It was the latter who, with a unit of imperial guardsmen, actually disposed of the tsar in his apartment within the fortified palace of Saint Michael. Here was regicide carried out by a court circle and supported by the victim's closest relatives in what seemed almost conscious imitation of late Roman and Byzantine episodes, the murder of Claudius or that of Nicephoras Phocas. Yet it was to be the last such murder of a ruler of the "Third Rome" by aristocratic assassins. History's remaining cases of assault upon Romanov tsars would feature very different sorts of activists.

The eighteenth century, in its last years and at its turning, appeared to renounce the very characteristics which had until then made its annals so distinctive a chapter in the history of political murder. The importance of the French Revolution in this resumption of purposeful violence is obviously great, but not all-enveloping. As the deaths of Gustav III and Paul I made clear, more traditional forms of regicide returned to the public arena alongside the work of revolutionary mobs and tribunals.

At London's Drury Lane Theatre in May 1800 another monarch, King George III, survived an attempt on his life. This one was much more dangerous than its predecessor fourteen years before, inasmuch as a shot from the pistol of James Hadley, a demented ex-soldier, struck a pillar in the royal box. The playwright and diplomat Richard Sheridan at once composed a new stanza, which was sung from the stage that very night as part of the national anthem:

> From every latent foe,
> From the assassin's blow,
> God Save the King!

Sheridan's words and the applause that greeted them testified to what a recent biography describes as the monarch's "immense popularity with his subjects."[44] Surrounded by other related incidents, however, the episode was a warning that regicide and assassination had taken, to use an admittedly paradoxical expression, a new lease on life.

10

The Nineteenth Century

An Old, but Widening Stage

In the uses of political murder Europe has been teacher to the world. The traditions and practices of other lands obviously played their part, but the Judeo-Greco-Roman legacy of ideas, interpreted and often ruthlessly translated into action by Europeans, dominated a millennium extending from what the West knows as the early Middle Ages until well past the crisis of 1789–1815. Not until the middle of the nineteenth century did events in the Western Hemisphere, East Asia, and elsewhere begin to break out of that established frame. Thereafter, developments in far places loomed larger and larger, until today a study of assassination couched in the earlier terms would be unthinkable.

Yet the focus did not abruptly shift away from Europe. Concurrently with expansion, geographically defined, came a quantitative increase in violence. Since the larger, global process was one of accretion, not substitution, Europe retained its place as a center of attention, where older impulses and modes of action refused to fade away as newer ones gained prominence. Religious passions illustrate the point. Queen Isabella of Spain was attacked by one fanatical priest in 1852, and Archbishop Sibour of Paris stabbed to death in 1857 by another (who believed, wrongly, that his victim had endorsed the newly enunciated dogma of the Immaculate Conception). In 1874 an enraged German Catholic attempted to shoot Chancellor Bismarck during the so-called *Kulturkampf* between church and state.

Added to these recurrent seizures of piety, the cumulative effect of nationalist, egalitarian, anarchist, and other secular causes can be seen in assaults upon monarchs, their relatives, and their ministers occurring at a rate unmatched even during the Wars of Religion. Twenty-one rulers in Europe were singled out as targets over the course of the nineteenth century; and that tally takes no account of duplication of attempts aimed at certain individuals, including Louis Philippe of France, Alexander II of Russia, and England's Queen Victoria.

Leading figues of less than royal rank found themselves in, if anything, greater danger still. Among those who perished were Prime Minister Perceval in England (1812), President Capodistrias in Greece (1831), and Premier Stambulov in Bulgaria (1895). The first of those deaths showed that traditional types of assassins—in this case the unbalanced loner, embittered over some real or imagined injustice—remained much in evidence. Such a man was John Bellingham, the ruined merchant and fugitive from a Russian debtor's prison who shot Spencer Perceval in the lobby of the House of Commons. Such, too, were Carl Sand in Germany and, at the end of the century, the Italian terrorist Luigi Luccheni, who in 1898 lay in wait on a Swiss boat dock for the French duke of Orleans, only to slay Empress Elizabeth of Austria-Hungary when his intended victim failed to appear.

Luccheni, for all his raving, belonged to a significant new category: doctrinaire anarchists committed to shaking the government, any government, because of their conviction that all authority is pernicious.[1] Sometimes the target was an entire institution, as when Auguste Vaillant threw his bomb into a plenary session of the French Chamber of Deputies in 1893. More characteristic, however, was Sante Caserio's fatal stabbing of President Sadi Carnot the following year at a Lyon trade fair. So were the killing of the Spanish premier Canovas del Castillo in 1897 and the two attempts made upon Emperor William I of Germany in 1878.

Was the mounting frequency of assassination proof of more repressive action by governments, or less?[2] No simple response is possible, in part because exposure to twentieth-century despotism has tended to modify older portrayals of the nineteenth in this regard. Consider the matter of capital punishment. Death sentences carried out against political opponents were not only far fewer in number per decade than they have been since 1918 but also less flagrantly abused than during previous epidemics of bills of attainder, treason trials, and condemnations by revolutionary tribunals.

At the same time, imprisonment or transportation to places as distant as Siberia and French Guiana unquestionably became increasingly common features of political conflict. While even in Russia governmental reliance on hanging and shooting accounted for fewer deaths than popular stereotypes suggest, other measures adopted by tsarist officials, as well as by Austrian authorities in Italy, English forces in Ireland, and a succession of nervous French regimes, helped to create heroes of insurgency and in some instances future assassins. One result of all this was that dynasties long considered virtually immune to physical attack—Hapsburgs, Hohenzollerns, Spanish Bourbons—provided their share of targets for would-be killers, eager to prove that crowns offered no protection against vengeance.

What about the rest of the world? The comparatist seeking to encompass the past of thinly documented societies faces serious problems, as witness the case of sub-Saharan Africa. Until well into the twentieth century the history of that region depended heavily on oral tradition, unevenly augmented by the accounts of explorers, traders, and missionaries. The study of political violence involving Africans leads inescapably to that of tribal warfare, without which another major phenomenon, the slave trade, could not have flourished as it did for centuries. Yet precisely this connection with slavery long made tribal warfare a subject taken up reluctantly, if at all, by observers more concerned with the role of alien forces, Arabs first and then Europeans. As a result, only now are African scholars beginning to illuminate the history of their continent, seen in its own terms.

Any effort to bring China into the emerging picture raises problems that are different, but no less formidable. The notion that the Chinese have indulged relatively little in political murder, despite the "cultural revolution" and its undeniable violence, continues to enjoy wide acceptance in the West. This tendency on the part of foreigners to confuse an established tradition of not glorifying assassins with a nearly total absence of the act itself has given rise to an amazingly bland impression of political behavior in a vast segment of the globe.

Attempting to quantify the history of assassination in China on the basis of practically nonexistent statistical data may do credit to the perseverance of social scientists, but its results have been disheartening. The chapter on China in the staff report to the United States National Commission on the Causes and Prevention of Violence (the Eisenhower Commission of 1969) offers a case in point.[3] It contains a table showing that in the period 1600 to 1644 there were 38 recorded "deaths of eminent Chinese," only *one* of whom is identified as having been slain with malice aforethought: the Ming emperor, T'ai-ch'ang, "in all likelihood the victim of a successful Court plot to poison him."[4] This single case is converted into a rounded figure of 3 percent of the deaths from all causes and then, in a more refined tabulation, leads to the conclusion that 5 percent of Han Chinese but 0 percent of Manchus were assassinated!

The report is somewhat more helpful with regard to the nineteenth century, though here, too, one is forced to reflect on the limitations of quantitative analysis. A table covering the entire period from 1645 to 1912 cites 5 assassinations among 365 deaths of eminent Chinese during the 267 years in question—less than one assassination every 50 years. The total of 5 is then broken down to reveal one in each of the subperiods 1645–1660, 1661–1680, 1701–1720, 1721–1740, and 1900–1912, leading to the conclusion that the nineteenth century, despite some executions and suicides, was wholly free of political murder. Whatever statistical significance may be attached to it, this phenomenon is not explained in the commission's study.

Japan is the Asian country in which European patterns of political violence seem to have been most nearly matched, beginning early in the history of the island empire. Though confirmation of episodes recounted by chroniclers is often difficult, Japanese literature serves as a corroborative source, testifying to a cultural tradition rich in sanguinary tales and images. Modern renderings, including the motion picture "The 47 Ronin," based on a legend about a band of assassins who slew countless victims and finally themselves, follow in a line from the plots of the *Bun-raku* theater. They present, as anyone who has attended Bun-raku performances will recall, a picture of familial and factional struggle to which Merovingian kings and medieval Scottish clansmen might have shown the respect reserved by one group of experts for the work of another.

Political murder in modern Japan has required no Western model, only a Western challenge. In one stretch of twenty-five years xenophobic assassins slew Prime Minister Naosuke in 1860, Defense Minister Musajiro in 1869, Prime Minister Toshimichi in 1878, and Education Minister Arinori in 1885, all on grounds of their alleged surrender to European and American influences. Even this onslaught, like other clusters of events occurring around the world prior to 1900, provided only a faint adumbration of waves of homicide still to come.

In two other regions, the Ottoman Empire and the Americas, European influence was stronger and more direct. The Turkish case, however, was also marked by reminders of an older, Eastern past, not least in Istanbul's customary measures for safeguarding the throne. In 1807–1808 Sultan Mustapha IV, true to time-honored strictures of prudence, had first his own sons and then an ex-sultan, Selim III, murdered, with a minimum of ill feeling—on Mustapha's part at any rate. In 1876 the never fully explained death of the recently deposed sultan, Abdul-Aziz, in the prison of Topkapi was followed by the slaying of one of his old opponents, Foreign Minister Hussein Avni.

Across the Atlantic, successor republics of New Spain produced murders at a rate which increased as the century went on. Apart from the defeated Hapsburg Emperor Maximilian, shot by a Mexican firing squad in 1867, other notable casualties included Santos Guardiola, president of Honduras (1862); Garcia Moreno, president of Ecuador (1875); El Salvador's former President Menendez (1890); and President Barrios, dictator of Guatemala (1898). Because these are only scattered illustrations of a considerable phenomenon, one might be inclined to blame the Spanish colonial heritage, had not the record of political violence in the United States during the final third of the nineteenth century overshadowed that of Latin America for the period in question.

And yet the increasing frequency of political murder throughout much of the rest of the world is not sufficient cause to neglect the pivotal role of nineteenth-century Europe. On the contrary, far from abating its demands on our attention, European history continued to provide a larger number of sensational cases than could be discussed in a single chapter. Instead, it has been necessary to single out four among them, taking us to Germany on the morrow of Waterloo; France in the reign of Emperor Napoleon III; tsarist Russia; and Ireland under English rule.

The Kotzebue Killing

In 1971 West German Radio telecast a historical dramatization entitled "Sand," with a scenario by Tankred Dorst. Dorst's script, later published in book form, is of more than passing interest, constituting not only an artistic evocation of the past but also a document expressing urgent concerns of the author's own time.[5] Its subject was the murder in 1819 of a well-known German playwright and publicist, August von Kotzebue, by the student Carl Ludwig Sand. The incident, as few TV viewers needed to be reminded, was acutely relevant to contemporary revolt in the universities and political terrorism being practiced by, among others, youthful members of the Baader-Meinhof gang.

The television program did not attempt to portray much of the agitation over nationalist and liberal demands with which Sand was identified, and the scenario ends abruptly with the murder itself, followed by only a brief epilogue showing an enterprising innkeeper as he trudges toward Heidelberg, carrying home Sand's execution chair to serve as a conversation piece in his taproom. Nothing is shown of the investigation, the trial, or the political uses to which the crime was put almost as soon as it was committed. Finally, while the protagonist's motives and personality are examined with considerable care, his victim appears only as the unsuspecting object of what amounts to a ritual homicide. These self-imposed limitations obviously reflect Dorst's wish to achieve a degree of dramatic unity within his medium's severe constraints. For our purposes, however, it is important to know more about the context of the deed, including the personality and significance of the man whose life it took.[6]

Kotzebue was born in 1761, the son of an official at the ducal court of Weimar, where Goethe, according to his own later account, met the young man when the latter was about fourteen. Goethe's judgment of the playwright's frivolous, generally risqué comedies, written and staged in profusion over the ensuing decades, was that they revealed a limited, but within its limits genuine, talent.[7] That Kotzebue became a popular writer, widely known outside as well as inside Germany, there can be no doubt. In the France of 1800, his play *Die deutsche Kleinstädter* was assigned in schools as an introduction to small-town speech and manners across the Rhine. And Jane Austen in *Mansfield Park* (1814) has her characters perform an impromptu country-house reading of what Kotzebue had entitled *Das Kind der Liebe* (The Natural Son), only to have it emerge in English as *Lovers' Vows*.[8]

It was his Russian admirers, however, including the mercurial Paul I in the period just before the tsar's own assassination, who most deeply affected the dramatist's life. Not only was he summoned to Saint Petersburg and, after being briefly exiled to Siberia, recalled in order to take over the direction of the German theater, he also received an estate in Courland as a reward for his services. Finally, in 1815 he returned to the Russian service by accepting from Paul's son Alexander I the title of privy councilor and a regular salary for composing monthly reports on cultural and political developments in Germany.

It was as "a spy of the tsar" that Kotzebue first attracted the hostile notice of more nationalistically inclined compatriots. In actuality, his commission to send regular newsletters to Saint Petersburg required nothing more of him than was being done by numerous other citizens of the newly formed German Confederation who served foreign governments in what were essentially consular posts. That his enemies realized this, even while making use of his alleged "treason" in public attacks, becomes clear when one considers the real reason why patriotic students burned his books at patriotic rallies of the Deutsche Burschenschaften. When Kotzebue's *History of the Germans* was flung into the great bonfire terminating the Wartburg National Festival, which was held to commemorate the defeat of Napoleon's France at the same time that it celebrated the tercentenary of the Reformation in 1817, the loudest cheers sprang from those who felt injured by its author's having ridiculed *them* in print. That much seems clear from numerous contemporary accounts, including some of the testimony given at Sand's trial.

Early in 1819, shortly after he had moved with his family from Weimar to what he hoped would be the more congenial atmosphere of Mannheim in the grand duchy of Baden, Kotzebue wrote for his magazine an editorial about disturbances at Göttingen University in Hanover. It concluded:

> We cannot convince ourselves that so-called academic freedom deserves to be considered either noble or liberal. Today every father has to tremble if a young man is quick and intelligent; for all about lie waiting for him the coral reefs of student provincial leagues and Burschenschaften, gymnastic clubs, even the very lecture halls where mindless professors tell him he is called upon to reform his country—and no one offers the anxious father any assurance that his son's expensive time will be put to proper use. Would it not be reasonable and useful if provisions were made for the youth to do what he came for?[9]

Students yearning for a "national Germany," with or without a liberal constitution, might dismiss petty princes as buffoons and public officials as venal creatures of *Kleinstaaterei;* but Kotzebue's literate sarcasm was unbearable.

Carl Ludwig Sand was such a student, a twenty-four-year-old candidate enrolled in theology at Jena until the spring term came to an end on March 9, 1819, the day he set forth on his mission to Baden.[10] Born in Wunsiedel near Bayreuth, the child of a lower court magistrate in the Prussian service, he had grown up in an atmosphere of Protestant piety and reverence for learning. Having volunteered for service in the Bavarian army near the end of the War of Liberation, he returned to civilian life in 1815 as a student, matriculating first at Erlangen, then at Tübingen, and finally at Jena. Although he attended the Wartburg festival as a member of the Jena Burschenschaft, he withdrew from even this loosely organized political union in the first weeks of 1819. By that time he apparently had no need of others to bolster his belief that Kotzebue (with whose very name he was seemingly obsessed) was an immoral hedonist and a corrupter of the "German idea"—in short, a self-convicted traitor.

Sand's diary, numerous draft memoranda, and eventual testimony under oath indicate that by the last weeks of 1818 (the diary ends on December 31), he had made up his mind to carry out the indicated execution. He continued to attend classes and even to fraternize with other students, but more and more of his time was devoted to solitary pursuits, devising cabalistic inscriptions and preparing the two daggers he later said were intended for assassination and suicide. Upon leaving Jena that March day, dressed in "old German" garb and under a heavy pack, he walked the few miles to Erfurt. There he took the first of several stagecoaches which, with stops of several nights each in Frankfurt am Main and Darmstadt, brought him on the morning of March 23 to Mannheim and the house of the enemy.

After taking a room at an inn, Sand hurried around to the privy councilor's door and made an appointment for late that afternoon. He then ate lunch at the common table of his hostelry and even hired a guide to show him the local sights; but nothing could keep him from his interview with Kotzebue. When the latter's man servant answered the door at five o'clock he found a presentable young traveler who gave the name "Heinrichs, from Mietau," a town well-known to the privy councilor from his time in Baltic Russia and well-calculated to avoid the suspicion that the arrival of a student from radical Jena would have aroused. Sand had planned cunningly in another respect as well, guessing correctly that once admitted he would have no trouble approaching his host, who despite his acerbity in print was known to be affable in social settings. Hence it was easy for the assailant to draw one of the daggers from a sleeve, feint in the direction of Kotzebue's face (a tactic rehearsed in advance), and then, when the older man's arms jerked upward in self-defense, drive two powerful knife thrusts into his chest. One of them severed a major artery, bringing death in a matter of moments.

Just as this was taking place, the victim's small son chanced to enter the room and began to scream, so that servants, followed by a group of women who had been paying a call on Frau Kotzebue, rushed in almost immediately. Despite this influx of witnesses, Sand later recalled how he took time to stare into the dying man's eyes and to slash at himself ineffectually with the other weapon before running unhindered to the street. There constables took him into custody. As they did so, he stabbed himself again, this time more seriously.

The immediate aftermath of the Kotzebue murder was dominated by a determined search for evidence of a wider conspiracy Baden's state government set up an investigative commission, which retained jurisdiction over the criminal charges per se even after it was ordered a few months later to forward all information to the Federal Diet's own commission of inquiry at Mainz. In November the local panel laid its findings of fact before the Supreme Court of Baden in Karlsruhe, the regular tribunal which in due course found Sand guilty of murder combined with high treason and sentenced him to death. He was publicly beheaded outside Mannheim's Heidelberg Gate on May 20, 1820, fourteen months after the crime.[11]

Before and during his trial, the defendant had been a voluble witness, explaining at length his virtuous motives, citing heroic role models of tyrannicide in the past, becoming guarded and seemingly devious only with respect to what he had planned to do if he managed to escape following the murder.* At least twice he contradicted himself regarding advice and money given him by friends before he left Jena, but nothing elicited from him by interrogation supported the notion of a real plot and none was subsequently uncovered.

Despite the lack of evidence pointing to a conspiracy, the states of the German Confederation moved with speed and unprecedented harshness against the exercise of academic freedom in political affairs. The Carlsbad Decrees, drafted by Prince Metternich in July 1819 and ratified by the Federal Diet at Frankfurt that September, not only established the investigating commission already mentioned but also encouraged member governments to increase their censorship of allegedly seditious expression of opinion and to provide for dismissal, even criminal prosecution of university teachers charged with propagating sedition. The one professor seriously implicated in Sand's crime, Carl Follen of Jena (the Baden commission possessed evidence that he had supplied his former student with travel money), had already fled the country to the United States, where he devoted the remaining

---

* Although Sand repeatedly compared himself with William Tell and Charlotte Corday, Brutus' name is hardly mentioned in his testimony—a curious fact, given the German secondary schools' heavy emphasis on classical history and literature. As for his thoughts of surviving the assassination of Kotzebue, Sand's self-inflicted wounds with the second dagger and his frequent references to martyrdom conflicted sharply with hints of an escape route contained in some of his letters, as well as with the four gold coins found sewn into the lining of his overcoat.

twenty years of his life to preaching in various churches, giving instruction in German at Harvard, and initiating the annual decoration of an outdoor Christmas tree on Cambridge Common.

Considering this official backlash, unaccompanied by any surge of revolutionary *élan* in Biedermeier Germany, the assassination of Kotzebue might appear to have been just one more example of counterproductive histrionics. Nevertheless, Sand's undertaking remains an uncommonly emphatic demonstration of political romanticism, or what a German writer in the 1920s defined as "subjectivized occasionalism."[12] The brooding Jena student, moved by the lectures of such teachers as Follen and by memories of book-burning at the Wartburg, sought and found his occasion for self-fulfillment in the wielding of a knife at Mannheim. In so doing, he found as well some vocal admirers not only in his own country but also abroad, especially in England, where emotional sympathy for foreign patriots—German, Greek, Polish, Italian, though generally not Irish—was just embarking on its erratic course. As early as August 1819, after the Kotzebue murder but before its perpetrator had come to trial, an anonymous *Memoir of Charles Louis Sand* appeared in London, accompanied by a *Defence of the German Universities.*[13] Beneath the volume's frontispiece, an idealized portrait of the assassin, appears the following from *King Lear:*

> The tempest of my mind
> Doth from my senses take all feeling else,
> Save what beats there.

Orsini in Paris, 1858

The incidents that serve best to connect Revolutionary with later manifestations of political homicide in France were clustered, as one would expect, around the figure of the first Napoleon, a nexus between past and future in this regard as in so many others. Although he was not toppled from power by an assassin's hand, he was twice the intended victim of serious attempts occurring within the space of a single decade.

The first, which took place on December 24, 1800, in a street between the Louvre and the Opera, involved a bomb explosion that took the lives of thirteen passersby. The minister of police, Joseph Fouché, who had been on the trail of earlier plots, immediately—and, as it turned out, correctly—suspected an inept circle of royalist diehards. The First Consul, on the other hand, seized the opportunity to launch an attack upon another set of old enemies, survivors of the radical Left. Some 130 of these, called by Bonaparte "the general staff of the Jacobins," were tried, convicted, and deported to the French penal colony in Guiana. Even when Fouché's investigation produced unblinkable evidence against the real culprits, all but one of whom were apprehended and guillotined, his implacable master pardoned none of the deported Jacobins, of whom he had said: "We banish these men for the massacres of September, for 31 May, for Prairial, for the conspiracy of Babeuf, for all they have done and all they still might do."[14]

Once crowned Emperor of the French in 1804, Napoleon often resorted to the exemplary execution of rebels in occupied lands, ranging from Madrid's unnumbered dissidents to the Tyrolean Andreas Hofer and the bookseller Palm in Nuremberg. As for threats to his life, however, a combination of immense vanity and understandable distaste for the very thought of assassination kept him from publicizing the issue. The military execution of an eighteen-year-old Austrian subject, Friedrich Staps, for having tried to stab the Corsican conqueror at Vienna in 1809 was not announced until some years later. The ease with which this pious son of a Lutheran minister had introduced a paper-wrapped knife into Schönbrunn palace, where Napoleon was residing after his victory on the battlefield of Wagram, nevertheless raised unanswered questions about other possible close calls along the imperial way.[15]

Nevertheless, not Napoleon I but his nephew, Louis Napoleon, was destined to personify, in the role of intended victim, a new world of motives and methods for committing political homicide. Elected president of the Second Republic in 1848, proclaimed emperor following a carefully orchestrated coup d'état in 1851, married to a Spanish beauty, Eugénie de Montijo, he took his place at the center of one of modern history's most startling dramas of assassination.

On the evening of January 14, 1858, Paris gave few indications of lingering regret over the murder of Archbishop Sibour the previous year.[16] There appeared to be little cause for concern in the *grand monde* over anything weightier than the winter "season" of galas, gossip, and theatrical performances, both on and off stage. The famous Opera, in its old building a short distance east of the present location, was decked out with festoons and additional lighting in honor of the retirement of the veteran baritone Eugène Massol. The night was unseasonably mild and a large crowd had assembled in the street to watch celebrities arrive. Napoleon III and his empress, the former's hesitations overcome by Eugénie's insistence, had decided to attend. Their carriage, escorted by thirty horsemen of the Garde de Paris, was no more than fashionably late; when it came clattering up to the entrance the orchestra had just begun the program with selections from Rossini's *William Tell*.[17]

The emperor's previous uneasiness might have increased had reports in the hands of subordinate officials been passed along more promptly to those responsible for his safety. Earlier that evening police agents on the lookout for Giuseppe-Andrea Pieri, a known "Mazzinian," as Italian revolutionaries were commonly known, had found him loitering not far from the Opera in the Rue Le Peletier, carrying on his person a knife, a revolver, and a small bomb of unfamiliar design. Yet nothing was done to alert the prefect of police, Giuseppe Maria Piétri, who has having dinner at a cabinet minister's home; and no plainclothesmen from the Sûreté had been added to the uniformed personnel routinely assigned to any public appearance of the imperial couple.

As the state carriage was rolling to a stop, three bombs were thrown in its direction, exploding at approximately ten-second intervals. Napoleon III, his nose grazed by a fragment, and the empress, whose left eye was slightly cut, were quickly attended to in the foyer and then escorted to their box. The audience, some of whose members had heard the explosions outside, registered its relief with loud applause. Soon thereafter, however, Prefect Piétri, belatedly summoned from his dinner party, was obliged to announce that 156 victims of the attack, 42 of them police officers or mounted guardsmen, lay injured in the street; 8 were to die of their wounds.

The task of reconstructing the crime, rumors of an immense conspiracy including official complicity notwithstanding, proved to be almost ludicrously easy. Pieri, already in custody but now reinterrogated with greater intensity, gave his address in Paris as a hotel in Montmartre and named a certain "Da Silva" as his roommate. The latter, arrested at the hotel, admitted that his real name was Carlo di Rudio, that he was a Venetian driven to illegal activity by his need for money, and that he had thrown one of the bombs. Another participant, Anthony Gomez, was picked up in a restaurant near the Opera, having attracted attention by babbling wildly in a heavy Neapolitan accent. This simpleminded hireling claimed to be the valet of an "English gentleman" named Thomas Allsop, presently residing in the Rue Monthabor. It was there that a team of detectives found the plot's ringleader—not an Englishman, but a well-known Italian patriot, Felice Orsini—lying in bed and weak from wounds received from the grenade he had hurled at the emperor's carriage.

The bombs, two of which were recovered unexploded (one when Pieri was arrested before the event, the other found undetonated at the scene of the crime), proved to be important in their own right. For one thing, they employed fulminate of mercury, a recent addition to the arsenal of war and terrorism. For another, their trail led back to previously unidentified figures in the plot. Investigation revealed that the grenades had been produced in England by a Birmingham metal expert, who explained to British authorities that the novel weapons had been ordered from him by the real Thomas Allsop, ostensibly for governmental use. Allsop, whose name Orsini had borrowed while hiding in France, was a sixty-year-old barrister and former Owenite; but by the 1850s he had passed from involvement in Chartist agitation to a belief in anarchism. Although acquainted with Orsini, whom he had met in Nice some years before, Allsop was linked to the assassination attempt through Dr. Simon Bernard, a French republican living in London. Another dissident clearly implicated was J. D. P. Hodge, a friend of both Bernard and Allsop. Together they constituted the "English wing" of the conspiracy.

The bombs procured in Birmingham had been smuggled to Paris by way of Brussels, where the swashbuckling Pieri had been sent from France to fetch them. While there, he moved in with a woman to whom he boasted of a grand action in the offing. She appears to have been a police spy, for the French minister in Belgium was soon able to send the warning which, though vague, led to Pieri's capture on the evening of the attempt. Thus, the weapons played an important part, if not in preventing the attack at least in building the case against its perpetrators.

The man at the center of the effort could lay claim to a long record of patriotic agitation, which had brought him considerable fame as an author and lecturer. Orsini, son of a Napoleonic veteran, was born in 1819, at Forli in the Romagna. He grew up with a loathing for local despots and Hapsburg overlords matched by his enthusiasm for the national cause, the *còsa italiana*. Though naturally attracted to revolutionaries as diverse as Buonarroti, Bakunin, and Mazzini, the young patriot first entered the political limelight in the role of what, with allowance made for the circumstances, could be called a champion of law and order. This was during the revolution of 1848–49, when his home district elected him a delegate to the assembly of the short-lived Roman Republic following Pope Pius IX's flight to Naples. In the spring of 1849 the deputy from Forli was named to restore order in Ancona, where local revolutionists were running amok. Vestiges of Orsini's initial distrust of terrorists and terrorism can still be found in his subsequent memoirs:

> During the latter years of the Pontificate of Gregory XVI, and the first years of Pius IX, political homicides multiplied fearfully; but as we always find it to be the case, when crime becomes habitual, and the passions have full latitude, many innocent persons were destroyed to gratify private hatred, or interest; persons who did not interfere in the least in political affairs.[18]

The irony inherent in this passage arises from the fact that had the bombs of January 1858 not left eight "innocent persons" dead in Paris, the sometime pacifier of Ancona might well have escaped the guillotine.

In Rome, Mazzinian eloquence and Garibaldian bravura had proved no match for papal diplomacy and French power. France's new president, Louis Napoleon Bonaparte, decided he must assuage Catholic opinion at home by sending a military force to restore Pius IX to power, so on July 3,

1849, French soldiers occupied the Eternal City. Garibaldi marched his troops off to the south; Mazzini roamed through the streets a while longer, unmolested but powerless; and Felice Orsini headed into the confused world of Austrian administrative provinces and puppet states, which, with the patrimony of the House of Savoy, made up northern Italy. With him he took a bitter sense of having seen his cause betrayed by the new Napoleon and a growing conviction that hope for Italian independence lay only in dramatic violence.

The fugitive's personal and political adventures in the years that followed are profusely, if not always lucidly recounted in his published works, which for a variety of reasons purposely left vague many chronological and operational details. Fortunately other sources exist including the memoirs of the Russian émigré Alexander Herzen, which help to fill in the story.[19] The tall, handsome Orsini, justifying himself with the insistence that his wife, a stunning but reportedly giddy Florentine, was unfaithful during her husband's long absences, made the most of his own attractiveness to women as he moved with apparent ease through the radical-chic world of Europe's bored but easily stimulated expatriates.

The Italian adventurer, basing himself first in Genoa, for a time sold illegal Mazzinian national bonds, with the help of an Englishwoman, Matilda Ashurst Biggs, who represented her family of four redoubtable sisters by imitating Georges Sand as closely as possible, including smoking cigars. He next took part in a revolutionary fiasco, an unsuccessful invasion of Modena and the Papal States by steamboat, using as port of embarkation Shelley's beloved La Spezia. During the early 1850s Orsini became acquainted in Nice with Herzen, with the German poet and romantic revolutionary Georg Herwegh, and, most important, with the latter's wife. Emma Herwegh, a wealthy heiress from Berlin, was to be for several years his most reliable source of help in adversity.

And help he would need. Late in 1854, having accepted Michael Bakunin's advice that he try to link Italian with other, especially Hungarian insurrectionary movements, Orsini was arrested by the Austrian secret police at Hermannstadt (Sibiu) in Transylvania, transported back to Italy, and, at Mantua, sentenced to death for high treason. The execution, fortunately for the condemned man, was delayed by bureaucratic confusion, and in the spring of 1856, with help sent by his devoted Emma in the form of smuggled saw blades and money, he managed to escape from the forbidding old prison of San Giorgio.

Orsini's successful flight led him first to the Herweghs' residence in Zurich, and thence in late May to England. There, before the year was out, appeared in translation the story of his imprisonment and escape—in a red, white, and green cover featuring the Mazzinian flag and the legend "Óra e sempre," Now and forever.[20] In 1857 a first volume of his memoirs was also published in English. By that time their author, between lecture tours, was apparently seriously contemplating the act that would serve as a climax to his career.

French indignation over his and his comrades' deed was vehement enough to produce an international crisis. Conservative groups denounced Italy, especially the Piedmontese-Sardinian kingdom of Victor Emmanuel and Cavour, as an intolerable source of revolutionary contagion. For many of those Frenchmen, and for others as well, a centuries-old hostility encouraged the belief that across the Channel lay, to use King Louis XVIII's words, "not merely the consoler of the distressed but also the refuge of sinners."[21] Both reactions troubled Napoleon III, who prided himself on the ability to maintain good relations with London and Turin alike. Count Cavour obligingly sent on behalf of Piedmont a message welcomed in Paris for the firmness with which it denounced as misguided the excesses of Italian patriots. England's response was quite different.

Lord Palmerston, to be sure, sought earnestly to prevent a rupture in relations between Her Majesty's government and that of the French Empire. Unable under British law to grant the latter's urgent request for the deportation of all refugees suspected of intriguing against Napoleon, the prime minister tried instead to rush through Parliament a Conspiracy Bill which would have greatly restricted the future activities of émigré enemies of foreign regimes. On his instructions Scotland Yard followed the trail of Orsini's bombs from Birmingham to the coast, arrested Dr. Bernard, the republican Frenchman fromn Toulouse, and launched a full-scale search for his English coconspirators, Allsop and Hodge. In late February, however, the House of Commons responded to the outburst of Anglophobia in France by voting down the Conspiracy Bill and thus forcing Palmerston to resign with his entire cabinet. This startling turn of events did not have a lasting effect within the United Kingdom, for Palmerston was back with his second ministry in only a few months. Nevertheless, it marked one of the low points in nineteenth-century relations between Paris and London.

Parliament's rejection of the Conspiracy Bill constituted refusal to extradite either Bernard or Allsop. Hodge had fled to Turin, whence the Sardinian government was willing enough to expel him, but could not turn him over to the French without his own government's consent—and that was not forthcoming. What the imperial regime in Paris could and did do, following the example set by the first Napoleon in 1800, was to strike at all anti-Bonapartist elements within its reach. This applied especially to its enemies on the Left. Under the General Security Law promulgated in February 1858 any dissident imprisoned, transported, or exiled between 1848 and 1851, but subsequently released or allowed to return to France, was now declared liable to resentencing upon proof of renewed political activity.

If this law had been the only official reaction to Orsini's deed and to

England's uncooperative stance, the aftermath might be classified merely as further proof that an assassination attempt, regardless of the outcome, can be prohibitively costly to the very interests it was supposed to benefit. But the sequel was so complicated that the bombs of Orsini have come to symbolize instead one of history's rare examples of a conspiracy to commit political murder that achieved at least some of its stated ends. To do so, it had to fail. For the emperor who had been spared appeared to be haunted by remorse over having abandoned the pro-Italian sentiments of his youth. In addition, he was upset both by Great Britain's denunciations of his government and by the reactionary swing in that government's domestic policies. The following year Louis Napoleon took France into a war against Austria in support of Piedmont (he had met secretly with Cavour in July 1858, a few months after the assassination attempt). After some of the bloodiest fighting to take place in Europe between Waterloo and the First World War, the Kingdom of Italy was proclaimed in 1861. Meanwhile the emperor had striven to achieve, if not a lasting rapprochement with England, at least the unprecedented Anglo-French commercial treaty of 1860. During the same brief period he also launched the program of internal reform destined to confer on the final decade of Bonapartist rule in France the title of "the Liberal Empire."

Unfortunately for the adventurer whose grandiose assassination attempt had caused its intended victim to make these major changes in policy, he did not live to rejoice in the victories of Magenta and Solferino. The trial of the four defendants, beginning on February 15, 1858, in Paris, aroused intense excitement and a crush of would-be onlookers much larger than the courtroom could accommodate. Most of the sympathy expressed by the audience was reserved for the ringleader, with his dark good looks and elegant black costume. Orsini also possessed a seeming asset in the person of his defense attorney, the most celebrated French orator of the day, Jules Favre. Favre was at a critical point in his own career, being viewed with suspicion from both the Right and the Left as a self-styled Liberal in 1848–49 who had since accepted favors from the Empire. He persisted, nevertheless, in calling himself a man of the opposition and would shortly win election as such to the Corps Législatif. Meanwhile, the public expected to be entertained.

Attorneys appointed to represent the other three prisoners offered little by way of defense except pleas of desperate poverty in Rudio's and Gomez's behalf, patriotism and his arrest before the fact in Pieri's. Efforts to exculpate their leader, on the other hand, promised to be more elaborate. Admirers in England had sent money for legal expenses and showered Favre with suggested strategies, ranging from a flat denial of involvement to a diversionary verbal attack on Pope Pius IX. Orsini freely admitted that no later than the previous October, following consultation with Dr. Bernard, he had resolved to kill Napoleon III, for Italy's sake and that of a European-wide revolution. At his first opportunity to speak from the dock, he put the matter quite succinctly: "I acted as Brutus did. [The emperor] killed my country; I decided to kill him."[22]

Favre agreed that there was no point in contesting the charges. In a long oration generally conceded to be among his most brilliant, he sounded at times like anything but a defense attorney, roundly condemning the dedication of certain "barbaric sects ... to assassination in the name of patriotism." Jettisoning the most common rationalization of all politically motivated crimes, he denied the right of anyone to say: "If I committed a murder, it was because society was faulty in construction."[23] What he claimed in extenuation of Orsini's act—and here he read from a letter sent by the accused to Napoleon III and read to the court with the latter's express consent—was the love for Italy shared by the assassin and the emperor: "Yes, gentlemen of the jury, Orsini ... now bows down; but he ignores the fact that he is going to die. From the edge of the grave he addressed this solemn request to the man for whom he feels no personal hatred, to the man who has been his country's enemy, but who can be its savior."[24]

This glowing tribute to pure patriotism having done more for the barrister's fame than for his client's personal future, the trial consumed less than two days. On February 26, after deliberating only about two hours, the jury found all four defendants guilty of parricide (not treason, since none was a French national). Half an hour later, amid groans from the visitors' gallery, the panel of judges pronounced sentence. Gomez, in view of his demonstrated mental incapacity, was given life at hard labor, the other three, death by decapitation.

Napoleon III expressed an inclination toward clemency, remarking, with reference to another would-be assassin executed in 1855, "Orsini is not a common murderer like Pianori. He is a man and has my respect."[25] The emperor's ministers, however, were implacable; despite the courtroom lamentations of a sympathetic minority, public opinion seemed overwhelmingly opposed to forgiving the deaths of the eight innocent bystanders outside the Opera. Only one penalty was altered, Rudio's death sentence being commuted at the last moment to transportation for life. After three years' confinement in French Guiana, he escaped to the United States, where he earned the rank of major in the Union army during the Civil War, then migrated to California where he died in 1913. Gomez served much longer in the penal colony but survived to spend his last years back in Naples. Orsini and Pieri, meanwhile, had long since perished. Early on the morning of March 13, 1858, they were guillotined before a huge crowd surrounding the Place de la Roquette in Paris. Pieri went first, singing a Girondin anthem from 1791, Orsini after him, shouting "Viva l'Italia! Viva la Francia!"[26]

The Tsar and "The People's Will"

Like most other famous assassinations, the murder of Alexander II on a snowy Sunday afternoon in Saint Petersburg has found its place in myriad works of history, political theory, and ethical discourse.[27] The year was 1881. The weapons were two hand grenades manufactured by filling glass tubes with nitroglycerin, the second of which killed both the victim and his slayer when it exploded practically at their feet. Alexander's death was intended to launch a new era of freedom for Russia's people, brought about by the overthrow of Romanov tyranny. Instead, it signaled the beginning of the end for a proudly enunciated but short-lived version of popular revolt.

The drama contained elements reminiscent of the past, combined with others that foreshadowed episodes still to occur in the course of the ensuing century. Increasingly powerful weaponry, admiration for elaborate statements explaining Orsini-like deeds, oscillation between concessions and repression on the government's part, and even the role of university students place the Russian episode squarely within a familiar modern European pattern. Yet Russia a hundred years ago was also idiosyncratic in ways too important to be overlooked. The tsar was not a Hapsburg or Bourbon or Hanoverian, exercising power based on centuries of haggling over feudal contracts and parliamentary claims. He was a Romanov, ruling by right of his ancestors' conquests, superimposed upon the Tartars' Asiatic despotism. The "father of his subjects" was also the supreme autocrat commanding the military, legal, and social forces designed to keep those subjects in their place.

It was the immense mass of the peasantry, generally submissive but capable at certain times and places of exploding into revolt, to which radical critics of the regime looked for support, particularly following the Emancipation Edict of 1861. In the eyes of such critics, the peasantry might have been freed in a legal sense by Alexander's proclamation, but former serfs remained landless and hence, in socioeconomic terms, without hope for any real improvement in their lives. This preoccupation with the agricultural sector placed an indigenous stamp upon Russian revolutionary doctrine in the second half of the nineteenth century. To call all the spokesmen of insurgency "nihilists" would be unfair to many of them. Even the term "anarchists," though no doubt applicable to a large proportion, attaches too much weight to the rebels' lack of any coherent theory of government, at the expense of accurately appraising their most widely shared beliefs. "Populism" expresses most cogently their emotional attachments, their yearning for mass support, and their ultimate failure to grasp the organizational and tactical realities of a changing political scene.

Together with the roles of the autocracy and the peasant problem, that of an official church quite different from either Roman Catholicism or Protestantism—in that it supplied not even occasional or local support to civil resistance—completes the trio of distinctively Russian ingredients of the crisis at the end of Alexander II's quarter-century-long reign. The Orthodox establishment could, and did, voice opposition to governmental measures perceived by its leadership as objectionable from the hierarchy's own point of view. That much it shared with Western Christian churches, as well as with Moslem and other clergies throughout history. Nevertheless, it would be difficult to name any Russian revolutionaries of the past hundred years or more who have turned to organized religion for either sustenance or inspiration.

The political setting for Alexander's assassination had been created by a historical progression of events extending at least as far back in time as the abortive Decembrist uprising of 1825. It included the hopes and disillusionment surrounding the end of legal serfdom, the government's erratic conduct of foreign affairs from the Crimean War to the Congress of Berlin in 1878, the tsar's seeming conversion to repressive measures, and, in the months immediately preceding his death a new series of conciliatory, reformist moves by the autocracy. The historical backdrop for the opposition featured the actions, ideas, and personalities of spokesmen for sharply differing revolutionary causes. Gaps and inconsistencies were integral parts of that legacy; but nobody could complain that it lacked richness born of variation.

Among the foreign prophets had been the "Jacobin socialists," Babeuf, Blanqui, and the tireless Italian apostle of revolution, Buonarroti, enthusiastically interpreted by Russian anarchists such as Michael Bakunin and the gentler Prince Kropotkin.[28] By midcentury, a more intellectual strain of Western influence, that of Saint-Simon, Fourier, and Hegel among others, was flowing eastward, thanks to Alexander Herzen. This sometime enthusiast for the Decembrists in Russia, as well as for French, Polish, and other rebels beginning in 1830, lived the life of a well-to-do émigré until his death at Paris in 1870. Long before then, however, he had become suspicious of those he called the "matadors of rhetoric." To Orsini's dreams Herzen brought a mixture of amused interest in the man and grave doubts concerning his common sense; but the increasingly acidulous tone in which he commented on the activities of Bakunin, Herwegh, and other fellow exiles carried with it none of the quizzical respect he conceded the Italian.[29] Yet the wealthy sojourner in France, Switzerland, and England continued for as long as he lived to endow Russian political criticism with a breadth of knowledge and an ironic gift wholly lacking in such ponderous works as Chernychevsky's didactic novel *What Is To Be Done?* (1863).[30]

At the opposite pole from Herzen's contribution was that of S. J. Nechaev (1847–1882). To his collaboration with Bakunin in the writing of nihilism's most extreme statement, the *Revolutionary Catechism* of 1869, the former factory employee and student at Saint Petersburg University temporarily residing in Switzerland brought a tone clearly set by the pamphlet's opening passage: "The revolutionary is a lone [i.e., doomed] man; he has no interests of his own, no cause of his own, no feelings, no habits, no belongings; he does not even have a name. Everything in him is absorbed by a single, exclusive interest, a single thought, a single passion—the revolution."[31] As he pointed out a few pages later: "We are guided by hatred for all who are not the people . . . We have an entirely negative plan, which no one can modify: utter destruction."[32]

Whatever his appeal to certain connoisseurs of expanded consciousness, when judged by any other standard Nechaev imposes himself as a thoroughly repugnant figure, an obsessive egotist who eventually murdered one of his own followers. The disgust he inspired in Herzen, whom he met in the course of his first trip West, can easily be imagined; and even for Bakunin, who had at first described him ecstatically in a letter to a friend— "they are magnificent, these young fanatics, believers without God, heroes without rhetoric!"—disillusionment was not long in coming.[33]

Returning to Russia in the late summer of 1869, Nechaev applied himself to organizing a Central Revolutionary Committee, whose center was the University of Moscow's strategically well-situated School of Agriculture, but whose size and importance were greatly exaggerated by its founder. Within less than three months he concluded that a student member named Ivanov would have to be executed for insubordination. When the mutilated corpse was found, all the executioners were quickly apprehended save Nechaev, who had fled to Switzerland once more. He was extradited in 1872 on evidence provided by his erstwhile henchmen, convicted of complicity in Ivanov's death, and sentenced to imprisonment for life in Saint Petersburg's Peter and Paul Fortress. Despite a momentary return to public notice on account of his published correspondence with the assassins of 1881, little notice seems to have been taken of his death in the old prison a short time later. Had not Dostoyevsky immortalized him as the murderer Verhovensky in *The Possessed,* it is unlikely that he would still be so widely remembered as the self-styled "apostle of destruction."

By the winter of 1880–81, developments on both sides of the figurative barricades seem to have been moving toward a climax. As viewed by the tsar and some of his chief advisers, neither the reform projects of the reign's first half—emancipation of the serfs, liberalization of the regime in Poland, moves toward greater local self-administration, improvement in court procedures, opening of the universities to numbers of poor students previously excluded, permission for women to study abroad—nor the tougher stand against political agitation in the 1870s had brought the domestic peace and public affection for which Alexander II yearned. He had remained throughout a despot, benevolent in his impulses but condemned to failure by the form of rule he had inherited no less than by the growing stridency of social-democratic demands. At last, in response to an unsuccessful attempt on the life of Alexander's new interior minister, General Count Loris-Melikov, in February 1880, the imperial regime decided to soften the policies of recent years and give the tactics of "amelioration" (as imperial spokesmen called them) a further chance.

On the morning of March 13, 1881, the tsar discussed at length with Loris-Melikov the minister's plan to call an assembly of notables for the purpose of discussing drafts of proposed legislation. The two men also reviewed recent intelligence reports of terrorist activities and considered the wisdom of canceling Alexander's customary Sunday afternoon drive to a military review at the cavalry stables. After some hesitation the tsar decided to go ahead with what was to be his final journey.

Those who killed him belonged to the most extreme faction within the so-called *Narodnaya Volya* (People's Will), an offshoot of the society called Land and Freedom. Since the summer of 1879, when in a secret conclave at Voronezh the older body had split over tactics, the People's Will had clung to a policy of regicide.[34] The failure of the populists' missionary effort to "go among the peasants" and of uncoordinated assassination attempts, beginning in 1878 with Vera Zasulich's wounding of the Saint Petersburg police prefect, demanded in the militants' view a more ambitious stroke against tyranny. Zasulich, the educated daughter of a wealthy family and an admirer of Nechaev, had been acquitted by a tearful jury amid tributes to the new Corday.[35] But neither her gesture nor the killings of General Mesentsov at Saint Petersburg later the same year and of General Kropotkin at Kharkov in 1879 had produced anything but increased governmental pressure on the rebels.

How intensive and widespread during this period was the violence, whether revolutionary or repressive? Certainly not so extreme as references to "waves of revolutionary terror" or "massive police brutality" seem to imply. Today's reader may be surprised by the restraint on both sides—one concerned over possible harm to innocent victims, the other by no means indifferent to the demands of due process. The incidence of assassination attempts did increase sharply from 1878 onward (in a country that had known very few such occurrences prior to that year); and the number of arrests and trials rose proportionately. Yet a tabulation produced by Narodnaya Volya itself and published by its sympathizers in Geneva indicates that the last four years of Alexander II's reign witnessed only 22 executions for "political" crimes, as defined by the insurgents, and some 160 sentences of forced labor, generally served in Siberian camps.[36] Use of the term "only" is not intended to minimize individual suffering but simply to contrast its scale with that of the French Terror in the 1790s, not to mention the sweeping purges effected by twentieth-century regimes including those of Lenin, Stalin, and Hitler.

To the young activists of the People's Will, comparisons with the past were irrelevant. For them the emperor and his minions represented a tyranny whose effects no statistical evidence could alter. In fairness to the conspirators, it must be said that very few of them shared Nechaev's sadistic fantasies. The memoirs of Vera Figner, who spent a score of years in prison before being released, still a relatively young woman, in 1904, are far more reliable that the *Revolutionary Catechism* with respect to the minds and values of her fellow revolutionaries.[37] Figner's recollections express anguish over the plight of the peasantry, disgust with the Russian government's backwardness judged by liberal-constitutional standards, and what appears to have been an almost total lack of any sense of proportion or probability. A scornful ignorance of history in particular served as a shield to fend off the faintest suggestion that there might conceivably be regimes even worse than an aging autocracy.

The fatal attack on the tsar was the tenth in a series, the last seven of which had been planned by Narodnaya Volya. Prior to that group's arrival on the political scene, Alexander had survived attempts by the nihilist Karakasov in 1866, by a Polish patriot named Berezowski at the Paris Exposition of 1867, and by a Russian schoolteacher, Alexander Solovyov, in the park of the Winter Palace in 1879. Later that year, at its Voronezh conference, the People's Will passed upon Alexander II a solemn sentence of death. This was done, Vera Figner points out, not because the membership saw in him an especially wicked man, but for two quite different reasons. One was that his mild personality and efforts at reform threatened to blunt the edge of radical demands; the other, that precisely because the tsar was a comparatively inoffensive ruler, his dying would help to dramatize the impersonal nature of the group's struggle against an entire political regime and the social order on which it rested.

Having embraced that logic, the members proceeded to launch a half-dozen assassination attempts over the course of the ensuing eighteen months. The first five revealed a common pattern: tunneling in order to plant subterranean explosive charges under what was expected to be the route of a train bearing the emperor. Failure twice resulted from changes in railroad routes, in two other attempts from inability to detonate the bombs (the second because an accomplice failed to show up on time with a vital part), and in the fifth from unexpected precautions taken by the tsar's bodyguards (who had changed the order of cars in the train before the blast went off, scattering across the countryside outside Moscow a shipment of preserved fruit from the imperial orchards in the Crimea).

By the winter of 1880–81, the plotters, especially the relatively mature Andrei Zhelyabov and Sophia Perovskaya, a child of privilege become a terrorist as determined as she was handsome, had concluded that blowing up trains would not achieve their purpose. They had already made one serious—and, as it turned out, tragic—attempt to kill the tsar by other means. In February 1880, at Saint Petersburg's Winter Palace, a charge of over one hundred pounds of dynamite, set in place and detonated by Stephen Khalturin, a member of Narodnaya Volya employed as a carpenter in the imperial residence, exploded in the cellar two floors below the state dining room and directly beneath an intervening guardroom. The emperor's party had not yet arrived at the banquet table when the blast occurred, but there were eleven deaths among off-duty guardsmen and other occupants of the building. Khalturin, who with Zhelyabov had watched the event from the iron fence surrounding the grounds, was arrested and executed soon thereafter, his fellow spectator having escaped capture for the time being.

When the morning of March 13, 1881, dawned over the capital, the dogged agents of the People's Will were set to act again. Still hoping to succeed through the use of buried explosives, they had dug yet another tunnel at a point the tsar would cross if his small procession followed the Nevsky Prospect. This time, however, they were prepared to use hand bombs should the route be altered. Security officials did in fact change course, so that the sleighs and Cossack cavalry escort safely avoided the dynamite charge, emerging instead onto a street that ran alongside the Catherine Canal. From the other side of the waterway Sophia Perovskaya signaled the two reserve "throwers." The nitroglycerin grenade of nineteen-year-old Nikolai Rysakov damaged the imperial sleigh, injuring only some passersby and one of the mounted Cossacks. But when Alexander climbed from his vehicle to survey the damage, he exposed himself to another bomb thrown directly at his feet by Ignaty Grinevitsky, a young nobleman enrolled as a student at the Technical Institute. Both men were fatally wounded, the tsar dying within an hour at the Winter Palace, to which he had been carried by his stunned retainers.

Although the similar attack by Orsini on Napoleon III had produced at least a partial victory, however unforeseen, for the cause of the would-be assassin, the killing of Alexander II, whatever momentary jubilation it elicited from portions of the Russian intelligentsia at home and abroad, qualifies as one of the most abysmal failures in the history of political homicide. Its immediate toll can be dismissed as no worse than the conspirators had expected. Six of the plot's chief architects were tried and sentenced by a military court. Five of them, including Perovskaya and Zhelyabov were hanged on April 15 in Semyonov Square before a crowd which, according to some estimates, numbered as many as 80,000 spectators. Gesia Gelfman, the only other woman brought to trial, was spared the noose because she was pregnant; but her baby died in a foundling home soon after its birth, and the mother succumbed in prison the following winter. The sixth execution was that of an ex-naval officer, Sukhanov, shot by a firing squad in 1882. Other suspects, including Vera Figner, served time in cells and labor camps following later arrest but lived to win eventual release by virtue of imperial clemency.

These trials and the return to autocratic repression under Alexander III, who began his reign by dismissing Loris-Melikov, constituted the official response to the bloodshed by the Catherine Canal. Far more important in a broader historical sense was the collapse of nineteenth-century Russian populism as an organized revolutionary movement. The Italian scholar Franco Venturi therefore chose to conclude his study of that movement with a chapter on Alexander's death. In its aftermath both the utopianism of Chernyshevsky and the nihilism of Nechaev gave way to Marxian analysis, substituting for primarily agrarian concerns the socialist politics of an industrial age. Young Nikolai Lenin mourned an older brother executed in 1888 on charges of plotting to kill Alexander III. But neither Lenin nor the comrades he led to power in 1917 sought to imitate the Populists (though for a time his unsuccessful rivals, the Social Revolutionaries, did so). To Bolsheviks the People's Will offered only a source of useful memories, replete with martyred heroes and heroines.[38]

Phoenix Park

Between the killing of Tsar Alexander and Europe's next major assassination, not much more than a year elapsed. In physical terms, however, the distance separating the events—one in Saint Petersburg, the other in Dublin—was far greater. So was the difference between their settings: a snowy Sunday in Russia and a warm spring evening in a beautiful urban park. The Russian emperor had died after alighting from a sumptuous sleigh, with his Cossack cavalry about him. Lord Frederick Cavendish and Thomas Henry Burke, the second- and third-ranking officials in Ireland, were cut down while strolling within sight of a cricket match. Yet the two scenes, at variance in so many ways, repeated a sinister note, audible at times against the background of the late nineteenth century's major themes.[39]

Cavendish had arrived in Dublin only that morning, May 6, 1882, to assume his duties as chief secretary for Ireland under the "viceroy," or more accurately lord lieutenant, Earl Spencer at the time. The victim-to-be, younger son of the duke of Devonshire and brother to another powerful Whig magnate, Lord Hartington, was also related by marriage to Gladstone, inasmuch as Lady Cavendish was a favorite niece of the prime minister's wife. Despite these connections and his own experience at the Treasury back in London, the new chief secretary, unlike the redoubtable "Buckshot" Forster he was replacing on only a week's notice, was more notable for his affability than for uncommon energy or expertise. Perhaps it was this very mildness that attracted Gladstone to him, given the prime minister's policy of conciliation in the matter of Home Rule. It is likewise conceivable that the same quality made him look threatening to Irish nationalists determined to block all efforts to arrange a lasting truce. In any event, the men who took his life that Saturday evening can have known little about him one way or another, lending credence to the possibility that not he but his companion, the permanent under-secretary, was their primary target.

Thomas Burke, Irish-born, a veteran of thirteen years in the position he then filled, cared about his country's welfare, as he conceived it. That much no one seems to have denied. To compatriots who saw themselves at war with the English queen, however, his devotion to duty in her service could be read only as traitorous collaboration. It may have been no accident that it was he, not the Englishman with him, who was attacked by the older and more highly motivated of the two dagger men.

If the under-secretary was the central figure, the drama of Phoenix Park takes on an added dimension of fatal chance. For Lord Cavendish had been on foot, enjoying the fresh air en route home from his new office in Dublin Castle, when Burke happened to overtake him in a cab along the Main Road, a broad central drive that still bisects the 1,700-acre tract. The under-secretary dismissed his hack, and the two walked on together. Both men had official residences, or lodges, within the park grounds, though the chief secretary would not live to set foot in his; and both were expected, later, at the viceroy's lodge for a dinner welcoming Cavendish. Deep in conversation, they strolled past three and then a group of four more figures lounging beside the carriageway, seemingly harmless loiterers but actually the murder gang already warned of Burke's approach by a confederate's signal. It was seventeen minutes past seven o'clock.

Each of the waiting groups parted to let the pair walk by, then suddenly, at a cry of "Ah, you villain!"—characteristic of Burke's assailant, according to later testimony—two of the bystanders fell on their victims from behind wielding long, razor-sharp knives designed for use in surgical amputations. Neither Cavendish nor Burke can have retained consciousness for more than a few seconds under the stabbing, slashing attack, though both were still choking out their lives when the first witnesses reached the spot. By that time three of the conspirators had leapt into a horse cab held in readiness by a fourth, while the remaining four, including the actual killers, hastily boarded another such vehicle. In all, nine participants were fleeing along lanes out of the park to the west and circling back into Dublin by a different route before effective pursuit could be organized. Most of their number spent the evening toasting their triumph at Davy's Tavern, though young Timothy Kelly, who had slain Lord Cavendish, took the first available tram to his home, where his mother, he was to testify, would have worried had he stayed out late.

This was the deed—swift, brutal, fortuitous in detail, but in purpose long matured. Its background included the grievances and mounting frustration of Ireland's population in the years preceding May 1882. From a more general European point of view, however, Phoenix Park assumed special importance because it brought together two of the nineteenth century's most

The bodies of Lord Cavendish and Thomas Henry Burke

powerful streams of discontent. One was nationalism, represented by previous advocates as diverse as Sand in Germany and Orsini in France. The other was the "land question," which affected a host of peasants and struggling tenant farmers from the Urals to County Clare. In Ireland both sets of issues were interwoven to form a resistance movement whose dimensions encompassed elements that were rural and urban, economic and psychological, and whose expressions ranged from prayerful to savage.

The Fenian Brotherhood, founded in New York City in 1858 to support Irish efforts to overthrow English rule, had dominated events for a time and imaginations for much longer.[40] In their first decade Fenians were able to claim credit for such projects as the "invasion" of Canada from the northeastern United States in 1866, the bombing of London's Clerkenwell Prison in 1867, and a series of widely rumored plots to abduct or even assassinate Queen Victoria. As the dates suggest, not only American money but a brief transfusion of Civil War veterans played a part in paramilitary adventures on both sides of the Atlantic. Despite this record, it was a mistake to assume, as some observers did, that Fenianism accounted for most of the violence occurring on the Irish scene in the early 1880s. Its legacy was discernible in the genesis of the Phoenix Park murders, but its role was probably less significant than were memories of the former "Ribbonmen," wearers of the green badge of enmity toward Orangemen in the campaign of rural violence that had reached its peak in the mid-1850s.

There was in the countryside a tradition of resistance to landlords, many of them absentee and English as well, a tradition far older than either Ribbonism or Fenian nationalism and strong enough to outlast them both. Its expressions included cattle-maiming, strikes by farm laborers, attacks on squires and overseers accused of rack-renting, and, beginning around 1800, the practice of "boycotting," that is, ostracizing, intimidating, and on occasion physically assaulting any tenant rash (or avaricious) enough to take over a farm from which another had been evicted. Rural grievances and tactics such as these may seem a far cry from the plot hatched by urban workers in a Dublin pub; but in the absence of detailed information about the background of especially the younger Phoenix Park conspirators—who their fathers were and where their forerunners had come from—it is tempting to speculate that some of them may have had familial ties to erstwhile Ribbonmen. The chronology would be right for the assassins of 1882 to have heard at first hand from elder relatives tales of cattle-maiming and lynchings carried out a generation before. That would help to explain not only their own acts but also their seemingly unclear motivation.[41]

Meanwhile, the demands of tenant farmers had been given increased form and direction by the founding, in 1879, of the Irish National Land League. Under its president, Charles Stuart Parnell, the Land League's executive council had quickly established itself as what amounted to a shadow government in many rural districts of rebellious Ireland.[42] Inasmuch as Parnell also headed the Home Rule Party and since 1875 had sat as its most eloquent spokesman in the British Parliament at Westminster, the patriotic motive was intertwined with the land question at a level of political action never before approached by either Ribbonmen or Fenians.[43] And it was Parnell, backed by his party and the Land League as well, who had the task of dealing with England's prime minister.

Gladstone had formed his second ministry in the spring of 1880, against the grim backdrop of the previous year's dreadful harvest in Ireland. He was committed in principle to the restoration of peace, with the land question at the heart of all issues, but the extent of concessions he might make in the name of the English government was the subject of fierce debate.[44] Shotgun Forster, as chief secretary in Dublin and opponent of any sign of appeasement, had won his unenviable nickname by urging the use of buckshot instead of solid ammunition in quelling riots. Yet he remained Gladstone's and his cabinet's "man in Ireland" for fully two years.

The final series of developments leading up to the events of May 1882 had begun the preceding August, when the prime minister's Irish Land Act was passed at Westminster. It promised tenants fair rents to be set by courts of arbitration; security of tenure for all who paid such rents once established; and, for those who would not or could not pay them, the right to sell out at an equitable price under a government guarantee that the true value of their share in ownership would be recognized. The framers had high hopes for this legislative package, though in retrospect its terms may seem to have clashed with such realities of farm life as the tactic of boycotting to discourage all transfers of tenancy, regardless of terms, and the often well-founded popular distrust of land records as a basis for determining equities. What was particularly frustrating for Her Majesty's Government was the Land League's stubborn opposition to the bill and Parnell's support of continued boycotting. In mid-October, after weeks of futile exchanges, he was arrested, with a number of other Irish spokesmen, and confined in Dublin's Kilmainham Gaol.

The "Kilmainham martyrs" lived in relative comfort, playing chess or cards, taking outside exercise, corresponding freely, and receiving visitors; yet it is unlikely that they intended to continue their defiance indefinitely. Quite the contrary, they began almost at once to negotiate with Gladstone, through intermediaries, and by the following spring a truce had been agreed upon. England's acceptance of the terms had been bitterly opposed by Chief Secretary Forster, who left Ireland for the last time in late April to argue the case against concessions from his seat in the House of Commons. He and those who agreed with him were overruled. On May 2, 1882, Lord Granville, speaking in Parliament for the entire cabinet, announced that the existing Coercion Act was annulled and that Parnell and his associates had been released from detention in return for assurances that they would repudiate further use of boycotting and would join the English Liberal Party in supporting the Land Act of the preceding summer. This was the Kilmainham Treaty, about which Parnell's (not to mention Gladstone's) admirers and critics have disagreed ever since.

Following Granville's statement to the House, the prime minister rose to reveal, amid praise for Mr. Forster's past services, that the chief secretary for Ireland had tendered his resignation. Two days later Gladstone made public his choice of a successor, Lord Cavendish; suggestions in favor of Parnell or Joseph Chamberlain had been dismissed. On the evening of Friday, May 5, the new appointee left London by train with Lord Spencer to catch the Irish night boat from Holyhead. Less than twenty-four hours later, following a day of introductions at Dublin Castle, he lay dead with Thomas Burke on the carriageway in Phoenix Park.

The men who had planned and carried out the assassination were, with a couple of exceptions, not known Fenians, though many of their supporters were. Nor was any of them a farmer directly hurt by the extortionate land practices of the past, whatever connection may have existed with the Ribbonmen of earlier times. Among the twenty-six defendants eventually tried only one was a public figure, building contractor and Dublin town councilor James Carey. The rest were artisans, clerks, teamsters, or men unemployed when the crime was committed. What they had in common was membership in the recently organized Invincibles, a society pledged to the use of violence and described by one of its founders in the autumn of 1881 as a group "that would make history."[45]

Despite the large circle of suspected conspirators, the Invincibles' shock troops were not only few in number and lacking in political organization, but also quite well known to informers and hence to government officials. When the euphoria inspired by the successful attack in Phoenix Park gave way to mounting apprehension over the quiet but relentless police work being directed from the Castle, the suspected culprits reacted first by seeking to eliminate or intimidate everyone they considered capable of identifying them. That impulse led to their undoing.

The greatest difficulty confronting officers of both the Royal Irish Constabulary and their rivals in the Detective (or "G") Division of the Dublin Municipal Police lay not so much in thinking of suspects or in reconstructing the crime as in finding credible witnesses willing to risk reprisals for turning Queen's Evidence and testifying in open court. Much has been written about one investigator in particular, the apparently able but also controversial superintendent of Division G, John Mallon, a Catholic from Armagh who claimed to support Home Rule but not assassination in its pursuit. An admiring English journalist credited Mallon with breaking the Phoenix Park case, as well as many others, almost singlehandedly.[46] On the other side, a knowledgeable (though increasingly disaffected) official at the Castle later wrote that the chief detective had unscrupulously consigned humble Invincibles to the gallows while maintaining close relations with Patrick Egan, the Land League's elusive treasurer who sent money and advice back to Ireland from his comfortable headquarters in Paris. The same source, with corroboration from a long-time English spy who knew Egan in France and later in the United States, believed that the treasurer was the actual architect of the Phoenix Park murders and that he escaped arrest on that charge, while on a dangerous visit to Dublin in 1883, only because of a timely warning from someone, probably Mallon, at the Castle.[47]

Nevertheless, there is little difference of opinion regarding Mallon's success in trailing suspects, assembling tips from informants, and eventually making key witnesses out of several of the defendants charged, to the mortal detriment of the others. His efforts on all these fronts benefited greatly from the bravado of the Invincibles themselves, especially the contemptuous openness with which they committed further crimes. In July following the assassinations a dockworker named John Kenny, one of the Castle's most reliable underground sources, was found slashed to death "by great knives" under the Seville Place railway arch in Dublin. It was this crime which finally, despite the recent withdrawal of the Coercion Act, led to the naming of a special magistrate to examine individual witnesses with the help of the superintendent of detectives. Yet even while this rather French style of inquiry was in progress, the principal suspects mounted further assaults. Two days after a police constable was cut down, Joe Brady and Tim Kelly, who had actually killed Cavendish and Burke, struck again. This time they narrowly failed in an attempt to murder a discharged juror who had voted for the conviction of another suspected terrorist (not directly connected with the Phoenix Park affair). Both men stabbed their victim repeatedly, at the doorway of his home, Brady repeating the cry "Ah, you villain!" within the hearing of witnesses and Kelly dropping his cap before fleeing with the help of one of the cab drivers who had been in Phoenix Park the previous spring. This time all three participants were firmly identified, and in the ensuing weeks Mallon was able to pull together the final strands of evidence. By January 13, 1883, twenty-one suspects had been arrested; five more were taken into custody soon thereafter, bringing to twenty-six the number of defendants charged.

Preliminary hearings were held from January 20 to February 19, and the trial ran for three weeks beginning on April 9. Among the witnesses called were four defendants who saved themselves, for the time being anyway, by giving evidence against the rest. Of these "approvers," the one whose testimony was by far the most damaging to the prisoners was James Carey, the Dublin town councilor, in whose home police had found two surgical knives and a Winchester rifle.*

The Invincibles, according to evidence produced at their trial, had begun planning a major assassination late in 1881, after learning of the arrest and confinement of Irish leaders in Kilmainham Gaol. Discussions had included fugitive Land League officials, several ex-Fenians, and at least two of Parnell's fellow MPs. Despite rumors to the contrary, Irish-American organizations such as the Clan-na-Gael appear to have had little to do with the plot, though there were loud demands from across the Atlantic that someone "show something" in the way of overt action.[48] The chief supplier from the English side was said to be Frank Byrne of the Land League of Great Britain, whose wife, or a woman claiming her identity, had smuggled the surgical knives from London. At the center of things, however, stood Egan, the collector and dispenser of funds in Paris.

Recruiting within Ireland was entrusted to a Directory of Dublin Invincibles, among whose members Daniel Curley and a well-known pub owner

---

* The danger in becoming a prosecution witness was illustrated by Carey's eventual fate. Having escaped incognito to South Africa after the trial, with the help the government had promised in return for his testimony, he was recognized aboard a steamer from Capetown to Durban by an ex-Fenian from Donegal who shot him dead as a matter of honor.

named James Mullet were especially successful in rounding up volunteers for whatever "brisk work" might be ordered by their superiors. One of these recruits was a powerfully built but reputedly kindhearted street-paver, Joseph Brady. Another was Tim Kelly, a twenty-year-old coach-builder who joined Brady to form the society's principal team of executioners. Though most of the Invincibles, with the exception of Carey, were poor men, their own statements and those of witnesses who knew them suggest that they were united less by class-consciousness than by Anglophobia and a craving to do "something considerable."[49]

Their original target appears to have been Shotgun Forster, until his departure for England in late April 1882. Thereafter, his long-time assistant Burke became the primary object of the society's hatred—though there was enough of that to include whoever might arrive, as Cavendish did, to replace the former chief secretary. The trial record does not suggest that the murders in Phoenix Park were motivated by a carefully weighed decision to break up the "threat" of a lasting compromise between Gladstone and Parnell (though both men, when informed of the event, seem to have arrived independently at that conclusion). Instead, when Carey, Curley, Brady, Kelly, and their companions met at Wrenn's tavern near the Castle on that fateful afternoon of May 6, they talked, so approvers testified in court, not about long-range political strategy but about their shared detestation of Forster, who had eluded them, and of Burke, who remained within reach.

The Dublin jury found most of the defendants guilty of murder or varying degrees of complicity. Five were sentenced to death and hanged at Kilmainham Gaol between mid-May 1883 and early June: Joseph Brady, his fellow knife-wielder Tim Kelly (who had to be retried twice before a unanimous verdict was reached), Daniel Curley, and two less prominent but heavily implicated men. Of the prison sentences imposed on others standing in the dock, several were for life. Five suspects who would in all likelihood have been convicted managed to escape to America, where one of them, Patrick Egan, made a fortune in milling and served for a time as United States minister to Chile. Frank Byrne and a fellow conspirator, arrested by French authorities in Le Havre at Britain's request, were later released and allowed to take passage across the Atlantic. (Thus was avenged England's refusal to extradite persons wanted in France after the Orsini bombing and again following the revolt of the Paris Commune in 1871.)

The Invincibles hanged in 1883 became martyrs in the eyes of Irish patriots. What else did their "victory" in Phoenix Park achieve? Certainly not the abandonment of Gladstone's conciliatory policy. Though the prime minister was compelled by English public opinion to suspend his efforts temporarily following the murders, by the mid-1880s the Kilmainham Treaty with Parnell resumed its significance as the Liberals' prescription for lasting peace. Later events would discredit it, leaving the terms to moulder with other vestiges of the tortured relations between Ireland and England. That outcome, however, was determined by such powerful forces as the pursuit of political independence and the demand for economic self-determination rather than by a single bloody act on an evening in May. In only one tragic sense can the Invincibles be said to have won. In the irregular but relentless escalation of bitterness and reciprocal violence between Ireland and England, Phoenix Park has remained the symbol of hatred least likely to be forgotten by either side.

PART THREE

The Modern World

THE PAST SIXTY or seventy years have seen a quantitative increase in assassination so great that, in combination with its geographical expansion, it poses a global problem.

Even during earlier centuries—especially the nineteenth, when there were numerous cases in Japan, Latin America, and the United States—political murders occurred in both hemispheres and on all continents. But that is not the point. It is one thing to acknowledge that every segment of the human race has known assassination in some form, beginning with the first experiments in government. It is quite another to observe its impact being registered and discussed all over the world.

Certain truths about political violence have been not so much discovered as demonstrated with unusual force in our own times. One is the relatively low rate of assassination while major wars are in progress, followed by a sharp rise in its frequency during a period marked by civil discord once hostilities have ended. Another significant correlation is that between the incidence of political murder and the formative stages of nation-building, characteristic of an age of disintegrating empires.

Particular subperiods make special claims on our attention: the 1920s as a seedtime of later terrorism; the 1930s when the Nazi and Soviet regimes, each in its own way, combined dogma with technology to create new dimensions for despotism. Between 1942 and 1945 several dramatic exceptions to the rule that wartime controls inhibit assaults on political figures occurred. The slaying of Reinhardt Heydrich in Prague and of Admiral Darlan in Algiers foreshadowed the bomb attempt against Hitler and the summary execution of Mussolini by Italian partisans.

Today's terrorism began to display its salient features in the 1960s. Prominent among them is the effort by terrorists to depersonalize murder in one sense, by making every bystander a potential victim, while claiming to indict whole classes and governmental systems on charges once reserved for individual tyrants. Paradoxical as this blending of symbolic acts with punitive claims may appear, it recalls the linkage of furious impulse and dispassionate justification encountered in much older formulas for tyrannicide. Another reminder of the past is the persistent role of madmen as assassins.

New elements include the unprecedented growth of international communication and cooperation among terrorists. Another is the sharing of techniques between practitioners of terror both official and revolutionary, between governors and insurgents in many parts of the world. Finally, there has been a less frequently remarked fading of any meaningful distinction between "rightist" and "leftists" activists, in power or out. Whatever differences in rationality or humanity of purpose may have seemed to exist a hundred years ago, the significance of ideology began to be blurred as early as the 1920s; by now, save in the most doctrinaire of analyses, it has disappeared.

What remains is behavior, stripped of polemical trappings. And of behavior that is murderous, whatever its partisan claims, one must ask: What about political life?

11

Civilization
in the Balance

Before 1914

In the years just prior to the First World War there was little to suggest that changes might be afoot in the matter of assassination. President William McKinley's death in 1901 reminded Americans of earlier presidents slain. The murders of King Carlos of Portugal and his son in 1908, Spain's liberal Prime Minister José Canalejas in 1912, and King George I of Greece in 1913 had about them a somber repetitiveness. Latin America, despite the shock waves of Spain's final exclusion from the hemisphere, remained without a major political slaying until President Francisco Madero of Mexico was killed, also in 1913. As for Asia, leaving aside for a moment the special case of India, there was not much to report save the death in 1907 of the Persian premier, Amin-es-Sultan (stabbed by a banker who claimed descent from the original *Hashishiyyin*), and that of his Japanese counterpart, Prince Ito Hirobumi, in 1909 at the hands of a Korean nationalist.

Eastern Europe, experiencing no radical departure from nineteenth-century patterns of behavior, continued to produce its seemingly established quota of violence. In Bulgaria one cabinet minister, M. Kanzchev, was killed in 1902 and another, Dimiter Petkov, in 1907; but neither those assaults nor the murder in 1908 of the Hapsburg governor of Polish Galicia, Count Andreas Potocki, aroused as much excitement as did the lurid slaying in 1903 of King Alexander I and Queen Draga of Serbia.

These palace murders in Belgrade were important for several reasons, among them the growing importance of the Serbian monarchy in European power politics. The death of Alexander, last of the Obrenovich rulers, also marked the end of the dynastic struggle between his family and that of Karageorgevich, dating from the revolt against Turkish rule a century earlier. The accession of Peter Karageorgevich brought to the throne a popular prince destined, in Rebecca West's opinion, to be "a great king" throughout his eighteen-year reign.[1] Miss West's enthusiasm is somewhat mystifying, for Peter I proved to be as weak as he was affable. Nevertheless, he served well to legitimate the maneuvers of his shrewd premier, Nikola Pašić, who by 1918 would secure for his sovereign the crown of "Greater Serbia," the future Yugoslavia.

Numbers alone were enough to make the rising a major revolt, inasmuch as almost a hundred army officers took part in the butchering of twenty victims during a single night of carnage.[2] Those slain included not only the royal couple but also two cabinet ministers and two brothers of the queen, one of whom she had bullied her husband into naming heir to the throne. The uprising resulted in part from intense and widespread hatred for Her Majesty, a well-known courtesan who had converted the king from an infatuated lover into an obedient spouse, before the eyes of his disillusioned people. Yet the officers who dragged the ruler and his consort from their hiding place within the palace, to be shot, stabbed, and finally thrown down into the troop-filled courtyard, were motivated by more than obsessive animosity toward "that whore in the king's bed." A poisonous atmosphere had developed around Alexander himself, born of his unpredictable fits of spiteful rage. At the level of policy he was accused of pandering to Austria's imperial interests in the Balkans, whereas Karageorgevich was committed to the intense nationalism of the Serbian war party. (This circumstance may explain Rebecca West's favorable judgment of the assassinations and of their beneficiary.)

Despite its serious implications, the Serbian blood bath retains an almost Graustarkian quality of *opéra bouffe,* especially seen against the background of contemporary events in the huge Russian Empire. There the turn of the century had been accompanied by a renewal of political homicide on a scale surpassing even that of the years before Alexander II's assassination. Consider the victims of these major attempts, selected from the annals of a single decade:

1901   Nikolai Pavlovich Bogolepov, minister of education, killed by an expelled student;

Konstantin P. Pobedonostsev, chief procurator of the Holy Synod, former tutor of the tsar, wounded in an unsuccessful attempt;

1902   Dimitri F. Trepov, chief of Moscow police, survived three attacks;

Dimitri Sergeevich Sipiagin, minister of interior, killed at Saint Petersburg by a student, S. V. Balmashov;

Wahl, military governor of Vilna, wounded by a Lithuanian patriot;

Prince I. M. Obolenski, governor of Kharkov, attacked twice within two months;

1903   N. M. Bogdanovich, governor of Ufa, killed in Kiev by a Social Revolutionary (SR) agent;

1904   Nikolai I. Bobrikov, governor-general of Finland, killed by a Finnish nationalist student;

Bogoslovski, governor of the Caucasus, killed by local separatists;

Viacheslav K. Plehve, minister of interior, killed in Saint Petersburg by an SR bomb team;

1905   Grand Duke Sergei Alexandrovich, uncle of the tsar, governor-general of Moscow, killed by an SR bomb;

Pavel Andreevich Shuvalov, prefect of police of Moscow, killed by an SR agent;

1906   Professor Mikhail Ia. Gertsenstein, member of the Duma, killed by a fanatical anti-Semite;

Peter A. Stolypin, prime minister, escaped an SR bomb attempt during visiting hours at his villa (fifty visitors and guards were killed);

1911   Stolypin, fatally shot in the tsar's presence at the Kiev opera by an anarchist-police spy double agent.[3]

The uneven spacing of these attacks might suggest a direct linkage between their peak of concentration in 1904–1905 and the most intense frustration among liberal-constitutional reformers, declining once the government agreed to convoke the first Duma. Contrary to that tempting explanation, however, many of the assassinations had little to do with demands for a Russian legislature. Assaults upon high imperial officials formed part of a very different course of development, beginning when the newly formed Social Revolutionary Party revived the memory of the People's Will and set out to surpass Narodnaya Volya's efforts at destroying the Romanov autocracy. In the process, the SR achieved a clear preeminence in the field of political murder, on behalf of a program too radical to be disarmed by the mere convening of the Duma.

The decline in frequency of assassination attempts after 1906 revealed a demoralizing crisis of confidence within the SR leadership. This crisis affected especially the high command of the "Fighting Section," the terrorist machine so carefully constructed by its fabled chief, Yevno Azev. Revelations that Azev was himself a double agent, serving not only as an underground strategist but also as a high official of the tsarist security police, the Okhrana, shattered the discipline of Social Revolutionary cadres and produced the seeming aimlessness still in evidence when Stolypin was killed four years later at Kiev. In the meantime, the Fighting Section's fallen leader was secretly tried and found guilty by a special commission of inquiry, which met in Paris and comprised not only the venerable anarchist Prince Kropotkin but also Vera Figner, that ghost from the days of Alexander II released from prison only a few years before. Azev, warned of the Paris deliberations, managed to escape his would-be executioners and lived out his life in exile, leaving behind him in Russia a temporarily disorganized band of SR Maximalists.

The Social Revolutionaries were not alone in agonizing over tactics in the years following the revolution of 1905. V. I. Lenin, from his refuge in Switzerland, reacted strongly to news of the Saint Petersburg riots. Although he still opposed attempts to slay prominent political figures as "inopportune and inexpedient," more disruptive of revolutionary than of government forces, he began to issue calls for a general arming of the people, if need be by killing soldiers and taking their weapons. His personal contribution to the new effort was the translation into Russian of a textbook on urban guerrilla tactics written by a French veteran of the Paris Commune.[4] Thus, in place of demonstrative assassinations, Lenin preached furtive assaults on local constabularies, combined with what he labeled "expropriation" of needed funds by robbing banks, trains, shopping places, and other centers of capitalist activity. To manage such actions there was nobody he came to rely upon more heavily than "our wonderful Georgian," Josef Djugashvili, also known as "Soso," "Koba," and more and more commonly "Stalin."[5] Thus, a distinctively Bolshevik style of underground terrorism emerged in opposition not only to the imperial government but also to other insurgents, especially the Social Revolutionaries, with their histrionic gestures after the manner of Orsini or Zhelyabov.

Repercussions of what was happening in the empire of Nicholas II made themselves felt in quite a different imperial setting, amid growing opposition to colonial rule. The place was India, where new stirrings had always to be seen against the backdrop of violence that had plagued the great subcontinent throughout its history. Between 1826 and 1836 British authorities, in the course of their struggle against Thugee, had unearthed evidence of no fewer than 90,000 ritual murders committed by the gangs of Thugs infesting routes followed by religious pilgrims and commercial travelers.[6] In theory these killings represented sacrifices to the pitiless goddess Kali, but the suppression of Thugee, like that of Suttee, widow-burning, undertaken at about the same time, rested on the belief that both were crimes and justified the fullest possible mobilization of police, courts, and the military. The Great

Mutiny, with its ferocious display of savagery on both sides, ensued at mid-century. Once the killing at Meerut and Cawnpore and Lucknow had subsided, however, there was a return to public apathy, expressive of the fatalistic sense that British domination was irremovable. Behind every colonial official there stood (or so it must have seemed to most Indians) a line of available replacements figuratively stretching from Delhi and Calcutta back to Westminster, Whitehall, and Haileybury College, England's preparatory school for service in India. Such isolated acts of defiance as did occur, including the assassination of the viceroy, Lord Mayo, by a Moslem prison inmate in 1872, produced nothing to challenge that belief.

The sources of a new Indian militancy, destined to culminate in independence, lay partly in the realm of ideas, in the vision of their people's destiny invoked in the late nineteenth and early twentieth centuries by Vivekananda, Chatterji, Tagore, and other prophets who echoed their message. Another source of inspiration for militant nationalists was found in foreign models. Word from Russia and from Ireland, countries whose secret leagues had interested Indians traveling in Europe or reading at home even during the years of greatest lethargy, was reinforced by rumors of experiments with high explosives being conducted in Paris by students from India with the help of French sympathizers.

The signal for a shift in political tactics—note the parallelism with Russia—was a split between moderates and extremists in the Surat Congress of patriotic parties immediately before the outbreak of assassination attempts beginning in 1907. These "Indian murders," as the British Sedition Committee Report of 1918 referred to them, produced a total of six fatalities among perhaps three times that many British officials attacked—not a large number judged by either contemporary Russian or subsequent twentieth-century standards, but considered shocking at the time.[7] If this reaction seems exaggerated, it should be noted that these figures reveal only one corner of a much larger canvas: the Englishmen slain constituted a small fraction of the eighty-two victims who died at the hands of members of the dreaded "Yungantar Group" or other bands of assassins, most of whose attacks were aimed at Indians.[8]

War in 1914 brought further changes in England and India alike, leaving this flurry of homicide to join the Great Mutiny in the sporadic prehistory of Indian independence. Only the figure of Mohandas K. Gandhi, in his late thirties and still a resident of South Africa when the Indian murders occurred, serves to connect them very directly with later events. Gandhi, like his almost exact contemporary Lenin in Russia, but for very different reasons, condemned political murder as practiced by either Yungantar or Social Revolutionaries. Lenin was converted by stages to successive forms of terror, which he employed both before and after he arrived in power, surviving his own brush with assassination along the way. Gandhi, by contrast, never retracted or ceased to reiterate his plea for passive resistance until he died, the victim of a religious fanatic, in 1948.

The First World War

International conflict in modern times has generally been accompanied, at least until its last, most desperate stages, by a relatively low rate of political murder. Although major wars, especially since about 1800, have contributed to increased domestic violence appearing in their wake, the aftermath has not as a rule been announced by any spate of assassination while hostilities were still in progress. The twentieth century's two world wars, like earlier conflagrations, both have exhibited this tendency, however inconsistent with their dreadful toll in battlefield casualties. Some of the most startling concentrations of political homicide in recent history must be attributed not to war itself but to defeat in war or to expectations aroused by victory only to be disappointed at the peace table.

It would be a mistake to treat this phenomenon as more paradoxical than it really is. When war breaks out there is almost certain to be an immediate tightening of security measures, including those designed to protect the lives of government leaders. Such precautions generally acquire additional force from the willingness of the population at large to share in seeing that they work. Even disaffected elements are often reluctant to pursue their grievances in ways that might be viewed as treasonable. In addition, organized combat against outsiders may serve as an outlet for impulses otherwise expressed through civil disobedience, including assassination attempts.

This suggestion will strike some as especially surprising when applied to the First World War, whose outbreak is commonly perceived as the result of a sensational assassination. There is no denying that the government of the Austro-Hungarian Empire seized upon the shooting of the heir apparent to the Hapsburg throne as its *casus belli* in 1914, and that the German emperor's personal sense of outrage played a key role in Berlin's decision to second the demands of the war party in Vienna. Yet even the briefest reflection casts doubt on the notion that the murder of Franz Ferdinand and his morganatic wife on a street in Sarajevo actually *caused* the vast tragedy to follow, if by causation is meant that without the intervention of an adolescent assassin the ensuing collision of forces and interests could have been indefinitely averted. Still more fanciful is the not uncommon claim that because (a) Gavrilo Princip and his accomplices were challenging Hapsburg control over Bosnia and Hercegovina and because (b) one of the Great War's results turned out to be the cession of those provinces to Greater Serbia, (c) the collapse of Austro-Hungarian power in the Balkans made this an example of "successful" assassination. Nothing could be further from the truth. For the assassins who had thought to advance the cause of Bosnian independence, the permanent replacement of one foreign ruler in Vienna by another in Belgrade could hardly be called a triumph. Their pro-Serbian enthusiasm in 1914 had been at once expedient and transitory.

In some respects what happened at Sarajevo was an old-fashioned kind of political assault. It had been preceded by at least four other attempts against high Austrian or Hungarian officials in the region of Bosnia and Croatia. Its single claim to novelty, the death of its victims while riding in an automobile, is diminished by the fact that two years before, in Zagreb, another Slavic patriot had tried unsuccessfully to shoot the Hungarian governor of Croatia, Count Cuvaj, as he sat in an open car. As for Princip and the five other members of Young Bosnia who went forth to kill the archduke that June 28, they were, like many other assassins before and after them, little more than boys. The five who were arrested (one eluded capture), were all spared the death penalty, even when tried in wartime by an Austrian court, because they were under age. Only the three older defendants found guilty of complicity before the fact were hanged. The conspirators' plan of attack, hastily devised and no better executed than most of Narodnaya Volya's efforts had been in Russia, succeeded despite the inability of one of the culprits to throw a bomb and a complete failure of nerve on the part of two others. Incredibly, the pair of hasty pistol shots fired by the almost untrained Princip each killed one of his victims, the archduke and Duchess Sophie, and then only because their driver had made a wrong turn off the Appel Quay by the Miljacka River and come to a stop in Franz Josef Street.[9]

There can be no denying the awful consequences of that act: the pretext afforded the war hawks in Vienna for a showdown with Serbia; the wrath of Kaiser Wilhelm when news of his friend's death reached him aboard the imperial yacht off the Baltic coast; the shocking evidence provided of seemingly irreconcilable hatred between Slav and German. The powder in two rounds of pistol ammunition was enough to set huge armies in motion and to detonate cannon fire around much of a world destined never to be wholly restored. But given the tensions of 1914, it is difficult to believe that some other spark would not have had the same effects, even had the archduke's chauffeur avoided his fatal detour.

The conspiratorial aspect of the young Bosnians' success was inflated by the furious reaction of Austro-Hungarian authorities at the time and by popular demand for a grand pattern of international intrigue to account for such events. Princip and Nedelko Cabrinović had met still another Bosnian, Milan Ciganović, in Belgrade a few weeks before the attempt and had returned home with weapons and information given to them during their visit to the Serbian capital. It remains likely, though never verified, that their sponsor there was "Union or Death," a secret fraternity founded in 1911 to combat Austrian penetration of the Balkans and called by its enemies "The Black Hand." Its leader was Colonel Dragutin Dimitrijević, alias Colonel

Cabrinović, Ciganović, and Princip (right) in a Belgrade park

Apis, one of the participants in the assassination of King Alexander and Queen Draga. For the Black Hand to encourage anti-Hapsburg Bosnians would have been natural. For the royal government under the wily Pašić to have exposed itself to charges of direct involvement would have been more surprising, given the delicate international situation in which Serbia found itself. There has long been a presumption that Pašić knew something of the plot; but it is hard to believe that the Black Hand, almost as hostile to his cautious regime in Belgrade as to the "enemy" in Vienna, invited him to participate.

In the spring of 1917 at Allied army headquarters in Saloniki, Colonel Apis and several others, including a Bosnian Muslim who had been the only Sarajevo assassin to escape capture three years before, were arrested and charged with having plotted to kill the Serbian crown prince as well as having engaged in treasonable activities on behalf of the German imperial government. The Black Hand's chief and his two closest aides were found guilty by a military court and shot immediately. Was his death, as some have insisted, designed to silence him concerning the events of 1914? Or was a fatal penchant for conspiring against people in power enough to explain his downfall? These, too, remain unanswered questions.[10]

The outbreak of war began a terrible new chapter in the history of mankind's capacity for wholesale killing, not only on the battlefield but behind the lines as well. An early example was the execution of more than 150 Serbian sympathizers in Austria's South Slavic provinces, carried out by troops who cared little for the due process being observed in the trial of Franz Ferdinand's actual assassins. These mass hangings in Bosnia and Hercegovina, however, were rather quickly forgotten by a world public subjected to daily reports of far greater atrocities, in Belgium, on the Eastern Front, and elsewhere. The grisly record of mounting brutality and disintegrating restraints makes all the more remarkable the comparative infrequency of personal assaults on civilian and military leaders between 1914 and 1918.

This is not to say that there were no such attacks, only that their number was no greater than might have been expected under peacetime conditions. In Paris on July 31, 1914, with formal hostilities about to begin, a young nationalist named Raoul Villain walked up to the open window of a café and through it fired the shots that killed Jean Jaurès, French socialism's acknowledged leader and an outspoken critic of military preparations. In one sense, the assassination of Jaurès, opponent of such measures as the 1913 Army Law, was a war-related act, for which Villain was acquitted when finally brought to trial in 1919 amid the patriotic effusions of victory. In another sense, however, his victim was mourned less as a pacifist than as a domestic politician of uncommon courage and eloquence. More than twenty years after the event, in 1936, Raoul Villain was shot to death on the island of Majorca by Spanish Republican gunmen avenging the murder of a socialist martyr.[11]

Portugal witnessed another wartime incident, the near-fatal shooting of Premier-designate João Chagas on May 16, 1915, which proves on examination to have had little beyond internal political significance. Chagas, whose serious wounds prevented him from assuming office, was known as a supporter of cooperation with the Allies in their conflict with Germany; but the attack on him was only one of many cases of essentially domestic violence following the end of the monarchy in 1910. His assailant, Senator João de Freitas, was gunned down on the spot by bodyguards, adding to the number of legislators and other government officials slain during the Portuguese Republic's early years.[12]

For an assassination much more clearly imbedded in Europe's military crisis, one must turn to the moribund empire of the Hapsburgs. On October 21, 1916, Austria-Hungary's prime minister, Count Karl von Sturgkh, was just finishing his lunch in a fashionable Viennese hotel dining room when he was approached by a scholarly-looking man who shot him dead with four rounds from a revolver fired at point-blank range. The culprit was disarmed and captured after a brief scuffle in the course of which one of the premier's companions was slightly wounded by a final shot from the murder weapon. The case came to trial, without jury, before a special court (*Ausnahme-gericht*), but not until the following May. The delay, although officially attributed to the mass of eyewitness, background, and psychiatric evidence to be put in order, resulted at least as much from the military and political vicissitudes of a tottering imperial regime.[13]

Even under the most untroubled circumstances, Friedrich Adler would have been no ordinary defendant. This thirty-seven-year-old son of Austrian socialism's "grand old man," Victor Adler, had not only earned a Ph.D. in mathematics, but also become secretary of the Social Democratic Workers' Party and editor of its monthly journal *Der Kampf* (The Struggle). During his two days in court he discussed the shooting with complete lucidity, leaving to his lawyers such technical matters as an unsuccessful challenge to the "exceptional" court's jurisdiction.

Adler's testimony confirmed what expert witnesses from the Medical Faculty of the University of Vienna had already reported: that he was sane by legal standards, that is, fully capable of perceiving the meaning and consequences of his deed, and that he had been motivated to attack Count von Sturgkh by two urgently felt needs. One was to protest the government's refusal to convene parliament, relax police restrictions, or ease wartime limitations on freedom of expression. His other stated purpose was to shame his own party, the Austrian Socialists, for their support of the war effort. Not surprisingly, the party's principal newspaper, the *Wiener Arbeiter-Zeitung,* under its editor Friedrich Austerlitz, began by criticizing the assassin for having broken with the movement's tradition of nonviolence. There could be no doubt, however, that Adler had awakened the accusing ghost of Jean Jaurès, and before the trial was over Austerlitz and his newspaper, admittedly now taking advantage of reduced censorship, were praising the courage and integrity of "Comrade Adler."

The prisoner, intent on defusing any suggestion of insanity whether chronic or temporary, had candidly explained his sense of moral obligation and his indifference to the price: "I have the duty to bear witness here to my convictions, which are to me a more essential matter than whether during this war one man is or is not hanged in Austria. I have committed this act in the full knowledge that through it my life is closed." As for his right to murder a personally inoffensive minister, simply as a symbol of repression, he added: "I am guilty in the same degree as any officer who in war has killed or given the order to kill—in no way less, but in no way more." And exuding a self-assurance at once disdainful and impersonal, he replied to the prosecutor's claim that homicide cannot be countenanced as a political weapon in an ordered polity [*in einem geordneten Staatswesen*]: "I agree completely. However, the premise which has here to be proven is that we are living in an ordered polity."[14]

Condemned on May 19 to die, as he and everyone else expected, Austria's "Brutus of the Left" greeted the verdict with a cry of "Long live international revolutionary socialism!" His readiness to face execution appears to have been genuine enough, but in the event he did not even have to spend very long in jail. During the interval between the assassination and the trial much had changed inside the empire and out. Franz Josef had succumbed in November 1916, after a reign of more than sixty-eight years. His timid, well-intentioned grandson, Emperor Karl, had quickly agreed to the calling of parliament as well as the relaxation of the more stringent restrictions affecting freedom of speech, publication, and assembly. Russia's revolution in March had coincided with signs of flagging confidence even in mighty Germany, where the Ludendorff dictatorship was unable to stifle counsels of "weakness" voiced in the Reichstag. No government, least of all that of Austria, would have been eager to create a socialist martyr at such a time, so, after months of official hand-wringing, the death sentence hanging over Count Sturgkh's assassin was commuted to imprisonment for eighteen years.

Not even that reduced penalty could survive the end of the Hapsburgs' empire and the birth of the Austrian Republic. On November 2, 1918, Friedrich Adler walked out of Stein Prison a free man and returned to a life of teaching and writing—the latter highlighted by a book denouncing Stalin and the Soviet purge trials.[15] He lived quietly until 1960, when he died at the age of eighty-one. Death found Adler in Switzerland, where he had moved a quarter-century before to escape the Nazis; but he was still a legal resident of Sonnenhofgasse 6 in Vienna, the address from which he had set out by streetcar to have lunch at the Hotel Meissl & Schadn in October 1916 and, having dined, to shoot the Empire's prime minister.[16]

Russian Shambles

To treat the collapse of the Romanov empire and the birth of the Soviet Union merely as subordinate features of the World War would be wholly inappropriate. Together they constituted, next to the war itself, the most important political event anywhere in the world during the first third of the twentieth century. What makes the Russian Revolution, including its immediate prologue, unique in the history of violence is not only the gigantic scale of its mass encounters on streets and battlefields but also the kaleidoscopic variety of personal assaults found in its annals. These assassinations, taken one by one, were classifiable in terms already familiar to students of the past. In combination, however, the sequence of an aristocratic murder plot, the brutal liquidation of an entire ruling family, successful attempts upon the lives of new power figures, and a failed assault upon the most powerful of all, occurring in the space of less than two years, constituted a phenomenon without precedent.

Gregory Rasputin, *starets* or holy man, confidant of the Empress Alexandra, alleged savior of her son from hemophilia, dabbler in high policy including the disposition of tsarist armies, had barely missed being killed on the eve of the First World War. The day before Franz Ferdinand's death at Sarajevo, June 17, 1914, Rasputin was attacked in his home village of Pokrovskoe in western Siberia by a female follower of the rival Orthodox monk Iliodor. This Kinia Guseva seems to have believed that with the help of Iliodor's own knife she could eliminate the Antichrist.[17] Her confidence proved ill-founded, for the victim, a powerful man at forty-two, survived after a fortnight in critical condition, and his assailant was committed to an insane asylum. The tsarina's fervent prayers apparently had been answered; but hatred of her spiritual adviser continued to grow, making it all but inconceivable that another attempt against him would not be born somewhere in the shadows of that Byzantine court.

When the murder came, it was the work not of a religious zealot or a moralist, outraged by the monk's lechery, but of a scarcely less jaded representative of the highest Russian nobility and several fellow courtiers. Prince Felix Yussoupov, immensely rich, was the descendant of forebears who since the eighteenth century had stood next to the throne itself. By the end of 1916 this last scion of the house of Yussoupov had concluded that Rasputin was an enemy of the empire and would have to die. Prince Felix, though married to a niece of the tsar, seems not to have let that interfere with a social life featuring transvestite orgies among other diversions. It was, in fact, after several all-night escapades in Rasputin's company that he claimed to have discovered the monk's aim to force Nicholas II's abdication so that the tsarevich might assume the crown, with Alexandra as regent and the starets, of course, as *éminence grise*.

Yussoupov, having settled upon December 29, 1916, for the execution, invited his prey to dine with him in the elaborately furnished basement playroom of his Moika Palace at Saint Petersburg. The episode, as fantastic as its carefully arranged setting, has been described countless times, recreated on stage, and, in the persons of the brothers Barrymore, captured on movie film: the midnight supper for two; the physician who had escorted the guest of honor to the feast also lacing with cyanide powder the sweet cakes Rasputin was known to love; the nervous host pretending to join in the carousal, while upstairs the other conspirators, including Grand Duke Dimitri, brother of the tsar, strained to hear encouraging sounds above the incongruous notes of George M. Cohan's recently imported "I'm a Yankee Doodle Dandy," playing on a gramophone.

Rasputin was murdered with a combination of savagery and incompetence Nechaev himself would have been hard put to improve upon. Poisoned, shot four times, beaten with a club as he tried to stumble away across the snow-covered courtyard, the holy man was at last rolled in a piece of window drapery and lowered through a hole hastily gouged in the ice covering the Neva River. When his body was recovered two days later water was discovered in the lungs, proof that only drowning had succeeded where poison, a Browning revolver, and repeated blows to the head had failed.[18]

Despite its elaborate mise-en-scène, Prince Yussoupov's supper party had little effect on Imperial Russia's war effort, or for that matter on the timing of the Revolution. In the mounting confusion there was no opportunity even to proceed with an orderly investigation of the incident. Nevertheless, it marked the beginning of a flood of political murder destined to engulf the entire dynasty, not to mention some who were the Romanovs' worst enemies.

The culminating event of what might be considered the imperial phase of the debacle was the shooting of Tsar Nicholas II, his wife Alexandra, their son Alexander, and their four daughters, the Grand Duchesses Olga, Tatiana, Maria, and Anastasia, together with their family doctor, the imperial chef, the emperor's valet, and the tsarina's personal maid. The date was July 16, 1918; the place, Ekaterinburg (now Sverdlovsk) in the Urals; and the killers, a hastily assembled firing squad led by one Jakov Yurosky, a local Bolshevik acting on orders issued by the Ural Soviet on instructions from the Politburo in Moscow. At various sites, beginning with the killing of Nicholas II's younger brother Grand Duke Michael several days before the tsar's own death, continuing on July 17 with the shooting of six more Romanovs, and concluding in January 1919 with that of the four remaining grand dukes, the imperial family was obliterated.

The tsar, the tsarina, and their children had been under arrest since March 1917. For sixteen months they were shuttled about, subject initially to humane conditions, but treated more and more harshly as the Revolution progressed, until they were summoned to meet their fate in a provincial dining room. At the beginning, as Kerensky's memoirs make clear, the pre-Bolshevik revolutionaries had betrayed their embarrassment over the question what to do with the tsar. The provisional government wanted him removed from command of the armies, as well as from politically volatile Saint Petersburg—but what then?[19] For a time even the Bolsheviks were perplexed. More than that, they were frightened. White Russian forces, with the support of the Czech Legion, were threatening the very region in which the world's highest-born prisoners were confined, seeking to capture Ekaterinburg as a key to the southern supply routes. All the arguments for and against putting a deposed monarch on trial were revived and considered, arguments as familiar, allowance made for problems of translation, to Robespierre and Danton as they had been still earlier to Cromwell.[20]

How the decision was finally made and why, is nowhere more candidly set forth than in the memoirs of Leon Trotsky, who explains that he personally had favored a courtroom drama:

> During one of my short visits to Moscow—I think a few weeks before the execution of the Romanovs—I incidentally mentioned in the Politburo that, considering the bad situation in the Urals, it would be expedient to accelerate the Tsar's trial. I proposed that we hold an open court trial which would reveal a picture of the whole reign, with its peasant policy, labor policy, national minority and cultural policies, its two wars, etc. The proceedings of the trial would be broadcast throughout the country (?) [question mark Trotsky's]; in the *volosts* [village districts], accounts of the proceedings would be read and commented upon every day. Lenin replied to the effect that it would be very good if it were feasible. But . . . there might not be enough time . . . No debate took place, since I did not insist on my proposal, being absorbed in other work . . .
>
> My next visit to Moscow took place after the fall of Ekaterinburg. Talking to Sverdlov, I asked in passing: "Oh yes, and where is the Tsar?" "It's all over," he answered, "he has been shot." "And where is the family?" "And the family along with him." "All of them?" I asked, apparently with a touch of surprise. "All of them!" replied Sverdlov, "What about it?" He was waiting to see my reaction. I made no reply. "And who made the decision?" I asked. "We decided it here. Ilyich [Lenin] believed that we shouldn't leave the Whites a live banner to rally around, especially in the present difficult circumstances."[21]

Despite his earlier hopes of serving as public prosecutor before a revolutionary tribunal, Trotsky concluded that the decision had been "not only expedient but necessary." His treatment of the matter concludes: "The severity of this summary justice showed the world that we would continue to fight on mercilessly, stopping at nothing. The execution of the Tsar's family was needed not only to frighten, horrify, and dishearten the enemy, but also to shake up our own ranks, to show them that there was no turning back, that ahead lay either victory or complete ruin."[22]

One of the reasons for Lenin's desire to avoid a regicide trial in Moscow or Petrograd may have been that Russia that summer was beset by other sorts of political murder. It was in many ways a terrible season for the new Bolshevik rulers. In March 1918, convinced that the country must have peace with Germany, they had accepted the humiliating treaty of Brest-

Litovsk. Thereafter, the Politburo had still to face the military threat of counterrevolution accompanied by charges of having capitulated to the hated Teutonic conqueror. Social Revolutionary spokesmen were particularly vitriolic, and though Lenin had managed to suppress, partly by physical intimidation, the abortive Constituent Assembly on which the SR had pinned its political hopes, he continued to encounter serious difficulty in posing as a Russian national spokesman.

The Social Revolutionaries, defeated on the parliamentary front, abandoned none of their disdain for the peace, choosing instead to revive methods once employed against Plehve and Stolypin, but now aimed at high German officials. On July 6, 1918, Count von Mirbach, the Kaiser's diplomatic representative in Moscow, was killed by SR gunmen. On July 30 in Kiev, Field Marshal von Eichhorn, commanding German occupation forces in the Ukraine, was slain by a young sailor to whom the "Left Social Revolutionary" leadership at the Kronstadt naval base had assigned that task. Defiance of the temporary victors was manifest. Attempts to punish the regime that had accepted defeat at Brest-Litovsk were soon to follow.

On the morning of August 30 at Petrograd, yet another SR agent, a student named Kenigiesser, shot and killed Moses S. Uritsky, local head of the Bolshevik security police (Cheka). In Moscow, Lenin learned of the murder before giving speeches at two workers' meetings. As he was walking back to his car after the second of these, a woman detached herself from the onlookers and fired three pistol shots at close range, hitting her target with two of them. Lenin's wounds, though serious, were kept well-concealed from the public, as was the crisis of leadership within his party which lasted until the release of an optimistic medical communiqué later that day. His assailant, Fanya Kaplan, who had been imprisoned for terrorism under the tsar, now claimed to be a follower of the Social Revolutionary leader Chernov and a foe of the Bolsheviks because of their betrayal of the Constituent Assembly. Little more is known about her, in part because she was promptly executed without trial.[23]

In a fashion reminiscent of Napoleon I's response to the Christmas Eve *attentat* of 1800, Lenin and his secret police avenged the 1918 attack by striking not only at the Social Revolutionaries but also at what Stalin, reporting from his command post in the south, described simply as "the bourgeoisie and its agents." The Moscow Cheka alone, according to a modest report from its director, shot "not more than six hundred people," and tidings from the hinterland boasted of successful purges made possible, again in Stalin's words, by "open, mass, and systematic terror."[24]

Rasputin was dead, the last victim of the old court and its intrigues. The imperial family had been wiped out. A German diplomat and a German field marshal had been slain, to no purpose, only months before the cause they had served collapsed, carrying with it into oblivion the terms of Brest-

Litovsk. A Bolshevik chieftain had been assassinated in Petrograd, and a far greater one wounded in Moscow. The time had come for the Revolution to counterattack, moving against its enemies wherever they might be.

The "Terrible Twenties": Two Ends of Europe

The years immediately following the Great War, like those after 1815, saw not just a resumption but a steep rise in the frequency of political homicide in Europe. That quantitative change, however, is not what made the Twenties different. Rather, it was the unexpected appearance of certain changes in behavior and in public response, still limited to a few locales but sufficiently ominous, within those confines, to mark the period between 1918 and the onset of the Great Depression as the seedtime of modern terrorism.

The overall record was, like past experience, uneven. In Latin America, Mexico emerged, if only briefly, as a scene of recurrent bloodshed, which had taken the life of Madero in 1913 and now claimed in succession those of the revolutionary leader Emiliano Zapata in 1919, President Venustiano Carranza in 1920, Francisco "Pancho" Villa in 1923, and the newly re-elected President Alvaro Obregón in 1928. Elsewhere in South and Central America, however, a sullen moratorium would continue with only sporadic interruptions until the onset of a new wave of violence in the 1940s. In Africa as a whole there was little recourse to assassination attempts, despite the slaying of the British Resident, Sir Lee Stack, in Egypt and the unsuccessful assault on that country's prime minister, Zaghloul Pasha, both in 1924. To the north and east, on the other hand, the collapse of the Ottoman Empire brought a flurry of political killings, especially in Syria and among officials of the Turkish Republic but also in other parts of the Middle East all the way to Afghanistan.

The rest of Asia witnessed the murders of two Japanese premiers, Takashi Hara in 1920 and Yūkō Hamaguchi in 1930 (both carried out by fanatical nationalists), as well as abortive attempts aimed at another prime minister, Admiral Takaaki Katō, in 1925 and at Crown Prince Hirohito the following year. As for China, foreign observers managed to glimpse only one assassination, that of General Chang Tso-lin, military governor of Manchuria, who was killed by a bomb while on a train between Peking and Mukden in 1928. Persistent reports at the time pointed to Japanese agents as responsible for eliminating the general, who had allegedly just renounced his former obedience to Tokyo's wishes. In India, despite anti-colonial feelings excited by the war, growing peasant insurgency against landlords, and serious communal strife between Hindus and Moslems, not a single attack upon a major political figure took place between Viceroy Hardinge's narrow escape in 1912 and Mahatma Gandhi's death in 1948.

So despite the best intentions—literally "in the world"—to broaden our camera angle, it is impossible to grasp the full importance of political homicide in the years after 1918 without paying special attention to Europe. Even there, many countries underwent their share of startling episodes without offering unmistakable portents of worse to come; but some of the scattered shocks appear to have been freighted with uncommon significance. Among these was the slaying in 1924 of an influential Italian journalist and socialist deputy, Giacomo Matteotti, by Black Shirts—harbingers of increased official terror under Mussolini's newly established dictatorship. Another was the proscription that accompanied the Russian civil war. Ominous though the latter may have been, however, its connection with later developments was not immediately discernible. Between Lenin's death in 1924 and Stalin's purge trials in the 1930s, the only known "Russian murders" of individuals were committed outside the Soviet Union; and some did not appear to involve Bolsheviks at all. In 1926, to cite an early example, Simon Petliura, a Ukrainian politician-in-exile living in Paris, was shot by another refugee, Simon Schwarzbart, as retribution for anti-Jewish pogroms in the pre-1917 Ukraine.

In most European nations, postwar violence followed a limited number of familiar patterns. Spain's premier, Eduardo Dato, was slain in 1921 by an anarchist determined to avenge the recent outburst of police brutality directed against other members of the movement, especially in Barcelona. The same year, in Portugal, former Prime Minister António Granjo and four other conservative politicians were murdered during one night of bloodshed by a combination of soldiers and civilian vigilantes. All of the victims had been involved with the wartime strongman, President Sidónio Pais, himself assassinated in December 1918, hardly more than a month after the Armistice. Whether or not Pais should be counted a casualty of the return to peacetime politics, no such doubt surrounds the death a few weeks earlier of Count Stephen Tisza, the Hungarian premier shot by embittered soldiers who had been discharged but not disarmed.

In contrast to the Iberian cases, some of those arising farther east, as the confusion over Tisza's end indicates, suggested a wider range of goals than anarchy or leftist revolution. It was right-wing extremists who in 1922 took the lives first of the Finnish interior minister Heikki Ritavuori and then of the president of Poland, Gabriel Narutowicz. More than its share of political killing plagued the expanded Kingdom of the Serbs, Croats, and Slovenes (Yugoslavia, as it was renamed officially in 1929). There casualties among public functionaries ranged from Minister of Interior Milorad Drašković by a Bosnian Communist in 1921 to that of the Croat Peasant Party leader, Stepan Raditch, and two of his fellow deputies, gunned down in 1928 on the floor of the national parliament by a Montenegrin separatist.

If this litany of personal and factional violence were all one could derive from the European record of the postwar years, there would be little reason to attach special importance to the "Terrible Twenties." Yet the decade's claim to that grim distinction is secure, largely because of events occurring in three countries. Two of them, Ireland and Bulgaria, are at opposite extremes of the European map, while the third, Germany, occupies a place at its very center. All three, however, form parts of a centerpiece for this entire chapter.

In one respect the Irish tragedy's twentieth-century phase has been marked by a special irony. The memory of Ribbonmen and Fenians, of Phoenix Park and the Easter Rebellion, along with that of English counterblows, should have been enough to exhaust the taste for violence in this beautiful island with its deceptively gentle landscape. Nothing could be further from the truth. The old hatred of England survived recognition in 1921 of the Irish Free State, with its newly won dominion status within the British Empire. That hatred was in some ways intensified by the six Ulster counties' remaining part of the United Kingdom as Northern Ireland. It was civil war between Irishmen, however, which in the 1920s brought bloodshed on a scale surpassing anything unleashed by the struggle of Erse and English, at least since the seventeenth century.[25]

Eamon de Valera's rejection of the 1921 settlement signaled the beginning of internecine strife on two fronts. The very next year Prime Minister Michael Collins was killed in an ambush staged by the Irish Republican Army on Irish soil. In London, only weeks before that event, a pair of young IRA gunmen "executed" Sir Henry Wilson, a Protestant Ulsterman and retired field marshal well-known for his support of a separate Northern Ireland. Wilson's assassins, captured and hanged in Pentonville Gaol, had had the satisfaction of knowing that their victim was one of the ancient foe. Not so the slayers in 1927 of Kevin O'Higgins, shot to death while serving as vice-president of the Free State, and its most influential leader. The IRA's murder of this popular Catholic spokesman at last brought a revulsion of popular feeling; but nothing could erase the memory of countless hostages and military prisoners shot in cold blood by Free State forces and rebels alike.

In Bulgaria, as in Ireland, there was a background of bitter memories and lethal violence. But the same was true of other states standing on the ruins of Ottoman and Hapsburg hegemony, so it is not readily apparent why Bulgarian political life should have been even more sanguinary than that of Yugoslavia or Poland. Part of the explanation may be that, to a complex of grievances and quarrels over land problems, religious differences, socialist agitation, and the role of an alien (German) royal family, there had lately been added for Bulgaria the humiliation of successive military defeats. They had come in 1913 at the hands of Serbia, Greece, Rumania, and Turkey, and in 1918 with the ruin of the Central Powers, King Ferdinand's ill-chosen partners in the Great War. This double legacy of hatred, poisoning relations with all Bulgaria's Balkan neighbors, was nowhere more starkly revealed than in disagreements over the "Macedonian question," to which the interested parties brought a seemingly limitless ferocity. If to these international problems are added the traditional arrogance of the Bulgarian officers corps and the emergence following the Russian Revolution of a particularly belligerent Communist movement, the resulting witch's brew of causes is quite adequate to account for the brutal drama about to unfold.[26]

The worst of that drama occupied a period of about two years beginning in 1923. On June 14, shortly after the assassination of a cabinet member named Nicola Genadiev, a second and more prominent political figure was struck down. He was Alexander Stambolisky, ousted from the premiership only the previous week by a right-wing junta under Alexander Tsankov. Stambolisky was a politician of national stature, founder of the Bulgarian Peasant Party before 1914, opponent of his country's wartime alliance with Berlin and Vienna, sponsor of the Green International of European agrarian parties, and vocal exponent of rapprochement with old enemies abroad, notably including the government of victorious Serbia. Following his fall from power on June 8, he attempted to escape through the mountains, only to be overtaken and killed by a detachment of his pursuers. Those directly to blame belonged to the so-called Macedonian independence movement, or IMRO, an organization actually committed to Bulgarian dominance there. IMRO, however, was by no means the only faction intent upon destroying the former prime minister. Also involved were the military, Communist, and other hostile party leaders, not to mention the anti-Yugoslav court party around King Boris III.

Stambolisky's imperious manner had swelled the ranks of his enemies; but the death of his generally well-liked successor as head of the Agrarian Party, Petko Petkov, shot to death one year later on a street in the capital, proved that personal geniality was no protection against the vagaries of Bulgarian politics. Again IMRO appeared to have engineered the murder, with various elements on both the right and the left registering at least tacit approval. Meanwhile, the Bulgarian-Macedonian movement was suffering casualties of its own—some of them self-inflicted, as when the IMRO leader Todor Alexandrov was killed by former confederates who suspected him of straying from a properly anti-Serb, anti-Greek, and anti-Rumanian position.

Thus far, despite the multiplicity of hatreds in evidence, the clearest battle line in Sofia had appeared to be drawn between Agrarians and nationalists of various stripes. In the period after the deaths of Stambolisky, Petkov, and Alexandrov, however, there came into full view a no less bitter conflict between, on the right, civilian and military forces controlling the national government and, on the left, the Bulgarian Communist Party. Pro-Soviet by definition and hence Russophile in Balkan affairs, insistent on socioeconomic change but contemptuous of agrarian strategies, the leadership of the CP under Giorgi Dimitrov brought a new intensity, and very soon, a novel set of tactics, to the country's many-sided competition for power.

The climax of the struggle came in the spring of 1925. On April 14 an unsuccessful attempt was made on the life of King Boris. The next day, as religious services of rejoicing over his escape were being planned, the nation's highest-ranking soldier, General Kosta Georgiev, was killed by unknown gunmen as he stepped from his car outside the war ministry. Instead of celebration, a state funeral for Georgiev had now to be held on April 16 in Sofia's Saint Nedelja Cathedral. While the service was in progress, with the king and most members of the government present, a tremendous explosion ripped through the church. The bomb was poorly placed, from the assassin's point of view, for Boris III and other high officials escaped unhurt; but the final death toll came to more than 125.

Charges were leveled against the Communists, Dimitrov's absence from Bulgaria at the time being taken in some quarters as proof of guilty foreknowledge. Other voices insisted no less loudly that the assault was a Nationalist crime, perhaps committed by agents of the Tsankov government itself. Most foreign observers were inclined to credit the theory that the survival of the king and his ministers was evidence of a right-wing plot to incriminate Dimitrov's party. A third view, less complicated but well-seasoned with recent experience, was that anything this bad must have been the work of the Macedonian movement.

It is unlikely that all shadings of individual and factional involvement in the atrocity will ever be established beyond doubt. Direct responsibility for the bombing, however, is no longer a subject of conjecture, thanks to a revelation made almost twenty-five years later by an unexpected but not unqualified source. On December 19, 1948, delegates to the Bulgarian Communist Party Congress were startled to hear from the chairman of their now triumphant movement, Georgi Dimitrov, that the incendiaries of 1925 had indeed been Communists, advocates of terrorism whose tactics he had deplored then and still considered "incorrect." To countless believers in the Party's innocence, Dimitrov's blunt announcement came as a distinct shock; but none could argue that the Communist leader, become his nation's ruler by the grace of the Red Army, had any reason to lie.[27]

Nothing can have contributed more to the disapproval with which Dimitrov recalled the episode than the massive damage his party suffered as a result. The Tsankov regime seized the opportunity to crush opposition in general, imprisoning not only scores of Communists but also selected Agrarians, summarily executing dissidents in various parts of the country, and in the process lending credence to the suspicion that it had been responsible for the blast in the first place. In reacting thus, the royal government rode a wave of popular outrage and apprehension. It could also cite demands by the postwar Allied Control Commission in Bulgaria that order be restored and that no further chances be taken with the threat of a Soviet-style revolution. None were, and none would be until 1945, by which time the Russian advance into the Balkans made the success of such a revolution no longer a matter of chance.

Weimar Germany

During the years after 1918 the Irish and Bulgarian experience found a parallel in only one major European power. For Germans, the defeat and dissolution of their once-proud empire had brought a number of traumatic blows, none harder to bear or even to comprehend than the shattering of domestic order, confidence, and a certain ponderous restraint in interpersonal relations with which the old Empire was associated in popular memory. The Wilhelmian Reich had not been wholly immune to assassination. Empress Elizabeth may have shared the Austro-Hungarian throne with a Hapsburg, but she had been born a Bavarian princess and was mourned as such throughout Germany after her senseless murder in 1898. William II, like his grandfather before him, had been the target of two assaults, the first by a Frau Schnapka, who threw a hatchet toward him in 1900, the other by a Bremen shipyard worker, who the next year struck the Kaiser in the face with another missile, this one a scrap of iron. Even in the heyday of anarchism, however, critics of the imperial regime seem, almost without exception, to have shared the view taken by the leaders of the Social Democratic Party (SPD), namely, that political violence was counterproductive and tyrannicide a fantasy unworthy of loyal subjects.

The Armistice that ended the Great War, though it marked the dissolution of Hohenzollern government, brought no civil war so protracted as Ireland's nor any instance of mass homicide comparable to the cathedral bombing in Sofia. What the young Weimar Republic suffered instead was a demoralizing wave of homicidal attacks, almost all occurring within the space of four years, affecting twelve of its most prominent political leaders, and bringing death to no fewer than eight of them.[23] The list that follows omits the names of many less notable figures who were objects of lethal attempts, more of them fatal than not.

1919   Karl Liebknecht and Rosa Luxemburg, leaders of the Spartacist League and of the newly formed German Communist Party, killed by right-wing Free Corpsmen during the January uprising in Berlin;

Kurt Eisner, Independent Socialist minister-president of Bavaria, shot to death by Lt. Count Arco-Valley in Munich the next month;

Erhard Auer, successor to Eisner, attacked with two colleagues in the Landtag building on the day of Eisner's death by a self-styled Majority Socialist workingman (one of Auer's companions, deputy Ösel, died of gunshot wounds);

Otto Neuring, Socialist War Minister of Saxony, killed in April by soldiers protesting a cut in pay as well as other decisions by the state government;

Hugo Haase, former leader of the Independent Socialists, slain the following autumn by right-wing gunmen;

1921   Matthias Erzberger, parliamentary leader of the Catholic Center Party and a signer of the Versailles Treaty, more recently Finance Minister in the national government, shot to death on October 26 by two young ex-officers, members of the nationalist *Organisation Consul,* while he was strolling with a fellow Reichstag deputy near a Black Forest vacation resort;

Karl Gareis, Bavarian Socialist Landtag deputy, shot to death on June 10 outside his house in Munich by an ex-officer and member of the paramilitary *Einwohnerwehr;*

1922   Philipp Scheidemann, former Social Democratic chancellor of the Republic and incumbent lord mayor of Kassel, attacked with Prussic acid by two Organisational Consul agents while walking with his family, but drew a pistol and escaped without injury when both assailants fled;

Foreign Minister Walther Rathenau, Jewish businessman and internationally respected administrator and diplomat, killed June 24 while being driven from his Berlin-Grunewald home to the Foreign Office—the decade's most highly publicized and widely condemned assassination (the two Organisation Consul killers, former naval officers, escaped after firing a machine pistol from their car and throwing a hand grenade into Rathenau's, but were cornered while attempting to flee the country, one succumbing to police fire, the other taking his own life);[29]

Maximilian Harden, prominent and controversial Jewish publicist, survived blows to head and body inflicted with an iron bar by two Organisation Consul members near his residence in Grunewald a little more than a week after the Rathenau murder;

1924   Heinz Orbis, pro-French separatist leader in the Rhenish Palatinate, shot to death with four colleagues by a team of four nationalist gunmen in a hotel restaurant at Speyer.

Walther Rathenau

These episodes, concentrated as they were, in the early years of the Republic, lend support to what has become a widely accepted method of dividing Weimar history into periods. Political assassination was rampant throughout the first years, a time of post-Versailles resentment and humiliation, French intervention in the Ruhr, local uprising in "Red Saxony" as well as "Black-Brown Bavaria," and runaway inflation. During the ensuing interval of relative stabilization in the middle and late twenties, political violence, if it did not disappear, lost for a time its grip on the lives and thoughts of the German citizenry. A terrible model, however, had been displayed, one capable of returning to threaten public confidence again when in late 1929 Germany's republican experiment entered its terminal crisis.

The majority of German terrorists after 1918 came from the right, in the sense that they chanted the slogans of a bitter irredentism in opposition to what they branded the twin threats of international socialism and classical liberalism. Some of the never fully demobilized Free Corpsmen, extolling the memory of the "heroes of 1813" as fervently as they cursed that of the "traitors" of 1918, filled the nationalist paramilitary cadres, whence came most of the era's known assassins. The left, too, had marching formations:

but the Social Democrats clung to their condemnation of murder, while the German Communist Party remained more seriously split than even its Bulgarian counterpart over the advisability of resorting to terrorism.[30]

It was not, however, the political coloration of the Organisation Consul and the underground tribunals, or even the specific, time-bound reasons they gave for assigning teams of members to slay "republican traitors" that proved to be their most important attributes. Instead, what has conferred on Weimar Germany its peculiar significance for this history of terrorism is that it presented to a startled world a number of features which were new in the 1920s but have since become familiar attributes of political murder as a global phenomenon.

First, there was the conscious adoption of military models, not only in the organization of street-fighting units (Lenin had advocated that in 1905) but also in the use of sophisticated weapons by assassins trained in the requisite tactics and technology while members of regular armed forces. Teams of such men, equipped with the latest in firearms, explosives, and lethal chemicals, rehearsed carefully in secluded parks and forests before setting out on predetermined missions.

A second feature was less operational than conceptual in nature. This was the claim, foreshadowed by only a few of the most extreme nineteenth-century nihilists—Nechaev among them—that the terrorists were at war with an entire system, primarily political in the Germans' case, more broadly social in a growing number of later ones. This claim that they were engaged in declared hostilities turned up among the enemies of the Weimar Republic, in their courtroom speeches, in secret pamphlets circulated to discussion groups of the already converted, in letters sent to newspapers for publication, and even in the pledges of fugitives abroad to "carry on the war" from places of exile.

The third element, the reference to "trials" and "executions" by those claiming credit for political murders, points to the survival of certain older, judgmental metaphors of classical tyrannicide amid the military jargon also frequently employed by members of the new order of assassins. This recourse to the language of a twisted judicature was not confined to the clandestine treason courts (*Femgerichte*) with their fantasies of medieval German proceedings. Other terrorists, although not formally enrolled in the Feme movement, boasted at times of having carried out death sentences in the name of a higher law than could be found in the miserable Republic's constitution.

These forerunners of today's urban guerrillas displayed additional characteristics that have since become familiar, including the tendency to disagree among themselves over the relative merits of purely destructive appeals and more explicit statements of a programmatic sort. Was it enough to "shake the system," or were concrete objectives needed? Not infrequently, as in trying to determine the stance to be adopted concerning early Nazi propaganda, they simply tabled the matter. In the short run, after all, actions not words were what drew the most widespread attention.

And not even the intimidation of government officials had a higher priority than public notice. In the nineteenth century occasional assassins, among them Carl Sand, Felice Orsini, and the Irish Invincibles, had enjoyed the support of scattered patrons together with varying amounts of public sympathy. Generally speaking, however, curiosity had been more prevalent than support, and newspapers of the pre-1914 era had all but unanimously condemned physical attacks on individuals, regardless of political reasons put forward by the attackers. After 1918 the response to Feme murders and comparable acts committed in Weimar Germany suddenly became more confused. Not only did private citizens frequently register their detestation of the "Paris Peace criminals," but certain foreign regimes, that of Hungary for instance, were adamant in their refusal to extradite German nationalist refugees, including the acknowledged killers of Matthias Erzberger.

Erzberger's assassination in 1921 had received favorable attention within Germany itself, especially from the conservative press. On the day after the murder one German-language newspaper in the Silesian town of Oletzko (now Olesno, Poland) remarked on its editorial page: "Erzberger . . . has suffered the fate which the vast majority of Germans had long desired for him. Erzberger, the man who is alone responsible for the humiliating armistice; Erzberger, the man who is responsible for the acceptance of the Versailles 'treaty of shame.' "[31] Prussia's Junker mouthpiece in Berlin, the venerable *Kreuzzeitung,* striving to maintain a more decorous tone, arrived at a not very different conclusion: "Nothing is cheaper than to condemn the assassins, whose motives are still unknown . . . Those who now praise Erzberger and attack his enemies seem to forget completely that the entire campaign against [him] has been essentially a defensive struggle."[32]

The 1930s: Terror and the State

Surprisingly, the incidence of major assassinations attempted between 1931 and 1940 (46 attempts, 35 of them fatal) was lower than in any other decade of the twentieth century except the first. The corresponding figures for the twenties had been 63 attempts and 44 fatalities, while those for 1941–1950 come to 85 and 64. The trouble with statistical comparisons of this sort is that they may, and in the present case do, run the risk of focusing on the wrong variables. For what imparted a special grimness to the years immediately preceding World War II was not the still substantial number of political murders, defined in traditional terms, but the scope and intensity of repression practiced by ostensibly legitimate regimes. It was this quality of the period that led a great French historian, writing in 1938, to abandon the once honorable Roman term "dictatorship" and to speak instead of an "era of tyrannies," of new despotism in which gangsters had achieved power over entire nations.[33]

Governmental terror has in one form or another played as large a part in political history, whether of Hellenistic kingdoms or of the Zulu empire in nineteenth-century Africa, as have violent acts of insurgency.[34] What distinguished the 1930s was that they witnessed a new level of state-authorized brutality, justified by doctrines of order or racial purity or class conflict, intensified by a combination of a bureaucratic efficiency and technological capabilities. In a very real sense, the concept of civilization itself seemed to be facing extinction.

Many individual assaults continued to recall earlier ones, with or without the occasional addition of novel features. In February 1936, when the French socialist leader Léon Blum was attacked and wounded by nationalist demonstrators along the Boulevard Saint-Germain, some of his countrymen were reminded of Jean Jaurès' death in 1914, dissimilar though the two cases clearly were. Like Jaurès, Blum offended some of his enemies as a pacifist, others as a socialist. Even the anti-Semitic feelings directed against him from the right-wing Action Française and the fascist Croix de Feu, though encouraged by contemporary racism, owed at least as much to an anti-Dreyfusard tradition handed down from an earlier France.[35] The deaths of Poland's chief of political police in 1932 and its interior minister in 1934, fit even more neatly into an existing mold of ethnic revolt, since both men were killed by Ukrainian activists. The list of Europeans slain in colonial outposts increased by only one, Ralph Cairns, a British police official in Palestine under the League of Nations mandate, who died in 1939 at the hands of the Jewish underground (*Irgun zwei Leumi*). (Marshal Rodolfo Graziani, Mussolini's viceroy in Addis Ababa, had escaped an attack by Ethiopian partisans two years before.)

Elsewhere the decade's record was spotty. In the Western Hemisphere, reserving for now Zangara's firing upon President-elect Franklin D. Roosevelt in 1933 and Senator Huey Long's death at Baton Rouge, Louisiana, in 1935, there was a relative lull. There were no assassinations of note in Mexico and only one south of the Isthmus of Panama, that of Peru's President Luis M. Sánchez Cerro in 1933. In Nicaragua in 1943 a national guardsman killed the rebel chief Augusto Sandino, his brother, and two political associates, bestowing on the country's future ruling party its name and its martyr. By comparative standards, however, the New World's list of political murder committed during those years is remarkably short. The same holds true for most of Asia, though, as in the past, the exception was Japan.[36]

In January 1931 Emperor Hirohito escaped a second attempt to kill him (the first since his accession to the throne), this time by a young Korean dissident. The year 1932 brought the assassination of Tsuyoshi Inukai, prime minister and leader of the majority Seiyuko Party, killed by three naval officers who were determined, as they put it, to "free the Mikado from evil advisers." Like the Hara and Hamaguchi murders in the 1920s, the Inukai slaying and an unsuccessful attempt upon the life of former Premier Reejiro Wakatsuki the following year were obvious milestones on the Japanese imperialists' road to war. The worst episode in that sequence, however, had yet to come. In 1936 a number of more or less moderate policymakers, among them Finance Minister Korekiyo Takahashi and a former premier, Admiral Makoto Saitō, died in an abortive putsch staged by young army officers seeking to block the proposed naval limitation agreement and any curtailment of the conflict with China.

The sanguinary drama unfolding in Japan and the attack on Blum in Paris owed much to the peculiar hysteria of the 1930s, but they remained rooted as well in the nationalist passions of the preceding century. Added proof of this marriage of old and new was furnished by a pair of sensational episodes from 1934. One was the double murder of Alexander I of Yugoslavia and French Foreign Minister Jean Louis Barthou on October 9, while they were riding in an open car through the streets of Marseilles following the king's arrival for an important state visit to France. The other had taken place less than two months before in Vienna, where Chancellor Engelbert Dollfuss was gunned down by one of a gang of pro-Hitler Austrians. Otto Planetta, convicted of firing the fatal shots at Dollfuss, was, like his victim, a conservative Catholic; but he was also a believer in the New Germany, as the chancellor was not. The Austrian National Socialist Party, on directions from Berlin, made Planetta a martyr without even waiting for his execution that autumn.

Nazism's role in the Austrian assassination might tempt us to contrast the Dollfuss case with that of Alexander and Barthou in France, calling the former new and the latter just one more eruption of "traditional" Balkan hatreds.[37] Upon closer examination, the distinction fades. The killer in Marseilles was to be sure a Bulgarian acting on behalf of Croatian opponents of Serbian rule. But he had trained for his mission in Italy, with the help of Mussolini's government; and Ante Pavelich, leader of the rebellious Croats (*Ustachi*), was already identifiable as a fascist puppet within the boundaries of Yugoslavia. Both crimes, that in Marseilles no less than the one in Vienna, were seen by their instigators as adding force to the "wave of the future," destined in their view to sweep away Europe's old order in its entirety.

The spreading effects of that wave were nowhere more unsettling than in Rumania, where Bucharest, in the sequel to Bulgaria's crisis of the previous decade, seemed to have replaced Sofia as the Balkans' most unpredictable storm center. On the face of things the Rumanian situation seemed very different from the Bulgarian, particularly with respect to external relations. King Carol II ascended the throne in 1930 as ruler of a nation that had tasted military victory, first in 1913, then in 1918, and had substantial territorial gains to show for its fortunate choice of allies in both wars. Despite the enmity of defeated neighbors, the Danubian–Black Sea kingdom looked forward to a future seemingly assured by continuing French support, membership in the Little Entente as a partner of Czechoslovakia and Yugoslavia, the nonaggression pact achieved with Russia in 1933 despite the unresolved question of the Soviets' "lost province" of Bessarabia, and promising negotiations with Turkey, Greece, and Poland.

Unfortunately for the Bucharest government, however, this array of foreign engagements was not matched by similar grounds for optimism at home. Liberals and peasant leaders remained committed to oppositional roles, nonviolent but unyielding. Still more disturbing to the monarch and his council was the xenophobic, anti-Semitic, and authoritarian program of the Iron Guard, with its green-shirted paramilitary formations.[38] Its leader, Cornelius Codreanu, having denounced literally every foreign alliance thus far concluded or projected by the regime, at last provoked a forceful response from the prime minister, Jon Duca. In December 1933 Duca issued a decree imposing serious restraints on the Guard as a party and virtually outlawing its uniformed brigades.

Codreanu's reaction was immediate. On December 30 Duca was shot to death by a five-man team of Iron Guardsmen on the platform of a railway station in Carpathia. Nevertheless, a like-minded successor replaced him, and during the ensuing couple of years it was the Guard that appeared to suffer most from confrontation and internal stife. Young Michael Stelescu had been the founder of the Brothers of the Cross, an order that had joined forces with Codreanu's League of Saint Michael the Archangel to constitute the Iron Guard. Undermining this combination was the fact that Stelescu remained anti-German, out of deference to Rumanian war memories; by 1936 he was issuing dramatic forecasts to the effect that an attempt would be made to kill him for opposing closer ties with Hitler. He even induced the party newspaper to publish a list of eight men he believed had been chosen by Codreanu for the task. Stelescu's information was accurate. On July 16, while hospitalized following an appendectomy, he was shot thirty-eight times by precisely the agents he had named in advance.

The government continued to pursue the Guard's remaining leaders, with the justice minister, Armand Calinescu, in charge of the campaign. By the fall of 1938 Codreanu and no fewer than seventeen of his henchmen, including all of Duca's and Stelescu's murderers, had been arrested, tried, and sentenced—in Codreanu's case to ten years in the salt mines. On the night of November 29–30, while in transit from one prison at Ramnicu to another in Jilava, all eighteen convicted Guardsmen were shot to death by a gunman referred to in the justice ministry's communique as "unknown and unapprehended." For the moment King Carol's regime was victorious. In September 1939, however, only three weeks after Hitler launched his war, Calinescu himself was assassinated, beginning the long series of acts of vengeance carried out by the Iron Guard with Nazi blessings.

In Rumania, as in most other countries of continental Europe, the advance of the German Wehrmacht and the lengthening shadow of National Socialism had rendered passé much that had been taken for granted about interwar politics. So ominous was this spreading revolution in the theory and practice of the state, and so central the role of Nazi Germany, that there persists even today a mental habit of treating Hitlerian rule as all but unique in what its own leaders called their movement's "world significance." That tendency to concentrate on a single powerful nation, instead of seeking to make too much of either totalitarianism or even fascism as a wholly reliable abstraction, has a good deal to recommend it, if the USSR is not ignored.

The Thirties: Russia and Germany

In many important respects the 1930s "belonged" to this pair of military giants arising from defeat in the First World War. Their success in creating models of lethal repression did most to give the decade its distinctive place in the history of political homicide. Other cases—Spanish, eastern European, even Italian—though they testify to the phenomenon's exportability, were either imitative in theory or limited in fact by a relative lack of power. Another kind of contrast applies to certain earlier regimes, for compared to the results achieved in Germany under Hitler and the USSR under Stalin, the levels of despotism observable in either the Napoleonic or the Romanov Empire, to cite only two examples, fade into the background colors of traditional autocracy, with all its capricious inefficiency.

The Soviet regime had not waited until the thirties before commencing to apply deadly pressure when threatened by domestic resistance. Judging from the police records of various other countries, however, sometimes corroborated by the testimony of Russian defectors, it was only after the 1920s that Moscow began to authorize large numbers of murders on foreign soil. Then the USSR surpassed even Nazi Germany in the use it made of assassination abroad. The government of the Third Reich may have instigated, and certainly welcomed, many acts of violence in other countries—the slaying of Dollfuss in Vienna being a case in point—but Hitler showed surprisingly little interest in any effort to destroy opponents outside the area of direct German control. Perhaps he was simply waiting. If so, this was not a preference shared by Stalin, who willingly employed secret police of the GPU and, after it, the NKVD to carry out "executions," some of them thousands of miles from Moscow.

The most celebrated of these was Leon Trotsky's murder at his home outside Mexico City in August 1940. Lest this be mistaken for an isolated occurrence, it should be recalled that Trotsky's son, Lev Sedov, had been eliminated two and a half years earlier by Soviet agents in Paris. That same year, 1938, in Rotterdam the GPU was credited with the death by explosives of Evhen Konovalets, an exiled Ukrainish spokesman. In September 1937 a similar technique had been employed in Switzerland to kill the ex-Communist Party functionary and intelligence officer Ignaz Reis; a fortnight before that slaying the GPU in Paris, using information from a White Russian informer well-known to the Sûreté, had abducted another prominent émigré, known only as "General Evgeni," who was never seen again.

To careful students of Soviet practice, therefore, the destruction of so prominent and embattled a figure as Trotsky came as no surprise. He had been hounded out of Norway in 1937, amid demands from the USSR for his extradition, and only by fleeing to Mexico postponed the fate which overtook his son. There an attempt by a squad of gunmen to surprise him at his house in suburban Coyoacán late in May 1940 failed; but three months later Ramón Mercador, alias Frank Jacson [sic], used an ice-chopper's axe to succeed where the earlier assassins had not. Recruited and briefed by the NKVD in New York, Jacson upon arriving in Mexico had ingratiated himself as a volunteer chauffeur and "admiring friend" of the Trotskys, to whose living quarters he thus had easy access when the time came.[39] By Soviet standards Trotsky and his son died not as murder victims but as condemned criminals, having been tried in absentia and sentenced to death for crimes against the revolution and its homeland. Their deaths were in that sense integrally related to the treason trials undertaken by the USSR in the mid-1930s.

Much of the controversy over the great Soviet purge has centered around the question whether or not it can properly be described as just one more example of judicial murder. Partisan impulses being what they are, merely to call a given case of trial and punishment "murder" does not automatically validate the label. There are, however, times when solemn forms of justice serve only as a mask for proscription by those who control the state's legal apparatus. In the seventeenth century this was what occurred in the case of the distinguished Dutch leader Oldenbarneveldt, as well as in those of England's Rye House hangings and the "Bloody Assizes." A similar expedient was applied by the French Revolutionary Tribunal in the 1790s, on a far vaster scale. As for the Moscow version of such proceedings, post-Stalinist leaders of the Soviet Union no longer insist that even the sixteen so-called "worst defendants," Kamenev, Zinoviev, and Radek among them, who were convicted and shot in 1937, had all been foreign agents. Similar misgivings surround the condemnation and execution of Marshal Tukhachevsky and other high military officers, beginning in June of that year, on charges of treasonable collaboration with the German and Japanese general staffs.[40]

Brushing aside questions of individual guilt or innocence, defenders of the Soviet procedure point to a higher political good. During the two decades following the Great October Revolution, so this argument runs, the USSR was struggling to survive in a hostile world, seeking at the same time to create a new social, political, and economic order within Russia itself. The need for harsh discipline purportedly accounts for the elimination of Social Revolutionaries, Mensheviks, and tsarist diehards by Lenin, Trotsky, and others of the first Bolshevik generation. The same necessity is cited to justify the subsequent liquidation of the unassimilable independent farmers, or *kulaks*. In this context the treason trials of the 1930s appear as a reaction to yet another threat, that of Nazi subversion and future aggression. Memories of secret Russo-German military collaboration in the 1920s served to reinforce other causes for distrust within the Kremlin, even after Hitler's abrupt termination of the arrangement. As for the civilian defendants, how could one be sure they had not slipped into deviationism or even criminal correspondence with agents of the capitalist West?

The trouble with the claim that Stalin "saved Russia" by cleaning out subversive elements prior to the outbreak of World War II is that it betrays a stubborn indifference to the lack of hard evidence against those accused, as distinct from their somnambulistic "confessions." It also ignores the dictator's own refusal in 1941 to credit reports of an impending German invasion and his stunned withdrawal into seclusion for nearly two weeks after the Wehrmacht attacked. There can be no denying that the Moscow trials suggest another historic case of rigged judicature as a subspecies of assassination. Yet despite the comparisons between Nazis and Bolsheviks drawn by observers as different one from the other as Friedrich Adler and Arthur Koestler, or the indictment of Soviet leaders expressed by Elie Halévy, who in 1937 wrote that "their tyranny . . . ends up looking very like the German or Italian," some important distinctions between the two regimes must be made.[41]

One of these stands by itself in appearing, however superficially, to favor Germany, in that it shows Hitler's government less inclined than Stalin's to send killers abroad. Paradoxically, during their movement's first years in power Nazis were the victims, not the perpetrators, of two sensational murders of Germans residing in foreign parts. On February 4, 1936, Landesgruppenleiter Wilhelm Gustloff, assigned to Switzerland for the purpose of organizing pro-Nazi activities there, was killed at Davos by a Jewish student, David Frankfurter. Serious as were the effects of this act on the position of Jews living in Germany under the recently promulgated Nuremburg Decrees, the second episode was a signal for still more brutal reprisals. On November 7, 1938, Ernst von Rath, an embassy official in Paris, was shot to death by another Jewish assailant, the seventeen-year-old Polish citizen Herschel Grynszpan.

Within the Reich, Rath's murder touched off officially sponsored terror on a scale previously unknown. A wave of pogroms culminated in the nocturnal orgy of beatings and destruction of Jewish shops, whose shattered windows inspired jubilant Nazis to name their triumph "Crystal Night," in mocking reference to a glistening winterscape. Hermann Goering, Hitler's special commissioner to assess more formal penalties, first imposed on the nation's Jewish community a fine of one billion marks, then confiscated for governmental use all insurance payments due owners of property destroyed or damaged on the *Kristallnacht,* and finally issued the climactic decree providing, as its title proudly announced, for "The Elimination of Jews from German Economic Life." Neither Frankfurter in Davos nor Grynszpan in Paris did his unfortunate coreligionists a favor; but even had no "Jewish atrocity" occurred, the regime would almost certainly have found another pretext for adopting the same course of action.

The National Socialists, from their beginnings in the wake of the First World War, had shown little interest in individual, demonstrative attacks after the manner of the Organisation Consul, preferring the kind of collective hooliganism Nazism would exploit so effectively along its road to power. Between 1930 and 1933 in particular, the Brown Shirts of the *Sturmabteilungen* (SA) disrupted the meetings of their Communist and Social Democratic rivals, bludgeoned, kicked, and sometimes murdered opponents on the streets or in the victims' home, vandalized the latter's property, and in general implemented Hitler's vision of a "double terror." This called for the purposeful creation of terror by the Nazis themselves, coupled with fervent efforts to enlist public support for the promised suppression of disorder (using methods still terrorist in nature). It was partly this tactic which led Franz Neumann to name his 1940 treatment of the regime *Behemoth,* after a huge beast of the Chaos.[42]

Once Hitler was ensconced in power, the next order of business was the silencing of dissent among the rowdier of the old Nazis, the soothing of uneasy conservative allies, including high army officers, and the crushing of a polyglot array of former opponents. All this he achieved on June 30–July 1, 1934, the "Night of Long Knives." In one burst of murderous assaults, synchronized but geographically scattered, stealthily organized commandos of the Führer's own bodyguard, or *Schutzstaffel* (SS), and the Secret State Police (*Gestapo*) killed more than fifty SA leaders, among them Ernst Roehm, the disgruntled commander of the Storm Troops. Victims who were not members of Roehm's organization included former Bavarian Minister President Gustav Kahr, Hitler's erstwhile ally turned enemy over the Beerhall Putsch attempt in 1923; Gregor Strasser, the "Nazi Left's" most eloquent critic of compromise with vested interests; two political generals, Kurt von Schleicher and Ferdinand von Bredow (the former Hitler's immediate predecessor as Reich chancellor); and assorted functionaries including two personal aides of former Chancellor Franz von Papen.

Here was political murder directed at individually selected targets and carried out on a scale exceeding even that of Stalin's treason trials. Between the two purges, however, the differences were at least as significant as the similarities. Whereas Stalin would make the fullest use of judicial trappings, Hitler on this occasion went straight to summary executions, wasting no time on formal criminal proceedings. His own creation, the People's Court (*Volksgerichtshof*), constituted only two months before the killing of Roehm, Strasser, and the rest in 1934, was destined to get full use against accused "traitors of July 20th" ten years later. During the intervening decade it pronounced innumerable death sentences, most of them carried out by decapitation or slow hanging in the grisly execution chamber of Berlin's Ploetzensee Prison. At the time of the Blood Purge, however, the relatively young dictatorship apparently did not trust this still younger tribunal to meet the pressing needs of the moment.

At that early stage in the National Socialist consolidation of power, tactics congenial to underground fighters continued to serve an ostensibly "legal" regime engaged in fastening its grip upon a population by turns frightened, misled, reassured, and exhilarated. Two vestiges of successful double terror survived to set their stamps as clearly on Nazi government as they had on Nazi disruption. One was the speed and unpredictability with which victims were struck down. The screaming klaxons of police cars and the clumping sound of regulation boots continued to be heard, but far more typical of Nazi practice were the unheralded approach of SS squads and Gestapo plainclothesmen in the night, protracted torture under questioning, and swift transportation to scaffold, block, or concentration camp without delays occasioned by any concern for due process.

The other element, no less unnerving, was the calculated blend of silence and anonymity, obliterating all dreams of purposeful martyrdom. No day in court, no speech prior to execution, no eloquent letters from prison save for the most privileged inmates—only pain and confinement, often terminating in a brutal, solitary end and an unmarked grave, or with the delivery to the next of kin of a small urn of unidentifiable ashes, accompanied by a letter of explanation referring solemnly to "death from natural causes while detained in the public interest." To this travesty of political existence the National Socialist despotism had brought its own people, even before setting forth to overwhelm or intimidate the rest of Europe.

12

World War II
and After

Some Noteworthy Victims

The Second World War resembled the First, up to a point at least, in producing rather fewer outright assassinations than the staggering level of other human losses between 1939 and 1945 might lead one to expect. Like its predecessor a quarter of a century before, the titanic struggle between the Axis Powers and their foes showed an increase in attacks on prominent individuals during its late stages, especially in nations faced with impending defeat. To that extent the two conflicts were clearly comparable. Where they differed was in the second's punctuation by certain major fatalities, occurring at irregular intervals throughout almost its entire course. This may have reflected the greater ideological diversity and bitterness of World War II, its unprecedented geographical sweep, the savage reach of its weapons, or a combination of these and other factors. In any event, its leading actors can never have felt as secure as Clemenceau or Ludendorff or Lloyd George had seemed in their day.

Even leaving aside the early Nazi murder of designated opponents swept up by the advancing Wehrmacht or the Soviets' massacre of Polish officers, functionaries, and intellectuals at Katyn (near Smolensk) in May 1940, as too indiscriminate to be called assassination in the strictest sense, plentiful evidence remains to show how soon the fortunes of war began to threaten governmental figures. For Rumania, to use just one example, the fall of France meant the collapse of an entire structure of alliances already undermined by Hitler's rape of Czechoslovakia. During the summer of 1940 the Nazi arbiter of Europe decreed Transylvania's return to Hungary and southern Dobruja's to Bulgaria—the USSR having already reannexed Bessarabia—and King Carol fled into exile. October brought German army units to secure the Ploesti oil fields. In November the pro-Axis strong man, General Ion Antonescu, signed the Rome-Berlin-Tokyo Pact for the government of Carol's son and successor, Michael V. The once outlawed Iron Guard reappeared, astride the ruins of the Rumanian monarchy. Its old political foes killed during that chaotic autumn alone are reliably estimated to have numbered at least four hundred. For two full years no attempt was made to restrain the Green Shirts, until a pair of their gunmen tried to eliminate Antonescu himself. Long before that occurred, in neighboring Yugoslavia the German invasion of April 1941 had elevated Ante Pavelich, Mussolini's long-time protégé and now Hitler's as well, to a position from which he could direct his Ustachi against former "Serbian oppressors" of an independent Croatia, with results that were if anything even more sanguinary than the reprisals going on in Rumania.

As the war continued, further attacks were launched against different sorts of targets in widely separated locales. Japan's vice-premier, seventy-five-year-old Baron Koiicchiro Hiranuma barely escaped death in August 1941 at the hands of Black Dragon Society gunmen. The attack at first appeared puzzling, since Hiranuma was a samurai, described in an article published at the time as the "darling of the Army extremists" (presumably including most of the Black Dragon's membership) and as "one of the first Japanese of high position to be labeled 'Fascist.' "[1] Since the outbreak of fighting in Europe, however, and especially after he joined Prince Konoye's cabinet, Hiranuma had reportedly become increasingly skeptical of the advantages his country might hope to derive from membership in the Axis alliance.

Other military and civilian officials died under circumstances ostensibly attributable to the fortunes of war. Some of these deaths, despite speculation on the part of politicians and journalists, appear to have occurred in the line of duty. Japan's loss of Fleet Admiral Yamamoto, shot down in the South Pacific on April 17, 1943, was considered in some circles to have been highly mysterious; but there is no longer reason to doubt that the "mastermind of Pearl Harbor" perished in a command aircraft intercepted by an American fighter pilot who was guided by intelligence derived from the famous breaking of the Japanese naval codes. An equally straightforward explanation exists for the death of German General Werner von Fritsch on a Polish battlefield in September 1939. Fritsch, deeply depressed since his removal as commander-in-chief of the army on Hitler's orders in February 1938—and despite his partial rehabilitation including assignment to a field command not long before Poland was invaded—was reported by his own aide-de-camp to have exposed himself to direct fire at the earliest opportunity.[2]

Another air crash, in some ways prefiguring Yamamoto's misadventure, has remained clouded by greater suspicion. It took the life of Marshal Italo Balbo on June 19, 1940, only a little more than a week after Mussolini declared war against England and France. The celebrated aviator who in 1933 had led a flight of seaplanes across the Atlantic bearing the Duce's greetings to the Chicago World's Fair was serving as both military commander and governor of Libya when a heavy bomber with himself at the controls went down near the Italian base at Tobruk, killing all on board. In London, despite the state of war, officials announced that no RAF planes had been in action over Tobruk on the day of the crash. Not only because of these British denials (the more convincing in a situation where claims of a military triumph might have seemed the natural response), but also because of Balbo's known distaste for cooperation with Germany, rumors began to circulate in Rome and elsewhere that he had been killed on orders from his own government. The official account, released after considerable delay, attributed the governor's death to Italian anti-aircraft fire resulting from his having failed to radio proper recognition signals.[3] This seems plausible, but not plausible enough to silence all controversy over the fate of so glamorous a figure.

Probably the most significant air casualty of the war years, considered in political terms, was General Wladyslaw Sikorski, premier of the Polish government-in-exile, who perished when the British bomber in which he was traveling plunged into the sea after taking off from Gibraltar on July 4, 1943. Almost at once suggestions were voiced to the effect that his disappearance seemed as timely, for Churchill's and Roosevelt's purposes, as his replacement by an ostensibly less anti-Soviet Polish leader, Stanislaw Mikolajczyk, appeared welcome.[4] Proponents of the murder theory point out how ticklish the Western Allies' dealings with the USSR had become by that "last summer with no invasion" and have noted that all four engines of the plane carrying Sikorski and his party were said to have failed without warning, after which the RAF pilot parachuted to safety. On the other hand, it must be pointed out that such abrupt, multiple engine failures are not inconsistent with power outages known to have afflicted World War II aircraft, and that the Polish premier had not been as hostile to Moscow during the weeks immediately preceding his death as certain contemporary reports alleged. On the contrary, his increasingly careful avoidance of outspokenly anti-Russian émigré elements in London had suggested a growing awareness of the delicacy of relations with the Soviet Union.[5]

Certain representatives of belligerent governments died under circumstances not open to serious argument. At Minsk on September 22, 1943, Wilhelm Kube, the German commissioner general for White Russia, was killed by an explosive device planted in his headquarters by Russian agents. This action carried out by the Soviet underground recalled the assassinations of two earlier German occupation officials in the East, Mirbach and Eichhorn, at the end of the First World War. Given its location and timing, however, it signified something at once more immediate and more ominous for the future of the Reich. Hitler acknowledged as much by violently denouncing the "outrage" and ordering, in addition to the customary mass reprisals, a lavish state funeral in honor of the fallen *Reichskommissar.*[6] What had occurred could not be dismissed as an isolated event; it was part of a developing trend in opposition to the Third Reich's despotism. And in the assaults upon German leaders and their collaborators could be discerned the long-obscured features of classical tyrannicide.

Heydrich, Darlan, and the Resistance

During a great international conflict seen on both sides as "total," tyranny assumes an extended meaning. To the traditional charges of illegitimacy, injustice, or ungodliness, war adds a further justification for the act of assassination. An enemy general or high civilian official becomes a tyrant of sorts, one whose destruction, whatever his personal attributes, may be seen as an act of patriotism committed in defense of one's home and fellow citizens. When in addition the target is identified with a particularly cruel and oppressive regime, the case for tyrannicide appears that much clearer. Inasmuch as this century's second great war involved, in the Third Reich, the quintessential example of such a regime, small wonder that its annals should record three attempts to kill power figures identified with the New Order. Two of these attempts were aimed, respectively, at a trusted German lieutenant and a former French ally of Adolf Hitler. Both succeeded. The third attempt, directed at his own person, failed.

In May 1942 thirty-eight-year-old Reinhard Heydrich, chief of the Reich Central Security Office (*RSHA*), commissioner-general of the Gestapo in occupied territories, and recently appointed coordinator of the Jewish extermination program—the "final solution" officially launched by Hitler's secret decree of August 24, 1941—was also serving as governor of Bohemia-Moravia. His record as "Reich Protector" of that unfortunate territory had been, without qualification, frightful, a reign of terror so widespread and so pitiless that it had caught the attention of a world press otherwise preoccupied with following the Russo-German conflict and with assessing the spreading consequences of Japan's dramatic entry into the war.

On the morning in question, the blond, hawk-featured Reich Protector was being driven from his country home outside Prague to his downtown office when the car was struck by a bomb explosion accompanied by gunfire. The Nazi leader clung to life for over a week at a local hospital before dying on June 4. Because Heydrich's killers, though Czechs, had been trained at a secret installation in Canada, given British weapons, and dropped back into their homeland from an RAF night bomber, Berlin called upon Nazi sympathizers in Czechoslovakia to join in mourning and condemning this "traitorous act of collusion with foreign enemies of the Reich."

Clearly, however, it had been more than that, as the Nazis conceded in their own macabre fashion. Their retaliation fell upon the entire Czech pop-

Heinrich Himmler, Reichsführer SS,
and his deputy, Reinhard Heydrich

ulation, treated not as wayward subjects owing allegiance to the Führer but as a national enemy of Greater Germany. In all, at least 1,300 people were slain by the Gestapo and special army units. Some of the victims were shot in their homes, others trapped and massacred en masse like the 120 resistants, probably including Heydrich's two assassins, who held out briefly in a Prague church. Still others were systematically registered for execution, as occurred in the case of all 173 male residents of the outlying village of Lidice, selected by Hitler for obliteration on the basis of what turned out to be a false report that one of its residents had been important to the plot. Lidice's women, 198 of them according to SS records, were transported to the Ravensbruck concentration camp, while 81 of the 98 children taken into custody were reportedly killed at Chelmno in Poland after being classified as "racially unsuitable" to live.[7]

That Heydrich had been a pitiless butcher is indisputable. What is open to question is whether his carefully planned assassination was worth the backlash it produced—and worth it to whom? To the Czechs? The British? The anti-Nazi underground throughout conquered Europe? Finding an answer is made no easier when one reflects that none of the programs for which the deceased had borne major responsibility, including the projected massacre of millions of Jews, was altered or even delayed by his death. Justification for the action in Prague can be sought only in the message of defiance and hope it was meant to convey.

Compared to Heydrich's, the other major assassination of that eventful year seems relatively purposeful, in that it may have affected political decisions. On the afternoon of December 24, 1942, Admiral Jean François Darlan, high commissioner for French North and West Africa, had just arrived at his headquarters in Algiers, the former summer palace of the beys, when he was fatally shot at close range. His assailant, a twenty-year-old Frenchman named Fernand Bonnier de la Chapelle, was given a summary trial by the Imperial Council of France, acting under the authority of the Anglo-American invaders, and was executed by a firing squad within forty-eight hours of the event. Until after the sentence had been carried out, the culprit's name and nationality remained closely guarded secrets.

This combination of haste and secrecy, to which were added public statements by President Roosevelt, Prime Minister Churchill, and Secretary of State Cordell Hull, lamenting Darlan's death and condemning the assassin, encouraged early rumors of German or Italian responsibility. With Axis forces retreating before the British Eighth Army in Libya and with Tunisia threatened by the Allied advance from Morocco and Algeria, it seemed possible that Hitler might have ordered reprisals against erstwhile Vichy officials such as Darlan, who had changed sides with self-serving facility.[8]

The truth, which soon emerged, was that the Axis Powers had not been involved. The cause of Darlan's death lay in his record as a collaborationist and as a hater of Hitler's enemies. Churchill's pronouncement in particular, had it been read with care, would have revealed between the terse lines of formal regret a clear absence of enthusiasm for the admiral's hastily revised estimate of how the war was going to end. Nevertheless, once Darlan had slipped out of France and announced his new allegiance upon reaching North Africa, American policy in particular favored using him to the full. Relations with General De Gaulle, as leader of the Free French, never easy, had become no better when the first large areas of France overseas—*la*

France d'outre-mer—began to be won back from Axis control. Many Allied officers, concentrating on the military problem before them, considered Darlan a welcome source of direct, continuous authority, a high-ranking French officer who had once sternly ordered resistance to the "Anglo-Saxons," but who now could save the lives of countless American and British soldiers by instructing his fellow countrymen to cooperate with the Allies.

The young man who killed him saw things in a wholly different light. Like many others at the time, he detested the admiral as a traitor to France in 1940, a toady to Hitler thereafter, and at last, if allowed to play out his opportunistic game, a double turncoat capable of discrediting the very idea of liberation. Bonnier, a student-patriot, was convinced that such a disgrace must be prevented. Once enrolled in an anti-Vichy society, Singers of Youth, which was pledged to support the Allied invaders when they came, he had become increasingly obsessed with a sense of his own special mission. His self-imposed task was, quite simply, to destroy the former collaborator. From a somewhat less visionary—and less French—point of view, Darlan's death could be seen as offering escape from the ill-advised, because shortsighted, American entanglement with hastily converted collaborationists. An outspoken journalistic critic of that course, Freda Kirchway, concluded a few days after Bonnier's deed: "The assassination of Darlan was a free gift to the United States. Everyone felt this, no matter what he said publicly."[9]

"The Führer Must Go!"

The century's greatest single instance of tyrannicide, tinged as in the past with desperate opportunism, would have been the assassination of Adolf Hitler. A target with clearer credentials for extinction would be difficult for anyone but the most thoroughly brainwashed Nazi to imagine. But precisely because the case against the Reich's all-powerful leader appears irresistible, it may invite suspicions of equations skipped en route to almost predetermined conclusions. There is no inclination here to revise the prevailing view of Hitler's place in history, but questions bearing on attempts to assassinate him—that of July 20, 1944, in particular—should be asked. They involve motives, options, and alternative outcomes both actual and imaginable. Matters of timing also arise. If the Führer had been killed or simply ousted before the outbreak of war in 1939, a balance sheet of costs and benefits would read quite differently from one devoted to an assassination carried out when the great conflict was in its final stages.

In the late spring and summer of 1945 Allied investigators, dependent until then on scattered intelligence reports and official Nazi announcements for knowledge of the previous year's bomb attempt, were able to institute on-the-spot investigations of their own. Despite the inherent problems of digging through the wreckage, psychological as well as physical, there was no lack of evidence to be considered: captured Gestapo files and court records, documents drafted by the conspirators and brought forward willingly once the Third Reich was no more, prisoner interrogations, and interviews with other suvivors.[10] A reasonably accurate picture of the plot and its ramifications therefore emerged without too much delay. That, however, as Peter Hoffmann has shown in his encyclopedic study of German opposition movements, was just a beginning.[11] Continuing research during the past forty years has unearthed additional information, in the process amplifying and, with regard to many particulars, correcting earlier approximations. Yet the initial reconstruction of the attempt and what led up to it has stood the test of time remarkably well. The most stubborn question, as difficult to answer today as it was in 1945, has nothing to do with details: if the Führer had met his end that afternoon, instead of the following April in the Berlin chancellery's underground bunker, would his assassination have done mankind, not only in 1944 but also in the future, more good than harm?

The attack on July 20 was not the first upon Hitler's life. It was, however, the first that involved a complex conspiracy and, at the same time, left reliable enough traces to rule out any doubts concerning its authenticity. The explosion on November 8, 1939, in one of Munich's famous beer halls, the Bürgerbräukeller, unquestionably occurred and was a very near miss indeed. But it was the work of an isolated individual, a former Communist named Georg Elser, disillusioned by the failure of leftist forces to produce any organized resistance and convinced that only a daring act by a single tyrannicide could eliminate the dictator. Elser had managed to spend several nights in the beer hall, by hiding there at closing time, and had made use of the opportunity to conceal a time bomb containing a powerful explosive (stolen from the stone quarry where he worked) inside a partially hollow pillar at one corner of the speaker's platform. On the night in question Hitler, obeying one of his frequent hunches, changed the schedule without notice and, having completed an address in honor of the 1923 putsch attempt, abruptly left the celebration. Minutes after his car drove away the explosion occurred, killing nine Storm Troopers and wounding some sixty others. Elser, arrested at Konstanz while attempting to escape into Switzerland later that night, was sent to a concentration camp, there to remain for more than five years without trial, his punishment held in abeyance because the Führer, now obsessed with the danger of assassination, apparently refused to have public attention drawn back to the Munich attempt.[12]

Numerous projects said to have been conceived by military groups are carefully scrutinized by Hoffmann. Even the most intriguing accounts, however, including a frequently repeated one concerned with a time bomb secreted in Hitler's airplane while he was visiting the headquarters of the Central Army Group on the Russian front in 1943, suffer from weaknesses that invite challenges to their credibility. In the *Heeresgruppe Mitte* case, for example, subsequent battle deaths and the execution of numerous officers later implicated in the 1944 plot have made it impossible to corroborate the story of a lone survivor, a former officer who had much to gain after 1945 from appearing well-informed about anti-Nazi projects.[13]

A shortage of testimony is not the problem with respect to the July 20 conspiracy. Instead, the very profusion of interest groups and individuals who were involved continues to complicate efforts at reconstruction, just as it endangered the participants while Hitler was still alive and in power. Such a loose coalition, viewed in retrospect, calls to mind Machiavelli's famous strictures on conspiracy and its weaknesses, not least among them the difficulty of maintaining secrecy.

Active participants came eventually to include prominent Nazis best represented by Berlin's chief of police, Count Wolf von Helldorf, who had begun his career as a Storm Trooper in the 1920s. At his trial, replying to Judge Roland Freisler's shouts of incredulity that an "old fighter" had betrayed the Party and its leader, Helldorf merely shrugged and said: "Abspringen müssen wir alle einmal!" (We all have to hop off sometime!) Other well-placed Germans, many of them still in uniform, had reached the same conclusion, that the Third Reich was a bus running out of control or a foundering ship, depending on the metaphor preferred. Still others were long-time—one might have said "natural"—enemies of National Socialism, including left-wing socialists such as Julius Leber and Adolf Reichwein; Social Democratic Party regulars represented by Wilhelm Leuschner and Gustav Dahrendorf; as well as a prominent Catholic labor leader, Jakob Kaiser.

In addition, there were pivotal figures whose depth of individual commitment is less easy to explain. Pastor Dietrich Bonhoeffer was a devout Protestant believer, not in politics but in the "inner light." Carl Goerdeler, former lord mayor of Leipzig and since the late 1930s the conspiracy's tireless "motor," might be dismissed as an embittered conservative politician swept from office by the Nazi wave; but he was too principled and too courageous, often to the point of foolhardiness, to be written off as merely vengeful or ambitious. The same integrity, touched by naiveté in some of its manifestations, informs the record of certain aristocrats—retired ex-diplomatists Ulrich von Hassell and Werner von der Schulenburg (former ambassadors to Italy and the USSR, respectively), as well as younger men such as Adam von Trott zu Solz, still active in the foreign service, and the youthful organizers of the anti-Nazi Kreisau Circle. This last-named, a discussion and action group some of whose members bore such famous Junker names as Moltke and Yorck von Wartenburg (Kreisau was Helmuth von Moltke's Silesian estate), shared utopian tendencies that were partly socialist in inspiration but also rooted in a much older "feudal paternalism" well known to students of Prussian history.

With all deference to these sincere opponents of Nazi tyranny, the mantle of the classic tyrannicide should be placed on the aging shoulders of Colonel General Ludwig Beck. A distinguished soldier, who had resigned as chief of the general staff in September 1938, hoping thereby to trigger a coup in opposition to Nazi plans for Czechoslovakia, Beck in July 1944 was aware that no help could be expected from the Allies. Nevertheless, he still voiced the firm belief that an attempt against Hitler must be made, regardless of the odds against its success. By insisting that in the motive, not the outcome, lay the moral justification for this "undertaking against a criminal system" and that for future survival the effort must come "from within the circle of the German people itself," Beck spoke the language of ancient Stoicism.[14]

In the event, the bomb smuggled into Hitler's East Prussian headquarters at Rastenburg on July 20 exploded on schedule beneath a heavy map table, killing several of the staff officers present but only wounding the Führer himself. From the adjoining air strip, Colonel Claus Schenk von Stauffenberg, the partially disabled army officer who had delivered the explosive in a dispatch case, watched the shed in which the "situation room" was located go up in the blast and then took off for the capital, confident that the most serious obstacle to the revolt had been removed. By 12:30 that night, however, Stauffenberg and three other officers captured by troops loyal to the government had been shot by a firing squad in the courtyard of the war ministry on Berlin's Bendlerstrasse. Their deaths had been hastily ordered by the Commander of the Home Army, General Friedrich Fromm, himself destined to be executed for having failed to report his prior knowledge of the conspirators' plans. By the time Stauffenberg died in the glare of an army truck's headlights, Hitler had already spoken to the nation by radio, vowing to destroy the "cowardly clique of reactionary officers" and all who had supported them in any way. By that time, too, General Beck had shot himself, not fatally, and received the coup de grâce from a Home Army officer.

The Nazis' vengeance was as terrible as their leader's promises. Through the rest of 1944 and on into the next year the executions continued by shooting, beheading, and strangulation, this last expressly ordered by Hitler in certain cases and carried out before movie cameras. Until the last German military resistance collapsed at the end of April 1945, prisoners sentenced by the People's Court were being dragged from cells and put to death before they could be saved by the converging Allied armies. The leading civilians—among them Goerdeler, Hassell, Schulenburg, Trott zu Solz, and Pastor Bonhoeffer—died alongside renegade National Socialists such as Count von Helldorf and the once-powerful *Reichskriminaldirektor* Arthur Nebe. No one can say with certainty how many members of the armed forces were executed, some in distant places after summary courts-martial, others, such as Field Marshal von Witzleben, following a lurid show trial before Judge Freisler in the People's Court. Even Germany's most renowned field commander, Erwin Rommel, the Desert Fox of Afrika Korps fame, committed suicide near his Württemberg home in October 1944 after Hitler sent two generals to offer him the choice of that (and a hero's funeral) or public trial on charges of high treason.[15]

Not all victims of the Reich's final convulsions had been recently arrested. According to surviving justice ministry files, of the 5,764 death sentences carried out "in due form" (that is, not in the gas chambers of mass extermination centers) through 1944 and the 800 less meticulously recorded for the first months of 1945, only about 200 were directly linked to the July 20 attempt, though an indeterminate number of others may have had some connection with it.[16] Like Bonaparte in 1800 and Lenin in 1918—and following the now vastly expanded pattern of his own Blood Purge in 1934—the Nazi Führer took the occasion to settle many older scores by striking down innumerable opponents left over from earlier years. Ernst Thälmann, the German Communist Party's candidate for the presidency of the Republic in 1925 and again in 1932, when he finished third behind Hindenburg and Hitler, was suddenly ordered shot at Buchenwald, after more than eleven years' confinement. Not until April 1945 was Dachau's SS commandant instructed to "liquidate" the 1939 beer hall bomber Georg Elser, using as cover the next Allied bombing raid.[17]

The attempt by Germans to rid Germany of Hitler had failed, at a cost in lives possible to estimate but, like much else in the history of the Third Reich, difficult to credit. For nine more months great armies and air armadas fought on, all hope of an earlier peace having vanished. Hitler, Goebbels, and Himmler died as suicides within that space of time, as did Ley and Goering soon thereafter. Other former Nazi leaders would end their lives on a scaffold at Nuremberg, as condemned war criminals. Tyrannicide, seen as an ideal and an effort, had played a part in the twilight of the German gods. As a completed act capable of changing the course of events, it had played none.

Should we conclude that the failure of the attempt against Hitler represented an unqualified disaster? An immediate disaster, of staggering dimensions, it assuredly was, considering the millions who died in battle, in concentration camps, in bombed cities and battle-torn villages between July 1944 and the end of April 1945. The continuing slaughter of European Jews in itself sufficed to make that period one of the most gruesome in recorded history. Not all, but very probably a large percentage of the victims could have salvaged some added years of life had the earlier date marked the end of the war in Europe.

A counterfactual hypothesis—in this case, "let us suppose the July 20 plot had been a success"—demands that its implications be pursued. The task is made no easier by the uncertainties attendant on any effort to compare the possible effects of an assassination, had it succeeded, with the known effects of its having failed. Measuring what did occur against what might have occurred seldom leads to ready agreement. What it involves is consideration of two scenarios. One stresses the benefits that might, in the short run, have accrued from a successful putsch. The other concentrates on a potentially dangerous legacy to the future. Both may be plausible, but which is more important for history?

Consider the first of these projections. Had Stauffenberg's bomb killed Hitler in the Rastenburg conference room, so runs the argument, only good would have resulted. The conspirators in the Bendlerstrasse might well have been able, using the military chain of command, to topple a demoralized Nazi hierarchy, defeat the SS, disarm the Gestapo, and establish a constitutional regime offering relief from the terror that for twelve years had gripped Germany. Assume further, if all that had taken place, the rapid conclusion of cease-fire agreements on both the western and eastern fronts, the imposition soon thereafter of peace terms upon the Japanese Empire, and the orderly return home of the world's armies, including countless "undefeated" Wehrmacht divisions from Scandinavia, the Low Countries, Italy, the Balkans, even parts of France. There is of course no assurance that things would in fact have worked out that way, especially given the Allies' flatly stated demands for unconditional surrender; but an end to the war, on whatever terms, could scarcely be described as anything but a blessing to suffering mankind.

The contrary position involves taking a longer and undeniably colder view. If those who tried to kill the Führer and seize control of the government in July 1944 had been able to do so, it must be assumed, according to this projection, that they would have (1) shortened the Second World War, (2) spared Germany the bombing and shelling of the ensuing autumn, winter, and spring, and (3) enabled the Wehrmacht to lay down its arms while still a powerful military force in being, something it no longer was by the time V-E Day finally arrived. More to the point, as in 1918, one German regime would have fought the war, while another had to assume responsibility for ending it. Capitulation in some form might have been recognized by most Germans at the time as unavoidable, even welcome. It might, however, have been transformed with the passage of time into a humiliating memory of "unnecessary surrender," like that of 1918.

The delayed message of a successful putsch, however unselfishly conceived and courageously undertaken, becomes in these terms the possible source of subsequent trouble. Its danger can best be expressed by repeating the phrase "stab in the back." For if Hitler himself, in his rise to power, could benefit from exploiting that caricature of Germany's defeat in World War I, how much more effectively might not future demagogues have used the image of another surrender brought about in 1944 by a "cowardly clique" of dissidents who had betrayed their nation's leader and sold out to its foes? A successful coup in 1939 would have been one thing, a revolt five years later quite another. By that time the only permanent solution was for the Third Reich to be left in ruins, its leaders trapped in the devastation they had brought. Only then, for Germans about to start building a new political life, was the road ahead unimpeded by doubts as to whose war it had been, or who had lost it.

This second line of argument should not be ruled out merely on grounds of exhibiting too little sensitivity to human suffering in 1944 and 1945. It has at least the virtue of forcing us to ponder the difficulties that arise from any effort to judge past adventures on the basis of a limited range of possible effects. Its weakness lies in relying too heavily on a presumption of historical recurrence. The end of the Second World War would have been far different from that of the First, even if Stauffenberg had had better luck with his bomb. The enormity of the Nazi disaster was already, by mid-1944, more apparent than the Second Empire's predicament had been to many Germans in 1918, and the problems of a successor regime made up of Beck, Goerdeler, and their associates would not have been the same as those with which the Weimar Republic was burdened.

It would be placing an extraordinarily high value on a single outcome—the peaceful internal development of postwar Germany—to suggest that such a result was worth the price of those last nine months of Hitler's war. Cost-benefit analysis alone will not dispel all feelings of regret over the reprieve granted by fortune to Adolf Hitler in 1944, or over the use he made of it.

Settling Accounts

Not all the leaders of the once irresistible Axis shared Hitler's temporary good fortune in escaping retribution at the hands of his own people. The demise of European Fascism's second most influential dictator, its first in seniority, was a case in point. Benito Mussolini, having spent the previous two years in increasingly abject dependence on his German sponsor, at last had to follow, with no greater success, the example of his son-in-law.* Accompanied by a number of political henchmen, as well as by twenty-five-year-old Clara Petacci, he made a futile effort to reach Switzerland through northern Italy. Following recognition and arrest by partisan forces near Dongo on April 27, 1945, the Duce, his young mistress, and sixteen other Fascist dignitaries were court-martialed and shot the following day, within sight of Lake Como and the Swiss Alps. All eighteen bodies were dumped into a moving van and by dawn on April 29 were displayed, hanging by the heels,

---

* Count Galeazzo Ciano attempted to escape to Switzerland in early January 1944, but was captured by Italian troops still loyal to Mussolini. The former Italian foreign minister was tried at Verona, declared guilty of treason, at the insistence of the Germans, and shot by a firing squad.

in Milan's former Piazza Loreto, newly renamed Piazza dei Quindici Martiri in honor of fifteen anti-Fascists executed there a few weeks before. Not until darkness had fallen were the battered corpses of Mussolini and Petacci, the targets all day of public abuse, removed for secret burial.[18]

With varying degrees of judicial solemnity, other European governments emulated Italy's anti-fascists in punishing former accomplices in Nazi war crimes. A few major culprits escaped. Hungary's ex-regent Admiral Nicholas Horthy fled to Spain, while the Croat Ante Pavelich succeeded in reaching South America. Marcel Déat made his way out of France to northern Italy, where he died in hiding. Many others, however, were captured and punished. The most notable executions in western Europe included those of Dr. Anton Mussert, Hitler's handpicked "Führer of the Netherlands People," and a second Dutch National Socialist, Max Blokzijl, both shot in the spring of 1945. It took Norway only slightly longer to pass judgment on a man whose very name had become synonymous with collaboration everywhere: Vidkun Quisling, tried on charges ranging from high treason to crimes against Norwegian Jews, found guilty on all counts, and put to death by a firing squad at Oslo's Akershus Fortress.

Further east the Rumanian strong man Antonescu and his erstwhile prime minister (of the same name, but no relation), were executed, as were two other incriminated premiers, the Hungarian László de Bardossy, garroted Magyar-style at Budapest, and the Slovak Bala Tuku. Czechoslovakia imposed the death penalty on its leading anti-Semite, Otomar Kula. In Yugoslavia the situation was complicated by the fact that the victorious partisans of Marshal Tito moved first against royalist rivals in the opposition, who had been abandoned by their English and American sponsors and in 1944 repudiated by King Peter himself. General Draja Mihailovich and eight of his principal henchmen were hunted down in their mountain retreats, tried on charges of countenancing Nazi atrocities while using their own Serbian *Chetnik* forces against fellow-Yugoslavs, and hanged at Belgrade on July 17, 1945. Not long thereafter, Marshal Sladko Kvaternik, wartime premier and in Pavelich's absence the highest-ranking Croatian separatist leader, was put to death in similar fashion.

Perhaps the most divisive of Europe's postwar purges took place in France. There, although Pierre Laval, ex-premier of both the Third Republic and the Vichy regime, was tried and shot in October 1945, Marshal Pétain, the actual chief of the *État Français* throughout its humiliating four-year life, received a sentence of "perpetual imprisonment," in recognition of his advanced age and his reputation, as resilient as it was dubious, for heroism at Verdun in 1916. Another well-known collaborator, Fernand de Brinon, following a long trial and an exceptionally stubborn defense, was convicted and finally shot in April 1947, as a number of less famous culprits had been before him.

No doubt inevitably, given its kaleidoscopic history of successive constitutions and differing regimes, France found the issue of collaboration-and-survival versus defiance-with-honor increasingly hard to disentangle from peacetime politics. One result was what an angry and highly vocal segment of the population considered the premature abandonment of proceedings against favored individuals. On the other hand, when in 1953 a military court sentenced nine French citizens to prison for participation in the shooting of hostages at Oradour near Bordeaux in 1944, public reactions included some that were equally critical of such stern punishment. The Oradour trial was especially painful because all the defendants were Alsatians who at the time of the massacre had been serving in German uniform, unwillingly according to their lawyers. The sensitivity of any issue affecting embattled Alsace may help to explain why their trial was the Fourth Republic's last significant action against French nationals accused of complicity in war crimes.

No such misgivings inhibited the prosecution of German and other Axis officials who had been captured by their erstwhile victims. Greece, for example, despite its own civil war between Communist and anti-Communist resistance forces, found time to execute two German generals in December 1946. Few nations could rival the Poles in their thirst for revenge, hardly surprising in a people who had been among the worst-treated victims of Nazi despotism—if gradations can be assigned to horror. Despite numerous executions of concentration-camp overseers at Óswiecim (Auschwitz), Majdanek, Treblinka, and other extermination centers, however, Poland was far from alone in imposing retribution. Yugoslavia, having disposed of its anti-Tito Chetniks, turned with apparent relish to other groups of prisoners. In February 1946 Colonel General Alexander von Loehr, once Hitler's Balkan commander-in-chief, was shot and five of his division commanders hanged as common criminals. The following November the sometime Hungarian chief of staff, General Ferenc Szombathely, was executed with a number of subordinates at Novi Sad for having organized the massacre of Serbo-Croatians perpetrated there in 1942. Finally, at the end of 1946 General August Meissner, former head of the Gestapo's regional bureau in Belgrade, was hanged in the company of eight other senior SS officers.

Additional punishments undoubtedly would have been carried out by individual governments had the powers of the victorious alliance not assumed a large part of that responsibility. Despite the odious record of judicial murders in centuries past, and at the risk of being blamed for imposing nothing but "winner's justice" upon a broken enemy, the Allies had been compelled to acknowledge that in the eyes of much of the world more than a few of the now captured war leaders were, quite simply, murderers. Not all, or even most, of the losing generals and admirals could be called such, but some could, as could numerous civil officials. Had the victors been satisfied to frame their indictments in the widely recognized language of criminal justice instead of inventing new categories of international misconduct, tribunals established by great-power agreement might have aroused less vehement controversy—about their legitimacy far more than their decisions.

There could be no argument about the centrality of the German venue. Some of the Third Reich's leaders had always assumed that the penalty for losing their kind of war would be death and chose not to await it on their enemies' terms. Hitler and Goebbels killed themselves in the Berlin chancellery's bomb shelter at the end of April 1945.[19] Himmler followed suit after being captured by British counterintelligence near Hamburg a few days later. Ley ended his own life with a cyanide capsule the following autumn, while awaiting trial. Twenty other individuals however, lived to constitute the first group of defendants arraigned before the newly seated International War Crimes Tribunal at Nuremberg. Almost a year later, on October 1, 1946, the Soviet, British, French, and American judges sentenced eleven of the accused to death by hanging:

> Hermann Goering, Reich marshal, supreme commander of the air force, Reich commissioner for Prussia;
> Joachim von Ribbentrop, minister of foreign affairs;
> Wilhelm Frick, minister of interior;
> Ernst Kaltenbrunner, chief of security forces (*RSHA*);
> Wilhelm Keitel, field marshal, chief of staff of the combined armed forces command (*OKW*);
> Alfred Jodl, colonel general, coordinator of Hitler's supreme planning staff (*Führungsstab*);
> Alfred Rosenberg, minister of occupied territories and Nazi party theoretician;
> Fritz Sauckel, "general plenipotentiary for work mobilization," that is, director of slave labor;
> Julius Streicher, editor of *Der Stürmer,* exponent of genocide;
> Arthur Seyss-Inquart, veteran Austrian Nazi, Reich commissioner for the occupied Netherlands;
> Hans Frank, governor-general of Poland.

On the morning of October 15, at Nuremberg Prison, ten of the condemned were executed by a U.S. Army detail, Goering having contrived to escape the gallows by swallowing poison the previous night.

Of the remaining defendants in the first trial, six received jail sentences to be served in Berlin's Spandau Prison under rotating four-power guard:

> Rudolf Hess, deputy Führer of the Nazi Party until his flight to Scotland in 1941 (life);
> Erich Raeder, grand admiral, supreme commander of the navy (life);
> Walter Funk, minister of economics (life);

Albert Speer, minister of armaments and munitions (twenty years);
Baldur von Schirach, director of Nazi youth programs (twenty years);
Karl Doenitz, admiral, chief of the submarine service, and Hitler's choice
    to succeed him in 1945 (ten years).

Finally, despite vehement protests from its Soviet member, the court acquitted Franz von Papen, former chancellor of the Weimar Republic, briefly
Hitler's vice-chancellor, thereafter ambassador successively to Austria and
to Turkey; Hans Fritzsche, radio propaganda director; and Dr. Hjalmar
Horace Greeley Schacht, Germany's financial czar in the 1920s and Funk's
predecessor as minister of economics under Hitler.

Subsequent cases involving capital charges brought to twelve the number of trials in Germany under Control Council Law No. 10. They produced
twenty-six additional death sentences, seven of which were carried out, the
balance being commuted to imprisonment, theoretically for life. The total
number of executions at Nuremberg thus came to seventeen out of thirty-
seven authorized by the court.[20]

Those who have dismissed the Nuremberg trials as mere additions to
history's long roll of judicial murders or as simply an application of *vae victis*
(woe to the vanquished) seem curiously lacking in ability to differentiate
among variant cases. To point out that Napoleon was not hanged after Waterloo (Prussian intentions notwithstanding) or that the Kaiser was permitted to live out his life in exile after 1918 is to demonstrate just one of a
number of the differences between the Third Reich and the former French
and German empires. Or, using seventeenth-century points of reference, it
requires no long reflection to realize that a Kaltenbrunner or a Streicher
bears no meaningful similarity to Oldenbarneveldt or Lord Jeffreys' victims
in the Bloody Assizes.

This is not to deny that the post–1945 war crimes trials raised serious
questions in the minds of many thoughtful observers. No appeal to a universal "sense" of justice could erase all misgivings about the validity of retroac-
tive definitions of wrongdoing. Although the most objectionable aspect of
wholesale indictments affecting countless humbler defendants—namely,
that they were categorical, citing memberships, offices, or associations in
place of specific evidence of criminal behavior—did not apply to the major
cases, in at least one of these the decision reached appeared not to rest on
clearly proven individual guilt. General Alfred Jodl, chief of the small
Führungsstab, received the death sentence and was hanged at least in part, it
would seem, because his judges considered him to be the most prominent
representative of a condemned organization, the German General Staff,
which he was not.[21]

Another problem arose from the language in which the indictments were
couched. It should be remembered that all the principal defendants were

tried on one or more of four counts: (1) conspiracy to wage aggressive war; (2) crimes against the peace; (3) violations of the rules of war; and (4) crimes against humanity. A world stunned by daily increments of evidence found in captured documents and liberated concentration camps was ready to accept for the time being such formulations, despite their undeniable redundancy. In the long run, however, direct charges of murder and conspiracy to commit murder would have been more susceptible of lasting proof. Much of the trouble lay in the anxious effort to invent a new legal vocabulary to meet terrible, but nonetheless transitory circumstances.

The international war crimes tribunal established in Tokyo, comprising judges from eleven different nations, differed from the German in important respects. Unlike the Third Reich, Emperor Hirohito's government retained certain powers under the terms of surrender; and its voice was heard, politely but insistently, at intervals throughout the course of the trials. The nature of the evidence entered in the Far Eastern cases bore primarily on military aggression and violation of the rules of war (Nuremberg's first and third counts). Crimes "against the peace" and "against humanity" were considered, but they received less attention than in Germany.

Despite their appearance of greater simplicity, the Tokyo trials were more protracted than those in Europe. This was not true of proceedings resulting from mass atrocities in outlying parts of the war-inflated empire. At Manila a special United States military commission, acting unilaterally, wasted little time in condemning General Tomoyuki Yamashita, the so-called "Tiger of Malaya," who was hanged in February 1946. General Masaharu Homma, former commander-in-chief in the Philippines, was also convicted and shot six weeks later. The following summer in Singapore, British authorities executed two groups of Japanese, a total of twenty-three individuals, for atrocities committed in the course of the Malayan campaign and subsequent occupation. Other jurisdictions on the Asian mainland and in the East Indies handed down comparable decisions with a minimum of delay.

In Japan itself, however, the main trial dragged on for fully two and a half years, from its opening in the spring of 1946 to the announcement of findings in November 1948. By that time one of the original twenty-seven defendants, wartime foreign minister Yosuki Matsuoka, had died of natural causes, while another had been pronounced hopelessly insane and committed to an asylum. These seven were sentenced to death:

Hideki Tojo, prime minister;
Koki Kirota, deputy prime minister;
Seishiro Itagaki, minister of war;
General Kenji Doihara, field commander in Manchuria;
General Iwane Matsui, charged with devastation of Nanking;

General Akira Muto, chief of staff in the Philippines, charged with primary responsibility for the 1942 "Bataan death march" of U.S. prisoners;

General Hitaro Kimura, chief of staff in Burma.

The remaining eighteen received prison sentences, sixteen of them for life. The hangings were carried out at Tokyo's Sugamo Prison on December 23, 1948, after which cases still on the international tribunal's docket were dropped. This abrupt closing of the books lent credence to the belief that in East Asia prosecution had never been intended to reach beyond the highest warlords of the defeated empire.[22]

While some nations enacted statutes of limitations on the amount of time that could elapse before instituting war crimes proceedings, others did not. As a result, arrests and indictments continued for years, even decades. One sensational case, that of Klaus Barbie, the former German SS official arrested in Argentina and returned to face trial before a French court, is still pending as these lines are written, almost forty years after he escaped from Europe with the connivance of American officials.

An earlier episode, also involving arrest in South America, remains the most dramatic example of patient pursuit and eventual reckoning. In May 1960 Israeli Prime Minister David Ben Gurion announced to Israel's parliament, the Knesset, that Adolf Eichmann, a former SS *Obersturmbannführer* and chief of the Gestapo's "Jewish Department," had been taken into custody and would be tried in Jerusalem under its 1950 law providing for punishment of Nazis and their collaborators. Shortly thereafter the Israeli government released details of how its investigators had seized Eichmann in Argentina and smuggled him out of that country to Tel Aviv. The ensuing trial, which consumed 114 sessions, lasted from February into June 1961. Conducted in the presence of a large press corps and officially designated foreign observers, it received in evidence more than 1,500 documentary exhibits, heard testimony from 120 witnesses, and produced a judgment some 180 pages in length. The sentence was death; but not until May 31, 1962, after the Supreme Court of Israel had refused after two sets of detailed hearings to overturn the decision or commute the death penalty, was the condemned man executed by hanging.

The Eichmann trial raised a number of objections, most of which had been expressed with regard to earlier trials conducted under other auspices. The applicability of national law to "international crime" was challenged once again, as were the validity of ex post facto legislation and the justice of holding an individual responsible for carrying out the orders of his superiors in a purportedly monolithic system. Other, less legalistic misgivings arose out of distaste for recalling better-forgotten horrors, especially since in the eyes of some critics the very concept of "crimes against the Jewish people" threatened to reinforce an appearance of exclusiveness that could only encourage anti-Semitic reactions in various parts of the world.

Most of those objections, reexamined more than twenty years later, appear to have lost whatever force they ever had. Eichmann, as the evidence clearly showed, had not just obeyed orders; he had interpreted, elaborated, and embellished them. He may have gone about his business without sinking to acts of personal brutality, organizing genocide with all the primness of a conscientious bureaucrat; but such behavior was wholly consistent with what Hannah Arendt, in an unforgettable phrase, called "the banality of evil."[23] Had he been caught in any of a number of European countries, Hungary or Poland for example, he would certainly have been executed as promptly as were other leading war criminals, in all likelihood without much critical comment from abroad. Such reflections will not answer all possible objections, but they rightly emphasize the scrupulous attention to due process displayed by the Israeli courts. As for the presumed danger of new outbursts of anti-Jewish sentiment in other countries, a cogent reply came from a Greek legal observer whose book is the best general account of the proceedings: "If the trial were followed by such a reaction, it would in reality be merely a pretext for a phenomenon far more complex and profound in its social and psychological causes."[24]

Such damage as the affair may have done to the cause of international justice arose less from the courtroom proceedings in Israel than from the defendant's forcible abduction from Argentina. Understandable though such intervention was, especially in view of France's earlier inability to secure the extradition of Marcel Déat and Belgian frustration in the parallel case of Léon Degrelle, it offered a troubling foretaste of methods soon to be applied by terrorist hijackers in transportation of hostages, Jews in particular, to such destinations as Entebbe and Mogadishu. In the Eichmann case it led in August 1960 to a carefully negotiated joint statement by the Israeli and Argentine governments, announcing that they had agreed "to regard as closed the incident that arose out of the action taken by Israeli nationals which infringed fundamental rights of the State of Argentina."[25]

The most important lesson to be learned from the era of retribution after World War II is that the concept of merely "political" crime is illusory, either as a reason for punishment, in the absence of clearer charges, or as an excuse for amnesty when such charges do exist. Murder is murder; and responsibility for it originates in provable, individual action.

As late as the summer of 1981, the relatively light sentences given eight German defendants found guilty of crimes committed at the Majdanek death camp aroused widespread indignation in Germany and abroad. The fact that the court in Düsseldorf had worked conscientiously for five and a half years over the evidence, some of it conflicting and all of it blurred by age, prompted Chancellor Helmut Schmidt to comment in public on both the verdict and the penalties imposed. Stressing the obligation of any state based on law to respect the principle of personal, not merely associational guilt, he concluded: "We cannot set aside this principle even if the weight of the crimes is immeasurable."[26]

Different Battles on Changing Lines

The prosecution of those charged with war crimes could not indefinitely monopolize world attention. For large portions of mankind it had always been a somewhat remote concomitant of the struggle between imperial powers, while within the newly expanded Russian sphere of influence it was rapidly superseded by issues having less to do with the bloodshed just concluded than with the entrenchment of Soviet satellite governments. Presiding over the latter process was the man Lenin had called "our wonderful Georgian," out of appreciation for his effective use of terror. The extension of Stalin's technique into the Balkans and east-central Europe can perhaps best be illustrated in terms of what it meant for two non-Communist politicians, Nikola Petkov in Bulgaria and Jan Masaryk in Czechoslovakia.

Petkov's was a family seemingly cursed with assassination. His father, Dimiter, had been shot to death on a Sofia street in 1907, while a member of the national cabinet. In 1924 Dimiter's elder son, Petko, like the father an agrarian leader, had been killed under similar circumstances, probably by Bulgarian-Macedonian nationalists. Nikola, the surviving son, emerged from World War II as secretary of the resurrected peasant party, one of the major components in the anti-fascist Fatherland Front. Increasingly, however, during the years after 1945 he used his influence in the national parliament (Sobranie) to oppose Russian demands. As a result, political disagreement developed into bitter personal enmity between him and Georgi Dimitrov, who, having survived the Bulgarian bloodshed of the 1920s and his trial in Germany following the Reichstag fire in 1934, had returned home to the secretary-generalship of his nation's Communist Party.

On June 6, 1947, Petkov was arrested in the parliament chamber and hustled off to jail. Brought to trial before the People's Court in August, he was convicted as an enemy of the state, despite a curious absence of specified charges, and executed by hanging the following month. The American and British governments attempted to save his life, citing legal as well as humanitarian grounds; and both condemned the execution in the strongest terms either had employed publicly against the behavior of their former ally. Dimitrov for his part proudly hailed Petkov's death as a triumph of the people's justice over "reactionary foreign attempts at interference." The statement by the Bulgarian Labor Union leadership concluded on a note less international than personal: "For a dog, a dog's death."[27]

Not half a year passed before the scene of violence shifted from Sofia to

Prague, and to a tragedy far more complex than Petkov's. In the interval Iuliu Maniu, the seventy-four-year-old leader of the Rumanian Peasant Party, had been arrested on charges of treason; he died in 1953 without having been brought to trial—or released from solitary confinement. By February 1948, especially in view of Stalin's brusque warning to the Czech government the preceding summer not to accept economic assistance from the United States under the Marshall Plan, there was good reason to expect political crisis in that nation as well.

From most points of view, the decisive blow to the hopes of non-Communist Czechs and Slovaks had come with the decision by the nation's ailing president, Eduard Beneš, to accept the resignations of four key ministers, all members of his own nationalist party. This occurred on February 25 and left the Communists, under Premier Klement Gottwald, in almost undisputed control of the state. To make sure they did not mishandle the opportunity, Valerian Zorin, the Soviet deputy foreign minister and Stalin's personal representative, had arrived from Moscow on February 19 and was keeping a close eye on the progress of the coup d'état. The only remaining ambiguity surrounded the figure of Jan Masaryk, minister of foreign affairs and son of Thomas Masaryk, founder of the Czechoslovak Republic in 1918. In the thirtieth anniversary year of that hopeful launching, Jan Masaryk, an affable, cosmopolitan moderate, who had broadcast from London to his homeland during the period of the German occupation, represented in the eyes of Western observers the embodiment of a degree of liberal continuity. As seen from Kremlin, he was a present embarrassment who might easily become a troublemaker. Particularly disturbing to the Politburo appears to have been evidence that he was preparing to leave Czechoslovakia again, this time to assume the role of an anti-Stalinist émigré spokesman.

On the morning of March 10, 1948, Masaryk's lifeless body was found in a courtyard of Prague's Czernin Palace, which housed not only the foreign ministry but also the minister's personal apartment, located three floors above the spot where his corpse lay. The official communique issued that day announced with regret the suicide of the popular leader, supposedly after a period of mounting depression. He was given a respectful funeral on March 13 and buried following emotional tributes from Gottwald and other Communist dignitaries. The rumor that he had been murdered had already begun to spread. It was inevitable that such an explanation should have received early and continuing credence, given the combination of the victim's ordinarily buoyant manner, the obvious embarrassment he represented to the executors of Soviet policy, and the fact that several key witnesses, including the doctor who was called to examine the body and a Czech police official centrally involved in the ensuing inquiry, died unexpectedly within a very short time.

Even now, despite the flurry of long-suppressed reports and new investigations during the months in 1968 before the Red Army and its Warsaw Pact allies moved into Czechoslovakia to end Alexander Dubcêk's efforts at liberalization and greater autonomy within the Eastern Bloc, the last word cannot be written concerning Masaryk's fate. In the aftermath of the "Prague Spring," however, Claire Sterling published a reconstruction of the events of March 9–10, 1948, in the Czech capital, together with their background.[28] In contrast to numerous efforts aimed at overturning official interpretations of sensational deaths in other countries, Sterling's book shows an unusual combination of thoroughness and candor. She does not insist that Masaryk was totally incapable of taking his own life; and the fresh evidence made available in 1968 is weighed against the possibility that suicide, not murder should in fact be the verdict. Nevertheless, when medical, political, biographical, and simply descriptive elements have all been taken into account, one is left with the strongest impression this side of certainty that the foreign minister was assassinated.

While the new Russian empire was asserting itself between the Elbe and the Black Sea, older forms of dominion widely scattered around the world, their foundations shaken by the Second World War, proceeded to crumble with increasing speed once it was over. This crumbling, and the resulting struggles for succession in territories released from European, Japanese, and American control, gave rise to an outburst of political murder which has yet to subside.

Nowhere did the postwar challenge to European domination announce itself earlier or more emphatically than in what since 1920 had been the British Mandate of Palestine. Neither Jewish nor Arab inhabitants had been satisfied with that disposition of the slice of land separating the Mediterranean from the River Jordan, and sporadic outbursts of violence had occurred with increasing frequency in the thirties. Not until the next decade, however, when the battles of World War II spread from North Africa to the edge of the Middle East, did the struggle for an independent Israel assume truly revolutionary force.

On February 12, 1942, at Tel Aviv, a Polish-born Jew by the name of Abraham Stern, who had been imprisoned in 1939 as an agent of the underground Irgun Zwei Leumi but was released when war broke out in Europe, was shot to death by a British military patrol. Stern by that time had broken with Irgun and its leader, his erstwhile prison comrade David Raziel, preferring to form the militant organization, perhaps two hundred strong, that bore his name. In death, however, he became an instant martyr for Israeli nationalists of all kinds.[29] The raid on his apartment, commanded by a security officer who had himself been the target of an unsuccessful ambush by the Stern Gang, proved to be a decisive step toward conflict between the occupiers and Jewish patriots.

For England of course the overriding consideration was the menacing advance of Rommel's Afrika Korps, about to attack Egypt from the west and seemingly quite capable of overrrunning the Levant, Iraq, and Iran at a time when Japan's forces were approaching Burma, and conceivably India as well, from the opposite direction. To an impatient minority of Palestinian Jews, on the other hand, not even the danger of a Nazi victory could offset the temptation to attack the British Mandate, gambling, as Lenin once had done at Brest-Litovsk, that in the long run the Germans would be unable to win the war. If their reasoning did not enlist the support of their coreligionists, it was because too many of the latter recognized the terrible risks involved.

Even after the British victory at El Alamein in late 1942, this uneasy truce survived until Axis power in North Africa had been destroyed. Only then did Israeli nationalism produce a stunning blow designed to hasten England's withdrawal from the region. On November 6, 1944, Walter Edward Guinness Baron Moyne, His Majesty's minister of state for the Middle East, was gunned down on the outskirts of Cairo by two members of the Stern Gang, Eliahu Bet Zouri and Elahu Hakim, aged twenty-two and seventeen respectively. Moyne's driver was also killed, but his military aide, though wounded, pursued the fleeing pair on foot until policemen overtook their bicycles.[30] Both were tried in Egypt and hanged the following March. Their act, however, started a chain of assassinations leading to the bombing of the King David Hotel two years later, as well as to the murder, also at Jerusalem, of Count Folke Bernadotte and his French fellow observer for the United Nations in 1948.

Concurrently with the trial and sentencing of Bet Zouri and Hakim, the anti-colonialist campaign in Egypt took a further turn, its motivation no less anti-British, but in other respects diametrically opposed to that of Moyne's slayers. On February 24, 1945, the Egyptian prime minister, Ahmed Maher Pasha, having just informed the Chamber of Deputies of his government's declaration of war against Germany and Japan, was fatally shot as he walked through the parliament building to repeat this announcement before the Senate. His assailant, a twenty-eight-year-old Moslem lawyer named Mahmoud Essawi, described himself as a patriot. Unlike the Israelis, however, he was also a Nazi sympathizer, who insisted during his trial (he was executed in September) that Maher had deserved to die for his "betrayal of Egypt's true friends." No other occurrence near the end of the great conflict was so clearly "war-connected," while at the same time looking ahead to the crusade against European control of the Maghreb, from the Nile to the Atlantic.

The same year that saw Count Bernadotte gunned down on a street in Jerusalem brought a still more shocking murder committed half a continent away, in India. On January 30, 1948, as he was walking through the garden of Birla House, his temporary residence in Delhi, on his way to evening prayers, the seventy-eight-year-old Mahatma Gandhi was fatally shot by Nathuram V. Godse, a Hindu newspaper editor. Godse and two accomplices were convicted and eventually hanged in November 1949. According to their testimony, they had acted out of a shared belief that their quarry must die for having denounced Hindu mob violence against Moslem fellow citizens.

Seen in terms of his assassins' motivation, Gandhi's death, like Sadat's in Egypt a third of a century later, takes its place in the annals of religious struggle. However, as part of the birth crisis of independent India, and indirectly of Pakistan, it was thoroughly political. The man who had passively but triumphantly resisted the British *raj,* without repudiating a lifelong commitment to nonviolence and without ceasing to plead for peace between the faiths in place of communal riots, had time only to call out twice to his god—"Hai Rama! Hai Rama!"—before he died. Less than twenty-four hours later, in accordance with Indian tradition and the leader's own instructions, his body was consumed on a pyre of scented logs beside the Jumna River. Ironically, as one biographer points out, final rites for the century's most celebrated pacifist were entrusted to the new Indian ministry of defense under its English commander-in-chief.[31] As a result, the funeral procession was dominated by units of all three armed services, including a squadron of military aircraft engaged in dropping roses upon the American-made weapons-carrier that bore the corpse. When the last of the fire had died, the Mahatma's ashes were consigned to the *Sangan,* the "sacred confluence" of the Jumna and the Ganges.

The year 1948, when Mohandas K. Gandhi died—after a career spent observing the effects of the Boer War on Africa and of the Government of India Act on his native land in 1919, serving sentences in English jails, vainly trying to convince British leaders that Hitler's Wehrmacht could be disarmed by the arts of nonresistance, and at the end charming Lord Mountbatten, the last of the viceroys—seemed to mark an uncommonly significant watershed in world history. It was the year when Communist victory was sealed in mainland China and imposed on Czechoslovakia; when, with President Harry Truman's support, Israel declared its independence; and when France, Great Britain, and the United States endorsed the creation of a central government for the three western zones of occupied Germany. Above all, it was the year when the last semblance of cooperation between the Soviet Union and its wartime allies disappeared, save for the most limited diplomatic and technical arrangements. World politics, accompanied as always by its most violent practitioners, moved on to other issues.

13

Recent Times

Mass and Location

Up to this point I have been able to discuss historical patterns of political murder with the help of a fairly limited number of illustrative cases. As one enters the realm of contemporary history, however, the task of selection becomes more difficult. Proximity in time alone makes for controversy over choices and judgments. But a far more important complication arises from the unprecedented rise in the number of assassinations attempted. Their incidence increased roughly tenfold between the nineteenth century and what has elapsed of the twentieth. More ominous still, the *rate* of increase has been steepest during the past three decades.

For about a century and a half prior to the 1790s the Western world and most of the rest of mankind witnessed, amid violence enough of other sorts, a prolonged respite from assassination. During the nineteenth century a noticeable resurgence produced some thirty-five to forty fatalities in Europe, including Russia, and a slightly smaller but comparable figure for non-European lands. Thus, allowing for occasional disagreement over labeling and tallying, the global total for the years 1801–1900 can be set at approximately 100 major attempts, of which between sixty-five and seventy succeeded. The corresponding figures for the period 1901–1980, as shown in the accompanying table come to almost seven hundred attempts, more than 70 percent of them fatal. No less startling than these composite figures is the fact that over half of the twentieth-century fatalities have occurred since 1950, at a rate apparently still accelerating.

Common sense advises a degree of caution in the treatment of such statistics. When contemplating the events of one's own day, it is easy to be moved by some whose memory will fade with the passage of time, as that of others has faded in the past. Furthermore, the effects of modern technology on the reporting and recording of violent scenes heightens their immediate

Major assassination attempts, 1901–1980 (number of intended victims; fatalities in parentheses).

Decade	Western and Central Europe	Russia and Balkans	Middle East and North Africa	Sub-Saharan Africa	Eastern and Southern Asia	Americas, excluding U.S.A.	United States of America	Total [% fatal]
1901–1910	7 (4)	16 (8)	3 (2)	—	3 (2)	—	6 (3)	35 (19) [54.3]
1911–1920	18 (11)	28 (22)	5 (4)	—	2 (2)	6 (5)	3 (1)	62 (45) [72.6]
1921–1930	34 (25)	12 (9)[a]	6 (4)	—	5 (3)	3 (2)	3 (1)	63 (44) [70.0]
1931–1940	17 (14)[b]	5 (2)[c]	4 (2)	1 (0)	10 (6)	4 (4)	5 (5)	46 (33) [71.7]
1941–1950	19 (14)[d]	5 (4)[e]	13 (12)[f]	—	26 (20)	15 (12)	7 (2)	85 (64) [75.3]
1951–1960	26 (18)	3 (1)	30 (21)	4 (0)	24 (8)	26 (13)	8 (4)	121 (65) [53.7]
1961–1970	10 (7)	5 (2)	25 (19)	18 (16)	24 (17)	30 (22)	16 (15)	128 (98) [76.6]
1971–1980	34 (30)	4 (3)	36 (27)	15 (12)	20 (14)	30 (24)	3 (1)	142 (111) [78.2]
Total [% fatal]	165 (123) [74.5]	78 (51) [65.4]	122 (91) [74.6]	38 (28) [73.7]	114 (72) [63.2]	114 (82) [71.9]	51 (32) [62.7]	682 (479) [70.2]

Number does not include victims of:
a. Sofia Cathedral bombing, 1925 (estimated fatalities: 125)
b. Nazi Blood Purge, 1934 (with exception of Roehm, G. Strasser, and Schleicher)
c. Soviet purge trials, 1937–1938
d. Post-July 20 reprisals in Germany, 1944–1945
e. Stalinist purges within USSR, 1945–1953
f. King David Hotel bombing, Jerusalem, 1946 (fatalities: 53)

impact on our consciousness. Nevertheless, in compiling the table an effort was made to include only episodes that, even if they had taken place before 1900, would in all likelihood be part of history as it is read today.

Side by side with the rise in total casualties, there has been a significant change in their geography. Long before the end of the nineteenth century, global imitation was under way, accompanied in many places by indigenous resistance and repression. There was as yet, however, little reason to predict the expansion shown in the table, beginning at both ends of Asia in the 1940s, extending into Latin America by the 1950s, and reaching Black Africa with the 1960s, which also brought the United States an abrupt increase in lethal assaults. Notice, referring once more to the table, that there has been no absolute decline in the frequency of assassination attempts in Europe, where the figure for 1971–1980 in western and central European nations matched (and in resultant fatalities actually surpassed) the previous high for a single decade, that of the "terrible twenties." In other words, political murder's greater prominence in some areas of the world has not been offset by its decline in others.

Two problems arise from the profusion and dispersion of political homicide. The first involves the need to distinguish between a given attack's location and the national or regional identity of its intended victim. The table has been constructed using the former criterion: it classifies events according to where they happened. This should not obscure the fact that many sensational killings originated far from where they were committed. West Germany, in addition to having local outbreaks, was the place where a former Azerbaijani officer in the USSR's Red Army was slain in 1954, to be followed by a fugitive Slovak diplomat (1955), two anti-Soviet Ukrainians (1957 and 1959), a female White Russian defector (1959), and a growing number of North African figures, including an ex-minister of justice from Tunisia (1961).

France, although it has suffered no such stunning tragedy as the massacre of eleven Israeli Olympic athletes by agents of the Palestinian "Black September" movement at Munich in 1972, has in recent years surpassed Germany in playing host to foreign assassins. Other countries have shared this unenviable experience: England, where a former Iraqi ambassador was assassinated in 1968 and where the Israeli ambassador was critically wounded by a Palestinian gunman in 1982; Sweden, in whose capital two German embassy officials were murdered by a squad of terrorists from the Federal Republic on April 24, 1975; and the United States, which has been the scene of fatal assaults upon prominent Chilean and Iranian exiles, as well as at least two Turkish diplomats.

The second problem of classification stems from having to employ a constant definition of assassination, in a world plagued by individual, multiple, and mass homicides. When in July 1982 a United States State Department spokesman announced that "political murders" were occurring in El Salvador at a rate of 300 per month, he presumably was trying to bring a message of hope—a leading news magazine having just published a figure of 4,383 deaths in that Central American Republic during the last six months of 1981.[1] Whatever its genesis, his statement reveals how imperative is the maintenance of consistency when making certain distinctions.

In one sense or another, deaths produced by random gunfire at a mass demonstration, the decimation of mutinous troops or civilian insurgents, genocidal massacres, efforts to starve an unwanted social class, even formally declared war between nations can all be accurately described as "political." For purposes of quantitative comparison with past *assassinations,* however, such categories are useless. As an African political scientist has repeated with timely emphasis, it is for some purposes necessary to concentrate on cases that concern the purposeful killing of "politically important" individuals "for reasons which are either political or unknown," that is, not manifestly personal.[2] It is only these cases that the table attempts to enumerate, for they alone are the subject of this book.

Independence and Nationhood

The frequently heard statement that "one man's terrorist is another's freedom fighter" is redundant in the sense that virtually all exponents of political violence have their admirers. The same observation is misleading, however, if taken to imply that all terrorists are alike and that any distinction drawn among them lies only in the eye of the beholder. An illustration of how unfounded such a claim would be is the difference that separates those militants who march to the familiar beat of a patriotic drum from those whose principal object of attack is their own government and the society it represents.

Most of the national liberation movements that flourished in the aftermath of the Second World War have long since been transformed, by success, into the ruling parties of sovereign states. Independent Israel, Syria, Algeria, Kenya, Indonesia, Bangladesh, and Vietnam are only a few of the nations now controlled by survivors and heirs of what were once militant rebel forces battling for liberation from colonial status. But the demands of certain other nationalist groups have not been satisfied, so their campaigns go on with unabated ferocity. Three such formations claim to represent the respective interests of non-Jewish Palestinians, Spanish Basques, and "separated" Irishmen living in the six Ulster counties that remain part of the United Kingdom.

Because of their place in the volatile and dangerous power politics of the Middle East, competing factions of Palestinian nationalists command more continuous attention and arouse more heated controversy around the world than does any comparable movement. Contributing to this nervous fascination is an awareness that Moslem (and to a lesser degree Christian) residents of the former Mandate can point to disappointed expectations based on British promises. There is also the anomaly of the Arabs' debt to Jewish militancy in the decade 1938–1948, dramatically recalled by the prominence of ex-premier Menachem Begin, a veteran of the Irgun Zwei Leumi and a memoirist who defended both the assassination of Lord Moyne and the bombing of the King David Hotel. More important than these historical considerations, however, is the savagery of the Palestinians' own campaign in recent times and the often bewildering struggle among their competing leaders, with control of the entire effort at stake.

At the center of that effort has stood the figure of Yassir Arafat and his Palestinian Liberation Organization, long only dimly perceived, then for a time apparently in the ascendant, but of late so beleaguered as to be unsure of even surviving. Alternately wooed and repudiated by leaders of various Arab and non-Arab states, attacked as too moderate by extreme elements within the independence movement, as well as by "foreign" Moslems including Syrians and Druses, the PLO chieftain has sometimes preached restraint and at other times launched strikes at his enemies, rival Palestinian leaders among them. A possible instance of the latter tactic was the murder of Jahir Mohsen on July 25, 1979. Mohsen, chief of military operations for both the PLO and a Syrian-backed guerrilla force, was shot by two unidentified assailants at Cannes, where he had arrived from Liberia under a false passport to direct a supposedly "interfactional" delegation at a meeting of the United Arab League. Although Mohsen was known to have opposed Arafat because of the latter's efforts to improve relations with Jordan's King Hussein, PLO and Syrian spokesmen at once blamed Israeli or, more vehemently, Egyptian agents for Mohsen's death.

Israel has nevertheless remained the Palestinians' principal enemy, from raids on Jewish border and coastal towns, through the Munich "Olympic massacre," to the killing of one Israeli diplomat in Paris on April 3, 1982, and the wounding of a second in London two months later. (These incidents triggered Israel's invasion of Lebanon that June). Particularly notable amid all these sanguinary exercises has been the eagerness of the Popular Front of the Liberation of Palestine (PFLP) to obtain help from foreign terrorists, Japanese in the case of the Lod Airport machine-gunning in 1972, Germans in that of the hijacking of a French jetliner to Entebbe, Uganda, in 1976, with 78 Jewish passengers among the 246 hostages aboard. No other terrorist movement has relied more heavily than the Palestinians on supplies (including money) funneled through Prague, Sofia, Tripoli, Damascus, and other distribution centers—and none has suffered more from rivalries among insiders and outsiders alike, affecting its internal councils.[3]

The Basques of Spain, separated from Latin culture by language, history, and customs, concentrated in a fairly distinct region of the Biscayan coast and the western Pyrenees, are the base for a particularist movement quite different from those of the Levant. The organization called "Basque Country and Freedom" (*Euskadi Ta Askatasuna*, ETA) was founded in 1959 to resist the centralist policies of Generalissimo Franco's Spanish dictatorship. It shared some of the concerns of another border province, Catalonia, and tended for a while to adopt certain Catalan positions, without really sharing many of its eastern neighbor's traditions or loyalties. ETA was at the outset a group committed to the cause not of social revolution but of Basque independence.[4]

That aim had involved certain difficulties, inasmuch as the logic of separatism would sooner or later not only lead to isolation from other Spanish opponents of the Franco regime but also call for a determined effort to incorporate French basques into a future autonomous state. Yet France was the refuge to which ETA militants looked for asylum from their Falangist enemies. Hence purely nationalist appeals were toned down in favor of stronger emphasis on the class war against Spanish and indeed world capitalism. While this developing change of front attracted some new recruits, it alienated many of the more conservative Basques. For all its elaborate organization under a general assembly, with an executive committee, specialized sections, and district leaders (*herrialdes*), ETA has been increasingly riven by disputes over social and political strategies.

The move to open violence, long discussed, began only in 1967, with a rash of ETA bombings of army barracks, police stations, Falangist newspaper offices, and other institutional symbols of Franco's rule. Thereafter, for some time ETA tactics were largely restricted to nonlethal sabotage within the Basque territory and as such received a great deal of popular support. Gradually, however, the killing of police and other officials increased, starting at lower and moving to higher ranks in the government, while certain young Basques showed a growing fascination with such foreign models of terror as the PLO and the Italian Red Brigades. By the early 1970s it was being remarked by well-informed observers that in this age group traditional Basque reading was rapidly being replaced by the teachings of Chairman Mao, Ho Chi Minh, and Ché Guevara.

Then, on December 20, 1973, in Madrid, a limousine carrying Spain's seventy-year-old premier and Franco's chosen successor, Admiral Luis Carrero Blanco, was destroyed by an explosion so massive that it hurled the car over a five-story building and into the courtyard of a church where the prime minister had just attended mass. He was of course killed instantly, as were his driver and a police bodyguard. The government's assertion that Basque activists based in France had planned the crime was greeted by the international press with considerable skepticism. A week later, however, Madrid's charges were confirmed in substance if not in every detail when four hooded men, identifying themselves as members of ETA, held a press conference in Bordeaux at which they claimed credit for the assassination.[5]

Although the accession of King Juan Carlos following Franco's death in 1975 brought a temporary shift of terrorist attention away from national dignitaries and back to officials serving in the four Basque provinces, the murder rate in fact increased. In October 1976, at San Sebastián, wild gunfire wounded ten people and killed five others, including Councilor of the Realm Juan María de Araluce Villar, whose death was the occasion for another triumphant ETA press conference in Bordeaux. Almost exactly one year later Augusto Anceta Barrenuechea, an ethnic Basque serving as president of the provincial council of Vizcaya, was shot to death at Guernica by rebels now publicly committed to the destruction of "all instruments of domination of the Basque country by the Spanish oligarchy." No longer was there any apparent inclination to wave anti-Falangist banners.

Beginning in May 1979, when General Luis Gómez Hortiguela, chief of staff of the army, was shot to death in Madrid, another alteration in strategy, back to assaults on central authorities in the Spanish capital, signaled the victory of youthful ideologues over traditional Basque separatists. The style of Hortigela's assassination—the general, two colonels, and their driver were killed in broad daylight by men who approached on foot, discharged more than fifty rounds of machine-gun fire and threw a hand grenade before escaping in a waiting automobile—is enough to suggest imitation of Italian and German techniques. The day after the Hortiguela murder, eight Madrid residents died and forty were injured when a bomb exploded in a crowded café, bringing to sixty-five the government's count of fatalities from political violence during the first five months of the year. That fall the provincial governor of Guipuzcoa was slain at San Sebastián, as were two other officials at Bilbao a few days later.

The political changes that have occurred in Spain during the past decade—whether the creation of an increasingly popular monarchy, or the movement to middle-of-the-road government under Leopoldo Calvo Sotelo and thence to one of the moderate left under Felipe González following the Socialists' electoral victory in 1982—have not caused the most radical segment of ETA to alter its behavior. Early in November 1982, while a triumphant González was preparing to assume the premiership, two motorcycle gunmen in Madrid riddled another staff car with automatic-rifle fire and rode away, having killed Victor Lago Roman, commander of the elite Brunete First Armored Division and the fifth general assassinated in four years. The toll of lower-ranking officials, in the capital and in the northern provinces, runs into the hundreds.[6]

While the Basque extremists, at least with respect to weapons and tactics, have become all but indistinguishable from the "Red commandos" of various other countries, their political strategy remains obscure. Some commentators insist that the leading insurgents have abandoned Basque independence as their primary goal, sacrificing traditional ethnic appeals in favor of an effort to disrupt Spain's social and economic system, as a whole and at any cost. Other experts believe that national liberation is still an aim, though perhaps an altered one to be pursued versus the Spanish crown and army, as well as the Catholic Church and the Socialist Party. Whatever ETA's intentions prove to be, the trials of democracy in Spain, threatened by both extremes of the political spectrum, are depressingly familiar to anyone acquainted with the history of Weimar Germany.

The growth of a terrorist *internationale* can be seen in efforts to encourage, arm, and incorporate less impressive independence movements in other parts of Europe. Reports that Libyan and Algerian representatives at a "summit conference" in 1976 had assumed responsibility for supplying not only Spanish Basques but also Corsican and Breton separatists within France, should, if nothing else, explain why Basques from Spain no longer enjoy the once hospitable guarantee of asylum in Paris or even in Bordeaux.[7] Meanwhile, elusive organizers such as "Carlos the Jackal" (a Venezuelan), George Habash (a Palestinian), and Antonio Dages Bouvier (with his false Ecuadorian passport and generous KGB bank account) have supplied funding and advice for undertakings scattered from the Irish coast to Munich and from Tel Aviv's airport to Entebbe's.[8]

All this raises the question of international ties in relation to the oldest of Europe's nationalist undergrounds, the Irish. When in 1971 the Dutch government intercepted four tons of illegal weapons in transit from Czechoslovakia to Northern Ireland, the inference was drawn in some quarters that this, combined with evidence of operational training given Irish Republican Army members abroad, proved that another national movement had been absorbed by world terrorism. Yet a tradition of political murders going back more than a hundred years to Phoenix Park would seem to relieve Ireland's twentieth-century dissidents of any need to seek tutelage from foreigners. Also the well-publicized flow of money sent by sympathetic Irish-Americans could easily account for direct and unconditional purchase of weapons from Czechoslovakia, or anywhere else. The most one can safely say is that there has been growing evidence of technical assistance from German terrorists in particular.

One indication that Irish affairs continue in part to follow their own course is statistical proof that underground violence in Ulster, unlike that in the Middle East, Central America, Spain, and a number of other places, has actually declined since its high point around 1972. During that gruesome year, according to figures gleaned from reports by the British army's Northern Ireland Office and the Royal Ulster Constabulary, there were 467 deaths (321 civilian, 146 military), followed by 216 (166, 50) in 1973 and 297 (245, 52) in 1974. By 1979 the corresponding total and subtotals had fallen to 113

(51, 62), and in 1981, they were 97 (57, 40). Nevertheless, even the most recent numbers are tragically high for six counties whose combined population is only slightly over 1,500,000; and the cumulative total for 1969 through mid-August 1983, 2,320 deaths in all, suggests not sporadic actions so much as civil war.[9]

The question continues to center not so much on casualty lists as on specific, individually significant assassinations. What, if anything, in contemporary Irish history can reasonably be compared with Lord Cavendish's and Thomas Burke's murders in 1882, or with those of Michael Collins, Sir Henry Wilson, and Kevin O'Higgins during the 1920s? The best response is to cite a cluster of deadly acts committed by the Provisional Wing of the IRA, the "Provos," in the space of less than four years. The fact that those same years saw the abovementioned decline in Northern Ireland's "combat deaths" more broadly defined illustrates once more the not uncommon lack of correlation between mass violence and more personalized attacks. It should be noted that none of the following murders occurred in Ulster, though all of them had their roots in its struggle. They are evidence of the IRA's confidence that it can strike down "enemies of Ireland" anywhere.

The first victim in the series was Ross McWhirter, coeditor of *The Guinness Book of Records* and a vocal proponent of stronger measures against Irish terrorism, who was shot to death at the front door of his house in London on November 27, 1975. Next to lose his life was Christopher Ewart-Biggs, the United Kingdom's ambassador to Eire, killed on July 21, 1976, in Dublin when an explosive charge was detonated beneath his car, presumably by three young men seen fleeing from a nearby hiding place immediately after the blast. With him died his secretary, while his driver and a high-ranking British civil servant on a visit from Belfast were injured. The Irish and English prime ministers joined in denouncing the bomb assault but avoided, wisely as events soon revealed, any promises to their constituents concerning the future.

Indirectly, though not immediately, the Ewart-Biggs slaying was prophetic of a third assassination, that of Richard Sykes, whom Prime Minister Callaghan had sent to investigate the 1976 murder. By March 1979 Sykes had been appointed British ambassador to the Netherlands, and it was at The Hague that he was fatally shot by a pair of Provo gunmen. Only days later, on March 30 to be exact, Airey Neave, a leading Conservative member of Parliament met his death in London much as Ewart-Biggs had in Dublin: the victim of a car-bomb explosion. Neave was a natural target by IRA standards, since he was his party's legislative spokesman on issues affecting Ulster and seemed certain to be named secretary for Northern Ireland in the likely event of a Tory victory in the approaching elections.

The slaying of Airey Neave, though it rocked Great Britain as had only a handful of previous assassinations in the country's history, was not the crest of the IRA's 1979 wave of terror. That came five months later, on August 27, when the calm of a summer afternoon on the west coast of Ireland was shattered by a tremendous explosion approximately a mile out to sea, bringing death to England's most famous surviving hero of World War II. Admiral Louis Mountbatten—Earl Mountbatten of Burma, India's last British viceroy, and cousin of the queen—with five family guests and a young hand signed on at the local village of Enniskillen had gone aboard the fishing boat from a dock near Mountbatten's vacation home in County Sligo. The murder weapon, which contained at least fifty pounds of powerful explosive, was detonated either by a timing device or more probably, according to investigators, by a radio signal from a hidden observation post. In addition to the seventy-nine-year-old admiral, three others were killed: his grandson Nicholas Knatchbull, aged fourteen; the fifteen-year-old "boat boy," Paul Maxwell; and Nicholas' paternal grandmother. Seriously injured were Nicholas' twin brother, his father, and his mother (Mountbatten's own daughter).

To heighten the shock effect of this stroke, another concealed bomb, combined with sniper fire, took the lives of eighteen British soldiers and an English tourist the same afternoon in a village some thirty-five miles from Belfast. The IRA Provisionals waited three days, presumably to let the news sink in, then on August 30 released a statement proudly claiming responsibility and calling the assassination "a discriminate act to bring to the attention of the English people the continuing occupation of our country." "For this," it concluded, "we will tear out their sentimental imperialist hearts."

An important aspect of what followed was the full involvement not only of English and Northern Irish authorities but also of Eire's police and courts as well, Prime Minister John Lynch having pledged as much in an emergency meeting with Margaret Thatcher, his British counterpart. It was the Irish Republic's detectives who, on the very day the Provos released their communiqué, announced the arrest of thirty-four-year-old Thomas McMahon, an IRA member who had been rounded up in a routine police check, almost by accident, but whose clothing yielded traces of nitroglycerine and ammonium phosphate, as well as green paint matching that on the fishing boat. Three months later McMahon was sentenced to imprisonment for life, without appeal, by a criminal tribunal in Dublin. The same court acquitted a second defendant, ruling that the chemical evidence in his case was inconclusive.

The IRA's members, based in a country already fully independent but ostensibly pledged to secure the "liberation" of a part of Ulster and its incorporation into a united Ireland, might more accurately be described as "irredentists" than as "rebels." Nationalists, however, they unquestionably are. The real distinction is between what "freedom for Ireland" meant to a host of nineteenth- and early twentieth-century patriots and what recovery of "the separated counties" means to the Provos today.[10]

The New Nihilists

Beginning in Europe during the 1960s and spreading with varying degrees of comprehension to other parts of the world, a purportedly new formulation of anarchist doctrine has given rise to a number of more genuinely novel expressions of terrorist resolve. Its sources range from legends of the wartime Resistance and exploits of the late Ché Guevara, especially as related by Régis Debray, to selections from Bakunin, Nechaev, and Carlos Marighella's *Handbook of Urban Guerrilla Warfare.*[11] Philosophical support was supplied at the outset by certain intellectuals, one of whom, Jean Paul Sartre, traveled to Germany in order to pay a sympathy call on the imprisoned Baader-Meinhof gang leaders. Not for the first time in history, however, philosophers as heroes have tended to wear out with disappointing rapidity amid the changing reactions of impatient audiences. The real inspiration demanded by small but painfully intense groups of alienated students in the 1960s came from an even smaller minority, composed of teachers they encountered in their universities—Antonio Negri at Padua, for instance—or radical journalists such as Ulrike Meinhof in Berlin. These academic sodalities offered reinforcement for daring opinions and the promise of mutual support when the time for action arrived. Financial help was necessary, and pending the organization of systematic fundraising by means of kidnaping and bank robbery, nascent terrorist cells benefited from philanthropists of whom perhaps the best known was the Italian multimillionaire Giangiacomo Feltrinelli, patron of the Red Brigades.

The New Left's extreme fringe displays a number of salient characteristics having more to do with organization and tactics than with ideology. One of these is a high degree of technological sophistication in the choice of weapons and means of communication. Involving communication in a different sense is the effective exploitation of mass media, television above all, that has dramatized the daring of self-styled "activists" while publicizing their apocalyptic message. With respect to personnel, the most striking innovation lies in the increased recruitment of women into terrorist formations, a phenomenon encountered during the period of Narodnaya Volya's greatest activity in Russia, but largely discontinued for at least sixty or seventy years thereafter. Demonstrations by suffragettes over that space of time gave scant warning of the behavior during the 1960s and 1970s of Meinhof, Gabriele Kröcher-Tiedemann, Gudrun Ensslin and other German women, Leila Khaled in the Middle East, or the Japanese Fusako Shigenobu.[12]

Nowhere more clearly than in Japan has political violence been traceable to widely differing motives. A particularly serious epidemic of attacks on public figures began in October 1960, when Inejiro Asanuma, chairman of the Socialist Party, was stabbed to death while delivering a televised address before a live audience of 3,000. His killer was a seventeen-year-old university student described as "ultrarightist" and "patriotic." Two Japanese premiers—Nobusake Kishi in 1960 and Hayato Ikeda in 1961 and 1963—survived similar attacks, as did a minister in Ikeda's government on the second occasion. When on March 23, 1964, U.S. Ambassador Edwin O. Reischauer was seriously wounded, the "emotionally disturbed" knife-wielder could not be linked to any organization. By that time radical opposition to the United States had become so intense that the Reischauer incident provoked a cabinet crisis in the middle of which the Japanese minister of public safety was forced to resign.

With the emergence, later in the sixties of the Japanese Red Army (*Sekigun,* or, when claiming to be a united federation, *Rengo Sekigun*), any ambiguity concerning political orientation largely disappeared. Sekigun's participation in airliner hijackings and individual murders quickly attracted worldwide attention. Reacting quickly, Japan's security forces whittled away at the new terrorism formations, making arrests and precipitating defections or escapes abroad, until by February 1972, when a group of diehards were surrounded in an abandoned hotel at Karuizawa, only a scattering of terrorists remained hidden elsewhere. When the Karuizawa "fortress" was stormed by police, the bodies of fourteen defenders were found already dead, killed as deviationists by the survivors in what one writer has described as "an orgy of self-purification."[13]

Nevertheless, on May 30 of the same year remnants of the Red Army produced another, still more terrible death spasm thousands of miles from their homeland. It occurred at Lod Airport outside Tel Aviv, when a team of three émigré Sekigun assassins, organized at Baalbek in Lebanon by Wadi Haddad, representing the PFLP, and flown to Israel via Rome, where they received Czech grenades and rapid-fire guns from Carlos the Jackal, shot to death twenty-six waiting airline passengers, sixteen of whom were Puerto Rican pilgrims to the Holy Land. One of the killers died in his comrades' crossfire, another shot himself on the spot, and the third was sentenced to life imprisonment by an Israeli military tribunal.[14] Surviving members of the Japanese Red Army still are glimpsed from time to time, around French, Dutch, and other hideouts, but the "pilgrims' massacre" at Tel Aviv, hailed by Sekigun's female chief of foreign operations, as a mission to "consolidate the international revolutionary alliance against imperialists of the world," remains her movement's last major victory.

It would be wrong to attribute to New Leftists all political murder in a world where military juntas and "death squads" of rightists continue to take their daily toll of victims, while a neofascist splinter group such as Italy's "Armed Revolutionary Nuclei" can inflict a tragedy as massive as the railway station bombing that killed more than eighty people in Bologna on August 2, 1980. The irreconcilably colonialist French Secret Army Organization (OAS) sought for years to match North African terrorists in the use of machine-gun and explosive *plastique* until Algeria was finally granted independence in 1962. Even after that, OAS plotters repeatedly tried to assassinate President De Gaulle in retaliation for what they saw as his betrayal of the French Empire. As late as 1976, Prince Jean de Broglie, a moderate Catholic politician who had earlier been deputy foreign minister, was shot to death in Paris by a youthful representative of the nationalistic Club Charles Martel as retribution for having supported the Algerian independence bill in the National Assembly *fourteen years before.* Finally, in Turkey, which since about 1977 has become, in the words of an undoubted authority, "the world's worst case of raging terrorist warfare," the struggle goes on between such groups as Colonel Arpaslan Turkes' nationalist Gray Wolves and the Turkish People's Liberation Army.[15]

Nevertheless, the growing predominance of the TPLA, with its PLO-trained elite and its European connections, illustrates the differing growth rates of revolutionary and reactionary movements in the twentieth century. Ultraleftist jargon is by now the true *lingua franca* of terrorism organized on a global basis. The "politicization" of ETA, relying heavily on such language, unsettled numberless Spanish Basques. Even more clearly, the rhetoric of Michael Farrell, the decision by Bernadette Devlin to join the Trotskyite "Fourth International" in 1969, and Seamus Costello's defection from the official wing of the IRA five years later in order to help found still another extremist National Liberation Army (INLA) along lines established at conferences he had attended on the Continent were unwelcome to more traditional Irish patriots.[16]

Historic Targets: Schleyer, Moro, and the Pope

Three recent episodes have served to illuminate some of contemporary terrorism's most repugnant features. In so doing, they have not only deeply affected the response of people close to the action but also altered the attitudes of millions less directly involved. One took place in West Germany, the other two in Italy—all within a span of less than four years toward the end of another "terrible decade."

In the spring of 1977 German terrorists, paying special attention to various cities along or near the Rhine, launched the most sustained campaign of political murder to be visited upon their country since the collapse of Hitler's Reich. It began in Karlsruhe, home of the nation's two highest courts, where on April 7 the chief federal prosecutor, Siegfried Buback, his driver, and a bodyguard were shot to death by two gunmen who arrived on motorcycles but escaped in a waiting car. Within two days the police had named their leading suspects, including Heidelberg attorney Siegfried ("Khaled") Haag, known to have succeeded to leadership of the Red Army Faction after Ulrike Meinhof's death and Andreas Baader's incarceration in

Stammheim Prison near Stuttgart.[17] Haag, too, had been caught and sent to jail, albeit more recently, for his role in the bloody seizure of the Stockholm embassy in 1975. When arrested he had been carrying a "hit list," which included Buback's name, together with several others, all referring to a strategy for winning the release of the prisoners in Stammheim. These prisoners no longer included the forty-one-year-old Meinhof, who had committed suicide in her cell on the night of May 8–9, 1976; whence the claim by the "Ulrike Meinhof" commando that its members had killed the chief prosecutor as retribution for her death.

While public excitement rose, along with criticism of the seemingly helpless federal government, Jürgen Ponto, chairman of the Dresdner Bank with headquarters in Frankfurt-am-Main, was killed at his home on July 30. Ponto's slayers, four women and one man, had secured easy entry because the father of one of the women named, twenty-six-year-old Susanne Albrecht, was a personal friend of their victim. According to surviving witnesses, the team's aim had been to abduct Ponto, but he resisted and was gunned down instead. The stage was now set for action against the next alternate whose name appeared on Siegfried Haag's list.

On September 5, 1977, at Cologne, Hanns-Martin Schleyer, president of both the West German Confederation of Employers' Associations and the Federation of West German Industries, was taken alive from his limousine, though his chauffeur and three police guards were machine-gunned to death by attackers whose van pulled alongside the industrialist's seemingly secure two-car motorcade.[18] The following day a letter, delivered in Wiesbaden and confirmed by telephone, set forth the RAF's demands: immediate release of eleven imprisoned colleagues, including Baader, Jan-Carl Raspe, and Gudrun Ensslin (since Meinhof's death the most prominent female terrorist in confinement), all serving life terms for murder. Also specified was the payment of 100,000 marks (about $40,000) and air transport to a destination yet to be specified.

The negotiating record of the Baader-Meinhof gang, now calling itself the Red Army Faction, had been uneven but by no means unencouraging from the abductors' point of view. In March 1975 a group of terrorists in Berlin, having kidnaped the Free City's Christian Democratic party chairman, Peter Lorenz, had demanded and obtained the release of five convicted prisoners, including the soon-to-be notorious Gabriele Kröcher-Tiedemann, in return for the release of Lorenz unharmed. On that occasion Chancellor Schmidt's federal cabinet in Bonn made the decision to surrender. The following month, however, when Haag and other organizers of the occupation of the German embassy in Stockholm had demanded the release of Baader, Meinhof, and twenty-four other prisoners from Stammheim, plus $20,000 for each liberated convict and a plane to fly them out of Europe, Bonn's answer was a flat refusal. Still, Schleyer's captors appear to have reasoned, the embassy incident in Sweden had really proven nothing inasmuch as the explosives used there had blown up accidentally only thirteen hours after seizure of the building. Who could be sure that pressure applied over a longer period of time would not persuade the chancellor and his associates to capitulate once more, following the example of the Lorenz case?

If that was in fact their reasoning in 1977, they were wrong. Chancellor Schmidt announced that there could be no concessions of any kind, even to save the life of his former economic adviser, and appealed for the public's help in apprehending those responsible for "this bloody provocation." Widespread expressions of indignation and grief over the killing of Schleyer's four companions suggested that the great majority of the Federal Republic's citizens were on the government's side.

Nevertheless, the deadlock continued for several weeks, until its scope was suddenly and dramatically expanded. On October 15 a Lufthansa airliner en route from Majorca to Frankfurt was commandeered by four Palestinians apparently intent on paying a debt of gratitude for help received in the past from their "German brothers and sisters." Among these favors presumably had been the joint German-PLO action in July 1976, when a planeload of hostages had been flown to Entebbe, Uganda, only to be freed by Israeli combat troops. This time the destination again was in Africa—Mogadishu, Somalia to be exact. First, however, the jet had to land at Aden for refueling, and there its pilot was shot in full view of the passengers and crew—"executed," his killers announced before dumping his body onto the airport runway. In point of fact Mogadishu was much less favorable a choice, for the hijackers' purposes, than Entebbe had been, since the Somalian government, unlike that of Idi Amin's Uganda, was sympathetic to the victims. On October 18 a unit flown from Germany entered the grounded aircraft and subdued the terrorists with the help of "stun grenades" of British provenance, killing three members of the commando and seriously wounding the fourth, a woman.

Before they were overcome at Mogadishu, the Palestinians had demanded freedom for the eleven prisoners already listed by the RAF in Germany. Consequently, failure in Africa had immediate repercussions at Stammheim where, within hours of learning the news, the most famous trio of inmates committed suicide: Gudrun Ensslin by hanging herself; Baader and Raspe with pistols secreted in their cells. Otto Schily, their principal defense attorney since the arrest of Siegried Haag, at once announced that Baader had been shot in the head *several times* and called for an international inquiry. In at least two countries, Italy and France, there were protest riots and fire bombings to the accompaniment of cries of murder.

Given the confusion of the ensuing months, it is not surprising that little notice was paid to the official report of the three autopsies or the testimony of two independent medical observers, one Belgian, the other Swiss, before a

Baden-Württemberg state commission investigating conditions in Stammheim Prison. The foreign doctors found it " 'most improbable' that the deaths were not suicide," an admittedly involuted but not really obscure conclusion. Only a few unusually astute commentators pointed out that the locations of the *single* gunshot wounds that had killed Baader and Raspe (whose corpses showed powder burns on the hands) were consistent with the directions given in a classified manual for terrorists written by Ulrike Meinhof prior to her own death under similar circumstances. There she had explained how it was possible to shoot or hang oneself in such a way as to throw suspicion on one's jailers.

The self-destruction of the remaining Baader-Meinhof leadership was only one part of the episode's grisly termination. On October 19, the day after the hostages were rescued in Africa, anonymous instructions received by telephone directed police to a designated spot on the French side of the Rhine, at Mulhouse in Alsace. There they found Schleyer's body. The man held captive for almost five weeks had died of three bullet wounds and a slit throat, "executed," in retaliation for Mogadishu and in memory of the "martyrs of Stammheim."

The discovery of his body set off the largest and most determined manhunt in the history of the Federal Republic. No fewer than sixteen suspects, ten of them women, were publicly identified and charged with various shares of complicity in the Buback-Ponto-Schleyer murders. What followed was an amazing disintegration of the allegedly impenetrable cadres of the RAF. On November 10, 1977, after a gun battle, Dutch police seized two fugitives from West Germany, one of whom, Christoph Wackernagel, was wanted for his part in the Schleyer kidnaping, which had included recording the victim's captivity on motion picture film. The other man arrested in the Netherlands was being sought for a bombing in Zweibrücken. That same day all four remaining suspects wanted for the Zweibrücken attack were arrested at Kaiserslautern, a disastrous break in the terrorists' shield of secrecy having virtually wiped out their "southwestern branch." Two days later, in Munich's Stadelheim Prison, Ingrid Schubert, another of the eleven Baader-Meinhof veterans whose release had been the asking price for Schleyer's return, joined the procession of suicides by hanging herself. On November 16 the French government agreed to extradite Klaus Croissant, Baader's former lawyer and accomplice. And finally, in December at Porrentruy, Swiss detectives picked up by now "most-wanted" Gabriele Kröcher-Tiedemann. When arrested, she had with her part of a ransom she and other German terrorists had to show for a kidnaping carried out in Austria. The balance was already in the hands of authorities, having been found on two other couriers arrested at the Swiss-Italian border en route to a rendezvous with the Red Brigades.

Italy's *Brigate Rosse* were already engaged in planning the abduction of an even better-known victim than Hanns-Martin Schleyer. Aldo Moro, taken from his car in Rome on March 16, 1978, by gunmen who killed all five of his bodyguards, was at the time his country's most respected political figure, one who had served as premier no fewer than five times. As leader of the Christian Democratic Party, he maintained cordial relations with the other parliamentary blocs, including that composed of regular Communists. Like the Schleyer case in Germany, this one involved an effort to liberate terrorists currently in governmental custody, specifically the fourteen Red Brigade members on trial before a court in Turin. No one was surprised, therefore, when the kidnapers' first telephone call included a confident demand for the immediate release of the "Turin Fourteen."

What did elicit widespread amazement was the public reaction in Italy, a country whose citizens had in the past wasted little sympathy on politicians, capitalists, or policemen, while showing a good deal of cynical acceptance of outlawry in general. This time the Italian people seemed to explode with indignation. On the evening of the bloody onslaught in Rome, a number of labor unions, adopting a tactic traditionally associated with struggle against the right, staged a symbolic strike to register condemnation of the killers. The following day a crowd estimated at more than 100,000 surrounded the scene of funeral services for the five slain bodyguards. In reply, the kidnapers released photographs and voice tapes of Moro begging for help and of their own spokesmen announcing his scheduled trial before a *Feme*-like "people's court." The ensuing weeks brought the usual confused reports, frustrated hopes born of false leads, and ungrounded speculation by the news media, as well as increasingly bitter statements from the victim's wife demanding that the government make the necessary concessions to his jailers. Painfully but stubbornly the Italian cabinet, like West Germany's educated by past extortion and repelled by the thought of endless repetition, clung to its position: no deal.

Failure to win freedom for even one of the "Turin martyrs" affected Red Brigade tacticians as defeat at Mogadishu had their German counterparts. Frustration brought sadistic rage. On May 5 another of their communiqués was published, this one announcing that Aldo Moro had been tried, found guilty of crimes against the people, and sentenced to death by "proletarian justice." On May 7 his wife received a final letter from the ex-premier, saying merely that he had now been told he would "be killed in a little while." On May 9 his bullet-riddled body was found in the trunk of a car parked between the Christian Democratic and Communist headquarters in the capital, where an anonymous phone caller had said it would be. At another mass meeting called to mourn the outcome, Rome's Communist mayor spoke from the podium, registering contempt for "cowardly anarchists." In the years since, the Brigate Rosse have made repeated gestures, among them the abduction of General James L. Dozier, rescued by a police assault team

a month later, in January 1982, and the murder in 1984 of another American, Leamon R. Hunt, head of the peacekeeping force for the Sinai Peninsula, by a splinter group calling itself the Fighting Communist Party. The
parent organization, however, has never recovered either the self-confidence
or the degree of public tolerance which it enjoyed prior to the Moro assassination.[19]

The third in this cluster of European sensations remains subject to such
intense controversy among journalists and spokesmen for various governments that it can scarcely be treated in historical terms at all. The very nature of the debate, including premises apparently shared without hesitation
by parties in disagreement over conclusions, says a great deal about the pervasive sense of terrorism's potential. Ever since May 13, 1981, when Pope
John Paul II and two onlookers were wounded in the great piazza of St.
Peter's Basilica by a twenty-three-year-old Turkish gunman, arrested on the
spot and since condemned to life imprisonment, the world has had to confront a deeply troubling set of possibilities.

It would be wrong to assume that prelates of the Catholic Church are
seldom targets for lethal violence. Christianity's long history contains too
many examples for any such illusion of immunity to persist; and from Cardinal Sibour in Paris (1857) to Cardinal Biayenda in the Republic of Congo
(1977) modern ecclesiastical princes have died as victims of assassination. At
Manila in 1970 a knife-wielding Bolivian artist, who later told reporters he
sought only to "save humanity from superstition," tried and failed to kill
Pope Paul VI during the pontiff's visit to the Philippines. Benjamin Mendoza y Amor Flores, like the man who in 1972 smashed with a hammer at
Michelangelo's Pietà in St. Peter's, was readily described in the mellifluous
Italian term *squilibrato*—"unbalanced." Whether the same word was appropriate for John Paul's assailant, however, was from the outset far less certain.

Mehmet Ali Agça's Turkish police record revealed that he had been a
member of the neo-fascist "Gray Wolves," imprisoned in 1979 for having,
by his own admission (later withdrawn), murdered a left-wing newspaper
editor, but successful in escaping a maximum-security prison with extensive
assistance, including funds for purposes of bribery, supplied by confederates
on the outside. The accused's own statements, made to the Italian court that
convicted him of attempted murder in 1981, supported the view that he was
a religious fanatic who saw in the pope an enemy of Islam, "the Commander
of the Crusaders" Agça once called him in a published letter. Italy's government, however, suspected a secular motive, as statements emanating from
the office of Judge Ilario Martella, the investigating magistrate, soon made
clear. In the summer of 1982 a magazine article by Claire Sterling launched
the explicit allegation that Agça had been a tool of Communist bosses, specifically Bulgaria's state-security police (DS), acting on orders from Mos-

cow.[20] Demands for the convicted gunman's release, purporting to originate with spokesmen for the Red Brigades, cast further doubt on the initial depiction of Agça as a conservative Muslim zealot.

On the strength of apparent leaks from Martella and his staff, the case for a "Bulgarian connection" gained steadily increasing attention in the Italian press. New evidence showed Agça to have been an international agent who had claimed membership in the Gray Wolves simply as cover for quite different activities. His wanderings included a long visit to Sofia in 1980 and extensive travels thereafter from Iran and Tunisia to West Germany. Charged by Italian authorities with having been his "controls" in Rome during the spring of 1981 were three junior Bulgarian functionaries, one an employee of Bulgaria's national airline and travel office, the other two officials in their country's Rome embassy. This trio is said to have given Agça money when he arrived in Italy, briefed him on Vatican security arrangements, and taken him on a scouting trip to the Piazza San Pietro, bringing him back there to carry out his mission on the morning of May 13. Yet only the airline representative, Sergei I. Antonov, was arrested in Rome; the two foreign service officers, Todor S. Aivosov and Major Zhelyu K. Vasilev, hurriedly returned to Sofia, where they remain safe from extradition.

The body of evidence, most of it disclosed in the form of officially inspired leaks to the press, is too substantial to be dismissed as just one more example of the unfounded conspiracy theories inspired by numerous political crimes during the past quarter of a century. Some important questions nevertheless remain unanswered. Why were the Bulgarians in Rome—even if, as has been strongly implied, they planned to kill Agça as soon as he had shot the pope—so incautious as to deal directly with the designated assassin instead of using less easily identifiable go-betweens? Why was the Italian government so slow to take formal steps against the suspects, while it permitted the gunman's statements to circulate freely and countenanced privileged speeches by cabinet members accusing Sofia and Moscow of direc involvement? And what would either of those governments, regardless of their previous record in earlier cases of assassination committed abroad, have gained from making the pontiff a martyr both of his church and of his native Poland?

To entertain doubts about the formal participation of the Bulgarian and Soviet governments in such a plot is, one must admit, to apply the rule of reason to an activity whose very nature often defies rational explanation. The possibility that subordinate officials took the lead without clear instructions from above, seeking to anticipate what they hoped were their superiors' real wishes, cannot be dismissed out of hand. Nevertheless, although the incriminating evidence, according to the most recent reports, totals some 25,000 of documentation, the case will not have been proven until it is tested in open court. The eagerly awaited trial began only in late May 1985, more than a year after the Martella report had recommended the indictment of Aivasov, Antonov, and Vasilev, as well as five alleged Turkish accomplices, and the reindictment of Agça, all on new charges of conspiracy to assassinate the pope.[21]

Post-Colonial Crises

Although spared the worst of Europe's "post-industrial" terrorism, nations created since the Second World War have tended instead to exhibit their own patterns of violence arising from difficulties inherent in the building of new states. The number of such states precludes any full enumeration of their experiences in this regard. The record, however, supports the observation that one reason why today's world contains so much political murder is because it contains so many governments.

As the assassination of Mahatma Gandhi gave notice, the former British empire in South Asia was not replaced by sovereign entities without lethal episodes. In point of fact, the largest of these new structures reared upon the foundations of very old societies, the Republic of India, has not suffered from as high a rate of politically inspired homicide as pessimists eying the bitterness of communal and other forms of strife in the 1940s were ready to predict. There have, to be sure, been periodic incidents such as the murder of Ao I, head of Naga State, shot by a local assassin in 1961, or that of Lalit Narayan Mishra, national minister of railways, killed by a bomb at Samastipur in 1975. As recently as April 1980, Prime Minister Indira Gandhi was narrowly missed by a knife-thrower in a crowd with which she was talking outside Parliament House at Delhi. Yet even Mrs. Gandhi's ill-fated experiment in autocracy, the Emergency of 1975–1977, for all its repressive measures and angry public response, did not lead to so great a loss of lives as many had expected.

All the most stunning, therefore, was the eruption of open warfare between Sikh dissidents and the government, culminating in the assassination of Prime Minister Gandhi by a pair of her own bodyguards on October 31, 1984. The previous June she had ordered Indian Army units to storm the Golden Temple of Amritsar, the Sikhs' holiest religious site but also the headquarters and arsenal for their separatist movement. Following that bloody engagement, explicit threats of vengeance were uttered at home and abroad by spokesmen for the embattled sect. On the morning of October 31, as she walked from her bungalow to another building in the residential compound at New Delhi, the prime minister was cut down in a hail of fire from the two Sikh guards. One of them, thirty-three-year-old Beant Singh, was a trusted veteran in her service. The other, a young constable named Satwant Singh, was a recent recruit who had just returned from a furlough spent in the troubled Sikh area. The immediate sequel was a wave of reprisals by Hindu mobs, which took the lives of at least a thousand Sikhs not involved in the crime. Within three months, however, the overwhelming electoral victory of Indira Gandhi's son Rajiv confirmed him in the office of prime minister and continued the line of direct succession from his grandfather Jawaharlal Nehru. It also testified to the ability of India to recover its political balance in the midst of tragedy. Whatever aims the Sikh executioners may have had, apart from retribution for Amritsar, a new lease on life for the house of Nehru cannot have been one of them.

The subcontinent's recent history includes much that occurred outside the boundaries of India per se. In September 1959 Solomon Bandaranaike, prime minister of Ceylon (since renamed Sri Lanka), was fatally shot by two Buddhist monks protesting his reform of hospital practices in defiance of Ayur-Vedic medical tradition. Bandaranaike's conversion to Christianity some years before had not saved his life—quite the contrary—but it had set the stage for the modernization program continued by his widow and successor, Sirimavo.

This murder at Colombo notwithstanding, Sri Lanka has been less seriously divided and rocked by violence than the other principal state of the region, Pakistan. The Islamic Republic, as it is officially named, despite its comparative homogeneity in terms of religion, has been almost continuously beset by regional divisions, tense foreign relations, endemic party strife, and frequent intervention in domestic politics by its proud, sometimes ruthless, military caste. Assassinations began soon after the death, from natural causes, of Mohammed Ali Jinnah, the "father of Pakistan," in 1948. Just three years later Prime Minister Liaquat Ali Khan, Jinnah's chosen political heir, was slain by a Moslem fundamentalist. Again in 1958 religious zealotry took the life of another premier, Khan Sahib, condemned by his more bellicose coreligionists for having sought to establish a quite pacific policy with respect to India. Revolt in East Pakistan not surprisingly claimed its quota of prominent victims, including the governor, Abdul Konem Khan, shot at Dacca in October 1971. This occurred on the eve of the ferocious "December war" with India, from which emerged the independent People's Republic of Bangladesh. At the other extreme of Pakistan's original boundaries, February 1975 brought the assassination of Hyat Mohammed Sherpao Khan, home minister of the Northwest Frontier Province, killed by an explosion while presiding over ceremonies at the University of Peshawar. Responsibility for the murder, according to the national prime minister, rested with Baluchistan's National Awami (Pathan separatist) Party, whose own leader, Abdul Achakzai Khan, had been slain at Quetta the previous year.

Zulfikar Ali Bhutto, Pakistan's most colorful leader after Jinnah, was also the victim of its most sensational execution, having been found guilty of complicity in murder. Bhutto was the son of a wealthy landowner and had been educated at Bombay's Cathedral School, the University of California, and Oxford, before being admitted to the English bar in 1953 at the age of only twenty-five. Returning home soon thereafter to launch a political career in the name of what he called "Islamic Socialism," this cosmopolitan young man revealed a special affinity for foreign affairs, especially those involving the great organized land masses of Asia: Indian, Soviet, and Chinese. During most of the dictatorship of General Ayub Khan, Bhutto showed a preference for appointive over elective office, serving in turn as minister of commerce, minister of information, and foreign minister (the last concurrently with representing his country at the United Nations in New York). Then followed a sharp break with Ayub's successor, Yahya Khan, a switch to parliamentary politics, and finally, when the army turned on its own representatives in government after the Bangladesh debacle, elevation to the presidency, a title he chose to exchange for that of prime minister under his new constitution of 1973.[22]

Bhutto in power showed himself still eager to capitalize on his international contacts but increasingly dependent on Red China's support, the only consistent feature of his foreign policy. He spoke much of friendship with Delhi but strove to overtake India in military terms, while angering the USSR by favoring Moslem insurgents in Afghanistan against the pro-Soviet leader there. In domestic affairs this aristocrat from Sind, who preached Islamic socialism, kept promising Baluchistan and the Northwest Frontier, the nation's two neediest provinces, more than he could deliver without hopelessly alienating his financial and commercial supporters, to say nothing of the ever-touchy officers' corps. At the end he seemed to be losing confidence in populist appeals and turning increasingly to autocratic means of governing.

Despite his difficulties, Bhutto's own Pakistan People's Party was generally expected to win, if not an overwhelming, at least a workable majority in the election of March 7, 1977, the nine opposition parties composing the Pakistan National Alliance having shown no capacity for concerted action. The premier, however, refused to settle for less than a crushing victory at the polls, something his slate achieved, but only at the cost of intimidation and bribery on a scale that shocked even friendly observers. By mid-March mass demonstrations against his methods had been matched by the announcement by all parties in the National Alliance that they would boycott the new session of the Assembly. In one three-day series of riots fifty-five died in the streets of Karachi and seventeen in Hyderabad. Worse was to come, as rebellion spread to other provinces. The Punjab rose in protest against the "southerner from Sind," while mobs in Baluchistan condemned the inadequacy of economic relief provided by the "rich man in Karachi." The prime minister's declaration of a state of siege was formally condemned by the national bar association, a telling blow to the prestige of its most illustrious member; and in mid-April Pakistani diplomats in Athens, Madrid, and other foreign capitals began to resign.

The military finally settled the issue. Whether it acted out of opportunism, principle, characteristic Punjabi animus, or a combination of all three, the officers' corps destroyed its erstwhile favorite as surely as it had made him in 1971. On July 5, 1977, urging the need to "defend the rights of the people and their holy religion," General Mohammed Zia ul-Haq, chief of staff, assumed full power, announced the removal from office of the entire cabinet, and promised new elections for October. No elections were held then, or have been since; and General Zia shortly assumed the presidential title in addition to that of Chief Martial Law Administrator.

At the head of the new regime's agenda was the matter of punishing the leaders it had overthrown. On September 3, following two months of close surveillance, Bhutto was arrested and charged with the murder of two political opponents during his time in office; General Zia subsequently added the name of another victim. In the long run only a single assassination attempt, and that one unsuccessful, figured in the indictment. Finally in March 1978 after a four-month trial punctuated at intervals by riots in support of the ousted premier, he and four codefendants, including his former security chief, were found guilty and sentenced to death by the Lahore High Court. The Supreme Court of Pakistan, after one brief stay of execution, confirmed the Lahore judgment, and on April 4, 1979, Zulfikar Ali Bhutto was hanged in Rawalpindi's central jail. General Zia, commenting some weeks earlier on urgent messages received from an impressively varied array of foreign leaders, including President Carter, Chairman Brezhnev, Chinese Communist chief Hua-Kuo-Feng, Prime Minister Callaghan in London, President Giscard d'Estaing in Paris, Yugoslavia's Marshal Tito, Pope John Paul II, and Libya's Muammar Khaddafi, remarked blandly: "All the politicians are asking to save a politician, but not many non-politicians have asked me for clemency."[23]

East Asia has had, to say the least, its share of political murder, affecting lands once dominated by a number of different imperial powers. Not all these former rulers were European—British, French, Dutch, Spanish, Portuguese—and even among those that were, no two systems of rule were exactly the same. Hence in the Far East the political legacies bequeathed by the era of dependency have varied markedly from one emergent nation to another.

The situation on the Korean Peninsula is a case in point. Liberation from Japanese control in 1945 was followed within five years by a bitter war between North and South, which drew the United States and China into the fighting and the uneasy truce concluded in 1953. In the southern Republic of Korea one of the byproducts of instability has been frequent eruptions of internal violence, including three attempts to assassinate iron-fisted old President Syngman Rhee in the space of only a little over the same number of years, between June 1952 and October 1955. The identities of the would-be killers in that trio of assaults show the range of animosities their target aroused: an ultranationalist in the first instance; a Communist sympathizer with North Korea in the second; and a member of the opposition Independence Party in the third.

Rhee was more fortunate than his successor, General Chung Hee Park. In August 1974, having survived attacks in 1963 and 1964, the President was wounded and his wife killed when a Korean emigrant to Osaka, belonging to a Japanese-based Korean Youth League there, fired on the speaker's platform at a Liberation Day celebration in Seoul. General Park's luck ran out on October 26, 1979, at a banquet comparable in some respects to a Borgian dinner in Renaissance Italy and in others to a scene from an American gangland movie. He and his chief security officer were shot to death, as were five bodyguards surprised elsewhere in the building by confederates of the plot's apparent leader. This was Kim Jae Kyu, head of Korea's Central Intelligence Agency and a longtime friend of his victim. Disagreement over his motives, variously alleged to have been personal ambition, principled opposition to Park's authoritarian regime, and a nervous breakdown resulting from mental exhaustion, was not publicly resolved at his trial, which ended with sentences of death for him and six other defendants. The KCIA director's execution was no surprise, but that of Kim Kae Won, chief of staff, left a host of questions unanswered, as they still remain.

The Philippine Islands, once part of the Spanish colonial empire but under American rule from the turn of the century until they achieved full independence on July 4, 1946, owed the end of foreign domination not to the outcome of the Second World War (despite the four-year interval of Japanese occupation), but to the progression through commonwealth status begun under U.S. auspices in 1935. Yet despite this relatively violence-free achievement of sovereignty, the Philippine Republic has suffered in the course of the past four decades from no less violence than its East Asian neighbors.

As in the case of Korea, assassination attempts upon Filipino leaders have come from various points of the political compass, further complicated in this instance by ethnic and religious differences. In 1949 Aurora Quezon, widow of the late President of the Commonwealth, was killed by insurgent Huk tribesmen. The flurry of assaults, arrests, and discoveries of hidden weapons, however, which reached its peak in 1971–1972, was centered around a two-pronged government offensive against both Moslem rebels on the huge island of Mindanao and hideouts of urban guerrillas loyal to the Maoist New People's Army. Assassination attempts directed against numerous officials before, during, and following that crisis have been repeatedly invoked as justification for the heavy-handed measures of President Ferdinand Marcos' regime, including cancellation of the presidential election scheduled for 1973.

A decade later, the death of Benigno Aquino, Jr., who had planned to oppose Marcos in that aborted election, made political murder a cause for debate more intense than any previously known in even the Philippines' stormy history. Aquino had been tried and sentenced to death for subversion during the period after 1973, but he was released from prison on orders from President Marcos in 1980 and allowed to travel to the United States for heart surgery. Having had his medical treatment, he spent some time at Harvard and the Massachusetts Institute of Technology, engaged partly in research and partly in organizing political support at home. Despite his own premonitions and pointed warnings from the presidential palace in Manila, he landed at the airport there on August 21, 1983, and was killed, together with his alleged assassin, almost immediately upon stepping from the plane. The Marcos government hurriedly explained that his murderer had been a leftist agitator dispatched on the spot by government troops detailed to protect the opposition leader.

This attempt by the regime to put an end to speculation about Aquino's death failed to stem the tide of doubt expressed by foreign correspondents in Manila or to satisfy diplomatic inquiries originating abroad. Jarred by negative reactions in foreign capitals, including President Reagan's decision to cancel a previously scheduled state visit, the Philippine government announced the creation of a special commission of inquiry. After a year's work that body reported in late October 1984 that in its estimation no fewer than twenty-six individuals (only one of them a civilian) were indictable for their parts in a conspiracy to murder the late opposition leader. Among the military personnel cited were three generals, including General Fabian C. Ver, chief of staff of the armed forces and chief of Philippine intelligence. Ver immediately requested and was granted a leave of absence to prepare a defense for his trial, which was scheduled for 1985.

In the other great Asian archipelago, that of the East Indies, the incidence of lethal attacks has been lower than that in the Philippines, despite several failed attempts on the life of the late President Sukarno between 1957 and 1962. (He died, presumably of natural causes, while under arrest in 1970.) The most notable assassination in those parts since World War II in fact occurred not within the sprawling national boundaries of Indonesia but in what was at the time still the British crown colony of Sarawak on the island of Borneo, since incorporated into Malaysia. There, Governor Duncan Stewart was fatally stabbed in December 1949, a time of frequent attacks on British representatives in mainland Malaya as well. Somewhat ironically, the other outbreak of violence involving East Indians took place far away, in the Netherlands, where in 1975 a tiny minority of the country's 35,000 South Moluccan refugees began a series of deadly attacks aimed at forcing the Dutch government to reconquer their lost Melanesian homeland.

Assassinations in both Thailand and Malaya have already been mentioned; but in Southeast Asia for more than thirty years it has been the

Indo-Chinese states—Vietnam, Laos, Cambodia—which have assumed tragic preeminence in the matter of political murder. To appreciate the full extent of this phenomenon, Americans must suspend their obsession with the United States' involvement there and give equal attention to atrocities beginning well before and continuing long after that fateful interlude.

The first major assassination in Cambodia's "liberation period" actually antedated complete independence from the French Union by some three years, occurring in 1950 when Ioe Koeux, chairman of the Democratic Party, was slain by political rivals. Later there were unsuccessful attempts on the lives of King Norodom Suramit and the premier, Prince Sihanouk, in 1959 and 1960 respectively. Later still, Sihanouk's uncle, Prince Sissowath, succumbed to a bomb attack at Pnompenh in 1971. Comparable incidents have been repeated almost annually since that time. Laos, by contrast, has had not so much steady attrition as periodic outbursts of assassination, the first of which came in 1963. That year no fewer than six separate attacks, all of them successful, took the lives of an inspector of education, an intelligence director, a high police official, a former army chief of staff, and two cabinet members, one of whom was the foreign minister, Quinim Pholsena. Some of these men were viewed as anti-Communist; others as anti-American. But although 1963 was a year of increasing U.S. "presence" in Vietnam, the same did not yet apply to Laos, where indigenous political motives still predominated.

The South Vietnamese situation between 1961 and 1973 was obviously different, being increasingly dominated by the spreading military operations and American involvement therein. It is nevertheless important to bear in mind that, during those same years, a substantial number of prominent civilians were assassinated, many though not all by North Vietnamese agents or sympathizers. A few such victims are mentioned by way of illustration: Tran Van Van, a leading member of the Constituent Assembly, shot to death on a Saigon street in 1966; South Vietnam's minister of education and, after him, the acting dean of the Saigon University Medical School, killed on successive days in 1969: Nguyen Van Bong, founder of the Progressive National Party, fatally wounded by a car bomb in 1971.

No other political murders in Vietnam have attracted, or are likely to attract, so much attention as the shooting of President Ngo Dinh Diem and his brother Ngo Dinh Nuh, chief of the secret police, in early November 1963. The activities of Diem and Nhu, not to mention those of the former's wife, had elicited increasingly hostile comment from American officials in both Washington and Saigon. But the extent of U.S. involvement in or even forewarning of the coup that took the brothers' lives less than three weeks before President Kennedy's own assassination remains a matter of dispute. To the extent that the case raises questions about American intelligence policy and about "special operations" in the heyday of CIA inventiveness, it will be discussed in a later chapter.

Africa Enters the Arena

The African continent as a whole is no more homogeneous in terms of politics and political murder than in economics, race, or religion. The Maghreb, that tier of nations extending along the Mediterranean's southern shore from Sinai to Tangier and thence down the west coast of Morocco, is closely tied by history and by current involvement to the affairs of Europe and the Middle East. Egypt's Anwar Sadat was an African, but his assassination in 1981 was an act rooted in Islamic piety and the power politics of the Arab world in general. Salah Ben Youssef had been a Tunisian minister of justice and General Mohammed Khider once headed the Algerian National Liberation Front; but the first was shot to death in 1961 at Frankfurt, Germany, where he was living in exile, the second outside his Madrid apartment in 1967, by a gunman believed to be acting on orders from President Houari Boumedienne's government in Algiers. Both before and after these events the Red Hand, Morocco's secret terrorist organization, took the lives of numerous victims, including high officials in the Spanish and French colonial services.

In Capetown, at the other extreme of the huge land mass, the fatal attack on Prime Minister Hendrik Verwoerd in the parliament chamber on September 6, 1966, occurred against a backdrop of racial tensions, specifically those of the Union of South Africa and its apartheid policies, which the premier had made his own during eight years in office. The assailant, Dimitrios Tsafenda, was routinely described in the government communique as "a mulatto passing for white." In other respects, however, Verwoerd's assassin was less deeply "African" than the government's terse characterization might suggest. He certainly differed from various black leaders who have succumbed in the Union's prisons. A forty-five-year-old drifter with a previous record of mental treatment in five different countries, including the United States, Tsafenda escaped the death penalty at Capetown because the defense mounted a successful plea of legal insanity.

These and other incidents that could be cited suggest nothing very special about the often deadly politics of the so-called Dark Continent. Really new departures must be sought elsewhere, in the forty-three independent nations south of the Sahara and north of the Transvaal. To appreciate what has happened there, the reader should return to the table at the beginning of this chapter, specifically to the column headed Sub-Saharan Africa. Notice that the region produced virtually no memorable assaults on public officials or other political figures until well after the twentieth century's midpoint. The same had been true of the nineteenth century as a whole. There was, to be sure, a great deal of cruelty and bloodshed under various native rulers during the 1800s, notaby on the island of Madagascar and in the Zulu Empire. There were also instances of brutal repression, including the killing of rebellious tribal leaders, by European forces—French, English, Boer, Belgian, Portuguese, German—extending well past the turn of the century. In Black Africa, however, to an even greater degree than in India and South-east Asia, subject populations seem to have accepted the futility of attacking the proconsuls of imperial powers certain to send replacements with orders to mete out condign punishment.

The wave of major assassinations that broke over the new African states at the beginning of the 1960s was, therefore, all the more startling. Possible explanations for its force have been suggested by Ali A. Mazrui, a Kenyan political scientist now living in the United States.[24] He argues that it originated in an unprecedented combination of new expectations and opportunities, but also fears and suspicions brought by independence. National boundaries in post-colonial Africa were in many cases drawn quite arbitrarily, with little or no regard for ethnolinquistic differences and older units of social organization. The result has been the simultaneous onset of two separate but closely related crises, one centering on the issue of national integration, the other on that of political legitimacy.

Integration, according to this view, is a problem in present-day Africa, as it was elsewhere in earlier times, "because different clusters of citizens do not as yet accept each other as compatriots."[25] Tribal divisions hamper the quest for a shared nationality, even in such relatively advanced states as Kenya and Nigeria, while proving more disruptive still in Zaire, Uganda, and other polities torn by harshly conflicting loyalties. The parallel crisis, that of legitimacy, involves vertical instead of horizontal relationships, in that it grows not out of a refusal to acknowledge a common national identity but out of the denial by some citizens that they have a government entitled to fill the vacuum created by the departure of colonial authority. In this second case, it is more a matter of "ruled against rulers" than of "neighbor against neighbor."

In January 1961, as a new decade began, Patrice Lumumba, former premier of the Democratic Republic of the Congo, was arrested with two political aides in Leopoldsville on orders from President Joseph Kasavubu and flown under guard to Elisabethville in the secessionist province of Katanga. This was tantamount to execution, for it delivered him into the hands of his mortal enemy, Moise Tsombe. Although the three bodies were never found, Lumumba's death was first rumored, then officially announced by Katanganese leaders in mid-February. Only after having been chosen in 1964 by Kasavubu to serve as the Democratic Republic's prime minister (the country was officially renamed Zaire in 1971) did Tsombe solemnly place a wreath on the monument honoring his late opponent. Later still, in 1966, the new president, General Sese Seko Mobutu, harnessed the dead hero's name to the service of both integration and legitimacy. In a speech following his own successful coup d'état, Mobutu suddenly launched into an encomium for "the first martyr of our independence, Patrice Emery Lumumba, who was the victim of the colonialist plot."[26] Thus, in death the man slain in Katanga, reportedly by a Belgian mercenary under Tsombe's orders, became what he had never been in life, a standard-bearer for the entire Third World.

Whatever its symbolic importance for worldwide ideological struggles, Patrice Lumumba's death signaled the beginning of sub-Saharan Africa's first major group of political assassinations. Many of the victims, especially in the initial cluster—two premiers of Burundi; Togo's President Sylvanus Olympio in 1963; several leading politicians killed during the Tanzanian revolt in 1964; and Nigerian leaders, including Prime Minister Balewa, slain in 1966—were put to death by rebellious army officers. There followed a brief respite during which Mazrui permitted himself the hope that these casualties of the "wave of militarism," might prove to have lent "the mystique of their ancient names to the slow growth of primary consensus."[27]

Unfortunately for such longings, the onslaught was resumed, more savagely than ever and with an ominously increased heterogeneity among assassins and motives. On July 5, 1969, Tom Mboya, the youthful hero of Kenya's struggle for independence and by this time minister of economic affairs in President Jomo Kenyatta's government, was fatally shot as he walked along a street in Nairobi. His accused murderer, hanged several weeks later, was a Kikuyu, a member of Kenyatta's tribe, and the most direct response to the shooting was an epidemic of running battles between other Kikuyus and the slain Mboya's fellow Luos.[28] Before the repercussions from Nairobi had subsided, Abdiraschid Ali Shermarke, president of the Republic of Somalia, was assassinated on October 15 while touring the drought area in the north of his country. Shermarke's killer, a young member of the national police, was tried and condemned to death. Meanwhile, however, on October 21, 1969, the day following the late president's burial, army and police forces took over Mogadishu, the capital, in a bloodless coup and, having arrested all members of the previous government, announced the creation of a Somali Democratic Republic.[29]

Once again, as in the period between Balewa's and Mboya's murders, after Shermarke was assassinated there occurred a pause of sorts, lasting for about two and a half years. Then political murder broke out afresh, bringing an ever-widening circle of territories and governments into its bloody scenario. The year 1972 brought the fatal shooting of Sheik Abeid Amani Karume, chairman of the Revolutionary Council for Zanzibar, and 1973 that of Amilcar Cabral, leader of the nationalist opposition in Portuguese Guinea. These attacks were followed in mid-1974 by the first round of "Ethiopian murders" in Asmara, Addis Ababa, and other centers. Between February 1975 and March 1977 military commandos took the lives of the Republic of Madagascar's president (himself a colonel), Nigeria's chief of state, and the president of the Congo Republic. In this last instance, the murder of President Marien Ngouabi at Brazzaville was followed by the trial and execution of his predecessor and six other convicted conspirators, as well as by the murder of Cardinal Biayenda, archbishop of Brazzaville, reportedly by relatives of the slain Ngouabi. Early in 1978 South Africa's minister of health for Namibia (former German Southwest Africa), Toivo Shiyanga, leader as well of the Ovambo tribe, was shot to death at Windhoek by Namibian "freedom fighters."

And so the toll of political homicides has continued to grow longer in Black Africa. Faced with the Ugandan horror under Idi Amin, Emperor Bokassa's tyranny in the Central African Republic, and the corruption followed by overthrow of Nigeria's government, the cautious optimism of some observers in the mid- and late-1960s has undergone a significant change. In the Reith Lectures delivered in 1979 on BBC television, Ali Mazrui seemed rather defensive in his insistence on a distinction between "just" and "unjust" terrorism, while reserving his sharpest criticism for what he considers Israel's overly harsh reprisals for PLO attacks. A distinctly pessimistic mood, however, appears in the choice of titles for lectures in the series: "A Garden of Eden in Decay," for instance, or "The Cross of Humiliation."[30]

Other analysts, among them American press correspondent David Lamb, have shown themselves equally depressed but markedly less forgiving toward certain factions—including, but not limited to the whites in South Africa. Lamb's recent account of his travels up and down the continent ends with what seems to have been almost the only African expression he found comforting: "Give us time. We are young."[31]

While waiting, friendly observers such as Lamb make no attempt to hide their consternation at the bloodbath that occurred in what had seemed an unlikely setting: Liberia. Events there deserve to be kept in mind when considering the distance much of Africa has still to go in its search for a political order at once stable and humane.[32] On April 12, 1980, at Monrovia, capital of Black Africa's oldest republic, an army coup led by Master Sergeant Samuel K. Doe overthrew the relatively mild, though undeniably venal government, killing President William R. Tolbert, Jr., and twenty-seven members of his entourage the first night, when Doe and a band of rebellious troops stormed the palace grounds. Vowing to end corruption, the twenty-eight-year-old conqueror ordered all important government officials who had survived the initial massacre tried before a five-man military panel, which would in turn report to the newly created People's Redemptive Council. Charges included high treason, peculation, and "gross violations of human rights." After formless and perfunctory hearings death sentences were handed down for thirteen of the defendants, among them the late government's ministers of foreign affairs, justice, finance, agriculture, and commerce, together with the former chief justice of Liberia's supreme court, the president of its senate, and the speaker of its house of representatives. On April 22 the condemned were bound to stakes along a beach on the Atlantic coast and shot by firing squads whose members then desecrated the corpses, reportedly to loud applause from the festive crowd of onlookers. Three days later President Doe, as he had now become, suspended his country's 133-year-old constitution.[33]

The Middle East

For all the histrionics of terrorists in Europe and the human cost of struggles for power in East Asia, the Indian subcontinent, and Black Africa, the Old World's true epicenter of political murder lies elsewhere. It is the predominantly Islamic domain stretching from the Hindu Kush westward to the Levant and thence across the immense expanse of North African desert and mountains. This vast region has the dubious distinction of surpassing all others, except perhaps Latin America, in the degree to which its component societies and governments are permeated by seemingly endemic violence. While much of the rest of Asia and Africa are preoccupied with personal and factional competition for control over newly independent states, and Europe with the sporadic assaults born of doctrinaire anarchism, in the Middle East these and other incentives are jumbled together in a potpourri of hatreds, most of them extremely old.

These lands, like the rest of the erstwhile colonial territories, have witnessed countless homicides inspired by power conflicts, both within and between nations. When in 1949 the president and the prime minister of Syria were killed, even before their country had achieved full independence, one of the Middle East's now familiar patterns of assassination began to assert itself. Such attempts were to be repeated incessantly, and often successfully, during the decades since then. The victims have in some cases been Muslim monarchs — King Faisal II of Iraq, slain with his uncle (and former regent) and the Iraqi premier, by a rebel general in 1958, or King Hassan II of Morocco, who survived at attack on his summer palace in 1971. The Moroccan ruler had another narrow escape the very next year, this one occurring when three escorting jet fighters of the Moroccan Air Force tried to shoot down the royal Boeing 727 as it was approaching Hassan's capital, Rabat. There another flight of air force planes made a strafing run even after he had landed.

In certain other cases the victims were former resistance leaders, become heads of state but still forced to resist foreign as well as domestic foes—as President Habib Bourguiba of Tunisia declared himself to be doing in 1962. Although his purge resulted in the trial of twenty-six defendants and the execution of ten, most of them Tunisian nationals, Bourguiba did not hesitate to accuse neighboring Algeria's leaders of having been the conspiracy's real instigators. Only six years later his Algerian counterpart, Houari Boumedienne, was wounded when his limousine was attacked by a single assailant firing a machine gun. A retired army major was charged, in company with several alleged accomplices.

To bitterly divided North and South Yemen, recent years have brought a series of savage personal attacks unequivocally linked to conflicts over foreign policy. Those attacks, which go back at least as far as the mid-sixties, reached a new level of ferocity in 1978. In June of that year, at Sana, North Yemen's capital, President Ahmed Hussein al-Ghashmi was slain while receiving the credentials of the new envoy from Soviet-backed South Yemen. The ambassador, whose briefcase exploded when he opened it to produce his documents, perished at the same time. Two days later in Aden, South Yemen's President Salem Robaiya Ali was unceremoniously deposed and executed by rivals within his own leftist National Liberation Front. Some observers at the time blamed both deaths on rival pro-Soviet factions in the South Yemeni regime. Others insisted that al-Ghashmi's had been planned by exiles from North Yemen living at Aden. Whatever the truth, it did not alter the fates of the two presidents.

Roughly contemporaneous and closely connected with this continuing Yemeni crisis was the upheaval in another arena of Soviet intervention, Afghanistan. Its setting had been created in 1973, when Mohammad Duad Khan assumed power (though no crown) from his brother-in-law King Mohammad Zahir, who had been deposed in favor of a republic while away on an ill-timed visit to Italy. The end of the monarchy opened an era of conflicting pressures from abroad. Urged by the shah of Iran to abandon his initially pro-Russian stance, Duad also faced the menace of Islamic rebels armed and encouraged by Ali Bhutto in Pakistan. The "founder of the Republic" having responded by making concessions to conservative religious interests, Afghanistan's Communist movement, with support from the Kremlin, overthrew him in April 1978 and installed the seemingly more pliable Mohammed Taraki. When the new premier, while insisting on his loyalty to Moscow, made conciliatory gestures toward the Muslim dissidents, he encountered the strident challenge of a younger Communist leader, Hafizullah Amin. By September 1979 Amin was ready to move, seizing power while Taraki was shot to death in the course of a coup d'état. Amin proved no more fortunate than his predecessors in his handling of conflicting demands within the country, and Brezhnev's government in Moscow turned against him in a matter of weeks. In December 1979 Amin was deposed and promptly executed for crimes against the state, to be replaced by a less colorful Communist leader, Babrah Karmal, in response to whose obedient "appeal" the Soviet invasion of Afghanistan was launched by the Red army and air force.

In a part of the globe where Lebanese Muslims and Christians have waged a religious war since the mid-1970s, while Jews battle the forces of Islam, which are bitterly divided into Shi'ite, Sunnite, and numerous smaller groupings, the role of sectarian hatred is not only incessant but obtrusive. Long before a bomb killed Lebanon's president-elect Bashir Gemayel with twenty-six fellow Christian Falangists at their party headquarters in September 1982, Kamal Jumblat, a prominent left-wing Muslim spokesman, had been shot to death outside Beirut in 1977, touching off vengeance riots in which sixty-six Christians reportedly lost their lives. That Moslem "victory" was avenged by the Christian militia, as was the Gemayel assassination several years later, when Falangist gunmen massacred several hundred Palestinian refugees in a camp outside Beirut in the autumn of 1982, while Israeli forces stood by without intervening.

The most sensational among recent Middle Eastern slayings, however, occurred not in the blood-soaked Levant but in a suburb of Cairo where, on October 6, 1981, Egypt's President Anwar Sadat was cut down by gunfire and shrapnel as he sat on a richly carpeted stand reviewing a military parade. According to the report of the investigating commission named by his vice-president and successor, Hosni Mubarak, the four men in army uniforms who leapt from a passing truck and attacked the dais with grenades and automatic firearms acted in what they proclaimed to be the service of Allah. Their ringleader, who had smuggled his three immediate accomplices

The assassination of Anwar Sadat

into the procession as substitute members of an anti-tank gun crew, was a Lt. Khaled Ahmed Shawky al Islambouli, whose brother belonged to a sect called Al Taqfir was Hijra (Atonement for Sin and Retreat), an offshoot of the fundamentalist Muslim Brotherhood. Al Taqfir's founder, Sayyed Kotb, had been executed in 1965 for an attempt on the life of the late dictator, Gamal Nasser; but on July 3, 1977, his spiritual followers kidnaped Mohammed Hussein al-Zahabi, former Egyptian minister of religious affairs, whose body was found in Giza four days later. Zahabi's murder had been the society's announcement of the campaign of terror that culminated in the slaying of Sadat, identified by his killers as a heretical borrower of Western ways and believer in detente with Israel, as witness the Camp David Accords.[34]

Amid war, competition for power, and religious strife, several struggles for independence have contributed to Middle Eastern bloodletting. Ironically, the Israelis' own success at guerrilla operations in dramatizing their national claims during and just after World War II supplied perhaps the most instructive model as well as the eventual enemy for the region's other liberation movements. Some of these, notably Nasser's in Egypt, the Syrian revolt against mandate status, and of course the struggle for a Free Palestine, have proceeded on the assumption that Israel was the principal enemy from the moment it attained sovereignty. The Armenian, Kurdish, Berber, and Greek Cypriot movements, on the other hand, have evinced little excitement over the "Jewish question." But all owe a debt to Irgun Zwei Leumi and the Stern Gang.

Kurds have assassinated Iranian officials and Cypriots, Turkish ones. But only the Armenians and Palestinians regularly attack selected targets far from the boundaries of their respective homelands. In the case of the self-styled "Justice Commandos for Armenian Genocide," still avenging early twentieth-century Ottoman atrocities while pursuing contemporary political aims, the victims chosen have regularly been Turkish diplomats on duty abroad. In 1975 alone Ankara's emissaries to Austria and France, as well as the first secretary of its embassy in Beirut, were slain by Armenian assassins, as was Taha Carim, Turkish ambassador to the Vatican, in 1977. After a brief lull, seven representatives of Turkey in foreign countries were shot, all but one of them fatally, within a period of less than a year and a half: the consul-general in Sydney, killed (December 1980); two embassy officials in Paris, killed (March 1981); a member of the consular staff in Geneva, killed (July 1981); the consul-general in Los Angeles, killed (January 1982); the commercial counselor in the Ottawa embassy, critically wounded (April 1982); the honorary consul-general in Boston, killed (May 1982).

As for the Palestinians, the far-flung activities of PLO agents—including those of its military arm, Al Fatah, and ultraextremist offshoots such as Black September and the PFLP—have already been discussed, as has their extensive collaboration with German, Latin American, Japanese, and other foreign allies. It remains only to recall that some of the leading players in the sanguinary contest between Arafat and his foes have themselves been victims of retaliatory strikes. Late in January 1979 Abu Hassan Salameh, a West Bank sheikh's son who became a Fatah chieftain and helped to organize Black September's European operations—in which capacity he was the principal planner of the massacre of Israeli athletes at the 1972 Olympics in Munich—was killed with four bodyguards and five passersby when a powerful bomb exploded alongside his car on a street in West Beirut. Salameh's father had been slain by Haganah explosives during the Arab-Israeli fighting in 1948; and the son, too, appears to have died at the hands of assassins sent from Israel.[35] The fact that the victim, as chief of security for Fatah, had provided protection for U.S. diplomats and CIA agents stationed in Beirut, while serving as his cousin Yassir Arafat's go-between in dealings with the Americans, did not render him immune in 1979 when Jerusalem decided to act.[36]

In August 1981 Mohammed Daoud Oudeh, known to fellow terrorists as "Abu Daud"—cofounder of Black September, mastermind behind the murder of Jordan's Prime Minister Wasfi Tal at Cairo in 1971 and that of United States Ambassador Cleo Noel at Khartoum in 1973—was shot and seriously wounded by an unknown assailant while visiting Warsaw with an assumed name and an Iraqi passport. Again the Israeli intelligence agency Mossad came under suspicion as the moving force. This time, however, there were several plausible alternatives, not excluding the PLO high command itself, given its recent internal conflicts and reversals of policy.

The case of Iran is special not only to Americans, by virtue of their government's long involvement with the late shah and the harrowing captivity of the hostages in the Tehran embassy, but also to observers, regardless of nationality, who in what once was Persia now see the entire region's special combination of forces on display. Nowhere else can the interaction of ethnic pride, Muslim religiosity, power-political conflicts (both domestic and international), economic and minority grievances, terrorist acts carried out in foreign places, and egalitarian rhetoric harnessed to the needs of authoritarian revolution be seen so clearly.

Long before the shah's abdication and the triumphant return from Paris of Ayatollah Ruholla Khomeini in the first week of 1979, the country, even its modern form, had known plenty of assassination. In 1951 Prime Minister Ali Rasman was shot dead while visiting a mosque, by a gunman whose comrades then killed the vice-chancellor of Tehran University as well. Other such attempts followed, but without another fatality of similar moment until 1965, when a second premier, Hassan Ali Mansour, was fatally wounded by a Muslim student. The year 1971 brought the murder of the chief of the Iranian Military Court, General Ziaddin Farsiou, characterized by police as the work of "Maoist terrorists." Iran played host to numerous violent incidents, but it was not on that account very different from other Middle Eastern and North African states during the same period.

At the beginning of 1979 the scene was drastically altered by the flight of Mohammed Riza Pahlavi, second *shah-in-shah* of his father's short-lived dynasty, and the homecoming of Khomeini, leader of the country's Shi'ite Islamic priesthood. The theocracy of ayatollahs (at once prelates and judges charged with applying the Koran's moral and legal strictures) has shown great eclecticism in its choice of means for political killing. In the use of lynching and other forms of mob violence, including the mobilization of "revolutionary students," the regime has had no dearth of past models. Murder by its agents of opponents abroad, on the other hand, is an essentially modern device, at least when employed on the scale of a Stalin or a Khomeini.

The slaying of Shariar Mustapha Chafik is a case in point. The thirty-four-year-old nephew of the shah was shot to death on December 7, 1979, near the Parisian apartment he shared with his sister, Princess Ashraf. Responsibility was promptly claimed by the Muslim Liberation Front's office in the French capital, but not before Ayatollah Sadegh Khalkali, president of Iran's own Islamic Revolutionary Tribunal, had issued a statement from far-off Qom in Iran, praising Chafik's Fedayeen killers for having carried out the sentence against an "absent criminal." European sources noted that General Hussein Fardust, chief of the new Iranian secret police (*Savama*), had just returned to Teheran from visits in Paris and London. Worldwide interest in General Fardust and his organization increased still further a few months later, when in July 1980 a former official of the shah's government, Ali Akbar Tabatabai, was gunned down at the door of his home in a suburb of Washington, D.C., by an assassin wearing a postman's uniform.

It was in the use of purge trials, however, that the new Iranian government most clearly established its right to a place in the Pantheon of terrorist regimes. Iranian purges since 1979 have not been uniformly intense, there having occurred at least one slackening, after the early stampede of prosecutions, convictions, and mass executions. By mid-1981, however, under the combined influence of war with Iraq, émigré activity in France and elsewhere (especially after the outlawed ex-President Abolhassan Bani-Sadr succeeded in escaping to Paris), persistent Kurdish revolts, growing economic confusion, and numerous assassinations of its own officials, the Khomeini government embarked anew on a program calling, to judge from its own announcements, for the trial and execution of hundreds of suspected traitors each month. One of the most notable casualties proved to be Sadegh Ghotbzadeh, still foreign minister during much of the American embassy hostage crisis, but shot by a firing squad in September 1982, having been convicted of participation in a plot to overthrow the government.

Whether or not Ghotbzadeh had in fact conspired against the ayatollahs, there can be no doubt that insurgency of various kinds began to challenge the regime almost as soon as it took power. In the spring of 1979 the Kurdish minority's Forghan Fighters made several assassination attempts. Following the temporary crushing of the Kurdish uprising in the north that March, when more than five hundred Kurds reported were shot by firing squads, the beleaguered chief of staff of the Iranian People's Army, General Mohammed Wali Qareneh, resigned. Laying down his command did not save his life; on April 23, 1979, he was fatally wounded by three gunmen in Tehran. Responsibility for his assassination, the first of a high official close to Ayatollah Khomeini, was claimed by Forghan, as was the killing a week later of Ayatollah Morteza Motahari, a leading member of the Revolutionary Council.

Gunplay over the Kurdish question was serious enough, especially when the government resumed its policy of shooting large numbers of prisoners. Yet proportionately the list of lethal assaults upon the Islamic Republic's leaders began to grow even faster. The Kurds remained defiant, but their place as the most dangerous rebels was by this time being taken by the radical Mujahedin-e-Khalq guerrillas, predominantly ethnic Iranians who fought openly with Khomeini's Revolutionary Guards in the street of Tehran while from Paris their émigré leader, Massoud Rajavi, proclaimed the creation of a transitional government-in-exile. By the summer of 1981 the rate of executions had resumed its earlier levels, but now it was being matched, if not in numbers at least in shock effect, by that of assassination. Here are the names and titles of fourteen leaders of the Islamic Republic who died in just five incidents during a three-month period:

June 28 (bombing)	Ayatollah Mohammed Beheshti, chief justice of Iran and leader of the Islamic Republican Party; with the ministers of environment, transportation, and power and the deputy minister of commerce;
August 5 (shooting)	Hassan Ayat, cofounder of the Islamic Republic Party;
August 30 (bombing)	Mohammed Ali Rajai, president of the Iranian Islamic Republic; Hojatolislam Bahonar, prime minister; Colonel Houshang Datsgerdi, police chief;
September 11 (hand grenade)	Ayatollah Assadollah Madani, friend and official aide of Khomeini;
September 29 (airplane crash)	Mussa Namja, minister of defense; Valiollah Falahi, acting chief of staff; Javad Fakuri, former air force commander; General Mohsen-Rahim Kolahdoz, commander of the Revolutionary Guards.[37]

The cause of the September 29 plane disaster, which killed a total of forty-one "heroes of the Abadan campaign" against Iraq, was disputed. From Paris the Mujahedin's head, Rajavi, for once denied all responsibility. He did not hesitate, however, to seize the occasion for issuing his announcement of a transitional government and for urging a boycott of the coming presidential election to choose a successor to the slain Ali Rajai. His and Bani-Sadr's pleas from abroad did not prevent the election of the Islamic Republic Party's chairman, Hojatolislam Khamenei, with 96 percent of the vote. The regime, however, was no nearer to solving a particular form of the problem of order—how to square its condemnation of violent protests with the incantations of a leader who came to power preaching death for all enemies of Allah and whose mildest threat against political opponents has regularly been that he would "cut off their hands."

Although the roll of assassinations recalled in the present chapter has been long, and continues to grow longer by the month if not the day, it has been limited to events occurring in Europe, Africa, and Asia (including Oceania). Before hazarding any reflections on political murder as a global phenomenon, therefore, we need to turn our attention to the American hemisphere and the characteristic patterns that have developed there.

14

The Americas:
Latin, British, and French

Where Does the "New World" Fit?

My decision to reserve consideration of the Americas in general and the United States in particular until almost the end of this inquiry was not lightly made, nor has its implementation been without cost. At many points along the way issues and episodes in the history of what is, after all, no longer a very New World could easily have been introduced into the continuing discussion of the Old. On balance, however, it has seemed better to accord America, both South and North, separate treatment after having described configurations of political murder elsewhere on the surface of the earth. Whereas many of the Western Hemisphere's most vividly remembered assassinations can be related to those encountered in the European record—and to such general problems as nation-building, anarchist doctrines, governmental repression, and, most recently, international terrorism—events on this side of the Atlantic exhibit certain characteristics undeniably their own.

Examining the political experience of any major region on earth creates an impression of pondering images familiar enough in certain respects, but images nevertheless altered, subtly in some cases, drastically in others, by the change of scene. So it is with the Western Hemisphere, whose relation to the European past can be fully understood only if these refractions are clearly acknowledged. But that is not the only combination of affinities and differences we must bear in mind. Quite as important as the historical divergence between the Old World and the New is that between, on the one hand, the erstwhile British and French colonial possessions and, on the other, the former Iberian empires, today's Latin America.

An array of sovereign states on the mainland, extending from Mexico to Cape Horn, seventeen of them Spanish in speech and an eighteenth primarily Portuguese, form a vast conglomeration of peoples and political entities. To them must be added the two large Spanish-speaking island nations, Cuba and the Dominican Republic (the latter sharing Hispaniola with French-speaking Haiti), as well as the nearly three million inhabitants of the Commonwealth of Puerto Rico associated with the United States. The crucial role of Iberian culture in establishing a measure of regional identity is obvious, but a number of other European languages and ethnic traditions are represented; Indian elements remain everywhere important, and the Black African component actually predominates in many of the constituent populations. This racial intermixture and the large number of separate governments in being give "Latin" America a political complexity approaching that of Africa, whose record of civil violence it greatly exceeds.[1]

Only the Middle East has produced more bloodshed from assassinations, wars, governmental terror, and virtually continuous underground operations than has Latin America since the 1950s. One of the most striking affinities between these two otherwise dissimilar areas is the combination of traditional and novel influences at work in both. In the once Luso-Hispanic colonies, not only certain characteristics of former imperial rule but also the memories of nineteenth-century revolt against Spain and Portugal must be borne in mind. Most of the Latin American wars of national independence were inspired and sustained by the mixture of militarism and a Bonapartist conception of constitutionalism that left its stamp on Europe as well during the post-Napoleonic period. The prominence of juntas and the vulnerability of civilian regimes are neither new nor are they peculiar to the Western Hemisphere.

One of the things insurgent movements such as Argentina's Montoneros, Uruguay's Tupamaros, and even Nicaragua's Sandinista Front have in common, apart from their euphonious Hispanic names, is a debt to the guerrilla tradition, beloved by Goya and by Ernest Hemingway, and latterly romanticized in the glorification of Ché Guevara as a martyred outlaw hero. Yet, like militant groups everywhere (including another former Spanish possession, the Philippine Islands), those of Central and South America obviously owe as much to "horizontal" connections with other elements in the twentieth-century terrorist complex as they do to history.[2] Given the chronic poverty and frequently heavy-handed autocracy that have afflicted the region, its violent fratricidal conflicts should scarcely be a cause of surprise. Perhaps less obvious is the variety of forms in which that violence has appeared. This, too, invites comparison with the Middle East.

Assassinations of a more or less traditional kind had been a fairly constant feature of Latin America's post-imperial republics, in which at least forty significant political killings occurred between the early nineteenth century and the middle of the twentieth. As indicated by the table in Chapter 13, however, the dramatic increase in such numbers has been comparatively recent. One of its earliest signals was an attempt in 1960 to kill

Venezuela's President Rómulo Betancourt. This barely failed, but it was followed a year later (June 1961) by the successful assault that ended the life of Betancourt's mortal enemy, General Rafael Trujillo Molina, former president of the Dominican Republic and still his country's dictator when he was cut down by machine-gun fire on a road outside the capital city bearing his name. Throughout the sixties such attempts, over two-thirds of them successful, continued to plague the southern part of the hemisphere, as they did the northern. An average of at least three episodes per year, two or more of them fatal, has been sustained ever since, even with the count limited to only the most significant instances.

Sometimes a single year has produced an atypically heavy concentration of major assaults, as when, in 1971, the following occurred:

April 1   Former Bolivian Director of Intelligence Roberto Quintanilla shot to death in West Germany, where he had been serving as consul general at Hamburg; the Bolivian National Liberation Army claimed responsibility;

April 19 Former Minister of Economic Affairs Alberto Larrea Humerez assassinated in Bolivia;

May 23   Maximilian Gómez, exiled general secretary of the left-wing Dominican Popular Movement, shot to death in Belgium two months after being freed from prison in Santo Domingo as one of twenty inmates involved in an exchange for a kidnaped U.S. official;

June 8   Edmundo Pérez Zujovic, former Chilean minister of the interior and leader of the conservative Chilean Christian Democratic Party, fatally shot in Santiago by three gunmen, one of whom was identified by the victim's daughter as a member of the Marxist Organized People's Vanguard (denounced by President Salvador Allende for its act of "deliberate provocation");

July 6   José Luis Arriaga Arriola, Guatemalan congressman representing the opposition Democratic Revolutionary Union, killed in Guatemala City following earlier murders of two political allies in January and retaliatory insurgent attacks on the British consulate as well as against a provincial police chief slain in March;

July 9   Argentine President Alejandro Lanusse and Uruguayan President Jorge Pacheco Areco objects of a plot to blow up the reviewing stand at the Independence Day parade in Buenos Aires (fourteen members of the Argentine-Uruguayan Revolutionary

People's Army were arrested and a large cache of arms and explosives uncovered);

August 22
and
September 15   Colonel Andrés Selich, Bolivian interior minister in the new rightist government of Hugo Banzer Suárez survived two bomb attempts blamed on (but not acknowledged by) the leftist Army of National Liberation.

Little would be gained by simply enumerating the monotonous roll of Latin American assassination attempts in recent years, their heaviest concentrations occurring in El Salvador, Nicaragua, and Guatemala to the north and Bolivia as well as Argentina at the extreme south, with a generous scattering in between. Certain cases are so startling as to demand special notice. One was the death of President Salvador Allende during the Chilean coup in 1973. Despite the widely held view that he was murdered by soldiers during the storming of the presidential palace at Santiago, a number of neutral observers are inclined to accept the theory that he died by his own hand rather than be captured and subjected to trial by his enemies. Nevertheless, whether Allende was a despairing suicide or a victim of murder, the military junta that overthrew him was responsible for his death. The same onus rests on the government of El Salvador for the shooting of Archbishop Oscar Arnulfo Romero y Galdames, a persistent critic of the regime until he was slain in 1980 while saying mass.

Alongside the tragic recurrence of individual assaults, mass executions, and seizures of hostages in a half-dozen or more countries must be placed another feature of Latin American political strife. This is the internationalization of a terrorism that is both imported and exported, governmental as well as revolutionary. Imports include the benefits, if such they can be called, of Cuban programs for bringing arms from the USSR's eastern European arsenals and tactical advice accompanied by group training offered in staging areas such as Lebanon and Libya. They also include the arming by the United States of numerous rightist regimes in power, as well as anti-Sandinista rebels (Contras) in Nicaragua.

With respect to exported terrorism, the balance between right-wing and left-wing elements appears less even. It is possible that rightist movements have aided likeminded groups outside of South America, although their resources for doing so are very limited. What is not seriously denied is that Cuban operatives have worked assiduously not only in the Western but also in the Eastern Hemisphere—from Africa, where major bases exist in the former Spanish colony of Equatorial Guinea and once-Portuguese Angola, to Europe, territory of Carlos the Jackal and of other only slightly less prominent Latin American "volunteers."[3]

Not that all such activity requires the explicit blessing of Castro's government in Havana. In 1976, when Norbert Kröcher, the German fugitive intent on winning freedom for Andreas Baader and other Red Army Faction leaders imprisoned inside the German Federal Republic, was assembling forces at Stockholm for the abduction of Sweden's minister of immigration, non-German recruits were indispensable. In the multinational gang of some fifty members he eventually brought into being, his principal accomplices proved to be one Armando Carrillo, a Mexican veteran of the Soviet-financed Movimiento de Acción Revolucionaria (previously trained in North Korea), Carrillo's Chilean wife, and three more Mexicans, two of whom flew from Havana to Stockholm at the urgent request of the third. Their travel, Swedish authorities discovered, had been arranged for by a Cuban-front organization, the so-called Junta for Revolutionary Coordination. Fortunately for his intended victim, Kröcher was himself surprised on a Stockholm street and arrested in the spring of 1977, before the minister could be kidnaped and secreted underground in a ventilated coffin as had been planned. Most of Kröcher's confederates, including the Latin Americans, disappeared from sight once more, at least for the time being.[4]

The worst violence exported by the Latin American Right has taken the form of murderous assaults upon former opposition leaders living abroad. The assassination of the Dominican exile Maximiliano Gomez at Brussels in 1971 has already been noted. Even more atrocious was the slaying of Orlando Letelier, former Chilean ambassador to the United States and for a time Allende's foreign minister. Letelier and Ronni Karpen Moffitt, his associate in the Institute of Policy Studies, died as victims of a car bomb explosion in Washington, D.C., on September 21, 1976; Mrs. Moffitt's husband, also in the limousine, survived. Letelier, following the overthrow of the Allende government in 1973, had first been arrested by the new junta and imprisoned for a year, then released and allowed to emigrate. Two books based on detailed investigative reporting have traced the planning of this assassination directly to DINA, Chile's secret police. No comparable incident has aroused such indignation in the United States against criminal intervention by a foreign government.[5]

"English Islands"

It is easy, when discussing North and South America, to fall into the terror of distinguishing between the United States, on the one hand, and Latin America, on the other, as though between them they exhaust the topic. Both in general and with respect to political violence, the former British colonial possessions, many now sovereign states but still members of the Commonwealth, are too important to be overlooked. Nor is it enough to concentrate on Canada alone, recent events in the Caribbean having pointed up the significance of those island republics in the Western Hemisphere that lie outside the bounds of Hispanic influence.

Large and populous Jamaica has played a central role in much of the region's stormiest history, from piracy through slave uprisings to the tumultuous events preceding the general election of 1980, when the leader of the winning party, now Prime Minister Edward Seaga, was exposed to danger from gunfire as late as the day before the polls opened. Nevertheless, the voting took place on schedule and with a decisive outcome, confounding the dire predictions of many experts, doubtless including the former premier whom Seaga defeated.

On March 10, 1973, the governor of the self-governing colony of Bermuda was shot to death while walking his dog outside the governor's residence in Hamilton. Slain with Sir Richard Sharples that evening was his aide-de-camp, Captain Hugh Sayers. Government spokesmen at first refused to offer any explanation of the killings, beyond conceding that they followed by only six months the assassination of the commissioner of police. On March 13 the Bermudian constabulary arrested six members of the Black Beret Cadre, an organization claiming—without a great deal of apparent justification—to represent the 33,000 blacks who constitute over 60 percent of the population. Two of the accused eventually were convicted of five murders, including those of Sharples, Sayers, and the police commissioner, and were hanged in December 1977, touching off street riots by several hundred black youths and occasioning the brief appearance of a small force of Commonwealth troops from Belize (the former British Honduras). Inasmuch as the four highest offices in the island government by this time were held by black leaders, the racial issue failed to excite continuing unrest. Nevertheless, the memory of the Sharples affair remains a grim reminder of what a well-armed minority, however small, can achieve before the rest of society recovers its balance.[6]

The other notable "island murder" formed part of the background of the U.S.-led intervention in Grenada, southernmost of the Windward Islands, in the autumn of 1983. Disagreement over that operation continues, both in the United States and abroad. No longer central to the issue are the presence of a uniformed Cuban contingent in Grenada, the large-scale construction work in progress to enlarge the airport's military as well as commercial capacity, and the existence of a cache of powerful weapons far exceeding anything one might have expected to find there. Argument has therefore shifted increasingly from the reality of a problem to the quality of Washington's response.[7]

Of primary interest for this book, however, is the "pre-American" situation, especially the death on October 19, 1983, of Maurice Bishop, the recently ousted prime minister. Bishop had been suspected in 1974 of plotting the assassination of the then premier, Eric Gairy; ordering the assassination of a member of the anti-communist Grenadian National Party a few weeks before; and arranging for a shipment of Soviet munitions from Czechoslovakia which had been intercepted by authorities on the island of Barbados.[8] Ironically, until almost the moment of his own overthrow he had continued to concentrate his oratory on "the threat from the U.S.A." In spite of his claim to represent the Grenadian revolution, he had fallen under increasingly heavy criticism from the left, and on October 13, 1983, he was abruptly replaced by the hard-line Communist deputy premier, Bernard Coard, who placed his fallen predecessor under close house arrest pending further decisions.

On October 19 Bishop was temporarily freed from confinement by a crowd composed of his own followers, only to be shot to death within a few hours, under circumstances not yet fully clarified. According to the official communiqué released the following morning, he had led his supporters into a bloody confrontation with government troops and was killed, one of many casualties. Testimony collected after Coard's fall a week later give a different version, in which Bishop was singled out for assassination by selected gunmen. Whatever the truth of the matter, Bishop's death made a profound impression on opinion, popular no less than official, in such important West Indian island republics as Barbados, Jamaica, and Dominica. Fidel Castro himself spoke from Havana on the 19th, deploring the former premier's demise and criticizing Coard's tactics.[9] History contains many "political" assassinations that can only be described as politically inconsequential, but Maurice Bishop's was not one of them.

Canada—and Quebec

Canada's encounter with terrorist bloodshed brings one directly back to comparisons with the European arena of the IRA, the German Red Army Faction, and the Italian Red Brigades. On the morning of October 5, 1970, James Cross, senior commissioner of the British Trade Commission at Montreal, was kidnaped from his home in suburban Westmount by two armed men who drove him away in their car before his housekeeper's calls for help could summon the police. Within hours the first of many numbered communiqués from the self-styled "Liberation Cell" of the Front de Libération du Québec (FLQ) was found on the campus of the University of Montreal, as specified by telephone. This document, like many others of its kind, listed a number of political prisoners, in this instance twenty, who were to be released and placed aboard a jet airplane with $500,000 in gold bullion, for safe passage to either Cuba or Algeria. It demanded further that the liberated men be accompanied by lawyers of their choice, as well as by two reporters representing French-language newspapers. As the number of dissidents to be set free suggests, the action came near the end of several months of intermittent bombings, police raids, and one aborted kidnaping plot. Nevertheless, Canadians in general were not prepared for the reality of

the Cross abduction. They were about to be shocked still more by what followed.[10]

While the federal government in Ottawa and provincial officials in Quebec were exchanging statements with the Liberation Cell, members of another tiny FLQ unit, the Chénier Fund-Raising Cell, decided, according to a
confession later attributed to its coleaders, that a second hostage was
needed. On October 10 the chief kidnaper, twenty-seven-year-old Paul
Rose, with his brother, aged twenty-three, and two other accomplices, seized
Pierre Laporte, Quebec's provincial minister of labor and immigration, at
gunpoint while he was playing football in a vacant lot across the street from
his house in another Montreal suburb, St. Lambert, and drove off with him
according to plan. The taking of Cross had thrust Canada into a difficult
struggle to save the life of a British diplomatic and commercial representative; Laporte's abduction involved a major figure in domestic politics, until
recently a rival of the Liberal Party, now one of the key ministers in its cabinet. The reasons for the terrorism obviously had broadened to include the
overwhelming defeat of René Lévesque's separatist Parti Québécois by Jean
Robert Bourassa's federalist Liberals in the provincial elections of April
1970. Such sympathy as the FLQ militants received at the beginning of the
new campaign stemmed primarily from French-Canadian frustration at this
apparent failure to send a stronger "message to Ottawa" from their polling
places.

As events unfolded, however, the tactics employed by the Laporte kidnapers destroyed the goodwill of any but the most fanatical separatists.
Tension between Prime Minister Trudeau's national government and
Bourassa's Quebec regime was, under the circumstances, inevitable. Nevertheless, the controversial decision by Trudeau on October 16 to invoke the
War Measures Act and to impose what amounted to martial law, while explicitly naming the FLQ in the proclamation and appended regulations, was
reached in direct response to written appeals from Quebec's own premier
and highest-ranking police officers, all stressing the urgent need for federal
support. It is also worth remarking that the two groups of kidnapers, in their
choice of language and apparent hatred of *all* legal authority, never bothered to draw any significant distinction between the national prime minister
(himself a French Canadian) and the provincial leaders.

The denouement followed quickly in one case, more tortuously and in-
decisively in the other. On the evening of October 17 (the day following the
proclamation of the War Measures Act) the latest in a seemingly endless
stream of communiqués, this one boasting of action by what it called the
"Dieppe cell (Royal 22nd)," informed a local broadcasting station that the
man sneeringly referred to as "minister of unemployment and assimilation"
had been executed and that his body could be found in the trunk of a green
Chevrolet at a gate leading into St. Hubert airport. Police discovered there
the remains of Pierre Laporte. According to the coroner's report, he had

been strangled, though the corpse showed other superficial wounds later explained by his killers as having resulted from an attempt he had made to escape through a window in the house where he was confined.

Meanwhile, Royal Canadian Mounted Police, with detectives and agents of the provincial as well as city police, continued to search for James Cross and his abductors. Finally, on December 2, acting first on tips and partial confessions from individuals arrested after the Laporte murder, then on their own observation of a dwelling in one of Montreal's working-class neighborhoods, the combined national, Quebec, and Montreal forces cordoned off six blocks of Montreal North where they had just arrested Jacques Cossette-Trudel and his wife, sister of Jacques Lanctot, now correctly believed to be the ringleader. Early the next morning, from the booby-trapped house where Cross was being held, the Liberation Cell opened negotiations to save themselves. Quebec's minister of justice, acting as chief negotiator for the government, and Ricardo Eschartín, the acting Cuban consul, who represented the FLQ cell members, reached an agreement to save Cross at the expense of losing custody of his captors. The latter, four in number, drove their prisoner in a (booby-trapped) car to the site of the forthcoming world's fair on St. Helen's Island. There they delivered him over to Eschartín in an exposition building declared Cuban territory for purposes of the exchange. A police helicopter then carried seven individuals, including the twenty-five-year-old Lanctot's wife and child as well as Mme. Cossetti-Trudel, to Dorval Airport. An air force plane flew them to Havana, where they were greeted by Cuban Foreign Ministry officials. Upon receipt of radioed assurance of their safe arrival, Cross, twenty-two pounds lighter than when he had been seized fifty-nine days before but otherwise unharmed, was released.[11]

With the Cross kidnapers beyond the reach of Canadian law, the search for Laporte's killers became the principal item of public business. On October 27 the authorities had received a "joint communiqué of the Chénier, Libération, and Dieppe Cells" to which Paul Rose had affixed his thumbprint and attached his passport. This statement of defiance, in addition to branding the previous spring's elections an outrage made possible by the "Anglophone vote," called for support from sons of "the boys who were massacred at Dieppe," and ended with the customary "We shall overcome."* The document contained nothing strikingly new, but it did focus attention once and for all on Rose, already considered, with his brother Jacques and two other men, Francis Simard and Bernard Lortie, to be among the prime suspects.[12]

---

* The claim that the ill-fated Dieppe landing on the German-occupied Channel Coast of France in August 1942 had been a senseless consignment of five thousand Canadian troops to death or capture as "guinea pigs" or "cheap labour" served to recall bitter memories of World War II, including opposition to the draft in Canada.

For another two months, until long after Cross had been released by his Havana-bound abductors, the self-styled "executioners" of Labor Minister Laporte remained at large, hidden by sympathizers in various refuges, until on December 27 they were finally captured in a subterranean hiding place beneath a farmhouse some twenty miles southwest of Montreal. After negotiations conducted on the fugitives' side by one of their admirers, Dr. Jacques Ferron, they surrendered to police early on the morning of December 28, 1970.

Paul Rose, found guilty of murder and of kidnaping by two separate juries in 1971, was sentenced to life imprisonment on each count. His appeal on both convictions was dismissed by the Quebec Appeal Court, and he and his counsel decided for political reasons not to pursue the matter before the Supreme Court of Canada. Jacques Rose was acquitted of murder and kidnaping but convicted of being an accessory to his older brother's crimes and sentenced to an eight-year prison term. Simard and Lortie were also found guilty, the former of murder, the latter of kidnaping, and received sentences of life and twenty years' imprisonment respectively; the remaining twelve defendants were given shorter terms.

The crisis of 1970 left a bitter legacy of recrimination, even as it cast a deep shadow across relations between Quebec and Ottawa in the aftermath of the spring elections. Some critics have insisted that Laporte's life could and should have been saved by the kind of concessions that led to the release of James Cross. Others continue to argue that the French-Canadian separatist movement was unfairly blamed for the excesses of a handful of extremists determined to imitate foreign models of terrorism.[13] Canada's crisis of 1970 did not herald the end of constitutional liberty, nor did the disservice done by the terrorists to the interests of Quebec's ethnic majority prevent the political resurgence of the Parti Québécois in the elections of 1976. Like other efforts to destroy the workings of parliamentary democracy in countries whose people have remained loyal to it, the recourse to violence had shaken the foundations of government but failed to demolish them.

15

The United States

"Conceived and Born in Violence"?

The phrase just quoted appears in a thoughtful essay devoted to the American past, but the metaphor is accompanied here by a question mark.[1] That the history of the United States contains much riot and more than a little bloodshed is undeniable. For a nation created by colonial rebellion and welded together by the nineteenth century's costliest war of unification, this was all but inevitable. Civilizations characterized by geographical expansion have generally been marked as much by the harshness and impatience as by the imagination and optimism of frontier society. So it was with the Greeks colonizing sites from the shores of the western Mediterranean to those of the Black Sea, with the Romans planting garrisons to defend distant borders, with Russians facing an inviting but embattled Asian hinterland—and so it has been with Americans carving out a republic a continent wide.

That much is familiar, but it does not tell the whole story, including some less commonly noted twists and paradoxes. Throughout the colonial period of more than one hundred and fifty years, for example, while the future United States witnessed many violent acts and demonstrations, these included no lethal assault upon a prominent representative of the British crown. In this sense our ancestors may be said to have shared, probably without being aware of it, in Europe's early modern respite from political murder. Even when contemplating two later concentrations of assassination in the United States, we should realize that the country's history has been more frequently influenced by group violence than by individual homicide. Its record in colonial times renders especially puzzling the choice of locale for the first performance (in 1859) of Verdi's "Masked Ball," an opera directly inspired by the assassination of King Gustaf III in 1792 but discreetly set by the composer not in Stockholm but in colonial Boston!

What did flourish in the colonies, and continued in the new nation, were popular outbreaks of the kind made famous by the angry Regulators of North Carolina in the 1760s, the North End Mob and South End Mob of Boston (this last best known for the tea party which actually was one of its milder exercises), and participants in the Whiskey Rebellion of 1794. More personalized, but still not equivalent to assassination by stealth or surprise, was dueling between gentlemen of honor, a practice that seems, rather surprisingly, to have involved politically prominent individuals more frequently in the New World than in the Old.[2] Not only did Aaron Burr kill Alexander Hamilton in 1804 on the heights of Weehawken, New Jersey, but both Andrew Jackson and Thomas Hart Benton took the lives of dueling adversaries before becoming, respectively, president of the United States and senator from Missouri. As late as 1859 David S. Terry, chief justice of the California Supreme Court, slew U.S. Senator David C. Broderick in a duel involving both a quarrel over patronage and conflicting political views, Broderick having been a vocal opponent of extending slavery into the Far West.[3]

Despite its survival in the sometimes almost ritualistic gunfights on the frontier, as well as in the blood feuds of the southern Appalachians and parts of Texas, dueling rapidly declined in popularity after about the middle of the nineteenth century, to be replaced by attempts at outright assassination. The latter phenomenon did not make its first appearance in the nation's history until January 30, 1835. When it did, perhaps appropriately the intended victim was that old duelist, President Andrew Jackson.[4]

The sixty-seven-year-old Jackson, almost halfway through his second term, walked out of the rotunda of the Capitol on the arm of his secretary of the treasury, Levi Woodbury, following a funeral service for a deceased congressman. Waiting for him among bystanders on the east portico was a former house painter, Richard Lawrence, who had been born in England around 1800 but, while still a boy, brought by his parents to live near Washington. By the time he reached his mid-thirties, he was prey to various delusions of grandeur, including the obsessive belief that he was really King Richard III and as such had valid claims against the British and U.S. governments, just payment of which was being thwarted by the administration's refusal to create a national bank. As the President emerged from the rotunda into the daylight, Lawrence from about eight feet away tried to discharge first one, then the other of two pistols he held aimed at the tall, but now painfully bent figure. Both misfired, their powder and balls having fallen out into the would-be assassin's pockets while the clumsy weapons were concealed there.

Jackson was momentarily enraged by the fiasco, which he at first blamed on political opponents, but he quickly recovered his poise and ordered that no harm should be done to Lawrence. That unfortunate, whose easily documented symptoms of what would today be called paranoid schizophrenia were matched by a family history of mental illness that included his father and an aunt, was apparently never in much danger of being hanged. Brought to trial in a courtroom where he continued his bizarre posturing, he was acquitted of attempted murder—not only the jury but the prosecutor, Francis Scott Key of "Star Spangled Banner" fame, being convinced of the defendant's incapacity—and was committed to a succession of asylums. He died a quarter of a century later, at Washington's Government Hospital for the Insane. When he did so, the nation was about to enter upon a terrible struggle, destined to end with a tragedy beside which his escapade in 1835 would shrink to the stature of a farce.

The Watershed of the Civil War

Concentrations of civil violence, including assassination, are less likely to coincide with major military conflicts than to precede or follow them. That generalization holds true for the United States just prior to the firing on Fort Sumter and after Lee's surrender at Appomatox. The rising passions of the 1850s over the slavery question, intertwined with that of federal authority versus states' rights, found expression not only in Justice Terry's shooting of Senator Broderick in distant California but also in South Carolina Representative Preston Brooks's severe beating of Charles Sumner with a heavy cane in the Senate chamber on May 22, 1856. Two days earlier the senator from Massachusetts had delivered an extraordinarily fervent abolitionist speech, which included a verbal attack on a relative of Brooks. The Southern congressman obviously viewed his response as a duel of sorts, though a less biased observer would have been bound to call it distinctly one-sided.

If such an incident could take place within the walls of the Capitol, small wonder that the prelude to war included murders committed from Kansas to Harper's Ferry. In effect, Northerners' praise of John Brown for his sanguinary exploits in Kansas and his famous raid, like their mourning over his execution in 1859, made him the United States' first political martyr.[5] He and his supporters appear to have assumed that the justice of their cause justified whatever cost in innocent lives his methods might entail. The first victim of Brown's attack on Harper's Ferry had in fact been a black freedman killed while doing his job as stationmaster.

There is a well-attested theory that great wars are often followed by eruptions of domestic violence, involving political as well as private acts, because the demobilization of armies releases on society veterans who have acquired an indifference to the value of life and a knowledge of how to take it. That explanation fits very well the part played by disgruntled veterans in Germany during the 1920s but not that of their successors in the twenty years or so immediately after 1945. As for the United States, although experience and training received during the Civil War may have contributed to much of the gunplay of the ensuing period, neither then nor later does the "veterans' connection" seem to have had anything to do with the making of presidential assassins, with one obviously important exception: Lee Harvey Oswald.

This is not to say that all these assassins, merely by virtue of lacking a military background, were solitary misfits, vengeful toward society, craving recognition, but indifferent to public issues. Quite the contrary; most of them gave evidence of being strongly affected by what one author has called the "political context" of their times.[6] John Wilkes Booth offers a case in point. In order to form any reliable estimate of his politics, it is necessary to dispense with some widely held misconceptions of his personality. The most popular of these has been that he was a failed actor, jealous of a more gifted father and elder brother, infatuated with the South only because his stage appearances had been well-received there, driven to kill Abraham Lincoln by a yearning for notoriety as a substitute for unachievable fame. Vain and self-regarding in some respects Booth clearly was, but personally charming as well, attractive to women, loyal to friends, and, above all, the opposite of a professional failure. One of the mostly highly paid and acclaimed actors of his day, enthusiastically reviewed in New York, Boston, Philadelphia, and other Northern cities at late as 1864, he had no need to rely on Southern audiences for his only applause.

Booth's devotion to the Confederacy appears to have been sincere enough, albeit grounded in emotion and melodramatically expressed. In the months following Gettysburg, and still more after the President's reelection in 1864, as Grant's and Sherman's armies applied ever more relentless pressure upon an exhausted South, Booth's anti-Union sentiments became correspondingly stronger. His hatred of Lincoln in particular drew added virulence from much that a biased and selective observer could pick up even in the North from an environment poisoned by the seemingly endless war, with its casualties, draft riots, shortages, and disappointments. In October 1864, just a month before Booth appeared for the last time on stage with his brothers, Edwin and Junius Brutus, Jr., playing the part of Mark Antony in *Julius Caesar* before an audience of two thousand at New York's Winter Garden Theatre, he began a series of trips to Montreal for clandestine meetings with Confederate representatives in Canada. There, in collaboration with desperate Southern agents, he conceived in its original form his plan to help reverse the tide of Union victories.[7]

The scheme Booth brought to Washington that winter called for its ringleader, with a few trusted accomplices, to kidnap the chief executive, conduct him handcuffed through Maryland to where he could be taken behind Confederate lines and held until exchanged for tens of thousands of Southern prisoners of war. In preparation for the undertaking—a wild one, but not wholly impracticable given the almost total lack of security precautions

The Booth brothers in *Julius Caesar:*
from left to right, John Wilkes, Edwin, and Junius Brutus, Jr.

in the nation's capital—Booth recruited five men he had come to know in various connections. One was an experienced Southern spy named John Surratt; two were discharged Confederate soldiers; and the remaining pair were anti-Northern civilians who declared themselves ready to help. On an evening in March 1865 this band intercepted a carriage in which they believed the President to be riding en route to a play at the Soldiers' Home on the edge of Washington. Lincoln, however, had decided not to attend, and the kidnapers, upon finding Secretary of the Treasury Salmon P. Chase alone in the conveyance, rode away in frustration.

The failure of the abduction attempt, combined with the announcement of General Lee's surrender on April 9, led to the adoption of a more desperate alternative. As Booth explained it to his not uniformly enthusiastic comrades, only by assassinating the Union's principal war leaders—President Lincoln, General Grant, Vice-President Johnson, and Secretary of State Seward (second to Johnson in presidential succession)—could they hope to demoralize the federal government and revive hopes for a negotiated peace. Booth was to kill Lincoln and Grant, whose attendance with their wives at a performance of "Our American Cousin" had been announced for April 14. The powerfully built war veteran George Atzerodt was assigned to murder Andrew Johnson. The other ex-Confederate soldier, Lewis Payne, with the help of the feebleminded nineteen-year-old David Herold, had the task of slaying Seward, known to be confined to his bed by injuries suffered in a carriage accident a few days before.

The disintegration of the venture would not have surprised Machiavelli. At the last minute Atzerodt decided not to assault the vice-president, a man he "had never even met." Payne, with Herold waiting outside, gained entry to Seward's residence and wounded not only the secretary, with a single pistol ball, but also his son and three other occupants of the house. The Grants had decided not to accompany Abraham and Mary Todd Lincoln to the theater, so Booth had only one target. And as the world knows, he did kill the President.

The immediate aftermath was as straightforward as the long-term effects were unfathomable. John Surratt escaped punishment by fleeing to Europe and then, after his arrest in Cairo the following year and extradition back to the United States, winning acquittal by a deadlocked jury in Washington. By that time his mother, Mary Surratt, though probably not privy to the actual plot, had been convicted as an accomplice and hanged on the same scaffold as Atzerodt, Herold, and Payne. Four other accused accessories received prison sentences but were pardoned by President Johnson in 1869. Descendants of Dr. Samuel Mudd, who had treated Booth's broken leg during his flight, eventually secured his full exoneration. Booth evaded capture for almost a fortnight spent in dodging, with the devoted Herold, from one hideout to another in a desolate, swampy section of Maryland. He was at last tracked to an old barn. On April 26, 1865, the surrounding troops set fire to the building; and Booth, having ordered Herold to give himself up for trial, apparently killed himself. The persistent rumor that he was struck down by a shot fired blindly through the barn's planking from thirty feet away by a sergeant who ignored the order to ground arms can only be termed implausible.[8]

The indignant tyrannicide, as he saw himself, had inscribed in his diary while in hiding after the murder: "I am here in despair. And why? For doing what Brutus was honored for—what made Tell a hero. And yet I, for striking down a greater tyrant than they ever knew, am looked upon as a common cutthroat."[9] There is no way of knowing what Lincoln's appeal for peace "with charity for all, with malice toward none" might have accomplished had he lived, but the cost to the assassin's beloved South of the President's untimely death was immense.

Part of the cost to the entire nation took the form of an epidemic of political murder. In the space of one decade, 1867–1877, according to the report of the Eisenhower Commission, a total of thirty-two political officials were attacked, twenty-three of them fatally.[10] The victims included a United States senator, two congressional representatives, three state governors, ten state legislators, eight judges, and eight other appointed or elected office-holders. In approximately one-third of these cases the motives appear to have been unknown or nonpolitical, that is, financial, sexual, or professional. Nevertheless, even "nonpolitical" assaults upon governmental officials say something about the restraint, or lack of it, with which figures of authority are treated in various periods of history.

A substantial number of the incidents took place in the former Confederacy: successive governors of Louisiana wounded in the seventies; an Arkansas congressman slain in 1868; five state legislators and six judges killed; and so on. Nevertheless, there were too many other atrocities committed in northern and western states during the same period to permit this worst shootout in U.S. history prior to the 1960s to be blamed entirely on motives or conditions peculiar to the South.

By the late 1870s the outburst was beginning to subside, unevenly to be sure, but undeniably. Looking ahead no farther than the start of the ensuing decade, however, today's observer can glimpse the outlines of another pattern of recurring homicide. Unlike that of the immediate post-Civil War years, this one was to be less random, but more obstinately focused on the highest office of all: the presidency.[11]

That Lincoln's murder was not destined to remain an isolated trauma became clear when President James A. Garfield, less than four months after having been inaugurated, was fatally shot by the self-styled "lawyer, theologian, and politician," Charles Julius Guiteau.[12] The thirty-nine-year-old assassin had been born in Illinois, briefly exposed to higher education at the

University of Michigan, and thereafter, at his devout father's urging, introduced to the Kingdom of God as visualized by organizers of the Oneida
Community in upstate New York. While still only twenty-four, the egocen-
tric and ambitious young man had broken with the Oneida elders and
moved to New York City. There he had intended to launch his own newspaper; instead, having had to take a desolate room in Hoboken, New Jersey, he
settled into an existence marked by failure and recriminations, debt, petty
crime, endless scribbling, and almost invariable rejection by women, whom
he pursued with an obsessive lubricity that seemed unaffected by discourag-
ing outcomes.

The political atmosphere before, during, and after the presidential campaign of 1880 was remarkably rancorous. Garfield, once elected, was
vouchsafed little or nothing in the way of a "honeymoon" during the first
months of his administration. The stridency of public discourse appears to
have been congenial, if overstimulating, to Guiteau, alternating between
self-advertisement and self-pity. He had hung around Republican headquarters in New York during the campaign, preparing at least one "address"
in support of the candidate, or so he assured Garfield after the latter's victory in November. Throughout the winter he continued to bombard the
president-elect and any other party leader he could think of with demands
for favors in recognition of his imaginary services to the winning cause. In
particular, he fancied himself as a likely appointee to a major consular post
in Europe. On March 5, 1881, the morrow of election day, he moved from
Hoboken to Washington, the better to oversee the nation's health while
pursuing his own career.

As the spring wore on, with no action on his consulship despite chance
encounters with both President Garfield and Secretary of State Blaine in the
corridors of the latter's office building, Guiteau began to express mounting
indignation and identified himself increasingly with the Stalwarts, who had
failed the previous year to get Grant nominated for a third term but were
represented in the administration by Vice-President Chester A. Arthur. In
the numerous letters, draft speeches, and fragments he wrote in preparation
for his star turn, Guiteau referred to himself as "a Stalwart of the Stalwarts,"
explaining that he bore his victim no ill will but was convinced that for the
good of the country "my friend Arthur" must become president.

On the morning of July 2, carrying a recently purchased revolver, a final
statement addressed "To the White House," and a letter to General Sherman concerning his own protection by troops while in prison, he made his
way to the Washington terminal of the Baltimore and Potomac Railroad.
Garfield arrived at the station to take a train to New York and thence north
to Williamstown, Massachusetts, for his twenty-fifth class reunion at Williams College. As the President walked toward the waiting room with Secretary Blaine, Guiteau shot him twice in the back at close range. The assassin

was quickly overcome, despite having hired a cab to take him directly to jail before he could be lynched. His victim clung to life for almost eighty days before succumbing in September.

Guiteau's long trial, which gave him the public stage he had longed for, provided plentiful evidence of his demented state.[13] In at least two respects the case can be viewed as an epilogue to the crisis of the Civil War and Reconstruction. First, it involved important figures of the sixties, Grant in particular, and a party structure that continued to bear the marks of the great crisis. Second, it seems likely that Guiteau would not have been hanged, as he was a year after firing the shots in the railroad station, had not his victim (unlike Jackson in 1835) died as a result and had the tragedy of 1865 not intervened between his insane act and that of Lawrence almost half a century before.

Madmen or Zealots?

A common assessment, stated frequently but not solely by European observers, is that the United States has had few if any genuinely political assassinations, inspired by motives at once rational and larger than self. Political impact, yes—so this argument runs—but no conception of ends and means worthy of a Brutus or an Orsini or a Stauffenberg. At the root of such skepticism is a widely held belief that the Republic's would-be tyrannicides have all been either addled lunatics or insignificant pawns in the service of labyrinthine conspiracies composed of shadowy "establishment figures."

The roll of major U.S. political crimes has been called too often and examined in too many books, articles, and official reports to call for detailed recapitulation here. It seems more appropriate to ask a few specific questions about a selection of principal episodes, all but three of them belonging to the twentieth century. Up to now nine presidents have been assaulted (one of them twice) as well as one president-elect (Franklin D. Roosevelt in 1933), three presidential candidates (Theodore Roosevelt in 1912, Robert Kennedy in 1968, George Wallace in 1972), and two other political figures of comparable national prominence (Huey Long and Martin Luther King.)[14] By limiting to sixteen the list of assailants it may be possible to give questions bearing on responsibility, motivation, and results the attention they deserve. How many of the assassins were subject to delusions or other cognitive and psychic disorders so extreme as to relieve them of legal culpability by reason of insanity? How many were impelled by aggression, exhibitionism, or self-pity so intense as to render them "unbalanced" by some reasonable if not clinically sophisticated definition, yet fully cognizant of the meaning of their actions? How many others, by contrast, despite obsessive ruthlessness, were committed to beliefs or purposes extending well beyond the demands of self-expression? And, finally, were there among them any whose motivation remains either unfathomable or at the very least subject to sharp and continuing disagreement?

The need to include the trio of incidents from the nineteenth century in order to achieve an overview of the past one hundred and fifty years is nowhere more apparent than in considering the small group of assassins who, on the basis of existing evidence, appear to have been hopelessly demented, possessed by fantasies of grandeur and persecution that effectively cut them off from the realities about them. One was a post-1900 figure: John Schrank, who in 1912 wounded Theodore Roosevelt outside Milwaukee's Hotel Gilpatrick, not, he explained at the time, because of any hatred for the former president but "as a warning to other third termers." Schrank's delusion had taken the form of a recurrent vision, which he first noted in 1901, of the murdered President McKinley in his coffin and calling for vengeance on his successor, "Theo. Roosevelt" as he is called in the dreamer's handwritten account. An almost identical dream apparently came to him again in 1912, a month before his grand gesture. Having been examined by a panel of alienists and declared unfit to stand trial, the seemingly amiable immigrant from Bavaria lived out his life as a model patient in a state mental hospital, where he died in 1943 at the age of sixty-seven.[15] The other two apparent psychotics come earlier in the succession of culprits—Richard Lawrence in 1835, earliest of all. The other, now generally conceded to have been legally incompetent, was Charles Guiteau, who nevertheless went to the gallows for having slain President Garfield in 1881.

Even these three, largely insulated as they were by their own madness, were not wholly unaffected by the political events of their lifetimes. Lawrence had heard and read enough about Jackson's struggle with the Second Bank of the United States to hold him responsible for British withholding of payments owed a reincarnated monarch. Guiteau had been greatly excited by the presidential campaign of 1880, and Schrank was offended by T.R.'s Bull Moose candidacy. In none of these cases, to be sure, were the political circumstances decisive in tilting the behavior of the men involved; but politics formed part of the backdrop for their desperate actions.

A considerably larger group of would-be assassins have shown signs of personality disorders without, however, losing touch with reality. Neurotic, lonely, vengeful, self-aggrandizing, they nevertheless took their cues quite directly from things occurring around them, not only in world and national affairs but also in the worlds of crime, rebellion, economic and social conflict, even motion pictures.

On February 15, 1933, in Miami, a thirty-two-year-old Italian immigrant bricklayer named Guiseppe Zangara discharged a volley of pistol shots in the direction of Franklin D. Roosevelt's open limousine, which was serving as a rostrum for an outdoor rally. Five persons were wounded, one of them, Mayor Anton Cermak of Chicago, fatally. All of this, according to Zangara's subsequent confession, had transpired because he held authority, embodied in his own father, in the president-elect, and in rich people generally, to be responsible for the agonizing stomach disorder he had suffered since childhood. At an earlier point in his career he had considered killing the king of Italy, and as recently as the week before he fired on F.D.R. he was still planning to assassinate President Hoover. Obsessive resentment over his physical pain seems to have been central, but Zangara had heard snatches of anarchist rhetoric, providing at least a rationalization of sorts for what he wanted to do. Although the Depression as such seems not to have bothered him—he preferred to work irregularly—it is likely that what he knew of the trial and execution of Sacco and Vanzetti in Massachusetts, soon after he immigrated in 1923, strengthened his belief that all Italian-American radicals were objects of persecution. He went to his death in the Florida State Penitentiary's electric chair for the murder of Cermak, still snarling defiantly: "Lousy capitalists . . . no pictures! . . . Go ahead. Push the button."[16] To the extent that he identified his hated father with kings, presidents, and plutocrats, and only to that extent, even Zangara was a political assassin.

The same mixture of sneering resentment and indifference to the exact identity of his victim informs the history of Arthur Bremer, the twenty-one-year-old Milwaukean who in Laurel, Maryland, on May 15, 1972, shot Governor George Wallace at an outdoor gathering honoring the Democratic presidential hopeful. Bremer, a perverse but by no means simpleminded loner, alternately brooding and excited, even giddy, had previously stalked the incumbent President Nixon to Ottawa, Canada, before starting to follow Wallace in Michigan about a week before the actual shooting. Bremer did not kill the flamboyant candidate from Alabama, but he did leave a formidable campaigner paralyzed from the waist down, thereby knocking him out of that year's race and dramatically altering the presidential election prospects in 1972. Despite the self-centered malice at the core of the gunman's behavior and the debt he says he owed to the sex and violence pervading his favorite movie, "A Clockwork Orange," he had also read with fascination books about Booth, Oswald, and Sirhan. Not surprisingly, he chose a political figure as a target.[17]

During the second week of November 1968, in Brooklyn, New York, the Federal Bureau of Investigation arrested three naturalized immigrants from Yemen, Ahmed Raget Namer and his sons Abdo and Hussein, charging them with conspiring to assassinate President-elect Richard Nixon.[18] Press coverage of this alleged plot was skeptical at the outset; and the Namers, although indicted almost at once, were acquitted the following July on all counts except that of illegally possessing two switchblade knives. What is ironical about this flimsy scenario (which is not included in the count of sixteen assassination attempts given above) is that its purported target was to be the object of a real, albeit harebrained plan more than five years later, without any opportunity being afforded for either him or the FBI to forestall its tragic denouement.

The leading role in 1974 was played by a thickset, reportedly friendly Philadelphian. Samuel Byck was, at forty-four, a failure in business, recently divorced by his wife, and rooming in a friend's modest home. In August 1973 Byck had begun writing angry letters to, among others, the Small Business Administration and Senator Richard Schweiker of Pennsylvania about the difficulties that supposedly prevented worthy applicants from securing SBA loans; the Federal Communications Commission denouncing a broadcast editorial endorsement of capital punishment; and the Israeli Consulate, urging (as a Jew who "cared") that Israel withdraw its army from the Sinai Peninsula. Side by side with Byck's deep feelings of persecution and isolation there appeared to exist a compulsion to be noticed and to be heard on public issues of the day, from the oil crisis to the Watergate affair.[19]

His secret project, grandiosely entitled "Operation Pandora's Box," he explained in one of many tape recordings, this one dictated on February 21, 1974. The next day, said Byck, having commandeered a commercial jetliner he would force the crew to fly toward the White House, after which he intended to shoot the pilot, seize the controls, and steer the plane into the executive mansion, killing the President and numerous others, obviously including himself and everyone else aboard his chosen projectile. Late that night, still dictating at intervals into the tape recorder, he set off from Philadelphia for Baltimore-Washington International Airport in his car with its layer of "Impeach Nixon" decals. The following morning he rushed the gate admitting passengers for a Baltimore-to-Atlanta flight, killing a security guard with two pistol shots in the process. Once inside the plane, he wounded the pilot and copilot, the latter fatally, before being hit by two rounds of sniper fire from outside. Defeated, lying on the floor of the aircraft, he shot himself in the temple with his own weapon. Although this double murder culminating in suicide momentarily startled the nation, it is probably the least-remembered such episode in United States history, its repercussions having been quickly drowned by the clamor over Watergate.

The cases of Lynette Alice ("Squeaky") Fromme, Sara Jane Moore, and John W. Hinckley, Jr., require less notice because of the publicity they received and because they occurred more recently. Fromme and Moore, the first American women charged with attempted assassination (leaving aside Mary Surratt's deeply flawed conviction as an accessory in 1865), were involved in separate incidents occurring within a two-and-a-half-week period in 1975. On September 5 Fromme aimed a pistol at President Gerald Ford as he was walking from the Senator Hotel to the California state capitol building in Sacramento. Moore, on September 22 outside San Francisco's St. Francis Hotel, fired a single revolver shot across the street as Ford was about to enter a limousine. The third attempt, that of Hinckley against President Ronald Reagan on March 30, 1981, was carried out under eerily similar circumstances, between a hotel (this one in Washington) and a waiting car, but with far more damaging effect. The President was struck in the chest by one bullet, his chief press aide in the head by a second, and one of the plainclothesmen in the arm and leg by two others. Squeaky Fromme and Sara Jane Moore were found guilty at their respective trials; both, having been judged competent, that is, legally responsible, are serving life sentences. John Hinckley was found not guilty by reason of insanity and ordered to undergo treatment in a mental hospital.[20]

The impression of inequity created by these sentences is strengthened by the fact that all three defendants had quite comparable, albeit highly individual complexes of personal derangement to which their actions could be traced. Squeaky Fromme was infatuated with the convicted Charles Manson, to whose band of youthful followers she had belonged.[21] By her own account he had been at once her lover and her surrogate father, an object of quasi-religious devotion, whether as a Christ figure or as an Antichrist did not seem to matter. Even his planning of the senseless Tate and LaBianca murders in 1969 was in her eyes only a necessary part of his crusade. She seems to have believed that the chance to have him called as a witness at her trial, giving him another chance to explain his vision to a court, justified pointing a gun at the President.

In the case of Sally Moore, a former suburban matron turned public accountant after five marriages (two of them to the same man) and the abandonment of three children to her parents for adoption back in West Virginia, the immediate causes for shooting at Gerald Ford were fear and an acute sense of isolation. Having volunteered to serve as a double agent between the Federal Bureau of Investigation and the San Francisco radical underground, she had been dropped from the list of FBI informers after confessing to her friends in the Movement that she had revealed their secrets. For at least two years before the assassination attempt her fear of retribution from the left had been growing, especially after the murder of Oakland's black school superintendent, Marcus Foster, by the Symbionese Liberation Army in the autumn of 1973. Firing at the President was a penance of sorts, and also a gesture of solidarity.[22]

Hinckley, when not brooding over grievances against his wealthy parents and an unresponsive society, spent much of his spare time writing love letters to his favorite movie actress, Jodie Foster, who had appeared in the film "Taxi Driver" before entering college at Yale. Such is the sometimes weird circularity of assassination, not to mention the suggestive power of the silver screen, that Robert DeNiro's role as the obsessed gunman in that picture was partially inspired by the biography of Arthur Bremer, Governor Wallace's assailant and himself a fan of movies concerned with violence.

For all their neuroses and fixations, this trio of performers in assassination's theater of the absurd had in common an exaggerated susceptibility to the political sensations and the ephemeral cultism of their time. Not only wars and presidential scandals but also terrible mass murders, usually divorced from politics but awash in sadosexuality, were reported in newspapers and on television screens with sickening frequency in the 1960s and 1970s. These must have provided the "consciousness-expanding" stimulation deviant personalities appear to receive from demonstrative violence. Whether international terrorism, approaching its pinnacle of media exposure when the Bremers, Bycks, and Frommes were forming their resolves, had a comparable effect on them is difficult to estimate. There is no evidence of specific linkages. On the other hand, the savage jargon of a nihilist crusade was obviously part of the general static.

The perceptions of neurotics must be distinguished, however, from the more purposeful, though not necessarily less repellent, ideological commitment shown by a few of America's most publicized assassins. All of these men were unbalanced to some degree, lacking the restraint dictated by common sense or ordinary kindness, as well as any rational calculus of either self-interest or the needs of a functioning society. At the same time, each of the figures in question displayed a resolute—in a limited sense self-sacrificing—devotion to some cause greater than his own ease and self-esteem.

What has just been said applied to John Wilkes Booth in 1865, Leon Czolgosz in 1901, the Puerto Rican nationalists who sought to shoot President Truman in 1950, and Sirhan Sirhan, Senator Robert F. Kennedy's assailant in 1968. Although the prospects of advancing the Southern cause by assassinating Abraham Lincoln were certainly much slimmer than those of making some difference by kidnaping him while the war was still in progress, his murderer was convinced that the shot fired in Ford's Theatre was a great service to the Confederacy. Booth, as already noted, was by no means a lonely, embittered failure. He was fully aware that he would be thought mad for throwing away a life in which "I have my friends and every thing to make me happy [and] where my profession has gained me an income of *more than* twenty thousand dollars a year" (italics his).[23] (One year he in fact earned over thirty thousand, a vast sum in the 1860s.)

Leon Czolgosz, the quiet, studious son of Central European immigrants to Michigan, who later moved to Pennsylvania and finally to Cleveland, Ohio, was only slightly older than Booth, twenty-eight to be exact, when he shot President William McKinley on September 6, 1901, at the Pan-American Exposition in Buffalo. The assassin had lived through some and read about more of the hardships suffered by factory workers in America's Northern industrial belt at the end of the nineteenth century. He had also attended anarchist meetings, though his inscrutability had aroused suspicions there that he might be a police spy—perhaps adding to his desire to prove himself by some dramatic gesture. The writings and speeches of

Emma Goldman in particular impressed him, as did a brief interview he had with her in Chicago during the summer of 1901. There is no suspicion that the fiery apostle of anarchism sought to incite him to violence; on the contrary, she expressed only grief at the outcome. For Czolgosz, however, the message of his times was clear, and the operative conclusion inescapable. "I don't believe in the Republican form of government and I don't believe we should have any rulers. It is right to kill them," he told attending alienists after the event, adding at another point: "I fully understood what I was doing ... I am willing to take the consequences."[24] He went calmly to the electric chair barely six weeks after his victim's death.

Equally convinced of the justice of their cause, and no less willing to die for it were Griselio Torresola and Oscar Collazo when they packed their bags in New York City, said goodbye to their wives, and took a train to Washington.[25] The next morning, October 31 1950, they strolled around Blair House, the temporary presidential residence across Pennsylvania Avenue from the White House during the latter's extensive restoration. After lunch they went to their modest hotel for the pistols they had left there, caught a taxi back to Blair House, and after separating so that they could approach its entrance from opposite directions, launched their attack. It was at best a makeshift operation, but it took the life of one member of the unsuspecting security force, injured two others, and ended with Torresola lying dead beside the ornamental shrubbery. Collazo got close to the front door but collapsed there as a result of wounds from which he shortly recovered. The danger of a still more serious outcome had been increased when President Truman thrust his head out of a second-floor bedroom window where his nap had been interrupted by the commotion.

There was no evidence that the President was an object of particular hostility on the part of Torresola and Collazo. He was, however, a symbol of United States dominance in Puerto Rico, where just the day before a serious uprising by members of the Nationalist Party had erupted in several places. Like their equally zealous wives and a number of friends in New York, the two amateur gunmen were convinced that "North Americans" did not appreciate the depth of Puerto Rican opposition to territorial status or to any intermediate form of home rule. Only a stunning demonstration would make the point. Six weeks before the Washington attack Torresola, who had been in the United States for two years (unlike Collazo, who had lived in New York since 1937), had gone back to the home island for a meeting with the Nationalist leader Albizu Campo. He returned with letters confirming his "leadership of the Movement in the United States" (Campo's words).[26] Neither attacker counted on surviving. Collazo did so, only to be sentenced to death by a court in Washington. His intended victim granted him executive clemency, commuting the sentence to life imprisonment. And in 1979 President Carter abruptly ordered that he be released from prison, along with the Puerto Rican Nationalists convicted in 1954 of the shooting affray in the Capitol that left five congressmen wounded. Jubilantly, amid vows to continue the battle, Collazo and three of the freed "heroes of House Gallery 11" flew home to San Juan.

Less clearly recognized, largely because at his trial both prosecution and defense seemed intent on conceding his impaired mentality, was the nationalist fanaticism of Sirhan Sirhan, killer of Robert F. Kennedy in the early hours of June 6, 1968. Like Governor Wallace in 1972, the senator from New York was a strong contender for the Democratic presidential nomination, probably the strongest in view of his success in the previous day's California primary voting. It was the emergence of this "middle Kennedy" as a possible next president of the United States that seems to have crystallized Sirhan's decision to strike a blow for his lost Palestinian homeland by keeping the man he saw as Israel's champion out of the Oval Office.[27]

Robert Kennedy's twenty-four-year-old slayer had not only seen but personally experienced, in the course of a literally blasted childhood before his family emigrated to America, more of the tragedy behind the grievances he expressed than had any previous assassin in this country with the possible exception of Czolgosz. Sirhan's hatred of Israel was deep, and his animus toward Kennedy, an assiduous bidder for Jewish votes from New York to California, while of more recent origin was sharply focused. Even the future killer's fragmentary and repetitive notebook entries written over a period of several months need not have been treated as a number of psychiatrists treated them: as evidence of hopeless insanity. Assuming a mixture of ethnic fanaticism and vindictive hatred in their author's personality, they can with equal plausibility be read as proving that he was consciously employing mind-control exercises to focus his resolve—and incidentally to prepare for confounding his interrogators after the event. Mind control, after all, had been what interested him most about the West Coast Rosicrucian group he had joined not long before the assassination.

In the foregoing, I have tried to illustrate the many combinations of delusional, obsessive, and rational behavior exhibited by individuals guilty of lethal assaults upon major American political figures. I have not suggested that in all of these cases mental disorder was decisive in causing murderous action, although it clearly played that role in some of them. When we reflect on the distance separating the perceptions and degrees of criminal responsibility of Guiteau or Schrank from those of Czolgosz or Sirhan, there is no choice but to abandon comfortable generalization in favor of careful differentiation. It might be convenient, but it would not be correct to conclude simply that "they were all mad."

Centers of Controversy: Weiss, Oswald, and Ray

The assassinations of Senator Huey P. Long, President John F. Kennedy, and Dr. Martin Luther King, Jr., have been omitted from the preceding discussion. This is because to an extent unmatched by any of the other twentieth-century American cases, and by none of the earlier ones save that of Abraham Lincoln, all three remain subjects of debate concerning motives as well as responsibilities and offer no promise of consensual agreement in the near future. In addition, they have all given rise to "conspiracy theories" varying a great deal in their degrees of credibility. Nevertheless, the episodes in Baton Rouge, Dallas, and Memphis must be looked at in markedly individual terms, for their distinguishing features are at least as important as their similarities.

The problem with respect to Dr. Carl Austin Weiss, the twenty-nine-year-old physician who shot Huey Long to death in a corridor of the Louisiana state capitol building on September 10, 1935, centers almost exclusively on his motivation. Only a few of the large number of the victim's constituents who initially believed that someone else had killed him seem to have clung to that opinion, so Weiss himself remains the principal object of ongoing debate.[28] A quiet, intelligent, and sternly moral young man, raised in a strict German Catholic household and happily married to a wife who had given birth to their first child (a son) only three months before the assassination, Weiss seemed the most unlikely of political assassins. Since he was killed on the spot by his victim's bodyguards, he was never interrogated or observed after the event, leaving the field open to those fascinated by the question Why did he do it?

Some of the answers suggested in the course of the past half-century have attributed to Weiss the traits of a pure tyrannicide, joined in spirit to the Austrian Friedrich Adler before him or the slayer of Admiral Darlan, still to come in 1942. For Oscar Jászi this was so because in his eyes Louisiana's "Kingfish" had been "a genuine tyrant of the classic type," an unscrupulous rabble-rouser and blackmailer who had "destroyed a superficially rooted constitution by ruse and corruption."[29] Despite the assassin's well-attested probity and unselfishness, another and less exclusively idealistic motive has won increasing credence among students of the region and the period until now it may enjoy more support than does any alternative hypothesis: namely, that Weiss had been chosen by lot from among a group of conspirators nursing various personal grievances. Even this explanation, however, fails to account for the assassin's observed behavior prior to the shooting. There remains only one alternative, at once simpler and more plausible in the circumstances.

Huey Long was hostile to Weiss's father-in-law, the influential Judge Benjamin Pavy of St. Landry and Evangeline parishes, and to the judge's brother, a member of the state legislature. Both of these French-Louisianan politicians were destined to be broken by the Long machine soon after its leader's death. But what, one might reasonably ask, had this family feud to do with the seemingly impulsive murder committed by a man who only hours before he drew a pistol in the capitol had appeared relaxed and cheerfully looking forward to a normal, indeed highly successful life? The answer, if there is only one, was advanced shortly after the assassination by an undoubted expert on Louisiana politics and further developed by the author of a more recent study concerned with such matters.[30] It is that Long, determined to drive the Pavy brothers out of their respective offices and not satisfied to rely solely on the tactic of gerrymandering, which he had already set in motion to that end, was about to carry out his privately uttered threat to "tarbrush them" as he had other opponents in the past. That is, the state's dominant political figure was about to make use of the news media under his control to launch the story that the Pavy family tree included one or more blacks.

Given the place and time, this would have been disastrous to the public careers of Judge Pavy and his brother. It also would have damaged the prospects of their descendants, including the three-month-old Weiss grandson. On the very evening of the killing the child's father could have heard confirmation of a forthcoming newspaper article featuring the racial allegations and reacted not necessarily out of furious impulse but certainly without long-matured premeditation, using a gun he kept in his car for protection when making medical calls late at night. That hypothesis might explain the apparently sincere incredulity of his family and friends at hearing him charged with a cold-blooded shooting. His earlier enmity toward Huey Long had, in the opinion of those who knew him best, been strong but general, and more intellectual than passionate. The "tarbrush theory" fits the historical circumstances in suggesting what it was that produced homicidal intent and suicidal resolve.

The debate over Long's possible plot against the Pavy family and Carl Weiss's reaction will probably never end, but it can no longer be seriously equated in terms of magnitude with that over President Kennedy's murder in Dallas on November 22, 1963. Yet even in that case the range of disputed issues has narrowed considerably over the course of the past couple of decades. This is the result not so much of public fatigue and indifference as of a profoundly felt need on the part of millions of people to believe in one or another complex explanation of the event, in itself so brutally simple, having slowly yielded to the pressure of evidence—or the lack of it.[31]

The event posed a series of challenging questions. How did John Kennedy's death affect American involvement in Vietnam? What would the record of the Kennedy administration have been, had its leader survived and been reelected to serve out a second term? To what extent did his slaying set the tone for one of the grimmest and most desperate decades in American history? All of these belong quite properly to the contemplation of murder in relation to politics. Yet none of the problems looms larger in difficulty or significance than does that of assessing public states of mind. And among the social-psychological issues involved, that of the urgent "need to believe" in some sort of conspiracy, remarked by innumerable observers then and since, has a special relevance to the theme of this book.

Part of the explanation for the yearning to complicate must be sought in a feeling of intolerable disproportion between the magnitude of what had happened and the incongruous jumble of personal impulses, timing, and geographical accident on which its narrative appeared to depend. Three shots from a mail-order Mannlicher-Carcano rifle, fired from a warehouse window at a passing motorcade, seemed unequal to the historic responsibility of having precipitated a massive political crisis and never-to-be-forgotten national shock. Added to the initial sense of outrage at seeing childish mischief elevated to high tragedy was the almost unbelievable sight of the sole suspect's own death the following day at the hands of yet another embodiment of opaque malice performing for the television cameras. Finally there has to be considered the desire of many if not all helpless onlookers to find an answer not only bearable in terms of due proportion but also reassuring in terms of their respective political leanings.

Lee Harvey Oswald insisted proudly that he was a Marxist, and the record showed that he had lived in the USSR for more than two and a half years prior to returning to the United States in June 1962. He had distributed pro-Castro literature on the streets of New Orleans, defended its contents on television, and tried unsuccessfully to secure a visa to enter Cuba by way of Mexico. At the very least, conservatives were quick to register relief that no reactionary businessman or Klansman seemed to be implicated. Thus, in a novel by John Updike, admittedly more concerned with suburban sin than with politics, one affluent character telephones another on the afternoon of November 22 (both having known of the assassination for several hours) to ask: "Did you hear? It wasn't one of ours, it was one of *theirs!*"[32] On the other hand, the American left was quick to insist that Kennedy's worst enemies had not been on its side of the ideological barricades and even quicker to begin production of librettos in which the finger of suspicion swung from big business to the FBI and CIA all the way to the former vice-president, and back again. The list of conspiracy theories was long and varied enough to offer something for nearly everyone. For less intensely political citizens the Mafia and other personifications of organized crime supplied a tempting alternative, especially since both Oswald and Jack Ruby, who shot him, were easier to envisage as nervous hit men than as subtle assassins.

When on January 2, 1979, the Select Committee on Assassinations of the United States House of Representatives, Louis Stokes, Ohio, chairman, presented a summary of its conclusions and recommendations, the opening paragraph came as a surprise. This document, as well as the full report which followed in March, had been prepared by a large staff, assisted by scores of technical consultants, under the overall direction of Chief Counsel G. Robert Blakey, who made no secret of his personal belief that the murder of John F. Kennedy, like that of Martin Luther King, Jr., had been the work of a major conspiracy.[33] Nevertheless, the committee introduced its findings on the Dallas tragedy with the following laconic sentences:

A. Lee Harvey Oswald fired three shots at President John F. Kennedy. The second and third shots he fired struck the President. The third shot he fired killed the President.

1. President Kennedy was struck by two rifle shots fired from behind him.

2. The shots that struck President Kennedy from behind him were fired from the sixth floor window of the southeast corner of the Texas School Book Depository building.

3. Lee Harvey Oswald owned the rifle that was used to fire the shots from the sixth floor window of the southeast corner of the Texas School Book Depository building.

4. Lee Harvey Oswald, shortly before the assassination, had access to and was present on the sixth floor of the Texas School Book Depository building.

5. Lee Harvey Oswald's other actions tend to support the conclusion that he assassinated President Kennedy.[34]

It is essential for the purposes of this book to keep clearly in mind the nature of the source just quoted. Its five-point summary does not come from the Warren Commission of 1963–64, accused by some of having dismissed too quickly the crime's possible complexities in its eagerness to reassure the country, while facilitating President Johnson's assumption of power.[35] It is the report of a later task force, seemingly determined to keep alive any possibility of a conspiratorial explanation. By agreeing to issue its list of basic conclusions, the Select Committee of 1976–1979 may not have achieved all its chief counsel had hoped, but it did sweep away as cleanly as any document could a fifteen-year accumulation of discredited evidence—ballistic, acoustical, and mnemonic—as well as a mass of fervently, and often profitably, disseminated theories devised with varying degrees of reference to such evidence.

Not all the criticism of the Warren Commission's findings deserve to be lumped together with the products of the "conspiracy seminars" and tendentious theorizing characteristic of the 1960s and early 1970s in particular. Edward Jay Epstein's book on the subject, published two years after the commission released its report, was a serious and thought-provoking attempt to point out the latter's procedural and conceptual shortcomings and to ask the kind of questions that would have arisen had Lee Harvey Oswald lived to stand trial.[36] (Jack Ruby's still not fully explained shooting of the accused assassin in the Dallas police station was referred to repeatedly by Epstein but does not figure prominently in his bill of particulars, save with respect to the puzzling treatment of that bizarre epilogue by members of the Warren Commission's staff.)

For the historian, who bears a responsibility different from that of either a prosecutor or a defense attorney, part of the difficulty lies in the fundamental difference between historical and judicial inquiry. Neither the historian nor the lawyer can lay claim to absolute and final truth. Both must rely on fallible human intelligence to make what it can of incomplete, conflicting, and seldom fully or uniformly credible testimony. The goal of a murder trial is to arrive at a verdict of guilty or not guilty, after counsel for both sides have exploited to the limit every possible means of establishing or undermining proof of guilt beyond a reasonable doubt. For the defenders of an accused killer, this means probing any alternative hypothesis to the limits of imagination, exploiting every flaw in the prosecution's case, whether substantive or procedural, and making full use of the mind's propensity for playing with "what if's," intriguing possibilities perhaps not very plausible or closely related to the apparent facts but nonetheless conceivable. The jury's decision may be reached with none of its members convinced by more than a margin of 51 to 49 percent; but once the decision has been recorded, barring later reversal, the final score for legal purposes is 100 to nothing.

Historical truth in the same case is not determined by the institutional requirement that it be announced, flatly, at a given point. Instead, it is truly "the daughter of time," in the sense that it is subject forever to possible revision in the light of new evidence not available to the framers of previous conclusions. The search is potentially endless; it is at any rate open-minded. There may be a temptation to say that because we don't know everything, we really don't know anything—we shall have to wait. That, however, seems irresponsible when discussing the meaning of major assassinations, the public understanding of which may, to a greater or lesser degree, influence the way in which other large political issues are addressed. With respect to the Kennedy tragedy, it seems not only sensible but also honest to conclude that the slain president really was the victim of a neurotic loner who needed no conspiracy to ghostwrite his essentially trivial scenario. That explanation may someday be proven inadequate, but such a reversal would demand additional information of a kind not accessible today, quite possibly because it does not exist.

One word more must be said about the findings of the Select Committee on Assassinations of the U.S. House of Representatives. Having laid out the five points contained in their opening paragraph, quoted already, the members proceeded to approve two more sections, summarizing in an obviously ambiguous fashion the conclusions they and their staff had reached regarding a number of other much-debated matters:

B. Scientific acoustical evidence establishes a high probability that two gunmen fired at President John F. Kennedy. Other scientific evidence does not preclude the possibility of two gunmen firing at the President. Scientific evidence negates some specific conspiracy allegations.

C. The Committee believes, on the basis of the evidence available to it, that President John F. Kennedy was probably assassinated as a result of a conspiracy. The committee is unable to identify the other gunman or the extent of the conspiracy.

1. The committee believes, on the basis of the evidence available to it [a qualification repeated in each of the ensuing three sentences], that the Soviet Government was not involved in the assassination of President Kennedy.

2. The committee believes . . . that the Cuban Government was not involved in the assassination of President Kennedy.

3. The committee believes . . . that anti-Castro Cuban groups, as groups, were not involved in the assassination of President Kennedy, but that the available evidence does not preclude the possibility that individual members may have been involved.

4. The committee believes . . . that the national syndicate of organized crime, as a group, was not involved in the assassination of the President, but that the available evidence does not preclude the possibility that individual members may have been involved.

5. The Secret Service, Federal Bureau of Investigation and the Central Intelligence Agency were not involved in the assassination of President Kennedy.[37]

With all due regard for the select committee's even-handedness in deciding that the preceding list of possible suspects should be ruled out, while at the same time asserting that the President was the victim of a conspiracy, these sections, when examined in conjunction with those in Section A seem, to me at least, to pose three serious difficulties. The first arises from the staff's apparently unshaken confidence in now discredited acoustical evidence (see Section B), despite the fact that some sounds originally thought to be gunfire have been proved to be the noise of gasoline engine backfires, and in some cases to have been recorded on tape far from the scene and possibly not at the time of the fatal shooting. The second point has to do with the seeming contradiction between the disclaimer contained in the second sentence of the preamble to Section C and the insistence, under subsections 3 and 4 that individual anti-Castro Cubans and/or representatives of organized crime "may have been involved." Third, and most puzzling, is the entire drift of the argument in the two sections taken as a whole, namely, that given a lack of crucial evidence and a sufficient accumulation of suspicions found by the committee to be individually unconvincing, one can arrive at a general probability that a conspiracy was the murder's efficient cause, and two presumably strong possibilities with respect to its membership. Clearly, the need in some quarters to believe in a "Kennedy conspiracy" is tenacious enough to survive any inquiry.

The murder of Dr. Martin Luther King, Jr., having been bracketed with that of President Kennedy in the congressional charge to Representative Stokes's committee in 1976, there was a tendency to assume that handling of the two cases would be similar and that the same misgivings would be excited by both. To believe so would be a great mistake. Although the two treatments reveal a strong predisposition in favor of conspiratorial explanation, their treatment of the evidence and of plausible uses of it are markedly different.

The famous black civil rights leader was fatally shot while standing on the balcony outside his second-floor room at the Lorraine Motel, where he was staying during a visit to Memphis, Tennessee. At London's Heathrow Airport sixty-five days later the most-wanted American fugitive, James Earl Ray, was arrested by British police and after brief but by no means perfunctory extradition proceedings was returned to the jurisdiction of the Criminal Court of Shelby County, Tennessee. There, on the strong urging of his attorney, Percy Foreman of Houston, Texas (who had volunteered his services), Ray pleaded guilty to first-degree murder and was sentenced, without a jury but in accordance with the prosecution's recommendation, not to death, as permitted by law, but to imprisonment for ninety-nine years in the state penitentiary.

The opening sections of the House committee's preliminary summary of findings read as follows:

A. James Earl Ray fired one shot at Dr. Martin Luther King, Jr. The shot killed Dr. King.

1. Dr. King was killed by one rifle shot fired from in front of him.

2. The shot that killed Dr. King was fired from the bathroom window in the rear of a roominghouse at 422½ South Main Street, Memphis, Tenn.

3. James Earl Ray purchased the rifle that was used to shoot Dr. King and transported it from Birmingham, Ala. to Memphis, Tenn., where he rented a room at 422½ South Main Street, and moments after the assassination, he dropped it near 424 South Main Street.

4. It is highly probable that James Earl Ray stalked Dr. King for a period immediately preceding the assassination.

5. James Earl Ray fled the scene of the crime immediately after the assassination.

6. James Earl Ray's alibi for the time of the assassination, his story of "Raoul," and other exculpatory evidence are not worthy of belief.

7. James Earl Ray knowingly, intelligently, and voluntarily pleaded guilty to the first degree murder of Dr. King.

B. The committee believes, on the basis of the circumstantial evidence available to it, that there is a likelihood that James Earl Ray assassinated Dr. Martin Luther King as a result of a conspiracy.

C. The committee believes, on the basis of the evidence available to it, that no private organizations or individuals, other than those discussed under Section B, were involved in the assassination of Dr. King.

D. No Federal, State or local government agency was involved in the assassination of Dr. King.[38]

Having placed these conclusions on record, the committee summarized (under Section B, as mentioned in Finding C, above) its investigation of no fewer than ten different sets of allegations purporting to implicate a considerable list of possible conspirators in the death of Dr. King, ranging from the Minutemen and the United Klans of America to representatives of organized crime including Sam Giancana and Carlos Gambino.[39] None of these possibilities, in the opinion of the staff and members, was supported by enough evidence to warrant charges that Ray had been involved with any of the organizations or individuals named.

What the committee did consider worth reporting was the likelihood that Ray had acted in conjunction with, or at the instigation of, members of the conspiracy discussed at length in the full text.[40] It was, if it existed at all, a very limited conspiracy, hardly comparable to the intricate constructions found in most conspiratorial fantasies of the period. It appears to have been a family affair, financed by a handful of outsiders. Therein, however, lies part of its plausibility. It does not posit elaborate connections with unlikely figures, but confines itself to providing a rationale for the assassin's behavior before and after the crime.

The reasons for doubting that Ray acted entirely on his own can be reduced to four. First, although the "Raoul" to whom the killer repeatedly alluded left no fingerprints or other discernible traces, such as sightings by witnesses, there is plentiful evidence that Ray was in regular contact with accomplices—specifically two of his brothers—beginning before his escape from the Missouri State Penitentiary in April 1967 and continuing throughout the ensuing year, much of which he devoted to planning the murder. Such evidence recurs constantly in the reconstruction of his jail break, the lucrative robbery of the bank in his home town of Alton, Illinois, and his extensive but seemingly purposeful travels, from Montreal to Los Angeles and a number of Southern cities, always keeping in touch with his brothers. Second, despite the efforts by two authors to prove the opposite, neither a desire for fame nor an all-consuming racial hatred has been convincingly established as Ray's basic motive.[41] Third, what does emerge from his record and from his behavior following the crime suggests that he was, in the words of the committee's report, "a financially motivated criminal," whose frequent scrapes with the law, like those of his brothers, John and Jerry, regularly involved lucrative crimes. Fourth, the most probable source of funds to be offered in payment for the killing of Dr. King can be identified in the person and associates of John Sutherland, a wealthy, eccentric St. Louis businessman, represented on good authority to have been active in nostalgic Southern causes and deeply antipathetic to any such public figure as Martin Luther King.

According to testimony which, if far from conclusive, is not easily dismissed, Sutherland had for some time let it be known through St. Louis underworld contacts with easy access to the Ray brothers that fifty thousand dollars would be easily earned by performing certain services. The notion that these consisted of the killing of Dr. King and keeping it simple fits what is known of Ray's attitudes far better than it would have those of Lee Harvey Oswald or Sirhan Sirhan. It also fits the assassin's determined and by no means hopeless effort to escape after firing his single fatal bullet at the balcony of the Lorraine Motel. Finally, assuming that he and his brothers were cheated of the reward once King was killed, it would help to explain the convicted killer's backtracking on his hasty plea of guilty and the not very heavily veiled threats of disclosure uttered by all three brothers at various times since his incarceration.

There is no discernible prospect of confirming the now famous "Byers evidence" concerning the St. Louis links and personalities. Both John Sutherland and John Kauffmann, the other principal suspect, had died—the former in 1970, the latter in 1974—well before this evidence was made public. J. Edgar Hoover's FBI, though it worked hard to capture the assassin in 1968, was apparently subject to no great pressure from above to pursue its prisoner's connections any further. In any event, the statute of limitations has long since intervened to preclude any judicial pursuit of alleged conspirators.

Official Connections

Throughout this book the roles placed by wielders of public power have intertwined with the acts of their opponents, whether rebels, competing peers, or psychopaths. The record of the United States is no exception. Indeed, Americans often find themselves speculating as to whether politial homicide in one form or another is not the work of their government as much as of its enemies. Before embracing too quickly the suspicions and inferences of an anti-authoritarian tradition, however, we should ask what the relationship is between constitutional guarantees and the application of violence. Hard-pressed regimes such as those of present-day Italy and the German Federal Republic have had to ponder that question. How could the United States hope to avoid it?

The state, in theory if not in fact, holds a monopoly over the supreme expression of purposeful violence, the waging of war. In addition, not only do the citizens of a republic concede to it the power to threaten force in order to protect them from criminals, to collect taxes, and to enforce the civil rights of groups and individuals, but its failure to do so would, like the appearance of private armies, be greeted as an intolerable failure of government. In short, the same act of authority may appear tyrannical in spirit and unlawful in form or it may seem an intervention of might on the side of right, depending on the aims and values of the citizen doing the judging in each particular instance.

In terms of this study lethal violence touches the United States government in three principal ways (apart from military hostilities). First, and most obviously, the majority of victims of assassination attempts have been incumbent officials, in the past usually attacked within the national boundaries though of late sacrificed with increasing frequency while on active service abroad. Second, there is the matter of judicial proceedings seen, by some observers at least, as political trials and capable, if capital punishment is involved, of eliciting cries of judicial murder. Third, the "special operations" of security and intelligence agencies invite scrutiny by an uneasy populace and its elected representatives.

Earlier in this chapter and in the table in Chapter 13 attention was drawn to the sharp fluctuations in frequency of lethal assaults on politically significant individuals, American peaks having occurred in the years 1865–1881 and in the 1960s and 1970s. That configuration, however, does not hold true as clearly for "presidential-level" assassination attempts as it does for a broader but still restricted listing of such victims as Louisiana justices Chase and Gray, killed in 1868, or San Francisco's Mayor George Moscone and Supervisor Harvey Milk, fatally shot by an embittered ex-supervisor in 1978. The variety of motives has rivaled that of targets, though there are concentrations of regional hostility after the Civil War and of gangland-type interventions during the Prohibition era.

Beginning in the 1960s and continuing since, slaying of Americans on diplomatic, military, or international service abroad has assumed a previously unknown importance. There were of course scattered episodes from about the turn of the century onward, but nothing to compare with the murders of British colonial officials in India prior to the First World War or French in North Africa during the 1950s. Noteworthy in the series of assassinations of U.S. diplomats in key positions was the fatal shooting of John G. Mein, ambassador to Guatemala, in 1968, by gunmen believed to be acting for the pro-Cuban Revolutionary Armed Forces. Then came the death of Rodger P. Davies, ambassador to Cyprus, killed on August 19, 1974, during a demonstration by Greek Cypriots outside the embassy. Less than five years later, in February 1979, Adolph Dubs, ambassador to Afghanistan, was fatally wounded in Kabul when a government assault team attempted to free him from the control of Muslim extremists who had kidnaped and were holding him prisoner.

The roll thereafter includes a mounting total of foreign service officers, together with other Americans singled out by virtue of their business, educational, or in some cases U.S.-related activities. Military commanders—General Maxwell D. Taylor twice (Korea in 1955, Vietnam in 1965), NATO Commander Alexander M. Haig near his headquarters at Mons, Belgium, in 1965, General James Dozier, rescued from Red Brigade abductors in Rome in 1981—had better than average luck, though a number of officers ranking below the top echelon have fared less well in Europe, Latin America, and elsewhere.

In most parts of the world a marked increase in the number of political assassinations has either accompanied or soon followed the proliferation of autonomous political regimes—in Latin America during the nineteenth century, in eastern Europe after 1918, in Asia and Africa since the end of World War II. The experience of the United States has been, if only in this one respect, very nearly unique. It has comprised the growth of big government, occurring at several different levels but always, especially since the Civil War, within a single national framework, with rising stakes and an audience growing from millions to tens of millions, to more than two hundred million citizens. Seen in that light, the mounting number of casualties among American representatives abroad becomes comprehensible as part of the price paid for the latest expansion of power. the adoption of a world role, and the enemies that come with it.

The second issue mentioned, the place of courts of law in the sometimes deadly game of politics, turns out to be less imposing than might have been supposed. Because the United States Constitution explicitly forbids passage of any bill of attainder, that early modern English device for arrogating to the legislature quasi-judicial power to condemn an official to death on essentially political grounds has played no part in this country's history since the Revolution. There has, accordingly, been no widespread practice of bringing defeated leaders to trial before regular criminal courts. The crucial test in this regard was the inability of the victorious North to prosecute Jefferson Davis, ex-president of the Confederacy after 1865, despite charges by some federal officials that, in addition to having betrayed the Republic. he had been directly implicated in Lincoln's assassination. Here again a constitutional prohibition played a major part, by requiring that a treason case be brought before a jury in the state, Virginia in this case, where the crime was alleged to have been committed. Davis was released on bail in 1867 and never tried on any count.[42]

"Political trials" in the United States have tended to be court cases in which the defendants claimed to be victims of politics or were at least seen as such by a large number of Americans. One such was Mary Surratt, hanged as an accomplice of John Wilkes Booth in July 1865. Others have included Nicola Sacco and Bartolomeo Vanzetti, convicted in 1921 of having murdered a factory paymaster and a guard during a payroll robbery in South Braintree, Massachusetts, on April 15, 1920, and finally executed in 1927, after prolonged hearings and numerous demonstrations in their favor. Most impassioned and persistent among charges of judicial murder, however, have been those leveled against the trial judge, the United States Supreme Court, and the President of the United States in the case of Julius and Ethel Rosenberg, culminating in their execution at Ossining, New York, in 1953 for the crime of conspiracy to commit espionage.

A distinction that must be drawn in both the Surratt and the Sacco-Vanzetti cases is one separating the issue of guilt or innocence per se from that of the justification for applying the death penalty. (The same question arises with respect to the Rosenbergs, but there the belief in their complete innocence has been limited to a relatively small number of commentators.) Certain historians, notably Dewitt in his emotional attack on Secretary Stanton, have argued that Mrs. Surratt was ignorant of the conspiracy to kidnap or to assassinate President Lincoln.[43] Many more argue that it is reasonable to assume some guilty knowledge, derived from her son John, Booth's closest associate in the undertaking, and more especially from conspiratorial meetings held first in her Maryland tavern ten miles outside Washington, then in the boardinghouse she set up on H Street in the capitol five months before the murder. Nevertheless, the degree of her involvement was never established by clear proof, and her being sentenced to death rather than imprisonment (like four of the other eight defendants) seems inexplicable save in terms of the grief and fury enveloping public as well as official opinion in the North.[44]

The problem with regard to Sacco and Vanzetti is more acute because the lines remain sharply drawn between those who believe that, irrespective of their Italian immigrant background and anarchist connections, they were guilty of murder in the first degree, and those who are convinced that they were innocent men hounded to their deaths because of their political beliefs in an era of intense anti-anarchist feeling. No attempt will be made here to pass judgment on the conviction as such, for there is no new evidence upon which to base a further revision of the mountainous literature dealing with the subject. Testimony offered in 1925 by a condemned hoodlum to the effect that not they, but a criminal gang of which they knew nothing, had committed the killings has been neither confirmed nor disproved. A three-man commission, comprising a retired judge and the presidents of Harvard University and Massachusetts Institute of Technology, advised Massachusetts Governor A. T. Fuller that in its opinion there would not be grounds for any grant of clemency on his part—in other words, that the condemned men were guilty as charged. The commission's members were "establishment types," in the words of their critics, but they were not known as vindictive Red-baiters and surely not as docile conformists. The aura of tragedy surrounding the episode results in part from its conclusion, after seven years of tortuous delays, and in part from the painful realization that no criminal case can be decided solely on its legal merits once these are engulfed in a flood of partisan rhetoric.[45]

That realization was destined to return with even greater force when the Rosenberg affair broke upon the nation in 1950. On March 6, 1951, in the United States District Court of New York, Judge Irving R. Kaufman presiding, Julius Rosenberg, his wife, Ethel, and their alleged accomplice, Morton Sobell, went on trial for conspiring to commit espionage. Although they had been indicted for having passed information to Soviet agents over the course of six years, the most sensational count was that in 1944 and 1945 they delivered top secret data concerning the as yet untested uranium atomic bomb. This information, according to the prosecution, had been obtained from Mrs. Rosenberg's brother David Greenglass, a machinist employed by the Manhattan Project in Los Alamos, New Mexico, and thereafter turned over to one Harry Gold, convicted in 1950 of complicity with the English atomic spy Klaus Fuchs.

The timing of the trial, opening a year and a half after the first nuclear explosion in Russia and nine months after the North Korean invasion of South Korea, guaranteed that the proceedings would be surrounded by intense public fear and indignation. Greenglass, the government's key witness, escaped with a sentence of fifteen years of which he served ten. On April 15, 1951, the jury having reached a verdict of guilty after several hours of deliberation, Judge Kaufman pronounced sentence on the three principal defendants. Sobell was given thirty years in prison. Both Rosenbergs were sentenced to death. On June 19, 1953, they were electrocuted, after a series of unsuccessful appeals by their attorneys and a public campaign on their behalf unmatched even by the uproar surrounding the Sacco-Vanzetti case.[46]

The Rosenbergs were not, prior to their arrest anyway, prominent national figures. Nevertheless, their trial assumed a major place in the political record of the United States after World War II and during the earliest, most emotional phase of the Cold War that succeeded it. What makes the trial and execution of the Rosenbergs important for a book concerned with death and politics is precisely the difficulties it posed for moderate observers striving to arrive at a fair conclusion. Much of that difficulty arose, and still arises, from confusion over which of the separate issues implicit in the Rosenberg affair was being debated. First there is the inescapable question of guilty or innocent *intent*. Second, one must face the problem of assessing as objectively as possible the amount of damage done by the alleged espionage, assuming that it had in fact been committed. Third, taking into account both these matters, as well as the jury's finding of fact, there remains the query: Was the death penalty justified?

As for the question of guilt or innocence, several observations are in order. The federal jury which found the Rosenbergs guilty cannot have escaped the overheated public atmosphere of the time. Even in a calmer setting, however, it would have been difficult to ignore the evidence that Julius and Ethel Rosenberg did believe it essential to help the USSR in its efforts to meet the American "atomic threat," and that they had been recruited by Soviet agents employing tactics about whose reality no student of the period could have serious doubts. A review of the voluminous bibliography does not leave one with the impression that the jury's verdict has been as seriously challenged by either legal or scientific experts as have other aspects of the affair. A balanced and painstaking study provides the following conclusion:

> Julius and Ethel Rosenberg and their accomplices were so captive to their blind adulation of Stalinist Russia that they failed to perceive the true implications of their espionage, much less to comprehend how their actions would discredit the Left in the eyes of their fellow Americans. The Rosenbergs' accusers, on the other hand, were oblivious to the fact that the danger to national security from ideologically motivated amateur spies—already a vanishing breed by the time of the trial—was far less than the damage that would be done by allowing American justice to serve as a handmaiden to Cold War politics. Partisans on both sides were convinced that they held a monopoly on truth and that the end justified the means.[47]

What remains to be said about the penalty imposed in the Rosenberg case must begin with Judge Kaufman's summation in April 1953:

> Your crime is worse than murder . . . In commiting the act of murder, the criminal kills only his victim. The immediate family is brought to grief and when justice is meted out the chapter is closed. But in your case, I believe your conduct in putting into the hands of the Russians the A-bomb years before our best scientists predicted Russia would perfect the bomb has already caused the Communist aggression in Korea with the resulting casualties exceeding 50,000 Americans . . . Indeed, by your betrayal, you have altered the course of history to the disadvantage of our country.[48]

Concerning this estimate of what the defendants had achieved, Judge Kaufman's reference to "our best scientists" notwithstanding, there remain a number of unresolved doubts, the most serious centering on the real importance of the sketches made by Greenglass and delivered to the Rosenbergs.

It was difficult for independent observers to argue this point at the time of judgment or for many years thereafter, since the courtroom exhibits were impounded following the trial and kept secret on grounds of security. When in 1966 the Greenglass notes were at last made available by court order and submitted by Morton Sobell's lawyers to several nuclear scientists, two of the latter concluded that the documents contained numerous errors and omissions, and as a result gave a "grossly false impression" of such crucial mechanisms as detonation by implosion. A third, Henry Linschitz, who had served on the Alamagordo research team, remarked about the supposedly decisive sketch by Greenglass: "It is not possible in any technologically useful way to condense the results of a two-billion dollar development effort into a diagram drawn by a high school graduate machinist on a single sheet of paper."[49]

Even assuming that the defendants were guilty and that their actions had been more damaging to their fellow citizens than the foregoing references suggest, there remains a third level of uncertainty. Judge Kaufman need not have imposed a sentence of death. Once he had done so, however, neither the United States Second Circuit Court of Appeals nor the Supreme Court saw fit to alter his decision. Both higher courts, the former in upholding the verdict of guilty, the latter in explaining its refusal to review the case, restricted themselves to the conduct of the trial, including the admissability of the evidence presented. In jurisprudential terms, such delimitation of what could and could not be appealed, pointedly excluding the ultimate sentence, was no doubt solidly based on precedent. The historian's conclusions, however, must take into account a wider range of possible objections and at least consider additional options. One thing seems clear: Had the Rosenbergs not been executed—Ethel Rosenberg as the first woman to die for a federal crime in almost ninety years—there would still have been protests against their conviction and legal efforts to secure their release from prison. But there could have been no cries of "murder."

The higher courts having declined to reconsider the death sentence, and the trial judge having refused to modify his decision, the possibility of commutation became solely a matter for the White House. Despite numerous appeals for clemency, including some published in the names of such distinguished physicists as Albert Einstein and Harold Urey, President Truman left office on January 20, 1953, without having taken action. Thus, the matter was left to his successor. Three weeks later, on February 11, President Eisenhower's response was announced to the news media in written form. It read in part:

> I have given earnest consideration to the records in the case of Julius and Ethel Rosenberg ... and am satisfied that they two individuals have been accorded their full measure of justice.
>
> There has been neither new evidence nor have there been mitigating

circumstances which would justify altering this decision, and I have determined that it is my duty, in the interest of people of the United States, not to set aside the verdict of their representatives.[50]

To a chief executive convinced, in the words used elsewhere in his statement, that the accused had "in fact betrayed the cause of freedom for which free men are fighting and dying at this hour," any other course of action would have been inconceivable. The Rosenbergs, however, had been found guilty neither of willful homicide nor, despite Judge Kaufman's strictures on the subject, of having directly caused the Korean War. That being so, the memory of their execution will continue to cast a long shadow across the history not so much of formal justice as of political discernment in the United States.

The final matter calling for attention under the rubric of "official connections" entails secret operations contemplated and sometimes apparently carried out by the United States Central Intelligence Agency, specifically by what in 1964 emerged under the title Covert Action (formerly Psychological and Paramilitary) Staff. Despite the information gleaned from the recollections of a substantial number of ex-KGB and other Soviet-bloc agents, supplemented by such books as Philip Agee's *Inside the Company,* the work of a former CIA official, confirmation of any assassination carried out at the behest of an identifiable national bureau, anywhere in the world, remains exceedingly difficult to document.[51] Even where the degree of probability is very high, as in murders allegedly directed from Tehran, Tripoli, and other capitals of nations making no great effort to hide their support of terrorism, hard proof in a particular case is rarely forthcoming.

To say that one knows little in detail is not to say that one knows nothing at all about trends and tendencies. There is no longer any serious doubt that political murder, during World War II selectively abetted by the British in the case of Reinhard Heydrich's assassination by the Czech underground and at least encouraged by American intelligence officers in that of the Twentieth of July conspiracy against Hitler, has come to occupy an assured place in the repertoire of today's shadow warriors, as they are called in the title of a recent book on the subject.[52] Clandestine operations, by their very nature and the mind set they encourage, invite a rich growth of fanciful theories, born of the "what would happen if?" mentality that is at a premium among secret planners. The trouble is that the same penchant manifests itself almost as frequently among people who write about them.

The shooting of Rafael Trujillo Molina, dictator of the Dominican Republic, on May 30, 1961, is a case in point. The Trujillo murder attracted wide attention at the time, partly because of the victim's despotic rule and his known unpopularity with the new Kennedy administration in Washington, but partly because the way in which he was slain, by seven assailants firing machine guns with which they were obviously very familiar, did not suggest the impulsive act of a Latin American tyrannicide.[53] The same event returned to public attention some fifteen years later, when Agee's book confirmed the multiplicity of "dirty tricks" proposed or attempted throughout his period of service with the CIA in Washington, Ecuador, Uruguay, and Mexico during the sixties. Although *Inside the Company* may have contributed to the resuscitation of old curiosity about the Trujillo case, however, it offers specific comment only about a quite different episode that occurred several months later in 1961. This was the arrest in Havana of Luis Toroella, subsequently executed for having plotted to kill Fidel Castro, according to Agee on orders from the CIA's Miami station.[54]

More complex in certain respects were the questions surrounding the South Vietnamese coup in early November 1963, which took the lives of President Ngo Dinh Diem and his brother Ngo Dinh Nhu, chief of security police and intelligence for the Republic of Vietnam. McGeorge Bundy, then special assistant to the president for national security, has given me permission to report his recollection of the episode. He still remembers most clearly President Kennedy's anger at the double assassination under circumstances that raised questions about a possible U.S. role in its background. It was no secret, especially in view of the growing distaste expressed in Washington for the brothers Dinh and their regime, that the administration reacted to the coup with some relief. The President, however, had forbidden any participation by American officials in their overthrow, let alone any physical action against them. Paraphrasing Kennedy's exasperated comments, Bundy recalls in particular his reference to King Henry II's famous line before the murder of Thomas Becket, approximately quoted as "Will no-one free me of this low-born priest?" The chief executive's conclusion appears to have been that it is not enough simply to issue a ban on dirty tricks—it must be repeated, emphatically, over and over.[55]

The most controversial experience of United States officials and the death of a foreign head of state in recent years grew out of the Chilean coup of September 11, 1973, in which President Salvador Allende Gossens was overthrown by a four-man military junta, as a result of which, according to the official account, he shot himself while barricaded in his office at Santiago's presidential palace. The controversy centers around two related but separable questions: Was the late president a suicide or was he killed by his enemies? What was the role of the United States government? The claim that Chile's beleaguered president took his own life rather than surrender was at first accepted even by his widow, according to statements she made before flying into exile in Mexico. Once there, however, and after talking with other survivors of the fallen regime, she repudiated that explanation and insisted that he would never have done such a thing. The alternative view, that he was shot down in cold blood during the army's seizure of his headquarters, has been adopted by virtually all émigré Chileans who oppose the Pinochet government still ruling their homeland. Such convictions became, if possible, even more fervent with the tragic death of Allende's former minister of foreign affairs, Letelier, on a Washington street in 1976.

Although good reason exists to be cautious about accepting the idea of Allende's suicide, certain responsible commentators on Chilean affairs give it credence, even while deploring the coup d'état.[56] There is less difference of opinion concerning the CIA's part in the program of destabilization carried out to increase the socialist Allende's troubles in the months and years preceding his overthrow. Agee, reflecting on the affair from his own place of exile, London, a month later, speaks of it as having increased his sense of urgency about publishing a book of revelations:

> Signs of preparations for the *coup* were clear all along. While economic assistance to Chile plummeted after Allende's election [in 1970], military aid continued: in 1972 military aid to the Chilean generals and admirals was the highest to any country in Latin America; the growth of the CIA station [in Santiago] . . . the murder of General Schneider [allegedly perpetrated in 1973 by opponents of Allende, but blamed on Marxist assassins as a provocation], the militancy of the well-heeled "patriotic" organizations such as Patria y Libertad; the economic sabotage; the truckers' strike of 1972 with the famous "dollar-per-day" to keep the strikers from working.[57]

This set of charges, written by a man already the self-appointed exposer of his erstwhile employers, as part of a passage which becomes more incoherent with emotion as it proceeds, is clearly not the last word on Allende's fate. Nevertheless, Agee's assumptions concerning Chile are fully consistent with his account of personal experience with covert operations in other Latin American countries. Furthermore, the same authority who accepts the suicide of a despairing Allende at the end credits without hesitation both the reality and purpose of official American efforts to destabilize his government prior to its downfall.[58] The point is not that the CIA or any other U.S. agency can be conclusively shown to have planned or even countenanced a murder which may in fact never have taken place. The point is that CIA tactics in general, including some that have never been denied by any official source, lend credence to charges that no thoughtful student of political violence can in conscience ignore.

Part of the purpose of this book has been to ask of world history whether assassination has shown itself to be good politics by either ethical or pragmatic standards. In case after case, with only the rarest exceptions, it has not. Its demonstrable tendency has nearly always been to besmirch the perpetrator's credentials, while undermining his chances of any lasting political success.

Conclusion:
Looking Backward
and Forward

A book such as this cannot end with finality greater than that of history itself. Too many unresolved puzzles and gaps in the available evidence remain to permit a smooth, tidy exit, with certainties set all in a row. If the bombing of the Sofia cathedral in 1925 had to wait until 1943 for Giorgi Dmitrov's authoritative confirmation of its authorship, small wonder that other riddles, among them the deaths of Martin Luther King, Jr., in 1968 and Salvador Allende in 1973, not to mention the shooting of Pope John Paul II in 1981, remain as yet unsolved. To leave the results of an inquiry provisional in some respects, however, is not to render it meaningless. If nothing else, each expedition of this kind leads to the establishment of new base camps, from which future quests for knowledge and understanding can be launched, using trails as yet unknown.

Many pages ago my Introduction raised some opening questions. Among them was one concerning the appropriateness of examining politics in the somber light of murder. What should by now be clear is that while assassination has generally failed to *direct* political change into predetermined channels, it has repeatedly demonstrated the capacity for affecting, often in the most drastic fashion, situations which, in the absence of lethal violence, might conceivably have developed very differently. Some of these interventions have seemed so fortuitous, so unrelated to rational grievances or purposes, as to deserve nothing better than inclusion among pure accidents of history, comparable to natural disasters, human illness and death by misadventure, chronological coincidence, and the like. On other occasions personalized violence has struck in the midst of an atmosphere so charged with hatred and foreboding that some such flash of deadly energy seemed then, and still seems in retrospect, all but inevitable. Whatever the variety of circumstances under which it has occurred, intentional homicide, committed for the purpose of seizing, retaining, or undermining power in the state, has been a chronic feature of political association itself.

It is no less important to acknowledge those intermittent remissions, periods in which assassination has been attempted with relative infrequency. The West has produced at least four notable respites of this kind: in mainland Greece throughout the otherwise turbulent fifth century B.C.; in Rome during roughly the first four hundred years of the Republic; in feudal Europe between about the mid-eleventh and early fourteenth centuries of the Christian era; and again in Europe from the middle of the seventeenth century until almost the end of the eighteenth. Other parts of the globe, including China and Black Africa in particular, appear to have produced comparable interludes, whatever other forms of violence those areas may have witnessed.

In practice this meant that a Roman consul of the third century before Christ had decidedly better prospects of living to a peaceful old age than did a Roman emperor four or five hundred years later, and that in a western or central European nation around 1700 a king had less reason to fear for his life, save possibly at the hands of his doctors, than had his great-grandfather. To what extent fluctuating rates of assassination have actually affected the willingness of qualified individuals to assume royal or ministerial power is hard to say, since throughout history the supply of candidates for high office has shown itself to be more constant than the number of people prepared to stab, poison, or shoot them. The record does show, however, that the human race is not incapable of doing better than it has done during its worse orgies of bloodshed and self-destruction.

A further question suggested by periodic peaks and valleys in the frequency curve for political murder is whether they correspond to any common characteristics worth noting. Do the "highs" reveal one set of institutional practices or social conditions (including popular attitudes) and the "lows" quite another? If so, do the correlations suggest any lessons for the future? If not, is it only because historians and social scientists have failed thus far to isolate the crucial variables?

It is easier to say what periods of rampant political murder were *not* than to identify relevant traits they appear to have had in common. Contrary to a good deal of recent belief, high assassination rates have not generally accompanied extremes of repression and perceived social injustice, any more than they have tended to coincide with major wars. That despotism at its most extreme has seldom paid the price for stifling freedom, though successor regimes may have, does not constitute a recommendation for that form of rule. It is simply an undeniable fact based on the records of great tyrannies, ancient and modern alike, at their respective pinnacles of power and self-confidence.

Conversely, assassination has burgeoned when such summits of autocracy have been passed, in times characterized by nervous concessions and partial reforms from above, of growing popular excitement, high expectations, and impatient demands for still more rapid change. With respect to individual motivation, such periods open long-neglected paths to power, inviting often ruthless competition among new aspirants hoping to ride waves of popularity. Thus, post-revolutionary, post-colonial, and postwar situations often have provided the most material for students of civil strife. The instances of nineteenth-century Europe (including Alexander II's Russia), Weimar Germany, Black Africa since about 1960, and most of the present-day Middle East come readily to mind.

Past remissions in political murder have not occurred in periods of release and intoxicating optimism nor have they been marked by the most pitiless repression. The latter may work for a time, but in most known societies not for an indefinite time; and even in those where it has, it is irrelevant to the discussion of a phenomenon, consensual restraint, which to have meaning must presuppose some degree of choice on the part of the ruled. Nor does the restraint appear to depend entirely on brilliant executives or busy legislatures, though sensible laws, leaders, courts, and citizens are obviously a great help. If one were to single out the most important characteristic shared by fifth-century Athens, the Roman Republic, the feudal monarchies of the high Middle Ages, and the governmental structures of the *ancien régime* in Europe, it would be no bad choice to settle on a certain quality of balance, as between authority and forebearance. This equilibrium between, on the one hand, a fairly high degree of respect for government as a social necessity and, on the other, the buffering effects of customary rights may not have been worked out in great theoretical detail in the minds of most contemporaries (the Greeks and Romans probably were more self-conscious in that sense than the later Europeans); but the benefits seem to have been appreciated.

One of the many corollaries, elusive but arresting in its implications, was an atypically high degree of awareness within each of the successive ruling groups concerning both its prerogatives and its responsibilities—abused as these often were by selfish men—combined with self-imposed limitations on personal aggrandizement. At the popular level, whatever dissatisfaction there may have been with things as they were, there appears also to have been a prevailing assumption that acts of violence offered no promising solution. The resulting compromises proved to be less than everlasting, yielding in time to the combined effects of economic and demographic change, external reverses, new aspirations, perhaps simple boredom. Yet while they lasted, they created institutional monuments still intriguing to contemplate.

A quite different question posed at the beginning of this book had to do with the relative importance throughout history of individual assassins acting alone or in small groups, as distinct from extended conspiracies. No conclusive comparison of these patterns is feasible, but conspiracy is certainly not the more common one despite the eagerness of many observers to find elaborate collusion even in cases where little or no evidence for it exists. In a clear minority of cases evidence of plots has turned up belatedly where previously there had seemed to be none. Far more often, however, ingenious conspiratorial explanations have failed for lack of confirmation.

The preponderance of individual actors over cabals has been most pronounced in cases of successful assassination. Reasons for this are as apparent now as they were to Machiavelli, who emphasized the weaknesses of group actions measured in terms of their frequent lack of secrecy, surprise, and common resolve. The only caveat to be added is a logical one, namely, that we can never be sure how many conspiratorial undertakings have gone undetected, because their participants stopped short of overt action. Offsetting this possibility, however, is the fact that such coups, when they do succeed, may alter governments or create new ones, thus guaranteeing their own visibility to the eye of history. The same is true if they are resounding failures or are prematurely exposed.

The relation between political murder and certain personal impulses not self-evidently political at all must be sought and followed through often complex episodes. Without the reinforcing impulse of religious zeal—be it transcendental, as in the Old Testament cases and those of sixteenth-century Europe, not to mention Islam throughout most of history, or secularized, as in so many nineteenth- and twentieth-century examples—it is difficult to imagine numerous assassinations' having been attempted at all. Sex, too, has often played a powerful role, not only in blatant expressions of lust and jealousy but also as a source of otherwise mysterious social and psychological animus. The phallic symbolism of dagger or pistol has not been lost on many theorists; and while the ancient Jewish heroine Jael or Charlotte Corday stabbing Marat to death in his bath cannot easily be portrayed as confusing their acts with copulation, they may well have taken pride in appropriating male weapons of conquest for thrusts of retribution.

Exhibitionism is an element in the records of so many known assassins that its very profusion tends to discourage an investigator seeking to reconstruct a crime in terms of what led to it. The same problem confronts a clinical psychologist hoping to prevent one. One form of self-dramatization, however, bears close watching. This is the self-destructive impulse discernible in many would-be assassins. The incidence of assassination in history bears little or no discernible relation to rates of private crime, popular unrest, or battlefield casualties. It has been suggested that a significant correlation does exist between suicides and political murders committed in certain societies, including those of Germany in the 1920s and Japan throughout much of its modern history. Counterexamples such as that of Sweden, however, force one to conclude that the linkage has yet to be established as a universal phenomenon.

Connections between history and other disciplines involved in the contemplation of political murder no doubt deserve more attention than limitations of space and scope have permitted here. Law, philosophy, art, literary fiction (including both the spoken theater and grand opera), anthropology, sociology, and psychology all offer insights of their own into the phenomenon of assassination. Philosophical and literary figures such as Jean Genêt and Maurice Merleau-Ponty, applauding terrorism with at least intermittent support from Jean-Paul Sartre, might discourage all deference to literary or philosophical figures in this regard. Yet those same pronouncements issuing from safe and comfortable Parisian apartments elicited an infinitely more profound response from Günther Grass, which alone was worth the candle.

More could be asked from sociology and social psychology than has yet been forthcoming with respect to the sources of political homicide. The tendency to blame a repressive society for lethal behavior on the part of even its most "unrepressed" members has already been remarked; nor does the willingness to denounce, instead of the entire "system," errant relations with parents, spouses, lovers, and other contemporaries seem likely to raise the argument to a level better than that of rationalization after the event. The essential quality of civic responsibility is too important to be suspended in favor of terrorism, seen as nothing worse than one among many expressions of reproach directed against the times.

It is from a different quarter, that of the law, that help may prove to be most urgently required, in at least two regards. The first involves the very meaning of "political crime" as interpreted and applied by the courts. For a historian it is easy to see in the murder of a political figure by a political opponent, for political reasons, an event posing special difficulties for a constitutional regime, including its judicial branch. But is a bank robber committed in order to fund political activities also definable as a political crime, requiring separate treatment? If mail fraud or tax evasion on the part of a candidate for office is definable as a crime, which it generally is, without regard to the identity of the accused, why should murder committed to dramatize a partisan cause be considered anything more or less than murder?

Queries and doubts concerning the reality of political crime as a legal category are by no means abstract, as witness the concrete problem of extradition. Extradition treaties and the law derived from them have achieved no high degree of coherence even after centuries of debate; and courts sometimes shy away from the task of imposing greater clarity. To the nonlegal mind, prima facie evidence of a felony, warranting trial under the law of both the nation requesting extradition and the one asked to grant it, would seem to establish a compelling case for recommitting the accused to the appropriate venue. Despite curious irregularity in findings, the courts do appear to accept, at least part of the time, this line of argument. In 1968, for example, British justice returned James Earl Ray to American jurisdiction, despite his lawyers' claim that he had no personal motive for killing Martin Luther King, Jr., and was thus unextraditable by virtue of being a "political prisoner." This action contrasts sharply with the repeated refusal by French and other courts in continental Europe to deliver arrested terrorists into the custody of countries having what seemed to be well-documented indictments pending against them.

The second legal question raised by hostage-taking, purposeful abduction, and certain other forms of demonstrative political violence is more delicate still, since it involves the issue of the death penalty. In one respect the relevance of capital punishment to the subject of this book is narrower than might at first be assumed. This is because a direct and more or less instantaneous act of assassination is indistinguishable, or should be, from any other murder and can therefore be punished only in accordance with the penal law, whether permitting or excluding the death penalty, which is in force at a given time and place. That is not complicated, and the division of opinion over punishment applicable to all murder will not be discussed here.

What brings political murder, in the form of calculated killing *after due deliberation,* into the center of the controversy is its comparability with two other troublesome categories; rape and kidnaping for profit or other private advantage. Applied to these three crimes, the logic employed by Beccaria more than two centuries ago, and invoked repeatedly by opponents of the death penalty ever since, ironically works in reverse, helping no doubt to explain why neither the Italian reformer nor the English legal commentator Blackstone before him was willing to condemn capital punishment without qualification. That logic rests on the twin assumptions that criminals in general are not stupid, insane, or incapable of reckoning incremental cost of various options and that the law should not unwittingly encourage murder as an adjunct to some other crime. Thus, if it is senseless, as Beccaria rightly pointed out, to hang a man for stealing a loaf of bread, whether or not he murders the baker in the process, it is equally irrational to promise the rapist, the kidnaper, or the political terrorist holding a hostage that he is assured of receiving the same treatment whether his victim lives or dies. Under such circumstances, why should he hesitate to eliminate the most dangerous witness?

To invite all the furious objections sure to be aroused by any attempt to draw distinctions among kinds of murder might seem to be courting unnecessary resistance, in a field lying outside the subject of this book, narrowly defined. The subject of political murder, however, is not narrow enough to justify denial of its relevance to one of the most profound legal, moral, and political dilemmas of our time. Like the unblinkable fact that countless imprisoned terrorists have supplied the pretext for further attacks designed to free them, at the cost of more innocent lives, the need to supply a compelling reason for not killing captives refuses to go away.

What well might be the most important issue is the claim that some political murders, admittedly a very few even in the present century so filled with others of all kinds, deserve the moral cachet of tyrannicide. Although it cannot be lightly dismissed, it must yield precedence to a broader question: not "Is assassination ever justified?" by some ethical standard, but "Does assassination work?" At this pragmatic level history's dispassionate judgment should have something to offer.

If the answer is that sometimes it does work, serving purposes not otherwise achievable because of repression or institutional inertia—or, if achievable at all, would be so at a cost far greater than the life of a single victim—then one would have to concede that it can be "good politics." The Koran proclaims that "if two khalifs live, one should be murdered, for murder is better than disorder." But is it? Has assassination proved that it can solve problems, not only in the short but also in the long run?

Put thus, the question whether or not political murder can also be good politics would seem to be susceptible of just one reply, subject to only minimal exceptions. The history of countless assassinations, examined with an eye to comparing apparent motives with actual outcomes, contains almost none that produced results consonant with the aims of the doer, assuming those aims to have extended at all beyond the miserable taking of a life. Gavrilo Princip and his comrades in 1914 no more got what they wanted, a Bosnia independent of Austria-Hungary and Serbia alike, than did John Wilkes Booth in making a martyr of Lincoln while calling down Northern vengeance at its most extreme on the Confederacy from 1865 onward.

Allowance made for the elimination of certain highly unattractive rulers in earlier times, two modern assassination plots appear to exhaust the category of exceptions to the rule. Orsini's attempt to murder Emperor Napoleon III in 1858, although it literally misfired, killing innocent bystanders and sending the Italian patriot and his principal accomplice to the guillotine, nevertheless led directly to the second Bonaparte's change of course with respect to Italy: the very next year he took France into war against Austria-Hungary in support of the kingdom of Sardinia and the cause of Italian unification. The other case involved the slaying of President Anwar Sadat by Moslem extremists at Cairo in 1981, which was followed by—if it did not cause—the shift in Egyptian policy away from détente with Israel. These outcomes unquestionably were welcomed by the movements for which the two sets of assassins claimed to have acted. Nonetheless, given the general pressures operating on the two governments—that of France in the nineteenth century and that of Egypt in the twentieth—Napoleon III and Sadat, or if not they then other leaders reasonably soon after them, might well have altered direction to a comparable degree, without need for the violent prompting.

Political murder is undeniably dramatic. It is also, given the impossibility of predicting with assurance the full range of its consequences, a highly unreliable expedient. More important, in a sense far deeper than that of expediency, it is a means that twists and dehumanizes its own ends. History has repeatedly demonstrated that assassination, including tyrannicide conceived in the most unselfish spirit, has tended to ignore man's hard-won regard for due process and to defeat the highest purposes of political life. If governments and their declared opponents were to act (or, sometimes better still, refrain from acting) in the light of that knowledge, a world facing a host of other problems would have at least one good reason to rejoice.

Notes

Index

Notes

Introduction

1. Bernard Lewis, *Encyclopaedia Britannica* (Chicago: Encyclopaedia Britannica, 1959), II, 554.

2. *The Oxford English Dictionary* (Oxford: Clarendon, 1933), I, 499.

3. *Encyclopaedia of the Social Sciences* (New York: Macmillan, 1937), I, 271.

4. *Newsweek,* November 12, 1984, p. 65.

1. Jehovah's Children and His Enemies

1. Herbert Butterfield, *The Origins of History* (New York: Basic Books, 1981), pp. 80–81.

2. A valuable guide to chronology, periodization, geography, and many points of modern interpretation is John Bright, *A History of Israel,* 2nd ed. (London: SCM Press, 1972).

3. Judges 3:9–11.

4. Ibid., 3:12. For wording of biblical quotations and for the spelling of proper names, I have relied on the *Revised Standard Version: Old Testament Section* (New York: Thomas Nelson and Sons, 1952).

5. Judges, chaps. 4–5 contains the story of Deborah, Barak, Sisera, and Jael.

6. Ibid., 5:21.

7. Ibid., 4:21.

8. Bright, *History of Israel,* p. 434, including n. 8, summarizes recent scholarly discussion concerning the composition of the Book of Judith. In the Anglican revision of the Bible, whose two volumes containing *Apocrypha* appeared in 1888 (London: John Murray), the Reverend C. J. Ball, editor for the section on Judith, I, 241–360, called it "a work of fiction."

9. Judges 8:22–23.

10. Ibid., chap. 9.

11. Ibid., 9:53–54.

12. Ibid., 9:57.

13. The Reverend John Taylor in Frederick C. Grant and H. H. Rowley, eds., *Dictionary of the Bible,* rev. ed. (New York: Charles Scribner's Sons, 1963), p. 5.

14. I Samuel 17:55–57.

15. For the account of Abner's fate, see II Samuel, chaps. 2–3.

16. Ibid., II Samuel 3:14.

17. Ibid., II Samuel 3:31–39.

18. Ibid., II Samuel 13:14.

19. Ibid., 13:28–29.

20. Ibid., 14:1–14.

21. Ibid., 14:26.

22. Ibid., chaps. 15–18, for the rebellion and defeat of Absalom.

23. Ibid., 16:22.

24. Ibid., 18:9.

25. Ibid., 18:33.

26. Ibid., 20:8–10.

27. Ibid., 20:13–22.

28. Ibid., 11:15–17.

29. I Kings, chaps 1–2, for Solomon's accession and Adonijah's rebellion.

30. Ibid., 1:52.

31. Ibid., 2:28.

32. Ibid., 2:46.

33. Ibid., 15:26.

34. Ibid., 15:28–29.

35. II Kings 1:1–17.

36. I Kings 16:30–34.

37. Ibid., chap. 19, for the struggle between Jezebel and Elijah. The story of Naboth appears in I Kings 21:1–16.

38. II Kings 3:2.

39. Ibid., 8:26.

40. II Chronicles 21:2–4.

41. II Kings 9:27–28.

42. Ibid., 11:1–3. For the story of Joash, see the balance of chap. 11.

43. Ibid., 11:20.

44. Ibid., 14:29, 15:8–14.

45. Ibid., 15:19–20. In this passage Tiglath-pileser is referred to as "Pul," the title he assumed after having taken Babylon.

46. Bright, *History of Israel,* p. 270, n. 5, cites an article by A. M. Honeyman in the *Journal of Biblical Literature,* 67 (1948): 24, which offers an interesting speculation concerning the close similarity, indeed for philological purposes the identity, between the name of the killer and that of his victim. If its author is right, Pekah took not only Pekahiah's life and throne but also his "throne name."

47. II Kings 15:30.

48. In commenting on this "Assyrian captivity," Bright, *History of Israel,* p. 274, cites the figure 27, 290 as the number of Israelite deportees claimed by Sargon. If nothing else, the reference further confirms what we have long known, that Assyrian inscriptions were remarkably specific as to details.

2. The Greeks

1. Herodotus (bk. VII, chap. 6) portrays Hipparchus as imposing, in his own name, a sentence of exile. *Herodotus,* trans. A. D. Godley (The Loeb Classical Library; Cambridge, Mass.: Harvard University Press, 1971), III, 307.

2. The figures of the assassins sculpted by Antenor and placed in the Agora were taken away by Xerxes when his Persian forces briefly occupied the city in 480 B.C. A second monument was then executed by Critias (Kritios) and Nesiotes, but a century and a half later Alexander the Great sent home the original work after his conquest of Persia. The two standing male nudes which survive in the Museo Nazionale at Naples may be not Antenor's but the second set or, more likely still, a mixed pair. See Ernest Arthur Gardner, *A Handbook of Greek Sculpture* (London: Macmillan, 1914), I, 185.

3. Herodotus, bk. V, chap. 55.

4. Ibid., bk. VI, chap. 123.

5. *Thucydides,* bk. VI, chaps. 54–59, trans. B. Jowett (Oxford: Clarendon, 1881), I, 14. While relying on the original Jowett translation, I have profited greatly in treating Thucydides from later assessments, including that by John H. Finley, *Thucydides* (Cambridge, Mass: Harvard University Press, 1942).

6. Ibid., bk. I, chap. 20.

7. Ibid., bk. VI, chap. 58.

8. Ibid., bk. VI, chap. 57.

9. *Constitution of Athens,* chap. 18:6, in *The Works of Aristotle,* ed. W. D. Ross (Oxford: Clarendon, 1921), vol. X. The translator of this item, Sir Frederic G. Kenyon, used the Latin title, *Atheniensium Respublica.*

10. Ibid., chap. 16:2.

11. Ibid., chap. 18:2.

12. Ibid., chap. 18:3.

13. Ibid., chap. 18:4.

14. Neither Thucydides nor Aristotle has much to tell us about Cimon's career as a whole. Plutarch was later to describe it in detail, however, comparing it, in the author's system of paired Greek and Roman biographies, with that of Lucullus. *Lives: The Dryden Plutarch,* rev. Arthur Hugh Clough (New York: Everyman's Library, 1910?), II, 181–200, 240–243.

15. *Thucydides,* bk. III, chap. 54; bk IV, chap. 56.

16. Aristotle, *Constitution of Athens,* chap. 25:1–4.

17. Ibid., chap. 27.

18. See note 9, above.

19. *Thucydides,* bk. V, chap. 17.

20. Ibid., bk. III, chap. 81.

21. Ibid., bk. VII, passim.

22. Regarding the "age of tyrants," see especially Helmut Berve, *Die Tyrannis bei den Griechen,* 2 vols. (Munich: C. H. Beck'sche Verlagsbuchhandlung, 1967); also Antony Andrewes, *The Greek Tyrants* (London: Hutchinson's University Library, 1956); Malcolm McLaren, Jr., "Tyranny," in *The Greek Political Experience* (Princeton: Princeton University Press, 1941), pp. 78–92; Hans Friedel, *Der Tyrannenmord in Gesetzgebung und Volksmeinung der Griechen* (Stuttgart: W. Kohlhammer, 1937);

and P. N. Ure, *The Origin of Tyranny* (New York: Russell & Russell, 1962). Two older treatments in German, which still retain their importance, are Hermann Gottlob Plass, *Die Tyrannis in ihren beiden Perioden bei den alten Griechen* (Bremen: Franz Schlochtmann, 1852), and "Über den Begriff der Tyrannis bei den Griechen," in *Eduard Zellers kleine Schriften* (Berlin: Georg Reimer, 1910), pp. 398–409. The most important of recent additions to this literature is Andrew Lintott, *Violence, Civil Strife, and Revolution in the Classical City, 750-330 B.C.* (Baltimore: The Johns Hopkins Press, 1982).

23. Berve, *Die Tyrannis*, I, 29.

24. In the first of his Pythian odes, Pindar remarks: "the kindly generosity of Croesus fadeth not away, while Phalaris, ruthless in spirit, who burned his victims in his brazen bull, is whelmed for ever by a hateful infamy, and no lyres beneath the roof-tree welcome him as a theme to be softly blended with the warbled songs of boys." *The Odes of Pindar,* trans. Sir John Sandys, rev. ed. (Loeb Classical Library; Cambridge, Mass.: Harvard University Press, 1968), p. 167.

25. Berve, *Die Tyrannis*, I, 131.

26. Plato's version of Syracusan events, and his own part in them, appears in the third, seventh, and eighth of his *Thirteen Epistles,* trans. L. A. Post (Oxford: Clarendon, 1925). See also "Dion" in the revised *Dryden Plutarch* cited in note 14, above; Cornelius Nepos, "Dion," trans. John Selby Watson, in *Justin, Cornelius Nepos, and Eutropius* (London: Henry G. Bohn, 1853), pp. 351–358; and George Grote, *History of Greece* (London: John Murray, 1853), XI, 75–180.

27. J. D. Bury, *Cambridge Ancient History* (Cambridge: Cambridge University Press, 1927), VI, 136.

28. Ibid., VI, 281.

29. Berve, *Die Tyrannis,* I, 259–260.

30. VI, 83.

31. On Clearchus of Heraclea see, in addition to Berve, Plass, and others, the work of the Roman historian, Justin, in the translation by Watson noted in note 26, above. Justin's treatment of the Heraclean crisis appears on pp. 146–149 of that volume.

32. *Isocrates,* trans. La Rue Van Hook, rev. ed. (The Loeb Classical Library; Cambridge, Mass.: Harvard University Press, 1954), III, 455.

33. Demosthenes, *The Crown, the Philippics, and Ten Other Orations,* trans. C. Rann Kennedy (New York: Everyman's Library, 1911).

34. The soldier who killed the king was alleged to have had a personal grievance, but many dark rumors were circulated concerning Olympias' role in instigating her husband's murder. *The Cambridge Ancient History,* VI, 269, follows Plutarch, who was cautious about offering any judgment (*Lives,* II, 471). Justin, on the other hand (bk. IX, chaps. 6–7), directs suspicion at the queen without producing anything more than circumstantial evidence.

35. Oscar Jászi and John D. Lewis, *Against the Tyrant: The Tradition and Theory of Tyrannicide* (Glencoe, Ill: The Free Press, 1957), p. 3, citing W. W. How and J. Wells, *A Commentary on Herodotus,* rev. ed. (Oxford: Clarendon, 1936), I, 278.

36. Herodotus, bk. III, chap. 80.

37. "Hiero," chap. 4, in *Xenophon's Minor Works,* trans. John Selby Watson (London: George Bell & Sons, 1891), p. 55.

38. Werner Jaeger, *Paideia: The Ideals of Greek Culture,* trans. Gilbert Highet

(New York: Oxford University Press, 1945), I, 252. Jaeger devotes bk. I, chap. 11, to "The Cultural Policy of the Tyrants," I, 223–233, before discussing Aeschylus and Sophocles in bk. II, chaps. 1–2.

39. Xenophon, *Memoirs of Socrates,* bk. IV, chap 6:12, trans. Hugh Tredennick (Harmondsworth: Penguin, 1970), p. 220. The same volume contains Xenophon's *Symposium: The Dinner Party.*

40. See, for example, Jászi and Lewis, *Against the Tyrant,* pp. 3–8; and Ure, *Origin of Tyranny,* pp. 302–303.

41. Plato, *The Republic,* trans. Benjamin Jowett, rev. ed. (New York: Colonial Press, 1901), pp. 267–271; and Aristotle, *Politics,* trans. Benjamin Jowett (New York: Modern Library, 1943), pp. 238–246. For Plato's views in particular, see Gerhard Heinzeler, *Das Bild des Tyrannen bei Platon* (Stuttgart: W. Kohlhammer, 1927).

42. In his quadripartite classification of monarchies (*Politics,* bk. III, chap. 14), Aristotle refuses to identify as tyrannies two primitive types of autocracy—kingship among barbarians, and the elective dictatorship or *Aesymnetia* of earlier Greek times—the former because barbarian kings relied on their own troops, not mercenaries, and the latter because an ancient Greek dictator was elected, hence legitimate.

43. See note 10, above.

44. Robert Nisbet, writing of "Anomie" in his *Prejudices: A Philosophical Dictionary* (Cambridge, Mass.: Harvard University Press, 1982), pp. 11–15, speaks with historical insight about *nomos* among the ancient Greeks.

45. Pierre Vidal-Naquet, *Le Chasseur noir: Formes de pensée et formes de société dans le monde grec* (Paris: Maspero, 1981).

46. *The New York Review,* March 3, 1983, p. 29.

3. Rome

1. Stewart Perowne, *Death of the Roman Republic* (Garden City, N.Y.: Doubleday, 1968), pp. xiv–xv.

2. F. E. Adcock, *The Roman Art of War under the Republic* (Cambridge, Mass.: Harvard University Press, 1940), pp. 4–14, passim.

3. A. W. Lintott, *Violence in Republican Rome* (Oxford: Clarendon, 1968), emphasizes the frequency of action by mobs, including some affecting the various assemblies. He points out, however, the late appearance in Rome of assassination as such.

4. Paul Liman, *Der politische Mord im Wandel der Geschichte* (Berlin: A. Hofmann, 1912), p. 145, confidently refers to the assassination of Lars Porsenna; but for a discussion of the difficulties involved in even identifying the supposed tyrant, see *Cambridge Ancient History,* VII, 397.

5. The best review of modern scholarship on this topic is the chapter by E. Badian, "Tiberius Gracchus and the Beginning of the Roman Revolution," in Hildegard Temporini, ed., *Aufstieg und Niedergang der römischen Welt* (New York: Walter De Gruyter, 1972), I, 668–731. Two works of particular narrative value are D. C. Earl, *Tiberius Gracchus: A Study in Politics* (Brussels: Collection Latomus LXVI, 1963), and Henry C. Boren, *The Gracchi* (New York: Twayne, 1968).

6. Ernst Badian, *Foreign Clientelae, 264–70 B.C.* (Oxford: Clarendon, 1958), pp. 173–174.

7. Plutarch, *Lives: The Dryden Plutarch,* III, 141.

8. Ibid., III, 157.

9. Lintott, *Violence in Republican Rome,* appendix A, pp. 209–216.

10. By the Julian calendar, shortly to be decreed by Caesar, the date was November 22–23, 50 B.C.; by the older Roman calendar it replaced, it was January 10–11, 49.

11. *Commentaries: The Civil War,* bk. III, chaps. 88–89, trans. W. A. McDevitte, and W. S. Bohn (New York: Harper & Brothers, 1898), pp. 365–366.

12. Sir Charles Oman, *Seven Roman Statesmen of the Later Republic* (1st ed., 1902; reissued Freeport, N.Y.: Books for Libraries, 1971), p. 287. Later and more detailed analyses of politics in the age of the Civil War include Ronald Syme, *The Roman Revolution* (Oxford: Clarendon, 1939), and Matthias Gelzer, *Caesar: Politician and Statesman* (Cambridge, Mass.: Harvard University Press, 1968).

13. Plutarch, *Lives,* II, 456.

14. Ibid., II, 457.

15. *Cambridge Ancient History,* IX, 735.

16. Plutarch's description of Caesar's death (*Lives,* II, 578) is corroborated by that of Gaius Suetonius Tranquillus, *The Twelve Caesars,* trans. Robert Graves (London: The Folio Society, 1964), p. 47, even to the number of stab wounds.

17. *Cambridge Ancient History,* X, 21.

18. Plutarch, *Lives,* III, 222–223.

19. For the death of Caligula, as for those of Claudius, Galba, Otho, Vitellius, and Domitian, see Suetonius, *The Twelve Caesars,* passim.

20. Tacitus, *The Annals,* bk. XII, chaps. 66–67, trans. A. J. Church and W. J. Brodribb (New York: Twayne, 1964), pp. 184–185, gives a more circumstantial and seemingly confident account of Claudius' demise than does Suetonius, *The Twelve Caesars,* p. 208, who refers to the use of poison only as a widely circulated rumor. M. P. Charlesworth concludes that "the fact is certain," in *Cambridge Ancient History,* X, 696, n. 4.

21. G. H. Stevenson's excellent chapter "The Year of the Four Emperors," in *Cambridge Ancient History,* X, 808–839, makes extensive use of both Tacitus and Suetonius.

22. On Caracalla's murder of Geta, see Dio Cassius, *Roman History,* epitomized by the eleventh-century Byzantine John Xiphilinus, bk. LXXVIII, chap. 206, trans. Earnest Cary (New York: Loeb Classical Library, 1927), IX, pp. 279–285. The account of Caracalla's own assassination appears in bk. LXXIX, chaps. 4–6 (Cary, IX, 347–353).

23. Ibid., bk. LXXX, chaps. 20–21 (Cary, IX, 477–479). Dio, the Roman historian, senator, and confidant of emperors, was an obviously well-placed, if superstitious and sometimes rather naive observer.

4. Other Peoples, Other Lands

1. II Kings 8:7–15.

2. Bk. I, chaps. 7–15, trans. A. D. Godley (Loeb Classical Library; Cambridge, Mass.: Harvard University Press [1926], 1969), I, 11–17.

3. Friedrich Hebbel, *Gyges und sein Ring* (Frankfurt-am-Main: Ullstein Bücher, 1965); first performed in 1856.

4. Polybius, *The Histories,* bk. I, chap. 24, trans. W. R. Paton (Loeb Classical Library; Cambridge, Mass.: Harvard University Press, 1922), I, 67, recounts the fate of the admiral, and in bk. II, chap. 36 (Paton, I, 33), that of Hasdrubal. Appian, *Roman History: The Wars in Spain,* chap. 2, trans. Horace White (Loeb Classical Library; Cambridge, Mass.: Harvard University Press, 1964), I, 151, asserts that Hasdrubal was killed by a slave whose master had been ' cruelly put to death" by order of the governor. The same slayings are discussed by Livy, *Summary,* bk. XVII, trans. B. O. Foster (Loeb Classical Library; Cambridge, Mass.: Harvard University Press, 1963), IV, 555, for Hannibal's crucifixion, and bk. XXI (Foster, V, 7), for the murder of Hasdrubal.

5. Livy, *Summary,* bks. LIV and LV, trans. A. C. Schlesinger (Loeb Classical Library; Cambridge, Mass.: Harvard University Press, 1954), XIV, 49–51, 55; also Appian, *Wars in Spain,* chap. 74, I, 253.

6. Sallust, *The War with Jugurtha,* trans. R. C. Rolfe (Loeb Classical Library; Cambridge, Mass.: Harvard University Press, 1971), pp. 131.–381. See also *The Dryden Plutarch,* II, 143, on Sulla's role.

7. Caesar treats his victory at Zela and the flight of Pharnaces in *The Alexandrian War,* chaps. 69–78, trans. A. G. Way (Loeb Classical Library; Cambridge, Mass.: Harvard University Press, 1955), pp. 121–135. For Asander's killing of Pharnaces, however, it is necessary to consult the *Cambridge Ancient History,* IX, 679.

8. Jack Lindsay, *Cleopatra* (London: Constable, 1971), p. 123.

9. G. S. Goodspeed, *A History of the Babylonians and Assyrians,* 2nd ed. (New York: Charles Scribner's Sons, 1906), pp. 206–207; Robert W. Rogers, *A History of Babylonia and Assyria* (Cincinnati: Abingdon, 1915), II, 262–266; and Leonard W. King, *A History of Babylon* (New York: Frederick A. Stokes, 1915), p. 267. All three works, though relatively old, remain helpful.

10. Bk. II, chaps. 161–169.

11. Jeremiah, chap. 27; Ezekiel, chap. 17.

12. *Cambridge Ancient History,* VI, 3, 139, n.1.

13. Ibid., IV, 187. On the Achaemenids in general, see Richard N. Frye, *The Heritage of Persia* (Cleveland: World, 1963), esp. pp. 74, 255, n. 37); also Roman Ghirshman, *Iran from the Earliest Times to the Islamic Conquest* (Harmondsworth: Penguin, 1954).

14. Demetrius C. Boulger, *The History of China* (London: W. Thacker, 1898), I, 28–36; Ch'en Meng'chia, "The Greatness of Chou (ca 1027–ca. 221 B.C.)," in Harley Farnsworth MacNair, ed., *China* (Berkeley: University of California Press, 1951), pp. 54–71.

15. George Sansom, *A History of Japan to 1334* (Stanford: Stanford University Press, 1958), esp. chap. 3, "The Yamato State." For other valuable observations, see Edwin O. Reischauer, *The Japanese* (Cambridge, Mass.: Harvard University Press, 1977), and Malcolm D. Kennedy, *A History of Japan* (London: Weidenfeld and Nicolson, 1963).

16. Narada Thera, *The Buddha and His Teachings* (Colombo: Vajirarama, 1964), p. 161; Hermann Oldenberg, *Buddha: His Life, His Doctrine, His Order,* trans. William Hoey (London: Williams and Norgate, 1882), pp. 160–161.

17. Oldenberg, *Buddha,* p. 161.

18. E. A. Wallis Budge, *History of Ethiopia* (London: Methuen, 1928), p. 280.

19. Jules Perruchon, ed. and trans., *Vie de Lalibala, roi d'Ethiopie* (Paris: Ernest Leroux, 1892), p. 85, n. 2.

20. E. A. W. Budge, ed. and trans., *The Queen of Sheba and Her Only Son Menyelek: ... A Complete Translation of the KEBRA NAGAST* (London: Martin Hopkinson, 1922).

21. Ephraim Isaac, "An Obscure Component in Ethiopian Church History," *Le Muséon* (Louvain), 85 (1972): 250–251.

22. Tadesse Tamrat, *Church and State in Ethiopia, 1270–1527* (Oxford: Clarendon, 1972), p. 283; see also Enrico Cerulli, *Il Libro etiopico dei miracoli di Maria* (Rome: Giovanna Bardi, 1943), I, 79–86.

5. Zealots, Barbarians, and Assassins

1. Both Books of Maccabees are technically apocryphal by Judaic and Protestant, though not by Catholic definition. Despite this qualification, the first of the two at least is to all appearances reliable, having been composed within a half-century of the events it records. Modern treatments include J. C. Dancy, *A Commentary on I Maccabees* (Oxford: Basil Blackwell, 1954), William R. Farmer, *Maccabees, Zealots, and Josephus* (New York: Columbia University Press, 1956), and E. J. Bickerman's work originally published in German, *The Maccabees,* trans. Moses Hadas (New York: Schocken Library, 1947).

2. I Maccabees 13:23, 16:16.

3. G. A. Williamson, *The World of Josephus* (London: Secker & Warburg, 1964), p. 58. See also Michael Grant, *The Jews in the Roman World* (London: Weidenfeld and Nicolson, 1973).

4. Herod's often devious role in Palestinian developments of the Roman Civil War period, including the murder of his father Antipater, the suicide of his brother Phasael, and finally his own succession in 37 B.C., is described in bks. XI–XIV of Flavius Josephus, *The Jewish War and Other Selections,* ed. Moses I. Finley, trans. H. St. J. Thackeray and Ralph Marcus (New York: Twayne, 1965), pp. 98–110.

5. Josephus, bk. II, chap. 13, cites as an example the murder of the high priest Jonathan, but elsewhere blames Herod.

6. Acts 21:38.

7. Farmer, *Maccabees, Zealots, and Josephus,* pp. 186–202, and Grant, *The Jews in the Roman World,* pp. 99–119, both discuss the question of "the historical Jesus" in this context.

8. Liman, *Der politische Mord,* p. 54.

9. *Historia [De gestis] Langobardorum, Monumenta Germaniae historica* (hereafter cited as *MGh*): *Scriptores rerum Langobardicarum et Italicarum* (Hanover: Hahn, 1878). There is now an English translation by William Dudley Foulke of Paul the Deacon's *History of the Lombards* (Philadelphia: University of Pennsylvania Press, 1974). See also L. M. Hartmann in *The Cambridge Medieval History* (hereafter cited as *Camb. Med. Hist.*), corrected ed. (Cambridge: Cambridge University Press, 1926), II, 195–196.

10. Tacitus, *The Germania,* trans. Hugh Mattingly (New York: Penguin, 1971).

11. Earlier, on Justinian's orders, Belisarius had attacked and defeated the

Vandals in North Africa. For the destruction of the Ostrogothic kingdom in Italy, see Charles Diehl, *Camb. Med. Hist.*, II, 14–18, who draws on such sources as [Bishop] Jordanes of Ravenna, *De Getarum sive Gothorum, MGh: Auctores Antiquissimi,* vol. V (Hanover: Hahn, 1882), and Isidore of Seville, *History of the Kings of the Goths,* now available in English, trans. Guidi Donini and Gordon B. Ford, Jr. (Leiden: E. J. Brill, 1966).

12. The fullest account of these struggles is, as remarked in the text, that by Gregory of Tours, ed. W. Arndt et al., *MGh: Scriptores rerum Merovingicarum,* vol. I (Hanover: Hahn, 1885). A modern French translation by Robert Latouche bears the title *Histoire des Francs* (Paris: Les Belles Lettres, 1963–1965). In addition, the Italian poet Fortunatus wrote stanzas to celebrate Sigebert's marriage to Brunhild, then went on to praise her future enemy, Fredegund, in an ode summarized by Christian Pfister, *Camb. Med. Hist.,* II, 120–123.

13. G. W. Bowersock, "LIMES ARABICUS," *Harvard Studies in Classical Philology* 80 (1976), 219–229, examines written and archaeological evidence of Roman defenses on this front.

14. Ibid., p. 226, n. 18. Bowersock cites I. Shahid (Kawar) on this incident, *Byzantinische Zeitschrift* (Munich), 53 (1960), 60. The original source was a Greek chronicler, Malalas.

15. For an excellent discussion of Muslim theories of religion and the state, see E. I. J. Rosenthal, *Political Thought in Medieval Islam* (Cambridge: Cambridge University Press, 1962).

16. This sequence of schisms is well summarized by Bernard Lewis, *The Assassins: A Radical Sect in Islam* (New York: Basic Books. 1968), chap. 2. See also G. S. Hodgson, *The Order of Assassins* (The Hague: Mouton, 1955), and Enno Franzius, *History of the Order of Assassins* (New York: Funk & Wagnalls, 1969).

17. Lewis, *The Assassins,* p. 32.

18. P. A. Mackay, "Patronage and Power in 6th/12th Century Baghdad: The Life of the Vizier Adud al-Din Ibn al-Muzaffar," *Studia Islamica* (Paris), fasc. 34 (1971), 27–56, recounts a particularly bloody cluster of political murders in the capital of the Caliphate before the latter was overwhelmed by Mongol invaders. These killings, related as they were to court struggles within the Sunni ruling group, cannot have been the work of Ismaili Assassins, who had no discernible stake in them.

19. St. Louis's great chronicler, Joinville, chap. 89, trans. Frank Marzials (New York: Everyman's Library, 1908), p. 248, has some pungent remarks to make about both the success of the Syrian Assassins in extorting money from various princes and their subsequent failure when confronted by the "faceless" Hospitallers and Templars, Christian orders able to replace any casualties as quickly as could their Muslim opponents. According to Lewis, *The Assassins,* p. 121, the Assassins themselves paid grudging tribute to these "Frankish" knights.

20. Bernard Lewis, "Saladin and the Assassins," *Bulletin of the School of Oriental and African Studies,* 15 (1953), 239–245.

21. *The Travels of Marco Polo,* chap. 22 (London: Everyman's Library, 1954), pp. 73–77.

22. Arnold of Lübeck, as quoted by Lewis, *The Assassins,* p. 4.

23. Ibid., p. 139.

24. Ibid., p. 96.

6. The High Middle Ages

1. Geoffrey Barraclough, *The Mediaeval Empire: Idea and Reality* (London: The Historical Association, 1950), p. 12.

2. Assassinations in the Eastern Roman, that is, the Byzantine Empire, are treated by authors of numerous modern studies, while some of the most important western European sources, including Gregory of Tours, Paulus Diaconus, and Isidore of Seville, have been mentioned in earlier connections. The Greek chroniclers are extensively cited in the *Camb. Med. Hist.*, new ed. (Cambridge: Cambridge University Press, 1966), vol. IV, pt. 1.

3. Quoted by Robert Lee Wolff, "How the News Was Brought from Byzantium to Angoulême; or, The Pursuit of a Hare in an Ox Cart," in *Byzantine and Modern Greek Studies: Essays Presented to Sir Steven Runciman* (Oxford: Basil Blackwell, 1978), IV, 142.

4. Ibid., pp. 142–143.

5. Ibid., pp.183–189.

6. See especially Marc Bloch, *Feudal Society,* trans. L. A. Manyon (Chicago: University of Chicago Press, 1961); David Herlihy, *The History of Feudalism* (New York: Walker, 1971); and Hans Kammler, *Die Feudalmonarchien* (Cologne: Böhlau, 1974).

7. H. F. Huchinson, *Edward II: The Pliant King* (London: Eyre & Spottiswood, 1971); and Caroline Bingham, *The Life and Times of Edward II* (London: Weidenfeld & Nicolson, 1973).

8. Galbert of Bruges, *The Murder of Charles the Good,* trans. and ed. James Bruce Ross (New York: Columbia University Press, 1960).

9. "Rome was subdued by the might of a woman's hand," wrote the contemporary annalist Benedict of San Andrea, in his *Chronicon,* quoted by C. W. Prévité-Orton, *Camb. Med. Hist.,* III, 154.

10. The struggle that reached its climax at Anagni has yet to be better described than by Ch.-V. Langlois, *Histoire de la France des origines jusqu'à la Révolution,* ed. Ernest Lavisse (Paris: Hachette, 1901), III, pt. 2, 158–166.

11. Outstanding for its sane judgments and meticulous handling of detail is a work by Richard Winston, *Thomas Becket* (New York: Knopf, 1967).

12. Ibid., p. 346.

13. I Peter 2:13–14. See Jászi and Lewis, *Against the Tyrant,* p. 12.

14. Romans 13:1–5.

15. Proverbs 8:15–16, quoted in *De Civitate Dei,* bk. V, chap. 19. The best English translation of *The City of God* is that by Henry Bettenson (Harmondsworth: Penguin, 1972).

16. From *Libri moralium in Job,* bk. XXII, chap. 24, quoted by R. W. and A. J. Carlyle, *A History of Mediaeval Political Theory in the West* (New York: Barnes & Noble, 1950), I, 153, n. 1.

17. C. H. McIlwain, *The Growth of Political Thought in the West* (New York: Macmillan, 1932), pp. 152–154; and Jászi and Lewis, *Against the Tyrant,* p. 14.

18. Ibid., quoting Isidore's *Etymologiae,* bk. IX, chap. 3.

19. Ibid., p. 15. Lewis, a specialist in medieval intellectual history, attaches great importance to this Stoic influence.

20. Ibid., p. 19. Of special interest in this regard is Marsilius of Padua, *Defensor Pacis,* ed. C. W. Prévité-Orton (Cambridge: Cambridge University Press, 1928).

21. Henry de Bracton, *Bracton On the Laws and Customs of England,* trans. and ed. Samuel E. Thorne, 4 vols. (Cambridge, Mass: Harvard University Press and the Seldon Society, 1968–1977), II, 33.

22. Armand A. Maurer, *Medieval Philosophy* (New York: Random House, 1962), p. 81. Maurer, a Thomist, devoted his sixth chapter to John of Salisbury before turning to Aquinas.

23. Question 93, 3rd Article, Reply to Objection 1, in *Introduction to Saint Thomas Aquinas,* ed. Anton C. Pegis (New York: Modern Library, 1948), p. 633.

24. *De Regimine Principum,* bk. I, chap. 15, cited by Jászi and Lewis, *Against the Tyrant,* pp. 21, 260, n. 16.

25. *Summa Theologica,* Question 97, "On Change in Laws," in *Basic Writings of Saint Thomas Aquinas,* ed. A. C. Pegis (New York: Random House, 1944), II, 800 ff. Saint Thomas founded this argument on ancient examples, not mentioning medieval bodies—church synods, law courts, assemblies of estates or notables—as having any such institutionalized role. See Ewart Lewis, *Mediaeval Political Ideas* (New York: Knopf, 1954), pp. 249–253.

26. *Commentum in IV Libros Sententiarum,* bk. II, di. 44, q. 2, a. 2, cited by Jászi and Lewis, *Against the Tyrant,* p. 261, n. 40.

27. *De Regimine Principum,* bk. I, chap. 6.

7. A New Age of Princes

1. Alfred Coville, *Jean Petit: La question du tyrannicide au commencement du XV^{e}siècle* (Paris: August Picard, 1932), offers an unusually full and scholarly study of the duke of Burgundy's defense and his advocate.

2. Ibid., p. 220.

3. Thomas Basin, *Histoire de Louis XI,* ed. and trans. Charles Samaran (Paris: Société d'Édition "Les Belles Lettres," 1963), I, 176–179, parallel Latin and French texts; translation mine.

4. W. H. Woodward, *Cesare Borgia* (London Chapman and Hall, 1913), pp. 179–182; M. E. Mallett, *The Borgias* (London: Bodley Head, 1969), pp. 176–178.

5. On Ferrante of Naples, see J. M. Batista i Roca and Cecilia M. Ady in *The New Cambridge Modern History* (hereafter cited as *NCMH*), vol. I: *The Renaissance* (Cambridge: The University Press, 1957), chaps. 11–12.

6. Vladimir I. Lamansky, ed., *Secrets d'état de Venise* (St. Petersburg: Académie Impériale des Sciences, 1884), pp. 9–10, states on the basis of his archival research that the Council of Ten's highly classified records list scores of assassination proposals received and discussed. Felix Gilbert, an authority on Renaissance Venice and its diplomacy, has confirmed by letter the existence of such lists, without being so confident as the Russian scholar about the precise numbers involved. In Jászi and Lewis, *Against the Tyrant,* pp. 40–41, note is taken of the Lamansky's assertion that included among the Ten's preparations for contingencies was a store of poisons kept in a hidden locker.

7. C. M. Ady, *Camb. Med. Hist.,* vol. VIII: *The Close of the Middle Ages* (Cam-

bridge: The University Press, 1936), p. 217, remarks that after the failure of the conspiracy, "Sixtus IV could not fight on alone, and in 1480 peace was restored," leaving his decrees of excommunication and interdict to be quietly rescinded.

8. Niccolò Machiavelli, *The Prince and the Discourses* (New York: Modern Library, 1940), chap. 8 of *The Prince,* pp. 31–35.

9. Ibid., p. 34.

10. G. F. Young, having treated the Pazzi affair in great detail, *The Medici* (New York: Modern Library, 1930), pp. 166–175, dismisses this 1513 episode as little more than a tragicomic replay of the real drama concluded twenty-five years before. His deprecating treatment is no longer widely accepted.

11. "Recitazione del caso di Pietro Paolo Boscoli," reproduced in *Archivio Storico Italiano* (Florence), 1 (1842), 296.

12. For a discussion of Girolamo Savonarola's influence, which helps to illuminate the conflict between Christian humility and admiration for pagan virtue in Boscoli's anguished appeal, see Felix Gilbert, *Machiavelli and Guicciardini* (Princeton: Princeton University Press, 1965), pp. 144–145 and n. 66.

13. *De Casibus Virorum Illustrium,* bk. II, chap. 15, quoted by Jacob Burckhardt, *The Civilization of the Renaissance in Italy,* trans. S. G. C. Middlemore (New York: Oxford University Press, 1944), p. 36. Also Coville, *Jean Petit,* pp. 186–187, for comment.

14. *The Encyclopedia Britannica,* 11th ed. (Cambridge: The University Press, 1910), XII, 685. For a more balanced view see Mark Phillips, *Francesco Guicciardini: The Historian's Craft* (Toronto: University of Toronto Press, 1977).

15. Gilbert, *Machiavelli and Guicciardini,* p. 118, n. 25, p. 137, in quoting this passage points out that its author used the formulation in two separate treatises.

16. Ibid.

17. John Addington Symonds, *The Age of Despots* (London: Smith, Elder, & Co., 1898), p. 132.

18. Francesco Guicciardini, *History of Italy and History of Florence,* ed. J. R. Hale (New York: Washington Square Press, 1964), p. 8.

19. Gilbert devotes close attention to similarities and differences between the two men in his *Machiavelli and Guicciardini.*

20. Machiavelli, *The Prince and The Discourses,* bk. I, chap. 10, p. 14. The *Discourses* are translated by Christian E. Detmold for this edition, with an introduction by Max Lerner.

21. Ibid., bk. III, chap. 6, p. 412.

22. Ibid., *The Prince,* chap. 7, p. 26. Translation by Luigi Ricci. See also Woodward, *Cesare Borgia,* pp. 278–285.

23. Niccolò Machiavelli, *The History of Florence and Other Selections,* trans. Judith A. Rawson with intro. by Myron P. Gilmore (New York: Washington Square Press, 1970), p. 262.

24. Machiavelli, *The Prince,* chap. 7, p. 27.

25. Machiavelli, *History of Florence,* bk. VIII, pp. 263–275.

26. Ibid., p. 263. Machiavelli treats this subject much more fully in the *Discourses,* bk. III, chap. 6, "Of Conspiracies," pp. 410–436, in the Modern Library version, one of the longest single chapters, if not the longest, in any of his major works.

8. Religious Warfare and Reason of State

1. Since the appearance of the discussion of monarchomachs and other oppositional polemicists in Jászi and Lewis, *Against the Tyrant,* pp. 48–74, the fine treatment by Quentin Skinner has been published, occupying most of his *Foundations of Modern Political Thought,* vol. II: *The Age of Reformation* (Cambridge: The University Press, 1978). See also Pierre Mesnard, *L'Essor de la philosophie politique au XVIe siècle,* 3rd ed. (Paris: J. Vrin, 1969), pp. 501–504; R. H. Murray, *The Political Consequences of the Reformation* (New York: Russell & Russell, 1960), pp. 93–273; and Walter Platzhoff, "Die Theorie von der Mordbefugnis der Obrigkeit im XVI. Jahrhundert," *Historische Studien,* no. 54 (Berlin: Emil Ebering, 1906).

2. Skinner, *Foundations,* II, 194–207, shows that between the start of Charles V's counterattack on the Reformation in 1529–30 and the conclusion of the Religious Peace of Augsburg in 1555, Lutheran theologians developed a body of resistance theory based on both constitutional and private-law arguments and more explicit than anything yet produced by the Calvinists. Among the latter, Beza in particular acknowledged his confession's debt to this often overlooked leadership provided by the older Reformers. After the compromise was reached within the Holy Roman Empire, however, the patriotic-loyalist aspects of Lutheranism came increasingly to the fore there, as well as in Sweden and Denmark. Almost simultaneously, developments in France, the Netherlands, and Scotland began to thrust members of the Reformed, or Calvinist, churches into the position of rebels, with which students of history most commonly identify them.

3. Roland H. Bainton, *Hunted Heretic: The Life and Death of Michael Servetus, 1511–1553* (Boston: Beacon, 1953).

4. Donald Nugent, *Ecumenism in the Age of Reformation: The Colloquy of Poissy* (Cambridge, Mass.: Harvard University Press, 1974), pp. 96–103.

5. On the *Politiques,* see especially Mesnard, *L'Essor de la philosophie politique,* pp. 473–548, and Julian H. Franklin, *Jean Bodin* (New York: Columbia University Press, 1963).

6. Roland H. Bainton, ed., *Castellioniana* (Leiden: E. J. Brill, 1951); and Donald M. Frame, *Montaigne: A Biography* (New York: Harcourt, Brace & World, 1965). Frame in addition edited several volumes of Montaigne's writings. See also Franklin L. Ford, "Dimensions of Toleration: Castellio, Bodin, Montaigne," *Proceedings of the American Philosophical Society,* 166 (1972): 136–139.

7. Coville, *Jean Petit,* p. 564.

8. Although the *Vindiciae contra Tyrannos* has never been fully translated into English, important selections appear in Francis William Coker, ed., *Readings in Political Philosophy,* rev. ed. (New York: Macmillan, 1938), pp. 349–365.

9. Geddes MacGregor, *Thundering Scot* (London: Macmillan, 1958), pp. 67–69; Jasper Ridley, *John Knox* (Oxford: Clarendon, 1968), pp. 171–180.

10. John Knox, *Works,* ed. David Laing (Edinburgh: James Thin, 1895; reprinted New York: AMS Press, 1966), IV, 349–422.

11. Ibid., III, 49, from "A Faithful Admonition to the Professors of God's Truth in England."

12. W. S. Hudson, *John Ponet: Advocate of Limited Monarchy* (Chicago: University of Chicago Press, 1942), pp. 111–112.

13. Quoted by Jászi and Lewis, *Against the Tyrant,* p. 54. Lewis' discussion of Buchanan in chap. V of that work is the best short treatment of the Scottish monarchomach known to this writer; but see also Skinner, *Foundations,* II, 343–345.

14. Harold Laski, ed., *A Defence of Liberty against Tyrants* (New York: Peter Smith, 1963), p. 5.

15. Leopold Ranke, *History of the Popes* (London: George Bell and Sons, 1891), I, 519–523; Marvin R. O'Connell, *The Counter Reformation, 1559–1610* (New York: Harper & Row, 1974), pp. 207–241.

16. Coville, *Jean Petit,* p. 565.

17. An old but still important study of the Jesuit monarchomachs is Franz Heinrich Reusch, "Die Lehre von Tyrannenmorde," in his *Beiträge zur Geschichte des Jesuitenordens* (Munich: C. H. Beck, 1894), pp. 1–58; see also Skinner, *Foundations,* II, 154–184.

18. Juan de Mariana, *The King and the Education of the King,* bk. I, chaps. 6–7, trans. George Albert Moore (Washington: Country Dollar Press, 1948), pp. 142–155.

19. For the narrative and interpretation of Scottish history in the sixteenth century, see especially Gordon Donaldson, *The Edinburgh History of Scotland,* vol. III: *James V to James VII* (New York: Frederick A. Praeger, 1966).

20. Lucien Romier, *Le royaume de Catherine de Médicis,* 2nd ed. (Paris: Perrin, 1922), and *Catholiques et Huguenots à la cour de Charles IX* (Paris: Perrin, 1924).

21. A compact account of Coligny's murder and what followed appears in Lavisse, *Histoire de France depuis les origines,* vol. VI, pt. 1, pp. 121–133. See also Alfred Soman, ed., *The Massacre of St. Bartholomew: Reappraisals and Documents* (The Hague: Nijhoff, 1974).

22. In *The Jew of Malta* (ca. 1589–1590), the prologue is delivered by an imaginary Machiavelli, who, "now the Guise is dead, is come from France." Marlowe's *The Massacre of Paris* apparently was written at about the same time. A recent biography is by Pierre Duhamel, *Henry of Guise* (Paris: Librairie Académique Perrin, 1974).

23. For the background of William the Silent's murder, consult two earlier classics: John Lothrop Motley, *The Rise of the Dutch Republic* (New York: Harper & Brothers, 1883), III, 598–614, and Pieter Geyl, *The Revolt of the Netherlands, 1555–1609,* 2nd ed. (London: Ernest Benn, 1962), pp. 192–194; as well as C. V. Wedgwood, *William the Silent* (New Haven: Yale University Press, 1944), pp. 248–253.

24. Herbert H. Rowen, ed., *The Low Countries in Early Modern Times* (New York: Walker, 1972), p. 79.

25. Works touching upon this aspect of Elizabeth's reign include Francis Edwards, *The Dangerous Queen* (London: G. Chapman, 1964); and Alan G. R. Smith, *The Government of Elizabethan England* (New York: W. W. Norton, 1967).

26. J. B. Black, *The Reign of Queen Elizabeth, 1558–1603* (Oxford: Clarendon, 1936), p. 144.

27. Smith, *Government of Elizabethan England,* pp. 28–30; see also Maurice Wilkinson, "St. Pius V and Elizabeth: The Bull 'Regnans in Excelsis,' " *The Month* (London), 155 (1930): 501–509.

28. For a perceptive examination of English Catholicism, including its response to tyrannicide theory, see Thomas H. Clancy, *Papist Pamphleteers: The Allen Persons*

Party and the Political Thought of the Counter-Reformation in England, 1572-1615 (Chicago: Loyola University Press, 1964).

29. For the narrative setting of Henry IV murder, see Mariéjol in Lavisse, ed., VI, pt. 2, 1-140. Further light is thrown on the king's foreign ventures and his assassination's impact abroad by Maurice Lee, Jr., *James I and Henry IV* (Urbana: University of Illinois Press, 1970).

30. Roland Mousnier, *L'Assassinat de Henry IV* (Paris: Gallimard, 1964).

31. Georges Mongrédien, *Léonora Galigai: Un procès de sorcellerie sous Louis XIII* (Paris: Hachette, 1968), pp. 141-174, devotes a full chapter to the slaying of his subject's husband prior to her own trial. Orest Ranum's remarks appear in "The French Ritual of Tyrannicide in the Late Sixteenth Century," *Sixteenth Century Journal*, 11 (1980): 63-81.

32. The most recent comprehensive biography is by Golo Mann, *Wallenstein: His Life Narrated,* trans. Charles Kessler (New York: Holt, Rinehart & Winston, 1976; German original, Frankfurt-am-Main: S. Fischer, 1971). This massive study does not, however, supersede Leopold von Ranke's classic, *Geschichte Wallensteins,* 4th ed. (Leipzig: Duncker & Humblot, 1880), or Heinrich von Srbik's Czech as well as German documentation in *Wallensteins Ende,* 2nd ed (Salzburg: O. Müller, 1952).

33. Robert Bireley, *The Peace of Prague (1635) and the Counterreformation in Germany* (Ann Arbor: University Microfilms International, 1976); abstracted in the *Journal of Modern History,* 48 (1976): iii.

34. Ranke, *Geschichte Wallensteins,* p. 338.

35. Richelieu, *Mémoires,* ed. C. B. Petitot (Paris: Collection des mémoires relatifs à l'histoire de France, 1823), VIII, 105; quoted by Mann, *Wallenstein,* p. 854.

36. "Récit particulier et véritable du procès criminel de monsieur le mareschal de Biron," pamphlet bound into second of three folio volumes, *Lettres et ambassade de messire Philippe Canaye, seigneur de Fresne,* Bibliothèque Nationale, Rés. Fol. Lg⁴.12.

37. Mongrédien, *Léonora Galigai,* pp. 175-206. A portion of her final interrogation has been analyzed and published by Charles Samaran. "Cursives françaises de XVᵉ, XVIᵉ et XVIIᵉ siecles," *Journal des savants* (July–September 1967): 143–152.

38. Louis André, ed., *Le Testament politique de Richelieu,* 7th ed. (Paris: R. Laffont, 1947), provides not only the most modern rendering of the text but also an excellent critical and historical introduction.

39. Rowen, ed., *The Low Countries in Early Modern Times,* pp. 116-126, nos. 25-26; Pieter Geyl, *The Netherlands in the Seventeenth Century,* pt. 1: *1609-1648,* rev. ed. (New York: Barnes & Noble, 1961), esp. pp. 62-63.

40. John de Tex, *Oldenbarnevelt,* trans. R. B. Powell (Cambridge: The University Press, 1973), offers the most complete and recent discussion of the constitutional issues.

41. John L. Motley, *The Life and Death of John Barneveld, Advocate of Holland* (New York: Harper & Brothers, 1902), II, 390.

42. C. V. Wedgwood, *The Trial of Charles I* (London: Collins, 1964), p. 10. See also documentation in *A Complete Collection of State Trials and Proceedings for High Treason,* ed. T. B. Howell (London: Longman, 1816), IV, 990-1154.

43. Wedgwood, *The Trial of Charles I,* p. 23.

44. Ibid., pp. 216-224, and *State Trials,* V, 947-1263.

9. The Early Modern Interlude

1. Portions of this chapter are adapted from Franklin L. Ford, "Assassination in the Eighteenth Century: The Dog That Did Not Bark in the Night," *Proceedings of the American Philosophical Society* (Philadelphia), 120 (1976): 211–215.

2. See Chapter 7.

3. Coville, *Jean Petit,* pp. 566–568.

4. See Chapter 6.

5. Claudio Aquaviva, S.J., Decretum de tyrannicidio, July 6, 1610, Archivum Romanum Societatis Jesui, Francia 32, fol. 431. The text of this document, as well as those cited in the ensuing two notes, has been made available through the great kindness of Robert Bireley, S.J., Loyola University of Chicago. For a letter of July 1611 in which Dudley Carleton, the English ambassador to Venice, warns his government of the "treacherous and bloody practices of Romanists and Spaniards," see Maurice Lee, Jr., *James I and Henri IV* (Urbana: University of Illinois Press, 1970), p. 178.

6. Archivum Romanum Societatis Jesui, Congregationes 59, fol. 129.

7. Ibid., fol. 133.

8. Louis Maimbourg, *Histoire du grand schisme d'occident* (Paris: S. Mabre-Cramoisy, 1686), pp. 480–481. Quoted by Coville, *Jean Petit,* pp. 574–575.

9. Pierre Bayle, *Dictionaire [sic] historique et critique* (Rotterdam, 1715), II, 232.

10. Gregorio Marañon, *El conde-duque de Olivares: La pasión de mandar,* rev. ed. (Madrid: Espasa-Calpe, 1952), remains the best existing biography, pending publication of John Elliott's comprehensive work on the subject.

11. Conversation and correspondence with John Elliott. See also his *The Revolt of the Catalans* (Cambridge: The University Press, 1963); and Eulogio Zudaire Muarte, *El conde-duque y Cataluña* (Madrid: Consejo Superior de Investigaciones Cientificas, 1964), concerning the most serious revolt within Spain.

12. See Chapter 8. Among general works see Carl J. Burckhardt, *Richelieu and His Age,* trans. Bernard Hoy, 4 vols. (London: G. Allen & Unwin, 1967–1971); V. L. Tapié's much older but only recently translated *France in the Age of Louis XIII and Richelieu,* trans. D. McN. Lockie (New York: Macmillan, 1974); and Philippe Erlanger, *Richelieu,* 3 vols. (Paris: Perrin, 1967–1971).

13. Pierre Chéruel, *Histoire de France pendant la minorité de Louis XIV,* 4 vols. (Paris: Hachette, 1879–1880).

14. Gulielmus Lamormaini, S.J., *Ferdinandi II Romanorum Imperatoris Virtutes* (Vienna: Gregorius Gelbhaar, 1638), p. 79. The same passage translated into German appears in *Die Tugenden Ferdinands des Zweyten Roemischen Kaysers* (Augsburg: J. B. B. Merz, 1791), p. 100.

15. H. Günter, *Die Habsburger-Liga, 1625–1635: Briefe und Akten aus dem General-Archiv zu Simancas* (Berlin: E. Ebering, 1908), pp. 120, 332.

16. Charles H. Firth, *Oliver Cromwell and the Rule of the Puritans in England* (New York: G. P. Putnam's Sons, 1900; new ed. 1947), p. 438.

17. Charles H. Firth, *The Last Years of the Protectorate* (London: Longman, Green, 1909), I, 33–40, 113–119, 219–236; also Antonia Fraser, *Cromwell, The Lord Protector* (New York: Knopf, 1973), pp. 584–585, 592–595.

18. Felix Gaiffe, *L'envers du grand siècle* (Paris: A. Michel, 1924), emphasizes

the "dark side" of the reign. Pierre Goubert, *Louis XIV and the Twenty Million Frenchmen* (New York: Random House, 1972), is also critical but less tendentious.

19. George Mongrédien, *L'affaire Fouquet* (Paris: Hachette, 1956), and *Madame de Montespan et l'affaire des poisons* (Paris: Hachette, 1953).

20. Herbert H. Rowen, *John de Witt, Grand Pensionary of Holland, 1625–1672* (Princeton: Princeton University Press, 1978), pp. 861–884.

21. John Philippe Kenyon, *The Popish Plot* (New York: St. Martin's, 1972); James Rees Jones, *The First Whigs: The Politics of the Exclusion Crisis, 1678–1683* (New York: Oxford University Press, 1961); and Kenneth H. D. Haley, *The First Earl of Shaftesbury* (Oxford: Clarendon, 1968).

22. Harold Armitage, *Russell and Rye House* (Letchworth: Letchworth Printers, 1948); Doreen J. Milne, "The Results of the Rye House Plot and Their Influence upon the Revolution of 1688," *Transactions of the Royal Historical Society*, 5th Ser. 1 (1951): 91–108.

23. Bryan Little, *The Monmouth Episode* (London: Werner Laurie, 1956); Peter J. Helm, *Jeffreys* (London: Hales, 1966); George Williams Keeton, *Lord Chancellor Jeffreys and the Stuart Cause* (London: MacDonald, 1965). J. G. Muddiman, ed., *The Bloody Assizes* (Edinburgh: William Hodge, 1929), uses Treasury documents now in the Public Record Office to tabulate 320 capital sentences, of which, however, fewer than half had been carried out at the time of reporting.

24. *English Historical Documents,* ed. Andrew Browning (New York: Oxford University Press, 1953), p. 122.

25. Sir George Clark, *The Later Stuarts, 1660–1714,* 2nd ed. (Oxford: Clarendon, 1955), pp. 184–185.

26. Ignaz A. Fessler, *Geschichte von Ungarn* (Leipzig: F. A. Brockhaus, 1867–1883), V, 61–65.

27. John Brooke, *King George III* (New York: McGraw-Hill, 1972), pp. 314–316, discusses both episodes.

28. *Supplément à l'Encyclopédie, ou Dictionnaire raisonné des sciences, des arts et des métiers* (Amsterdam: M. M. Rey, 1776–1777), I, 653a–654a.

29. Ibid., III, 333b–340b. See also the original *Texte* (Paris: Briasson, 1751–1765), VIII, 250b–253b; IX, 529b; XVII, 439b–444a.

30. Coville, *Jean Petit,* pp. 576–579.

31. Ibid., pp. 579–583.

32. David Hume, *The History of England,* new ed. (Boston: Little, Brown, 1849–1850), V, 48.

33. Edward Gibbon, *The History of the Decline and Fall of the Roman Empire* (New York: Everyman's Library, 1936), VI, 24.

34. Mouffle d'Angerville, *Vie privée de Louis XV* (London: J. P. Lyton, 1781), III, 108.

35. Frantz Christoph Khevenhiller [sic], *Annals Ferdinandei, oder wahrhaffte Beschreibung Käyser's Ferdinandi des Andern ... Geburth, Aufferziehung und ... Thaten* (Leipzig: M. G. Weidmann, 1721–1726). Assassination scenes appear in II, 332–333; III, 676–677, 748–749; IV, 1331–1332; VI, 3002–3003; VII, 311–312; XII, 1158–1159. Weidmann published an additional two volumes of copperplates, *Conterfet kupferstich deren jenigen regierenden grossen herren* (Leipzig, 1721–1722). John

Elliott and others have made extensive use of Khevenhüller's *Annales*, especially as a source for the Thirty Years' War period.

36. Edmond Jean François Barbier, *Chronique de la régence et du règne de Louis XV, 1718–1763* (Paris: Charpentier, 1857–1885), VI, 511–512, reproduces the advocate general's *réquisitoire*, demanding suppression of the pamphlets. For the case in general, see François N. N. Ravaisson, ed., *Archives de la Bastille* (Paris: A. Durand & Pedone-Lauriel, 1866–1904), XVI, 423–484; *Pièces originales et procédures du procès fait à Robert François Damiens* (Paris: Pierre-Guillaume Simon, 1757); and Dale K. Van Kley, *The Damiens Affair and the Unraveling of the Ancien Régime* (Princeton: Princeton University Press, 1984).

37. H. V. Livermore, *A History of Portugal* (Cambridge: The University Press, 1947), pp. 362–366, 380–385. The most recent monograph in any language is by Guilherme G. de Oliveira Santos, *O caso dos Távoras* (Lisbon: Libraria Portugal, 1958). For relevant documents, see Pedro de Azevedo, ed., *O processo dos Távoras* (Lisbon: Publiacoes da Biblioteca Nacional, 1921), Ineditos I.

38. *Gespraech in dem Reiche der Todten zwischen dem Urheber der Zusammenverschwoerung wider den Koenig in Portugall Joseph de Mascarenhas, ehemaligen Herzog von Aveiro, und Robert Franz Damiens, bekannten Koenigsmoerder in Frankreich, usw.* (Frankfurt-Leipzig, 1759); Widener Library copy, Harvard University, 47534.11.

39. Jean Epois, *L'affaire Corday-Marat: Prélude à la Terreur* (Les Sables-d'Olonne: Cercle d'Or, 1980); also John Fisher, *The Elysian Fields: France in Ferment, 1789–1804* (London: Cassell, 1966; U.S. printing entitled *Six Summers in Paris*, New York: Harper & Row, 1966), pp. 155–157.

40. Michael L. Walzer, ed., and Marian Rothstein, trans., *Regicide and Revolution: Speeches at the Trial of Louis XVI* (New York: Cambridge University Press, 1974); David P. Jordan, *The King's Trial* (Berkeley: University of California Press, 1979); and Albert Soboul, *The French Revolution, 1787–1799,* Alan Forrest and Colin Jones, trans. (New York: Random House, 1974), pp. 272–285.

41. Donald Greer, *The Incidence of the Terror during the French Revolution* (Cambridge, Mass.: Harvard University Press, 1935), p. 165.

42. Despite more recent works such as Beth Hennings, *Gustav III: En Biografi* (Stockholm: Norstedts, 1957), and Gardar Sahlberg, *Den aristokratiska ligan* (Stockholm: Bonniers, 1969), the most detailed account of the plot, Anckarström's act, and the aftermath remains that of L. Léouzon Le Duc, *Gustave III, roi de Suède* (Paris: Amyot, 1856), pp. 318–344.

43. Paul I's assassination naturally receives attention in all studies of the Russian empire during the Napoleonic epoch, as well as in dynastic histories of the Romanovs. The brief treatment here follows that of Nicholas V. Riasanovsky, *A History of Russia* (New York: Oxford University Press, 1963), pp. 305–306.

44. Brooke, *King George III,* p. 315.

10. The Nineteenth Century

1. Important treatments of anarchism in the nineteenth and twentieth centuries include James Joll, *The Anarchists* (London: Eyre & Spottiswoode, 1964), and Walter Laqueur, *Terrorism* (Boston: Little, Brown, 1977), though the latter, as its title suggests, covers much else.

2. On insurgency and repression in this period, see Charles Tilly, Louise Tilly, and Richard Tilly, *The Rebellious Century, 1830–1930* (Cambridge, Mass.: Harvard University Press, 1975).

3. *Assassination and Political Violence,* vol. VIII of *A Report to the National Commission on the Causes and Prevention of Violence,* ed. James F. Kirkham, Sheldon G. Levy, and William J. Crotty (Washington: U. S. Government Printing Office, 1969).

4. Ibid., Supplement C: "Political Assassination in China, 1600–1968," by Daniel Tretiak, pp. 505–508.

5. Tankred Dorst, with Ursula Ehler, *Sand: Ein Szenarium* (Cologne: Kiepenheuer & Witsch, 1971).

6. Works devoted to Sand's victim and published after the assassination begin with a hasty translation of his autobiography, *Life of Augustus von Kotzebue* (London: Boosey & Sons, 1820), with an added chapter by an anonymous writer describing the event in Mannheim. Much later one of his descendants, Wilhelm von Kotzebue, edited an interesting collection, *August von Kotzebue: Urtheile der Zeitgenossen und der Gegenwart* (Dresden: Wilhelm Baensch, 1831). Concerning his literary career, without regard to his sensational demise, see Frithjof Stock, *Kotzebue im literarischen Leben der Goethezeit* (Düsseldorf: Bertelsmann Universitätsverlag, 1971).

7. Freiherr Woldemar von Biedermann, "Goethe und Kotzebue," in Kotzebue, ed., *August von Kotzebue,* pp. 26–27; also Stock, *Kotzebue,* pp. 36–40.

8. Ibid., p. 9. Mrs. Inchbald's translation of the play, as performed by the Theatre Royal at Covent Garden in 1798 is an appendix to Jane Austen, *Mansfield Park* (London: Oxford University Press, 1966).

9. *Literarisches Wochenblatt* (Weimar), 2 (1819), no. 18; translation mine.

10. Among numerous studies of Sand and his deed, two works stand out. One is the almost contemporary study by a Berlin law professor, Carl Ernst Jarcke, *Carl Ludwig Sand, usw.: Eine psychologisch-criminalistische Eroertung aus der Geschichte unserer Zeit* (Berlin: Ferdinand Dummler, 1831); the other is a twentieth-century monograph, Alexander von Müller, *Karl Ludwig Sand* (Munich: Beck, 1925).

11. Jarcke, *Carl Ludwig Sand,* pp. 245–376, based on von Hohnhorst, *Vollstaendige Uebersicht der gegen Carl Ludwig Sand, wegen Meuchelmordes veruebt an dem Kaiser(lichen) Russischen Staatsrath v. Kotzebue gefuehrten Untersuchung* (Stuttgart-Tübingen, 1820), British Library copy 5511. cc. 19.

12. Carl Schmitt, *Politische Romantik,* 3rd. ed. (Berlin: Duncker & Humblot, 1968).

13. *Memoir of Charles Louis Sand* (London: G. & W. B. Whittaker, 1819).

14. Michael J. Sydenham, "The Crime of 3 Nivôse (24 December 1800)," in J. F. Bosher, ed., *French Government and Society, 1500–1850. Essays in Memory of Alfred Cobban* (London: Athlone, 1973), p. 309.

15. Despite the interest aroused by Ben Weider's and David Hapgood's colorful book, *The Murder of Napoleon* (New York: Congdon & Lattès, 1982), it is difficult to accept their claim that the emperor's death on Saint Helena in 1821 resulted from arsenic administered by Count Charles-Tristan de Montholon, allegedly a royalist agent serving the future king of France, Charles X. The theory itself is not new. Sten Forshufvud, Swedish dentist, serologist, and toxicologist, whose cooperation the authors acknowledge, spelled out most of the case more than twenty years ago in a

work entitled *Wem mördade Napoleon?* (Stockholm: A. Bonnier, 1961), also published in English as *Who Killed Napoleon?* (London: Hutchinson, 1962). Forshufvud and Weider subsequently wrote *Assassination at St. Helena* (Vancouver: Mitchell Press, 1978).

Between the earliest and the most recent of these books, advances in atomic mass spectrometry made it possible to achieve greater precision in the chemical analysis of various objects, including human cadavers exhumed long after burial. Basically, however, the Forshufvud hypothesis has remained unaltered. It rests on the unexpectedly well-preserved state of Napoleon's corpse when it was removed from its island grave for transfer to Paris in 1840 (considered significant because arsenic is a preservative commonly used by taxidermists), and on traces of arsenic reliably identified in samples of his hair.

The thesis that the emperor must have been intentionally poisoned raises a number of serious doubts. Foul play is supposed to have begun either around 1812, after which deteriorating health is blamed for his losing battles, or quite the reverse, only after 1815 when, following what is referred to as "a lifetime of robust health," he is purported to have mysteriously sickened and died. An obvious difficulty lies in the fact that the subject's symptoms of physical decline—growing obesity, fits of lethargy, unnatural pallor—had been remarked by contemporaries with increasing frequency beginning before his coronation in 1804. A further weakness in the case is that it assumes the presence of arsenic in hair and body tissue to be evidence of only one thing: purposeful homicide. In fact, the powdered mineral was widely used in the nineteenth century as a specific for various complaints, notably for dyspepsia, from which Napoleon was known to be a chronic sufferer. Arsenic may have contributed to his death in any of a number of ways, but from that possibility one can scarcely conclude that it was the sole or even the principal cause, let alone that it could only have been administered with intent to kill, imputed to a shadow assassin whose motives are never clearly spelled out.

The charge against Montholon would seem to spring from nothing more substantial than his acknowledged unreliability in both personal and public business, combined with the fact that he was personally acquainted with the Bourbon heir presumptive, a tireless intriguer. If Napoleon was seen as a threat to the restored monarchy, he could have been eliminated more expeditiously than by small doses of arsenic sprinkled on his food over a period of six years—years during which he was doing his successors the one disservice possible from his place of exile: writing his highly polemical memoirs. Security arrangements on the lonely island were not so strict as to preclude any number of accidents quicker and more dependable than gradual poisoning. (My thanks to Matthew Ramsey and Leonard Groopman, M.D.)

16. Roger L. Williams, *Manners and Murders in the World of Louis-Napoleon*, chap. 2, "Death Comes to the Archbishop" (Seattle: University of Washington Press, 1975), pp. 44–67.

17. An important source is the contemporary collection of documents, as well as illustrations engraved by Charles Metais, *L'Attentat du 14 janvier 1858* (Paris: Gustave Barba, [1858]). More recent treatments include Adrian Dansette, *L'Attentat d'Orsini* (Paris: Editions Mondiales, 1964); and Williams, *Manners and Murders*, chap. 3, "Felice Orsini's Defenders," pp. 68–101. The most comprehensive work remains Michael St. John Packe, *The Bombs of Orsini* (London: Secker & Warburg, 1957).

18. *Memoirs and Adventures of Felice Orsini, Written by Himself,* trans. George Carbonel (Edinburgh: Thomas Constable, 1857), p. 74. Selections from Orsini's correspondence with Mazzini and Garibaldi in particular appear in *Letere edite ed inedite de Felice Orsini* (Milan: Francesco Sanvito, 1962).

19. Alexander Herzen, *My Past and Thoughts,* trans. Constance Garnett, abridged ed. (New York: Knopf, 1973), pp. 367–374. This version does not include Herzen's account of the seduction of his own wife by Herwegh, which appears as a novella of sorts, "A Family Drama," in the complete four-volume Garnett translation (New York: Knopf, 1968), II, 932–950, accompanied by additional references to Frau Herwegh and Orsini.

20. Felice Orsini, *The Austrian Dungeons of Italy,* trans. J. Meriton White (London: G. Routledge, 1856).

21. Williams, *Manners and Murders,* p. 68.

22. *Gazette des Tribuneaux,* 26 February 1858, quoted in Williams, *Manners and Murders,* p. 81.

23. Ibid., p. 82, quoting the *Gazette des Tribuneaux,* 27 February 1858. The full text of Favre's celebrated closing speech to the jury appears in G. L. Chaix-d'Est-Ange, ed., *Discours et plaidoyers* (Paris: F. Didot, 1862), I, 439–460.

24. Williams, *Manners and Murders,* p. 88.

25. Roger L. Williams, *The Mortal Napoleon III* (Princeton: Princeton University Press, 1971), p. 289.

26. Packe, *The Bombs of Orsini,* pp. 281–282.

27. Excellent treatments of the background and narrative appear in Franco Venturi, *Roots of Revolution* (London: Weidenfeld & Nicolson, 1960), trans. Francis Haskell from the Italian original, *Il Populismo Russo* (Turin: Giulio Einaudi, 1952); and Ronald Hingley, *Nihilists: Russian Radicals and Revolutionaries in the Reign of Alexander II, 1855–81* (London: Weidenfeld & Nicolson, 1967). Older but still valuable is Sir Donald Mackenzie Wallace, *Russia on the Eve of War and Revolution,* ed. Cyril E. Black (New York: Vintage, 1961), the original edition having been published in 1877 under the title *Russia.*

28. Joll, *The Anarchists,* pp. 67–96; also E. H. Carr, *Michael Bakunin* (London: Macmillan, 1937), and *Bakunin on Anarchy: Selected Works by the Activist-Founder of World Anarchism,* ed. Sam Dolgoff (New York: Knopf, 1972).

29. See note 19 above; also Martin Malia, *Alexander Herzen and the Birth of Russian Socialism* (Cambridge, Mass.: Harvard University Press, 1961), esp. pp. 372–387. The best work in English on radical violence and its doctrinal basis in late tsarist Russia is Adam Ulam, *Ideologies and Illusions* (Cambridge, Mass.: Harvard University Press, 1976).

30. Nikolai Gavrilovich Chernyshevsky, *What Is To Be Done?: Tales about New People,* trans. Benjamin R. Tucker and L. B. Turkevich (New York: Vintage, 1961). See also W[anda] Bannour, ed. and trans., *Les Nihilistes russes, textes choisis de N. Tchernyechewski, N. Dobioloiubov et D. Pisarev* (Paris: Bibliothèque Sociale, 1974).

31. Venturi, *Roots of Revolution,* p. 365. The full text of the "Catechism," differently translated, appears in Robert Payne, *The Life and Death of Lenin* (New York: Simon & Schuster, 1964), pp. 24–29.

32. Venturi, *Roots of Revolution,* p. 373.

33. Ibid., p. 364; see also Carr, *Michael Bakunin,* chap. 28, "The Affaire Nechaev," pp. 375–393.

34. Astrid von Borcke, "Violence and Terror in Russian Revolutionary Populism: The *Narodnaya Volya,* 1879–83," in Wolfgang Mommsen and Gerhard Hirschfeld, eds., *Social Protest, Violence and Terror in Nineteenth- and Twentieth-Century Europe* (London: Macmillan, 1982), pp. 48–62.

35. Barbara Alpern Engel and Clifford N. Rosenthal, eds. and trans., *Five Sisters: Women against the Tsar* (New York: Knopf, 1975), pp. 59–94, for Vera Zasulich's memoirs.

36. *Kalender des Volkswillens für* 1883 (Geneva, 1883), pp. 135–145, summarized in tabular form by Alphons Thun, *Geschichte der revolutionären Bewegungen in Russland* (Leipzig: Duncker & Humblot, 1883), p. 375. Thun was a professor at the University of Basel.

37. Vera Figner, *Memoirs of a Revolutionist,* trans. A. S. Kaum (New York: International Publishers, 1927; repr. Greenwood Press, 1968). Other famous reflections include those by Sergei Kravchinsky, killer of General Mesentsov in 1878, published under the pseudonym "Stepniak," *Underground Russia: Revolutionary Profiles and Sketches from Life* (New York: Scribner, 1883; repr. Westport, Conn.: Hyperion, 1973).

38. Adam Ulam, *The Bolsheviks* (New York: Macmillan, 1965), esp. pp. 92–95, on the effects of Alexander II's murder; also Norman M. Naimark, *Terrorists and Socialists: The Russian Revolutionary Movement Under Alexander III* (Cambridge, Mass.: Harvard University Press, 1983).

39. Tom Corfe, *The Phoenix Park Murders: Conflict, Compromise and Tragedy in Ireland, 1879–1882* (London: Hodder & Stoughton, 1968).

40. E.R.R., "The Fenians," *History Today,* 8 (1958): 698–705; also William D'Arcy, *The Fenian Movement in the United States, 1858–1886* (Washington: Catholic University Press, 1947).

41. John V. Kelleher has offered a number of helpful suggestions with respect to the possible roots of the Invincibles and on other points as well.

42. N. Dunbar Palmer, *The Irish Land League* (New Haven: Yale University Press, 1940); and relevant portions of Conor Cruise O'Brien, ed., *The Shaping of Modern Ireland* (London: Routledge & Kegan Paul, 1960).

43. Conor Cruise O'Brien, *Parnell and His Party, 1880–1890* (Oxford: Oxford University Press, 1957); also Jules Abel, *The Parnell Tragedy* (London: Bodley Head, 1966).

44. J. L. Hammon, *Gladstone and the Irish Nation* (London: Longmans, 1938). In addition, the Irish Question receives attention in more general works, ranging from John Morley, *Life of William Ewart Gladstone* (New York: Macmillan, 1903), to Philip Magnus, *Gladstone: A Biography* (London: John Murray, 1954), and Peter Stansky, *Gladstone: A Progress in Politics* (Boston: Little, Brown, 1979).

45. Corfe, *The Phoenix Park Murders,* p. 139.

46. Frederick Moir Bussy, *Irish Conspiracies* (London: Everett, 1910).

47. Leon Ó Broin, *The Prime Informer: A Suppressed Scandal* (London: Sidgwick & Jackson, 1971), based on the memoirs and other writings of William Henry Joyce (1850–1928), pp. 31–33. The corroborative source referred to in the text is "Major Henri Le Caron" (Thomas Beach), *Twenty-five Years in the Secret Service: The Recollections of a Spy,* 4th ed. (London: William Heinemann, 1892), pp. 160–170, 228–230.

48. Ibid., pp. 207–208.

49. Corfe, *The Phoenix Park Murders,* pp. 135–145. Another contemporary source of considerable value, despite the author's pompous claims, is the book by "Number One" as he styled himself, P. J. P. Tynan, *The Irish National Invincibles and Their Times* (New York: Irish National Invincible Publishing Co., 1894).

11. Civilization in the Balance

1. Rebecca West, *Black Lamb and Grey Falcon* (New York: Viking, 1941), I, 11–12.

2. Liman, *Der politische Mord,* pp. 106–120.

3. The list printed here is derived in part from that found in Vladmir Dedijer, *The Road to Sarajevo* (New York: Simon & Schuster, 1966), pp. 449–451, supplemented by contemporary memoirs and newspaper accounts, as well as by Roland Gaucher's work, *The Terrorists: From Tsarist Russia to the O.A.S.,* trans. Albin Michel (London: Secker & Warburg, 1968), pt. I.

4. Gustave Paul Cluseret, *Mémoires,* 3 vols. (Paris: Jules Lévy, 1887–1888); V.I. Lenin, *Collected Works,* trans. Bernard Isaacs and Isidor Lasker (Moscow: Progress, 1962), VIII, 237–238.

5. Adam Ulam, *Stalin: The Man and His Era* (New York: Viking, 1973), pp. 96–113.

6. George Bruce, *The Stranglers: The Cult of Thugee and Its Overthrow in British India* (London: Longmans, 1968); also Geoffrey Moorhouse, *India Britannica* (New York: Harper & Row, 1983), pp. 92–95.

7. *Report of the Committee Appointed to Investigate Revolutionary Conspiracies in India,* Parliamentary Papers, No. 9190 (London: H. M. Stationery Office, 1918).

8. Manmathnat Cupta, *History of the Indian Revolutionist Movement* (Bombay: Somaiya Publications, 1972), pp. 1–53; Sir H. Verney Lovett in *The Cambridge History of India* (Cambridge: The University Press, 1932), VI, 550–559; and W. H. Moreland and Atul Chandra Chatterjee, *A Short History of India,* 4th ed. (London: Longmans, 1957), pp. 448–451.

9. Harry Wilde, *Politische Morde unserer Zeit* (Frankfurt-am-Main: Societäts Verlag, 1966), pp. 107–115. For a detailed reconstruction of the actual assassination, see Roberta S. Feuerlicht, *The Desperate Act* (New York: McGraw-Hill, 1968). With regard to the background and aftermath, see Dedijer, *The Road to Sarajevo,* and R. W. Seton-Watson, *Sarajevo: A Study in the Origins of the Great War* (London: Hutchinson, 1925).

10. Robert Lee Wolff, *The Balkans in Our Time* (Cambridge, Mass: Harvard University Press, 1956), pp. 96–97.

11. Gordon Wright, *Insiders and Outliers: The Individual in History* (San Francisco: W. H. Freeman, 1980), pp. 78–80.

12. Douglas L. Wheeler, *Republican Portugal: A Political History, 1910–1926* (Madison: University of Wisconsin Press, 1978), pp. 122–125, 129–130.

13. *Friedrich Adler vor dem Ausnahmegericht,* ed. J. W. Brügel (Vienna: Europa, 1967); also Julius Braunthal, *Victor und Friedrich Adler: Zwei Generationen Arbeiterbewegung* (Vienna: Wiener Volksbuchhandlung, 1965), pp. 225–245; and Ronald Florence, *Fritz: The Story of a Political Assassin* (New York: Dial, 1971).

14. *Adler vor dem Ausnahmegericht,* pp. 10, 64.

15. Friedrich Adler, *The Witchcraft Trial in Moscow* (New York: Pioneer, 1937); first published in London, 1936.

16. *Adler vor dem Ausnahmegericht,* pp. 57–58.

17. Colin Wilson, *Rasputin and the Fall of the Romanovs* (London: Arthur Barker, 1964), pp. 154–155.

18. Ibid., pp. 190–195.

19. Alexander Kerensky, *Russia and History's Turning Point* (New York: Duell, Sloan & Pearce, 1965), pp. 328–338.

20. Adam Ulam, *The Bolsheviks* (New York: Macmillan, 1965), pp. 426–428.

21. Leon Trotsky, *Diary in Exile, 1935,* trans. Elena Zarudnaya (Cambridge, Mass.: Harvard University Press, 1958), pp. 80–81.

22. Ibid., p. 81.

23. Ulam, *The Bolsheviks,* pp. 428–430.

24. Quoted by Ulam, *Stalin,* p. 174.

25. Gaucher, *The Terrorists,* pt. 3, takes up the Irish rebellion and civil war as one of several "struggles for independence," the others being those in Macedonia, Israel, and Algeria.

26. Wolff, *The Balkans in Our Time,* pp. 111–114.

27. Ibid., p. 113.

28. E. J. Gumbel, *Vier Jahre politischer Mord* (Berlin: Malik Verlag, 1922); Gustav Radbruch, "Staatsnotstand, Staatsnotwehr und Fememord," *Justiz* (Berlin), 5 (1929): 125–129. On the most important regional case, see Allan Mitchell, *Revolution in Bavaria, 1918–1919* (Princeton: Princeton University Press, 1965); Richard Greenberger, *Red Rising in Bavaria* (New York: St. Martin's, 1973); and Heinrich Hillmayr, *Roter und weisser Terror in Bayern* (Munich: Nusser, 1974).

29. Count Harry Kessler, *Walther Rathenau: His Life and Work* (New York: Harcourt, Brace, 1930), pp. 341–361; and Peter Berglar, *Walther Rathenau: Seine Zeit, sein Werk, seine Persönlichkeit* (Bremen: Universitätsverlag, 1970).

30. Eve Rosenhaft, "The KPD in the Weimar Republic and the Problem of Terror during the 'Third Period,' 1929–33,"in Mommsen and Hirschfeld, eds., *Social Protest, Violence and Terror,* pp. 342–366.

31. *Oletskoer Zeitung,* August 27, 1921, quoted in Klaus Epstein, *Matthias Erzberger and the Dilemma of German Democracy* (Princeton: Princeton University Press, 1959), p. 388.

32. Ibid., quoting the *Kreuzzeitung,* August 28, 1921.

33. Élie Halévy, *L'ère des tyrannies* (Paris: Gallimard, 1938); trans. R. K. Webb, *The Era of Tyrannies: Essays on Socialism and War* (New York: Anchor Books, 1965).

34. Eugene Victor Walter, *Terror and Resistance: A Study of Political Violence, with Case Studies of Some Primitive African Communities* (New York: Oxford University Press, 1969), pp. 109–219.

35. Joel Colton, *Léon Blum: Humanist in Politics* (New York: Knopf, 1966), pp. 115–117.

36. Edwin O. Reischauer, *Japan: The Story of a Nation* (New York: Knopf, 1970), pp. 179–217; Hugh Byas, *Government by Assassination* (New York: Knopf, 1942); Ivan Morris, ed., *Japan, 1931–1945: Militarism, Fascism, Japanism?* (Boston: D. C. Heath, 1963).

37. For example, Stoyan Pribichevich, *World Without End: The Saga of Southeastern Europe* (New York: Reynal & Hitchcock, 1939), p. 118, on the murders of four Serbian rulers, beginning in 1804 and ending with Alexander III's death in 1934; see also Stephen Graham, *Alexander of Yugoslavia* (New Haven: Yale University Press, 1939).

38. Henry L. Roberts, *Rumania: Political Problems of an Agrarian State* (New Haven: Yale University Press, 1951), pp. 175–241; see also Wolff, *The Balkans in Our Times,* pp. 192–195; and Gaucher, *The Terrorists,* pp. 144–150.

39. Jan van Heijenoort, *With Trotsky in Exile: From Prinkipo to Coyoacan* (Cambridge, Mass.: Harvard University Press, 1978).

40. Ulam, *Stalin,* pp. 435–490; Nikita Sergeevich Krushchev, *Krushchev Remembers,* trans. and ed. Strobe Talbott (Boston: Little, Brown, 1970), pp. 75–89.

41. Adler, *The Witchcraft Trial in Moscow;* Arthur Koestler, *Darkness at Noon,* trans. Daphne Hardy (London: J. Cape, 1940); Halévy, *The Era of Tyrannies,* p. 283.

42. Franz Neumann, *Behemoth: The Structure and Practice of National Socialism* (New York: Oxford University Press, 1942).

12. World War II and After

1. *Time,* August 25, 1941, p. 29.

2. Peter Hoffmann, *The History of the German Resistance, 1933–1945,* trans. Richard Barry (Cambridge, Mass.: MIT Press, 1977), pp. 41, 543, n. 32.

3. *New York Times,* June 30, July 1–4, and July 8, 1940.

4. *Time,* July 12 and 19, 1943.

5. For an excellent treatment of the political setting, see Sarah M. Terry, *Poland's Place in Europe: General Sikorski and the Origin of the Oder-Neisse Line* (Princeton: Princeton University Press, 1982).

6. *New York Times,* September 30, 1943, p. 1. Alfred Rosenberg, representing Hitler at Kube's funeral, spoke of the growing threat of attacks upon German dignitaries.

7. Vojtech Mastny, *The Czechs under Nazi Rule: The Failure of the National Resistance, 1939–1942* (New York: Columbia University Press, 1971), pp. 207–221.

8. *Time,* January 4, 1943, pp. 24–25; see also Jászi and Lewis. *Against the Tyrant,* pp. 179–181.

9. *The Nation,* 156 (1943): 3.

10. Franklin L. Ford. "The Twentieth of July in the History of the German Resistance," *American Historical Review,* 51 (1946): 5–17.

11. The English translation of Hoffmann's book, mentioned above, is from *Widerstand, Staatsstreich, Attentat,* 2nd ed. (Munich: R. Piper, 1970).

12. Hoffmann, *History of the German Resistance,* pp. 256–258. See also his monograph *Hitler's Personal Security* (London: Macmillan, 1979).

13. Fabian von Schlabrendorff, *Offiziere gegen Hitler* (Zurich: Europa, 1946); English trans. *They Almost Killed Hitler,* ed. Gero von Gaevernitz (New York: Macmillan, 1947).

14. Hoffmann, *History of the German Resistance,* pp. 526–531.

15. A personal account by Rommel's son Manfred is appended to *The Rommel Papers,* trans. Paul Findlay (New York: Harcourt, Brace, 1953), pp. 495–506. See

also Hans Speidel, *Invasion 1944: Rommel and the Normandy Campaign*, trans. Ian Colvin (Chicago: Regnery, 1950), pp. 151–160.

16. Günther Weisenborn, *Der lautlose Aufstand: Bericht über die Widerstandsbewegung des deutschen Volkes, 1933–1945* (Hamburg: Rowohlt, 1962), p. 240.

17. Hoffmann, *History of the German Resistance*, p. 258.

18. Sir Ivone Kirkpatrick, *Mussolini: Study of a Demagogue* (London: Odhams Books, 1964), pp. 615–635; Roy Macgregor-Hastie, *The Day of the Lion: The Life and Death of Fascist Italy, 1922–1945* (New York: Coward-McCann, 1963), pp. 350–354.

19. H. R. Trevor-Roper, *The Last Days of Hitler* (London: Macmillan, 1947).

20. United States Chief of Counsel for the Prosecution of Axis Criminality, *Nazi Conspiracy and Aggression*, 8 vols. (Washington: U.S. Government Printing Office, 1946), and *Final Report to the Secretary of the Army on Nuernberg War Crimes Trials under Control Council Law No. 10;* see also Telford Taylor, *Nuremberg Trials: War Crimes and International Law* (New York: Carnegie Endowment for International Peace, 1949).

21. *Nazi Conspiracy and Aggression*, II, 565–575.

22. Philip R. Picigallo, *The Japanese on Trial: Allied War Crimes Operations in the East, 1945–1951* (Austin: University of Texas Press, 1979). Postwar international tribunals in East Asia have in general received more critical treatment than their European counterparts, as witness the serious work by Richard H. Minear, *Victors' Justice: The Tokyo War Crimes Trial* (Princeton: Princeton University Press, 1973).

23. *Eichmann in Jerusalem: A Report on the Banality of Evil* (New York: Viking, 1964; rev. ed. Penguin, 1976).

24. Peter Papadatos, *The Eichmann Trial* (New York: Frederick A. Praeger, 1964), p. 101.

25. Ibid., p. 60, n. 54.

26. *German Press Review* (Washington: Embassy of the Federal Republic of Germany, 1981), no. 81–27, p. 1.

27. Wolff, *The Balkans in Our Time*, pp. 300–303.

28. Claire Sterling, *The Masaryk Case* (New York: Harper & Row, 1969).

29. Gaucher, *The Terrorists*, p. 207.

30. Gerold Frank, *The Deed* (New York: Simon & Schuster, 1963). See also Yehuda Bauer, *From Diplomacy to Resistance: A History of Jewish Palestine, 1939–1945*, trans. Alton M. Winters (New York: Atheneum, 1973); and Menachem Begin, *The Revolt: Story of the Irgun* (New York: Henry Schuman, 1951).

31. Geoffrey Ashe, *Gandhi* (New York: Stein & Day, 1968), pp. 380–385.

13. Recent Times

1. *Newsweek*, July 26, 1982, p. 40.

2. Ali A. Mazrui, "Thoughts on Assassination in Africa," *Political Science Quarterly*, 83 (1968): 45.

3. Claire Sterling, *The Terror Network* (New York: Holt, Rinehart and Winston, 1981); see also Christopher Dobson, *The Terrorists: Their Weapons, Leaders and Tactics* (New York: Facts on File, 1979).

4. Gerhard Brunn, "Nationalist Violence and Terror in the Spanish Border

Provinces: ETA," In Mommsen and Hirschfeld, eds., *Social Protest, Violence and Terror,* pp. 112–136.

5. Julen Agirre, *Operation Ogro: The Execution of Admiral Luis Carrero Blanco,* trans. Barbara Probst Solomon (New York: Quadrangle New York Times Books, 1974).

6. *Newsweek,* November 15, 1982.

7. Claire Sterling, "The Terrorist Network," *The Atlantic,* November 1978, p. 42.

8. Sterling, *The Terror Network,* pp. 3, 126, 146.

9. *The Boston Globe,* August 28, 1983.

10. Peter Laffan, "Violence and Terror in Twentieth-century Ireland: IRB and IRA," in Mommsen and Hirschfeld, eds., *Social Frotest, Violence and Terror,* pp. 155–174. Fuller treatments include Conor Cruise O'Brien, *States of Ireland* (New York: Pantheon, 1972), and J. Bowyer Bell, *The Secret Army: The IRA, 1916–1979,* rev. ed. (Cambridge, Mass.: MIT Press, 1980).

11. For selections from Marighella's "minimanual," as it came to be called, and other important texts, see Walter Laqueur, ed., *The Terrorism Reader* (Philadelphia: Temple University Press, 1978).

12. Despite published fragments by other female terrorists, the only full text available in English is Leila Khaled's *Autobiography* (London: Hodder & Stoughton, 1973).

13. An account of this episode appears in Christopher Dobson and Ronald Payne, *The Carlos Complex: A Study in Terror* (London: Coronet Books/Hodder & Stoughton, 1977), pp. 187–191.

14. Ibid., pp. 191–194.

15. Sterling, *The Terror Network,* p. 228. See also Jacob M. Landau, *Radical Politics in Modern Turkey* (Leiden: E. J. Brill, 1974).

16. Ovid Demaris, *Brothers in Blood: The International Terrorist Network* (New York: Charles Scribner's Sons, 1977).

17. Jillian Becker, *Hitler's Children: The Story of the Baader-Meinhof Terrorist Gang* (Philadelphia: Lippincott, 1977), deals at length with the origins of the RAF and its roots in the Baader-Meinhof gang.

18. Kai Hermann and Peter Koch, *Entscheidung in Mogadishu: Die 50 Tage nach Schleyers Entführung* (Hamburg: Grunner, 1977).

19. Yonah Alexander, *Terrorism in Italy* (New York: Crane, Russak, 1979; Giovanni Spadolini, *Diario del dramma Moro* (Florence: Le Monnier, 1978).

20. *New York Times,* August 17, 1982, referring to a prepublication copy of Miss Sterling's article, "The Plot to Murder the Pope," *Reader's Digest,* 121 (September 1982): 71–82.

21. Paul B. Henze, *The Plot to Kill the Pope* (New York: Charles Scribner's Sons, 1983); Claire Sterling, *The Time of Assassins* (New York: Holt, Rinehart & Winston, 1983). Edward Jay Epstein's review of these two works in *The New York Times Book Review,* January 15, 1984) summarizes the present state of the evidence, including its gaps. On June 10, 1984, the *New York Times* reported in detail Judge Martella's recommendations calling for nine indictments.

22. Dilip Mukerjee, *Zulfikar Ali Bhutto: Quest for Power* (Delhi-Bombay: Vikes Publishing House, 1972).

23. *Facts on File,* 1979, p. 116.

24. Mazrui, "Thoughts on Assassination," pp. 40–58.

25. Ibid., p. 52.

26. *Africa Digest* (London), 14 (1966): 22–23.

27. Mazrui, "Thoughts on Assassination," p. 58.

28. *Facts on File*, 1979, p. 431.

29. Ibid., p. 673.

30. Ali A. Mazrui, *The African Condition: A Political Diagnosis* (Cambridge: Cambridge University Press, 1980). Comparable uneasiness informs the essay by Victor T. Levine, "Problems of Political Succession in Independent Africa," in Ali A. Mazrui and Hasu H. Patel, eds., *Africa in World Affairs: The Next Thirty Years.* (New York: Third Press, 1973), pp. 79–103.

31. David Lamb, *The Africans* (New York: Random House, 1982), p. 342.

32. Ibid., pp. 126–131.

33. *Facts on File*, 1980, p. 353.

34. *Newsweek,* October 19, 1981, pp. 26–31. David Hirst and Irene Beeson, *Sadat* (London: Faber and Faber, 1981), completed—except for a last-minute prologue—just before its subject's death, supplies background for that event by sympathetically reviewing Arab and Egyptian criticisms of his détente with Israel.

35. Michael Bar-Zohar and Eitan Haber, *The Quest for the Red Prince* (New York: William Morrow, 1983).

36. James M. Markham, "Life and Death of a Terrorist," *The New York Times Book Review,* July 10, 1983.

37. Based on a tabulation and commentary published in *Newsweek,* October 12, 1981, pp. 53–54.

14. The Americas: Latin, British, and French

1. Karl M. Schmitt, "Assassination in Latin America," in Kirkham et al., *Assassination and Political Violence,* pp. 537–543.

2. Alex Schubert, *Stadtguerrilla: Tupamaros in Uruguay, Rote Armee Fraktion in der Bundesrepublik* (Berlin: Wagenbach, 1971), illustrates the comparative analysis of terrorism.

3. Sterling, *The Terror Network,* pp. 248–250.

4. Ibid., pp. 95–112; also Hans Hederberg, *Operation Leo* (Stockholm: Raben & Sjogren Boktorlag, 1978).

5. John Dinges and Saul Landau, *Assassination on Embassy Row* (New York: Pantheon Books, 1980); Taylor Branch and Eugene M. Propper, *Labyrinth* (New York: Viking Press, 1982).

6. *Facts on File*, 1973, p. 206; 1977, p. 935; *The New York Times,* March 11, 14, 1973.

7. Chris Searle, *Grenada: The Struggle against Destabilization* (London: Writers and Readers Publishing Cooperative Society, 1984), is a sharply critical discussion of U.S. policy.

8. *Facts on File*, 1974, p. 312.

9. Ibid., 1983, p. 871.

10. John Saywell, *Quebec 70: A Documentary Narrative* (Toronto: University of Toronto Press, 1971), an excellent circumstantial summary. See also Gustav Morf, *Terror in Quebec: Case Studies of the FLQ* (Toronto: Clark, Irwin, 1970).

11. *Facts on File,* 1970, p. 896.

12. Saywell, *Quebec 70,* pp. 121–122.

13. Pierre Vallières, *The Assassination of Pierre Laporte: Behind the October '70 Scenario* (Toronto: James Lorimer, 1977).

15. The United States

1. Richard Maxwell Brown, "Historical Patterns of American Violence," in Hugh Davis Graham and Ted Robert Gurr, eds., *Violence in America: Historical and Comparative Perspectives,* rev. ed. (Beverly Hills, Calif.: Sage Publications, 1979), p. 20.

2. William O. Stevens, *Pistols at Ten Paces: The Story of the Code of Honor in America* (Boston: Houghton, Mifflin, 1940); pp. 147–165 treat Hamilton's duel with Aaron Burr.

3. Brown, "Historical Patterns," mentions the Terry-Broderick affair but incorrectly gives its date as 1857.

4. Robert J. Donovan, *The Assassins* (New York: Harper & Brothers, 1955), pp. 63–79.

5. Stephen B. Oates, *To Purge This Land with Blood: A Biography of John Brown* (New York: Harper & Row, 1970).

6. *American Assassins: The Darker Side of Politics* (Princeton: Princeton University Press, 1982), p. 9.

7. Donovan, *The Assassins,* pp. 216–292, and Clarke, *American Assassins,* pp. 19–39, do not diverge in most respects, though they disagree about Booth's character.

8. William Hanchett, *The Lincoln Murder Conspiracies* (Urbana: University of Illinois Press, 1983), reviews a number of highly imaginative works setting forth conspiracy theories of one kind or another. These include David Miller DeWitt, *The Assassination of Abraham Lincoln, and Its Expiation* (New York: Macmillan, 1909); Lloyd Lewis, *Myths after Lincoln* (New York: Readers Club, 1941); and Otto Eisenschiml, *Why Was Lincoln Murdered?* (New York: Grosset & Dunlap, 1937). As early as December 1866 the judge advocate general of the United States Army, Joseph Holt, whose Bureau of Military Justice had been charged with investigating the crime, wrote President Johnson that the complicity of former Confederate President Jefferson Davis and others in his government was a "matter of solemn record, and this record stands unimpeached" (Hanchett, p. 81). A more widely believed charge was that Secretary of War Stanton stood at the center of an elaborate plot to eliminate his own commander-in-chief. Neither hypothesis is given much credence by present-day scholarship, although the "Stanton theory" in particular continues to appear in occasional works.

9. Clarke, *American Assassins,* p. 36. Booth's diary is in the National Archives, Attorney General's Papers, Lincoln Assassination, RG No. 60.

10. Kirkham et al., *Assassination and Political Violence,* table 1, pp. 12–19; tables 4–10, pp. 24–41.

11. Ibid., pp. 49–112, "Assassination Attempts Directed at the Office of President of the United States."

12. Donovan, *The Assassins,* pp. 14–62; Clarke, *American Assassins,* pp. 193–214.

13. Charles E. Rosenberg, *The Trial of the Assassin Guiteau* (Chicago: University of Chicago Press,1968).

14. Although Clarke's precise classification of subjects into four basic types (plus two "atypicals") in *American Assassins* has not been adopted here, this section owes a debt to his treatment of case studies and his effort to distinguish degrees of insanity.

15. Donovan, *The Assassins,* pp. 127–147; Clarke, *American Assassins,* pp. 214–222; Oliver E. Remy et al., *The Attempted Assassination of Ex-President Theodore Roosevelt* (Milwaukee: Progressive, 1912).

16. Clarke, *American Assassins,* p. 173.

17. Arthur H. Bremer, *An Assassin's Diary* (New York: Harper's Magazine Press, 1972). Clarke, *American Assassins,* pp. 174–193, makes extensive use of trial documents.

18. *Facts on File,* 1968, p. 609; 1969, p. 454.

19. Clarke, *American Assassins,* pp. 128–142.

20. *Facts on File,* 1981, pp. 209–211, 212–213; 1982, pp. 449, 587.

21. Ibid., 1975, pp. 661, 957; also Clarke, *American Assassins,* pp. 144–156, relying for background on a widely read book concerning the Manson gang, Vincent Buglione, with Curt Gentry, *Helter Skelter* (New York: W. W. Norton, 1974).

22. *Facts on File,* 1975, pp. 701, 958; 1976, p. 23; Clarke, *American Assassins,* pp. 156–165.

23. Ibid., p. 31, citing a letter from Booth to his brother-in-law, written while contemplating the abduction of the President, now with his diary in the National Archives (see note 8 above).

24. Ibid., p. 59, citing Joseph Fowler et al., "Official Report of the Experts for the People in the Case of the People v. Leon F. Czolgosz (1901)," in John D. Dawson, ed., *American State Trials* (St. Louis: Thomas Law Book Co., 1923), 14: 169–170.

25. Donovan, *The Assassins,* pp. 169–215; Clarke, *American Assassins,* pp. 64–76.

26. Ibid., p. 67, quoting FBI documents.

27. Robert Blair Kaiser, *"RFK Must Die!" A History of the Robert Kennedy Assassination and Its Aftermath* (New York: Dutton, 1970); Godfrey Jansen, *Why Robert Kennedy Was Killed* (New York: Third Press, 1970).

28. Harnett T. Kane, *Louisiana Hayride: The American Rehearsal for Dictatorship* (New York: W. Morrow, 1941), pp. 135–137.

29. Jäszi and Lewis, *Against the Tyrant,* p. 176.

30. Kane, *Louisiana Hayride,* pp. 134–135; Clarke, *American Assassins,* pp. 224–239.

31. An example of the earlier tone, at once suspicious and inconclusive, survives in an article by Christopher Lasch, "The Life of Kennedy's Death," *Harper's,* October 1983, pp. 32–40, which concludes: "John F. Kennedy was killed, in all likelihood, not by a sick society or by some supposedly archetypal, resentful common man but by a political conspiracy his own actions may have helped set in motion."

32. John Updike, *Couples* (New York: Knopf, 1968), p. 299.

33. For an unofficial indication of Blakey's views, see G. Robert Blakey and Richard N. Billings, "The Plot to Kill the President: An Expert's Theory," with comment by columnist Jack Anderson, *Parade Magazine,* November 16, 1980, pp.

5-7. This article directs suspicion at two Mafia leaders, Carlos Marcello and Santo Trafficante, claiming that organized crime had several reasons for wanting the chief executive dead. It cites rumors of Joseph P. Kennedy's relations with criminal elements during the 1930s, reports of an affair between President Kennedy and Judith Campbell, former mistress of Sam Giancana, and the reality of Attorney General Robert F. Kennedy's highly publicized campaign against racketeers. The chief strength of Blakey's explanation consists in trying to make at least hypothetical sense of Ruby's gangland-style murder of Lee Harvey Oswald the day following the assassination. An offsetting weakness is that the coauthors continue to speak confidently of the mysterious "fourth shot from the grassy knoll" at Dealey Plaza in Dallas, a shot whose very existence has ceased to be accepted as proven.

34. *Report of the Select Committee on Assassinations, U.S. House of Representatives, Ninety-fifth Congress, Second Session: Findings and Recommendations* (Washington: U.S. Government Printing Office, 1979), p. 1. See also its *Hearings,* vols. 1-12 (Washington: USGPO, 1978).

35. *Report of the President's Commission on the Assassination of President John F. Kennedy,* and *Hearings,* vols. 1-26. (Washington: U.S. Government Printing Office, 1964). Examples of "anti-Warren Report" works include Thomas Buchanan, *Who Killed Kennedy?* (New York: Putnam, 1964); Mark Lane, *Rush to Judgment* (New York: Holt, Rinehart & Winston, 1966); Richard Popkin, *The Second Oswald* (New York: Avon, 1966); and more recently, pursuing the "Russian connection," Edward Jay Epstein, *Legend: The Secret World of Lee Harvey Oswald* (New York: McGraw-Hill/Reader's Digest Press, 1978).

36. Edward Jay Epstein, *Inquest: The Warren Commission and the Establishment of Truth* (New York: Viking, 1966).

37. *Select Committee* (1979), pp. 1-2.

38. Ibid., p. 3.

39. Ibid., pp. 373-380, 404.

40. Ibid., pp. 325-374.

41. William Bradford Huie, *He Slew the Dreamer* (New York: Delacorte, 1970); George McMillan, *The Making of an Assassin* (Boston: Little, Brown, 1976).

42. Hanchett, *The Lincoln Murder Conspiracies,* pp. 74-82; also Roy Franklin Nichols, "United States vs. Jefferson Davis, 1865-1869," *American Historical Review,* 31 (1926): 266-284.

43. David Miller Dewitt, *The Judicial Murder of Mary E. Surratt* (Baltimore: John Murphy, 1895).

44. Hanchett, *The Lincoln Murder Conspiracies,* pp. 61-71.

45. *The Sacco-Vanzetti Case: Transcript of the Record of the Trial of Nicola Sacco and Bartolomeo Vanzetti in the Courts of Massachusetts and Subsequent Proceedings, 1920-1927,* vols. I-V, and Supplement (New York: Henry Holt, 1928-1929).

46. A strongly anti-government recapitulation of the narrative, containing some striking quotations, is the *Fact Sheet in the Rosenberg Case* (New York: National Committee to Secure Justice in the Rosenberg Case, 1953). Outwardly judicious but actually a partisan treatment is Walter and Miriam Scheir, *Invitation to an Inquest* (Garden City, N.Y.: Doubleday, 1965). Preferable, albeit older, is Malcolm P. Sharp, *Was Justice Done?: The Rosenberg-Sobell Case* (New York: Monthly Review Press,

1956). Most of the previous literature has been superseded by the excellent study of Ronald Radosh and Joyce Milton, *The Rosenberg File: A Search for the Truth* (New York: Holt, Rinehart & Winston, 1983).

47. Radosh and Milton, *The Rosenberg File,* pp. 453–454.

48. *New York Times,* April 6, 1951.

49. Ibid., August 26, 1966.

50. Ibid., February 12, 1953; repeated in slightly different form in the subsequent statement issued on the day of the Rosenbergs' execution, *New York Times,* June 20, 1953.

51. Philip Agee, *Inside the Company: CIA Diary* (New York: Stonehill, 1975); see also Victor Marchetti and John D. Marks, *The CIA and the Cult of Intelligence* (New York: Knopf, 1974).

52. Bradley F. Smith, *The Shadow Warriors: O.S.S. and the Origins of the C.I.A.* (New York: Basic Books, 1983), a work which, despite its arresting title, seems curiously overweighted on the side of "politicking" within the Office of Strategic Services, at the expense of clarity or comprehensiveness in discussing that organization's relationship to its partial successor, the Central Intelligence Agency.

53. The interim report of a select committee of the U. S. Senate charged with a study of governmental intelligence activities, *Alleged Assassination Plots Involving Foreign Leaders* (Washington: U. S. Government Printing Office, 1975), p. 191, summarizes its findings in the Trujillo case as follows:

> Trujillo was a brutal dictator, and both the Eisenhower and Kennedy Administrations encouraged the overthrow of his regime by Dominican dissidents. Toward that end the highest policy levels of both Administrations approved or condoned supplying arms to the dissidents. Although there is no evidence that the United States instigated any assassination activity, certain evidence tends to link United States officials to the assassination plans.

> Material support, consisting of three pistols and three carbines, was supplied to various dissidents. While United States' officials knew that the dissidents intended to overthrow Trujillo, probably by assassination, there is no evidence that the weapons which were passed were used in the assassination.

There follow several sentences explaining that the select committee had no conclusive evidence on which to base a judgment as to how high in either administration information concerning assassination plots had been passed prior to Trujillo's death in May 1961, but that permission from above was known to have been refused for four machine guns to be delivered to the dissidents. The summary concludes:

> The day before the assassination a cable, personally authorized by President Kennedy, was sent to the United States Consul General in the Dominican Republic stating that the United States Government, as a matter of general policy, could not condone political assassination, but at the same time indicating the United States continued to support the dissidents and stood ready to recognize them in the event they were successful in their endeavor to overthrow Trujillo.

54. Agee, *Inside the Company,* pp. 195–196.

55. Interview with McGeorge Bundy, April 21, 1983.

56. Arthur P. Whitaker, *The United States and the Southern Cone: Argentina, Chile, and Uruguay* (Cambridge, Mass.: Harvard University Press, 1976), p. 329. See also Francisco Orrego Vicuña, ed., *Chile: The Balanced View: A Recopilation [sic] of*

Articles about the Allende Years and After (Santiago University of Chile Institute of International Affairs, 1975), clearly a propaganda document but it reproduces serious essays by various American and British observers. On the other side, see Judy White, ed., *Chile's Days of Terror: Eyewitness Accounts of the Military Coup* (New York: Pathfinder Press, 1974), which offers plentiful testimony to the bloodshed and violence surrounding Allende's ouster and death.

57. Agee, *Inside the Company,* p. 583.
58. Whitaker, *The United States and the Southern Cone,* pp. 413–417.

Index

425